REFORM AND RESPONSIVENESS

Readings in American Politics

REFORM AND RESPONSIVENESS

Readings in American Politics

Edited by DENNIS S. IPPOLITO and THOMAS G. WALKER

Emory University

ST. MARTIN'S PRESS   New York

ACKNOWLEDGMENTS

The editors would like to thank Miss Mary Wilkins for her editorial assistance, and
Mrs. Elaine Marta, who accomplished the difficult task of securing permissions. The
editors are also grateful to those authors whose articles have been reprinted here.

p. 6 "Controls and Influence in American Elections (Even 1968)" by Gerald M.
Pomper is reprinted from *American Behavioral Scientist,* Volume 13, Number 2
(November/December 1969), pp. 215-230, by permission of the Publisher, Sage
Publications, Inc., and the author.

p. 17 "Direct Popular Election of the President" by William T. Gossett is reprinted
from *American Bar Association Journal,* 56 (March 1970), 225-231, by permission
of the *American Bar Association Journal* and the author.

p. 29 "Regulating Campaign Spending" by John Gardner, U.S. Senate, Communications Subcommittee of the Committee on Commerce, *Federal Election Campaign
Act of 1971.* Report No. 92-6, 92nd Congress, 1st Session, 675-678.

p. 34 From *Polls, Television and the New Politics* by Harold Mendelsohn and
Irving Crespi (San Francisco: Chandler, 1970), pp. 297-314, 317. Reprinted by
permission of Intext Educational Publishers.

p. 52 "Some Determinants of Political Apathy" by Morris Rosenberg is reprinted from *Public Opinion Quarterly,* 18 (Winter, 1954/1955), 349-366, by permission of *Public Opinion Quarterly* and the author.

p. 69 "Protest as a Political Resource" by Michael Lipsky is reprinted from the
American Political Science Review, 62 (December 1968), 1144-1158, by permission
of the *American Political Science Review* and the author.

p. 89 "The Federal Government and Protest" by David Mars is reprinted from
The Annals of the American Academy of Political and Social Science, 382 (March
1969), 120-130, by permission of The American Academy of Political and Social
Science and the author.

p. 100 "A Postscript for Peace Workers: Some Concrete Advice" by Ralph K.
White. From Milton J. Rosenberg, Sidney Verba, and Philip E. Converse, *Vietnam
and the Silent Majority* (New York: Harper & Row, 1970), pp. 133-155. Reprinted
by permission of Harper & Row, Milton J. Rosenberg, and the author.

p. 121 "The End of American Party Politics" by Walter Dean Burnham. Copyright
© December 1969 by Transaction, Inc., New Brunswick, New Jersey. Reprinted by
permission of the publisher and the author.

p. 134 "Television and the Loyal Opposition" by Joseph Califano, U.S. Senate,
Communications Subcommittee of the Committee on Commerce, *Public Service*

CONTENTS

INTRODUCTION

> ... [M]oralists, who are not necessarily idealists, have always
> been hell on the rest of us. A moralist refers everything back to
> himself, and that is what makes ... [him] so stupefyingly dull.
> Politics needs not be a demanding profession, which is one reason it
> attracts the people it does, and the moralists among the politicians
> usually have been found on the Right. Strom Thurmond, for example,
> is uncluttered with either ideas, or a sense of ambiguity, but he has a
> high sense of purpose, and he is a moralist. The liberals, however
> grievous their other faults, are more cynical about things, and they
> lack that high sense of purpose, which makes them
> easier to get along with.

—John Corry[1]

> When you're young it's easy enough to streak appeals across the
> sky like rockets. But as you get older you feel increasingly responsible
> for those traveling the road your rocket lights. What if you've led
> them wrong? You grow wary of making reckless appeals, and a
> sense of responsibility must be tempered above all with analysis and
> reflection. Relentless analysis alone, not childish shouting,
> embodies the true appeals.

—Yevgeny Yevtushenko[2]

This volume presents literature dealing with the reform of national political institutions. It examines proposals for altering the relationship between the public and government in such a manner as to increase governmental responsiveness—that is, the ability of government to respond readily and effectively to legitimate public needs and preferences.

THE PROBLEM OF CONFIDENCE

Many people believe that the public problems affecting the United States today are of unprecedented severity. During the past decade, the United States has been particularly prone to a "crisis psychology" rooted in such distressing events and circumstances as the war in Southeast Asia, racial problems, urban decay, the degradation of the physical environment, and the disaffection of young people. The traditional optimism of the American people about their nation's destiny has been tempered by the realization that the threats of international and domestic violence have not diminished as the United States has achieved greater military power and material affluence. The problems confronting American society are indeed serious, and they represent intellectual as well as institutional challenges.

If there is one judgment which appears to unite people scattered across the political spectrum, it is that the performance of government in meeting these challenges has not been distinguished. As Peter Drucker expressed it, "The greatest factor in the disenchantment with government is that government has not performed."[3] And this comes at a time when the pace of social and economic change necessitates effective governmental action.

Agreement dissolves, however, over questions about what should be done. Much of the political "debate" in recent years has consisted of sloganeering rather than reasoned political analysis. This is, in part, a reflection of what John Bunzel calls "anti-politics"—a hostile and contemptuous view of politics in a democratic society.[4] Thus conspiratorial theories about politics abound on the extreme Right and the extreme Left, along with equally bizarre solutions for political problems.[5] A disinclination to deal with real politics also characterizes the spokesmen for cultural "revolution" who assume that politics will be subsequently transformed through some mysterious but nevertheless inevitable process. And then, of course, one finds people whose political philosophy consists of the belief that the media, campus "freaks," minority groups, and permissive parents are responsible for all problems.

Meanwhile, political leaders have added to the confusion by driving the government's credibility to a distressingly low level. Even before the publication of the "Pentagon Papers" in June of 1971, many Americans were disinclined to believe government statements, particularly those relating to Southeast Asia.[6] Indeed, official political rhetoric has ofttimes been as banal, as mindless, and as self-serving as the more whimsical critiques from the extreme Right and the extreme Left. Even when it is not wholly untrue, the language of politics is too often insincere, adding to other offenses the debasement of language. George Orwell's indictment of a generation ago still holds:

> In our time, political speech and writing are largely the defense
> of the indefensible. . . . Thus political language has to consist largely
> of euphemism, question-begging and sheer cloudy vagueness. . . .
> The inflated style is itself a kind of euphemism. A mass of Latin
> words falls upon the facts like soft snow, blurring the outlines and
> covering up all the details.

It is extremely unlikely that the political "debate" of recent years has done much for the public's understanding of what needs to be done to improve the conduct of government. This may explain, at least in part, the popularity of apocalyptic solutions among certain groups. But the most prevalent effect has probably been to turn people away from politics altogether. When politics seems to ignore reason, the only defense may be resignation.

Sloganeering will not do much to improve politics or to solve the very serious problems which face American society, and it is improbable that a revolution will soon occur in the United States. In the long run, it has been noted, we are all dead, and this fact necessitates some greater attention to real politics, which is specific programs and policies. If there is to be any significant improvement in American politics during the 1970's, it will probably result from a program of rational, if not very romantic, political reform.

This does not mean, of course, that the pressures and demands occasioned by social change either should be resolved or can be resolved exclusively by government. There are some obvious practical limits on what government can expect to accomplish under even the most favorable circumstances. And it would appear that the dislocations of contemporary society are not well understood, nor is there widespread agreement on ends. But the immediate task remains of restoring public confidence in political institutions. And this may require that political institutions be altered in such a way that they can respond more effectively to the enormous problems of a national society.

RESPONSIVENESS AND DEMOCRATIC GOVERNMENT

Alexander Hamilton opened the defense of the proposed Constitution in Federalist Paper No. 1 by asking what he called the important question —". . . whether societies of men are really capable or not of establishing good government from reflection and choice, or whether they are forever destined to depend for their political constitutions on accident and force."

Since the establishment of the Constitution, America's political institutions have undergone considerable change. Technological developments, alterations in the social and economic context within which government operates, and the efforts of individuals with a variety of motives have had a significant impact on the size and scope of the federal government. With the notable exception of the Civil War, political institutions have in the past proved to be sufficiently flexible to adapt with some degree of success to the conflicts and tensions produced by social change.

These conflicts and tensions are obvious today, and an effective institutional response is necessary if they are to be managed. But the reform tradition in American politics indicates that the intrepid reformer should proceed with caution. Through most of our history, the reform debate has been dominated by what might be termed a populist predisposition—the idea that more democracy means better government. On the one hand, this has involved a long-term expansion of the suffrage. On the other, it has led to some rather questionable institutional arrangements.

The Progressive movement during the early part of the twentieth century provides some good examples of both these types of responses. First, the right to vote was extended to women, and direct popular election of senators was instituted. These were laudable achievements. Second, some "imaginative" institutional arrangements were adopted in many states—the direct primary, the referendum, initiative, and recall—to encourage greater public participation not only in party affairs but also in policy-making. The result of these innovations has usually been the reverse of what was hoped. Turnout in primary elections and referenda is considerably lower than turnout for general elections. Primaries, for example, often attract only 20-25 percent of the potential electorate or about half that participating in general elections. And while voter turnout in referenda varies greatly with the kind of issue involved, referendum issues typically attract fewer voters than regular elections, even when they are on the same ballot.[7] Rather than promoting majority rule, therefore, these devices have often functioned as the tools of minority pressure.

Reform is unlikely to achieve desired ends when it stems from narrow perspectives or from unwarranted assumptions about the electorate's interest in and information about politics. As E. E. Schattschneider has stated:

> *The problem is not how 180 million Aristotles can run a democracy, but how we can organize a community of 180 million ordinary people so that it remains sensitive to their needs. This is a problem of* leadership, organization, alternatives, and systems of responsibility and confidence.[8]

Politics is, after all, complex and ambiguous. It defies attempts at reducing serious questions to moralisms, and this means that proposals for reform must involve an understanding of how politics operates and of the utility of action in different areas and of varying magnitude. Professor Schattschneider's list of problems illustrates the broad perspective from which any serious analysis must proceed. And from this broad perspective, "power to the people" represents as empty a response as "the President knows best."

Democratic politics is bound to be undistinguished in the face of public indifference and mediocre leadership. The relationship between the public and government constitutes a major test for a democracy. As the authors of *The Real Majority* stated:

> *It is now the task of responsible politicians to attune themselves honestly to the legitimate desires of the voters and, in attun-*

ing themselves, reestablish their ability to lead. For the first task of democracy is to be responsive to the real majority of voters—without being repressive to minorities.

To lead the people, to lead the people in wisdom, is a fine day's work but a tricky business.[9]

Democratic government, then, must be responsive in the sense that it attempts to satisfy the legitimate demands of the governed. This does not mean that government must mirror precisely public opinion, nor does this mean that leadership is unnecessary. What is required is that effective links exist between public preferences and governmental action, that there be "concern in good faith by governments for public preferences and in dedication to mass interests."[10] To state the ethical imperative of democratic theory is simple, but to translate it into the real world of American politics is somewhat more difficult.

In his 1971 State of the Union message, President Nixon told Congress, "Let us give the people of America a chance, a bigger voice in deciding for themselves those questions that so greatly affect their lives." In an interview with C. L. Sulzberger of *The New York Times,* which was reported on March 10, 1971, the President seemed considerably less enthusiastic about the blessings of self-government:

I am certain a Gallup poll would show that the great majority of the people would want to pull out of Vietnam. But a Gallup poll would also show that a great majority of the people would want to pull three or more divisions out of Europe. And it would also show that a great majority of the people would cut our defense budget. Polls are not the answer.[11]

Even after one makes the customary allowances for political rhetoric, these two statements are clearly contradictory. They do, however, illustrate the difficulties which simplistic statements about "government by the people" are bound to raise.

There are certain procedures, such as the referendum, where the people can directly decide issues of public policy. Policy referenda, however, are not possible under the federal Constitution. And even in states and localities which allow referenda, relatively few questions are decided through the referendum procedure. In most cases, citizens do not directly carry out the public business. Instead, they empower others—elected and appointed officials—to perform this business for them.

RESPONSIVENESS AND INSTITUTIONAL LINKAGES

Direct democracy, then, is not the customary decision-making procedure in the United States, particularly at the national level. Thus the relationship between governmental decision-makers and the public represents the critical interactive process in a democracy. In his classic study of public opinion, V. O. Key described an analytical approach to the study of this interaction process:

> *At the outset one must discard simplistic concepts, such as the notion that in some way public opinion exudes from the mass of men and produces guide lines for governmental action. A complex interaction occurs, with government (and other centers of influence as well) affecting the form and content of opinion; and, in turn, public opinion may condition the manner, content, and timing of public action. Again, opinion may be of no effect, for many public actions seem to be beyond popular concern or influence. . . . Yet some of the relations between opinion and government are institutionalized. . . . [Among] these formalized means for give and take between government and opinion [are]: elections, political parties, pressure groups, and representative procedures.*[12]

Interaction can occur in a variety of ways, many of which are included in the formalized linkages to which Key refers. Responsiveness can be viewed as largely dependent upon the effectiveness of these linkages. It should be noted, however, that responsiveness involves not only the quality of public participation but also the nature of political leadership. The approach utilized here, then, is to look at some of the more important linkages involving individual political activities, group activities, and political leaders and decision-makers.

Individual Participation

There are innumerable ways in which individual citizens can participate in politics and thereby hope to influence government. One can, for example, vote in elections—the most prevalent type of formal participation. And, in recent years, there has been considerable change concerning the right to vote. The passage of the 1965 Voting Rights Act, for example, has resulted in the registration of approximately 1.5 million blacks in the South, and this has had a decided impact on national politics as well as on southern politics.[13] In 1971, the ratification of the 26th Amendment enfranchised about 11 million 18-20 year olds. One of the more intriguing questions relating to the 1972 elections concerns the possible impact of this youth vote. In all, some 25 million persons under age 25 will be potential first-time voters in 1972. There is debate about how many will actually vote, but the weak party ties and rather disparate political attitudes evidenced within this age group suggest that there will not be a bloc vote. Indeed, the youth vote may be even more polarized than is the case for older voters.

Other types of direct action vary from attempts to communicate one's preferences to attempts to compel certain types of official behavior. They include writing letters to or petitioning public officials; participating in demonstrations; contributing money to candidates or causes; bringing suit against public officials or agencies, and so on. In recent years, direct action has often taken the form of disruptive or even violent protest. The impact of this type of confrontation has been profound if not necessarily desirable. As with other forms of direct action, the politics of protest or of confrontation is a political strategy which seeks to influence governmental action. Whether such a strategy is efficacious or counterproductive, therefore, depends upon the governmental response. And it becomes particularly important to analyze these types of direct action as long-term strategies, since protest activity appears to be highly unstable.

The seeming attraction of protest politics points out one of the problems relating to individual participation. The opportunities for individual participation are quantitatively impressive. Many people feel, however, that individual activity has little effect upon governmental action. Thus not only are there significant numbers who are politically apathetic, but some critics maintain that even those who do participate have little real influence on government. Part One of this book will examine some of the important questions related to individual political activity and its effect on government.

Group Participation

Political parties and interest groups provide a second type of linkage between the public and government. By bringing together individuals with similar interests and policy preferences, parties and interest groups can serve as effective mechanisms for political action.

The political party, at least theoretically, offers an efficient mechanism for converting popular preferences into governmental action. First, it provides the electorate with a set of candidates who advocate certain common policy proposals. Second, if its appeal is successful and a sufficient number of its candidates are elected to provide control of the government, the party can enact these policy proposals. In the United States, of course, this conversion process is not nearly so efficient. Indeed, the performance of the two major parties, in terms of their relationship with the electorate and their ability to govern, has come under very serious attack. The linkage provided by the party system is, according to some observers, especially weak.

The interest group operates somewhat differently from the political party, and the criticism of some interest groups is that they are too effective. The interest group does not seek control of the government as such. Rather, it engages in a number of related activities designed to influence governmental policy. Interest groups can, for example, provide financial support to candidates. They can work continuously with executive agencies and congressional committees in developing public policy. They can resort to the courts to check executive or congressional actions.

The attacks on interest-group activities generally focus on the effects which these and similar activities have upon the democratic process. The organization and financial resources of certain groups may provide them with influence disproportionate to their numbers. In addition to the inequality of group activities and pressures, many people do not belong to special interest groups, and the question arises as to how they are to be represented in a political process which is heavily influenced by interest-group activities. The importance of interest-group linkages, then, raises questions about power, representativeness, and techniques. Group activity linkages will be studied in Part Two.

Leaders and Decision-Makers

Responding to the legitimate preferences of the public while at the same time providing leadership is, of course, a delicate and difficult job. It requires perception, competence, and an acceptance of democratic norms and procedures.

The relationships between the public and the several branches of government differ. The judiciary and the bureaucracy are more insulated from public scrutiny than the President or members of Congress. Each of these "branches," however, plays a significant role in policy-making, so each is involved in the effecting of responsiveness.

First, of course, the relationships among the branches provide for certain types of reciprocal control. When these controls become imbalanced, political responsibility is diminished. For example, the President's power to make war can be checked by Congress' exercise of its constitutional powers, including the power to declare war, to raise and support the armed services, and to provide monies for the conduct of military operations. Most members of Congress are now convinced that the failure of the House and Senate to exercise these fundamental constitutional duties seriously in the past has led to a severe imbalance in effective foreign policy powers between the White House and Capitol Hill.

In a similar sense, the bureaucracy presents problems of responsibility and control. While the President heads the executive branch, his effective control of bureaucratic behavior is reduced by congressional and interest-group influence upon executive agencies.

The linkage between the public and government, then, is dependent first upon the relationships among the various branches of government, particularly the adequacy of reciprocal controls, since these factors affect political responsibility.

Second, institutional characteristics and procedures affect the linkage process. In Congress, for example, the seniority system and filibuster are anti-majoritarian devices. It has been suggested that the advisory channels in the White House insulate and isolate the President so that his perception of public opinion is distorted. Even the most well-intentioned leadership will inevitably become less responsive if it operates under conditions which serve to blur public needs and preferences.

To summarize, the internal characteristics of each branch and its relationships with other branches of the government affect its responsiveness. In Part Three, some problems and proposed solutions relating to leadership and governmental decision-making will be examined.

NOTES: INTRODUCTION

1. John Corry, "The Politics of Style," *Harper's* (November, 1970), p. 62.

2. Yevgeny Yevtushenko, "Being Famous Isn't Pretty," *Harper's* (July, 1971), p. 58.

3. Peter F. Drucker, "The Sickness of Government," *The Public Interest,* No. 14 (Winter, 1969), 7. Moreover, a recent study found that Americans believe that the country has slipped badly in the last five years, and almost one-half of them fear that current unrest and lack of unity are serious enough to endanger its survival. A. H. Cantril and C. W. Roll, Jr., *Hopes and Fears of the American People* (Potomac Associates, 1971).

4. John H. Bunzel, *Anti-Politics in America* (Vintage Books, 1970), p. 3.

5. One misses the full and fantastic flavor of these groups by not reading their literature. Nice second-hand treatments, however, are available in Bunzel, *Anti-Politics in America,* especially chapters 2 and 3, and in Daniel Bell, *The Radical Right* (Doubleday, 1963).

6. A CBS poll, taken after the Laos "incursion" of early 1971, found that a majority of respondents did not believe the Nixon administration's claim that no American ground troops were involved. "Credibility" problems also characterized the Johnson administration during much of its tenure.

7. See Frank J. Sorauf, *Party Politics in America* (Little, Brown, 1968), pp. 185-186.

8. E. E. Schattschneider, *The Semi-Sovereign People* (Holt, Rinehart and Winston, 1960), p. 138.

9. Richard M. Scammon and Ben J. Wattenberg, *The Real Majority* (Coward-McCann, 1970), p. 304.

10. V. O. Key, Jr., *Public Opinion and American Democracy* (Knopf, 1965), p. 412.

11. As quoted in "I. F. Stone's Bi-Weekly," XIX (March 22, 1971), 1.

12. Key, *Public Opinion and American Democracy,* pp. 409-410.

13. See Congressional Quarterly, *Civil Rights: Progress Report 1970* (1971), pp. 67-74.

Part One
INDIVIDUAL PARTICIPATION

ELECTIONS

*In America the people appoints the legislative and the
executive power. . . . The American institutions are democratic,
not only in their principle but in all their consequences. . . .
The people is therefore the real directing power; and although
the form of government is representative, it is evident that the
opinions, the prejudices, the interests, and even the passions of the
community are hindered by no durable obstacles from exercising
a perpetual influence on society.*

—Alexis de Tocqueville[1]

Free elections are the distinguishing features of a democracy. They represent constitutionally prescribed procedures for conferring power, and they
are the basis for democratic legitimacy. In the United States, over half a
million officials are elected to local, state, and national government posts.
There are elections for legislative, executive, and, in a majority of states,
judicial posts, as well as for numerous boards and authorities. Moreover,
general elections are not the whole story, for there are primaries and referenda, and occasionally the initiative or recall election. It is probable that
"no electorate in the democratic world is more frequently driven to the polls
than is the American."[2]

In addition to the large number of elections in which Americans are
expected to participate, there has been a gradual erosion of the legal and
extra-legal barriers to voting. During the first half of the nineteenth century, property and tax-paying qualifications for voting were eliminated by
the states. The twentieth century has seen the franchise extended to women;
the right to vote has finally become a reality for many black citizens; the
voting age has been lowered to eighteen in federal elections and state elections; the poll tax has been abolished; state residence requirements for
voting in presidential elections have been eased.

For many years, the operative question regarding elections was "who
should be allowed to vote." As more and more groups have won this right,
the discussion has moved to the character and significance of elections.
Despite the quantitative impressiveness of American elections, there are a
number of basic criticisms relating to their democratic character.

Measuring turnout in the United States is complicated by difficulties
in defining the eligible electorate with any exactitude. If turnout is measured in terms of the percentage of adult citizens participating in elections,
however, certain facts are apparent. First, turnout varies by type of elec-

tion, with presidential elections attracting the highest turnout (between 60 and 70 percent). Second, even in elections which attract a large percentage of eligible voters, turnout varies by social group. It is higher among upper status groups (those who are better educated, earn higher incomes, and hold a higher occupational status). The incidence of non-voting among persons with a grade-school education, for example, is almost three times higher than that for college-educated persons.[3]

The potential influence of elections is sharply reduced by these variations in turnout, since the least powerful groups—in social and economic terms—are the least likely to use the ballot. One interpretation is that these groups do not feel that the ballot represents an effective mechanism for improving their lives.

One begins, therefore, with the fact of unequal participation, and it is probable that psychological as well as administrative factors must be considered in trying to account for this.[4] The essay by Gerald Pomper adds another dimension to the problem faced by lower status groups. In his analysis of electoral behavior and party platforms, Pomper argues that elections are effective control mechanisms and that they do provide for indirect popular influence upon governmental elites. At the same time, however, elections represent only a limited means for effecting social change, so that the problems of racial discrimination, urban decay, and foreign wars require a commitment of political will by the public and the elite if they are to be solved.

Elections represent, then, only a partially effective mechanism for governmental responsiveness, since the influence involved is largely indirect. Responsible government is also diminished, however, by institutional features which lead to inequality in people's votes. Until the Supreme Court established the "one-man, one-vote" principle for the apportionment of seats in the House of Representatives, malapportioned districts served to exaggerate the influence of rural areas and diminish the impact of the urban vote.

A similar type of inequality, with a reverse bias, continues to exist under the electoral college system for electing the President. Not only does the electoral college distort the relative influence of very large and very small states, but the winner-take-all system effectively cancels minority votes in every state. The article by William T. Gossett, a member of the American Bar Association's Commission on Electoral College Reform, presents the case for direct election of the President. Mr. Gossett challenges the arguments against direct election and argues that direct election would increase voter equality and that its side effects (particularly on the party system) would also be positive.

Perhaps the most important questions concerning federal elections and particularly presidential elections relate to the impact of television. First, and most obvious, television has produced enormous increases in campaign spending. According to the most comprehensive study of campaign financing yet completed, campaign costs increased by 43 percent between 1952 and 1964 and by 50 percent between 1964 and 1968.[5] Total campaign spending was estimated at $300 million in 1968.

The costs of presidential campaigns reflect most clearly the impact of television, but some Senate races have also reached extraordinary limits. According to the FCC, over $58 million was spent on political broadcast advertising in 1968 (this is considered a conservative figure). In the California Senate race, over $1 million was spent on TV alone.[6] Campaign costs of this magnitude have at least two obvious effects. First, there is not even reasonably equal access to public office. Second, except for extremely wealthy candidates, an individual running for office must usually rely upon big contributors. Whatever else one might wish to conclude, this type of electoral bankrolling is inevitably corrupting. The statement by John Gardner, chairman of Common Cause and former Secretary of HEW, deals with three aspects of the campaign financing problem—subsidy or reduction of campaign costs to the candidate; ceilings on giving and spending; and full disclosure—and suggests how they might be handled.

Television also has usurped many of the functions previously assigned to the party organizations, and it has certainly added a new dimension to the national nominating conventions. The selection by Mendelsohn and Crespi deals with the problems noted here and suggests some possible solutions, with a particular emphasis on realizing some positive benefits from polls and television.

The importance of free elections in a democracy is inestimable. One does not have to be a utopian, however, to realize that some rather fundamental problems characterize the electoral process. Even with the reforms discussed in this section, elections alone cannot guarantee governmental responsiveness. If elections in the United States constituted programmatic mandates, voters could directly affect government policy. For this to occur, certain conditions would need to be fulfilled: "(1) Governmental institutions would facilitate the implementation of popular verdicts in official policy; (2) voters would be concerned primarily with future policy questions; (3) majority preferences on these questions as expressed in elections could be ascertained."[7] "However," as Professor Pomper goes on to note, "in the United States at least, none of these three conditions is substantially satisfied."[8]

CONTROLS AND INFLUENCE IN AMERICAN ELECTIONS (EVEN 1968)

Gerald M. Pomper

In the Presidential election of 1968, many doubted the efficacy of their choice. The Committee of Inquiry, formed to endorse a candidate responsive to black interests, declined to choose among Humphrey, Nixon, or Wallace. Opponents of the Vietnam war, deprived of the target of Lyndon Johnson, saw little difference between the Democratic and Republican policies or candidates. After the death of Robert Kennedy and the defeat of Eugene McCarthy, the alienation of thousands of the young increased.

These events have raised again perennial questions of the meaning, and desirability, of elections. Voting is clearly one of the principal means by which elites are related to masses.

THE ROLE OF ELECTIONS

There have been two broad and opposing positions on the effects of elections on policy outputs. One position sees elections as directly controlling public policy. In the fullest elaboration of this theory, elections are considered as mandates, or binding popular determination of future governmental programs. The opposing position sees elections as indirect influences on public policy, which are particularly important as protections of the vital rights and interests of the voters.

In the American institutional context, direct control of a mandate is difficult to imagine. The impact of any or many elections is limited by the diverse checks and balances of the national government, the "multiple cracks" of a federal system, the proliferation of nonelected public authorities, the powers of bureaucracies and courts, and the undisciplined party system. However, the very dispersal of power which makes control unlikely also makes influence more probable. In the conflicts and bargaining of branches, states, authorities, bureaucracies, courts, and parties, some agency is likely to support the vital interests of any significant number of voters.

Voting studies lead to similar conclusions. Voters do not make general policy choices in elections. Asked to describe the parties and their policies, only a small minority spontaneously evaluate them in terms of a political ideology. Depending on the looseness of the definitions employed, only 2.5% to 15% of the electorate can be considered ideologues who "clearly perceived a fundamental liberal-conservative continuum on which various of the political objects could be located."[1] Moreover, there is no meaningful coherence in mass attitudes toward specific policy questions. Opinions on federal aid to education, for example, show no correlation to opinions on federal aid to housing. Among many individuals, indeed, opinions on the same questions show only random consistency over short periods of time.

By contrast, the voting studies do yield evidence consistent with the alternative theory of elections as means of protecting vital interests. For 45% of the electorate, Democrats and Republicans are liked or disliked because of the group benefits they provide. As a whole, the electorate lacks conceptual clarity .in regard to public policies. On particular programs, however, there are concentrated "issue publics" which are knowledgeable and able to defend their specific interest. Concern for these special interests can even overcome the great influence of party identification. In the South in 1964, for example, whites expressed increased loyalty to the Democratic Party. The perceived threat to segregation nevertheless brought a marked change in "party image" and a greatly increased Republican vote.

Furthermore, while the voters are not prepared to decide policy questions prospectively, they are ready to judge the parties retrospectively on the basis of their performance. For a fourth of the population, politics is viewed in terms of the nature of the times. A party in power during periods of peace and prosperity is praised; a party associated with depression or war is condemned. Voting provides a means by which groups can effectively provide feedback and gain attention to their demands. Thus, as V. O. Key argued, "Governments must worry, not about the meaning of past elections, but about their fate at future elections."[2]

Given American institutions and voting behavior, ballots are unlikely to be means of direct control, but can be a method for indirect influence over policy. Elections are best considered as control mechanisms. In regard to policy, their principal function is to set boundaries—to provide legitimation for elite initiatives, to prevent actions which infringe on perceived vital interests, and to pass a retrospective judgment on these programs. Voting does not define the entire political system. It is one, but only one, vital input, an input most readily used by unorganized and unprivileged masses in attempts to gain attention to their needs and wants. This function can be fulfilled in various ways.

Often, elections are most important for the actions they deter elites from undertaking. Thus, de Tocqueville found democracies hobbled in conducting foreign policy. Changing public moods made it difficult to "regulate the details of an important undertaking, persevere in a fixed design, and work out its execution in spite of serious obstacles." Defenders of a long-term American involvement in Vietnam could easily agree. For better or worse, electoral pressure in 1968 made inevitable the withdrawal of United States troops.

Similarly, the threat of popular reprisal may limit the ability of elites to make basic, although desirable, changes in existing practices, such as British union rules, Indian caste practices, or American racial discrimination. More satisfying is the restraint electoral power places on arbitrary treatment of the enfranchised. Police protection of Negroes, for example, has been most evident where and when blacks voted, while police brutality and condoning of lynching has been most frequent where and when blacks were disfranchised. Positive actions have not always been stimulated by the ballot, but fairness and restraint have been encouraged.

In particular elections, the significant effect of the vote is the popular legitimation of party coalition. The electorate chooses a party as well as a candidate, and the composition and commitments of the winning coalition will greatly shape the course of future events. The voters thus indirectly affect governmental action by supporting or rejecting the men associated with these actions.

A majority party coalition does not exist for one election only in most instances. American history typically has seen the domination of one party over long periods of time, such as the period of Republican hegemony from 1896 to 1928, or the era of Democratic dominance since the New Deal. During these periods, whatever the outcome of particular contests, the basic party coalitions and their voting support by geographic areas and social groups remain relatively constant.

On some occasions, more extensive and long range changes take place. The basic voting support of each party shifts, resulting in a "critical election." The majority party is now supported by a new coalition of voters. It must recognize different demands from the past. Voters intervene decisively to change the political terms of reference. Victory in a critical election does not provide detailed policy instructions for the winning party, but it produces an opportunity to meet the new needs of the time and the desires of the new coalition.

Another effect of elections is the manner in which they condition the policy initiatives of party elites. Attempting to win votes, the parties offer proposals to the electorate in their party platforms. Indirect popular influence over policy can be facilitated in two ways through the platforms. First, the documents may provide a means by which the voters deliberately choose parties and their policies. Second, the platform may be significant even if not widely read. The campaign manifesto may reflect program initiatives made by parties in anticipation of voter needs and demands. The electorate's choice of a party would then become a choice of policies as well.

To be significant, platforms must be specific, policy-oriented, and relevant to the voters' concerns. Since voters tend to make their party choices on the basis of performance, they would facilitate a comparison of the two parties' positions and actions, with special attention to the merits and defects of the incumbents' record. They would also indicate the future positions of the party, specifically enough to be meaningful to the voter, particularly on issues of immediate concern.

The Presidential election of 1968 offers valuable data for analysis of the effects of elections. These data suggest that the period of 1964-1968 contains a pair of critical elections, changing the political shape of the nation. An analysis of the major party platforms of 1968 provides further evidence of this change, while also allowing some insight into the nature of platforms and elite-mass linkages.

A CRITICAL ELECTION IN 1968?

The concept of a critical election, first introduced by Key, is well-known. Such decisive contests "reveal a sharp alteration of pre-existing cleavages within the electorate. Moreover, and perhaps this is the truly differentiating characteristic of this sort of election, the realignment made manifest in the voting in such elections seems to persist for several succeeding elections."[3]

A major difficulty with this definition is the restraint it places on any attempt to classify contemporary elections. The investigator may suspect that he is living in a critical period, but the established criterion requires him to wait many years before he can make a definite judgment. By the time enough elections have passed to demonstrate persistence of an electoral change, the conclusion that such realignment has indeed occurred is almost trivial. For example, it requires no great insight for present-day scholars to assert that critical change occurred at the time of the New Deal. It is more risky, but more useful, to be able to make assertions about the character of the elections of 1964 and 1968.

To attempt such analysis, five statistical indicators of critical elections were developed. All measure the continuity in the geographical state-by-state distribution of the Democratic party vote for President. A critical election would be indicated by: (1) a low linear correlation between the election results in the given year and the preceding election year; (2) a low correlation between the results in the given year and the average results in the four preceding elections; (3) low correlations between the results in the given year and those in a consecutive series of preceding or succeeding elections; (4) a high (absolute) mean difference between state results in the given year and state averages in the preceding four elections; and (5) a high standard deviation of these differences.

By these standards, the election of 1964 appeared in earlier analyses to be a critical election. Correlation to the election of 1960 yielded a coefficient of only .31, and correlation to the previous four elections provided a correlation of $-.44$. There were no high correlations to previous consecutive elections. The average mean difference of state results was 16.82%, and the standard deviation was 9.00%. The significance of these figures may be better grasped by comparing them to the results for an election such as 1940, in which party loyalty was unchanged and dominant. Correlation to the previous election was .92, and to the previous four elections was .94. Furthermore, the 1940 results were highly correlated to two previous elections and to two succeeding elections. The average mean difference of state votes was only 7.78%, and the standard deviation but 4.16%.

Aside from these statistical indicators, there were other manifestations of critical change in the 1964 election. Detailed study of the South and the Northeast indicated great changes within the electorate of these areas. The intensely ideological character of the Goldwater campaign suggested a basic alteration of the practice of American politics, and the most thorough study of this campaign[4] discovered some meaningful changes in party identification as well. The overwhelming victory of Lyndon Johnson and the legislative innovations of the 89th Congress duplicated the pattern of previous critical elections which led to policy innovations.

The election of 1968 now provides data to test the persistence of the upheavals of the Goldwater-Johnson contest. If the 1964 election were but a quirk in American politics, it should stand alone statistically. If it did change the shape of the system, it would be revealed by continuity between the 1964 and 1968 results. The data support the latter hypothesis.

When the Humphrey Democratic vote is compared to the Johnson returns, there is a high degree of continuity. The correlation coefficient is .86, indicating that the sources of Democratic and Republican strength remained relatively unchanged from 1964 to 1968. The overall results were quite different, of course, as the entire nation moved considerably away from the party of Johnson and Humphrey. The important point, however, is that the character of each party's geographical coalition did not change greatly, although the size of the coalitions changed.

The other indices also indicate increased stability in the political system. Correlation to the four-election average rose to .37, the average state difference decreased to 9.44%, and the standard deviation dropped to 7.70%. The figures are still historically high, but this result is inevitable since a four-election average includes contests before 1964. The movement toward more normal figures is the more significant result.

The vote for George Wallace has a significant effect on these measures. If we artificially reunite the Democratic party by combining the Humphrey and Wallace vote, we then find a negative relationship between the combined 1968 Democratic vote and the 1964 vote for Johnson (r = −.37). This combined vote, however, shows a stronger relationship to the four-election averages than the Humphrey vote alone. The correlation to the four-election average is .48, the average mean difference is but 7.26%, and the standard deviation is 8.29%.

What do these statistics mean? They indicate that Wallace and Humphrey divided the old Democratic coalition into two parts. If they could be recombined in fact, as we have done statistically, there would have been no critical election in 1964, and the Democrats would continue their majority status on the same basis as has existed from the New Deal. In reality, the parts are divided. Part of the old Democratic coalition, represented by the Wallace vote and concentrated geographically in the South, has left the party, probably permanently. This element voted for Goldwater in 1964 in large numbers, and then for Wallace in 1968. The result is a transformation of the Democratic Party in 1964 and the persistence of that transformation in 1968. Despite the change in the environment and in events during the four-year period, the geographical basis of the party remained relatively constant, with new strength particularly in the Northeast and with unusual weakness in the South.

Evidence in support of these conclusions is offered in table 1, which shows the correlations between the results in 1968, as well as 1964 and 1960, with selected previous elections. The similarity of the Johnson and Humphrey votes is evident. The sectional character of the change is emphasized by comparisons of the latter-day votes with earlier sectional elections, such as 1948, 1896, and 1860. The division of the former Democratic coalition is shown by the relatively high correlations of the combined Humphrey and Wallace votes with the elections of the New Deal period. The Kennedy vote of 1960 is seen as transitional.

TABLE 1. CORRELATION OF DEMOCRATIC VOTE IN PRESIDENTIAL ELECTIONS, 1960-1968

Previous Elections	Humphrey 1968	Humphrey+ Wallace 1968	Johnson 1964	Kennedy 1960
1964	.86	-.37	1.00	.32
1960	.32	.46	.32	1.00
1956	-.42	.65	-.47	.38
1952	-.33	.84	-.39	.56
1948 (Truman only)	.39	-.44	.65	.17
1948 (Truman+Thurmond)	-.57	.76	-.68	.21
1944	-.54	.79	-.68	.30
1940	-.60	.75	-.67	.27
1936	-.68	.60	-.74	.15
1932	-.69	.58	-.72	.09
1928	-.38	.66	-.56	.22
1896	-.66	.23	-.68	-.16
1860 (Douglas only)	.44	-.40	.40	-.01
1860 (Douglas+Breckinridge)	-.71	.42	-.61	.00
1856	-.74	.38	-.60	-.06

Statistical evidence thus provides some reason for inferring that a critical election occurred in 1964 and that the pattern established in that year has persisted to 1968. It is still not clear whether the Democrats or Republicans are now the majority party. Both have won one of these two elections, and either result theoretically could be a deviation from the new norm. It would appear most likely, however, that the Democrats remain the majority party, subject to any innovations of the Nixon administration. The distribution of party identification still heavily favors the Democrats, although there have been major changes within the voting coalition. New voters have been won in suburban areas, among professionals and among blacks, replacing the votes lost among manual workers and Southerners. It should also be underlined that the Democrats nearly won the 1968 election, although short-term influences—urban riots, Vietnam, the Chicago convention, a third party movement, and the Humphrey candidacy—were severely unfavorable. Only a dominant party could be expected to survive and nearly overcome such disadvantages.

THE PLATFORMS OF 1968

Change in the parties can also be seen in their platforms, which are studied by means of content analysis. Each sentence of the major party manifestos is placed in one of three major categories, which are further subdivided into eleven minor categories. The categories are:

(1) Rhetorical or factual statements; (2) evaluations of the parties' records and past achievements, divided into four subcategories: general approval, general criticism, policy approval, and policy criticism; and (3) statements of future policies, divided into six subcategories, in order of increasing commitment and specificity: rhetorical pledges, general promises, pledges of continuity, expressions of goals and concerns, pledges of action, and detailed promises. The pledges of future action are also grouped into nine substantive areas.

The platforms of 1968 show both similarities to and differences from the platforms of the previous twenty years. In the general distribution of platform statements, presented in table 2, somewhat greater emphasis is placed on the pledges of future action, particularly in the Republican party.

TABLE 2. CONTENT DISTRIBUTION OF SELECTED PARTY PLATFORMS
(In percentages of designated platform)

Category	1968 Dem.	Rep.	1964 Dem.	Rep.	1960 Dem.	Rep.	1948 Dem.	Rep.	1948-64 Median
Rhetoric	21	13	20	11	20	21	12	23	16.5
Evaluations									
General approval	9	5	14	5	4	7	11	3	6
General criticism	1	6	1	12	7	1	3	4	4
Policy approval	14	2	48	2	4	13	10	8	10.5
Policy criticism	1	9	1	25	11	1	8	1	5
Future Policy	53	65	15	44	53	56	56	61	47.5
Number of Statements	822	536	941	414	795	519	205	159	5200

This pattern is due in part to the G.O.P.'s platform theme, "We must think anew and act anew." It is also a reflection of the changing demands placed on the parties by the unusual events and problems faced by the nation in 1968.

In their evaluations of the past, the parties followed an established pattern. As was true in almost all previous documents of the previous twenty years, the emphasis was on the record of the incumbent party. In 1968, as in the earlier period, the frequencies of platform statements assumed the following order: approvals by the in-party, criticisms by the out-party, approvals by the out-party, criticisms by the in-party. The debate is over the record of the executive party. It is not a contrast between two different sets of policies argued during the past four years.

This pattern is in keeping with the voters' own characteristic emphasis on retrospective judgments. The voters pass on the actual policies which they have experienced. The platforms are an aid to this consideration, praising or damning those policies as is respectively appropriate for the in-party and the out-party. It should also be noted that, as in the past, policy evaluations predominate over general comments on parties and leaders. Voters are thereby helped to see if the parties have acted to provide the group benefits and protection which they seek.

Continuities and changes are also evidenced in the pledges of future action made in the 1968 platforms. The topical distribution of pledges presented in table 3 is distinctive in the last three categories of welfare, government, and civil rights. By 1968, issues concerning black voters were no longer the matters of legal equality and nondiscrimination included in the heading of civil rights. Instead, they consisted of welfare questions, such as anti-poverty programs and aid to the cities. By 1968, the new issue of "law and order" had arisen, and this change is also reflected in the increased concern for governmental questions.

TABLE 3. TOPICAL DISTRIBUTION OF FUTURE PLEDGES IN SELECTED PLATFORMS (in percentages of designated platform)

Topic	1968		1964		1960		1948		1944-64
	Dem.	Rep.	Dem.	Rep.	Dem.	Rep.	Dem.	Rep.	Total
Foreign	12	17	11	26	19	14	18	22	17
Defense	5	5	10	20	4	10	5	6	7
Economics	18	15	13	11	15	14	17	20	15
Labor	4	5	11	3	5	5	7	2	5
Agriculture	9	6	6	7	7	9	12	7	10
Resources	7	7	9	5	13	8	10	9	11
Welfare	25	24	24	8	18	19	17	12	15
Government	18	18	8	13	10	10	8	17	11
Civil Rights	2	2	8	7	7	11	6	5	9
Number of Pledges	439	350	145	183	425	289	114	97	2,245

A key question about platform pledges of future policy is their degree of specificity. Those with meaning to the voters tend to be concentrated in the four subcategories from pledges of continuity to detailed promises. In past manifestos, pledges of this character have constituted 62% of the category, and this proportion was continued in both parties' programs for 1968 (61% of the Republican and 64% of the Democratic platforms). Detailed comparisons can be made by constructing a "mean pledge weight" for each topic in each platform. The resulting statistic can vary from 1.0, if all pledges were rhetorical, to 6.0, if all promises were detailed. The calculated figures are presented in table 4.[5]

The Democratic platform for 1968 shows a familiar pattern. Pledges are most definite in the areas of immediate and tangible interest to the voters —welfare, labor, agriculture, and natural resources, with civil rights in a middling position. Areas involving intangible and more ideological questions, such as foreign policy, defense, government, including law and order, and broad economic policy are handled through more vague statements. In this case, the party has responded to the particularistic interests of voters by including specific pledges on these topics in its platforms. Such pledges are the documentary expression of its concern for popular needs, and its recognition of the importance of group benefits in motivating the voters.

TABLE 4. "MEAN PLEDGE WEIGHTS," BY TOPICS, FOR SELECTED PLATFORMS

Topic	1968 Dem.	1968 Rep.	1964 Dem.	1964 Rep.	1960 Dem.	1960 Rep.	1948 Dem.	1948 Rep.	1944-64 Mean
Foreign	3.4	3.6	3.5	3.7	2.8	3.0	3.8	2.2	3.0
Defense	2.8	3.2	2.9	3.5	3.3	3.3	2.2	3.0	3.0
Economics	3.2	3.6	2.4	3.3	3.5	3.4	2.4	2.7	3.2
Labor	4.8	3.0	3.8	3.8	3.9	4.0	5.2	3.0	4.1
Agriculture	3.7	3.5	3.7	3.9	3.2	3.8	3.9	3.0	3.5
Resources	4.0	4.1	3.8	4.0	3.9	4.1	4.2	4.0	3.8
Welfare	3.9	3.8	3.3	4.4	4.2	4.2	4.6	3.3	4.0
Government	2.5	3.2	2.9	3.0	3.0	3.7	2.7	3.0	3.2
Civil Rights	3.5	2.3	2.8	2.2	3.8	4.1	4.7	4.4	3.3
Platform Mean	3.4	3.5	3.3	3.6	3.5	3.7	4.0	3.0	3.4
Number of Pledges	439	350	145	183	425	289	114	97	2,245

The Republicans present a different pattern in some respects. While there has been some change from the strongly ideological effort of 1964, echoes of that campaign are audible in the 1968 platform. In the areas of tangible benefits, there actually has been a decrease from the specific pledges of 1964, although these changes are generally in the direction of moderating and obscuring previously forthright conservative positions. In the more general areas, continued specificity is evident. The notable vagueness and neglect of the 1964 platform on civil rights is continued, with the only specific points relating not to Negroes, but to the immigration laws.

Further comparisons can be made between the parties by noting differences in the amount of attention they devote to different topics. Attention is gauged by adding to the "mean pledge weight," a figure indicating the relative percentage of the platform devoted to a particular topic.[6] In 1968, Democrats devoted more attention than Republicans to the more tangible issues of labor, agriculture, and welfare. Again, Republicans showed a greater concern for the more ideological issues of foreign, defense, and general economic policy, as well as issues of government, particularly law and order. Although similar to past patterns, the 1968 platforms indicate that the Democrats are becoming increasingly a party composed of a coalition of discrete interests, and the Republicans more one of ideological unity.

A sharp break from the past is apparent in the pledges on civil rights, although the small number requires caution in interpretation. In the past, the parties have matched one another in the degree of specificity, and often the content, of their pledges in this area. In 1968, the Democrats presented pledges of some specificity, although they made few statements. The Republicans not only made few promises, but they were almost entirely rhetorical in character. The platforms may be another indication of the new character of the Republican party, particularly its reliance on a strong Southern element. Both the earlier analysis of the changing geographical distribution of the vote and this analysis of civil rights provisions lends support to the belief that the Republicans have turned to a new base below the Mason-Dixon line and that they will no longer openly seek black votes.

Two major conclusions can be drawn from the study of the 1968 major-party platforms. First, as in previous years, the platforms provide a possible linkage between elite and mass. They present to the voters differing evaluations of the record of the incumbents. They concentrate on policy questions rather than the mindless rhetoric commonly assumed. In their future promises, pledges tend toward a meaningful degree of specificity, particularly in regard to those tangible benefits of most concern to the voters.

The 1968 platforms in particular also reveal the responsiveness of the parties to innovations in American policies. The relative attention devoted to the various subjects has been modified, reflecting new interests and demands by voters. In a time of change, more stress is placed on promises of future action. The altered coalitions of the parties, previously suggested in analysis of the voting returns, is also reflected in the emphases and contents of their platforms. Democratic party stress on economic, welfare, and racial benefits, and increased Republican attention to foreign policy and governmental questions indicate the development of new party alignments.

CONCLUSIONS

This analysis of the 1968 election provides some evidence of the indirect influence of elections on policy outputs. Statistical measures indicate that the voters are dissolving the bands of political loyalty which have constrained them since the New Deal. New coalitions of voters began to form in the 1964 election, and the new coalitions have been continued into the 1968 elections. These changes on the part of the voters can provide the popular support for a new elite coalition to initiate policies to meet the evident public needs of the nation.

The parties have also begun to display some responsiveness to public demands. The 1968 platforms were not simply repetitions of old and unfulfilled promises. The parties showed some awareness of the real problems of American society and some awareness of the existence of new voter alignments. In these two ways at least, elections have been shown to be a linkage between the mass and the elite.

In a time of crisis for the political system, however, it would be foolish to close on a note of complacency. Those unhappy with the choices and results of the 1968 campaign surely had good cause for their discontents. If changes are evident, it is not yet clear that innovations will be sufficiently rapid and decisive to meet the problems. It is not yet clear if there is enough political will in either mass or elite to meet the problems of racial division, urban decay, and foreign wars. It is not yet clear whether the Nixon administration will be any more successful than the Johnson administration in redeeming its most critical promises to diminish poverty and to end the war in Vietnam.

Even if these questions are successfully resolved, elections will remain a limited, although vital, means of effecting social change. Ultimately subject to the control of popular majorities, elections are not a sufficient means of achieving the goals of a distinct and permanent minority, particularly black voters in America. In a capitalist economy, votes and governmental action alone cannot assure economic progress. In a society of inevitably unequal status, the egalitarianism of the vote is only one resource for progress. Elections do provide a link between governed and governors, but forging a grid of interdependent relationships remains the unfinished business of American democracy.

DIRECT POPULAR ELECTION OF THE PRESIDENT

William T. Gossett

One of the most vital issues facing our nation is reform of the process by which the President and Vice President of the United States are elected. The House of Representatives has given an overwhelming 339-to-70 approval to a constitutional amendment embodying the recommendations of the American Bar Association's Commission on Electoral College Reform, which were adopted by the Association's House of Delegates in 1967 and which provide for the direct popular election of the President and Vice President.

President Nixon, who favored the direct election reform but considered it politically unachievable, now has said, "It is clear that unless the Senate follows the lead of the House, all opportunity for reform will be lost this year and possibly for years to come." The direct election amendment now is before the Senate, where action is needed to send it to the states for ratification.

The Presidential election of 1968 demonstrated the potential hazards of our present electoral college system and confirmed the conclusion of the Association's commission that the "electoral college method of electing a President of the United States is archaic, undemocratic, complex, ambiguous, indirect, and dangerous."

If there had been a shift of a relatively few popular votes in Ohio and Missouri, or if President Nixon had lost California, or if George C. Wallace had carried three border states, no Presidential candidate would have had a majority of the electoral votes. The electors pledged to Mr. Wallace would have held the balance of power, and he would have been tempted to play the role of President-maker. If he had decided against that role and his electors had voted for him, then the choice of President would have shifted to the House of Representatives under an inequitable one-state, one-vote formula susceptible to political wheeling and dealing and frustration of the popular will. The twenty-six least populated states, representing 16 per cent of the nation's total population, would have had the power to elect the President. It is conceivable that no candidate might have been able to obtain the votes of twenty-six states by inauguration day and that a Vice President selected by the Senate would have had to assume the powers and duties of the President. It is also conceivable that the House and Senate might have selected a split ticket by inauguration day. It is also conceivable that neither house might have been able to make a choice, in which event the Speaker of the House of Representatives would have become the Acting President.

The subject of electoral reform is not new. No sooner was the Constitution adopted than proposals were introduced in Congress to reform the electoral college. The first was introduced in 1797, and since then more than 500 proposals have been offered. The major plans of reform—the district, proportional, automatic and direct-vote plans—have their roots in proposals introduced in Congress during the nineteenth century.

The workings of the electoral college over the past 190 years show that it is something completely different from the institution envisioned by the Framers. Not until the final weeks of the Constitutional Convention was the electoral college adopted. Election by Congress was rejected because it was believed that the President would be subservient to the legislative branch and it opened the door for "intrigue, cabal or faction."[1] A direct vote by the people was criticized on the grounds that the people were too "uninformed" and would be "misled by a few designing men." One delegate said that an election by the people would be like referring a "trial of colours to a blind man."[2] What seemed to move the delegates to accept the electoral system were certain practical considerations, dictated not by political ideals but by the social realities of the time—realities that no longer exist.

The electoral college was envisioned by the Framers as a kind of elite gathering in which the most distinguished and talented persons in the various states would participate. These electors would deliberate and cast an informed and independent vote for President.[3] Because the large states would have considerable influence in the electoral voting, the Framers, in an effort to allay the fears of the small states, provided for the House of Representatives to choose the President, with each state having the same influence, when no candidate received a majority of the electoral votes. The convention debates indicate that many of the Framers were of the view that most elections would be thrown into Congress.

The design of the Framers in creating the electoral college was not fulfilled. Political parties appeared and the electors' role became a purely mechanical one of voting for their party's candidate. As they became partisan functionaries, their names and reputations became far less known to the citizens than those of the candidates. The Constitution having left to the states the right to determine the manner of selecting the electors, in the first elections a number of states gave the right of choice to the members of their legislatures rather than to the people. It was not until late in the nineteenth century that every state had entrusted the right of choice to the people. Today, of course, due to state law, the people choose the electors, who are expected to register the will of their constituents in the electoral college.

DEFECTS OF PRESENT SYSTEM SHOWN BY EXPERIENCE

Experience has shown that the electoral college is riddled with defects that could operate to frustrate the will of the people.

First, the popular will of the majority of the nation can be defeated by mathematical flukes. Under the winner-take-all or unit-vote rule for allocating a state's electoral votes, a candidate could win an electoral victory and yet receive fewer popular votes than his opponent. Success in twelve key states alone will give a candidate an electoral majority, regardless of his margin of victory in those states and regardless of whether he has received any votes in the other thirty-eight states. Three times in our history—1824, 1876 and 1888—the popular vote loser was elected President. In fifteen elections a shift of less than 1 per cent of the national vote cast would have made the popular-vote loser President.

Second, the choice of the President can be thrown into the House of Representatives, where each state has but a single vote. While it has been 144 years since the House of Representatives has had to choose a President, we have had seven narrow escapes since then, including the elections of 1948, 1960 and 1968. A shift of less than 1 per cent of the popular vote in a few key states would have thrown those elections into Congress, with the consequent risk of political deals and possibly the election of a President who was rejected by a majority of the voters. This feature of our system is clearly a political monstrosity, fully distorting the most elementary principles of self-government.

Third, Presidential electors can take matters into their own hands and reject the will of the people who chose them. The so-called constitutional independence of electors can take various forms. It can take the form of pledged electors defecting, as in our most recent election, and in 1956 and 1960; of unpledged elector movements, as in 1960; or third-party electors being instructed by their Presidential candidate to vote for one of the major candidates. Under the electoral college system, the decision of the people is meaningless unless it is approved by, in effect, another body of government. Such a barrier between the people and their President is both anachronistic and abhorrent.

The electoral college system violates fundamental democratic principles in other ways:

The winner-take-all feature of the system suppresses at an intermediate stage all minority votes cast in a state. The winner of the most popular votes in a state, regardless of his percentage of the votes cast, receives all of that state's electoral votes. The votes for the losing candidates are in effect discarded, while those for the winner are multiplied in value.

The present system discriminates among voters on the basis of residence. While a small state voter might seem to enjoy an electoral vote advantage because his state receives two electoral votes regardless of size, a large state voter is able to influence more electoral votes, and it is in the large industrial states that Presidential elections are usually won or lost. There is no sound reason why every citizen should not have an equal vote in the election of our one official who serves as the symbol and spokesman for all the people.

The electoral college system fails to reflect the actual strength of the voter turnout in each state. Under the system each state casts its assigned electoral votes regardless of voter turnout. Thus, voters in states where the turnout is small are given a premium. It is not uncommon to find a great disparity in the voter turnout in states having the same number of electoral votes.

DIRECT POPULAR ELECTION IS RECOMMENDED

To remedy these evils, the American Bar Association's Commission on Electoral College Reform proposed a system of direct popular election of the President and Vice President, and the House of Delegates of the Association endorsed the commission's recommendations at its Midyear Meeting in February of 1967. Here are the major features of the proposal:

A candidate must obtain at least 40 per cent of the popular vote to be elected President or Vice President. The commission concluded that a majority vote requirement was not desirable because it would frequently happen that no candidate had a majority and therefore a second election would be required to decide the outcome. In this regard, it should be noted that one third of our Presidents received less than a majority of the total popular vote cast. Additionally, the commission feared that a majority-vote requirement might encourage proliferation of the parties, since a small group might have the potential to cause the election to be resolved under the machinery established for a contingent election. In arriving at a 40 per cent plurality, the commission was of the view that it was high enough to furnish a sufficient mandate for the President and low enough so that the first election probably would decide the contest.

The Association recommends that in the event no candidate receives at least 40 per cent of the popular vote, a national runoff election should be held between the top two candidates. The commission believed that a runoff was preferable to an election by Congress because it would avoid the possibility of political wheeling and dealing and assure the election of the popular vote winner. The commission also believed that a national runoff, together with a 40 per cent plurality requirement, would operate to discourage proliferation of the parties. The commission reasoned that it would rarely occur that no major candidate had at least 40 per cent, even with minor party candidates in the field. However, if that happened, the people would choose between the top two.

We recommend that the President and Vice President be elected jointly by a single vote applicable to both offices. The purpose of this recommendation is to eliminate the possibility of a split ticket.

Congress should be empowered to establish the days for the original election and any runoff election, which should be uniform throughout the United States. Under our recommendation, Congress would set the date for the election by statute, as it does at present. This recommendation is similar to what now appears in the Constitution with respect to Congress's establishing the day on which the electors shall vote for President and Vice President.

Under the Association's proposal the places and manner of holding Presidential elections and the inclusion of the names of candidates on the ballot would be prescribed by the state legislatures, subject to a reserve power in Congress to make or alter such regulations. This is similar to provisions now in the Constitution governing elections for representatives and senators. The reason for giving Congress the residual power to legislate on the question of appearances on the ballot is to insure that the people of every state have the right to vote for major party candidates.

We recommend also that the qualifications for voting in a Presidential election be the same as those for voting in a Congressional election. The qualifications for voting for members of Congress being defined by state law and tied in with the qualifications for voting for members of the most numerous branch of the state legislature, the commission concluded that this would make substantially uniform the voting qualifications in both federal and state elections. Under the recommendation, states would be specifically authorized to establish special residence qualifications for voting in Presidential elections. This recommendation is premised on the fact that a majority of the states already have passed laws relaxing the residence requirement and that these laws are desirable in this day of great mobility among our people. The commission also recommended in the area of voting qualifications that Congress be given the reserve power to establish uniform age and residence qualifications.

Finally, we recommend that a constitutional amendment on direct election embody the necessary provisions for remedying gaps caused by the death of a candidate.

ADVANTAGES OF DIRECT ELECTION OVER OTHER PROPOSALS

The advantages of direct popular election over other proposals are numerous. It is the only method that can assure that the candidate with the largest number of popular votes will be elected President. It is the only method that would eliminate once and for all the principal defects of our system: the "winner-take-all" feature and its cancellation of votes, the inequities arising from the formula for allocating electoral votes among the states, the anachronistic and dangerous office of Presidential elector, and the archaic method by which contingent elections are handled. There would no longer be "sure states" or "pivotal states" or "swing voters," because votes would not be cast in accordance with a unit rule and because campaign efforts would be directed at people regardless of residence. Factors such as fraud and accident could not decide the disposition of all a state's votes. Direct election would bring to Presidential elections the principle that is used and has worked well in elections for senators, representatives, governors, state legislators, mayors and thousands of other officials at all levels of government. Under a popular vote system, Presidential elections would operate the way most people think they operate and expect them to operate.

Objections to the proposed reforms have arisen, however. Any suggestion to change old ways of doing things always invites vigorous objections—a healthy enough tendency in matters calling for constitutional amendment.

ANSWERING THE ARGUMENTS AGAINST DIRECT ELECTION

The main arguments raised against direct election may be grouped under three headings: (1) large or small-state advantage, (2) threats to the two-party system, and (3) vote counting procedures.

1. Will Either Large or Small States Lose a Present Advantage?

(a) The Small State Advantage Argument.   In the past, too many have dismissed direct election proposals without reaching their merits, claiming that such an amendment could not possibly be ratified by three fourths of the states, because thirty-six of them have added weight in the election of the President by reason of the electoral college system.

Behind this is a deceptively simple mathematical view of relative voter strength in Presidential elections. Based on the 1960 census, Alaska has one elector for each 75,389 persons; at the other extreme, California has only one electoral vote for each 392,930 persons. The easy inference is that an Alaskan has five times the weight of a Californian. By the same method, each Nevadan (one elector per 95,093 persons) has four times the weight of each New Yorker (one elector per 390,286 persons). Thirty-five states and the District of Columbia have a more favorable ratio than the national average of one elector per 333,314 persons.

In a law journal article inserted in the *Congressional Record*, direct election was opposed recently on the theory that it will deprive small states of a present advantage. It was noted that Alabama casts 2 per cent of the nation's electoral votes, while casting less than .9 per cent of the national popular vote; and the writer concluded that New York had only four times the electoral power of Alabama, even though it had ten times as many voters. Similar figures were shown for the twenty-five least populated states, and it was concluded that the American Bar Association's proposal "will not sell" to the less populated states. Reserving for a moment the mathematical issue, let us examine the view that the citizens of small states cannot be sold on the principle of voter equality in Presidential elections.

First, this prophecy is not justified by the positions of their elected leaders. No public official has a higher duty to represent the interests of a state in national politics than does its United States senator. It is noteworthy, therefore, that senators from smaller states are increasingly prominent among those who are sponsoring direct election proposals. They include Senators Gravel of Alaska, Inouye of Hawaii, Magnuson and Jackson of Washington, Hatfield and Packwood of Oregon, Bible of Nevada, Church of Idaho, Mansfield and Metcalf of Montana, Burdick of North Dakota, McGovern of South Dakota, Pearson of Kansas, Bellmon of Oklahoma, Randolph and Byrd of West Virginia, Ribicoff of Connecticut, Pell of Rhode Island, Aiken of Vermont, McIntyre of New Hampshire, and Smith and Muskie of Maine.

But what of the legislatures of these small states? Here, too, we are not left to speculation. In 1966 Senator Burdick of North Dakota polled state legislators on their preferences among the various proposals for electoral college reform. A surprisingly high return, 2,500 of 8,000 polled, showed 58.8 per cent in favor of direct election. It was supported by 50 per cent or more of the legislators replying from forty-four states. Most significantly, there was little variation between large and small states. Among the most heavily populated states, California legislators voted 73.5 per cent for direct election; New York legislators, 70.0 per cent; Pennsylvania, 55.8 per cent; Michigan, 52.4 per cent; and Ohio, 57.1 per cent. In the five smallest states—those with only three electoral votes—Vermont voted 60.9 per cent for direct election; Nevada, 62.5 per cent; Wyoming, 55.5 per cent; Delaware, 53.8 per cent; and Alaska 50.0 per cent.

The House of Delegates of the American Bar Association, a cross-section of American lawyers, approved its commission's recommendations by a three-to-one margin. Direct election has also been endorsed by other organizations representing wide segments and sections of American life, including the AFL-CIO, the United States Chamber of Commerce, the United Auto Workers and the National Federation of Independent Business. Public opinion polls show that 79 to 81 per cent of people throughout the country favor our proposal. Thus, those who accept the principle of popular election of the President should not assume that citizens of small states do not accept it.

The small state advantage argument is diametrically opposed by a plausible theory that it is large states who profit from the present system.

(b) The Large State Advantage Argument.   In a curious cross fire, direct election is also opposed by some champions of large states' interests. They claim that the small state advantage in ratio of electors to population is more than offset by the advantages accruing to large states from the winner-take-all laws. One such observer recently wrote that the features of the present system

> *have bred in moden times the decisive influence in Presidential elections of the large, populous, heterogeneous states, where bloc voting, as by ethnic or racial minorities or other interest groups, often determines the result. Much of the popular vote in the smaller, relatively homogeneous states, is simply wasted. Politicians and political scientists have at any rate long assumed that the Presidency is won or lost in the large states . . . we can now establish mathematically why modern Presidents have been particularly sensitive to urban and minority interests. . . . And only men who can be so responsive are generally nominated and elected.[4]*

The mathematical proof referred to is John Banzhaf's analysis of voter power,[5] which calculated by computer the individual voter's chances of affecting the outcomes in both his state and the national totals. This is a functional view of voting power; it is defined simply as "the ability to affect decisions through the process of voting." Mr. Banzhaf found that an individual voter in states such as New York and California has more than two and a half times as much chance to affect the ultimate Presidential outcome as a resident of a smaller state. This results from the fact that the large state voter influences a much larger unit of electoral votes. Each New Yorker now votes for forty-three electors and thus participates in casting fourteen times as many electoral votes as does a Nevadan.

This analysis confirmed what scholars and national politicians had sensed for many years. The historical record was updated recently when Delaware, joined by twelve other states, unsuccessfully sought United States Supreme Court relief to invalidate the state general ticket laws. Delaware alleged:

> *Sixteen of the two parties' 50 nominations for the Presidency from 1868 through 1964 have gone to New Yorkers. Of the total of 100 nominations for President and Vice-President, citizens of New York have been nominated in 24 instances. Six large states (New York, California, Illinois, Indiana, Massachusetts and Ohio) account for 68 of the total of 100 nominations, while the citizens of 26 states, including Plaintiff, have been totally excluded from the nominations. Plaintiff is one of eight of the original 13 states (Connecticut, Delaware, Georgia, Maryland, North Carolina, Rhode Island, South Carolina and Vermont) which has never elected one of its citizens President in the 45 elections conducted in our 177-year history and these citizens have been totally excluded from nomination for either President or Vice President during the past century. . . . Plaintiff and other small states as virtual bystanders do little more than watch while the large states serve as the fields of contest in national elections.[6]*

The present system obviously cannot favor both large and small states. But it is impossible to justify any system on the ground of voter inequality. Both arguments are unsound in principle. As a matter of constitutional structure, surely no citizen's influence upon his President should depend upon his geographical location within the United States. Only direct election will achieve this voter equality.

2. Effects Upon the Two-Party System

This question of parties occupied much of the commission's attention, and it adopted its position with confidence that direct election carries no risk of producing a multiparty system. Nonetheless, such objections have been raised. They are difficult to answer to the opposition's satisfaction because none of us can prophesy future political events with absolute certainty—including those who predict dire consequences to the two-party system. We can, however, project probabilities upon the basis of relevant experience and expert opinion. This we did in 1967; and recent reappraisals in light of the 1968 election only strengthen our position.

Those who oppose direct election on third-party grounds labor a hard oar after the 1968 election, which demonstrated most dramatically the potential for third-party leverage under our present system. I have mentioned three contingencies which in 1968 could have prevented any candidate from winning a majority of the electoral votes. Direct election would fully cure the defects in our system that the Wallace candidacy sought to exploit. It also would remedy other faults that could magnify third-party efforts. Close analysis proves that direct election will actually strengthen the two-party system—not weaken it—by removing special incentives to third parties and equalizing all voters throughout the nation.

Analytically, there are three distinct types of third-party efforts—local, regional and national. The first two would undoubtedly be weakened by direct election. Local, or intrastate, parties now may sometimes have a pivotal power to tip a state's electoral bloc for or against one of the major candidates. Under direct election the votes of a splinter group would count only for what they are worth in numbers of persons; and votes for major candidates would always count nationally.

Regional or sectional parties may generate a plurality of popular votes in a few states, deliver large blocs of electoral votes and possibly produce a balance-of-power position in the electoral college. Under direct election all votes would be counted as cast, and a third candidate could receive no disappointing leverage from being able to carry a few states.

The final type of third-party effort, the national one, is more difficult to analyze. Some argue that national third-party efforts would be encouraged by direct election merely because all state popular vote totals would be reflected in the national totals, whether or not any states were carried. This question was studied in depth by our commission. We found little evidence that elimination of the electoral college would harm the two-party system and concluded that direct election is more likely to strengthen it.

Among the voluminous materials studied by the commission was a collection entitled "Why Two Parties?", which was furnished us by the commission's adviser, John D. Feerick of the New York Bar. After personally exhausting the literature on the subject, Mr. Feerick selected for study by the entire commission excerpts from the writings of ten political scientists who have given special attention to the causes and functioning of political party systems. We learned that no single factor accounts for the two-party system and that there is considerable disagreement as to its major causes.

Among the causes listed as accounting for our American commitment to the two-party system are: persistence of initial form; election of officials from single-member districts by plurality votes; the normal presence of a central consensus on national goals; cultural homogeneity; political maturity; and a general tendency towards dualism. Some of the experts list the electoral college as a factor that may contribute; others ignore it; and some suggest that it is functionally opposed to two-partyism and that our party system may have survived despite the electoral college rather than because of it.

The experts are virtually in agreement on one point, however. It is that election of legislators and executives by plurality votes from single-member districts is the chief cause of two-partyism. This is the one element that all two-party systems have in common. No one proposes to alter our practice of electing members of Congress and state legislators, governors and mayors on this basis. To the extent that these elections undergird our two-party system, that support will continue. Furthermore, our proposal essentially places Presidential elections on the same basis and thus perfects and extends that feature which best serves the two-party system.

This has been apparent to the great majority of political scientists who have analyzed the American Bar Association recommendations. We concur in the following conclusions of Hugh LeBlanc of George Washington University:

> *The present system does discourage the rise of minor parties, but not because of its electoral college features. It is because the President runs for all intents and purposes in a single-member, national constituency in which minor party candidates have little hopes of winning.*
>
> *The assertion that a national plebiscite would contribute to the development of minor parties . . . will not withstand analysis. Parties are most likely to offer candidates when they have some hope of electoral victory. Thus under a system of proportional representation, minor parties have an inducement to compete because they are rewarded by representation proportionate to their strength. Under single-member, plurality elections, no such incentives are present. This is precisely the system that would apply if the President were directly elected from a nationwide constituency. It is of no matter that the votes collected in all States contribute to a total. The mere accumulaion of votes is meaningless except insofar as it cuts into the support that otherwise might have gone to support a major party candidate. In this regard, it might influence an election*

outcome. But is this threat any greater than that which now exists from a minor party whose electoral strength is geographically concentrated? I think not.[7]

Other political scientists who have reached similar conclusions include Paul David of the University of Virginia, David R. Derge of Indiana University, Joseph Kallenbach of the University of Michigan, Paul Piccard of Florida State University, and Robert S. Rankin of Duke University. Two elements of their analysis deserve emphasis:

First, the two-party system is not served by the electoral college as it is constitutionally structured but as the two national parties have caused it to function by extra constitutional devices. If present methods serve the two-party system, it is because they normally are expected to function as equivalent to national popular election. In this respect the direct election proposal will perfect, not damage, the electoral device that serves the two-party system.

The second point is that the functioning of a real two-party system in Presidential elections actually should be strengthened by direct election. By eliminating the disfranchisement of state minorities, it will prevent any votes from being written off as worthless. The result will be genuine two-party competition in every state.

Nonetheless, we were sufficiently concerned by the possibility of weakening the two-party system that a major provision of our proposal is directed largely at supporting it. This is the provision requiring runoff elections when no candidate obtains 40 per cent of the popular vote. This avoids peculiar evils of both majority and simple plurality requirements. A majority requirement would make runoffs the rule rather than the exception and positively encourage splinter candidacies. A simple plurality rule would enable a candidate to win with as little as one fourth or one third of the total vote—hardly a sufficient mandate to govern. This might encourage third and fourth parties. The 40 per cent rule incorporates our historical experience as a future norm.

Somewhat ironically, the runoff provision has been used to oppose the direct election proposal through an argument that runoff provisions encourage multiple candidacies and make runoffs more likely. Studies of nominating primaries in some Southern states are cited as proof. These were considered by the commission. Analysis shows that they are not comparable to national Presidential elections for three important reasons:

A. The Southern primaries involved competition within a one-party system, which is hardly equivalent to elections occurring against the backdrop of an established two-party system.

B. The Southern primary campaigns involve multiple candidacies of individuals, not parties. We always have a few individuals who seek personal expression as nominal Presidential candidates, but individuals without party organizations are no threat to the system.

C. Most important, the Southern primary experiences are caused mainly by majority requirements for nomination. The commission profited from these examples when it chose a plurality, rather than a majority, requirement. True, the plurality must reach a certain level; but it is one likely of attainment, and the tendency of majority requirements to cause third-party efforts is eliminated.

3. Vote-Counting Procedure

Another objection made to direct popular election is that it could delay the certification of a President for a long period of time due to vote-counting procedures. This objection is addressed to the mechanics of a system of direct election and not to the principle. The vote-counting problems that are likely to be encountered under such a system, such as recounts, fraud, challenged ballots and the like, are really no different in kind from those that exist in the election of a governor or United States senator. Any system of direct election requires an accurate, rapid and final vote count. These requirements have been satisfied in the direct election of officials at other levels of government, and we see no reason why they cannot be satisfied in a direct election for President. In the larger states millions of votes are now cast and counted in state-wide elections held in areas of thousands of square miles.

There are now procedures in the various states for certifying the results of popular elections for other offices that could be adapted to a system of direct election of the President. Under the direct election recommendations, the operation and regulation of Presidential elections would be left to the states, with a reserve power in Congress to legislate in the field. The states thus would have the flexibility to adopt and change election procedures in the light of experience. It is foreseeable that the states might adopt a uniform state law standardizing the procedures for handling recounts and challenged ballots and that Congress might create an election commission with responsibilities in the vote-counting area.

The trend toward better regulated and more scientific vote counting has reduced and will continue to reduce the possibilities of irregularities while expediting the final outcome. With a co-operative effort on the part of the states and Federal Government, we are confident that procedures and methods can be adopted to assure an effective system of direct popular election of the President.

DEMOCRATIC PARTICIPATION SHOULD BE ENLARGED

The trend of our political system is toward direct democratic participation of the people at every level. That trend has been reflected in the Fifteenth, Seventeenth and Nineteenth Amendments to the Constitution. It should now be reflected in an amendment providing for popular election of the President.

REGULATING CAMPAIGN SPENDING

John Gardner

I speak for Common Cause, an organization of more than 100,000 members which believes that our political system can be made more responsive to the public interest than it is today. A reform of present campaign spending practices is essential to our purpose.

Due chiefly to the heavy investment in television advertising considered essential to modern campaigning, costs to the candidate have become unbearably high. In most states and districts no citizen of ordinary means can run for office without placing himself under very heavy obligation to sources of wealth.

The likelihood, indeed certainty, that a few wealthy individual donors will enjoy favored access to public officials taints our entire electoral process and makes the word "politics" a term of contempt for all too many Americans. Common Cause's previous public statements and the lawsuit we have brought against the major political parties should leave no question about the depth of our concern.

My testimony is based on a study Common Cause has made of bills [presented for consideration by] Congress and of the various commission reports and academic findings that have been issued on this subject. I will describe the priorities we have set in the regulation of campaign spending and the principles we think such regulation should embody. Our position involves three basic approaches: 1. Subsidy or reduction of campaign costs to the candidate; 2. Ceilings on giving and spending; 3. Full disclosure.

1. SUBSIDY OR REDUCTION OF CAMPAIGN COSTS TO THE CANDIDATE

(a) First, we believe that blocks of broadcast time ("Voters' Time") should be provided without charge to each candidate for federal office in a general election and that these programs should include substantial live appearances by the candidate.

We would like to see this principle extended to primary elections as well as general elections, but we recognize the practical difficulties of such a provision. Senators Gravel and Pearson have suggested a legislative mandate to the FCC requiring a recommendation for an equitable and workable Voters' Time formula in the primaries. We are reluctant to accept the delay that will necessarily result from this approach, but it may be the only reasonable solution.

We feel, with Senators Gravel and Pearson, that the stations should bear the cost of Voters' Time. This is a fair demand to make on the stations in return for the profits they derive from public broadcast privileges.

If no other provision but this were enacted, we would have made a great advance toward equalizing competition for elective office. Voters' Time would provide a generous base of exposure on which a candidate could build the rest of his campaign. It would give him ample opportunity to explain his position to the voters. It would give the voter full opportunity to evaluate the intellectual talents and personalities of the candidates, however unequal their financial backing. If voters were given this opportunity to draw informed judgments, I suspect that they could weather whatever storms of packaged propaganda the campaign might otherwise churn up.

The objection has been made that it would be inconvenient to broadcast appearances by Congressional candidates in a metropolitan area where several Congressional districts lie within the range of a single station. We agree there are difficulties here but believe they can be overcome. One solution would be to distribute the burden of carrying campaign programs among the several stations serving an area so that different Congressional candidates would appear on different stations at different times. The inconvenience to the viewer would be negligible and the benefit to the voter immense.

Voters' Time would require repeal of Section 315 of the Communications Act of 1934 requiring equal broadcast time for all candidates for an office. This repeal would also permit debates between major candidates. Equal Time serves no good purpose today. It does not provide exposure to minor candidates, and it does stifle discourse between the major candidates. We urge its repeal.

(b) Another step we recommend is to broaden the financial base supporting the candidate by encouraging numerous small contributions. In this way one would hope to diminish the influence of large contributors and reinforce the candidate's sense of obligation to his entire constituency.

Public opinion polls indicate that if people were asked to contribute, many more would contribute than do now. People should be encouraged to view political contribution as a legitimate and honorable exercise of their responsibilities as citizens. Common Cause would also like to see a brief bipartisan appeal to contribute "to the candidate of your choice" included in each Voters' Time program.

(c) Still another means of easing the financial burden on candidates would be a reduction in media prices for political candidates. . . .

(d) Finally, Common Cause proposes a special campaign mailing frank to be available to House and Senate candidates in the 35-day period before both general and primary elections. We think that every major candidate for federal office should have the opportunity to put into the hands of the registered voters in his district a statement of his views on the issues. Congressional mailing privileges are so frequently used as vehicles for campaign publicity that we consider this provision necessary to restore a fair equilibrium to electoral competition.

2. CEILINGS ON GIVING AND SPENDING

(a) A gallup poll conducted in December of last year revealed that 78 per cent of the American people favor a limit on spending. Rarely has there been greater public consensus on a single issue. This is a mandate that none of us can ignore.

In view of the difficulty of enforcing a blanket limit on all spending and in view of the greater cost per constituent in House races than in Senatorial and Presidential races, Common Cause endorses the approach taken by Congressman Anderson of Illinois. He proposes a ceiling of 30¢ per registered voter in House races, 20¢ in Senatorial races, and 10¢ in Presidential races. We would add, however, that no ceiling should be set lower than $40,000.

Congressman Anderson also places these limits over five selected media which together carry almost all the financial burden of political advertising and which are susceptible to close surveillance. These media—radio and television, magazines and newspapers, telephones, postage, and billboards—are supplied by a few visible providers at published, standardized rates. In view of the stiff disclosure requirements that Common Cause also advocates, we think that these spending limitations would be observed. The ceilings are realistic and violations would be easily detected.

Last fall both houses of Congress passed a limitation on television spending by a majority exceeding two-thirds, but the President vetoed it. The objections he advanced were: (1) that the limitation was not extensive enough, that it "plugged only one hole in the sieve," and, (2) that the limitation discriminated against challengers.

We are advocating limitations that will meet his first objection. We are plugging all the important holes in the sieve. Of course, the President can still fall back on his second objection—that these limitations inhibit the challenger—but the point is debatable. It is true that during the election period a challenger for an office may need to spend more than the incumbent to attain the visibility the incumbent already enjoys. But in most cases the incumbent has built loyalties and obligations among the powerful interests in his constituency, and ordinarily he is the one who can expect the fat campaign treasury. The limitations we propose restrict the incumbent to a level of media expenditures that lies within the means of most challengers. Thus in the great majority of instances it serves to limit the natural advantage of the incumbent rather than to perpetuate the disadvantage of the challenger. In choosing between a situation where the challenger in theory can spend more than the incumbent but in practice can rarely spend as much, and a situation where in practice both are able to spend equally, we think the latter choice is clearly superior.

When we preserve the theoretical ability of a challenger to spend to the hilt we protect only the extremely wealthy challenger, a breed which for that reason is becoming more and more common. What does this mean to the incumbent? It engulfs him increasingly in a frenzied search for campaign funds. It distracts him from the public good and turns his eyes toward private sources of wealth.

[Senator Pastore's bill requires] that no media expenditures be made in a candidate's behalf without his authorization. We endorse this provision. We understand that objections can be raised to it on the grounds that it might infringe upon freedom of speech. But I believe that it is the only enforceable way to limit expenditures. On balance such a provision would serve the values of public political discourse that the First Amendment seeks to further.

Senators Gravel and Pearson avoid the First Amendment question by permitting unauthorized political committees to spend in behalf of a candidate, apparently without limit, as long as they clearly advertise that they do not have the candidate's authorization and that he is not responsible for their activities. The obvious difficulty here is that this provision offers a gaping and irresistible loophole. The candidate could publicly clear himself of affiliation with a particular group by shunting it onto the unauthorized list while he privately solicits its contributions and thereby incurs a political debt just as compelling as an "authorized" debt. This objection may seem cynical, but the history of campaign finance does not warrant trusting expectations. If a candidate believes that his job and his political future depend on his exploiting a loophole, I think it likely and understandable that he'll do just that.

We suggest that two separate rates be set for primary elections and general elections. If one limit is placed over both primary and general elections, the incumbent is placed at a disadvantage. He would wish to spend sparingly in the primary, conserving most of his quota for the general election. A challenger in the primaries, however, would view a victory over the incumbent as a political prize worth winning even if he were left penniless for the general election. He would be tempted, then, to run all out in the primary. The Gravel-Pearson bill, by setting separate ceilings on primary and general elections, meets this difficulty in what seems to us to be a reasonable manner. It encourages responsible campaigning in both primary and general elections, and as such does service to the two-party system.

Although this committee meets to consider regulations over communications only, I would nonetheless like to describe here the other type of limitation on campaign financing we consider essential.

We feel that ceilings should be placed on the amount any individual can contribute or spend in behalf of any single candidate. This restriction, combined with reporting and registration requirements, should be phrased to prevent the present evasion of ceilings through the use of "dummy committees."

In order to take account of the different magnitudes of finance involved in different types of elections we favor a graduated set of ceilings. A $10,000 limit on contributions for Presidential and Vice Presidential campaigns, a $5,000 limit on Senatorial campaigns, and a $2,500 limit on

House campaigns seem to us reasonable. These ceilings permit substantial donations by those who are able and willing to offer large sums, but they prevent donors from buying a controlling interest in any candidate's campaign.

3. FULL DISCLOSURE

Our third approach to the control of campaign financing also carries us beyond the jurisdiction of this Committee, but I shall mention it for the sake of completeness. We support the principle that all political committees must register with an independent elections commission as proposed in the Gravel-Pearson bill and must disclose fully all campaign receipts and expenditures. The loopholes in the Corrupt Practices Act should be eliminated by requiring intra-state and District of Columbia political committees to register and report. Full exposure of the sources and size of a candidate's financial backing permits the public to draw informed conclusions about the obligations and likely behavior of the candidate.

Lifting the shroud of secrecy from political finance removes many of the sinister suspicions associated with politics. If one of our goals in campaign reform is to broaden the base of political contribution and to draw as many citizens as possible into all stages of the electoral cycle, then any means that increases the respectability and attractiveness of political contribution deserves our warm support.

Disclosure seems to us a necessary corollary to ceilings on expenditures. The principal agent of enforcement for such ceilings will be the opposing candidate, and he can perform this function effectively only if he has access to disclosures candidly made and adequately publicized.

Finally, . . . let me express Common Cause's appreciation for the interest [Senator Pastore has] taken in improving this nation's campaign practices. We are pleased that the need for reform is so deeply felt in Congress by both parties, and we are confident that the legislation that emerges will be wise and constructive. Thank you for letting us share our views with you.

TELEVISION AND THE NEW POLITICS

Harold Mendelsohn and Irving Crespi

.

The cover of the November 1968 issue of *Psychology Today* depicts a political candidate standing on the rear observation platform of an old-fashioned whistle-stop train. He is confronted with a serious dilemma of the times. On his right an eager mother lifts a baby for him to kiss. To his left, a television camera is held up to him. No conflict. The politician leans over to plant a buss upon the video camera.

This image highlights the orientation of value-priorities of candidates working in the new politics: Get on television if you want to win. The illustration suggests that television's job is simply that of garnering votes during campaigns. The old hypodermic-needle concept of the influence of mass communications is still at work. What is difficult to realize is that had the hypodermic power of television been anywhere close to its alleged potency, Richard Nixon—who, as a candidate for the Presidency in 1968, spent more money for television exposure than any previous Presidential candidate—should have won the election by a far greater plurality than his 43.3 percent (which, incidentally, was just some four percentage points above the popular-vote percentage that obliterated the candidacy of Barry Goldwater in modern America's greatest Presidential defeat).

Regardless of whether television does or does not cause voters to switch their votes during campaigns, it has spawned four major changes in traditional American politics: 1. It has altered the processes of nominating candidates at party conventions; 2. It has altered campaigning; 3. It has altered traditional party structures and functions; 4. It has helped to encourage the questioning of the traditional ways of choosing and electing candidates, and, as a consequence, will aid in ushering in the new politics of the future.

Sophocles opined, "None loves the messenger who brings bad news." In its coverage of the Democratic nominating convention in 1968, television indeed appeared to bear bad news. It spoke to the electorate, who voiced amazement and shock at what they witnessed on their television screens, and, even more importantly, it spelled near-tragedy to many professional politicians, whose very political lives were put into jeopardy by television's incisive scrutiny into one of America's most cherished political institutions.

As will be recalled, not only were viewers at home treated to the simultaneous swirl of events that engulfed the Democratic gathering in Chicago, but delegates to the convention, confined in the security-tight Chicago Amphitheatre, were made painfully aware of the impact-laden occurrences that were taking place outside by the television recording of the clashes that involved the Chicago police, the Illinois National Guard, and the anti-Vietnam war and anti-Humphrey demonstrators at Chicago's Conrad Hilton Hotel.

As they were actually taking place, these events, because of the presence of television, affected both the viewing public and the delegates to the convention. Thus they served as immediate inputs into the convention itself. Recall, as one case in point, Senator Ribicoff's direct address to Mayor Daley in which he referred to the "Gestapo tactics" of the Chicago police, and the Mayor's fist-shaking response.

Reactions to the Chicago Democratic convention by the professional politicians were swift and predictable. Because they did not particularly like what they and the voters saw on the television screen, and probably because they wished to divert public attention from suddenly apparent major flaws in the political process, they immediately sought out television as their prime scapegoat. As a result, television itself became an important issue in the 1968 Presidential election. A newspaper article headlined "Dirksen Calls TV's Convention Coverage Outrageous: Urges Ban on Cameras," and by-lined by the late Minority Leader of the United States Senate, Everett McKinley Dirksen, is illustrative. Wrote Senator Dirksen:

> *The Miami Beach convention moved us to penetrating thought about TV reporting. The Chicago convention crystallized it. From Miami Beach, the TV people told the nation how boring it all was. From Chicago they pulled the switch and helped make it interesting indeed—and tragic and nauseating.*
>
> *A television person has no more right to force his tricks and his opinions from the floor of a convention than a newspaperman has a right to print his editorials right there on the convention floor.*
>
> *The television coverage of the two recent conventions is an outrage against the democratic process. . . .*[1]

The trade publication *Broadcasting* noted the following on page 44 of its September 9, 1968, issue:

> *Political Washington last week returned from convention combat and members of both parties turned to a common foe—the news media. In the inevitable post-mortems, controversy raged about the role of media and especially network television in its coverage of the battle of Chicago. During the week most of the slings and arrows levelled at broadcasters were oratorical, but more substantial moves were in the works.*
>
> *Focus of the anti-media (and pro-law-and-order) uproar was the Congress which devoted a good part of its first day back in session to denunciations of coverage of the Democratic national convention and surrounding disorders.*

Out of these congressional discussions grew the 1969 Senate Communications Subcommittee hearings that were held in February and March of that year under the chairmanship of Senator Pastore. The Senate subcommittee took advantage of the situation that arose in Chicago to launch into a broad-based, far-afield "investigation" of television's "responsibilities" in areas relating to self-regulation on matters of both violence and sex in its entertainment fare! The 1969 hearings shed very little light on what had been a primary issue in 1968—network coverage of national nominating conventions. The motivations of Congress in selecting out the television medium as a prime target for its wrath were placed under serious suspicion, as indicated in this remark attributed to Senator Russell B. Long: "We won't actually do anything to you (the media), you understand; we just want your consciences to hurt a little."[2]

As one consequence of the 1968 television coverage of both the Republican and Democratic conventions, and particularly the latter, an awesome spectre threatened to show itself on the American political scene—direct governmental intervention in the news-gathering and reporting processes. Jack Gould, the respected *New York Times* Television Editor, noted:

> . . . under one guise or another government is showing an inclination to intrude in the specifics of reportage, to reach a judgment on what is right or wrong to put on the screen, to assert itself with respect to program content. Private TV may have its faults, but they are insignificant in comparison with the possibility of government sitting in the editor's chair in television. For substantiation of such a consequence there is one place to look: French television under De Gaulle.[3]

It is most unlikely that future nominating conventions will resemble those of the past, at least as the electorate will be able to witness them via television. Ever since the late President Eisenhower launched his bitter attack upon the news media at the 1964 Republican convention and stated his subsequent recommendations for changes in convention procedures there has been a growing demand for modifications in this particular institution.

It is quite conceivable that conventions of the future will be considerably more subtly "managed" than heretofore, that they will be considerably shorter in duration, and even that television may be barred from conventions or so subject to control that it will refuse to cover these events. If the public is denied entree into the convention process either by the manipulation of the conventions themselves or by the barring of television from such meetings as they actually occur, it is similarly quite conceivable that the nominating convention as we have known it will no longer exist in the age of the new politics.

Immediately following the 1968 nominating conventions, Senator Gaylord Nelson called for drastic changes in the convention nominating process, observing in an Associated Press release on September 2, 1968, that ". . . a majority of the American public, regardless of party, is fed up with our quadrennial political party conventions." Nelson suggested that a new federal commission be established to come up with reforms in the nominating procedures for the Presidency. As of this writing his call has gone unheeded, despite the observation of Harry S. Ashmore that "[it] has taken a cycle of three national elections to prove the point, but there seems to be little doubt now that the communications revolution has reduced political conventions to essential irrelevancies."[4]

The impact of television on Presidential campaigning has [already] been discussed at length. . . . A footnote to how dead the old-style, east coast to west coast, whistle-stop approach really is is the fact that Richard Nixon travelled some 51,000 miles by jet aircraft in contrast to a mere 375 miles by whistle-stop train across Ohio in the 62 days of his 1968 formal campaign effort. It is quite probable that even the jet airplane will be displaced by television in the future. The Gallup Poll of November 23, 1968, reported that nearly half (44 percent) of the Americans sampled would not care if the entire campaigns were conducted by radio and television only. Right now one of the prime reasons that Presidential candidates go scooting about the country is simply to provide footage for both local and national television newscasts—footage whose only differentiating quality is the physical locale serving as a backdrop for the predictably unenlightening "speech" that makes no news.

Three aspects of the influence of television upon Presidential campaigning are worth reiterating in a somewhat different light. These aspects are related to the issues raised by the overwhelming commercialization of Presidential campaigning via television, to the problems that are raised by the high costs of commercial televised campaigning, and to the issue of precampaigning campaigning in the effort to attain a high degree of television exposure.

As has been indicated, the 1968 campaign was primarily oriented toward image-making. Thus communications in all three political camps were oriented toward the creation of affects—emotional responses to consciously fabricated mood stimuli. Little emphasis was placed on the cognitive or rational processes that are involved in serious decision-making of consequence. Thus even the tepid attempt to introduce some semblance of rationality into the campaign by affording a temporary suspension of Section 315 of the Communications Act, which would have allowed for direct debates among the major candidates, fell in ignoble defeat in Congress. The understandable reluctance of candidate Nixon to engage in direct debates plus the irresponsibility of Congress' reluctance to afford voters even this small token to rational political decision-making have caused much concern among citizens, scholars, and responsible politicians alike regarding television's responsibilities in the political process. In an interview with the *Chicago Daily News* several days prior to the 1968

Election, former FCC Chairman Newton Minnow observed ". . . the tragedy of the 1968 campaign on TV and radio is that what we are getting is each candidate's own appeal (paid political broadcasts) without confrontation to draw a comparison."

In a letter to Dr. Frank Stanton, President of the Columbia Broadcasting System, dated October 25, 1968, Thomas Hoving, Chairman of the National Citizens Committee for Broadcasting, wrote, "There is nothing to prevent a more thorough job of covering the campaign except the financial interests of the networks." Hoving continued, noting that candidates, "are being seen primarily in paid political announcements—commercials—where they are shown to their best advantage. With the great majority of electioneering being done this way, the institution of free elections in this nation is being reduced to the level of selling soap suds and dog food."

The apparent lack of responsibility in the 1968 Presidential campaign cannot be placed solely upon the commercial broadcasters. Currently there are more than 175 so-called educational television stations on the air throughout the United States. They make up what the Carnegie Corporation euphemistically designates as "public broadcasting" in America. These "educational" stations operate under the same FCC regulations that govern commercial broadcasters, with one important exception —a good portion of their financing is derived in one way or another directly from public taxes.

Preliminary findings from a study being conducted by Harold Mendelsohn and Melvyn Muchnik of the University of Denver's Communication Arts Center indicate that the "public broadcasting" sector did very little indeed to enlighten the voting public regarding the issues and the candidates in the 1968 election campaigns. Certainly there is no evidence from this study to indicate that public broadcasters suffered enough pangs of responsibility to make any significant attempt to fill the apparent gaps in informing the public, gaps which were left open by the nation's commercial broadcasters during the 1968 campaigns. Hobbled by politically cautious school boards, state legislatures, and university trustees who represent the majority of public television's licensees, station managers in the nation's "educational TV" enterprise generally stayed clear of political "controversy" in 1968, either hiding nervously behind the "fairness" and "equal time" doctrines that have managed to cover many sins of the commercial broadcasters or behind the rationalization of not "competing" with their commercial counterparts. If the record of commercial broadcasting's role in the 1968 election campaigns is suspect, the record of public broadcasting in that critical political year was nothing less than shameful.

If any semblance of rationality is to be recaptured in the nation's electioneering process, television-communications reforms are urgently needed. It is obvious that a major overhauling of the FCC's regulatory role in political broadcasting is necessary. Coupled with this necessity is the need for controls requiring balances between the amount of paid time that bona fide candidates will be allowed and the amount of free time that will be made available to legitimate candidates on commercial broadcasting outlets. Perhaps the most drastic reform proposal yet put forth comes from the pen of Harry S. Ashmore who recommends that either through congressional legislation or by FCC regulation, commercial broadcasters simply be prohibited from accepting paid political advertising, since such advertising cannot be considered to be truly in the public interest.

> *The proper use of television for direct political campaigning would require that the station play no role beyond that of common carrier, and would provide that the actual conduct of political broadcasts be arranged and supervised by an appropriate public agency. This implies no restriction on news coverage and commentary; on the contrary, it should free the broadcasters of some of the more inhibiting effects of the FCC's so-called fairness doctrine. The only objection the station owners could bring to such a requirement would be that it might cost them some money and cause them some inconvenience, and this is less than compelling in the case of an industry that derives phenomenal profits from government-granted monopolies on broadcast channels. Nor could the worn theoretical objections to any kind of interference with private enterprise be taken seriously in this instance; if any human activity can be properly classified as public it must be an election.*[5]

Additional proposals for regulating commercial political broadcasting—at least during Presidential elections—have been forthcoming. In this regard, the Twentieth Century Fund's independent commission on campaign costs has suggested that "voter's time" programs be purchased by the federal government at half the usual broadcast-time charges (at an estimated cost of $265,000 per thirty-minute program) and aired on all radio and television stations simultaneously at prime time. Under the proposal six half-hour broadcasts would be allotted to candidates of major parties. Minority-party candidates who managed to poll at least one eighth of the popular votes in a preceding national election and who are on the ballot in seventy-five percent of the states would be allowed two thirty-minute programs. A bill introduced in the Senate in the fall of 1969 by Senators Philip Hart and James Pearson (S-2876) would require broadcasters to provide air time for senatorial and congressional candidates at approximately thirty percent of usual commercial rates. The bill proposes that these rates apply to a total of one hundred and twenty minutes of prime air time to be afforded senatorial candidates plus sixty minutes of prime air time to congressional hopefuls during the five weeks immediately preceding the date of election.

It appears clear that the role of public broadcasting in the political process must be carefully reappraised so that it no longer remains absolved from its true public responsibility. Until the time when changes are made, by whatever means, in the manner in which commercial broadcasters are allowed to handle political campaigning, the public broadcasting sector must indeed be made to serve truly in its self-proclaimed role as an "alternative" to commercial television.

One immediate step that can be taken is for the FCC to encourage public broadcasting channels to make massive amounts of time (time that ordinarily is devoted to such "educational" matters as the preparation of Quiche Lorraine, interviews with reformed dope addicts, discussions of the "real tragedy of James Fenimore Cooper," and serious debates on whether the community needs more meter maids or not) available to *all* bona fide political candidates throughout a given national election year. Failure to do this should result in reappraisals of public broadcasters' licenses in terms of the criterion of serving the public interest. It is altogether apparent that we need a new gutsy public broadcasting endeavor that addresses itself seriously to the serious aspects of politics in the nation. The public broadcasting sector has the further obligation of making its time, talent, and facilities available to all legitimate local and state candidates who presently cannot afford the high costs of commercial television. In an era where "involvement" and "relevance" are rallying cries for the development of a more rationally oriented new political system, the public broadcasting sector must play its educational role. Public broadcasting must be taken out of the hands of wall-hugging boards of directors that are dominated by professional educators and placed into the hands of the voting public in order that this medium can be used for the political enlightenment of that public.

For years now political observers have been sounding alarms regarding the monumentally escalating costs of political campaigning—costs that, for the most part, represent the utilization of television. Current estimates suggest that a congressional candidate in an average race in a populous area requires some $100,000 to make an effective run. In 1966 a minimum of $5 million was spent on Nelson Rockefeller's campaign for the governorship of New York with an estimated 75 percent of that sum going to the broadcast media. In 1968, American labor unions poured some $30 million into the Presidential campaigns, with industry matching and outmatching that sum in kind. The scandalous lack of publicly available, reliable figures on *actual* total expenditures by political candidates and their supporters makes accurate tallies of total expenditures nearly impossible to discern. What does remain apparent is that political campaigning in the age of television is tremendously costly—to put it mildly.

As things stand presently, without significant reforms in our present system political offices will remain reserved for either the very affluent or those who are willing to accept substantial financing from groups or individuals representing special interests. Contributors of large sums are not completely altruistic in their giving. They expect something in return, and more often than not they get it.

Federal curbing of excessive campaign spending is supported by more than two-thirds of the American public. On this score, a Gallup Poll reported in *The New York Times* on November 24, 1968, revealed that sixty-eight percent of its sample of Americans favored a "law which would put a limit on the total amount of money which can be spent for or by a candidate in his campaign for public office." Twenty-four percent expressed opposition to such a reform, and eight percent held no opinion on the matter.

Somehow changes in financing high-cost political campaigns will come about. Such changes have been needed for decades, and perhaps the demands of paid political broadcasting will serve as an impetus for developing them. Among the various proposals concerning the financing of political campaigns in the future one element is common—namely, the necessity for broadening the base of financing across all sectors of the electorate spectrum. Whether this comes about through income tax allowances for voluntary contributions to political parties, or through nominal dues to be paid for membership in the political parties (which can be deducted from income taxes), or from some other source, the increasing costs of political broadcasting will some day result in promoting more direct participation in the election process by larger numbers of ordinary voters.

If nominating conventions have turned into political "irrelevancies" as a consequence of television, campaigning itself may become similarly insignificant. Such a consequence is predictable if costs continue to spiral in near geometric progression; if campaigns degenerate into one steady stream of commercials, and voters simply become bored; if reforms are instituted regarding the amount of paid political broadcasts that are allowed; and if the quaint fiction that campaigns alone win elections is quietly phased out. If it has not actually become irrelevant, campaigning already has taken on an air of sheer ritualism. The real political game is being played more and more *between* formal campaigns rather than during them. The playing field is the television screen, and the name of the game is "exposure."

The new politician is a creature of the amount and kind of television exposure he manages to get well before any formal hat-in-the-ring tossing takes place. Without considerable television exposure there can be no "build-up," and without a proper "build-up" there can be no serious candidacy. "Exposure" and "build-up" via television are on-going political processes in our time. No sooner are the polling booths closed down on Election Day than the speculations regarding who the candidates will be "next time" begin to circulate. Will there be a Muskie-Kennedy ticket in 1972, or a Kennedy-Muskie slate? Will Nixon go with Agnew again, or is the dump-Agnew movement already in progress? Speculations regarding Wallace's role in the 1972 Presidential lists were resolved by Wallace's own announced intention to try once again, not more than sixty days after the inauguration of President Nixon. And so it goes. Every move of the

President who was elected in 1968 will be dissected and analyzed to detect what impact it will have on his candidacy in 1972.

It is unlikely that we have heard the last of cries of "news management" and "credibility gaps." The contenders within the out-party will spend great amounts of effort and energy jockeying for television exposure, very much like packaged-goods manufacturers maneuvering for favorable shelf-space in the supermarkets. And throughout the quadrennial hiatus separating 1968 and 1972, the voter-viewers will be making assessments, judgments, evaluations, and even decisions well before the formal 1972 campaign is actually launched. (As early as February, 1969, the Gallup Poll was investigating public receptivity to Edward Kennedy as a Presidential prospect, and on May 4 it issued the results of a Nixon-Kennedy-Wallace "trial heat.")

Calls for reforms in the political process generally narrow down to calls for controlling formal campaigns. The problems involved in pre-campaign campaigning are generally overlooked, even though by comparison they loom as monumental. Still, it remains a fact of political life that, abetted by the sheer presence of the television medium, the precampaign campaign is a formidable fixture in the new politics.

Although American political parties have been vested with a variety of functions by scholars, politicians, and voters—functions that include serving as a super-employment agency for use by winning candidates faced with the task of filling new jobs, recruiting and grooming suitable candidates, mediating between opposing political ideologies, providing information regarding the pulse of the electorate, and fund-raising for the candidates—the fact remains that, as Clinton Rossiter has put it, "The primary function of a political party in a democracy such as ours is to control and direct the struggle for power."[6]

Despite the fact that the American political-party system has developed and has been nurtured outside the parameters of the Constitution, the American political-party system up until 1932, when Franklin D. Roosevelt became a Presidential candidate, managed to be the dominant element in the nation's political structure. Developing refinements in political information-gathering and in the means of mass communications have been eroding that dominance ever since 1932. Prior to that year it was the political party that sought to create candidates in its own image. Since then, the ability to take the electorate's pulse directly through the use of political-opinion polls and the ability to communicate directly and dramatically with voters in their own homes without the mediation of the party allowed strong candidates to emerge on their own. From 1932 on, political parties, for the most part, have desperately been attempting to shape themselves in the images of their candidates. The struggle of political parties to "control and direct the struggle for power" has been slowly shifting away from the parties and towards the strongly individualistic candidate and his management teams. In recent years, the management teams, emerging in response to developments in public-opinion polling and in the means of mass communication through the electronic media, have not only applied their management skills to candidates, but they have applied them as well to the political parties which ostensibly are responsible for the candidate's nomination. The consequence of this application of management skills, has been the near disappearance of functioning political parties on the American scene. Witness this observation by Ashmore:

> *Whatever the intent of the founders and their successors in the places of power, it is quite evident that the political parties no longer perform the functions assigned to them. The protracted and chaotic Presidential nominating process still takes place through primaries and conventions that bear the traditional labels, but the candidates use them principally as a means of dramatizing individual appeals beamed directly at the public at large. As they barnstorm through the scattered primary states the contenders take along their own fund-raising, public-relations, and grass-roots organizing machinery, and they determine their stand on issues by consulting public opinion polls, not local party leaders.*[7]

That potential and actual Presidential candidates can make substantial inroads into the electorate's vote-giving propensities without the support of the formal Republican and Democratic party structures has been more than peripherally demonstrated by the political efforts of John F. Kennedy (in his primary campaigns), Nelson Rockefeller, Robert F. Kennedy, Eugene McCarthy, and George Wallace. In each of these instances the candidate sought to shape his party's posture and orientation to what *his* beliefs were, and consequently was forced to operate outside the formal structure of either major party. In John Kennedy's case the attempt to sway the party was successful. For the rest it was not. Nevertheless, in this age of politics by polls and television it has become ever more evident that the days of the change-resistant, strong two-party structure of American politics have passed. The glowingly optimistic, romantic prognostications that political parties will continue doing business *status quo ante,* expressed by expert observers such as Clinton Rossiter, are made without adequate account taken of the impact that the innovations in electronic media have made on traditional party politics in this land.

> *As far as my own weak eyes can see into the future, the parties look like the parties of today [1960]—loose, supple, overlapping, decentralized, undisciplined, interest-directed, and principle-shunning enterprises in group diplomacy that are encircled and penetrated by a vigorous array of interest groups. They will be—in short, what they have always been—parties that aspire seriously to majority rule in a vast and motley democracy.*[8]

The candidate of the winning party in 1968 did not win by virtue of a numerical majority mandate. The 1968 "Constitutional crisis" brought on by the Wallace challenge heralded as a serious possibility the emergence of a pluralistic party system. The successes achieved in the primaries by

Eugene McCarthy in 1968 and his subsequent failure to win his party's nomination have touched off a rash of introspective exercises in the Democratic Party which virtually guarantee that that particular organization will *not* always be what it has been.

Exactly what the functions of the political party in the new politics will be are difficult to predict. The optimists say that nothing will change substantially. The old party structures will simply absorb the pressures for change and continue as of old. The pessimists predict the complete disappearance of political parties, and, as Marshall McLuhan has already declared, there will follow the emergence of all-powerful "tribal chieftains" who will come to power on their own via television and will rule by direct, computerized, daily plebiscites.

Observers of the moderate stripe see the functions of contemporary national political parties being reduced to simple fund-raising and doorbell-ringing among the local grass roots unless constitutional reforms of the entire election process are quickly instituted. Generally, suggestions for reform concern themselves mainly with the standardization of procedures in the primaries, with opening up popular caucuses for the selection of delegates to nominating conventions, with making nominating conventions more responsive to minority points of view, with either modifying or eliminating the Electoral College system, and with controlling or eliminating private financing of political campaigns.

Again, no matter what happens, the national political parties of the future will no longer be the same as in the past. Television has made the voter's home the campaign amphitheater, and opinion surveys have made it his polling booth. From this perspective, he has little regard for or need of a political party, at least as we have known it, to show him how to release the lever on Election Day.

After two decades of experiential learning from political television there is evidence throughout the land that the electorate has not been particularly entranced by what it has been viewing. Cries for reforms of all sorts in the political process echo from living rooms throughout the republic. The sense of simulated involvement in the American political process that has been induced through exposure to televised politicking has begun to be translated into the reality of sentiment. More and more Americans appear to be expressing the view that if they are in fact participants in the political process, which before television was merely an abstraction to most, they want more *actual* participation than was afforded to them previously.

At this point, the urgency for broadening actual participation in the political process reflects itself in the support for reforms that are designed to correct some of the more obvious faults of the politics of old. Testimony to such support are the results of various public-opinion polls that have been conducted since the 1968 Presidential election. As examples, the Gallup Poll reported that the proportion of Americans who say they would support a black candidate for the Presidency rose from thirty-eight percent in 1958 to sixty-seven percent in February, 1969. Majorities also now endorse lowering the voting age to eighteen and favor the selection of Presidential candidates via a nationwide primary instead of a political-party nominating convention.

On the matter of direct reform in the election process itself, it has previously been reported that, in view of the problems that are raised by ever-mounting campaigning costs, nearly seven in ten Americans would look favorably upon some federal controls regarding the amounts of money spent in any given political campaign for office. Another method for cutting down the costs of Presidential campaigns was suggested by sixty percent of a national sample of adults who told Gallup Poll interviewers during the days immediately following the 1968 election that they would favor "shortening Presidential campaigns to five weeks" instead of the customary ten. Whether economy or boredom are the motivational forces behind this public suggestion, the electorate is expressing a degree of distaste with campaigns as they have been waged in our most recent televised past, a disenchantment that cannot be disregarded.

Perhaps the most startling of all public expressions regarding the current reformist mood of the nation's electorate comes from the findings of a November 23, 1968 Gallup Poll as reported in *The New York Times*. The *Times'* story begins with this lead:

> The Gallup Poll reported today that 81 per cent of the public favored basing the election of the President on the popular vote throughout the nation rather than the present system where a candidate can be elected President even though he runs behind in the primaries.
>
> This new post-election percentage represents a dramatic rise in the proportion in favor of such a change since a September (1968) survey. That survey showed 66 per cent in favor.
>
> The American public has approved reform of the Electoral College on 18 different occasions. Majorities in every survey—as long as 1948—have either favored abandonment of the present system or a radical change to make it reflect more accurately the sentiment registered at the polls.

It appears that the vicarious political participation by voters in the United States that has been induced by exposure to television has created a paradox. The greater the degree and intensity of vicarious participation that is induced by merely watching political events, the greater seems to be the cry for realistic participation in them. Whether this demand is real or whether it merely reflects a new set of political clichés is difficult to ascertain at this point. What can be noted with certainty is the fact that the communications revolution that television has induced in American society indeed has within it the makings of a new politics.

Thus, to understand the new politics we must first understand the new communications. If we persist in equating the effects of political television with simple vote changes we are overlooking the essence of this barely understood communications force—its total impact upon our total lives. We must begin to take seriously the warning of Marshall McLuhan:

> *Today, in the electronic age of instantaneous communication, I believe that our survival, and at the very least our comfort and happiness is predicted on understanding the nature of our new environment, because unlike previous environmental changes, the electronic media constitute a total and near instantaneous transformation of culture, values, and attitudes. This upheaval generates great pain and identity loss, which can be ameliorated only through a conscious awareness of its dynamics. If we understand the revolutionary transformations caused by new media, we can anticipate and control them; but if we continue in our self-induced subliminal trance, we will be their slaves.*[9]

We must also take into account the synergistic effect of the broadcast-communications technology in combination with the survey method for information-gathering. Since the 1930s a radically new style of politics has been evolving as a direct consequence of the use of these techniques by some politicians, a style that came into full flower in the 1960s. Franklin D. Roosevelt pioneered the use of both broadcast communications and polls in American politics, and almost every Presidential candidate of the 1960s, successful or hopeful—including John F. Kennedy, Richard Nixon, Lyndon B. Johnson, Barry Goldwater, Hubert Humphrey, Robert F. Kennedy, Nelson Rockefeller and George Romney—has followed in his path.

As a direct result of the use of television and polls by these Presidential aspirants in the 1960s, the old-line party mechanism has become obsolescent and irrelevant. The past decade has witnessed the emergence of personal followings controlled and directed by technical specialists who report to the candidates themselves. To the extent that top echelon party functionaries have accommodated themselves to this development by becoming part of a candidate's entourage, they have been able to maintain their political viability. However, the process of institutional change creates tensions that will erupt into conflict unless and until new forms come into being that are adequate to control these tensions. In 1968 the old, expiring political forms had reached the point where they were no longer capable of containing conflicting political factions. In this light the "children's crusade" for Eugene McCarthy, the upheavals at the Democratic convention in Chicago, and the partial success of George Wallace's demagoguery are best understood as *symptoms* of political change rather than as the change itself.

The twin impacts of instantaneous communications and mass playback via opinion polls were first to foster and then to intensify and underscore the impotency of the old politics. Whether the new institutional forms will prove adequate to the task of generating an orderly politics that maintains democratic values is still a moot question. The potential of television and polls for unprincipled manipulation and phoney participation, as we have seen, is ever-present. On the other hand, there is no intrinsic reason why the use of polls and television should lead to these negative consequences. The challenge is to create institutional controls that will inhibit such developments and foster genuine two-way communications between political leaders and citizens in accordance with democratic principles. That challenge remains to be met.

NOTES: ELECTIONS

Introduction

1. Alexis de Tocqueville, *Democracy in America,* Volume I (Schocken, 1961), pp. 193-194.

2. Frank J. Sorauf, *Party Politics in America* (Little, Brown, 1968), pp. 183-184.

3. Fred I. Greenstein, *The American Party System and the American People* (Second Edition; Prentice-Hall, 1970), pp. 18-23.

4. See President's Commission on Registration and Voting Participation, *Report* (U. S. Government Printing Office, 1963), esp. pp. 5-14.

5. Herbert E. Alexander, *Financing the 1968 Election* (Citizens' Research Foundation, 1971).

6. Congressional Quarterly Weekly Report, XXVIII (April 17, 1970), 999.

7. Gerald M. Pomper, *Elections in America* (Dodd, Mead, 1968), p. 247.

8. *Ibid.*

Gerald M. Pomper

1. A. P. Campbell *et al., The American Voter.* New York: John Wiley, 1960, pp. 227-234.

2. V. O. Key, Jr., *The Responsible Electorate.* Cambridge, Mass.: Harvard University Press, 1966, p. 77.

3. V. O. Key, Jr., "A Theory of Critical Elections." *Journal of Politics,* Vol. 17, February, 1955, p. 4.

4. J. Kessel, *The Goldwater Coalition.* Indianapolis: Bobbs-Merrill, 1968, Chapter 9.

5. The method is simple. The content categories, from "rhetorical" to "detailed" are assigned arbitrary weights from one to six. The number of pledges in each category is then multiplied by the appropriate weight, and the sum of the products is then divided by the total number of statements.

6. The adjusted percentage is the proportion of the platform devoted to the topic in a given year, divided by the percentage devoted to that topic in all platforms from 1948 to 1964. If no particular emphasis is placed on the topic in the given year, the resulting ratio will be one. Increased or decreased emphasis will be reflected in ratios above or below one. The measure of attention **varies generally from 2.0 to 7.0.**

William T. Gossett

1. See 1 Farrand, *Records of the Federal Convention of 1787,* at 175 (1937 ed.); 2 Farrand 29, 34, 500.

2. 2 Farrand 31, 114.

3. *The Federalist* No. 68 (Hamilton).

4. Bickel, *The New Age of Political Reform* 5-7 (1968).

5. Banzhaf, *One Man, 3.312 Votes: A Mathematical Analysis of the Electoral College,* 13 Vill. L. Rev. 303 (1968).

6. *Delaware* v. *New York,* 385 U. S. 895 (1966) (complaint, pages 12-13).

7. *Hearings on Election of the President Before Subcommittee on Constitutional Amendments of the Senate Committee on the Judiciary,* 89th Cong., 2d Sess.; 90th Cong., 1st Sess. at 623.

Harold Mendelsohn and Irving Crespi

1. *Denver Post,* October 13, 1968.

2. *Broadcasting* (September 9, 1968), p. 44.

3. *The New York Times,* November 17, 1968.

4. Harry S. Ashmore, "Electoral Reform: What Can Be Done When Everybody Loses?" *The Center Magazine* (Santa Barbara, California: a publication of the Center for the Study of Democratic Institutions, January, 1969), p. 4.

5. *Ibid.,* p. 8.

6. Clinton Rossiter, *Parties and Politics in America* (Ithaca, New York: Cornell University Press, 1960), p. 39.

7. Ashmore, *op. cit.,* p. 4.

8. Rossiter, *op. cit.,* p. 164.

9. "Playboy Interview: Marshall McLuhan—Candid Conversation," *Playboy* (March, 1969), p. 56.

DIRECT ACTION

Violence has no constitutional sanction; and every government from the beginning has moved against it.

But where grievances pile high and most of the elected spokesmen represent the Establishment, violence may be the only effective response.

—William O. Douglas[1]

Although the voting booth may be the most commonly frequented arena of political activity, it also represents the form of individual participation requiring the least effort and imagination. While there is a certan majesty about millions of Americans dutifully expressing candidate preferences at the polls, too often the fifteen minutes which the average citizen devotes to casting his ballot is the extent of his personal efforts to mold the national government to his liking. This is unfortunate given the numerous ways in which the individual may attempt to affect the political system directly.

The forms of direct personal action provide almost unlimited opportunity for the citizen to inject his views into the governmental process. Direct action by the individual may be oriented toward formal political institutions (writing to a congressman) or toward fellow citizens (doorbell ringing in behalf of a candidate or cause); it may call for extensive efforts (circulating petitions) or be relatively effortless (affixing a political bumper sticker); it may be legal (peacefully demonstrating or filing a suit), or extralegal (bribery). Each of these possible forms of direct action shares the advantage of not requiring formal organization with others. Most may be carried out by a single individual. None are strictly confined to any particular time of the political year. And some can be potentially effective.

The greatest single roadblock to the extensive use of direct personal action is inertia. Institutionalized notions of civic responsibility may draw a citizen to the polls on the appointed day, but there is no corresponding force urging people to direct political action. The predictable result is inactivity. Governmental bodies can only be responsive if the citizenry makes demands. Morris Rosenberg's essay which appears below analyzes factors contributing to political apathy. It is a perceptive examination of why political activity plays such a minor role in the life of the typical American.

When an individual is moved to political action, his efforts are commonly short-lived and of relatively minor consequence. Sustained political action requires a commitment of time which the average person is unwilling or unable to make. The result is that displaying bumper stickers, writing letters, and having political discussions with family and friends are the most frequent forms of personal political action other than voting.

Individuals who do attempt to influence the government through direct action tend to be dissatisfied with the state of public affairs. When political attitudes and governmental policies are significantly at variance or when a person's disadvantaged plight is largely ignored by the political establishment, the situation is ripe for direct personal action. Due to this fact direct action is usually aimed at effecting a change in public policy. It is not unusual to observe automobiles adorned with "PEACE NOW" or "VICTORY IN VIETNAM" stickers, but very unusual for a person to advocate publicly no change in the administration's war policy. Similarly, the Congressional Mail Service delivers thousands of constituent letters each day urging representatives to vote a particular way. But it is rare for a person to be spurred into thanking a congressman for his voting record. The status quo is simply an insufficient force to move an individual to political activity.

Likewise, persons who engage in direct action tend to be the disaffected of society, those whose opinions are not being reflected by governmental policies. The more disaffected the citizen is the more extreme form his direct action will assume. The textile mill operator whose economic interests are adversely affected by foreign imports is disaffected in a relatively minor way. Personal action which he takes will assume rather traditional forms. The ghetto black whose disaffection may well approach being total is much more likely to resort to extra-legal political activity. Individuals such as Sirhan Sirhan or Lee Harvey Oswald, whose political and psychological estrangement may never be clearly understood, are moved to execute the most serious form of direct action, assassination.

The response of governmental bodies to individual demands depends largely upon the nature of the demand and the technique by which the demand is articulated. A basic assumption of a democratic society is that responsible officials will react positively to reasonable demands expressed in a rational manner. Many incidents of direct action, of course, do not promote reasonable goals and, therefore, the governmental response is a negative one. A good example is provided by former Representative Steven McGroarty's answer to a constituent's letter:

> *One of the countless drawbacks of being in Congress is that I am compelled to receive impertinent letters from a jackass like you in which you say I promised to have the Sierra Madre mountains reforested and I have been in Congress two months and haven't done it. Will you please take two running jumps and go to hell.*[2]

However, it might well be argued that presenting reasonable demands in a rational manner is an inadequate means of inducing a favorable governmental response. The work of the early civil rights and poverty movements quietly presenting demands to the national government had little payoff in terms of concrete policy changes. But the government did respond to more activist forms of protest, picketing, sit-ins, economic boycotts, and even violent demonstrations. Learning from this experience, protest movements of a more recent vintage, the Chicanos, the Indians, and segments of the peace movement, have taken a much more militant stance.

Two of the selections included in this section speak to the issue of direct action through political protest. In "Protest as a Political Resource," Michael Lipsky analyzes the utility of political protest in attempts to change public policy. The article examines the roles played by the communications media, protest leadership, and material and symbolic rewards. Lipsky concludes that relatively powerless groups cannot use protest with a high probability of long-range success. The second article dealing with this subject is "The Federal Government and Protest" by David Mars. This essay concentrates on the reaction of the government to the political protests of recent years and provides insights to the question of why and how the government responds to such protests.

While the protest movements of the last decade have been aimed primarily at effecting a change in the policies of governmental actors, a good deal of direct action concentrates on altering the political thinking of fellow citizens. The objective of this activity is to affect public policy by changing public opinion. The key question becomes one of how an individual can be most effective in convincing others to change their political views on issues of importance. At no time has this been such a great problem as in recent attempts by peace workers to convince Americans that the war in Indochina is destructive and immoral. No matter how valid the arguments of the young antiwar forces, most citizens find unacceptable anything supported by persons they perceive as communists, dope addicts, traitors and long-haired ingrates. Rhetoric couched in terms such as "fascist," "pigs," "racist establishment," destroys from the outset any possibility of gaining converts to the antiwar fold. Social psychologist Ralph K. White analyzes this problem in his article, "A Postscript for Peace Workers: Some Concrete Advice." Although this essay is directed specifically at the antiwar problem, its application can be generalized to all situations involving direct action geared toward convincing persons to alter their political views.

SOME DETERMINANTS OF POLITICAL APATHY

Morris Rosenberg

It has been observed that political apathy is a very widespread phenomenon in American culture. Whether one measures apathy by the criterion of political involvement, knowledge or activity, the number of people who satisfy the culturally defined desiderata of participation is small.

There are those who consider this a serious malfunctioning of democracy. If men are to maintain control over their political destinies, they must be aware of what is going on, and must take a hand in determining public policy. On the other hand, there are some political theorists who find such apathy a favorable, rather than an unfavorable, sign. They interpret it to mean that the society is fundamentally contented, is characterized by consensus rather than by broad cleavages, and is basically stable.

If we accept the view that the democratic ideal encourages political interest and participation, then the question naturally arises: what are the factors which bring about this absence of political interest and activity? In order to cast some light on this question, an exploratory study, designed to reveal the range and variation of factors which contribute to political apathy, was undertaken. Seventy qualitative interviews were conducted with a non-random sample of respondents, most of whom resided in Ithaca, New York. The interviews were of an unstructured type, designed to encourage the respondent to reveal his views regarding the political process with a minimum of direction and a maximum of spontaneity. We did not undertake to obtain statistically reliable data but, rather, sought to gather ideas and hypotheses for more systematic research. The results presented here, therefore, lay no claim to representing scientific proof, but are designed to serve as suggestive hypotheses.

Limitations of space prohibit a discussion of the total range of factors which were revealed in these interviews and which appeared to contribute to political indifference and inactivity, but three general factors merit discussion: (1) the threatening consequences of political activity, (2) the futility of political activity, and (3) the absence of spurs to interest and participation. Let us note how these factors are expressed concretely in the interviews.

THE THREATENING CONSEQUENCES OF POLITICAL ACTIVITY

It is generally felt that any restriction on the individual's right to express his political views freely represents a violation of the value of freedom of speech. It is assumed that the uninhibited airing of ideas, viewpoints, and facts is conducive to the attainment of rational democratic decisions. It may thus be argued that loyalty investigations which frighten innocent people into silence represent a limitation on freedom of speech.

The issue of freedom of speech is usually posed in terms of whether the *government* applies pressure on the individual to restrain him from expressing his political views. Yet there are social factors which may be far more significant than governmental restraint in limiting the expression of social and political ideas. The sociological issue of freedom of speech boils down to the question of whether one is willing to take the *consequences* of expressing one's political ideas and working in their behalf; governmental restraint, expressed in physical coercion, is only one such possible consequence.

Our predominantly middle class respondents expressed many fears of presenting their own political views freely, but very rarely were these fears of political authority. . . . One respondent, it is true, carefully checked on the identity of the interviewer; he was reluctant to express his political views frankly to an unknown person who, for all he knew, might actually be an official investigator trying to draw him out. This is a telling commentary on how . . . governmental investigations may immobilize certain people from the very minimum of political action. But such people proved to be rarities. The reason probably is that in any society, authoritarian or democratic, the individual is always free to stand up and express his views frankly in favor of the government; it is only when people desire to express views which challenge constituted authority that freedom of speech becomes an issue. Most of our respondents were Republicans or Democrats, and it did not appear to occur to them that *their* rights might be threatened by such investigations. Whether different results would appear among a more representative sample of respondents is a question requiring further research.

Our particular respondents, however, did express many fears of uninhibitedly expressing their political views, but the threats they mentioned tended to be of a social or psychological sort rather than of a political nature. The point to be stressed here is that political participation does not simply involve the relationship of the citizen to his government. Political participation may to a considerable extent involve *interpersonal interaction*. Consequently the dynamics of interpersonal relationships may have important implications for the operation of the democratic process.

In this paper we will use the term "political activity" in a broad sense to include political discussion, consumption of political communications, interest, voting, and participation in political organizations. It would be important in future investigations to analyze those manifestations of activity separately .

Threats to Interpersonal Harmony

One of the characteristics of politics in a democracy is that they are *controversial*. This establishes potentialities for interpersonal disagreement which may threaten the individual in many ways—particularly when the individual has an image of himself as a likeable, agreeable personality. Similarly, there are those who are so insecure that they are terrified of aggression or hostility of any sort directed against them.

Political discussion may threaten to alienate one's friends and neighbors.

> *Some of my friends are (active in politics). Some are avid Democrats, but most of my friends are not active. We don't discuss politics much. I think it's sort of like religion. It's personal, and I don't like to get into arguments. . . . When politics comes up in conversation, I always say—"Let's talk about something else," . . . especially when ————— is around. She's such a Democrat and gets so riled up.*

Political discussion posed threats to a recent marriage:

> *I personally want to be informed because my husband holds different political beliefs. We don't discuss politics very often because when we do we are likely to disagree violently. Right now I want to avoid friction—we were just married last June—so we try not to get into political discussions."*

Political discussion may endanger one's position in a group and threaten one's sense of belongingness. For example, a woman who was very much wrapped up in the ————— organization feared that political discussion might jeopardize her position there. When asked why she did not discuss politics more, she replied: "Well, you see, a lot of local political wives are in ————— and I have to be careful."

The manner in which social pressure may be applied to insure political conformity in a small community is illustrated in the following story:

> *I remember one time going to a city council meeting when I was back in Minnesota. I was disagreeing with one of the commissioners on an important town issue. Why, the next day I received calls and a visitor asking me what exactly it was all about and what I was up to. After that I just didn't go to meetings of that sort.*

Thus people may impose a powerful self-censorship on political expression in order to avoid threats to friendship, marriage relationships, and group solidarity. While they are legally free to say what they please, many are unwilling to face the interpersonal consequences of such expression. Whether the situation is actually threatening or whether it is simply interpreted as such by the individual, the effect is the same.

Threats to Occupational Success

The economic processes of production and exchange in a complex industrial-commercial society involve interpersonal relations at almost every point. If political discussion has a potentially divisive and disharmonious interpersonal effect, then it may be avoided because of its threats to the important area of occupational success. This is particularly likely to occur among those engaged in the sale of products where the salesman must maintain harmonious relations with his customer; it is not, however, restricted to this area. In brief, politics fosters argument and dispute, whereas business success thrives on harmony and good will. Consequently, people may fear to talk politics because of the threat it poses to their occupational success.

Political discussion may threaten the harmonious relations essential to economic production.

One respondent refused to tell the interviewer how he had voted. When asked for his reason, he replied:

> *Well, it's a personal subject . . . You see, in my field, there is no harm in avoiding unnecessary conflicts, and politics are subject to strong sentiments . . . I have to maintain relations among employees and management, and I try to avoid trouble points. I've always felt it wise policy to be quiet about how I vote.*

One respondent, a manager of a plant, was asked whether he had helped any candidates in the most recent campaign. He replied:

> *No, because I never like to express my political views in public. . . . Since I have to deal with so many men, both in the plant and in the buying of (raw materials), there is no sense in making people angry at you over a local election.*

One respondent was asked directly whether the fact that he conducted his business in a small town did not make public support of a candidate or party an economic danger. He replied:

> *Absolutely; for that reason I register* No Mark. *Actually I'm a Republican. But in the case of* ————, *it's different. He's a friend of mine . . . and* everybody *knew I'd support him anyway. Besides, he lives in* ———— *where I have my business, and (his opponent) is over in* ———— *(a different town). I don't sell much over there anyway.*

In other words, the man engaged in commerce cannot afford to alienate *either* Democrats or Republicans; in this sense business is not merely apolitical but anti-political. Similarly an employer may be reluctant to alienate his workers, and a worker may be unwilling to jeopardize his job, in defense of his political principles. These factors may be extremely significant deterrents to the free expression of political ideas.

Threat of Ego-Deflation

While political discussion may ostensibly represent a form of intellectual intercourse designed to evaluate alternative principles, it cannot escape implicating the self. An attack on a man's principles may often be seen as a blow to his self-esteem. While some people may enhance their egos through victory in political argument, there are others who, facing the prospect of revealing factual ignorance or committing gross logical errors, seek to avoid the feeling of defeat, abashment, humiliation, or other discomfiture by staying far away from such discussions. An individual with a highly vulnerable ego may impose a censorship upon himself which is as rigid as any imposed in an authoritarian state.

One woman, observing that her husband and in-laws discussed politics, was asked whether she joined in these discussions. "No, since I don't understand too much about politics, I just keep my mouth closed." When asked if she discussed politics with anyone, she answered: "Very little, because . . . well, I really don't understand too much about politics. People should know what they are talking about and this takes an education which goes beyond the high-school level."

> *I don't think I'm capable enough to take an active part (in politics). I just feel I lack the ability . . . I don't know what would be required of me.*
> *My husband and I talk it over, of course, but I don't talk about it in public because I don't know enough. I wish I knew more. Sometimes I'd like to say something.*

Although these statements reflected a faith in expertism, combined with a rational insistence that a person should have some basis for his expressed opinions, they suggest that an individual may prefer to avert the danger of exposing himself to public ridicule rather than to freely and openly express his political ideas.

To summarize, the democratic right of freedom of speech does not insure that people will feel free to express their political convictions publicly at all times. Threats of governmental action will deter some. Others will be blocked from talking or acting in behalf of their political beliefs out of fear of losing friends, alienating neighbors, endangering marriages, jeopardizing their positions in groups, losing business, jeopardizing their jobs, endangering production in their plants, facing community pressures, or exposing their feelings of self-esteem to threat. These are consequences which many people are unwilling to face and, to avoid these consequences, they impose a self-censorship on their political expression, participation, and even emotional involvement. One factor in the political structure which sets the conditions for these results is the multi-party system. In a democratic society, politics are *controversial,* and controversiality, while it may encourage interest, also has potential interpersonal consequences which may foster political inactivity.

THE FUTILITY OF POLITICAL ACTIVITY

In most cases a precondition for political activity is the conviction that what one does will make a difference, will have an effect of some sort. It is true, of course, that people may engage in some noninstrumental, goal activity such as political discussion simply because they are interested in the subject and enjoy talking about it. In most cases, however, political participation beyond the level of discussion probably has the aim of *getting one's will translated into political action*. But, people tend to be motivated to action only if they feel that this action leads to the desired goal.

One general factor contributing to political apathy is the feeling that activity is futile. The individual feels that even if he were active, the political results he desires would probably not come to pass. There is consequently no point in doing anything.

In expressing this sense of futility, the individual can focus on either the subject or the object of action. On the one hand, he can focus on certain characteristics of himself; e.g., he is insignificant, powerless, or incompetent. On the other hand, he can focus on the characteristics of the objects to be influenced; e.g., political representatives pay no attention to him, political machines run things just as they please, and so on. But if his representative pays no attention to him, this may be either because *he* is too unimportant or because *the representative* is unresponsive to the public will. In other words, each "reason" for feeling that political activity is futile implies both a characteristic of the individual effort and a characteristic of the agents to be influenced. For analytical purposes it is important to distinguish between reasons phrased in terms of the self and those phrased in terms of the nature of the political structure, although these should not be interpreted as representing alternative reasons.

Futility Based on the Sense of Personal Inadequacy

It is rather easy to see why, in a mass society characterized by broad disparities in power, an individual may tend to develop a sense of personal insignificance and weakness.

The feeling of the futility of action, deriving from a sense of personal insignificance, is likely to be particularly strong when the individual feels himself to be either (a) only one in relation to a great many, or (b) a weak person in relation to strong and powerful forces.

Simmel has noted that as the size of the group increases, each individual alone makes less of a difference to the totality. Although the proportion of potential voters who actually go to the polls in the United States is relatively small, the absolute number is extremely large; the 1952 national elections attracted over sixty million voters. Many of our respondents appeared overwhelmed by this huge number of participants and felt that their vote would have little effect on the outcome of the election one way or the other.

> *Voting doesn't make that much difference. What can an individual do about it? He can't really do much.*
> *My vote will always count, yet one vote one way or the other doesn't make much difference.*

One respondent considered herself politically unimportant for the following unexpected reason:

> *One vote doesn't mean much. The way it is set up now with the electrical or electoral college, I can't see we actually vote a person into office. I don't know too much about it. I think we should have each person voting and his vote counted separately. We should have just straight balloting.*

This sense of political impotence was expressed still more clearly by this respondent when she said:

> *There is no real justice in the present system. You don't have too much to say, right or wrong. You can feel or think, but that's about all.*

People may also tend to consider any serious political efforts on their parts as futile because they feel that they have very little individual power. They feel that their own voices are too weak, their own strength too puny, to make much political difference. One respondent felt that politics are

> *all right, but it is always the big guy he (the politician) is interested in helping. . . . The only thing I have against them is that they are too damn narrow-minded (and that politics) keep the little man down.*

Switching his attention to cities, this respondent felt that there was too much vote-buying in cities and that

> *the little man in cities is afraid to go against the party. He either votes right, or he doesn't vote.*

He felt the courts, too, were not fair; witnesses were bought off. "It's the same as in politics. . . The little guy has nothing to do about it."

Another respondent was asked what part the average man played in politics. "Not much of a part," he replied; "the little man votes and that's all. . . The party usually takes over pretty much. They don't think too much about the little man."

> *What does the working man care about politics, anyway? What can he do, even if he did care? That's probably it . . . What can he do? Nothing should bother him anyway. The country will still go on just the same for the average working man.*

One respondent, asked how much influence people like her had on the way the government was run, answered: "None—well, that isn't the right answer. I vote; is that what you mean by it?"

> *Well, it seems almost useless to do a lot of work for the national group when there are so many other people for it and when you really won't have much to say about what happens anyway.*

A lot of those people are a lot better than I am, and a lot of them have more pull.

In some cases, the *individual's self-image* does not correspond to his picture of the requirements of political activity. His sense of inadequacy is based on special personality characteristics.

One respondent was asked whether he would care about campaigning.

No, I don't think so. Unless I felt strongly enough about something, I would. I'm not much of a salesman. I never cared about buttonholing.

I don't really go in for it that much. I don't know. I guess I'm more of a listener in that line.

The Unmanageability of Political Forces

Many of the respondents who expressed a sense of futility that their own political action would culminate in a desired political result placed less stress on their own impotence and more on the unresponsiveness of political powers to their pressure. The feeling was that (1) the political representative, (2) the political machine, (3) the "government," or (4) some anonymous agencies of power simply ignored the will of the people; they made their own decisions almost completely uninfluenced by the people.

Under these circumstances, political activity was viewed as futile. Respondents expressing these views tended to feel that they had lost control over the political decision-making process; their political destinies lay in the hands of others.

Many people felt that their *elected representatives* were unconcerned with, and unresponsive to, the will of the people.

Once they (the politicians) get elected, they don't give a goddamn.

You got to know the man who does good, not your friend. You could be a good man but if the people don't like you, it's no good. You say to a guy, "I don't like you; I'm not going to vote for you." He say, "If you vote for me I'm your friend, and if you don't vote for me, I'm still your friend." But if he get elected, he don't do nothing for you. . . . This politics is really a funny thing.

Many respondents appear to feel that once the *political machines* gain power, the citizens' control over the political process tends to be lost.

The machine is too strong to do what you want.

The machines run things all around . . . Working to stop the machine could go on and on and still get no place. They'll always be there.

The centralization and concentration of government may produce a sense of remoteness from the decision-making process. The individual feels that he cannot maintain control over political decisions made by powerful figures hundreds and even thousands of miles away.

This phenomenon was highlighted by the respondents who contrasted the type of effectiveness he could have at the local level with his potential influence at the national level.

> *In local government, if things aren't really clear, you can usually find out the facts. Go back to knowing persons. You can't say that I can't get something out of some aldermen I know. If something is going wrong in the city, I can see one of them. In the case of senators, I can't go down to Washington and see my senator every time something goes wrong. In local, I think I can find out, whereas in national government, I don't feel I can.*

One respondent was asked whether world peace was important to him. He replied:

> *It's an important problem, yes, but there isn't much we can do about it in a meeting downtown. We're concerned about it, naturally, everyone is; but just about all we can do is sit by and watch what happens. Washington does all the deciding, and we've put men there for the purpose . . . I know what it entails to pick up garbage, but I haven't the foggiest notion of what it takes to put over a treaty between two countries. I don't know whether the men in Washington are doing the best possible job or not.*

Finally, there are some people who feel that action is futile because the basic political decisions are in the hands of certain *powerful anonymous forces*. The citizen cannot influence them, not simply because they are remote or unresponsive, but because he does not even know who they are.

> *The masses feel it's controlled by certain groups.*
>
> *We say we live in a democracy because we elect our representatives. But if the people we elect are in turn chosen by people who are outside our control, then our democracy is only relative and not as pure as we think it is. . . . I think that the higher levels of party organization are closed to ordinary citizens.*
>
> *Today most of the platforms of both parties are about the same. The people it really matters to are those who are looking for special favors. Just take the issue of tidelands' oil and take a list of the visitors of the General the day before he signed the bill!*
>
> *A couple of men get together in some room . . . and when they come out, the party nomination has been made. You never know.*

Thus some people feel it is futile to seek to influence those who make political decisions, because they feel that the locus of power lies in the hands of unknown powerful forces.

It is relevant to note the influence of the time factor in politics. At election time the citizen's sense of power and incentive for action is likely to be maximal. If the individual wishes to get his will translated into political action, he can do something about it, secure in the conviction that he is making some contribution toward that end. Not only may he vote for the candidate who propounds his views and position, but he may also seek to persuade others to do the same. He may thus feel some sense of control over the political process.

However, the *periodicity* of American elections requires the citizen to exercise his power at arbitrarily predetermined times, not when it suits his mood. Thus the individual who is angry at an incumbent or enthusiastic about a candidate may often have to wait a year or more before he can vote again. It is difficult for the human organism to maintain a high level of emotional ardor and involvement over a long period of time. The more characteristic reaction, therefore, is to withdraw one's emotional involvement from politics. Once emotion is withdrawn, of course, vigorous political activity becomes difficult. In other words, *electoral periodicity is not resonant with human reactions*. The individual has power at election time but tends to consider action futile at other times.

> Anyway, politics has really stopped until next fall. We won't start till next fall. A guy figures "what the hell?" People aren't interested when there's no election.
> Once a man is elected and he turns out no good, it is too late to do anything about it.
> They might not do what they say. Either they can't do it, or they say, "I'm in now, so I don't have to do it."

The citizen thus feels a *discontinuous* sense of control over the political process. He has some power at the periodic intervals of election time, but most of the time he sees no relationship between his desires and action and actual political results. In addition, he cannot work to translate his will into action immediately, but must "save up" his irritations, desires, or enthusiasms until the next election. This characteristic of the political structure may often cause him to feel that there is no point in getting excited or doing anything about political matters, i.e., it encourages apathy. It is true, of course, that citizens can write to their congressmen or participate in pressure groups, but these alternatives seldom appeared to have occurred to our respondents.

The Foregone Conclusion
The sense of futility generated by activity designed to translate one's will into action is likely to be strongest, of course, when one has reason to believe that such action will never come to pass. When a party has no more than a theoretical chance of victory, when the election is a foregone conclusion, then the rather vague incentive of an "impressive defeat" is little spur to vigorous political activity.

The individual feels that no matter how hard he works, the candidate he supports will not be elected in any case. This is particularly likely to be the case when a state or local community has a well-established and virtually unchangeable tradition of electing candidates from one party. Many people prefer to remain inactive, or at least uninvolved, rather than to face the frustration stemming from the certain defeat of their candidates or principles.

This is the situation in Ithaca. The town normally registers and votes overwhelmingly Republican. The Democrats often encounter difficulty in obtaining a slate of candidates, and the Liberal Party characteristically supports the Democratic candidate. A Democrat was elected mayor some years ago, but died before taking office, (the cause being, it is facetiously rumored, the terrible shock of his victory). Usually, however, a primarily Republican slate is returned.

> Nobody realizes how hard the Democratic Party around here does work. We'd like to get a higher caliber man to run but it's just impossible. Everybody knows the Republican will win and nobody wants to waste his time.
>
> Everyone votes Republican here whether they are good, bad or inefficient (sic) . . . In many town, local and county elections, one party dominates the area. There is not enough spirit of competition to arouse interest.

The Gap Between Ideal and Reality

Thus far we have focused on the individual's feeling of futility regarding the possibility of attaining some practical political goal. It is also possible, however, that if the goal itself is too remote or too difficult to attain, the individual will give up hope of trying to reach it. The level of social aspiration may be so very high that, rather than serving as an incentive to action, it may discourage and immobilize the individual.

For example, some people may sincerely embrace the social values of democracy, honesty in government, etc. We might thus expect them to be politically active in behalf of these principles. However, these values may be so high and pure, and the facts of political life so low and base, that they abandon any hope of bridging the gap between the normative and factual orders. Indeed it is often precisely the people who embrace the value of democracy most fervently who suffer the greatest disillusionment. One respondent explained,

> You gotta realize, life doesn't go the way you learn it in high school, or college, or the Constitution—It isn't that way.

This gap between the factual and normative orders of society is expressed clearly in this respondent's pungent statement: "The United States is great on paper."

> Everyone who goes to the polls wants democracy. They all consider themselves democrats with a small d. By the time the idea is represented, it ends up far afield from the original ideals. . . . Un-

fortunately, in spite of the need to vote, not only in America but in any democratic country, very rarely is the democratic objective accomplished.

It is true, of course, that even where the ideal is very low, the reality may be considered so remote from it as to render an effort to bridge the gap futile. The wider this gap, however, the more discouraged the individual is likely to be.

In sum, many people may be deterred from political activity by the conviction that their efforts will be futile. An individual may feel that he is but one among so many; that he is a very "little man" compared with very much more powerful agents; that the agents of political decision—representatives, machines, "the government," certain powerful anonymous forces—are unable or unwilling to heed his voice or follow his will; that the political reality is hopelessly remote from the ideal; or that the hopelessness of political victory makes any effort pointless. It may be observed that these consequences of apathy derive from the particular nature of the social and political structure. The *mass nature of the society,* characterized by wide disparities of power, promotes the sense of personal insignificance; the *centralization of government* fosters a sense of remoteness from the key decision-making processes; the *periodic elections* produce a discontinuous exercise of power; the *system of representation* draws power from the citizen and grants it to the representative; and so on. In other words, a political structure established with the aim of implementing democracy may unwittingly establish the conditions for political apathy.

ABSENCE OF SPURS TO ACTION

In illustrating the fact that people may be reluctant to be political participants out of fear of the potential dangers of such activity or because they consider it futile, we have stressed the *deterrents* to participation. However, it is also relevant to examine the question of apathy in the light of the absence of influences, stimuli, or appeals which might encourage participation. Theoretically there is no limit to the number of factors which can *fail* to stimulate an individual to political activity. Nevertheless, it seems relevant to cite certain factors, as they appeared in the interviews, which might have been influential in stimulating participation.

It would appear appropriate to analyze this section in terms of the concept of *attributes and influences.* Under the heading of "attributes" would be included those reasons given by respondents which indicated that it was some characteristic of politics which lacked appeal or which did not seem to offer any gratification. Certain factors which appeared among some of our respondents are: (1) The fact that the subject-matter of politics is not psychologically compelling; (2) The act or process of political activity lacks non-instrumental gratifications, fails to offer immediate satisfactions; and (3) The instrumental *results* of political activity do not appear to satisfy urgent and direct needs or provide important satisfactions. Under the heading of "influences," we refer to those cases in which people or groups fail, either by direct thrust or by shining example, to activate or inspire the respondent. Obviously these attributes and influences are not alternative determinants of apathy; for purposes of analysis, however, it is essential to consider them separately.

The Subject Matter of Politics Is Often Not Psychologically Compelling

Since the political institution deals with problems of the total society, involving subjects of general interest and concern, it tends to have an *abstract* or *impersonal* quality. However much the mass media seek to concretize and personalize political matters, they still remain, for many people, dull, remote and uninspiring.

One respondent mentioned that he did not pay much attention to national politics in the newspapers. When asked why, he replied:

> *Well, I'm not interested enough. I don't take the time to read such matters. I like to read more exciting things, such as kidnap cases, and I also like the sports' section a lot.*

Another respondent cited the many newspapers and news magazines he read. Asked what he read first, he replied: "Well, I always read the sports first, since that's what I'm most interested in."

> *People like to be entertained . . . and get away from the troubles of the day; and if you get them to start worrying about England and France and everything else in the world, they're just not interested. They've got enough troubles of their own without carrying the weight of the world.*
>
> *Well, I would say politics are dull in comparison to other news.*

When asked to be more specific, this respondent pointed to the local newspaper.

> *Well, like this here—I see much more excitement in this story about the plane crashes than in this story about Eisenhower and the story on farm supports.*

In other words, for many people the relatively abstract, impersonal, serious, and often complex, subject matter of politics cannot compete successfully with the simple, personal, emotional appeal and excitement of kidnapping and sports and more entertaining subjects of the mass media.

Absence of Noninstrumental Gratifications

The individual's incentive to political activity is often dulled by the absence of direct and immediate satisfactions to be derived from the activity itself. Just as people may engage in work not exclusively for the prestige and monetary rewards to be obtained from it but also because the work itself is satisfying, so people might conceivably engage in political activity because they enjoyed it, even if the goals they sought were not attained. Many people, however, find their current activities much more directly gratifying than political activity.

One respondent compared the gratifications she obtained by working with the Girl Scouts with the gratifications to be anticipated from political work. When asked, "Do you think your work as a Girl Scout leader more worth-while than political work would be?" she replied:

> *Yes, I think it's better to do something which has direct results. I don't know how party politics go or anything, and maybe I'm wrong, but it seems that you end up doing little things like telephoning or licking stamps. You don't have any control over things because everything is decided by party leaders, and you don't have much to say about what goes on. You don't get any direct results. In Girl Scouts, you see these results; you have a chance to shape the characters of the girls. I think that's more important.*

One respondent was asked why she happened to miss the campaign speeches:

> *R. I didn't have the time. If I had had the time, I would have been more interested. I work each day at the Community Center and it takes up most of my free time. I also devote many evenings to work there. I feel my work there is much more important than politics.*
> *I. Can you say why?*
> *R. I feel I'm really able to help people directly through my work at the Center, but I don't think I have much power to help others through politics.*

Political Results Meet Few Direct and Urgent Needs

Most people, concerned with the immediate and imperative needs and exigencies of day-to-day life, do not conceive of political action as a vehicle for the satisfaction of these needs. Politics may be viewed as a moderately interesting spectacle, but one that is remote from the direct concerns of daily life. The man who wants an apartment usually does not attempt to get one by lobbying vigorously for federal housing projects; rather, he consults agents, newspapers or friends. A woman who wants lower food prices ordinarily does not attempt to achieve it by joining a citizens' committee striving to apply pressure on Congress to restore price controls; rather, she goes several blocks out of her way to shop at a super-market whose prices are lower than those of the neighborhood grocer. Lack of concern with politics is understandable when viewed in this light.

One woman, asked if she were interested in politics, said: "I don't follow the news too much. I feel the world will go on without me, no matter." At a later point, asked if she felt that politics had any importance in her life, she replied: "No, we go on and politics has nothing to do with us. . . . I think most people go along from day to day and take what comes. I don't think they are much interested."

One respondent said: "Most of our serious issues are voted on in town meetings." Asked if he attended, he replied: "Only once in a while, for laughs. They really don't accomplish much, but they are nice to have around."

Another respondent, asked what effect she thought politics had on her everyday life, replied, "Don't think it has any, to tell the truth."

"I don't think politics or election results will or do affect my own life very much. Regardless of who is in power, I'll keep my job and my home."

> *I realize that politics does affect me, but it still doesn't seem to really touch me. I think we must be educated to a degree to think about it as something personal. . . . I think the fundamental thing is that we don't feel directly related or affected. . . . It doesn't concern us inwardly.*

The following conversation occurred with a Republican who was a member of the school board.

> *I. Do you think the Republican Party is as important as the school board?*
> *R. Goodness, no!*
> *I. Why?*
> *R. Because the school board directly affects my children.*

To many people, then, governmental action is considered irrelevant to their lives. They do not conceive of the government as an agent which can solve their immediate and pressing problems. It is, then, no wonder that these people fail to feel any urgent incentive to participate actively in political affairs.

People Often Lack a Personal Thrust to Action

Empirical studies of politics have shown that personal influence may be of great importance in determining political attitudes and behavior. Our data suggest that the interpersonal factor may operate in several different ways to promote apathy or discourage participation.

Potential participants may not be contacted by friends or party organizations.

One respondent claims that she would have been active had the stimulus been available. She was the friendly, cooperative type, always willing to lend a hand. When she was asked whether she had worked, she said:

> *No, I wasn't asked to do anything. Many of my friends were asked to help—ring doorbells, stamp envelopes, and things like that. But I wasn't asked to do anything. Had I been asked, I would have been glad to help.*

Another respondent said that she wasn't interested in politics, but that she would be active if asked to because, "I like to cooperate. It's like the school. I cooperate with them, too."

> Well, I might have helped if they'd really wanted me to, and if it didn't take too much time. . . . Besides, no one asked me to help out, so I didn't volunteer. I could have worked a little, though.

These respondents were certainly apathetic at the outset, but, as relatively compliant personalities, they might have been induced to participate. Such activity might in turn have led to increased interest. The absence of initial personal stimulation, however, ruled out the possibility that a start toward participation would be made.

Those who might consider it a social responsibility to participate politically may be reassured by the observation that most other people are apathetic. It also provides a very convenient rationalization for apathy.

> You can probably class me as apathetic, except when it's brought right to my attention, but I think most people are the same way. They are not aware of, or they ignore, corruption in government until a McCarthy-type seizes it and makes a big thing out of it.

Another respondent was asked about the political interest of her friends.

> Well, a few of our friends belong to some political groups. But I wouldn't call them our most intimate friends. Not many of our close friends belong.
>
> As a matter of fact, besides the professors' wives, I don't think too many women know much about politics. Even though a lot of them are active on the election board—canvassing and things like that—they still don't seem to know too much about politics—especially national politics.
>
> I guess everyone else is even more passive than I am. They're all busy with household things.

Thus, many people are not motivated because of the absence of a shining example by others. Furthermore, whatever guilt they feel may be assuaged by the observation that others (including the most respectable) are equally apathetic. It is reasonable to speculate, incidentally, that an individual who might be ready for action would be discouraged by the spectacle of such widespread apathy; he might feel that he could not carry the burden with so little help. Thus apathy may become self-reinforcing.

People may be members of groups in which apathy is a positive group norm. A young person became associated with a group of cynics who considered concern with political affairs an expression of philistine conformism. She remained inactive partly out of fear of the scorn and ridicule which would greet any manifestation of social responsibility.

Thus, interpersonal factors may operate in several ways to promote political apathy. In the first place, the individual may receive no positive encouragement from others to participate. In the second place, the guilt feelings arising from an individual's inactivity may be assuaged by the observation that others in the community are also inactive. An individual, ready for action, may be discouraged by the observation that the apathy of other people increases his own burden of political work. Finally, the individual may be a member of a group in which political apathy is a *positive group norm*—a group which would discourage political action.

Apathy may thus be circular and self-reinforcing. The apathetic individual is not encouraged, and actually may be discouraged, from being politically active. Each individual may thus be reassured and reinforced in his political non-participation by the observation that others behave in a similar fashion. Thus the individual who, by virtue of his own apathy, encourages apathy in others, may also be influenced in a similar fashion by them.

AREAS FOR FURTHER RESEARCH

In this paper we have suggested several factors which in some cases contribute to political apathy. That these factors have some significance is clearly suggested by the data, but their relative importance, their statistical distribution among various population sub-groups, and their interrelationships must remain subjects for more systematic research.

Space limitations prevent us from discussing in detail a number of additional factors which our data suggest might contribute to political apathy. It appears worth noting, however, that some people are apathetic because they feel there is no need to do anything; they are contented with the social and political system, have faith in their representatives, and see no need for change. This basic contentment tends to be linked with a confidence in the basic stability of the society. There are others who would favor change, but who feel that there is no real difference between the two major parties; the outcome of elections, therefore, lacks significance. Some people do not participate actively because of the incertitude of their political convictions; to them politics may be confused, complicated, contradictory; political communications may be rejected as propaganda; or the individuals may be uncertain regarding their own political activity. Others may be too exhausted by the pressure of other activities to pay much attention to it. Certain women express the attitude that political activity would be out of keeping with their social roles. Some people's reluctance to think about political matters ranges from a certain degree of mental laziness to a phobia toward serious thought which borders on the pathological. These and other factors would have to be examined before an adequate understanding of the determinants of political apathy could be achieved.

It is also necessary to bear in mind that apathy is a variable rather than a dichotomous attribute. Thus the reason a non-voter does not go to the polls is likely to be quite different from the reason a party worker who devotes his weekday evenings to the cause does not spend his weekends at it too. Further analysis would require an examination of the obstacles to action as it operates differentially at these various levels.

To those who consider political apathy a symptom of the malfunctioning of democracy, the important next question would be: What can be done about it? This is obviously a crucial area for social research. It is our conviction, however, that the phenomenon must first be thoroughly understood before fruitful research for its solution can be undertaken.

Finally, of course, the common observation that many people are not politically apathetic, that they do participate actively, virtually dictates an investigation into the factors which induce them to participate as much as they do.

PROTEST AS A POLITICAL RESOURCE

Michael Lipsky

The frequent resort to protest activity by relatively powerless groups in recent American politics suggests that protest represents an important aspect of minority group and low income group politics. At the same time that Negro civil rights strategists have recognized the problem of using protest as a meaningful political instrument, groups associated with the "war on poverty" have increasingly received publicity for protest activity. Saul Alinsky's Industrial Areas Foundation, for example, continues to receive invitations to help organize low income communities because of its ability to mobilize poor people around the tactic of protest. The riots which dominated urban affairs in the summer of 1967 appear not to have diminished the dependence of some groups on protest as a mode of political activity.

This article provides a theoretical perspective on protest activity as a political resource. The discussion is concentrated on the limitations inherent in protest which occur because of the need of protest leaders to appeal to four constituencies at the same time. As the concept of protest is developed here, it will be argued that protest leaders must nurture and sustain an organization comprised of people with whom they may or may not share common values. They must articulate goals and choose strategies so as to maximize their public exposure through communications media. They must maximize the impact of third parties in the political conflict. Finally, they must try to maximize chances of success among those capable of granting goals. The tensions inherent in manipulating these four constituencies at the same time form the basis of this discussion of protest as a political process. It is intended to place aspects of the civil rights movement in a framework which suggests links between protest organizations and the general political processes in which such organizations operate.

I. "PROTEST" CONCEPTUALIZED

Protest activity as it has been adopted by elements of the civil rights movement and others has not been studied extensively by social scientists. Some of the most suggestive writings have been done as case studies of protest movements in single southern cities. These works generally lack a framework or theoretical focus which would encourage generalization from the cases. More systematic efforts have been attempted in approaching the dynamics of biracial committees in the South, and comprehensively assessing the efficacy of Negro political involvement in Durham, N.C. and Philadelphia, Pa. In their excellent assessment of Negro politics in the South, Matthews and Prothro have presented a thorough profile of Southern Negro students and their participation in civil rights activities. Protest is also discussed in passing in recent explorations of the social-psychological dimensions of Negro ghetto politics and the still highly suggestive, although pre-1960's, work on Negro political leadership by James Q. Wilson. These and other less systematic works on contemporary Negro politics, for all of their intuitive insights and valuable documentation, offer no theoretical formulations which encourage conceptualization about the interaction between recent Negro political activity and the political process.

Heretofore the best attempt to place Negro protest activity in a framework which would generate additional insights has been that of James Q. Wilson.[1] Wilson has suggested that protest activity be conceived as a problem of bargaining in which the basic problem is that Negro groups lack political resources to exchange. Wilson called this "the problem of the powerless."[2]

While many of Wilson's insights remain valid, his approach is limited in applicability because it defines protest in terms of mass action or response and as utilizing exclusively negative inducements in the bargaining process. Negative inducements are defined as inducements which are not absolutely preferred but are preferred over alternative possibilities. Yet it might be argued that protest designed to appeal to groups which oppose suffering and exploitation, for example, might be offering positive inducements in bargaining. A few Negro students sitting at a lunch counter might be engaged in what would be called protest, and by their actions might be trying to appeal to other groups in the system with positive inducements. Additionally, Wilson's concentration on Negro civic action, and his exclusive interest in exploring the protest process to explain Negro civic action, tend to obscure comparison with protest activity which does not necessarily arise within the Negro community.

Assuming a somewhat different focus, protest activity is defined as a mode of political action oriented toward objection to one or more policies or conditions, characterized by showmanship or display of an unconventional nature, and undertaken to obtain rewards from political or economic systems while working within the systems. The "problem of the powerless" in protest activity is to activate "third parties" to enter the implicit or explicit bargaining arena in ways favorable to the protesters. This is one of the few ways in which they can "create" bargaining resources. It is intuitively unconvincing to suggest that fifteen people sitting uninvited in the Mayor's office have the power to move City Hall. A better formulation would suggest that the people sitting in may be able to appeal to a wider public to which the city administration is sensitive. Thus in successful protest activity the *reference publics* of protest *targets* may be conceived as explicitly or implicitly reacting to protest in such a way that target groups or individuals respond in ways favorable to the protesters.

It should be emphasized that the focus here is on protest by relatively powerless groups. Illustrations can be summoned, for example, of activity designated as "protest" involving high status pressure groups or hundreds of thousands of people. While such instances may share some of the characteristics of protest activity, they may not represent examples of developing political resources by relatively powerless groups because the protesting groups may already command political resources by virtue of status, numbers or cohesion.

It is appropriate also to distinguish between the relatively restricted use of the concept of protest adopted here and closely related political strategies which are often designated as "protest" in popular usage. Where groups already possess sufficient resources with which to bargain, as in the case of some economic boycotts and labor strikes, they may be said to engage in "direct confrontation." Similarly, protest which represents efforts to "activate reference publics" should be distinguished from "alliance formation," where third parties are induced to join the conflict, but where the value orientations of third parties are sufficiently similar to those of the protesting group that concerted or coordinated action is possible. Alliance formation is particularly desirable for relatively powerless groups if they seek to join the decision-making process as participants.

The distinction between activating reference publics and alliance formation is made on the assumption that where goal orientations among protest groups and the reference publics of target groups are similar, the political dynamics of petitioning target groups are different than when such goal orientations are relatively divergent. Clearly the more similar the goal orientations, the greater the likelihood of protest success, other things being equal. This discussion is intended to highlight, however, those instances where goal orientations of reference publics depart significantly, in direction or intensity, from the goals of protest groups.

Say that to protest some situation, A would like to enter a bargaining situation with B. But A has nothing B wants, and thus cannot bargain. A then attempts to create political resources by activating other groups to enter the conflict. A then organizes to take action against B with respect to certain goals. *Information concerning these goals must be conveyed through communications media* (C, D, and E) to F, G, and H, which are B's *reference publics.* In response to the reactions of F, G, and H, or in anticipation of their reactions, B responds, *in some way,* to the protesters' demands. This formulation requires the conceptualization of protest activity when undertaken to create bargaining resources as a political process which requires communication and is characterized by a multiplicity of constituencies for protest leadership.

A schematic representation of the process of protest as utilized by relatively powerless groups is presented in Figure 1. In contrast to a simplistic pressure group model which would posit a direct relationship between pressure group and pressured, the following discussion is guided by the assumption (derived from observation) that protest is a highly indirect process in which communications media and the reference publics of protest targets play critical roles. It is also a process characterized by reciprocal relations, in which protest leaders frame strategies according to their perception of the needs of (many) other actors.

In this view protest constituents limit the options of protest leaders at the same time that the protest leader influences their perception of the strategies and rhetoric which they will support. Protest activity is filtered through the communications media in influencing the perceptions of the reference publics of protest targets. To the extent that the influence of reference publics is supportive of protest goals, target groups will dispense symbolic or material rewards. Material rewards are communicated directly to protest constituents. Symbolic rewards are communicated in part to protest constituents, but primarily are communicated to the reference publics of target groups, who provide the major stimuli for public policy pronouncements.

The study of protest as adopted by relatively powerless groups should provide insights into the structure and behavior of groups involved in civil rights politics and associated with the "war on poverty." It should direct attention toward the ways in which administrative agencies respond to "crises." Additionally, the study of protest as a political resource should influence some general conceptualizations of American political

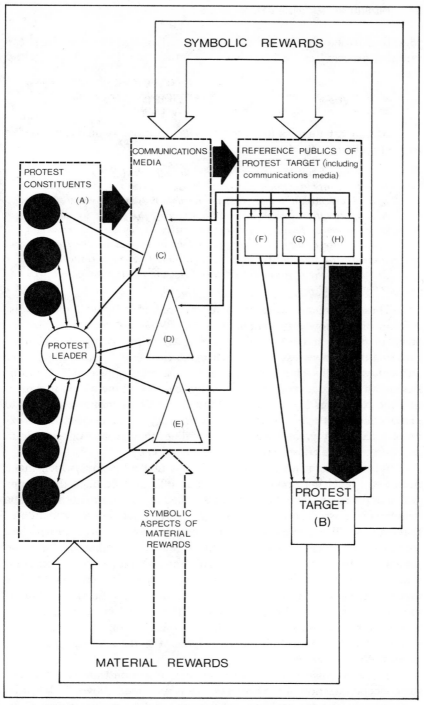

FIG. 1. SCHEMATIC REPRESENTATION OF THE PROCESS OF PROTEST
BY RELATIVELY POWERLESS GROUPS.

pluralism. Robert Dahl, for example, describes the "normal American political process" as

> one in which there is a high probability that an active and legitimate group in the population can make itself heard effectively at some crucial stage in the process of decision.[3]

Although he agrees that control over decisions is unevenly divided in the population, Dahl writes:

> When I say that a group is heard "effectively" I mean more than the simple fact that it makes a noise; I mean that one or more officials are not only ready to listen to the noise, but expect to suffer in some significant way if they do not placate the group, its leaders, or its most vociferous members. To satisfy the group may require one or more of a great variety of actions by the responsive leader: pressure for substantive policies, appointments, graft, respect, expression of the appropriate emotions, or the right combination of reciprocal noises.[4]

These statements, which in some ways resemble David Truman's discussion of the power of "potential groups," can be illuminated by the study of protest activity in three ways. First, what are the probabilities that relatively powerless groups can make themselves heard effectively? In what ways will such groups be heard or "steadily appeased"?[5] Concentration on the process of protest activity may reveal the extent to which, and the conditions under which, relatively powerless groups are likely to prove effective. Protest undertaken to obstruct policy decisions, for example, may enjoy greater success probabilities than protest undertaken in an effort to evoke constructive policy innovations.

Second, does it make sense to suggest that all groups which make noises will receive responses from public officials? Perhaps the groups which make noises do not have to be satisfied at all, but it is other groups which receive assurances or recognition. Third, what are the probabilities that groups which make noises will receive tangible rewards, rather than symbolic assurances? Dahl lumps these rewards together in the same paragraph, but dispensation of tangible rewards clearly has a different impact upon groups than the dispensation of symbolic rewards. Dahl is undoubtedly correct when he suggests that the relative fluidity of American politics is a critical characteristic of the American political system. But he is less precise and less convincing when it comes to analyzing the extent to which the system is indeed responsive to the relatively powerless groups of the "average citizen."

The following sections are an attempt to demonstrate the utility of the conceptualization of the protest process presented above. This will be done by exploring the problems encountered and the strains generated by protest leaders in interacting with four constituencies. It will be useful to concentrate attention on the maintenance and enhancement needs not only of the large formal organizations which dominate city politics, but also of the ad hoc protest groups which engage them in civic controversy. It will also prove rewarding to examine the role requirements of individuals in leadership positions as they perceive the problems of constituency manipulation. In concluding remarks some implications of the study of protest for the pluralist description of American politics will be suggested.

II. PROTEST LEADERSHIP AND ORGANIZATIONAL BASE

The organizational maintenance needs of relatively powerless, low income, ad hoc protest groups center around the tension generated by the need for leadership to offer symbolic and intangible inducements to protest participation when immediate, material rewards cannot be anticipated, and the need to provide at least the promise of material rewards. Protest leaders must try to evoke responses from other actors in the political process, at the same time that they pay attention to participant organizational needs. Thus relatively deprived groups in the political system not only receive symbolic reassurance while material rewards from the system are withheld, but protest leaders have a stake in perpetuating the notion that relatively powerless groups retain political efficacy despite what in many cases is obvious evidence to the contrary.

The tension embraced by protest leaders over the nature of inducements toward protest participation accounts in part for the style adopted and goals selected by protest leaders. Groups which seek psychological gratification from politics, but cannot or do not anticipate material political rewards, may be attracted to militant protest leaders. To these groups, angry rhetoric may prove a desirable quality in the short run. Where groups depend upon the political system for tangible benefits, or where participation in the system provides intangible benefits, moderate leadership is likely to prevail. Wilson has observed similar tendencies among Negro leaders of large, formal organizations. It is no less true for leadership of protest groups. Groups whose members derive tangible satisfactions from political participation will not condone leaders who are stubborn in compromise or appear to question the foundations of the system. This coincides with Truman's observation:

> Violation of the "rules of the game" normally will weaken a group's cohesion, reduce its status in the community, and expose it to the claims of other groups.[6]

On the other hand, the cohesion of relatively powerless groups may be strengthened by militant, ideological leadership which questions the rules of the game and challenges their legitimacy.

Cohesion is particularly important when protest leaders bargain directly with target groups. In that situation, leaders' ability to control pro-test constituents and guarantee their behavior represents a bargaining strength. For this reason Wilson stressed the bargaining difficulties of Negro leaders who cannot guarantee constituent behavior, and pointed out the significance of the strategy of projecting the image of group soli-darity when the reality of cohesion is a fiction. Cohesion is less significant at other times. Divided leadership may prove productive by bargaining in tandem, or by minimizing strain among groups in the protest process. Further, community divisions may prove less detrimental to protest aims when strong third parties have entered the dispute originally generated by protest organizations.

The intangible rewards of assuming certain postures toward the political system may not be sufficient to sustain an organizational base. It may be necessary to renew constantly the intangible rewards of partici-pation. And to the extent that people participate in order to achieve tan-gible benefits, their interest in a protest organization may depend upon the organization's relative material success. Protest leaders may have to tailor their style to present participants with tangible successes, or with the appearance of success. Leaders may have to define the issues with con-cern for increasing their ability to sustain organizations. The potential for protest among protest group members may have to be manipulated by leadership if the group is to be sustained.

The participants in protest organizations limit the flexibility of protest leadership. This obtains for two reasons. They restrict public actions by leaders who must continue to solicit active participant support, and they place restraints on the kinds of activities which can be considered appro-priate for protest purposes. Poor participants cannot commonly be asked to engage in protest requiring air transportation. Participants may have anxieties related to their environment or historical situation which dis-courages engagement in some activities. They may be afraid of job losses, beatings by the police, or summary evictions. Negro protest in the Deep South has been inhibited by realistic expectations of retribution. Protests over slum housing conditions are undermined by tenants who expect land-lord retaliation for engaging in tenant organizing activity. Political or ethical mores may conflict with a proposed course of action, diminishing participation.

On the other hand, to the extent that fears are real, or that the larger community perceives protest participants as subject to these fears, protest may actually be strengthened. Communications media and potential allies will consider more soberly the complaints of people who are understood to be placing themselves in jeopardy. When young children and their parents made the arduous bus trip from Mississippi to Washington, D.C. to protest the jeopardizing of Head Start funds, the courage and expense represented by their effort created a respect and visibility for their position which might not have been achieved by local protest efforts.

Protest activity may be undertaken by organizations with established relationship patterns, behavior norms, and role expectations. These organizations are likely to have greater access to other groups in the political system, and a demonstrated capacity to maintain themselves. Other protest groups, however, may be ad hoc arrangements without demonstrated internal or external relationship patterns. These groups will have different organizational problems, in response to which it is necessary to engage in different kinds of protest activity.

The scarcity of organizational resources also places limits upon the ability of relatively powerless groups to maintain the foundations upon which protest organizations develop. Relatively powerless groups, to engage in political activity of any kind, must command at least some resources. This is not tautological. Referring again to a continuum on which political groups are placed according to their relative command of resources, one may draw a line somewhere along the continuum representing a "threshold of civic group political participation." Clearly some groups along the continuum will possess some political resources (enough, say, to emerge for inspection) but not enough to exercise influence in civic affairs. Relatively powerless groups, to be influential, must cross the "threshold" to engage in politics. Although the availability of group resources is a critical consideration at all stages of the protest process, it is particularly important in explaining why some groups seem to "surface" with sufficient strength to command attention. The following discussion of some critical organizational resources should illuminate this point.

Skilled professionals frequently must be available to protest organizations. Lawyers, for example, play extremely important roles in enabling protest groups to utilize the judicial process and avail themselves of adequate preparation of court cases. Organizational reputation may depend upon a combination of ability to threaten the conventional political system and of exercising statutory rights in court. Availability of lawyers depends upon ability to pay fees and/or the attractiveness to lawyers of participation in protest group activity. Volunteer professional assistance may not prove adequate. One night a week volunteered by an aspiring politician in a housing clinic cannot satisfy the needs of a chaotic political movement. The need for skilled professionals is not restricted to lawyers. For example, a group seeking to protest an urban renewal policy might require the services of architects and city planners in order to present a viable alternative to a city proposal.

Financial resources not only purchase legal assistance, but enable relatively powerless groups to conduct minimum programs of political activities. To the extent that constituents are unable or unwilling to pay even small membership dues, then financing the cost of mimeographing flyers, purchasing supplies, maintaining telephone service, paying rent, and meeting a modest payroll become major organizational problems. And to the extent that group finances are supplied by outside individual contributions or government or foundation grants, the long-term options of the group are sharply constrained by the necessity of orienting group goals and tactics to anticipate the potential objections of financial supporters.

Some dependence upon even minimal financial resources can be waived if organizations evoke passionate support from constituents. Secretarial help and block organizers will come forward to work without compensation if they support the cause of neighborhood organizations or gain intangible benefits based upon association with the group. Protest organizations may also depend upon skilled non-professionals, such as college students, whose access to people and political and economic institutions often assist protest groups in cutting across income lines to seek support. Experience with ad hoc political groups, however, suggests that this assistance is sporadic and undependable. Transient assistance is particularly typical of skilled, educated, and employable volunteers whose abilities can be applied widely. The die-hards of ad hoc political groups are often those people who have no place else to go, nothing else to do.

Constituent support will be affected by the nature of the protest target and whether protest activity is directed toward defensive or assertive goals. Obstructing specific public policies may be easier than successfully recommending constructive policy changes. Orientations toward defensive goals may require less constituent energy, and less command over resources of money, expertise and status.

III. PROTEST LEADERSHIP AND COMMUNICATIONS MEDIA

The communications media are extremely powerful in city politics. In granting or withholding publicity, in determining what information most people will have on most issues, and what alternatives they will consider in response to issues, the media truly, as Norton Long has put it, "set . . . the civic agenda."[7] To the extent that successful protest activity depends upon appealing to, and/or threatening, other groups in the community, the communications media set the limits of protest action. If protest tactics are not considered significant by the media, or if newspapers and television reporters or editors decide to overlook protest tactics, protest organizations will not succeed. Like the tree falling unheard in the forest, there is no protest unless protest is perceived and projected.

A number of writers have noticed that the success of protest activity seems directly related to the amount of publicity it receives outside the immediate arena in which protest takes place. This view has not been stated systematically, but hints can be found in many sources. In the literature on civil rights politics, the relevance of publicity represents one of the few hypotheses available concerning the dynamics of successful protest activity.

When protest tactics do receive coverage in the communications media, the way in which they are presented will influence all other actors in the system, including the protesters themselves. Conformity to standards of newsworthiness in political style, and knowledge of the prejudices and desires of the individuals who determine media coverage in political skills, represent crucial determinants of leadership effectiveness.

The organizational behavior of newspapers can partly be understood by examining the maintenance and enhancement needs which direct them toward projects of civic betterment and impressions of accomplishment. But insight may also be gained by analyzing the role requirements of reporters, editors, and others who determine newspaper policy. Reporters, for example, are frequently motivated by the desire to contribute to civic affairs by their "objective" reporting of significant events; by the premium they place on accuracy; and by the credit which they receive for sensationalism and "scoops."

These requirements may be difficult to accommodate at the same time. Reporters demand newsworthiness of their subjects in the short run, but also require reliability and verifiability in the longer run. Factual accuracy may dampen newsworthiness. Sensationalism, attractive to some newspaper editors, may be inconsistent with reliable, verifiable narration of events. Newspapers at first may be attracted to sensationalism, and later demand verifiability in the interests of community harmony (and adherence to professional journalistic standards).

Most big city newspapers have reporters whose assignments permit them to cover aspects of city politics with some regularity. These reporters, whose "beats" may consist of "civil rights" or "poverty," sometimes develop close relationships with their news subjects. These relationships may develop symbiotic overtones because of the mutuality of interest between the reporter and the news subject. Reporters require fresh information on protest developments, while protest leaders have a vital interest in obtaining as much press coverage as possible.

Inflated reports of protest success may be understood in part by examining this relationship between reporter and protest leader. Both have role-oriented interests in projecting images of protest strength and threat. In circumstances of great excitement, when competition from other news media representatives is high, a reporter may find that he is less governed by the role requirement of verification and reliability than he is by his editor's demand for "scoops" and news with high audience appeal.

On the other hand, the demands of the media may conflict with the needs of protest group maintenance. Consider the leader whose constituents are attracted solely by pragmatic statements not exceeding what they consider political "good taste." He is constrained from making militant demands which would isolate him from constituents. This constraint may cost him appeal in the press. However, the leader whose organizing appeal requires militant rhetoric may obtain eager press coverage only to find that his inflamatory statements lead to alienation of potential allies and exclusion from the explicit bargaining process.

News media do not report events in the same way. Television may select for broadcast only thirty seconds of a half-hour news conference. This coverage will probably focus on immediate events, without background or explanatory material. Newspapers may give more complete accounts of the same event. The most complete account may appear in the weekly edition of a neighborhood or ethnic newspaper. Differential coverage by news media, and differential news media habits in the general population, are significant factors in permitting protest leaders to juggle conflicting demands of groups in the protest process.

Similar tensions exist in the leader's relationships with protest targets. Ideological postures may gain press coverage and constituency approval, but may alienate target groups with whom it would be desirable to bargain explicitly. Exclusion from the councils of decision-making may have important consequences, since the results of target group deliberations may satisfy activated reference publics without responding to protest goals. If activated reference publics are required to increase the bargaining position of the protest group, protest efforts thereafter will have diminished chances of success.

IV. PROTEST LEADERSHIP AND "THIRD PARTIES"

I have argued that the essence of political protest consists of activating third parties to participate in controversy in ways favorable to protest goals. In previous sections I have attempted to analyze some of the tensions which result from protest leaders' attempts to activate reference publics of protest targets at the same time that they must retain the interest and support of protest organization participants. This phenomenon is in evidence when Negro leaders, recognized as such by public officials, find their support eroded in the Negro community because they have engaged in explicit bargaining situations with politicians. Negro leaders are thus faced with the dilemma that when they behave like other ethnic group representatives they are faced with loss of support from those whose intense activism has been aroused in the Negro community, yet whose support is vital if they are to remain credible as leaders to public officials.

The tensions resulting from conflicting maintenance needs of protest organizations and activated third parties present difficulties for protest leaders. One way in which these tensions can be minimized is by dividing leadership responsibilities. If more than one group is engaged in protest activity, protest leaders can, in effect, divide up public roles so as to reduce as much as possible the gap between the implicit demands of different groups for appropriate rhetoric, and what in fact is said. Thus divided leadership may perform the latent function of minimizing tensions among elements in the protest process by permitting different groups to listen selectively to protest spokesmen.

Another way in which strain among different groups can be minimized is through successful public relations. Minimization of strain may depend upon ambiguity of action or statement, deception, or upon effective inter-group communication. Failure to clarify meaning, or falsification, may increase protest effectiveness. Effective intragroup communication may increase the likelihood that protest constituents will "understand" that ambiguous or false public statements have "special meaning" and need not be taken seriously. The Machiavellian circle is complete when we observe that although lying may be prudent, the appearance of integrity and forthrightness is desirable for public relations, since these values are widely shared.

It has been observed that "[t]he militant displays an unwillingness to perform those administrative tasks which are necessary to operate an organization. Probably the skills of the agitator and the skills of the administrator . . . are not incompatible, but few men can do both well."[8] These skills may or may not be incompatible as personality traits, but they indeed represent conflicting role demands on protest leadership. When a protest leader exhausts time and energy conducting frequent press conferences, arranging for politicians and celebrities to appear at rallies, delivering speeches to sympathetic local groups, college symposia and other forums, constantly picketing for publicity and generally making "contacts," he is unable to pursue the direction of office routine, clerical tasks, research and analysis, and other chores.

The difficulties of delegating routine tasks are probably directly related to the skill levels and previous administrative experiences of group members. In addition, to the extent that involvement in protest organizations is a function of rewards received or expected by individuals because of the excitement or entertainment value of participation, then the difficulties of delegating routine, relatively uninteresting chores to group members will be increased. Yet attention to such details affects the perception of protest groups by organizations whose support or assistance may be desired in the future. These considerations add to the protest leader's problem of risking alienation of protest participants because of potentially unpopular cooperation with the "power structure."

In the protest paradigm developed here, "third parties" refers both to the reference publics of target groups and, more narrowly, to the interest groups whose regular interaction with protest targets tends to develop into patterns of influence. We have already discussed some of the problems associated with activating the reference publics of target groups. In discussing the constraints placed upon protest, attention may be focused upon the likelihood that groups seeking to create political resources through protest will be included in the explicit bargaining process with other pressure groups. For protest groups, these constraints are those which occur because of class and political style, status, and organizational resources.

The established civic groups most likely to be concerned with the problems raised by relatively powerless groups are those devoted to service in the public welfare and those "liberally" oriented groups whose potential constituents are either drawn from the same class as the protest groups (such as some trade unions), or whose potential constituents are attracted to policies which appear to serve the interest of the lower class or minority groups (such as some reform political clubs). These civic groups have frequently cultivated clientele relationships with city agencies over long periods. Their efforts have been reciprocatd by agency officials anxious to develop constituencies to support and defend agency administrative and budgetary policies. In addition, clientele groups are expected to endorse and legitimize agency aggrandizement. These relationships have been developed by agency officials and civic groups for mutual benefit, and cannot be destroyed, abridged or avoided without cost.

Protest groups may well be able to raise the saliency of issues on the civic agenda through utilization of communications media and successful appeals or threats to wider publics, but admission to policy-making councils is frequently barred because of the angry, militant rhetorical style adopted by protest leaders. People in power do not like to sit down with rogues. Protest leaders are likely to have phrased demands in ways unacceptable to lawyers and other civic activists whose cautious attitude toward public policy may reflect not only their good intentions but their concern for property rights, due process, pragmatic legislating or judicial precedent.

Relatively powerless groups lack participation of individuals with high status whose endorsement of specific proposals lend them increased legitimacy. Good causes may always attract the support of high status individuals. But such individuals' willingness to devote time to the promotion of specific proposals is less likely than the one-shot endorsements which these people distribute more readily.

Similarly, protest organizations often lack the resources on which entry into the policy-making process depends. These resources include maintenance of a staff with expertise and experience in the policy area. This expertise may be in the areas of the law, planning and architecture, proposal writing, accounting, educational policy, federal grantsmanship or publicity. Combining experience with expertise is one way to create status in issue areas. The dispensing of information by interest groups has been widely noted as a major source of influence. Over time the experts develop status in their areas of competence somewhat independent of the influence which adheres to them as information-providers. Groups which cannot or do not engage lawyers to assist in proposing legislation, and do not engage in collecting reliable data, cannot participate in policy deliberations or consult in these matters. Protest oriented groups, whose primary talents are in dramatizing issues, cannot credibly attempt to present data considered "objective" or suggestions considered "responsible" by public officials. Few can be convincing as both advocate and arbiter at the same time.

V. PROTEST LEADERSHIP AND TARGET GROUPS

The probability of protest success may be approached by examining the maintenance needs of organizations likely to be designated as target groups. For the sake of clarity, and because protest activity increasingly is directed toward government, I shall refer in the following paragraphs exclusively to government agencies at the municipal level. The assumption is retained, however, that the following generalizations are applicable to other potential target groups.

Some of the constraints placed on protest leadership in influencing target groups have already been mentioned in preceding sections. The lack of status and resources that inhibit protest groups from participating in policy-making conferences, for example, also helps prevent explicit bargaining between protest leaders and city officials. The strain between rhetoric which appeals to protest participants and public statements to which communications media and "third parties" respond favorably also exists with reference to target groups.

Yet there is a distinguishing feature of the maintenance needs and strategies of city agencies which specifically constrains protest organizations. This is the agency director's need to protect "the jurisdiction and income of his organization [by] . . . [m]anipulation of the external environment."[9] In so doing he may satisfy his reference groups without responding to protest group demands. At least six tactics are available to protest targets who are motivated to respond in some way to protest activity but seek primarily to satisfy their reference publics. These tactics may be employed whether or not target groups are "sincere" in responding to protest demands.

1. Target Groups May Dispense Symbolic Satisfactions. Appearances of activity and commitment to problems substitute for, or supplement, resource allocation and policy innovations which would constitute tangible responses to protest activity. If symbolic responses supplement tangible pay-offs, they are frequently coincidental, rather than intimately linked, to projection of response by protest targets. Typical in city politics of the symbolic response is the ribbon cutting, street corner ceremony or the walking tour press conference. These occasions are utilized not only to build agency constituencies, but to satisfy agency reference publics that attention is being directed to problems of civic concern. In this sense publicist tactics may be seen as defensive maneuvers. Symbolic aspects of the actions of public officials can also be recognized in the commissioning of expensive studies and the rhetorical flourishes with which "massive

attacks," "comprehensive programs," and "coordinated planning" are frequently promoted.

City agencies establish distinct apparatus and procedures for dealing
with crises which may be provoked by protest groups. Housing-related departments in New York City may be cited for illustration. It is usually the
case in these agencies that the Commissioner or a chief deputy, a press
secretary and one or two other officials devote whatever time is necessary
to collect information, determine policy and respond quickly to reports of
"crises." This is functional for tenants, who, if they can generate enough
concern, may be able to obtain short-cuts through lengthy agency procedures. It is also functional for officials who want to project images of
action rather than merely receiving complaints. Concentrating attention on
the maintenance needs of city politicians during protest crises suggests that
pronouncements of public officials serve purposes independent of their
dedication to alleviation of slum conditions.

Independent of dispensation of tangible benefits to protest groups,
public officials continue to respond primarily to their own reference publics.
Murray Edelman has suggested that:

> *Tangible resources and benefits are frequently not distributed
> to unorganized political group interests as promised in regulatory
> statutes and the propaganda attending their enactment.[10]*

His analysis may be supplemented by suggesting that symbolic dispensa-
tions may not only serve to reassure unorganized political group interests,
but may also contribute to reducing the anxiety level of organized interests
and wider publics which are only tangentially involved in the issues.

2. Target Groups May Dispense Token Material Satisfactions.   When
city agencies respond, with much publicity, to cases brought to their attention representing examples of the needs dramatized by protest organizations, they may appear to respond to protest demands while in fact only
responding on a case basis, instead of a general basis. For the protesters
served by agencies in this fashion it is of considerable advantage that
agencies can be influenced by protest action. Yet it should not be ignored
that in handling the "crisis" cases, public officials give the appearance of
response to their reference publics, while mitigating demands for an expensive, complex *general* assault on problems represented by the cases to
which responses are given. Token responses, whether or not accompanied
by more general responses, are particularly attractive to reporters and
television news directors, who are able to dramatize individual cases convincingly, but who may be unable to "capture" the essence of general
deprivation or of general efforts to alleviate conditions of deprivation.

*3. Target Groups May Organize and Innovate Internally in Order to Blunt
the Impetus of Protest Efforts.*   This tactic is closely related to No. 2

(above). If target groups can act constructively in the worst cases, they will then be able to pre-empt protest efforts by responding to the cases which best dramatize protest demands. Alternatively, they may designate all efforts which jeopardize agency reputations as "worst" cases, and devote extensive resources to these cases. In some ways extraordinary city efforts are precisely consistent with protest goals. At the same time extraordinary efforts in the most heavily dramatized cases or the most extreme cases effectively wear down the "cutting-edges" of protest efforts.

Many New York City agencies develop informal "crisis" arrangements not only to project publicity, as previously indicated, but to mobilize energies toward solving "crisis" cases. They may also develop policy innovations which allow them to respond more quickly to "crisis" situations. These innovations may be important to some city residents, for whom the problems of dealing with city bureaucracies can prove insurmountable. It might be said, indeed, that the goals of protest are to influence city agencies to handle every case with the same resources that characterize their dispatch of "crisis" cases.

But such policies would demand major revenue inputs. This kind of qualitative policy change is difficult to achieve. Meanwhile, internal reallocation of resources only means that routine services must be neglected so that the "crisis" programs can be enhanced. If all cases are expedited, as in a typical "crisis" response, then none can be. Thus for purposes of general solutions, "crisis" resolving can be self-defeating unless accompanied by significantly greater resource allocation. It is not self-defeating, however, to the extent that the organizational goals of city agencies are to serve a clientele while minimizing negative publicity concerning agency vigilance and responsiveness.

4. Target Groups May Appear To Be Constrained in Their Ability to Grant Protest Goals.   This may be directed toward making the protesters appear to be unreasonable in their demands, or to be well-meaning individuals who "just don't understand how complex running a city really is." Target groups may extend sympathy but claim that they lack resources, a mandate from constituents, and/or authority to respond to protest demands. Target groups may also evade protest demands by arguing that "If-I-give-it-to-you-I-have-to-give-it-to-everyone."

The tactic of appearing constrained is particularly effective with established civic groups because there is an undeniable element of truth to it. Everyone knows that cities are financially undernourished. Established civic groups expend great energies lobbying for higher levels of funding for their pet city agencies. Thus they recognize the validity of this constraint when posed by city officials. But it is not inconsistent to point out that funds for specific, relatively inexpensive programs, or for the expansion of existing programs, can often be found if pressure is increased. While constraints on city government flexibility may be extensive, they are not absolute. Protest targets nonetheless attempt to diminish the impact of protest demands by claiming relative impotence.

5. Target Groups May Use Their Extensive Resources To Discredit Protest Leaders and Organizations. Utilizing their excellent access to the press, public officials may state or imply that leaders are unreliable, ineffective as leaders ("they don't really have the people behind them"), guilty of criminal behavior, potentially guilty of such behavior, or are some shade of "left-wing." Any of these allegations may serve to diminish the appeal of protest groups to potentially sympathetic third parties. City officials, in their frequent social and informal business interaction with leaders of established civic groups, may also communicate derogatory information concerning protest groups. Discrediting of protest groups may be undertaken by some city officials while others appear (perhaps authentically) to remain sympathetic to protest demands. These tactics may be engaged in by public officials whether or not there is any validity to the allegations.

6. Target Groups May Postpone Action. The effect of postponement, if accompanied by symbolic assurances, is to remove immediate pressure and delay specific commitments to a future date. This familiar tactic is particularly effective in dealing with protest groups because of their inherent instability. Protest groups are usually comprised of individuals whose intense political activity cannot be sustained except in rare circumstances. Further, to the extent that protest depends upon activating reference publics through strategies which have some "shock" value, it becomes increasingly difficult to activate these groups. Additionally, protest activity is inherently unstable because of the strains placed upon protest leaders who must attempt to manage four constituencies (as described herein).

The most frequent method of postponing action is to commit a subject to "study." For the many reasons elaborated in these paragraphs, it is not likely that ad hoc protest groups will be around to review the recommendations which emerge from study. The greater the expertise and the greater the status of the group making the study, the less will protest groups be able to influence whatever policy emerges. Protest groups lack the skills and resource personnel to challenge expert recommendations effectively.

Sometimes surveys and special research are undertaken in part to evade immediate pressures. Sometimes not. Research efforts are particularly necessary to secure the support of established civic groups, which place high priority on orderly procedure and policy emerging from independent analysis. Yet it must be recognized that postponing policy commitments has a distinct impact on the nature of the pressures focused on policy-makers.

IV. CONCLUSION

In this analysis I have agreed with James Q. Wilson that protest is correctly conceived as a strategy utilized by relatively powerless groups in order to increase their bargaining ability. As such, I have argued, it is successful to the extent that the reference publics of protest targets can be activated to enter the conflict in ways favorable to protest goals. I have suggested a model of the protest process which may assist in ordering data and indicating the salience for research of a number of aspects of protest. These include the critical role of communications media, the differential impact of material and symbolic rewards on "feedback" in protest activity, and the reciprocal relationships of actors in the protest process.

An estimation of the limits to protest efficacy, I have argued further, can be gained by recognizing the problems encountered by protest leaders who somehow must balance the conflicting maintenance needs of four groups in the protest process. This approach transcends a focus devoted primarily to characterization of group goals and targets, by suggesting that even in an environment which is relatively favorable to specific protest goals, the tensions which must be embraced by protest leadership may ultimately overwhelm protest activity.

At the outset of this essay, it was held that conceptualizing the American political system as "slack" or "fluid," in the manner of Robert Dahl, appears inadequate because of (1) a vagueness centering on the likelihood that any group can make itself heard; (2) a possible confusion as to which groups tend to receive satisfaction from the rewards dispensed by public officials; and (3) a lumping together as equally relevant rewards which are tangible and those which are symbolic. To the extent that protest is engaged in by relatively powerless groups which must create resources with which to bargain, the analysis here suggests a number of reservations concerning the pluralist conceptualization of the "fluidity" of the American political system.

Relatively powerless groups cannot use protest with a high probability of success. They lack organizational resources, by definition. But even to create bargaining resources through activating third parties, some resources are necessary to sustain organization. More importantly, relatively powerless protest groups are constrained by the unresolvable conflicts which are forced upon protest leaders who must appeal simultaneously to four constituencies which place upon them antithetical demands.

When public officials recognize the legitimacy of protest activity, they may not direct public policy toward protest groups at all. Rather, public officials are likely to aim responses at the reference publics from which they originally take their cues. Edelman has suggested that regulatory policy in practice often consists of reassuring mass publics while at the same time dispensing specific, tangible values to narrow interest groups. It is suggested here that symbolic reassurances are dispensed as much to wide, potentially concerned publics which are not directly affected by regulatory policy, as they are to wide publics comprised of the downtrodden and the deprived, in whose name policy is often written.

Complementing Edelman, it is proposed here that in the process of protest symbolic reassurances are dispensed in large measure because these are the public policy outcomes and actions desired by the constituencies to which public officials are most responsive. Satisfying these wider publics, city officials can avoid pressures toward other policies placed upon them by protest organizations.

Not only should there be some doubt as to which groups receive the symbolic recognitions which Dahl describes, but in failing to distinguish between the kinds of rewards dispensed to groups in the political system, Dahl avoids a fundamental question. It is literally fundamental because the kinds of rewards which can be obtained from politics, one might hypothesize, will have an impact upon the realistic appraisal of the efficacy of political activity. If among the groups least capable of organizing for political activity there is a history of organizing for protest, and if that activity, once engaged in, is rewarded primarily by the dispensation of symbolic gestures without perceptible changes in material conditions, then rational behavior might lead to expressions of apathy and lack of interest in politics or a rejection of conventional political channels as a meaningful arena of activity. In this sense this discussion of protest politics is consistent with Kenneth Clark's observations that the image of power, unaccompanied by material and observable rewards, leads to impressions of helplessness and reinforces political apathy in the ghetto.

Recent commentary by political scientists and others regarding riots in American cities seems to focus in part on the extent to which relatively deprived groups may seek redress of legitimate grievances. Future research should continue assessment of the relationship between riots and the conditions under which access to the political system has been limited. In such research assessment of the ways in which access to public officials is obtained by relatively powerless groups through the protest process might be one important research focus.

The instability of protest activity outlined in this article also should inform contemporary political strategies. If the arguments presented here are persuasive, civil rights leaders who insist that protest activity is a shallow foundation on which to seek long-term, concrete gains may be judged essentially correct. But the arguments concerning the fickleness of the white liberal, or the ease of changing discriminatory laws relative to changing discriminatory institutions, only in part explain the instability of protest movements. An explanation which derives its strength from analysis of the political process suggests concentration on the problems of managing protest constituencies. Accordingly, Alinsky is probably on the soundest ground when he prescribes protest for the purpose of building organization. Ultimately, relatively powerless groups in most instances cannot depend upon activating other actors in the political process. Long-run success will depend upon the acquisition of stable political resources which do not rely for their use on third parties.

THE FEDERAL GOVERNMENT AND PROTEST

David Mars

Abstract: During the late 1950's and the 1960's, the federal government took substantial action in dealing with injustices in the area of civil and political rights. Five major enactments were processed in the years between 1957 and 1968, dealing with a variety of matters, including voting rights and open housing. The same kind of accomplishments cannot be reported, however, for legislation designed to deal with perceived injustices in the social and economic fields. This is true partly because of the inherent difficulty in legislating for these areas and partly because progress in such legislation must be preceded by major societal attitudinal changes and the mood of the United States public has become more conservative and cautious during the past few years. This conservatism stems, in part, from reaction to the various protests of the 1960's. Protest, then, must be viewed in its strategic dimension: it is necessary in order to demonstrate that a condition exists and in order to win support, but engaging in protest often alienates many, including the very people whose support is sought.

Early in April 1968, on one Los Angeles radio station's two-way-radio-conversation program, a caller asked an interesting question. She wanted to know why the various civil rights acts and related measures which had been enacted during the past several years had been put on the books only after great struggles and widespread protest, rather than having been based on principle and "what was right." The commentator (or "communicaster," in the local-communications-media jargon), whose opinions were rather conservative, tried to respond to the question, remarking finally that more civil rights legislation had been passed in the past few years than had been passed in the entire previous history of the nation. To this, the caller answered quietly that we have also had more protest during the past few years than at any other time in the nation's history.

The relationship between protest and response to protest is an interesting and very important one to explore; it is also frequently a relationship extremely difficult to establish. On many occasions, it is almost impossible to discover whether an action undertaken by a governmental
body is indeed a response to protest or whether it was actuated by an
altogether different motive.

BASIC NATURE OF THE RIGHT TO PROTEST

In a fundamental sense, the right to protest lies at the very basis of a free
and democratic system of government. The revolutionary leaders who
played such an outstanding role in the civil rights movements of the 1770's
and 1780's, and those who were responsible for moving the amendments
which subsequently became the Bill of Rights, seemed to be well aware of
the connection, at least insofar as it extended to nonviolent protest. Hence,
they enshrined this right in the First Amendment, together with the other
basic rights of free speech, free press, and free religion (both in its exercise and in freedom from state-established religions).

Significantly, these early leaders were apparently not interested in
protecting a merely academic right of protest. They realized that for protest to be meaningful, there must be an expectation that the reasonable
demands stated and embodied in the protest will be responded to and
dealt with meaningfully by the state. Thus, while free speech, free press,
free exercise of religion, and freedom from established religion stand
alone as rights (and are connected by *or*), the right of protest was linked
closely with the right to expect implementation of steps designed to meet
the protest (and connected by *and*). Accordingly, the First Amendment
speaks of "the right of the people peaceably to assemble, and to petition
the government for a redress of grievances."

It hardly needs to be emphasized that the Constitution clearly does
not countenance violent protest, nor does it guarantee a right to the type
of protest which has come to be called civil disobedience.

The connection between protest and democracy is as clear and as
important today as it was in the earliest days of the Republic. Within the
past year, we have seen the statement made boldly and unflinchingly that
"when a presumably democratic government fails to respond to dissent or
protest, it has become a dictatorship."[1]

CIVIL VERSUS SOCIAL RIGHTS

The record of the federal government's response to protest during the
1960's has, in general, been marked by presidential and congressional
concern for, and action in, the field of civil and political rights, and by

considerably less action in the field of social and economic rights. By the late 1960's, there was general recognition that the civil rights struggle, bitter and protracted though it had been, would prove to be far less difficult than the achievement of social and economic justice for all Americans. The civil rights movement had focused largely on the black communities of the United States, where political inequality, and the injustices related thereto, had been long-standing, patent, and a very obvious blotch on America's image, both at home and abroad. In contrast, the question of social and economic justice was clearly not limited to one racial community. Though a large percentage of America's poor are, in fact, black people, by no means all of them are. In addition, the condition of poverty was—and is—not as apparent to many Americans as earlier civil and political abuses and malpractices (for example, lynchings, exclusion from the franchise, and the like) had been: witness such expressions as "the other America" and "the invisible poor." Finally, while the color of one's skin could not be hidden, one's economic condition could be, and frequently was, as a matter of pride and self-respect: it was demeaning to admit that one was poor.

Martin Luther King had been fond of pointing out that it had not cost one cent to desegregate lunch counters and other public facilities (he might have also mentioned housing in the same category, except that congressional action here did not occur until after his murder), and predicted that the struggle to win social and economic rights would be a far more difficult one.

A major reason for the difference in difficulty of achieving civil rights and social-economic rights is that the latter will require substantial attitudinal changes. It is one thing to permit a person with a different skin to vote in the same election (and have his vote counted equally), or to serve on a jury: it is a totally different thing to permit him to put his children into the same school as one's own children, or to dig deep into one's pocket to pay the taxes necessary to support a decent living standard for him.

President Johnson had recognized that though legislation in the area of civil rights was an important step along the path toward "liberty and justice for all," it was not the only step. In his 1968 civil rights message to the Congress, he said: "The more we grapple with the civil rights problem . . . the more we realize that the position of minorities in American society is defined not merely by law, but by social, educational, and economic conditions."

We will focus here on three points: (1) the civil rights legislation of the period 1957-1968, especially those enactments viewed as being particularly in response to protest, (2) the report of the National Advisory Commission on Civil Disorders, and (3) the Poor People's March and the action by Congress in 1968.

CIVIL RIGHTS LEGISLATION

Of the three branches of the federal government, the Congress was the slowest to move in the field of civil rights. During the 1940's and 1950's, both the Supreme Court and the President took substantial action to try to end racial discrimination and segregation. But the Congress did not move until 1957, when the Civil Rights Act of that year was adopted, the first federal legislation in the field since the days of the post-Civil War Reconstruction era. During the decade since then, a number of other civil rights measures were enacted: in 1960, in 1964, in 1965, and in 1968.

In one sense, perhaps none of this legislation was a direct response to protest. In another sense, at least three of the measures do seem to have borne some relation to previous actions of protest. We shall look at all the measures briefly, focusing particularly on those three which may be said to have constituted responses to protest. It is a tragic irony that, in two of these cases, the assassination of a very prominent American political leader played a part in the final passage of the legislation.

Of great interest also is the point that the three statutes which appear to have been responses to protest were the more recent enactments. Thus, it might be concluded that the Congress has been growing more responsive to protest. As will be shown below, however, Congress' very recent action —or inaction—raises some doubts on this point, or at least suggests that there is still a long way to go.

(1) The Civil Rights Act of 1957 was an outgrowth of President Eisenhower's proposals of 1956, embodied in his State of the Union message of that year and in a draft program submitted to the Congress in April. The package as finally approved by the Congress was somewhat narrower than the President's. The major contribution of the act to civil rights was the provision designed to enforce the right to vote, by empowering the Attorney General of the United States to seek an injunction in every instance where an individual was deprived, or was about to be deprived of his right to vote. Also important was the creation of the Commission on Civil Rights and of the Civil Rights Division of the Department of Justice, the latter to be headed by an Assistant Attorney General.

Of significance were the series of political events which took place in 1956, including the adoption of civil rights planks in the two major party platforms of that year: the Republican plank specifically endorsed and supported enactment of Eisenhower's civil rights program. Another important political event was the national election, in which the Negro vote reached substantial proportions. The Act may thus be viewed as having been, at least in part, a response to the visibly increasing political power of the Negro, though not specifically a response to actual protest.

(2) In early February 1959, President Eisenhower submitted a seven-point civil rights program to the Congress. The only legislative action taken by the Congress during 1959 was an extension of the life of the

Civil Rights Commission for two years (until November 1961). But the stage was set for the enactment of the next piece of civil rights legislation: the Civil Rights Act of 1960. This Act simply amended and supplemented some of the provisions of the earlier Act. The major new provision authorized judges—after a proceeding in which a pattern or practice of depriving Negroes of their right to vote had been determined—to appoint referees to help these Negroes to register and to vote. Among the other provisions of the Act were criminal penalties for obstruction of court orders, transportation of explosives with the knowledge that they would be used to explode vehicles or buildings, use of interstate facilities to threaten bombings, and crossing state lines to avoid prosecution or punishment for bombing or burning vehicles or buildings. (These provisions were not tied specifically to racial incidents.)

CIVIL RIGHTS ACTS AS RESPONSES TO PROTEST

(3) The Civil Rights Act of 1964 was the first enactment by the Congress during the period 1957-1968 which may be said to have been, at least partially, a direct response to protest. During 1963, demonstrations and boycotts by Negroes had taken place in eight hundred communities across the nation. The climax of these demonstrations came on August 28, when 200,000 persons, black and white, participated in the "March on Washington for Jobs and Freedom." It was on that occasion that Martin Luther King delivered his most famous speech, when he spoke of his dream of an America rid forever of racial inequality, with blacks and whites living peacefully together and sharing in the nation's opportunities and abundance.

Prior to this, however, the federal government had begun to take steps to process the protests. These protests had not been confined to Negro groups: many white persons, especially church groups and college students, had made common cause with the Negroes, and had expressed themselves forcefully in favor of racial justice and equality. In June, President Kennedy greatly broadened his civil rights program (originally submitted to the Congress in February), proposing rather sweeping legislation. He was fully conscious of the need for legislation to respond to the protests. In a nationwide television address, given a week before submitting his legislative package to the Congress, he had warned of the dangers in a situation in which legal remedies were ineffective or nonexistent. In these cases, he said: "Redress is sought in the streets, in demonstrations, parades and protest which create tensions and threaten violence—and threaten lives."

By late November, the bill incorporating the civil rights package had been formally reported but had not been cleared for floor action. On November 22, 1963, President Kennedy was assassinated in Dallas. In one of his first actions as President, Lyndon Johnson pressed for enactment of the legislation, saying: "No memorial oration or eulogy could more eloquently honor President Kennedy's memory than the earliest possible passage of the civil rights bill for which he fought so long."

Despite the urging of the new President and the connection of the proposed legislation with the martyred President, it was not until mid-year that the legislation finally cleared the Congress (and was signed by the President on July 2).

The Civil Rights Act of 1964 was the most comprehensive piece of civil rights legislation enacted in the country's history. In eleven titles, the act broadened the guarantees of the Negro's right to vote; barred discrimination in public accommodations; authorized suits by the federal government to desegregate public facilities and schools; broadened the responsibilities of the Civil Rights Commission and extended its life for four years; barred discrimination in any program or activity receiving federal assistance; outlawed discriminatory practices in employment and created the Equal Employment Opportunity Commission to enforce these provisions; and created a Community Relations Service to aid communities in resolving disputes growing out of discriminatory practices.

Though designed originally as a response to protest, the question may be fairly raised whether the Civil Rights Act of 1964 would have been so sweeping—or would have passed at all—without the additional political and sympathetic impetus provided by the assassination of President Kennedy.

(4) The Voting Rights Act of 1965 is the second of the three civil rights enactments of the 1960's which may be regarded as responses to protest. In fact, it represented the most direct response of the three. In this instance, the response was to a series of demonstrations protesting voting discrimination in the South. Though demonstrations, marches, and sit-ins were held in various places throughout the country in early 1965, the main focus of the protests was Selma, Alabama, where peaceful demonstrations soon gave way to violence, which, in turn, aroused much public attention and sympathy for the civil rights cause.

The depth of this sympathy, as well as the direct and obvious connection between the protest and the response, may perhaps be measured best by regarding the relative speed with which the Congress moved. On March 17, President Johnson submitted a draft voting-rights proposal to the Congress, and by August 4, the bill had cleared both houses: it was signed by the President on August 6.

The Voting Rights Act of 1965, considered to be the most sweeping such bill of modern times, contained a number of provisions bearing upon the right to vote. The most important provision, constituting a departure from the pattern of earlier civil rights legislation, was that calling for direct action by the federal government in the electoral process. This action took the form of authorizing federally appointed examiners to determine individuals' qualifications to vote, and to enroll voters, after specified findings made by a federal court or by the Attorney General, or after certain facts had been established.

Five days after the President signed the Voting Rights Act of 1965, Watts exploded into bloody violence, in the worst racial disorder in American history. The six days of violence caused 34 deaths, 856 injuries, over 3,000 arrests, and nearly $200,000,000 in damages.

THE CIVIL RIGHTS ACT OF 1968

(5) For those persons who were getting accustomed to a new piece of civil rights legislation every year, 1966 must have been a disappointing year. The key section of the administration-backed civil rights bill of that year, a provision calling for open housing, quickly aroused a great deal of controversy, and became the focal point for the opponents of the bill. It was to prove the proposal's undoing. Though the bill passed the House (by a roll-call vote of 259-157), a group of Republican senators, led by Senator Dirksen, focused their attack on the open-housing provision, and prevented passage by the Senate.

The next year, the first year of the Ninetieth Congress, was to prove almost as disappointing to civil rights supporters. The only action taken by Congress in this area during 1967 was to extend the life of the Civil Rights Commission for five years.

President Johnson's 1967 civil rights package, in substance, closely resembled the comprehensive bill introduced in 1966, which the Congress had turned down. However, in an attempt to win Congress' approval of the rights legislation in 1957, separate bills were proposed for each item. The law extending the life of the Civil Rights Commission was regarded as the least controversial of the items in the President's civil rights package. Two other parts of the package were passed by either the House or the Senate, but not by both.

In January 1968, President Johnson's civil rights message asked the Congress to enact five measures not acted upon during the previous year, including open housing, which subsequently was attached as an amendment to a civil rights bill passed by the House in 1967. Since the Congress appeared to be in a more conservative mood than it had been while passing the rights legislation of 1964 and 1965, most observers felt that the civil rights bill of 1968, especially since it contained an open-housing provision, would not pass.

After the Senate had approved it by a generous margin (71-20), the bill ran into trouble in the House. The dramatic switch which eventuated in the final passage of the bill came in the Rules Committee. First, the committee voted to delay the bill. After the delay, the committee was scheduled to vote on whether to approve the Senate-passed version or to send the bill to a conference committee. Before this next action could be taken, however, Martin Luther King, Jr., was assassinated in Memphis, and violence broke out in over a hundred American cities. The vote in committee was taken on the same day on which King's funeral was held in Atlanta. Republican John B. Anderson (Illinois) decided that sending the bill to a conference committee would seriously jeopardize its chances of passage, and unexpectedly switched his vote to favor bringing it to the floor of the House. On the next day, the House approved the bill, putting on the books the first federal open-housing legislation since 1866.

What effect King's death and the resulting disorder had on the vote is impossible to gauge accurately. It is possible that the bill would have passed eventually anyway, without the tragic events of April; it is also possible that the rioting subsequent to King's death lost supporters for the bill in Congress. Commenting indirectly on the possibility of such a "backlash" effect, Representative Anderson, who had played such a key role in the passage of the bill, said at the time of his vote, "I legislate today not out of fear but out of deep concern for the America I love."

In general, it was felt that King's death did contribute positively toward the bill's enactment. As in the 1964 act, the legislation came to be viewed as a fitting monument to a fallen political leader.

It is interesting to record that the Civil Rights Act of 1968, though it did incorporate the first federal open-housing legislation in over a century (and dealt with other rights as well), also included some antiriot provisions and penalties for specified riot activities.

THE REPORT OF THE KERNER COMMISSION

The work of the National Advisory Commission on Civil Disorders (Kerner Commission) and the fate of its report provided an interesting and revealing story. The creation of the Commission itself was clearly a response to protest, which, in this instance, had been articulated in the violent civil disorders which had swept through 128 American cities during the summer of 1967.

Commission members were so impressed with the urgency of the racial problem in the United States, and with the likelihood that the summer of 1968 would bring more violent protest in the mode of the previous summer, that they released their final report earlier than had been anticipated. Originally appointed by the President on July 29, 1967, members of the Commission had been instructed to make an interim report on its findings of fact by March 1, 1968, and a final report by July 29, 1968. Instead, they issued their final report on March 1, five months before the date that it was due. They expressed themselves as having "worked together with a sense of the greatest urgency" and, as a result, having decided that the "gravity of the problem and the pressing need for action are too clear to allow further delay in the issuance" of the report.

The report and its urgent tone apparently touched a responsive chord in the American people. Within the short space of three weeks, 740,000 copies of the report were sold (mostly on newsstands), probably qualifying it for the record of the fastest-selling book in history.

In sharp contrast, the response by both the President and the Congress was generally disappointing. The President's noncommital statement (some persons described it as cool) at the time of the release of the report disappointed many who felt that major changes were needed in order to alleviate the situation in the nation. Several weeks later, the President was asked at a press conference to comment on the report and on the criticism that he was not acting quickly enough on the recommendations contained therein. At that time, he elaborated on his view of the report, indicating that he found it to be very thorough and very comprehensive, and that it included many good recommendations. His extended remarks, however, again failed to reflect any urgency, and again disappointed many persons.

In a television broadcast about two months after the report was published, an attempt was made to trace its short history and its fate. Governor Kerner of Illinois, who had chaired the commission, expressed keen disappointment at the general lack of action on the recommendations which had been made, pointing out that, up to that time, there had been no discussion of it, either in Congress or in congressional committees. Mayor Lindsay of New York City, the commission's vice-chairman, agreed. He felt that the country was not moving fast enough, or far enough, to process the recommendations. He also felt that there had been insufficient action by the federal government, a failure which he identified as the responsibility primarily of the Congress.

Perhaps the most eloquent appraisal of the report—and a cogent comment upon protest in the American system—was made by a black resident of Newark, one of America's most riot-torn cities, who said: "The riot commission report didn't change anything: it's the riots that changed things."

THE POOR PEOPLE AND THE CONGRESS

The very day on which the words here were being written (in July 1968) brought an announcement from the Ninetieth Congress of the United States that that body, in which is vested "all legislative powers" granted by the Constitution, had announced that, in order to make possible an early adjournment, no further legislation authorizing new programs or commitments would be considered. The early adjournment was, of course, being contemplated with a careful eye on the calendar, for 1968 was a presidential election year, and the supreme legislative body of the nation had to cede the spotlight and the forefront of the stage to the national nominating conventions, to be held in August.

Earlier, the Congress had approved a twofold measure designed to check inflation: an income tax surcharge and a cut in spending by the federal government. It was widely felt that the measure would result both in increased unemployment (at a time when unemployment was a critical problem in urban ghettos) and cuts in domestic social welfare programs (at a time when it was becoming increasingly clear that the money committed to such programs had not been adequate to do the job).

In short, in the summer of 1968, the Congress of the United States had indicated that its stance toward protests based on pleas for social and economic justice would be: business as usual.

Reflective of this stance was Congress' reaction to the outstanding nonviolent protest made during the second half of the decade: the Poor People's March and Demonstration, in May and June of 1968, which was originally conceived by Martin Luther King as a dramatic move to symbolize the plight of the poor people of America. The leadership of the protest march and demonstration had devolved upon Ralph Abernathy, King's disciple and assistant, who had taken over the latter's role as leader of the Southern Christian Leadership Conference (SCLC), a major sponsor of the march. Abernathy possessed neither King's control over SCLC, nor his ability to evoke the confidence of the poor people, nor his level of political skill. It is clear that, in many ways, the Poor People's March and Demonstration, and their experience in the construction and management of Resurrection City, were badly handled by a divided and mutually suspicious group of leaders. Most to the point here is Abernathy's lack of political skill, as exhibited in his presenting the national government with what was generally regarded as an inordinate and impossible set of demands. We can speculate that King would have made demands which would have been easier to obtain, would have achieved some success in getting a fair number of these demands met, and then would have been able to ride out the protests of the militants among the poor, who would have been unsatisfied with the partial success.

But whatever the internal problems of the Poor People's March, our main point of concern here is the response by the federal government, and particularly the Congress, since it was the Congress which was the focal point of the protest. One newspaper commentator appraised the over-all accomplishments reflected in Congress' response, dealing with the question on two bases for measurement: measured against the demands made by the poor, he termed the record "abysmal"; measured against the President's proposed program for the poor, he characterized the record as "modest."[2]

In fact, the Congress did manage to take some action in mid-1968 in the fields of social and economic welfare, some of which action was presumably in direct response to the poor people's protest activities. In a number of instances, the Congress went even beyond the President's request, or took action without specific suggestion by the President. For example, in early July, the Congress added $28 million to a presidential request, in order to provide more summer-job and educational opportunities for the underprivileged than the President had programmed. Further, the Model Cities Program, designed to spur upgrading and redevelopment of urban ghetto communities, was given more generous financial support in 1968 than it had received the previous year. In addition, as this article is being written, there has been affirmative action by one house of Congress, and final action is expected before adjournment, in a number of other areas, including a large new program of housing subsidies and a large addition to the federal budget to provide free or low-cost school lunches to needy children.

In considering the positive steps taken by Congress during mid-1968 in response to protest, two separate points need to be made, the former pragmatic, the latter philosophical or a matter of policy. This first point is that the President has been charged by Congress with reducing federal spending by $6 billion during the next fiscal year. Accordingly, regardless of the number and the variety of programs which have been enacted and budgeted, the real question of how much federal money will be actually *spent* in their implementation has not yet been settled. It is clear that a spending cut of $6 billion cannot be effectuated without severe cuts in many federal programs, and we can predict that at least some of these cuts will come in the social welfare area.

The second point, setting aside the question of the looming spending cuts, is whether the action taken by Congress in 1968, parts of which were described briefly above, were, in fact, sufficient, in light of the real needs of the nation. These needs were perhaps most graphically portrayed in the Poor People's March (and in the activities and statements which preceded and accompanied it), and were also reflected in the grim statistic that by mid-year, 1968, serious disturbances related to racial conflict and the cause of the poor had occurred in over two hundred cities and towns across the United States.

The question of whether Congress' action in 1968 was sufficient raises still another question, even more fundamental: whether the people of the United States, taken at large, have reacted or responded sufficiently to the needs of the nation, particularly the disadvantaged portions, as expressed in the various protest movements. Both questions are closely interwoven and cannot, in fact, be separated, given the basic assumption of a democratic representative government. The question thus becomes: Could the Congress have done more than, in fact, it did, given the present level of concern and commitment of the American people? The answer is: Probably not. While there is a significant role for leadership by a representative body in a democratic system, that role must be delicately played, and can never be permitted to grow too far beyond the bounds set by majority opinion.

We might conclude with the opinion that, by mid-1968, the American people had not yet been aroused to that level of concern and commitment which would bring them to exert consistent pressure on federal legislators, executives, and administrators, to cause these, in turn, to undertake the major—and very costly—changes required to meet the present challenge and to respond to the protests of the 1960's. Until that concern and commitment are widespread and at a high level, we can expect little success in bringing about these major changes.

A POSTSCRIPT FOR PEACE WORKERS: SOME CONCRETE ADVICE

Ralph K. White

Effective persuasion . . . requires two things: First, *to build up inconsistency in the person's attitude structure*. For peace workers this means getting through with new arguments and information and also making more vivid and inescapable the reasons the person already has for being against the war. Second, *to remove or reduce the forces that hold him to his original attitude*. For peace workers this means such things as changing the person's perception of the social pressures that hold him in line and providing him with action possibilities. It means other things as well, and one of the most important is altering the person's distorted stereotypes of "the peace movement."

Every particular recommendation and guideline offered here is an aid to one or both of these two basic tasks in the persuasion process. More particularly, each recommendation points toward concrete and potent ways of achieving those conditions (whether communicator credibility, evocation of latent inconsistency, reduction of social supports, and so on) that have been shown to be especially important in arousing inconsistency or reducing barriers to evaluative change.

The main intent of this postscript, then, is to . . . show how [this practical theory] can be directly implemented—how it can be put to work in the great national debate over Vietnam and Southeast Asian policy.

Previous chapters have already shown that many in the ostensible silent majority are close to the threshold of basic change in their stated views. If they can be drawn across the threshold, the consequences for our immediate national welfare and our long-range style in foreign policy should be considerable. Those consequences would be effected through many different translations of attitude change into influence upon policy. But, clearly, the first and most likely translation would be through elections. With this in mind we turn, at the very beginning of this survey of concretely practical guides, to persuasion, to some points about the uses of persuasion in election campaigning—though our interest in changing the views of the silent majority is wider than the pre-election effort. Also we shall often be addressing the young (though not only the young), because they exceed many of their elders in the energy they can bring to the great national debate now in progress, while certainly matching them in depth of concern. Concerning elections, a basic distinction needs to be made between *canvassing*, which is the most important thing you can do to bring out the vote for a peace candidate, and *persuading* people to change their views on basic issues.

The two things don't mix very well. An effective door-to-door canvasser usually has little time to talk about issues. His main job is to bring to the polls those who are already leaning in his candidate's direction. During the short time that he can afford to spend in a particular house or on a particular doorstep, his time is usually occupied with inquiring politely into the ideas of the person who opens the door, making sure the person knows the candidate's name and (if he shows a leaning toward peace) being certain he knows the candidate *is* a "peace candidate." In the process, he usually finds out whether the individual, or his wife, needs transportation or a baby-sitter in order to vote.

This kind of unspectacular but essential work on the part of thousands of young, dedicated workers contributed greatly to the spectacular victories of Eugene McCarthy in New Hampshire and elsewhere. [It rests on the proposition] that basic values and assumptions are relatively constant and hard to change, while specific attitudes and actions, such as voting for a not too familiar candidate, are often easier to change. Also, it is rooted in the experience of political professionals. They know that door-to-door canvassing on a sufficiently large scale can supply the margin of the additional 5 per cent to 10 per cent that is needed in a close election to put one candidate over the top. They know, too, that it is not likely to be done on a sufficiently large scale if the canvassers are overoptimistic about changing unrelenting "hawks" into "doves" and spend more than a few minutes in an average household. (Whether or not this is true depends partly on how many canvassers are available to do the job.)

Since there are already available in print some excellent discussions of the art of canvassing, and since political professionals are usually available to provide the necessary coaching, the remainder of this postscript will be devoted not to canvassing but to the other relevant activity:

persuading people to change their views on relatively basic issues such as the Vietnam war. The demonstrated non-solidity of the "silent majority," the evidence that many of them already are experiencing considerable inconsistency of the sort that precedes attitude change—both of these suggest that while canvassers canvass, others should be at the more difficult but equally important task of trying to persuade the as yet unpersuaded.

This is something that all of us can do some of the time. Most of us have been trying to do it, whenever an opportunity offered, for at least five years. The Cambodian invasion, by its generation of further inconsistency and doubt, has simply given us a better opportunity to do effectively what we have been trying to do all along. Canvassers can do some of it in their spare time, or when they run into a particularly receptive on-the-fence voter, and the rest of us can do it when, for instance, we find ourselves talking with someone who seems basically peace-oriented but who believes that President Nixon is "withdrawing as fast as he can."

Such persuasion can also be done by persons who are willing to give it all or a large part of their time, and, with proper preparation, to talk with groups rather than individuals. This includes the use of TV and other mass media. It can be done both by qualified older people and by qualified younger ones who are willing to undertake what is required. Basically, two things are required: the first is some deepened understanding of the nature of the persuasion process and its basic principles. This, the authors have tried to provide in the fourth chapter. The second general requirement is to know how to use all available opportunities—and to maximize all the particular conditions which will help get the force of one's arguments and facts across so that inner-attitudinal inconsistency is established in a way that leads toward attitude change. That is where the guidelines offered here may be especially useful.

These guidelines should not be taken as rigid rules, even though (for the sake of clearness and compactness) they are stated in the imperative form as a series of do's and don'ts. Since you will meet an endless variety of persons and situations, the guidelines should be flexibly interpreted on the basis of your own experience and common sense.

THE PEOPLE YOU TALK WITH

Effective persuasion begins with knowing whom you stand a fair chance of persuading and knowing also who, given your limited time, is most worth persuading.

. . . Those who are close to the threshold for basic change in their stated views. . . . are the ones who are already troubled by the existence of potential inconsistency within their attitude structures. They are the ones with whom your main job is simply to make more vivid and inescapable the reasons they already have for being against the war. They are the ones who can be most easily drawn across the threshold—and, . . . there are a great many of these people in the "silent majority." Here, then, are some guidelines on how to reach them:

1. *Work in Your Own Community or Neighborhood If Possible.*   Your contacts there will give you an entrée, direct or indirect, to many of the individuals you would most like to reach, and the fact that you are already known in certain groups will make you more acceptable to group members. As a rule, an older person is likely to be more effective in speaking to older people, a black in speaking to blacks, a Pole in speaking to Poles, a Catholic in speaking to Catholics, a country-club member in speaking to country-club members, and so on.

2. *Seek Contact, Wherever Possible, with the Influential "Core" Members of the Groups You Want To Influence*   —the presidents or respected members of clubs of all sorts; priests, ministers, and influential lay members of church groups; labor leaders, business executives, farm organization leaders, veterans' organization leaders; active members of lodges, women's groups, and so on. The local editor is likely to be a particularly good informant as to who these individuals are. Some of these people— sometimes in unexpected places—are likely to be wholeheartedly on your side already; they can help you in devising ways of persuading the others in their own groups.

This is directly in line with the general principle that it is better if the people you influence are themselves influential. For instance, it is good if the people you talk with are the kind who might have direct contact with congressmen.

3. *Use One Contact To Get Others.*   If you want a contact with the president of the Rotary Club, for instance, and don't know him but do know a respected lawyer who knows him, it is better to get the lawyer to introduce you to him than to make the initial contact yourself, coming at him "cold."

4. *Other Things Being Equal, Work with Groups That Are Likely To Be Receptive Already.*   For instance, the survey evidence indicating that women tend to be more peace-oriented than men is a good reason to seek opportunities to persuade women's groups. One might think the opposite: that there is no use talking to those who are on your side already. But the general principle that is applicable here is one that has already been noted: where inner-attitudinal inconsistency already exists, you have a good opportunity to heighten it further and move people toward true attitude change. You want to reach as many people as possible who have already come part way to your position (or who accept your position without much conviction) and who will listen receptively. This is true especially if you want to recruit activists.

5. *But Don't Pass Up Any Good Opportunity To Meet with a Group, No Matter How Unreceptive You Might Expect It To Be.* It is important to remember, as pointed out above, that there are a considerable number of peace-oriented, realistically skeptical individuals in *all* groups and on every economic level. This is true of Catholics as well as Protestants, of "ethnics" as well as WASP's, of blue-collar workers as well as managerial and professional people, of patriotic societies and luncheon clubs as well as churches. A group that you might regard as relatively unreachable on the basis of such demographic characteristics may not really be prowar as much as it is anti-peace movement because of its stereotypes about that movement. It is probably reachable if one is sensitive to this problem. Such sensitivity is discussed in the next section.

6. *Reaching Groups Is Very Important, but Don't Forget the Tremendous Potential of Face-to-Face Discussion with One Other Person.* When you deal with groups, you are tailoring what you say to some approximate ideas about what most of them feel and think. But when you deal with one other person, you can, if you remain sensitive to the challenge of searching out his values and beliefs, develop some particularly effective ways of reaching him with the facts and arguments that can get him to re-examine his own attitudes. And remember that one man who achieves real attitude change will probably ultimately affect a number of others who are close to him.

STYLE

To be an effective persuader, it is often useful to make a conscious choice between the "expressive" and the "instrumental" approach. In the expressive style, the purpose is to vent or express one's own feelings; in the instrumental, it is to achieve or move toward a goal. In the present context, the distinction is between the "expressive" gratification of putting your own strongest feelings into words, getting them off your chest, and the "instrumental" satisfaction of actually communicating with others and perhaps influencing them. This is instrumental in that it considers communication as a means to an end, the end being effective persuasion.

There may be a paradox here, particularly for the student involved in peace work. While the life-style most characteristic of the present student generation is highly expressive, a considerable segment of that generation is now undertaking a task of persuasion that is, by its very nature, instrumental. It may be a difficult thing for some of those who do so to face up to the nature of the conflict that it involves.

Probably the chief difficulty lies in the feeling that an instrumental approach means insincerity. Actually, it does not need to mean that at all. A wholly sincere, candid person can set out deliberately to persuade others when something as important as peace is at stake, and can consider rationally what kind of appearance and manner and style of argument will best serve that end, within limits set by his unwillingness ever to say or do anything that he does not consider authentic.

To those who regard themselves as radical, in the sense of going to the roots of things, this decision is likely to be especially hard. To them, "expression" is likely to be an even more paramount value than it is for others of their generation. They are likely to admire the courage of those who are willing to stand up and be counted, taking whatever personal risk may be involved in expressing an unpopular view openly. They may feel that there is something evasive and even cowardly in discussing Vietnam without stressing the basic characteristics of our society—the economic system and the power structure—which, as they see it, are at the root of the Vietnam war, the arms race, poverty, racism, and other evils. Whether such persons are right in their diagnosis of the causes of war is not the issue here. Nor is it possible in all good conscience to advise that one suppress or hide what one believes. What we would hope is that in choosing among arguments, or in choosing among styles of argumentation, the peace worker would have the courage to face the real dilemmas involved. Then he will not choose the easy illusion that he can have it both ways.

When seen in this light, the following guidelines may seem fairly elementary:

1. *Dissociate Yourself, in Every Way That You Honestly Can, from the Distorted Public Stereotype of the Peace Demonstrator.*   The potency of this distorted stereotype was evident as the United States approached the 1970 Congressional elections. For example, Senator Yarborough, a staunch liberal, had lost to an opponent whose most effective technique was to show on television a film depicting unkempt, long-haired students demonstrating for Eugene McCarthy in Chicago, to link them with Yarborough by quoting a statement of his supporting McCarthy, and then to ask: Is this the sort of person you want in Washington? Other candidates had taken Yarborough's experience to heart. Senator Gore and others had actually asked students not to campaign in their behalf.

What meaning can be drawn from such recent signs? Their most immediate import is simply to remind us that the great majority of the American people are intensely antagonistic to what they conceive to be the typical student peace demonstrator. Even antiwar people, as was shown earlier, are usually hostile toward organized public protest against the war. The reader need only recall that most of the public sided with the National Guard in the Kent State episode.

The sources for this antagonism are many, but it is not our purpose to explicate the generation gap or to explain, condemn, or defend this antagonism. That goes well beyond our task. The connection between the peace movement and the more general culture conflict between the "hip" and the "straight" styles of life may be largely a historical accident of the time period in which Vietnam took place (though the connection is more complicated than that). Our only concern is to point out that such a connection may do the peace movement little good.

On the other hand, the vast talent and energy of American youth is probably the greatest single potential resource that the peace movement possesses. The way out of this dilemma lies in recognizing that if student support is to be as positive an asset as it can be, those involved have some hard decisions to make. The first of these is a decision about the purpose of the whole operation. For those who have undertaken to work as members of a team to elect a peace candidate, the essential purpose should be clear. It is not—except in the long run—to stop the war. It is to get a certain candidate elected.

This doesn't mean getting a crew cut, and it doesn't mean wearing an American flag on your shoulder. It certainly doesn't mean saying anything you don't wholly believe. It does mean accepting fully the 1970 equivalent of your own group, and of the people organizing that group, as to what compromises are necessary in appearance, style, words, and actions. Anything less than this would mean a less than honest relation to the people you are working with and to the candidate you are working for. Two psychological reasons prompting this advice should be recognized. It is partly a question of "communicator credibility and acceptability." You can't get in the door or bring people to a meeting or keep them listening open-mindedly if they are turned off because they associate you with their distorted stereotype of the peace demonstrator. There is also the need to remove or reduce the forces holding the person to his original attitude. If his distaste for the peace movement—as he conceives it—has been keeping him from identifying with peace policies, a significant change in his conception of the movement will help to start the process of attitude change.

We will not detail here the many choices available for regulating appearance and communicative style so as to gain greater communicator acceptability while at the same time altering the other person's stereotyped conception of the peace movement. Any reader capable of making the effort to see himself as various kinds of others see him can analyze his own situation for himself. The key issue for the individual is that of maintaining sincerity and authenticity while pursuing efficacy.

2. *Don't Downgrade Patriotism.* For a good many, a genuine conflict between total candor and considerations of persuasiveness comes up in connection with the concept of patriotism. There is a real difference between a humanist value system which respects the dignity and welfare of *all* human beings, whether they are American or not, and a narrower nationalist value system which, for example, treats American lives as inherently more important than Vietnamese lives. There is also a real difference between those who see a narrow nationalism as a major cause—

perhaps as *the* major cause—of war in the twentieth century and those who
do not. To many Americans, not accustomed to making any distinction
between nationalism and patriotism, such a diagnosis might in itself seem
like a lack of patriotism, confirming all their worst fears as to the softness
and the disloyalty of students and other intellectuals in the United States.
Does this mean that total candor on the part of a peace worker would
antagonize these people and lead them to shut their ears even if he were
arguing that America, in its own self-interest, should get out of the war?

That danger does exist, and some thought is clearly needed in order
to avoid it. But surely the problem is soluble in principle, since peace persuasion is *not* inconsistent with enlightened patriotism. In fact it is required
by it. If real American interests were now pitted against the interests of
others, there might be a conflict, but that is not the case. The interests of
Americans, of Vietnamese, and of the world as a whole are on the side of
peace. Therefore we can without insincerity meet even the most national-
istic American on his own ground and argue for peace mainly or entirely
on the basis of American interest: American lives, a healthy economy
here at home, reducing the danger of nuclear war in the future, and so on.

Are there ways of clearing the air at the very outset by actively
reassuring people as to our concern with American interests and American values? Perhaps not, but some illustrative possibilities deserve to be
at least thought about:

a. To stress "the kind of country we want America to be."

b. To begin a talk with some frank discussion of the peace-demon-
strator stereotype, including flag-burning, and to make a statement (but
only if it is a true statement) such as, "I feel the same way you do about
that sort of thing."

c. To cite Abraham Lincoln's opposition to the Mexican War as an
example of patriotic, principled opposition to a war.

d. To quote Carl Schurz: "Our country, right or wrong. When right,
to be kept right; when wrong, to be put right."

e. To invoke, against this war, the American principle of respect for
the independence of small nations.

3. *Avoid Terms That Grate Needlessly on Your Listeners' Ears.* This is
not a plea for being less than candid about actual convictions. It is a plea
for not using needlessly any term that involves no gain in accuracy in con-
veying your feelings (and possibly an actual loss, if you really don't mean
what is associated with a certain term in the listeners' minds) and that
consequently "turns off" the listener.

Some examples of what I mean are summarized in the following
table. They are illustrations, and many more could be given. It might well
be worth while to construct such a table of your own. You know best what
goes on the right-hand side for you.

Instead of . . .	*You might say . . .*
liberation	independence, freedom
imperialism	intervention, domination
the system	the military-industrial complex (with a somewhat different meaning)
the Establishment	the military-industrial complex, the Administration, the people who are now in power
revolution (if you really mean it)	basic change (and specify what kind; e.g., cultural rather than political)
prowar	in favor of the President's policy
superpatriotism	nationalism
radical (as something good)	fundamental
like	for instance, approximately, about
y'know	uh, maybe, I think, well, what's the word I want?

4. *It Is Important That You Separate the Issues.*   As already indicated, one important finding from the data on attitudes toward the war is that they do not necessarily form a neat and consistent bundle with attitudes on other subjects. Those who are opposed to the war (or who look as if their approval of the war has now been undermined by enough doubt to make them good candidates for your persuasion efforts) may not have liberal views on the race issue or on poverty or on a host of other subjects. This may be true particularly in some segments of society that feel threatened by rising taxes, increasing welfare costs, and black militancy.

It is easier to feel certain of the validity of this generalization than of what to do about it. The peace worker may consider these other issues of equal importance or greater importance. Under such circumstances, one cannot in good conscience advise him to "talk Vietnam" and ignore these other subjects. All that can be done is to suggest sensitivity to the situation and to warn the reader that he ought not to assume that he knows a man's attitudes on any other subject when he knows where he stands on the war. At any rate, the facts about issue separation are worth remembering if you are really concentrating on peace persuasion. If your own standards will allow you to approach the peace issue "separately" with those who probably disagree with you on many other issues, you may avoid an outcome that could negate all your efforts: namely, getting yourself typed as a "radical" because of views expressed on other issues, in a situation in which you cannot make headway on those issues and can lose the rapport you need in order to make headway on the peace issue.

5. *Cite the Great Number of Leaders and Authorities Who Oppose the War.* As we have seen, when individuals have little information, they are likely to depend upon authorities. And they are unlikely to change their attitudes if it will make their position inconsistent with that of some authority they respect. This is the basis of power in the role of President. It also suggests that the effective persuader will invoke those authorities who have turned against the war. There are now many such authorities—senators from both political parties, leading businessmen, lawyers, and bankers, leading newspapers, such as the *Wall Street Journal* and the *New York Times*, and former advisers to President Johnson, who should certainly have inside knowledge of the war. Which figures an individual is likely to find authoritative will vary from person to person. Businessmen are likely to be influenced by the views of other businessmen, lawyers by lawyers, workers by labor leaders, Republicans by Republicans, and Democrats by Democrats. For some, the *Wall Street Journal* may be an authority, for others not. "Find an authoritative source" is a general principle the specific application of which depends upon the particular circumstance. Fortunately, support for the war has eroded so widely that one can probably find authoritative sources to cite in almost every walk of life.

6. *Listen Before You Talk.* A good listener is likely to open ears that an appearance of arrogance would close. The atmosphere should be that of equal give-and-take, not of "I am enlightening you." Also, listening will help you understand the particular views and assumptions you have to respond to—it will help you map the inner structure and content of the attitude you hope to change.

7. *Acknowledge—If You Honestly Can—Some Truth in the Views of Those Who Disagree with You.* As the experimental evidence has shown, it is usually more effective to argue in a "two-sided" way, acknowledging some validity in the position of the other side, than in a "one-sided" way, as if you thought you had a monopoly of the truth. This is true especially when the other person starts out disagreeing with you; before he will really listen, he has to be given the feeling that you are leveling with him and listening to him, and are trying to see the facts in a balanced, objective way rather than simply trying to win an argument.

This is so especially in the light of the generally ambivalent views of the American people toward the war. Few people have clear-cut black and white views on the subject and many vacillate from one position to another. An approach that was insensitive to this, that could not concede the possibility that reasonable men would have an alternative position, is not likely to be effective. The individual who once thought the war was reasonable or who still has friends and relatives who think the war is reasonable will more easily change his position to an antiwar one if in so doing he is not required to acknowledge the total unreason of his previous position or of the present position of others he respects. The persuader for peace who concedes a little may gain a lot.

CONTENT

This has not been a book focused on the substantive issues of the war in Vietnam. Nor do we intend to provide a neat repertoire of arguments to be made in relationship to the war. The literature on the war itself is vast, and nothing can substitute for the intensive homework that one will have to do before one faces an individual or group in the role of a semi-expert on peace issues. An effective persuader needs to be prepared and needs to be informed. He must anticipate counterarguments and have the facts to answer them. Take an example. The individual with whom one is trying to communicate says that we must fight against aggression and that the North Vietnamese were the aggressors against the South. An effective persuader will not be one who replies in vague generalities or who simply asserts the other is wrong. Rather, he is one who knows the facts about the onset of the war and can cite chapter and verse. He can show that the assumption that this is a case of simple aggression from North to South is false. And if he can show that effectively, he will have gone far toward undercutting the other's belief in the war.

The reader will find such arguments for himself in the literature on the war. We can, however, use our knowledge of public opinion to make three essential suggestions about content. They are suggestions at different levels—but, reasoning from the available public opinion data, each seems particularly useful. The first concerns the definition of the Vietnam issue, the second draws upon what this book has already discussed about the main, latent inconsistency in the attitudes of Americans who still endorse our Vietnam involvement, and the third reinforces the single most important general point of advice that has already been given in this volume.

1. Make a Clear Distinction Between an Irreversible, Time-Limited Withdrawal (*the Pro-Peace Congressmen's Minimum Position*) *and the President's Reversible, No-Time-Limit Withdrawal.* For a person to be able to make an evaluative shift after sufficient inconsistency arousal has occurred, he often needs a new, and more acceptable, way of defining the position he previously rejected. This is very relevant to the present debate between the Administration and many of its "moderate" critics. When involved in real debate a supporter of the present policy is likely to attempt to fend off inconsistency arousal with the question: "The President *is* pulling out, isn't he?" It is important, therefore, to make a clear distinction between the kind of withdrawal the President wants and the kind pro-peace congressmen and candidates want, and to make plain what is wrong with the President's kind. His November 3 [1969] speech successfully blurred this distinction in the minds of a great many Americans. When he claimed that the only alternative to his kind of withdrawal is an immediate, "precipitate" withdrawal he was simply ignoring the intermediate policy of allowing a reasonable time for withdrawal but definitely getting out by a specified date as required, for example, in the McGovern-Hatfield amendment.

Ever since the beginning of the war, a great many Americans have supported their government's policy, not because they had any stomach for the war (or for the Saigon government), but because they "couldn't see any alternative." It is important therefore to clarify and to make real for them the alternative that many peace advocates are now presenting. (This is related also to a point made [in an earlier chapter] that "one should show the person that there are immediately available action alternatives that are open to him as a way of expressing his altered attitude." Here the "action" is vicarious, but the person at least can be given a clearly structured, easily defended type of national action that he can define and advocate in conversation with others).

2. *Your Single Most Effective Argument Is Likely To Be the Disastrous Effects of This War Upon the United States, Especially Its Economic Impact.*   Attitude change theory tells us that people will try to deny and avoid uncomfortable information. But the data on attitudes toward the war suggest that people have not been able to avoid Vietnam as an issue because it has intruded so thoroughly and overtly into life in the United States. The most direct intrusion has been in the economic realm—and this can easily be supported. Naturally this means being able to cite facts and figures on unemployment, inflation, and so on, and also to trace the connections between them and the war. The very large per cent of the national budget going to past and present wars, as compared with general welfare (i.e., unmet needs in housing, education, transportation, medical care, etc.) is a particularly impressive item.

There is much reason to think that this argument is, if anything, even more potent on those with lower levels of education than among the more educated with whom you may be more familiar. It is tangible, concrete, close to home, and is likely to seem relatively more important to those for whom foreign affairs are somewhat far away and unreal.

The effective persuader will take advantage of this. Also he will stress the disastrous effects of the war on other, related aspects of American life— on the "quality" of the American community as reflected in crime rates, vastly increased use of harmful drugs, campus despair, and regression to unfocused violence, the new bitterness between young and old, rich and poor, black and white. These economic and "quality of life" matters are ones that Americans of all class levels are most immediately and intensely troubled about. They are, therefore, the things around which one can most readily invoke support for an antiwar appeal.

Again, each person's shoe may pinch in its own way. The falling market may pinch the businessman, rising prices the housewife, unemployment the worker, cuts in federal spending the poor city dweller, increasing violence the parent.

3. Effectiveness Depends upon Understanding and, in a Sense, Sharing the Other Person's Values. As was pointed out [earlier], the effective persuader achieves credibility by demonstrating that he shares characteristics and values with the person he is trying to persuade. This is relevant to the *content* of the persuasion as well. For . . . most Americans—including those opposed to the war—have a deep commitment to America and its symbols, are generally if not intensely anti-Communist, are worried about campus violence and the general decline in values they hold dear. The persuader for peace whose words or manner suggest any condescension toward such values is more likely to lose than gain support for peace.

Are we suggesting that the individual who considers such values silly or pathetic or dangerous should feign support for them to gain the confidence of those he would persuade? The question has been raised before in this book—and again the answer must be obviously not—for such support would be insincere and probably self-defeating in the end. But we would suggest that the peace worker who does initially react with estrangement from the apparent values of some of the pro-policy people he contacts should try to put himself in the place of the average American and try to understand sympathetically why and how such values are held. The individual who cannot empathize cannot communicate effectively.

It has been said before at a number of points in this book, and it bears repeating as the last sentence and as the one point that should be most strongly urged upon all workers for peace: *Respect for, and comprehension of, the other man's concerns is the beginning and the basis for lasting political persuasion.*

NOTES: DIRECT ACTION

Introduction

1. William O. Douglas, *Points of Rebellion* (Vintage, 1970), pp. 88-89.

2. Quoted in John F. Kennedy, *Profiles in Courage* (Harper and Row, 1956), p. 10.

Michael Lipsky

1. "The Strategy of Protest: Problems of Negro Civic Action," *Journal of Conflict Resolution,* 3 (September, 1961), 291-303.

2. *Ibid.,* p. 291.

3. *A Preface to Democratic Theory* (Chicago, 1956), pp. 145-146.

4. *Ibid.*

5. *Ibid.,* p. 146.

6. *The Governmental Process* (New York, 1951), p. 513.

7. Norton Long, "The Local Community as an Ecology of Games," in Long, *The Polity,* Charles Press, ed. (Chicago, 1962), p. 153.

8. James Q. Wilson, *Negro Politics* (New York, 1960), p. 225.

9. Wallace Sayre and Herbert Kaufman, *Governing New York City* (New York, 1960), p. 253.

10. *The Symbolic Uses of Politics* (Urbana, Ill., 1964), p. 23.

David Mars

1. James W. Douglass, "Politics Without Violence?" *Christian Century,* June 28, 1968, p. 836.

2. Vincent J. Burke, *Los Angeles Times,* July 7, 1968, sec. G, p. 1.

Part Two
GROUP PARTICIPATION

POLITICAL PARTIES

> *In terms of the larger political system, the parties are
> conservative. They are not "the first by whom the new is tried."
> Over the course of American history, this party passiveness
> before social change has probably had a salutary effect, contributing
> to the capacity of the parties to perform a "peacemaking" or
> "reconciling" function. But in a period of exceptionally rapid and
> extensive change—and none has been more pronounced in this
> regard than our own—it also has the adverse effect of
> heightening the sense of unresponsiveness in the political system.*
>
> —Everett Carll Ladd, Jr.[1]

Apart from some academics and professional politicians, there are few people who will publicly admit any great fondness for America's version of political parties. A generation is now coming to political maturity whose perceptions of the parties are at least partially tainted by the crudities and banalities of the 1968 conventions.[2] P. T. Barnum is reputed to have said, "Nobody has ever lost money by underestimating the taste of the American people." During the 1968 campaign, three parties were spending millions in an apparent attempt to prove Barnum wrong.

The contemporary disenchantment with the parties is not unprecedented. The fact is that Americans have always displayed a curious ambivalence about them. On the one hand, the parties have been attacked as corrupt, undemocratic, and irresponsible. Urban machines and county courthouse rings have been among the chief villains of American politics for many decades. On the other hand, Americans have not only tolerated party dominance of the electoral process but have consistently identified in majority proportions with the two major parties. If America's parties are inadequate, the public has been quite willing to accept this inadequacy. Indeed the major thrust of party reform has characteristically been to weaken rather than to strengthen party organization. One of the major contributions of the Progressive era—the direct primary—certainly did reduce the party's control of nominations. And a number of states even prohibit official party committees from making pre-primary endorsements of candidates.

Despite the popular ambivalence about parties, American scholars have generally assumed that a competitive party system is essential to a democracy. Samuel Eldersveld explains:

> *It is accepted as incontrovertible truth that the historical de-*
> *velopment of democracy would have been impossible without the*
> *concomitant appearance of political parties. Representative, pop-*
> *ular government could not have been implemented without inter-*
> *vening political groups to support legislative leadership, mobilize*
> *voters, and agitate for alternative programs and policies.*[3]

Thus the contemporary challenges facing the parties concern their ability to perform these broad functions adequately, particularly given their decreasing ability to dominate each of these functions.

The mobilization of voters illustrates some of the difficulties which the parties now face. There is little question that the major American parties have been and are preoccupied with the electing function, more so than parties in most parliamentary democracies. It is also apparent that national elections have been virtually monopolized by candidates of the Democratic and Republican parties. Much of this dominance has resulted from these parties' ability to maintain the political loyalty of substantial portions of the population and at the same time to control political resources and political skills.

Party control of each of these elements of political currency, however, is eroding. The use of the direct primary for major offices in most states limits party control of nominations. The growing importance of the mass media in campaigning and the high costs of media campaigns have lessened party control of election campaigns. Potential candidates can secure party designation in primaries and need not depend on the party for advice on mapping a campaign, for running a campaign, or for funds to pay for a campaign. As Sorauf states, "The new campaign skills are freely available to whoever can afford them, and they can easily, therefore, serve individuals and organizations who would like to diminish the control of the party organizations over the contesting of American elections."[4] Moreover, the American electorate appears to be in a state of transition. Among young voters in particular, the incidence of "Independent" identification has increased over the past two decades.

At the same time, the economic and ethnic bases of party loyalty have also been shifting. Walter Dean Burnham's essay examines some of the shifts in party loyalties and argues that a major electoral realignment is necessary if the parties are to remain viable intermediary institutions. Burnham's analysis does not suggest that the parties will simply disappear, but it foresees only minimal organizational and symbolic functions for the parties of the future unless they confront some basic intellectual problems. And, of course, the electorate must confront the very same problems, particularly the question of whether strong, centralized, and vital parties are desirable. This really represents something which political debate about the parties generally ignores—whether or not the people in fact want majority rule.

Any real improvement in the conduct of party politics, therefore, must involve a redefinition of the relationship between the parties and the public, one which will enable the parties to address themselves to contemporary problems with some seriousness. In order for the electorate to respond to party appeals, however, the party should make a reasonably clear statement of what it intends to do, and its candidates should be committed to that statement. This represents a minor version of what is known as responsible party government.

For some twenty years, political scientists have been debating the possibility and desirability of responsible party government in the United States.[5] The arguments against party responsibility have usually focused on the inability of voters to understand politics in consistent, programmatic terms; the decentralization of the parties and their consequent inability to enforce discipline among officeholders; and the effect of institutional arrangements, such as the separation of powers, federalism, and the direct primary.

It is, however, taken for granted that an incumbent President speaks for his national party. Whether or not this has much impact among his fellow partisans in Congress will vary from issue to issue. But one can assume that presidential pronouncements are at least reasonably reliable indicators of party policy. For the opposition party, however, there is no acknowledged spokesman. The problems faced by the opposition party in providing effective and responsible alternatives are formidable, and they have been magnified by the President's access to the media and particularly by his ability to use television.

During the early part of the Nixon administration, the Democratic party working through its national committee and members of Congress launched an attack on the President's "monopolization" of the media, demanding equal time for opposition party rejoinders to presidential policy statements. This ultimately involved the networks, the FCC, and the Congress. The testimony by Joseph Califano, counsel to the Democratic National Committee and formerly an adviser to Lyndon Johnson, deals with some of the problems of public-service time for the political opposition. It should be noted that political opposition relates not only to the out party but also to the Congress vis-à-vis the President. Thus Califano's testimony touches the broader question of congressional responses to presidential pronouncements on foreign policy.

It is inevitable that any discussion of party reform must deal with the national conventions, given the nature of the 1968 experience, but this is part of a larger problem. The limited control which party organizations exert over nominations at all levels has debilitated the parties. A party which cannot control its nominations is not likely to be able to control its officeholders. For that reason alone, the direct primary makes party responsibility difficult. At the same time, limited access to party organizational positions may result in charges of "boss domination" which fueled the Progressive movement at the turn of the century and which were leveled at the Democratic convention in 1968.

The response to Chicago and, to a lesser extent, Miami was some discussion of nationwide presidential preference primaries. This proposal represents the kind of thinking which characterized the Progressive movement—the cure for democracy's ills is more democracy. It is unlikely that such primaries would help the parties any more than the direct primary has. Alexander Bickel's analysis of convention reform not only explores the importance of the conventions as deliberative institutions but also deals with substantive issues which confront the Democratic convention in 1972.

The subject of party reform has not received much attention in recent years, and this might simply indicate that the parties are no longer considered important institutions. It might also result, however, from growing uncertainty about the respective roles of the President and Congress. Party reform has usually been advocated by liberals seeking to enhance presidential leadership with respect to Congress, but the combined effects of the war in Southeast Asia and the Johnson and Nixon presidencies have forced a serious reexamination of whether such enhancement is at all desirable. In effect, a redefinition of the relationship between the parties and the public inevitably involves changes in relations between the parties, the President, and Congress. The selections presented here assume that the parties have an important role to play. If they are to do so, changes in the party electorates, party organizations, and the parties in government must take place. If not, it is difficult to see how governmental responsiveness can do anything but decline. According to Everett Ladd, "The responsiveness of party leadership in the 1970's in style, rhetoric, and policy commitments appropriate to the new agenda will in significant measure determine how easy or how painful the transition to the new society will be."[6]

THE END OF AMERICAN PARTY POLITICS

Walter Dean Burnham

American politics has clearly been falling apart in the past decade. We don't have to look hard for the evidence. Mr. Nixon is having as much difficulty controlling his fellow party members in Congress as any of his Democratic predecessors had in controlling theirs. John V. Lindsay, a year after he helped make Spiro Agnew a household word, had to run for mayor as a Liberal and an Independent with the aid of nationally prominent Democrats. Chicago in July of 1968 showed that for large numbers of its activists a major political party can become not just a disappointment, but positively repellent. Ticket-splitting has become widespread as never before, especially among the young; and George C. Wallace, whose third-party movement is the largest in recent American history, continues to demonstrate an unusually stable measure of support.

Vietnam and racial polarization have played large roles in this break-down, to be sure; but the ultimate causes are rooted much deeper in our history. For some time we have been saying that we live in a "pluralist democracy." And no text on American politics would be complete without a few key code words such as "consensus," "incrementalism," "bargaining" and "process." Behind it all is a rather benign view of our politics, one that assumes that the complex diversity of the American social structure is filtered through the two major parties and buttressed by a consensus of middle-class values which produces an electoral politics of low intensity and gradual change. The interplay of interest groups and public officials determines policy in detail. The voter has some leverage on policy, but only in a most diffuse way; and, anyway, he tends to be a pretty apolitical animal, dominated either by familial or local tradition, on one hand, or by the charisma of attractive candidates on the other. All of this is a good thing, of course, since in an affluent time the politics of consensus rules out violence and polarization. It pulls together and supports the existing order of things.

There is no doubt that this description fits "politics as usual," in the United States, but to assume that it fits the whole of American electoral politics is a radical oversimplification. Yet even after these past years of turmoil, new efforts have been made to appraise the peculiar rhythms of American politics in a more realistic way. This article is an attempt to do so by focusing upon two very important and little celebrated aspects of the dynamics of our politics: the phenomena of critical realignments of the electorate and of decomposition of the party in our electoral politics.

As a whole and across time, the reality of American politics appears quite different from a simple vision of pluralist democracy. It is shot through with escalating tensions, periodic electoral convulsions and repeated redefinitions of the rules and general outcomes of the political game. It has also been marked repeatedly by redefinitions—by no means always broadening ones—of those who are permitted to play. And one other very basic characteristic of American party politics that emerges from an historical overview is the profound incapacity of established political leadership to adapt itself to the political demands produced by the losers in America's stormy socioeconomic life. As is well known, American political parties are not instruments of collective purpose, but of electoral success. One major implication of this is that, as organizations, parties are interested in control of offices but not of government in any larger sense. It follows that once successful routines are established or reestablished for office-winning, very little motivation exists among party leaders to disturb the routines of the game. These routines are periodically upset, to be sure, but not by adaptive change within the party system. They are upset by overwhelming external force.

It has been recognized, at least since the publication of V. O. Key's "A Theory of Critical Elections" in 1955, that some elections in our history have been far more important than most in their long-range consequences for the political system. Such elections seem to "decide" clusters of substantive issues in a more clear-cut way than do most of the ordinary varieties. There is even a consensus among historians as to when these turning points in electoral politics took place. The first came in 1800 when Thomas Jefferson overthrew the Federalist hegemony established by Washington, Adams and Hamilton. The second came in 1828 and in the years afterward, with the election of Andrew Jackson and the democratization of the presidency. The third, of course, was the election of Abraham Lincoln in 1860, an election that culminated a catastrophic polarization of the society as a whole and resulted in civil war. The fourth critical election was that of William McKinley in 1896; this brought to a close the "Civil War" party system and inaugurated a political alignment congenial to the dominance of industrial capitalism over the American political economy. Created in the crucible of one massive depression, this "System of 1896" endured until the collapse of the economy in a second. The election of Franklin D. Roosevelt in 1932 came last in this series, and brought a major realignment of electoral politics and policy-making structures into the now familiar "welfare-pluralist" mode.

Now that the country appears to have entered another period of political upheaval, it seems particularly important not only to identify the phenomena of periodic critical realignments in our electoral politics, but to integrate them into a larger—if still very modest—theory of stasis and movement in American politics. For the realignments focus attention on the dark side of our politics, those moments of tremendous stress and abrupt transformation that remind us that "politics as usual" in the United States is not politics as always, and that American political institutions and leadership, once defined or redefined in a "normal phase" seem *themselves* to contribute to the building of conditions that threaten their overthrow.

To underscore the relevance of critical elections to our own day, one has only to recall that in the past, fundamental realignments in voting behavior have always been signalled by the rise of significant third parties: the Anti-Masons in the 1820s, the Free Soilers in the 1840s and 1850s, the Populists in the 1890s and the LaFollette Progressives in the 1920s. We cannot know whether George Wallace's American Independent Party of 1968 fits into this series, but it is certain—as we shall see below—that the very foundations of American electoral politics have become quite suddenly fluid in the past few years, and that the mass base of our politics has become volatile to a degree unknown in the experience of all but the very oldest living Americans. The Wallace uprising is a major sign of this recent fluidity; but it hardly stands alone.

Third-party protests, perhaps by contrast with major-party bolts, point up the interplay in American politics between the inertia of "normal" established political routines and the pressures arising from the rapidity, unevenness and uncontrolled character of change in the country's dynamic socioeconomic system. All of the third parties prior to and including the 1968 Wallace movement constituted attacks by outsiders, who felt they were outsiders, against an elite frequently viewed in conspiratorial terms. The attacks were made under the banner of high moralistic universals against an established political structure seen as corrupt, undemocratic and manipulated by insiders for their own benefit and that of their sup- porters. All these parties were perceived by their activists as "movements" that would not only purify the corruption of the current political regime, but replace some of its most important parts. Moreover, they all tele- graphed the basic clusters of issues that would dominate politics in the next electoral era: the completion of political democratization in the 1830s, slavery and sectionalism in the late 1840s and 1850s, the struggle between the industrialized and the colonial regions in the 1890s, and wel- fare liberalism vs. laissez-faire in the 1920s and 1930s. One may well view the American Independent Party in such a context.

The periodic recurrence of third-party forerunners of realignment— and realignments themselves, for that matter—are significantly related to dominant peculiarities of polity and society in the United States. They point to an electorate especially vulnerable to breaking apart, and to a political system in which the sense of common nationhood may be much more nearly skin-deep than is usually appreciated. If there is any evolu- tionary scale of political modernization at all, the persistence of deep fault lines in our electoral politics suggests pretty strongly that the United States remains a "new nation" to this day in some important political respects. The periodic recurrence of these tensions may also imply that—as dynami- cally developed as our economic system is—no convincing evidence of *political* development in the United States can be found after the 1860s.

Nationwide critical realignments can only take place around clusters of issues of the most fundamental importance. The most profound of these issues have been cast up in the course of the transition of our Lockeian-liberal commonwealth from an agrarian to an industrial state. The last two major realignments—those of 1893-1896 and 1928-1936—involved the two great transitional crises of American industrial capitalism, the economic collapses of 1893 and 1929. The second of these modern realignments produced, of course, the broad coalition on which the New Deal's welfarist-pluralist policy was ultimately based. But the first is of immediate concern to us here. For the 1896 adaptation of electoral politics to the imperatives of industrial-capitalism involved a set of developments that stand in the sharpest possible contrast to those occurring elsewhere in the Western world at about the same time. Moreover, they set in motion new patterns of behavior in electoral politics that were never entirely overcome even during the New Deal period, and which, as we shall see, have resumed their forward march during the past decade.

As a case in point, let me briefly sketch the political evolution of Pennsylvania—one of the most industrially developed areas on earth—during the 1890-1932 period. There was in this state a preexisting, indeed, preindustrial, pattern of two-party competition, one that had been forged in the Jacksonian era and decisively amended, though not abolished, during the Civil War. Then came the realignment of the 1890s, which, like those of earlier times, was an abrupt process. In the five annual elections from 1888 through November 1892, the Democrats' mean percentage of the total two-party vote was 46.7 percent, while for the five elections beginning in February 1894 it dropped to a mean of 37.8 percent. Moreover, the greatest and most permanent Republican gains during this depression decade occurred where they counted most, numerically: in the metropolitan areas of Philadelphia and Pittsburgh.

The cumulative effect of this realignment and its aftermath was to convert Pennsylvania into a thoroughly one-party state, in which conflict over the basic political issues were duly transferred to the Republican primary after it was established in 1908. By the 1920s this peculiar process had been completed and the Democratic party had become so weakened that, as often as not, the party's nominees for major office were selected by the Republican leadership. But whether so selected or not, their general-election prospects were dismal: of the 80 statewide contests held from 1894 through 1931, a candidate running with Democratic party endorsement won just one. Moreover, with the highly ephemeral exception of Theodore Roosevelt's bolt from the Republican party in 1912, no third parties emerged as general-election substitutes for the ruined Democrats.

The political simplicity which had thus emerged in this industrial heartland of the Northeast by the 1920s was the more extraordinary in that it occurred in an area whose socioeconomic division of labor was as complex and its level of development as high as any in the world. In most other regions of advanced industrialization the emergence of corporate capitalism was associated with the development of mass political parties with high structural cohesion and explicit collective purposes with respect to the control of policy and government. These parties expressed deep conflicts over the direction of public policy, but they also brought about the democratic revolution of Europe, for electoral participation tended to rise along with them. Precisely the opposite occurred in Pennsylvania and, with marginal and short-lived exceptions, the nation. It is no exaggeration to say that the political response to the collectivizing thrust of industrialism in this American state was the elimination of organized partisan combat, an extremely severe decline in electoral participation, the emergence of a Republican "coalition of the whole" and—by no means coincidentally—a highly efficient insulation of the controlling industrial-financial elite from effective or sustained countervailing pressures.

IRRELEVANT RADICALISM

The reasons for the increasing solidity of this "System of 1896" in Pennsylvania are no doubt complex. Clearly, for example, the introduction of the direct primary as an alternative to the general election, which was thereby emptied of any but ritualistic significance, helped to undermine the minority Democrats more and more decisively by destroying their monopoly of opposition. But nationally as well the Democratic party in and after the 1890s was virtually invisible to Pennsylvania voters as a usable opposition. For with the ascendancy of the agrarian Populist William Jennings Bryan, the Democratic party was transformed into a vehicle for colonial, periphery-oriented dissent against the industrial-metropolitan center, leaving the Republicans as sole spokesmen for the latter.

This is a paradox that pervades American political history, but it was sharpest in the years around the turn of this century. The United States was so vast that it had little need of economic colonies abroad; in fact it had two major colonial regions within its own borders, the postbellum South and the West. The only kinds of attacks that could be made effective on a *nationwide* basis against the emergent industrial hegemony—the only attacks that, given the ethnic heterogeneity and extremely rudimentary political socialization of much of the country's industrial working class, could come within striking distance of achieving a popular majority—came out of these colonial areas. Thus "radical" protest in major-party terms came to be associated with the neo-Jacksonian demands of agrarian small-holders and small-town society already confronted by obsolescence. The Democratic party from 1896 to 1932, and in many respects much later, was the national vehicle for these struggles.

The net effect of this was to produce a condition in which—especially, but not entirely on the presidential level—the more economically advanced a state was, the more heavy were its normal Republican majorities likely to be. The nostalgic agrarian-industrialist appeals of the national Democratic leadership tended to present the voters of this industrial state with a choice that was not a choice: between an essentially backward-looking provincial party articulating interests in opposition to those of the industrial North and East as a whole, and a "modernizing" party whose doctrines included enthusiastic acceptance of and co-operation with the dominant economic interests of region and nation. Not only did this partitioning of the political universe entail normal and often huge Republican majorities in an economically advanced state like Pennsylvania; the survival of national two-party competition on such a basis helped to ensure that no local reorganization of electoral politics along class lines could effectively occur even within such a state. Such a voting universe had a tendency toward both enormous inbuilt stability and increasing entrenchment in the decades after its creation. Probably no force less overwhelming than the post-1929 collapse of the national economic system would have sufficed to dislodge it. Without such a shock, who can say how, or indeed whether, the "System of 1896" would have come to an end in Pennsylvania and the nation? To ask such a question is to raise yet another. For there is no doubt that in Pennsylvania, as elsewhere, the combination of trauma in 1929-1933 and Roosevelt's creative leadership provided the means of overthrowing the old order and for reversing dramatically the depoliticization of electoral politics which had come close to perfection under it. Yet might it not be the case that the dominant pattern of political adaptation to industrialism in the United States has worked to eliminate, by one means or another, the links provided by political parties between voters and rulers? In other words, was the post-1929 reversal permanent or only a transitory phase in our political evolution? And if transitory, what bearing would this fact have on the possible recurrence of critical realignments in the future?

WITHERING AWAY OF THE PARTIES

The question requires us to turn our attention to the second major dynamic of American electoral politics during this century: the phenomenon of electoral disaggregation, of the breakdown of party loyalty, which in many respects must be seen as the permanent legacy of the fourth-party system of 1896-1932. One of the most conspicuous developments of this era, most notably during the 1900-1920 period, was a whole network of changes in the rules of the political game. This is not the place for a thorough treatment and documentation of these peculiarities. One can only mention here some major changes in the rules of the game, and note that one would have no difficulty in arguing that their primary latent function was to ease the transition from a preindustrial universe of competitive, highly organized mass politics to a depoliticized world marked by drastic shrinkage in participation or political leverage by the lower orders of the population. The major changes surely include the following:

The introduction of the Australian ballot, which was designed to purify elections but also eliminated a significant function of the older political machines, the printing and distribution of ballots, and eased a transition from party voting to candidate voting.

The introduction of the direct primary, which at once stripped the minority party of its monopoly of opposition and weakened the control of party leaders over nominating processes, and again hastened preoccupation of the electorate with candidates rather than parties.

The movement toward nonpartisan local elections, often accompanied by a drive to eliminate local bases of representation such as wards in favor of at-large elections, which produced—as Samuel Hays points out—a shift of political power from the grass roots to citywide cosmopolitan elites.

The expulsion of almost all blacks, and a very large part of the poor-white population as well, from the southern electorate by a series of legal and extralegal measures such as the poll tax.

The introduction of personal registration requirements the burden of which, in faithful compliance with dominant middle-class values, was placed on the individual rather than on public authority, but which effectively disenfranchised large numbers of the poor.

BREAKDOWN OF PARTY LOYALTY

Associated with these and other changes in the rules of the game was a profound transformation in voting behavior. There was an impressive growth in the numbers of political independents and ticket-splitters, a growth accompanied by a sea-change among party elites from what Richard Jensen has termed the "militarist" (or ward boss) campaign style to the "mercantilist" (or advertising-packaging) style. Aside from noting that the transition was largely completed as early as 1916, and hence that the practice of "the selling of the president" goes back far earlier than we usually think, these changes too must be left for fuller exposition elsewhere.

Critical realignments, as we have argued, are an indispensable part of a stability-disruption dialectic which has the deepest roots in American political history. Realigning sequences are associated with all sorts of aberrations from the normal workings of American party politics, both in the events leading up to nominations, the nature and style of election campaigning and the final outcome at the polls. This is not surprising, since they arise out of the collision of profound transitional crisis in the socioeconomic system with the immobility of a nondeveloped political system.

At the same time, it seems clear that for realignment to fulfill some of its most essential tension-management functions, for it to be a forum by which the electorate can participate in durable "constitution making," it is essential that political parties not fall below a certain level of coherence and appeal in the electorate. It is obvious that the greater the electoral disaggregation the less effective will be "normal" party politics as an instrument of countervailing influence in an industrial order. Thus, a number of indices of disaggregation significantly declined during the 1930s as the Democratic party remobilized parts of American society under the stimulus of the New Deal. In view of the fact that political parties during the 1930s and 1940s were once again called upon to assist in a redrawing of the map of American politics and policy-making, this regeneration of partisan voting in the 1932-1952 era is hardly surprising. More than that, regeneration was necessary if even the limited collective purposes of the new majority coalition were to be realized.

Even so, the New Deal realignment was far more diffuse, protracted and incomplete than any of its predecessors, a fact of which the more advanced New Dealers were only too keenly aware. It is hard to avoid the impression that one contributing element in this peculiarity of our last realignment was the much higher level of electoral disaggregation in the 1930s and 1940s than had existed at any time prior to the realignment of the 1890s. If one assumes that the end result of a long-term trend toward electoral disaggregation is the complete elimination of political parties as foci that shape voting behavior, then the possibility of critical realignment would, by definition, be eliminated as well. Every election would be dominated by TV packaging, candidate charisma, real or manufactured, and short-term, ad hoc influences. Every election, therefore, would have become deviating or realigning by definition, and American national politics would come to resemble the formless gubernatorial primaries that V. O. Key described in his classic *Southern Politics*.

The New Deal clearly arrested and reversed, to a degree, the march toward electoral disaggregation. But it did so only for the period in which the issues generated by economic scarcity remained central, and the generation traumatized by the collapse of 1929 remained numerically preponderant in the electorate. Since 1952, electoral disaggregation has resumed, in many measurable dimensions, and with redoubled force. The data on this point are overwhelming. Let us examine a few of them.

A primary aspect of electoral disaggregation, of course, is the "pulling apart" over time of the percentages for the same party but at different levels of election: this is the phenomenon of split-ticket voting. Recombining and reorganizing the data found in two tables of Milton Cummings' excellent study *Congressmen and the Electorate*, and extending the series back and forward in time, we may examine the relationship between presidential and congressional elections during this century.

Such an array captures both the intial upward thrust of disaggregation in the second decade of this century, the peaking in the middle to late 1920s, the recession beginning in 1932, and especially the post-1952 resumption of the upward trend.

Other evidence points precisely in the same direction. It has generally been accepted in survey-research work that generalized partisan identification shows far more stability over time than does actual voting behavior, since the latter is subject to short-term factors associated with each election. What is not so widely understood is that this glacial measure of party identification has suddenly become quite volatile during the 1960s, and particularly during the last half of the decade. In the first place, as both Gallup and Survey Research Center data confirm, the proportion of independents underwent a sudden shift upwards around 1966: while from 1940 to 1965 independents constituted about 20 percent to 22 percent of the electorate, they increased to 29 percent in 1966. At the present time, they outnumber Republicans by 30 percent to 28 percent.

Second, there is a clear unbroken progression in the share that independents have of the total vote along age lines. The younger the age group, the larger the number of independents in it, so that among the 21-29 year olds, according to the most recent Gallup findings [in 1969], 42 percent are independents—an increase of about 10 percent over the first half of the decade, and representing greater numbers of people than identify with either major party. When one reviews the June 1969 Gallup survey of college students, the share is larger still—44 percent. Associated with this quantitative increase in independents seems to be a major qualitative change as well. Examining the data for the 1950s, the authors of *The American Voter* could well argue that independents tended to have lower political awareness and political involvement in general than did identifiers (particularly strong identifiers) of either major party. But the current concentration of independents in the population suggests that this may no longer be the case. They are clearly and disproportionately found not only among the young, and especially among the college young, but also among men, those adults with a college background, people in the professional-managerial strata and, of course, among those with higher incomes. Such groups tend to include those people whose sense of political involvement and efficacy is far higher than that of the population as a whole. Even in the case of the two most conspicuous exceptions to this—the pile-up of independent identifiers in the youngest age group and in the South—it can be persuasively argued that this distribution does not reflect low political awareness and involvement but the reverse: a sudden, in some instances almost violent, increase in both awareness and involvement among southerners and young adults, with the former being associated both with the heavy increase in southern turnout in 1968 and the large Wallace vote polled there.

Third, one can turn to two sets of evidence found in the Survey Research Center's selection studies. If the proportion of *strong* party identifiers over time is examined, the same pattern of long-term inertial stability and recent abrupt change can be seen. From 1952 through 1964, the proportion of strong Democratic and Republican party identifiers fluctuated in a narrow range between 36 percent and 40 percent, with a steep downward trend in strong Republican identifiers between 1960 and 1964 being matched by a moderate increase in strong Democratic identifiers. Then in 1966 the proportion of strong identifiers abruptly declines to 28 percent, with the defectors overwhelmingly concentrated among former Democrats. This is almost certainly connected, as in the increase of independent identifiers, with the Vietnam fiasco. While we do not as yet have the 1968 SRC data, the distribution of identifications reported by Gallup suggests the strong probability that this abrupt decline in party loyalty has not been reversed very much since. It is enough here to observe that while the ratio between strong identifiers and independents prior to 1966 was pretty stably fixed at between 1.6 to 1 and 2 to 1 in favor of the former, it is now evidently less than 1 to 1. Both Chicago and Wallace last year were the acting out of these changes in the arena of "popular theater."

Finally, both survey and election data reveal a decline in two other major indices of the relevance of party to voting behavior: split-ticket voting and the choice of the same party's candidates for President across time.

It is evident that the 1960s have been an era of increasingly rapid liquidation of preexisting party commitments by individual voters. There is no evidence anywhere to support Kevin Phillips' hypothesis regarding an emergent Republican majority—assuming that such a majority would involve increases in voter identification with the party. More than that, one might well ask whether, if this process of liquidation is indeed a preliminary to realignment, the latter may not take the form of a third-party movement of truly massive and durable proportions.

The evidence lends some credence to the view that American electoral politics is undergoing a long-term transition into routines designed only to fill offices and symbolically affirm "the American way." There also seem to be tendencies for our political parties gradually to evaporate as broad and active intermediaries between the people and their rulers, even as they may well continue to maintain enough organizational strength to screen out the unacceptable or the radical at the nominating stage. It is certain that the significance of party as link between government and the governed has now come once again into serious question. Bathed in the warm glow of diffused affluence, vexed in spirit but enriched economically by our imperial military and space commitments, confronted by the gradually unfolding consequences of social change as vast as it is unplanned, what need have Americans of political parties? More precisely, why do they need parties whose structures, processes and leadership cadres seem to grow more remote and irrelevant to each new crisis?

FUTURE POLITICS

It seems evident enough that if this long-term trend toward a politics without parties continues, the policy consequences must be profound. One can put the matter with the utmost simplicity: political parties, with all their well-known human and structural shortcomings, are the only devices thus far invented by the wit of Western man that can, with some effectiveness, generate countervailing collective power on behalf of the many individually powerless against the relatively few who are individually or organizationally powerful. Their disappearance as active intermediaries, if not as preliminary screening devices, would only entail the unchallenged ascendancy of the already powerful, unless new structures of collective power were somehow developed to replace them, and unless conditions in America's social structure and political culture came to be such that they could be effectively used. Yet *neither* of these contingencies, despite recent publicity for the term "participatory democracy," is likely to occur under immediately conceivable circumstances in the United States. It is much more probable that the next chapter of our political history will resemble the metapolitical world of the 1920s.

But, it may be asked, may not a future realignment serve to recrystallize and revitalize political parties in the American system?

The present condition of America contains a number of what Marxists call "internal contradictions," some of which might provide the leverage for a future critical realignment if sufficiently sharp dislocations in everyday life should occur. One of the most important of these, surely, is the conversion—largely through technological change—of the American social stratification system from the older capitalist mixture of upper or "owning" classes, dependent white-collar middle classes and proletarians into a mixture described recently by David Apter: the technologically competent, the technologically obsolescent and the technologically superfluous. It is arguable, in fact, that the history of the Kennedy-Johnson Administrations on the domestic front could be written in terms of a coalition of the top and bottom of this Apter-ite mix against the middle, and the 1968 election as the first stage of a "counter-revolution" of these middle strata against the pressures from both of the other two. Yet the inchoate results of 1968 raise some doubts, to say the least, that it can yet be described as part of a realigning sequence: there was great volatility in this election, but also a remarkable and unexpectedly large element of continuity and voter stability.

It is not hard to find evidence of cumulative social disaster in our metropolitan areas. We went to war with Japan in 1941 over a destruction inflicted on us far less devastating in scope and intensity than that endured by any large American city today. But the destruction came suddenly, as a sharp blow, from a foreign power; while the urban destruction of today has matured as a result of our own internal social and political processes, and it has been unfolding gradually for decades. We have consequently learned somehow to adapt to it piecemeal, as best we can, without changing our lives or our values very greatly. Critical realignments, however, also seem to require sharp, sudden blows as a precondition for their emergence. If we think of realignment as arising from the spreading internal disarray in this country, we should also probably attempt to imagine what kinds of events could produce a sudden, sharp and general escalation in social tensions and threatened deprivations of property, status or values.

Conceivably, ghetto and student upheavals could prove enough in an age of mass communications to create a true critical realignment, but one may doubt it. Student and ghetto rebellions appear to be too narrowly defined socially to have a *direct* impact on the daily lives of the "vast middle," and thus produce transformations in voting behavior that would be both sweeping and permanent. For what happens in times of critical realignment is nothing less than an intense, if temporary, quasi revolutionizing of the vast middle class, a class normally content to be traditionalists or passive-participants in electoral politics.

Yet, even if students and ghetto blacks could do the trick, if they could even begin, with the aid of elements of the technological elite, a process of electoral realignment leftward, what would be the likely consequence? What would the quasi revolutionizing of an insecure, largely urban middle class caught in a brutal squeeze from the top and the bottom of the social system look like? There are already premonitory evidences: the Wallace vote in both southern and nonsouthern areas, as well as an unexpected durability in his *postelection* appeal; the mayoral elections in Los Angeles and Minneapolis this year, and not least, Lindsay's narrow squeak into a second term as mayor of New York City. To the extent that the "great middle" becomes politically mobilized and self-conscious, it moves toward what has been called "urban populism," a stance of organized hostility to blacks, student radicals and cosmopolitan liberal elites. The "great middle" remains, after all, the chief defender of the old-time Lockeian faith; both its material and cultural interests are bound up in this defense. If it should become at all mobilized as a major and cohesive political force in today's conditions, it would do so in the name of a restoration of the ancient truths by force if necessary. A realignment that directly involved this kind of mobilization—as it surely would, should it occur—would very likely have sinister overtones unprecedented in our political history.

Are we left, then, with a choice between the stagnation implicit in the disaggregative trends we have outlined here and convulsive disruption? Is there something basic to the American political system, and extending to its electoral politics, which rules out a middle ground between drift and mastery?

The fact that these questions were raised by Walter Lippmann more than half a century ago—and have indeed been raised in one form or other in every era of major transitional crisis over the past century—is alone enough to suggest an affirmative answer. The phenomena we have described here provide evidence of a partly quantitative sort which seems to point in the same direction. For electoral disaggregation is the negation of party. Further, it is—or rather, reflects—the negation of structural and behavioral conditions in politics under which linkages between the bottom, the middle and the top can exist and produce the effective carrying out of collective power. Critical realignments are evidence not of the presence of such linkages or conditions in the normal state of American electoral politics, but precisely of their absence. Correspondingly, they are not manifestations of democratic accountability, but infrequent and hazardous substitutes for it.

Taken together, both of these phenomena generate support for the inference that American politics in its normal state is the negation of the public order itself, as that term is understood in politically developed nations. We do not have government in our domestic affairs so much as "nonrule." We do not have political parties in the contemporary sense of that term as understood elsewhere in the Western world; we have anti-parties instead. Power centrifuges rather than power concentrators, they have been immensely important not as vehicles of social transformation but for its prevention through political means.

The entire setting of the critical realignment phenomenon bears witness to a deep-seated dialectic within the American political system. From the beginning, the American socioeconomic system has developed and transformed itself with an energy and thrust that has no parallel in modern history. The political system, from parties to policy structures, has seen no such development. Indeed, it has shown astonishingly little substantive transformation over time in its methods of operation. In essence, the political system of this "fragment society" remains based today on the same Lockeian formulation that, as Louis Hartz points out, has dominated its entire history. It is predicated upon the maintenance of a high wall of separation between politics and government on one side and the socioeconomic system on the other. It depends for its effective working on the failure of anything approximating internal sovereignty in the European sense to emerge here.

The Lockeian cultural monolith, however, is based upon a social assumption that has come repeatedly into collision with reality. The assumption, of course, is not only that the autonomy of socioeconomic life from political direction is the prescribed fundamental law for the United States, but that this autonomous development will proceed with enough smoothness, uniformity and generally distributed benefits that it will be entirely compatible with the usual functioning of our antique political structures. Yet the high (though far from impermeable) wall of separation between politics and society is periodically threatened with inundations. As the socioeconomic system develops in the context of unchanging institutions of electoral politics and policy formation, dysfunctions become more and more visible. Whole classes, regions or other major sectors of the population are injured or faced with an imminent threat of injury. Finally the triggering event occurs, critical realignments follow, the universe of policy and of electoral coalitions is broadly redefined, and the tensions generated by the crisis receive some resolution. Thus it can be argued that critical realignment as a periodically recurring phenomenon is as centrally related to the workings of such a system as is the archaic and increasingly rudimentary structure of the major parties themselves.

PARTY VS. SURVIVAL

One is finally left with the sense that the twentieth-century decomposition of partisan links in our electoral system also corresponds closely with the contemporary survival needs of what Samuel P. Huntington has called the American "Tudor polity." Electoral disaggregation and the concentration of certain forms of power in the hands of economic, technological and administrative elites are functional for the short-term survival of nonrule in the United States. They may even somehow be related to the gradual emergence of internal sovereignty in this country—though to be sure under not very promising auspices for participatory democracy of any kind. Were such a development to occur, it would not necessarily entail the disappearance or complete suppression of subgroup tensions or violence in American social life, or of group bargaining and pluralism in the policy process. It might even be associated with increases in both. But it would, after all, reflect the ultimate sociopolitical consequences of the persistence of Lockeian individualism into an era of Big Organization: oligarchy at the top, inertia and spasms of self-defense in the middle, and fragmentation at the base. One may well doubt whether political parties or critical realignments need have much place in such a political universe.

TELEVISION AND THE LOYAL OPPOSITION

Joseph Califano

MR. CALIFANO. . . .
It is a privilege for me, as general counsel to the Democratic National Committee, to be invited to testify during the course of this committee's

study of the fairness doctrine and the problem of securing access to the broadcast media for the expression of differing points of view on controversial isues of public importance.

This Nation must face up to the dominant political fact of our generation: The name of the deadly serious game of national and statewide politics in the 1970's is television. If anyone doubts that axiom, he had better recognize the implications of a few recent events:

With one 30-minute broadcast of a speech, television turned Spiro Agnew into the best known Vice President in our history.

Through a television blitz, a relatively unknown businessman soundly defeated a national hero in the Democratic senatorial primary in Ohio.

Broad-based concern about the Vietnam war is due in no small measure to the fact that it is fought in every American living room every night.

Lenore Romney based her Senate primary campaign largely on a color television movie which The Wall Street Journal characterized as "a living color snow job, a masterpiece of that rapidly developing branch of the cinema, aimed at creating desirable images for politicians."[1]

So essential is television to national and statewide political campaigns that it is more important for a candidate to have a television adviser, a first-rate FCC lawyer and television monitors than to have loyal precinct captains and doorbell ringers. In my judgment, there is no more important pending hearing in the Senate; for the problem of television in politics goes to the very core of our democracy.

The problem with which this committee is concerned is as complex as any presented by the advent of electronics in our society. The Democratic National Committee's formal interest is directed at Presidential and national party politics. But our concern as citizens involves the broad social, political, legal and economic ramifications of television that profoundly affect our society today, with enormous power to alter the society of our children tomorrow. The problem is not a partisan one. Nor is it even limited to the right of the Congress, as a coequal branch of the Government, to have access to television time dominated by the President who happens to be in office.

In any examination of the fairness doctrine, the current state of television and the fragile state of our political system, we must recognize the problem of television access for a wide variety of groups and individuals, not necessarily affiliated with any party and yet representative of large segments of our population: the blacks and chicanos, the students, the peace demonstrators, the Wallaceites and the hard hats.

These significant minorities, who feel increasingly powerless in the wake of post-industrial society, have turned more and more often to the streets to demonstrate visually their support for or opposition to one policy or another, at a time when access to television is otherwise denied them, and such access is critical if they are to develop nationwide constituencies of significant political force and effect. In short, it is the problem of the communication of ideas, the exchange of viewpoints—infinitely magnified by the pervasive presence of television. The Thomas Paine of the 1970's must do his pamphleteering on television.

THE FCC PETITIONS OF THE DEMOCRATIC NATIONAL COMMITTEE

The central concern of the Democratic National Committee has been the viability of the two party system in the age of television. We believe that the survival of the two-party system depends upon access to television on some equitable basis for the party out of power. For months, the Democratic National Committee has written polite letters to the networks in an attempt to gain access to television for a presentation of the views of the Democratic Party. Sometimes the requests were made by the National Committee, sometimes by elected Members of Congress. Without exception, the requests were turned down. Accordingly, we determined that the time had come to file legal petitions before the FCC.

These petitions dealt with the right of response to Presidential statements on controversial issues of public importance and the right of the Democratic Party to purchase time:

With respect to the free time issue, we requested a ruling that when a network or licensee broadcasts a presentation by the President of the United States of a viewpoint on a controversial issue of public importance, that network or licensee has an affirmative obligation to seek out responsible persons or entities with significant contrasting viewpoints on the controversial issue and afford them equal opportunities to present their views.

In the pay time area, we requested a declaratory ruling that under the first amendment and the Communication Act, a broadcaster may not, as a general policy, refuse to sell time to responsible entities, such as the Democratic National Committee, for the solicitation of funds and for comment on public issues.

THE FREE TIME PETITION

We recognize, of course, the unique status of the Presidential office in our system of Government. I would be the last person to advocate anything that might impair the integrity or effective leadership essential for the conduct of that office. I would oppose vigorously any measure which would restrict the President's ability to communicate with our citizens and thereby help him lead and govern the Nation.

On the other hand, we must recognize that the combination of the President of the United States—the most powerful individual in the free world—and television—undoubtedly the most effective communication medium ever devised by man—has an impact on public opinion that is difficult to exaggerate. Moreover, the most cursory analysis demonstrates that every televised Presidential address or press conference presents the President's self-interested viewpoint on controversial issues of public importance. A televised statement by the President of the United States simply by the force of the office and the impact of the medium, draws instant and massive attention, respect and belief. As one distinguished commentator has said:

> . . . *Television has put the President himself in control of what image he will project to the country and enabled him to project it farther and more favorably than was ever possible before, with less competition from Capitol Hill and less interference from the press.*[2]

This fact, like the problem it presents for our democracy, is not partisan. It applies to Democratic and Republican Presidents alike. Each President since Harry Truman has extended and innovated in the use of television. There is every reason to believe that the imaginative use of prime time television will increase with each succeeding President. We must recognize that there will be further Presidents, shrewder and more experienced in the exploitation of television, who will use it as an increasingly effective political tool in an attempt to mold the minds of our citizens in favor of their particular policies.

What this committee or this Congress does in 1970 must be looked at not in terms of the present alone; but in terms of the importance of preserving, indeed, enhancing, the democratic nature of our society; in terms of making the electronic medium work for democracy, instead of against it; in terms of recognizing that the most powerful social and political force abroad in our land today is not the hostility and disillusionment of youth, not the raging divisiveness of race or the Vietnam War, but rather television and the unparalleled amount of power it places at the fingertips of any President who picks up the telephone and tells the three networks he wants to go on television in prime time tonight, or any other night.

THE TELEVISION PRESIDENCY OF RICHARD NIXON

In his [first] 18 months in office, President Nixon . . . made 37 live nation-wide television appearances, more of them—14—in prime time than in any previous 18-month period in our history. In [one 3-month period] alone, the President . . . made five prime-time televised presentations devoted primarily to justifying his controversial policies and actions in Vietnam and Cambodia.

Like his predecessors, Mr. Nixon has had, upon request, an instant, captive prime-time audience. He has complete control over the timing, format and content of his presentation. He has unlimited freedom to augment his presentation with any devices he chooses, such as maps and, most recently, selected films. Above all, the President has been free to say anything he likes on any subject, secure in the knowledge that no spokesman would be afforded anything remotely approaching a comparable opportunity to correct misstatements of fact or to present a contrasting point of view.

President Nixon has made considerable use of this freedom. He has made partisan attacks on Congress, previous Democratic administrations and individuals. Yet, the networks almost invariably refuse to permit effective replies.

For example, the President requested and received prime time from the networks to explain his veto of the $20 billion appropriations bill for the Departments of Labor and Health, Education, and Welfare. Although attacked as irresponsible and inflationary, Members of Congress were not permitted air time to explain their decision to support the measure.

I might mention [that Congressman] Albert . . . requested that time on behalf of the democratic leadership in the House and was turned down by all three networks. Sometimes the attacks are undisguised, as where the President has said, and I am quoting from various press conferences:

> *This Congress has the worst record in terms of appropriations bills of any Congress in history. (News conference December 8, 1969: Weekly compilation page 1725, column 1).*
>
> *The previous administration tried, through jawboning . . . to put the blame on business for price increases, the blame on labor for wage increases. It (jawboning) is hypocritical . . . dishonest (and) most important . . . ineffective. (News conference September 26, 1969, Weekly compilation page 1330, column 2).*
>
> *We found that in the year, the full year, in which he (Clark Clifford) was Secrtary of Defense, our casualties were the highest of the whole five-year period and, as far as negotiations were concerned, all that had been accomplished, as I indicated earlier, was that we had agreed on the shape of the table . . . (News conference June 19, 1969; Weekly compilation page 879, column 2).*
>
> *I will follow the practice as President of the United States and as leader of the Republican Party of endorsing all Republican nominees. Therefore, I will endorse Senator Marchi and the other Republican nominees on the city ticket in New York. (News conference June 19, 1969; Weekly compilation page 879, column 1).*

More often his attacks were subtle, but the meaning is clear and unmistakable to the American people. Thus, when the President blames problems such as inflation and crime on the "last five years" or "the Federal Government in the 1960's," or "this Congress" no one can doubt his partisan meaning. For example, the president has said:

> *A review of the stark fiscal facts for the 1960's clearly demonstrates where the primary blame for rising prices must be placed. In the decade of the sixties the Federal Government spent $57*

> *billion more than it took in in taxes . . . Now millions of Americans*
> *are forced to go into debt today because the Federal Government*
> *decided to go into debt yesterday. (State of the Union Message*
> *January 22, 1970; Weekly compilation, page 61).*
>
> *Seventeen months ago . . . there were actually four roads open*
> *to us. One was the road of runaway inflation—to do nothing about*
> *Government spending and rising prices, to let the boom go on*
> *booming—until the bubble burst. That was the road the Nation*
> *was taken on in the sixties, and the people who suffered most along*
> *that road are the millions of Americans living on fixed incomes.*
> *(Address on Economics June 17, 1970; Weekly compilation,*
> *page 775).*
>
> *When this administration came in, all that had been decided*
> *(at the Paris Peace Talks) was the shape of the table. Now we are*
> *down to substance. (News conference June 19, 1969; Weekly*
> *compilation, page 879).*
>
> *When you get to the domestic issues, the crime package . . ., the*
> *inflation package, and the tax bill and the rest . . . I am going to fight*
> *just as hard as I can here, because this Nation wants this Congress*
> *to get to work and give us the tools to deal with narcotics, and deal*
> *with crime, to deal with all of these problems. We cannot do it until*
> *we get this legislation passed. (Congressional Breakfast November*
> *5, 1969; Weekly compilation, page 1560).*

Obviously, there are other significantly contrasting viewpoints on these matters—and these I might say are only a few selected examples. Yet they are never permitted to be aired in a comparable forum. Some take the position that balanced coverage is provided by affording an opposing Senator or Congressman one or two sentences on the next day's news program—where the President's words are repeated—or providing a panel program with both advocates and opponents of the President's views. As we stated in our brief to the FCC:

> *To equate a President's unfettered presentation during prime*
> *time to a brief off-the-cuff reply carried during a newscast or a*
> *tightly controlled debate is like equating Neil Armstrong's first*
> *moon step from the Apollo XI spaceship to a Shirley Temple*
> *two-step on the Good Ship Lollipop.*

Some argue that news commentators can satisfy the fairness doctrine by presenting contrasting points of view within their own news summaries. But, as the Supreme Court recently observed, quoting John Stuart Mill:

> *"[It is not] enough that [one] should hear the arguments of*
> *adversaries from his own teachers, presented as they state them, and*
> *accompanied by what they offer as refutations. That is not the way*
> *to do justice to the arguments, or bring them into real contact with*
> *his own mind. He must be able to hear them from persons who*
> *actually believe them; who defend them in earnest, and do their very*
> *utmost for them."*[3]

The rule which the DNC has proposed to the FCC would establish procedures which would tend to assure that the American electorate receives not only the President's views on controversial issues of public importance, but also the significant contrasting views of appropriate, responsible spokesmen.

We believe that the rule we have proposed will help balance the one-sided view of the policies of the administration in power that we have seen [since it took office]. Under our proposal, the respondent would have the same freedom of format as the President. Thus, where the President requests and is granted time by the networks to do whatever he wishes, the same courtesy would be accorded the respondents. Where a Presidential news conference is televised, the same format would be available to the respondents. The respondents would have the same time period and the same type of time—for example, prime time where the President uses prime time.

Two difficulties are raised by opponents of this proposal: One relates to the designation of the appropriate spokesman for response; the other hypothesizes an endless chain of responses to responses.

SENATOR PASTORE. What if the President of the United States took time on television and explained his policies with reference to the Middle East? Do you think that others who disagree with that policy have a right to be heard? If he enunciates the policy?

MR. CALIFANO. Where we are talking about significant differences of opinion, Mr. Chairman, yes. In the Nixon administration, as you know better than I, there was great concern among many Senators and Congressmen on both sides of the aisle about whether or not the Nixon administration was going to support peace and the Israeli Government in the way they thought appropriate. And I would think that if the announced policy for example were we were going to abandon Israel or something else, the people who felt the opposite way should have an opportunity to express their views. It is the idea, as you indicated, it is the controversial issues which should be fully aired.

SENATOR PASTORE. Let's go back to October 1962, the Cuban crisis, when President Kennedy went on television and explained the policy of the country with reference to Cuba. Do you think that the people who disagreed with him should have been given equal time?

MR. CALIFANO. There are obvious——

SENATOR PASTORE. I am making a distinction there between a political barrage and one that is within the confines of the Presidency of the United States. I hope we don't go so far here as to create a sort of a scramble that would actually defeat the public purpose rather than assist it. I mean we have got to bring this thing within certain guidelines to have it make sense. For instance, if, as you pointed out here, and I go along with you, if the President of the United States says something derogatory about the Congress, where the implication is clear that this was a rebuke of the fact that it was a Democratically controlled Congress, you might have a point. As a matter of fact, it would suffice to say you do have a point. But you have got to make a distinction between what the President of the United States may say without challenge as the President of the United States, merely because he is reporting to the people. I mean he is not looking for a debate. He is giving a report to the people. I think we have to make a distinction here, otherwise this will confuse: don't you think?

MR. CALIFANO. Yes; Mr. Chairman, I agree.

SENATOR PASTORE. The mere fact the President appears and has exposure, I hope we don't get into the Lar Daley case where the mayor of the city went out to meet a dignitary and because he got that exposure, his opponents felt he should be given the same amount of equal time. To me that was a little silly. You will agree with that; won't you?

MR. CALIFANO. Absolutely.

SENATOR PASTORE. It is what is said and how it is said that might raise a controversial subject whereby someone who disagrees with him thinks that he in fairness to the public and for the illumination of the public should be given a chance to state a contrary view. We are agreed on that; aren't we?

MR. CALIFANO. Yes; we are, Mr. Chairman. There are obviously national crises and a rule of reason.

SENATOR PASTORE. Yes; I wouldn't want to get into anything that would deter the President of the United States from reporting to the American people, no matter whether he is a Republican or Democrat. I mean we don't want to get into that.

MR. CALIFANO. I agree with that, sir.

SENATOR PASTORE. I hope that day never comes. I think the President of the United States as you say has a responsibility to report. And we have a responsibility to criticize him if we disagree with him. The big question is who is the individual who does this. Are you going to touch on that?

MR. CALIFANO. Yes, sir.

SENATOR PASTORE. All right.

MR. CALIFANO. I believe the designation of the appropriate spokesmen should be left in the first instance to the networks and licensees, under a rule of reason. Should an aggrieved party believe that he has wrongly been denied access, he would have the right, as now, to appeal to the FCC. In most cases the appropriate spokesmen will be obvious: the leadership in the Congress, the concerned committee chairman, the opposing party chairman. By ad hoc determinations, the FCC and the courts are eminently qualified to evolve a sound doctrine in this area.

The second purported difficulty—the infinite chain of response hypothesis—is specious. In the evolution of the fairness doctrine over the past several years, the FCC and the broadcasters have been able to meet and resolve this problem. As is the case throughout the common law, rules of reason must guide commissions and the courts. So far as I can tell, the basic sources for this imaginary horror are the networks and licensees, who are unwilling to give up any more revenues than the minimum required for political debate. They have raised problems of this kind at every step in the development of the fairness doctrine. Yet, over the years, applying a rule of reason, the FCC and the courts have evolved a fairness doctrine under which networks and licensees have been able to discharge their obligations as trustees for the public without any undue burden.

As for the petition of the Republican National Committee chairman to respond to Chairman O'Brien's July 7 [1970] response to President Nixon, I think it is wholly without merit. By White House reckoning, . . . since he took office, the President has appeared in prime time, simultaneously on all three networks, 14 times for a total of 7 hours, 3 minutes and 18 seconds. In response, the Democratic National Committee has been granted 25 minutes by one network—CBS—on one occasion to date.[4] To grant any additional time to the Republican Party would only aggravate the grave imbalance which already exists.

THE PAY TIME PETITION

During the past year, the DNC began to develop an extensive television and radio campaign to inform the electorate and to promote wider citizen participation in political affairs. By reaching large numbers of persons, the party believed it could encourage small contributions and stem the unhealthy trend of dependence of candidates and political parties upon large contributors. To make such a campaign effective, it was essential to use the broadcast media to reach large numbers of citizens. We had planned to broadcast issue-oriented programs and spot announcements of varying duration, some designed in part to solicit funds.

Through a variety of conflicting policies and practices, the networks and local stations denied the DNC access to the public's airwaves and frustrated our projected media campaign. Since there are over 7,000 individual radio and television stations in the Nation, with a wide variety of policies and practices, it was apparent that our national media campaign was doomed to failure unless we were assured of access on a broadly based scale.

We conducted a thorough analysis of the pertinent law, including, in particular, the Supreme Court's . . . landmark decision in the Red Lion Broadcasting case.[5] On the basis of that analysis, we concluded that the Constitution and the Communications Act prohibited the broadcasters from erecting arbitrary barriers which denied responsible entities, such as the DNC, the right to purchase time to discuss public issues and to solicit funds. Accordingly, last May we filed, with the Federal Communications Commission, a request for a declaratory ruling that would guarantee us access for our television campaign.

As we noted in that petition, "There is a critical question of public policy as well as constitutional law, involved here: Are the public airwaves —the most powerful communications media in our democracy—to be used to solicit funds for soap, brassieres, deodorants, and mouthwashes and not to solicit funds to enhance the exchange of ideas?"

CONCLUSION

Television is the most profound influence on our political system today. It can and should be a central tool in the communication of ideas and to inform the electorate. The whole concept of our democracy is based on the inherent good sense of the majority of our people to make sound judgments, if only they are informed. The political judgments of a population will never be better than the information on which they are based. And part of that information is the wide exposure of political ideas and personalities to the scrutiny of the American people.

The essence of our democracy is the vigorous debate of political issues, not the lopsided presentation of a single point of view to the American people. It is no accident that television is the critical tool of Government in George Orwell's frightening classic, 1984. Two-way television was the essential force needed by Big Brother to run Orwell's utterly dehumanizing totalitarian state. One-way television may not be as effective for the operation of a dictatorship; but, improperly used, it is certainly sufficient to plant the seeds of totalitarianism in our society.

SENATOR PASTORE. Thank you very much, Mr. Califano. I understand you have an exchange of letters here that you would like to have inserted in the record?

MR. CALIFANO. Yes, Mr. Chairman; the comments that were made earlier about having Mr. O'Brien use the first 25-minute portion of the Loyal Opposition show, I think it is important to clear the record that we talked to the CBS people about placing Congressional Members on that television show and the bureau chief of CBS in Washington informed us that no Members of Congress who were candidates for office could appear on the Loyal Opposition show, which effectively eliminated the House of Representatives and Senators Mansfield and Kennedy, our two top leaders in the Senate.

As a result—we had 10 days in which to put that show together—as a result, on June 29, I wrote to the bureau chief in Washington and protested that decision, said I wanted to make it clear we found that intolerable, we thought that Congressmen and Senators should be on the Loyal Opposition shows and, finally, on July 16 of this year, I received a letter from the attorney at CBS in New York indicating that CBS had changed its policy and would permit us to put Congressmen and Senators, even though they were candidates, on the show.

I would like to place those letters in the record.

SENATOR PASTORE. Thank you very much.

(The documents follow:)

ARNOLD & PORTER,

Washington, D.C., June 29, 1970.

MR. WILLIAM J. SMALL,

News Director and Bureau Chief, CBS, Washington, D.C.

DEAR BILL: As I understand it, last Wednesday, June 24, you called John Stewart, Director of Communications of the Democratic National Committee, and informed him that the Democratic Party could not have on its July 7 free time broadcast, or in any such subsequent broadcast, any person who is a candidate for public office.

As I indicated to Don Richardson in your absence, we believe that this is inconsistent with the network's obligations under the Communications Act and with our right of access to the broadcast media under the fairness doctrine and under the First Amendment to the Constitution of the United States. The effect of your rule would be to eliminate from any such broadcast all the members of the House of Representatives and a large number of Senate Democratic leaders during whatever period they are considered to be candidates.

At this time, it is not clear whether this CBS policy will become an issue in connection with the July 7 broadcast. However, we would like to make it absolutely clear that as far as we are concerned, we do not consider the arbitrary and unjustifiable exclusion by CBS of all Democratic members of the House of Representatives and a large number of Democratic Senators to be consistent with the Constitution of the United States and the Communications Act. Indeed, it is quite inconsistent with the spirit of the public announcements and background statements that CBS, through its president and other spokesmen, has given to the American press and the American public in the past few days. We believe such a policy is patently unfair and inconsistent with our legal rights and your legal responsibilities.

Sincerely,

JOSEPH A. CALIFANO, JR.,

General Counsel for the Democratic National Committee.

COLUMBIA BROADCASTING SYSTEM, INC.,

New York, N.Y., July 16, 1970.

JOSEPH A. CALIFANO, JR., Esq.,

General Counsel for the Democratic National Committee,

Washington, D.C.

DEAR MR. CALIFANO: This is in reply to your June 29, 1970 letter to William J. Small concerning the appearance of candidates for public office on the "Loyal Opposition" broadcasts to be prepared by the Democratic National Committee.

As you may know, the appearance of legally qualified candidates for public office on these broadcasts would appear to require under existing FCC interpretations of Section 315 of the Communications Act that stations broadcasting these programs afford "equal time" to all legally qualified opponents (including minor party opponents) of such candidates in their broadcast area. Thus, for example, if a Democratic Senator who was a candidate for re-election appeared on a "Loyal Opposition" broadcast, affiliates serving his state would have "equal time" obligations to all of his legally qualified opponents. Candidates taking advantage of this "equal time" right would, of course, be free to discuss any issue whether of local or national concern and whether or not such issue was related in any way to the subject discussed on the "Loyal Opposition" broadcasts.

CBS will not object to the inclusion of Senators or Representatives as spokesmen for the Democratic National Committee on these "Loyal Opposition" broadcasts provided that the Democratic National Committee informs CBS of such an appearance sufficiently in advance of the scheduled broadcast to enable those of our affiliates who might be affected by such an appearance to exercise their options. Those options would include not carrying the broadcast or offering "equal time" to the Senator's or Representative's opponents or securing waivers from such opponents.

Sincerely,

RALPH E. GOLDBERG, *General Attorney.*

SENATOR PASTORE. Of course, you differ somewhat with Mr. Fulbright's argument. He thought that the Congress, on its own, should make its own selection as to who should answer in the case of controversy. You take the position that should be left up to the broadcasting industry?

MR. CALIFANO. Mr. Chairman, I say that, in a general way, I fully agree that Congress, as a coequal branch, independent of any right to respond under the fairness doctrine, just as a coequal branch of the Government, must have access to television in a format that the Congress determines.

SENATOR PASTORE. But yours is apart from this, you are getting into the controversial aspects of it.

MR. CALIFANO. That is correct, Mr. Chairman. And I thought your suggestions today were excellent. Why not try it, let the Congress give the time to the Congress and let the Congress use the time and see what happens.

SENATOR PASTORE. On a voluntary basis you mean?

MR. CALIFANO. Yes, sir; immediately.

SENATOR PASTORE. Do you have any questions?

SENATOR SCOTT. Mr. Califano, have you commented on Dr. Stanton's testimony to the effect that your proposal would require that whenever the President delivers a state of the Union address, equal time to respond would have to be given to other groups with respect to each of the many issues upon which he touched, and that that grant would not suffice to satisfy the proposed rule, that equal time would also have to be given to other significant contrasting views, whether from the principal opposition party, the President's own party, or other segments of the general population, just as long as they were responsible, but it is not stated to whom or for what and there would be no end of responsible persons or entities asking for equal broadcast time.

MR. CALIFANO. Senator, we indicate in our brief, which we would like to insert in the record, that there is a rule of reason. With respect to the state of the Union, every state of the Union that President Johnson gave, I can remember going back to the White House and watching the Republican leadership in Congress for the half hour or hour immediately following the state of the Union address answering it.

We certainly thought that was sufficient. I would think the kind of time which was given to the Democratic leadership this year, after President Nixon's state of the Union, was the appropriate way to handle the state of the Union address. As you know better than I, FCC and its courts have been dealing with this problem for years and they have managed, through results of reason, to deal with this in a reasonable manner.

SENATOR SCOTT. Do you happen to have the dates when the Republican Party responded to the State of the Union address?

MR. CALIFANO. I don't have the dates: I can supply them for the record. In some cases it was the very night of the broadcast, in some cases about a week or 2 later. I will be happy to supply them for the record.

SENATOR PASTORE. You mean Mr. Ford and Mr. Dirksen?

MR. CALIFANO. That is correct, Mr. Chairman.

SENATOR SCOTT. Were they in every instance given equal free time? Do you recall?

MR. CALIFANO. I don't remember, you know——

SENATOR SCOTT. It is my impression the last time there was equal free time it was in 1963, 7 years ago, but I am not sure. How do you deal with the problem of the minorities? They would like to be heard perhaps to respond. You have mentioned that they turn to the streets to demonstrate their opposition. Are you sure that either political party could speak for the various significant minorities?

MR. CALIFANO. Not always, Senator. I think this is an enormously difficult problem. But I would much rather see the television stations, the networks, both [in] local community programing and nationally, provide time for some intelligent discussion by the president of the National Students Association, for example, or some black leaders, rather than have my children and your children and lots of Americans subjected to what is essentially aboriginal activity. The shooting at Kent State, the riots in some of our cities are not . . . reasoned discussion, and people [who] see that every night on television obviously get a jaundiced point of view of these situations.

Now, I am not saying that every time the President criticizes the college students or some other group that they immediately have a right to talk on television and speak for an hour. But I think the combined impact of saying some college students are bums, and looking on television and seeing college students in what really is a very small part of their activity when they are in a demonstration or riot on campus, is very bad for this country.

I would much rather see a half hour a month of discussion by college students campus presidents or some television show than that kind of activity.

SENATOR SCOTT. You would prefer the approach that you mentioned then to the demonstrations that we had in Chicago in the summer of 1968 also; would you not?

MR. CALIFANO. I certainly would, Senator.

SENATOR SCOTT. Yes; I would think you would. Dr. Stanton says this enactment would for the first time in American history provide that incumbent members of the Federal legislature have the privileged status over all other American citizens in or out of office in utilizing organs of information which he believes would be highly repugnant to the American people.

What do you think of that?

MR. CALIFANO. Is that a comment on our petition or the Fulbright resolution?

SENATOR SCOTT. I am quoting what Dr. Stanton said, that this proposed legislation would give incumbents a privileged status over all other American citizens.

MR. CALIFANO. I would assume, Senator, that if that incumbent was a candidate for office, and he appeared on one of the congressional television shows, and that appeared in his State, that his opponent in that State would have a chance to respond. For example, when Senator Mansfield appeared in response to the President on the economic message, his opponent in Montana had a chance to respond.

SENATOR SCOTT. I was going a little ahead of that. The criticism is that this bill would give a privileged status to incumbent members of the Federal legislature over all other American citizens. Actually it is discriminatory perhaps in another way, 35 Senators who are candidates for reelection, so if you choose from the Senate and don't choose one of the 65, you open yourself up to equal time as to the other 35, is that right?

SENATOR PASTORE. So there is discrimination there. But how do you decide whether you respond by a member of the legislature or by the chairman of the National Committee?

MR. CALIFANO. Well, Senator, I think the legislature, the Congress, as a coequal branch, has a right of access to television independent of response. I don't think it makes any difference in a Democratic controlled Congress whether the president is a Democrat or a Republican. The point is the Congress should have some opportunity to present their views in a format that they consider the most favorable.

I think the issue of the rights, so to speak, of the Democratic or the Republican party to respond to the statements of the President in power is an issue to be handled under the fairness doctrine in discussing and responding to statements on controversial issues of public policies.

SENATOR SCOTT. But one of the responses came from a Senator, another came from the chairman of the Democratic National Committee. My question was how do you decide who is to respond?

MR. CALIFANO. In terms of the Democrats deciding how its Democrats respond, I really don't think we have a serious problem. We have worked closely with Senator Muskie, who is chairing a television committee for the Democratic Policies Committee, Senator Mansfield responded, as I understand it, because there were so many statements in the economic message of the President dealing with the actions either not taken by the Congress that the President thought the Congress should take, or being taken by the Congress that the President thought the Congress should not take. When we put Mr. O'Brien on as I indicated we had hoped in that broadcast to put Senators and Congressmen on, but CBS would not let us place anyone who was a candidate for office on the program at that time. And, Senator, just before you came in I put letters in the record in which we protested that and CBS has changed its policy.

SENATOR SCOTT. I believe I recall that the Republican National Committee asked for equal time which would be national. On my behalf, I thought Mr. O'Brien said any political party which was responsible for the perpetuation of our involvement in Vietnam was not fit to govern, or words to that effect, and I thought he had probably eliminated the need for the Republican National Committee to reply.

But that is a matter of opinion. What about the proposal of the Senators sponsoring an amendment to end the war to supply time to any substantial group of Senators opposing the President's views? Do you think that that should be granted?

MR. CALIFANO. I would, I haven't really looked in detail at their brief. We limited the legal discussions in our briefs to the problems of the two major political parties. [That's] the kind of problem that the people have talked about all day today here[—]who speaks for the Congress and how does the Congress determine it.

I think that is something for the Congress to determine.

SENATOR SCOTT. Well, I would solicit your attention to a bill I introduced today which would provide a requirement for not less than four televised sessions of each House of Congress during certain time periods. Perhaps there the opposition could be well heard. I would like you to give some deliberation to that. I have proposed that and it seems to me it might be a viable alternative——

SENATOR PASTORE. You mean coming into the Chamber?

SENATOR SCOTT. Yes; coming into the Chamber and a requirement of not less than four times a year.

SENATOR PASTORE. On important issues?

SENATOR SCOTT. On important issues, things of that kind. But I really wonder how any Senator can be designated as fully representing the views of his party. I think that is part of the difficulty. With regard to another comment you made, regardless of who is President, or which party controls the Congress, have you ever in your life heard of a Republican Congressman demanding equal time for a Republican President or a Democratic Congressman demanding equal time in reply to a Democratic President?

MR. CALIFANO. No, Senator, but the point was not necessarily in response. I can certainly see that even in 1968, in terms of . . . the majority of the Senate's apparent view of the Vietnam war, that there were arguments that the Senate should have some opportunity to express its views of that conflict when President Johnson was expressing his view of that conflict on television.

SENATOR SCOTT. You are not arguing that the Democratic National Committee should have equal time to answer an address by the President in addition to the time provided to the Senate and House under S.J. Res. 209, are you? Not in addition?

MR. CALIFANO. I think they are two different questions, Senator. I think that if you take the Congress and assume the President—one of the quotes in my statement was that President Nixon said last year "This Congress has the worst record on appropriations of any Congress in the history of the Union." Well, I think that aside from the Democratic National Committee or anybody else, the Congress would have the right to point out that the appropriations bills came up later than they ever did before, that——

SENATOR SCOTT. And in a Democratic Congress. That is just bad housekeeping.

MR. CALIFANO. Whatever it is, it is not that simple a case. As Senator Muskie pointed out this morning, with respect to the tax legislation, the President can rail against the delay in passing the tax surcharge, the Congress obviously made a judgment, both sides of the aisle in that area, both Chairman Mills and Mr. Burns and in the Senate that a tax reform bill should be a part of that package and there was an extended debate on that. I would much rather have an appropriation bill delayed, for example, and have a thorough ABM debate than have an appropriations bill come through on time. I think those are problems of the Congress[—]of how you run the Congress as the leader for the Republicans and Senator Mansfield for the Democrats. I think Senator Fulbright's resolution would not in any way affect, in my judgment at least, and in line with the briefs we filed with FCC, our rights to time as we see it, to respond to the President's comments on controversial issues of public importance.

SENATOR SCOTT. As far as a caucus of the two parties in the Senate, I am keeping it just to one house to simplify it—it was decided that the reply by a responsible authority to the state of the Union address of the President should be made by a Republican Senator. Would that lead you on behalf of the Democratic committee to feel you had been ruled out under this law, if it became a law?

MR. CALIFANO. I think it would depend on what was said in the state of the Union addresses. In virtually all of President Johnson's and the [first] one of President Nixon, it seems to me that Congress would be the appropriate entity to respond.

Now there are two levels of disagreement here. I mean if the President attacks Clark Clifford because he was Secretary of Defense when casualties were highest during the Vietnam war, Clark Clifford has a right to respond, independent of the Congress, Democratic National Committee or anybody else. To use a very simple case, the Congress may also want to comment on that. President Johnson may want to comment on that. The Democratic National Committee may want to comment on what the policies are. There has to be some rule of reason.

SENATOR SCOTT. I think that is all, Mr. Chairman.

SENATOR PASTORE. Thank you very much.

REFORM AND CONTINUITY

Alexander M. Bickel

THE REFORM MOVEMENT

The Democratic National Convention of 1968 had before it a study and recommendations made in the summer of that year by an unofficial, privately funded Commission on the Democratic Selection of Presidential Nominees, of which the then governor, now Senator, Harold E. Hughes of Iowa was chairman. This commission was brought together on the initiative of a few delegates who were members of the convention's credentials and rules committees.

While accepting the value of the winner-take-all primary in a few states, the Hughes commission recommended absolute abolition of the unit rule at all levels of the delegate selection process, and abolition also of the practice in convention states of electing delegations by successive majority votes, thus denying representation to minority views. It recommended further that all systems of direct appointment of delegates, in whole or in part, by state party committees or other officials be abandoned, and that no members of the Democratic National Committee elected at prior conventions be seated at the convention. More affirmatively, the commission recommended that delegates be selected by procedures which "permit meaningful popular participation" within a period of "not more than six months before the Convention itself." Meaningful participation, the commission said, required "clarity of purpose for the voter at all levels of the nominating process such that he may register his choice for delegate-candidates without having thereby to select the same individuals as state party officers," and fair apportionment of a state's delegation.

The 1968 Democratic convention addressed itself to some of the issues raised by the Hughes commission. The convention decided no longer to enforce the unit rule in balloting at the convention itself. Thus it effectively abolished it at that level. Somewhat to everyone else's surprise, and perhaps also to its own, the convention went on as well to declare its understanding that "in selecting and certifying delegates and alternates to the Democratic National Convention" a state Democratic party "thereby undertakes to assure that all Democrats of the State will have meaningful and timely opportunities to participate fully in the election or selection of such delegates and alternates." Then, on August 27, 1968, the convention capped the edifice of reform, and the general surprise, by adopting the following resolution offered by a minority of its Rules Committee:

> *It is understood that a state Democratic Party, in selecting and certifying delegates to the National Convention, thereby undertakes to assure that such delegates have been selected through a process in which all Democratic voters have had full and timely opportunity to participate. In determining whether a State Party has complied with this mandate, the Convention shall require that:*
>
> *(1) The unit rule not be used in any stage of the delegate selection process; and*
>
> *(2) All feasible efforts have been made to assure that delegates are selected through party primary, convention, or committee procedures open to public participation within the calendar year of the National Convention.*

This was, to all appearances, a substantial part of the Hughes commission's recommendations. Plainly most professional appointment practices were now out, although appointment of some delegates, as in New York, by a state committee itself elected in the year of the convention remained possible. The unit rule was out, indeed doubly out, but whether minority-exclusion practices in convention, let alone in primary, states were also abolished was questionable. And the phrases, "full and timely opportunity to participate," and "procedures open to public participation" were certainly not entirely self-explanatory. At any rate, as the Hughes commission also suggested, the chairman of the Democratic National Committee was instructed to set up a special committee charged with helping the states implement the new policies.

Such a committee was appointed in February 1969 by Senator Fred R. Harris of Oklahoma, then chairman of the Democratic National Committee. It was called the Commission on Party Structure and Delegate Selection, and was headed by Senator George S. McGovern of South

Dakota as chairman, and by Senator Harold E. Hughes of Iowa, chairman of the earlier study commission that bore his name, as vice-chairman.

In November 1969, the McGovern commission issued a set of guidelines to state Democratic parties. The commission viewed most of the provisions of its guidelines as implementing the decisions of the 1968 convention, and as binding on state parties, unless reversed or modified by the 1972 convention. Hence the commission *required* state parties to comply with these provisions, warning that noncompliance would constitute grounds for refusing to seat a delegation at the 1972 national convention. If compliance proved impossible without changes in the statutory or constitutional law of a state regulating the delegate-selection process, then the commission required state parties to make "all feasible efforts" to achieve the necessary changes.

The commission *required* state parties to adopt and make readily available "statewide party rules and statutes which prescribe the state's delegate selection process with sufficient details and clarity"; in all but rural areas, to see to it that party caucuses and other meetings, as well as other party events, such as enrollment periods, take place on uniform dates, at uniform times, and in easily accessible places; to abolish proxy voting; to set "quorums at not less than forty per cent for all party committees involved in the delegate selection process"; whenever other party business is mixed in with delegate selection, as it always is under a system of committee appointment, and sometimes in convention systems, "to make it clear to voters how they are participating in a process that will nominate their party's candidate for President"; to give every candidate for delegate or for membership on a body that chooses delegates "the opportunity to state his Presidential preference on the ballot at each stage of the delegate selection process," and to list him as "uncommitted" if he so chooses; "to prohibit any practices by which officials elected or appointed before the calendar year [of the national convention] choose nominating committees or propose or endorse a slate of delegates—even when the possibility for a challenge to such slate or committee is provided"; to limit the portion of any delegation to the national convention chosen by committee procedures to "not more than ten per cent of the total number of delegates and alternates"; to ensure that slates of candidates for delegate, if any, are made up openly, with adequate public notice, and "that the right to challenge the presented slate is more than perfunctory and places no undue burden on the challengers"; to forbid use of the unit rule, strictly defined as "the practice of instructing delegates to vote against their stated preferences at any stage of the delegate selection process"; to prohibit the designation of ex-officio members of a delegation to the national convention; to see to it that alternates for delegates to the national convention are selected by the same method by which the delegates are selected, and to fill vacancies on a delegation by action of the state committee, of a convention, or of the delegation itself; not to make any mandatory financial assessments on delegates or alternates to the national convention; to keep costs, such as filing fees, to a maximum of ten dollars; and to hold the number of signatures needed on petitions entitling a person to be a candidate for delegate to not more than one per cent of Democratic strength in the state.

Without purporting to impose a binding requirement on the state parties, the McGovern commission *urged* them to dispense with fees of all sorts in the delegate selection process, otherwise to seek to ease the financial burden on delegates and candidates for delegate, and to end entirely the practice of committee appointment of delegates. In addition, the commission's guidelines dealt also, by way both of requiring and urging action, with the practice of electing delegations by successive majorities and thus foreclosing representation of minority views; with the problems of access to the party and apportionment within a state of its delegation to the national convention; and with the need to represent racial and ethnic minorities, women, and the young in the national convention. Here is a cluster of complex issues, of rather a different order of magnitude than most of the other provisions of the guidelines, and they call for separate and more extended treatment.

REPRESENTATION OF MINORITY VIEWS

Party professionals often maintain that the main object of the national convention is to achieve cohesiveness of the party, and the greatest degree of unity behind a ticket. Therefore, they say, while it is necessary at each stage of the delegation selection process to give a full hearing to all opinions, and to permit any view to prevail, it is equally essential at every stage to let a majority decide, and select the delegates who will represent it. Thus fragmentation of the convention is avoided. And thus the principle of majority rule, which is traditional in American politics, is vindicated.

No doubt, majority rule must obtain at final decision-making stages in our politics. But that very principle itself can be perverted by a too-early insistence on it at preliminary decision-making stages. If at such preliminary stages in the delegate selection process successive majorities are allowed to prevail and to represent only themselves, and if the representation of minorities is not carried forward to the national convention, then it is quite possible, it is in some circumstances likely, that the final majority of delegates which prevails at the convention will represent a minority, and not a majority, of the Democratic voters in the country at large.

In three or four large states, for example, 51 per cent of the Democrats may command a very substantial bloc of delegates to the national convention, selected on the principle of majority rule in each state, who favor presidential candidate A. The delegations from these states may then outvote on the floor of the convention the delegates selected by a nearly equal number of Democrats in several other states in which candidate B may have been preferred by a greater margin. Now candidate B may also have been supported by a losing 49 per cent of the Democrats in the three or four states which candidate A carried. This losing percentage of support, plus candidate B's winning margin in other states, may constitute the true majority. Yet it may not be reflected in the convention, and may be frustrated. The difficulty is aggravated when delegates from some states represent, not a majority, but only a plurality of the Democratic voters.

Thus it is possible to defeat the principle of majority rule by closely adhering to it in the delegate selection process. Just so, the present electoral college system, operating under the unit rule, could produce a winner who had fewer popular votes than his leading opponent. And it might be said for a national convention consisting entirely of delegates voting by the unit rule, or chosen by the successive-majorities method, that like the electoral college, it would be weighted in favor of the large states. But the justification for such a double weighting is not easily found. It certainly cannot be the same justification as that which supports using the electoral college to choose a president who will function jointly with a Congress oriented toward a different constituency, especially since the fact that in the general election the college gives the large states a disproportionate voice is itself a consideration affecting the judgment of any convention, whatever its composition. But the conclusive answer to this analogy rests on the difference in functions between the electoral college and the national convention.

There are, as I have been implying all along, two sorts of multi-member democratic institutions: the representative, deliberative assembly, and the body meant to register a single prior decision of its constituency. Congress is an institution of the former sort, the electoral college of the latter. (He did not "choose Samuel Miles to determine for me whether John Adams or Thomas Jefferson is the fittest man for President of the United States" said a Federalist voter of a member of the electoral college in 1796. "No, I choose him to act, not to think.")[1] Institutions meant to act by registering the decision of a majority of their constituents should consist of members responsive to that majority, and of no one else. Deliberative institutions, charged also to think, should contain within themselves as many of the significant factions in the total constituency as possible. That is why all American legislatures are districted. None is elected at large, to be a creature wholly of the majority. It is exceedingly rare also for any state to send to Congress an entire delegation elected on a statewide basis.

The national convention must be a deliberative, not a registering institution, else it is a poor and unseemly substitute for a national primary. And it is particularly necessary to represent minority views, indeed to reflect a wide variety of views, in a deliberative assembly like the convention, which sits briefly and only periodically, and has as its sole object the composition of a governing coalition. The minority must be there, quite simply, in order that some portion of it may be coalesced with; or to put it in other terms, no relevant majority exists for purposes of constituting such a deliberative assembly until the assembly's own majority-building work is done, and that work can be done only if the total or near-total constituency is present through its delegates. Moreover, even if they do not form part of the ultimate coalition, minorities are more likely to share a sense of the legitimacy of the convention, are less likely, although dissatisfied, to be disaffected, if they were present and had access.

It follows that the practice in convention states of building a delegation by successive majority votes from the precinct up is unacceptable. It follows also that while a state-wide preferential primary which binds no delegates and has only symbolic significance presents no problem, being essentially unrelated to the delegate selection or delegate instruction process, winner-take-all primaries, such as California's, in which a plurality or majority of the voters elects an entire slate committed to one candidate, or preferential primaries such as those of Massachusetts and Indiana, in which the preference of a plurality or majority of the voters binds an entire delegation, or part of it, for one or more ballots—such primaries do foreclose the representation of minority views. But there may be good reasons for retaining some of them as exceptions to an otherwise applicable principle of minority representation.

The state-wide, winner-take-all primary has attributes that are lacking in convention systems. It is a trial heat, a shakedown cruise for candidates, and a preview for the public. It catches attention and generates interest throughout the country, even though the level of voter participation in the primary itself is not always higher than in some convention systems that start with small precinct caucuses.

Politics is an educational endeavor before it is anything else, and in this endeavor the major state primary helps. The drama is heightened for all concerned by the winner-take-all feature; for the candidate with little support from the professionals, the attractiveness of the primary is enhanced, as for the public is its authenticity as a preview. And the winner-take-all primary injects into the convention's process of judgment a prediction that is more than a guess, and more reliable than a poll, of what the party faces in the general election.

But the state-wide, winner-take-all primary as universal practice would avoid few of the shortcomings of a national primary. And it would add some of its own. If a reasonably obvious national winner was turned up, the convention would be supposed merely to register the choice; or else, if as would more often happen, the state primaries produced no conclusive winner, the convention's task would be what it is today, but its composition would be most unsuited to a satisfactory, deliberative performance of that task.

It would be as unwise to eliminate the handful of state-wide, winner-

take-all primaries as it would be to opt for any nation-wide, rigidly uniform system of delegate selection. As one special element in the mix of a
convention which is otherwise faithful to the principle of minority representation, winner-take-all primaries such as California's serve a useful
purpose. One may be considerably more dubious about preferential polls
such as that of Massachusetts (as well as Oregon's, Indiana's, and even
Pennsylvania's attenuated one), which are divorced from the delegate
selection process itself, but bind all or part of a delegation for one or more
national convention ballots. Such primaries, like the elemental unit rule,
may cause delegates to act against their own convictions. They often bring
men into the convention wearing masks, so to speak, and unable to play a
deliberative role until they are free to shed their masks. The winner-take-
all primary, on the other hand, brings in delegates who represent a popular
majority's preferences in their proper persons, and who are likely to identify with that popular majority as does a legislator with his constituency.

Assuming the desirability of retaining winner-take-all primaries on
the California model, the question nevertheless arises whether they can be
kept to a handful, as they must be if they are to constitute a valuable element in the convention. It may be that if minority representation is required in convention states but not in winner-take-all primary states, the
former will feel discriminated against, because they will view the latter as
exerting greater influence in the convention. And it may be that convention states will be tempted to adopt the winner-take-all primary as a measure of self-protection. But party organizations in nonprimary states may
as likely continue to see advantages for themselves and for their constituents in the convention system, much as they have done when, despite the
possibilities of using the unit rule or the successive-majorities method, they
often arrived at the convention with divided delegations, and yet did not
stampede in self-protection to the winner-take-all primary. Nor have the
Republicans shown any inclination to flock to the winner-take-all primary
even though the unit rule for voting in the convention was repudiated by
their party as long ago as 1880.

The minority representation principle may be implemented either by
the method of proportionality or the method of districting. Proportionality
can be achieved in an elective system by various techniques, with varying
degrees of precision. It has been tried on occasion, but has never gained
widespread acceptance in American elective politics, chiefly because it
overly fragments legislatures. For a legislature to be effective, a good bit of
coalition formation needs to have taken place before the legislature con-
venes. But this consideration has little, if any, application to a convention
that sits only once, and that has as its sole task the formation of a coalition.

In a caucus and convention system, proportionality of one or another
degree of precision can be achieved by taking straw votes, which indicate
the range of opinion in an assemblage, and by then at each stage assigning

proportionate membership in intermediate and final delegations to the various groups, and perhaps allowing each group separately to select members to represent it.

Attempts to achieve minority representation by the method of proportionality will tend to direct attention to presidential preferences, and to de-emphasize other views and attitudes having to do with issues more than with personalities; and this may be considered a drawback, since, as was particularly evident in 1968, the convention plays a role in committing the party on issues, as well as in choosing the presidential nominee, and a delegate's stand on issues may be as significant as his preference for a candidate. Moreover, at the time at which a delegate is selected, not all the candidates who will be in the running may as yet be known, and some states may for this reason wish to select some uncommitted delegates. Yet the method of proportionality will tend to focus the proceedings on candidate preferences, no matter if premature.

Districting is a way of achieving a rough measure of minority representation. It is the method by which we represent minorities in our legislatures and in Congress. Districting can be used in a caucus and convention system as well as in an elective system, but—and this is of the essence—it can be used meaningfully only if intermediate and final state conventions do not operate on the principle of majority rule, but reflect the minority representation that districting may have achieved; this is to say that a caucus and convention system can achieve minority representation by virtue simply of being districted only if majority rule does not prevail in intermediate or state conventions, and the final state delegation is made up by assigning membership in it to the different opinion groupings that districting has produced in proportion to their strength.

For a primary or convention system to achieve any measure of minority representation by districting, the districts should be relatively small. If delegates are selected in large, multi-member districts, then minority representation may be ensured by adopting a system of proportionality in the district election. Districting, of course, raises issues of apportionment and of gerrymandering.

The Hughes commission, as we saw, answered in the affirmative the question—as formulated subsequently by Congressman Donald M. Fraser of Minnesota, a member of both the Hughes and McGovern commissions —whether "minority views should be preserved to the highest level of the nomination process, to the floor of the convention itself." A strong argument can be made that an affirmative answer to this question, applicable to convention states, or even to both convention and primary states, is implicit in the decision of the 1968 national convention to abolish the unit rule at all levels of the delegate selection process. For to permit successive majorities to govern that process is to achieve precisely the effect of the unit rule. As John Schmidt and Wayne Whalen have made clear, "instead of requiring all of the delegates from a particular county to cast their votes together in a state convention, the state party can simply allow the majority in the county to choose all of the delegates to the state convention in the first place. This is functionally indistinguishable from forcing all of the county's votes to be cast the same way. If [abolition of the unit rule] is to have its intended impact, this procedure . . . must be prohibited."[2] The only difference is that the elemental unit rule may force one or another individual to cast a vote against his conscience.

This difference impressed itself on a substantial majority of the McGovern commission. The successive-majorities practice in delegate selection did not seem to the McGovern commission to be quite the functional equivalent of the unit rule, and the commission found no implication of condemnation of the former practice in the decision of the 1968 convention to abolish the latter rule. The McGovern commission, moreover, had great difficulty distinguishing, as the Hughes commission had done, between the successive-majorities practice in convention states and the winner-take-all feature of state-wide primaries such as California's. It tended to view these two as functional equivalents, and could not bring itself to believe that it had a mandate from the 1968 convention to forbid winner-take-all primaries. And so the McGovern commission concluded that the decision of the 1968 convention abolishing the unit rule related only to the practice of requiring an entire delegation, after it has been selected, at whatever level, to vote as a unit in accordance with the wishes of a majority of its members, and did not in any way touch the process of delegate selection, or the question of representation of minority views in a delegation.

Although it thus concluded that it had no mandate to lay down requirements to state parties concerning representation of minority views, the McGovern commission nevertheless expressed its belief "that a full and meaningful opportunity to participate in the delegate selection process is precluded unless the Presidential preference of each Democrat is fairly represented at all levels of the process." The commission, therefore, *urged* the state parties "to adopt procedures which would provide fair representation of minority views on Presidential candidates," and it recommended that the 1972 convention "adopt a rule requiring state parties to provide for the representation of minority views to the highest level of the nominating process."

In the meantime, the commission did *require* state parties with convention systems "to select at least 75 per cent of their delegations to the national convention at Congressional district or smaller unit levels." This being one not ineffective method of ensuring representation of minority views, it can certainly be said that the McGovern commission, despite its doubts about its mandate, met the issue halfway, and quite possibly better than halfway. The rest is up to the 1972 convention.

ACCESS TO THE PARTY AND APPORTIONMENT OF DELEGATIONS

Since the function of the major party and of its convention is to form a broad-based coalition taking in diverse elements, access to the party is obviously crucial; it becomes necessary to define the party, and to be clear about the meaning of adherence to it.

One aspect of this problem emerged in the loyalty oath controversies that have bedevilled the Democratic party for a generation. The implications for the loyalty oath issue of the nature and function of the American major party, which the Democrats ultimately accepted, are that it is hardly consistent to require any group, as a condition for coming to the convention and engaging in the coalition-making process, to promise beforehand to abide by the result, even though, as may happen, it is affirmatively excluded from the coalition. The convention is the occasion of forming the party for a particular election, and no one can say with detailed assurance beforehand what kind of a party it will be. Hence, although the issue was fudged somewhat in a patchwork compromise about the Alabama and Georgia delegations at the 1968 convention, the Democrats by and large require only that delegates promise to use their influence to see to it that the nominees of the convention are listed as Democratic nominees on the ballot in their states, not that they promise necessarily to support the nominees.

The implications for procedures of delegate selection should be similar. It ought not to be necessary, as in many states it is, to have been a registered Democrat or Republican at a prior election in order to participate in a Democratic or Republican primary, or in party caucuses and conventions. The party ought each year to be open to all those groups which in that year wish to enter into the process of forming the coalition that will be the Democratic or Republican party. If the parties were as open as they should be, large numbers of people who had voted Democratic in the past might in 1968 have moved to form in the Republican party a coalition around Nelson A. Rockefeller, or around a Charles Percy or John Lindsay, oriented more to the right in some respects than would normally suit them, but more satisfactory to them in that year than what they foresaw as the Democratic combination. Or else anti-Vietnam Republicans might have helped put together in the Democratic party an alliance turning on the war issue, under such a candidate as Eugene McCarthy.

But there are difficulties, more serious in primaries than in local caucuses and conventions, and more serious in precinct caucuses than in state, let alone national, conventions, with their larger membership, more demanding activities, and greater exposure. The trouble is that each party is periodically a new coalition, all right, but each is also, and ought to be, an organism with a continuous existence, particular characteristics, and a corps of permanently loyal supporters. And the two parties must compete, else there will soon be one, and then many, whether in the guise of parties or factions. What can happen when the permanent loyalists are free to float is exemplified in states that do allow crossover of voters, or that might allow, as California did until just recently, cross-filing by candidates.

The upshot in California in primaries for state office was the nomination, not infrequently, of the same man in both primaries. This destroyed party competition rather effectively. Nor is competition apt to flourish when there is a crossover of voters intent in selecting the candidate most desirable from the other party's point of view, the weakest candidate, easiest to beat. The crossover voter may also be happy with the probable (or certain, if there is no contest) outcome in his own party, and go into the other primary in search of, as nearly as possible, the same result. This is not coalition building, but coalition duplicating. It is too nearly the same as the joint nomination of a single man through cross-filing. The two parties would not discharge their function if they did not overlap, or if they assumed polar positions, but though the ground on which they maneuver for differentiation is narrow, they must remain distinct in order to remain two. Party caucuses open to everyone are also subject to being captured by forces wishing to short-circuit party competition.

Nothing in the resolutions adopted at the 1968 Democratic convention suggests a way out of this dilemma. The McGovern commission, in its guidelines, stated it. The commission declared its belief that party membership must be open to all persons "who are not already members of another political party," but that "a full opportunity for all Democrats to participate is diluted if members of other political parties are allowed to participate in the selection of delegates to the Democratic national convention." And the commission wound up somewhat ambiguously, and too restrictively, urging state parties to allow "non-Democrats" and "unaffiliated voters" to join easily.

One of the commission's worries was that in the South, where often there are no registration laws, Wallace voters and Republicans are enabled to dominate both the Democratic and Republican parties. But the alternative is to induce blacks and liberals in the South to build a permanent-minority Democratic party there, a kind of private preserve resembling Southern Republican parties of old, never in power and hardly visible locally, except as it surfaces quadrennially at the national convention. That is not a fruitful future.

For the country as a whole, and in the long run for the South as well, the open party, with its risks, ought to be the prime objective. Party habits are still fairly strong, and at any rate, Machiavellian crossovers, while they occur, are not the norm. What is common and should be encouraged, as the McGovern commission did agree, is unaffiliated floating by voters who, if excluded at the nominating stage, are apt to be disaffected by the limitations of choice in the general election. And what ought equally to be encouraged, as the McGovern commission failed to see, is the easy shifting from one party to another of voters without strong party loyalty, who do freely switch, of course, in the voting booth on general election day, but who should be able to do it so as to influence nominations as well.

Each party should, accordingly, be open in each election year, in primaries and caucuses, to everyone willing at that time to register as a member. Registration should be easy. The McGovern commission, while cautious about allowing previously affiliated voters to cross over and enroll as Democrats, did urge state parties to eliminate burdensome laws and practices such as annual registration requirements, lengthy residence requirements, short, untimely or infrequent registration and enrollment sessions, and even literacy tests.

Free registration regardless of previous affiliation would be largely symbolic and would not exclude cross-overs, if for no other reason than that it would be as impossible as it would be ill-advised to try to bind individuals to vote the party ticket in November. But the symbolism would be endowed with some consequences. Certainly it should be provided that a voter may participate in the nominating process of only one of the major parties in any given year.

No state party which has not in some fashion resolved the problem of its own definition and of access to itself can sensibly address the question of fair apportionment of its delegation to the national convention. It is easy enough to fall into the prevailing apportionment rhetoric and conclude that the proper governing principle is one Democrat, one vote. But who is a Democrat? A Democrat, one may say, is a person who registered as such at some prior point in time, or who voted the Democratic ticket at the last presidential, gubernatorial, or congressional election. Hence a delegation ought to be apportioned within the state on the basis of registration or voting statistics, or of a combination of both. Yet so to apportion is necessarily to opt for a relatively closed party, the more closed as local election statistics are emphasized over those of the presidential election, and still more closed, in some places, as registration figures are preferred over voting statistics.

The open party defies apportionment with any approach to precision. For the open party is not defined until after its delegate selection process has been completed. That is the process by which, for the time being, it defines itself. It has no recourse but to take account of gross population figures. Yet if it bases its apportionment on population figures alone, it is certain to reach a distorted result, since its core strength does have some stability, and it will vary in different parts of the state. The open party must make a guess, therefore, combining population figures with registration and voting statistics.

So the McGovern commission concluded. It required "state parties which apportion their delegation to the national convention to apportion [on the basis of] a formula giving equal weight to total population and to the Democratic vote in the previous Presidential election." The require-

ment applies, it will be noted, to state parties "which apportion their delegation." States which select their delegations at large, as in a winner-take-
all primary, have no apportionment problem. But they fail to represent
minority views. And to insist on fair apportionment may be to invite—
because it is the easy way out—at-large selection of delegates. This is
where the objectives of fair apportionment and representation of minority
views are in tension.

The McGovern commission did not consider that it had a mandate
to forbid at-large selection in primaries or by state committees themselves
elected in the year of the national convention, although it did forbid selection of more than 10 per cent of a delegation by committee, and did
recommend abandonment altogether of committee selection systems, and
adoption everywhere of methods to ensure representation of minority
views. So far as convention states were concerned, the commission required that 75 per cent of delegations be selected "at Congressional district or smaller unit levels." So the at-large option is foreclosed to a very
substantial extent. The commission required also, with respect to apportionment of district and other local conventions, and of state conventions
or committees selecting those delegates who are still permitted to be
selected at large, that a formula be adopted "for each body actually selecting delegates to state, district and county conventions which is based upon
population and/or some measure of Democratic strength. Democratic
strength may be measured by the Democratic vote in the preceding
Presidential, senatorial, congressional or gubernatorial election, and/or
by party enrollment figures."

In sum, then, states which do not select an entire delegation at large
in a primary must use an apportionment formula based on population and
the vote at the last presidential election. In convention states, this formula
must control distribution over various parts of the state of at least 75 per
cent of the total number of delegates allocated to the state. For primary
states, the McGovern commission prescribed no percentage of delegates
who must be selected by district or smaller unit and may not be selected at
large. In convention and committee states, the state convention or committee which selects at-large delegates—no more than 10 per cent by committee or 25 per cent by convention—or the smaller unit convention which
selects the districted delegates, must itself be fairly apportioned over the
area it covers, except that here the formula need not take account of population, and may use other election statistics than the last presidential ones.

RACIAL DISCRIMINATION AND UNDERREPRESENTATION
OF WOMEN AND THE YOUNG

If it is essential that minority views find representation in the national convention, it is equally crucial that distinct groups within the population, par-

ticularly racial ones, be represented. Neither party dare permit its definition to run along hard and fast group, let alone racial or ethnic, lines.

Although racial discrimination in the delegate-selection process is not a generalized abuse found in all parts of the country, it has a long history in both parties. At the 1964 Democratic convention in Atlantic City, an all-white Mississippi delegation was challenged not merely on the obvious ground that Negroes were unrepresented even though Mississippi has a considerable black population, but on the basis also of extensive proofs that by concerted and deliberate action, the Mississippi Democratic party had excluded Negroes from its affairs. Blacks were often effectively deterred from attending precinct meetings by threats of economic and physical harm. Information of the times and places of meetings was withheld from them, and if they somehow did show up, they were denied parliamentary rights.

Moreover, the Mississippi Democratic party openly proclaimed racist principles, as did also the Republicans in Mississippi. In 1964, both the Democratic and Republican state platforms endorsed segregation. Since the Mississippi election law provides that "no person shall be eligible to participate in any primary election unless he . . . is in accord" with the state platform of the party in whose primary he wishes to vote, blacks were quite plainly invited out of both the Democratic and the Republican parties. The absence of any Negro on the Mississippi delegation to the 1964 Democratic convention merely dramatized these grievances.

With the mediating assistance of the then Senator Hubert Humphrey, the 1964 convention adjudicated the Mississippi challenge retroactively by reaching a compromise, and prospectively by adopting a strong statement of principle. Two Mississippi blacks were seated as delegates-at-large, and the all-white regular delegation was also seated. But for the future, Mississippi and all other states were required to afford to all voters, regardless of race, "the opportunity to participate fully in party affairs." Mere contrived representation of Negroes on state delegations would not do in the future. That much was in effect ordered retroactively for the 1964 delegation itself.

The decision of the 1964 convention did not—as would the 1968 resolutions—prescribe democratic methods of delegate selection. It did not, indeed, have specific reference to the process of delegate selection, and certainly not exclusive reference to it. It meant that, as a condition to being seated in 1968, state parties had to give free and full opportunity to Negroes to participate at all levels of party activity, at all times, whatever the method might ultimately be by which delegates were selected, and whatever sort of delegation that method ultimately produced.

This, if with a bit of backing and filling, was the understanding of a Special Equal Rights Committee set up by the Democratic National Committee to implement the 1964 decision. A report of the Special Committee in April 1966 still found vestiges of discrimination, and put the state parties on notice that none would be seated in 1968 which failed to change "rules, laws, and procedures" tending "to bar full party participation." There was no suggestion that the inclusion of some token blacks on a delegation could purchase legitimacy from the national Democratic party in 1968. Nor was there any such suggestion in a letter of July 1967 to all state party chairmen from a new chairman of the Special Equal Rights Committee, Governor Richard Hughes of New Jersey. This letter set forth "minimal prerequisites" for any program of implementing the decision of the 1964 convention. All public meetings, at all levels, it said, must be open to party members regardless of race. And the times and places of public meetings at all levels and the procedures for selection of party officers must be fully publicized.

Any narrower understanding of the intent and coverage of the 1964 decision, limiting it somehow to the delegate-selection process rather than viewing it as applicable to party affairs in general, on all levels, at all times, hardly seemed possible. For in most states, prior to the sort of reforms set in train at the 1968 convention, no easy distinction could be taken between party affairs in general and those directly related to the delegate-selection process. Party officials influenced the choice of delegates, to say the least, and it was not altogether unusual, as we have seen, for state committees to select delegates directly, without submitting their choices to anyone's ratification. Hence meaningful participation in the choice of the state's delegation to the national convention had to be participation at a much earlier stage of party affairs. A 1968 report of the United States Civil Rights Commission quotes a South Carolina NAACP official as saying: "If you don't get in at the precinct meeting, you are out."[3]

The 1968 convention, at which Governor Richard Hughes of New Jersey (who had headed the Special Equal Rights Committee of the Democratic National Committee) was chairman of the convention's Credentials Committee, seeing that nothing had changed in Mississippi since 1964, excluded the regular Mississippi delegation. In a compromise action, the 1968 convention also unseated half of the regular Georgia delegation. But the United States Civil Rights Commission's 1968 report, based on investigations of the 1966 and 1967 elections in Southern states, had found substantial evidence of exclusion and other kinds of discrimination against Negroes in party affairs also in Alabama and South Carolina.

In Barbour and Montgomery Counties, Alabama, measures were taken to prevent election of Negroes to the Democratic county executive committees, and in Choctaw County, Alabama, to prevent their serving as election officials. In Dallas County, Alabama, of which Selma of 1965 fame is the seat, the Democratic county executive committee is self-perpetuating, the members filling vacancies. This is a system which, of course, locks in all past discriminations against Negroes. It has precisely the vice of requirements, long since declared unconstitutional by the federal courts, that any new voter be vouched for by an old one. The effect in places where no, or very few, Negroes voted in the past is obvious. In South Carolina, the Civil Rights Commission found evidence that Negroes were excluded from some precinct meetings in Dorchester and Williamsburg Counties. And in Alabama as well as Georgia, state party officials declared to commission interviewers that they were powerless to deal with discrimination within the Democratic party at the county level.

Conceivably these abuses in Alabama and South Carolina were remedied to the satisfaction of the Credentials Committee of the 1968 convention. More probably, they were considered relatively minor, and were overlooked. The Alabama and South Carolina delegations were in any event seated. But the antidiscrimination policy first adopted by the 1964 convention, and implemented in 1968 in something of a spirit of gradualism, became part of the mandate of the McGovern commission.

That commission's guidelines required state parties to add to their rules, and to apply, six detailed antidiscrimination standards promulgated in January 1968 by the Democratic National Committee. State parties were further required to "overcome the effects of past discrimination by affirmative steps to encourage minority group participation, including representation of minority groups on the national convention delegation in reasonable relationship to the group's presence in the population of the state"—the commission adding its understanding that "this is not to be accomplished by the mandatory imposition of quotas."

The Hughes Commission on the Democratic Selection of Presidential Nominees had recommended in 1968 that in the case of a challenge to a delegation to the national convention based on credible evidence of racial discrimination—such as a showing of one or more instances of exclusion on grounds of race at any level of party activity, or a showing that the representation of blacks on the delegation is grossly disproportionate to their percentage of the population of the state—the burden of proof before the Credentials Committee of the convention should shift from the challenger to the challenged delegation. An analogous shift in the burden of proof was a technique central to the enforcement machinery provided in the Voting Rights Act of 1965. Under Section 4(a) of that act, a state or county wishing to reinstitute a literacy test for voting, for example, which was suspended by the act, had to come into federal court and prove that for a period of five years no such test had been used for the purpose, or with the effect, of discriminating against black voters. Relying on the strong substantive requirements it laid down, the McGovern commission, however, did not adopt this procedural recommendation.

The McGovern commission required state parties to overcome, not only the effects of past discrimination against blacks, but also the effects of what is assumed to have been past discrimination against women and young people—the latter "defined as people of not more than thirty nor less than eighteen years of age." Again, with the understanding that no mandatory quotas were to be imposed, the commission required that the representation of women and the young be encouraged in reasonable relation to their proportion of a state's population.

APPORTIONMENT OF VOTING POWER IN THE CONVENTION

Delegate-selection methods are not the only feature of the convention that leaves something to be desired. Another is the complicated formula for apportioning voting power among the states. It begins in both parties—and has done so since conventions came into being in 1832—with the electoral college scheme. In the 1968 Democratic convention, for example, states received three votes for each vote they have in the electoral college. In addition, every state has two votes on the Democratic National Committee, and it got a convention vote for each of these. The next step in both parties is a bonus system, as it is called. In the 1968 Democratic convention, one bonus vote was awarded for each 100,000 popular votes cast in a state for the Democratic nominees at the last presidential election, and on top of that there was a ten-vote bonus if the Democratic nominees carried the state.

The end result is a considerable, if helter-skelter, departure from the population standard of representation. It is not that all the larger states are handicapped, although many of them were in 1968, or that any single region is favored or disfavored, although that will happen if the last previous ticket had some marked regional strengths or weaknesses, as the Republican ticket did in 1964; it is just that from the point of view of representing population there is considerable disarray.

The peculiar purpose that the electoral college system serves in the general election could be fulfilled in the convention only if all delegations were chosen in winner-take-all popular primaries, and happily—as noted earlier—they are not. So this purpose is simply irrelevant to the convention. There is a certain fitness, and little harm in a body so large, in following the electoral college scheme to the extent of giving the smaller states something of an advantage; the composition of the Senate does so in Congress. There is no justification however, for giving them an additional bonus by letting them vote their two representatives on the Democratic National Committee also.

Again, a flat ten-vote reward for carrying the state for the Democratic nominee—the same whether for New York or Montana—is a further unjustified weighting of representation in favor of the smaller states, especially since there is a proportional bonus for having attracted more popular support, namely, one convention vote for each 100,000 popular votes cast for the ticket. The Hughes commission recommended elimination of the extra votes for the Democratic National Committee membership and of the flat ten-vote bonus.

The 1968 Democratic convention did not respond directly to this recommendation of the Hughes commission, nor to other suggestions for revising the rules by which the convention is formed and conducted. But it did pass a resolution calling for appointment by the chairman of the

Democratic National Committee of a Rules Commission to study and evaluate proposals for reforming the rules, and to report to the 1972 convention. Such a commission was appointed by Chairman Fred R. Harris in February 1969, when he also constituted the McGovern commission. Headed by Congressman James G. O'Hara of Michigan, the Rules Commission entered upon its task.

CONVENTION MANAGEMENT, FLOOR PROCEEDINGS, AND SIZE

The Hughes commission also had some suggestions concerning the management of the convention and proceedings on the floor. Among them were these: that voting within the Democratic National Committee, which exercises vast powers in planning and controlling the convention, be weighted in proportion to the convention votes of each state; that chairmen of convention committees, such as Rules, Platform, and Credentials, be appointed well in advance of the convention and be provided with adequate staff; that the votes of members of these committees, in which the coalition-building process really begins in earnest, and on which the states are now equally represented, be weighted in proportion to each state's voting power in the convention itself; that if a challenge to a delegation is supported by at least a 10 per cent minority of the Credentials Committee, that delegation not be permitted to vote on any question before the convention until the challenge has been resolved, barring only the case where an opening would thus be given for an attempt to pack the convention, as when challenges are directed at a number of delegations which together comprise more than 20 per cent of the total voting power at the convention; that the party pay a per diem expense allowance to delegates, so that persons of moderate means may find it less burdensome to accept service as members of the convention; and that a roll-call vote be obtainable not only, as at present, at the request of eight delegations, but also at the request of 20 per cent of the delegates, so that a roll call can be forced by a minority that is dispersed geographically, as well as by minorities that are concentrated regionally.

Each of these recommendations is aimed at correcting practices that prevail in closely similar form in the Republican party, too, although in the Eisenhower-Taft contest at the 1952 Republican convention, delegations under a challenge supported by more than one-third of the Credentials Committee were not permitted to vote at all before final resolution of the challenge on the convention floor. In its first action, in November 1970, the O'Hara rules commission recommended that the membership of the convention's Rules, Platform, and Credentials committees be revised so as to reflect the size of each state's delegation to the convention. The O'Hara commission also recommended changes in the procedures followed by the Rules, Platform, and Credentials committees.

Another serious flaw is the elephantiasis of the conventions, and it is greatly and increasingly more serious in the Democratic than in the Republican party. There were 2,477 delegates to the 1956 Democratic convention, casting 1,372 votes, many of them, obviously, fractional. The Republicans had 1,323 delegates, all of them entitled to a full vote. That is still a great many, but the size of the Republican convention has remained fairly stable. The Democrats in 1968 nearly doubled the number of votes—to a total of 2,622—in an effort to eliminate fractional voting. The end result was an increase not only in votes but in membership. There are, in addition to voting delegates, alternates, who at the 1968 Democratic convention numbered almost again as many—2,512.

No parliamentary body can operate effectively as a parliament—it can operate as something else, but not as what it ought to be—even at the size of the Republican convention, let alone at the preposterous one the Democrats have let themselves arrive at. The idea initially, in the 1830s, was of a body more or less the size of Congress. Under present conditions, as David, Goldman, and Bain have justly charged, both individual delegations and the convention as a whole "provide apt illustration" of Madison's remark in the 58th *Federalist* "that in all legislative assemblies the greater the number composing them may be, the fewer will be the men who will in fact direct their proceedings."[4] And assuredly the general atmosphere of the convention—about which the less said, the better—and the inconsequence as well as disingenuousness of much that goes on at it are in part the results of undue size.

No doubt, one reason why the number of delegates has risen steadily is that the more seats and votes there are to distribute around, the more groups and interests—and the more contributors, dignitaries, and just fashionable friends—can be accommodated. The objectives of having a convention of suitable parliamentary size and keeping it adequately representative do pull somewhat in opposite directions. But they are not irreconcilable. And a drastic reduction in the present size of the conventions, and particularly of the Democratic convention, is imperative. What we have now is a mass meeting in a bull ring. It behaves that way, and we treat it that way.

The issues touched on in the two sections immediately preceding must be addressed honestly and intelligently—and soon—and the recommendations made by the McGovern commission, as well as the requirements it laid down, must be implemented by the Democrats and considered by the Republicans, too, if the at once disorderly and over-controlled, and inadequately representative convention that we now have is to become the responsive, responsible, and respected deliberative institution it must be to survive.

NOTES: POLITICAL PARTIES

Introduction

1. Everett Carll Ladd, Jr., *American Political Parties* (Norton, 1970), pp. 307-308.

2. The best journalistic account of the 1968 conventions is Norman Mailer, *Miami and the Siege of Chicago* (World Publishing, 1968). The incredible events transpiring in Chicago are thoroughly recounted in Daniel Walker, *Rights in Conflict: Report to the National Commission on the Causes and Prevention of Violence* (Dutton, 1968).

3. Samuel J. Eldersveld, *Political Parties: A Behavioral Analysis* (Rand McNally, 1964), p. 21.

4. Frank J. Sorauf, *Party Politics in America* (Little, Brown, 1968), p. 224.

5. A very good summary of this debate can be found in Sorauf, *Party Politics in America,* ch. 16.

6. Ladd, *American Political Parties,* p. 311.

Joseph Califano

1. *The Wall Street Journal,* June 23, 1970, p. 16.

2. R. MacNeil, *The People Machine: The Influence of Television on American Politics* (1968), p. 292.

3. *Red Lion Broadcasting Co.* v. *FCC,* 395 U.S. 367, 392, n. 18 (1969), quoting J. S. Mill, *On Liberty,* 32, R. McCallum ed., 1947.

4. The ABC network, on May 9, covered a speech by Chairman O'Brien in Milwaukee as a news event, with only 45 of its 160 affiliates carrying it, along with its five owned and operated stations.

5. *Red Lion Broadcasting Co.* v. *FCC,* 395 U.S. 367, 1969.

Alexander M. Bickel

1. Quoted in American Bar Association, *Electing the President* (1967), p. 23.

2. See J. R. Schmidt and W. W. Whalen, "Credentials Contests at the 1968—and 1972—Democratic National Conventions," 82 *Harvard Law Review* 1438, 1459 (1969).

3. United States Commission on Civil Rights, *Political Participation* (Washington, D.C., 1968), p. 60.

4. *The Politics of National Party Conventions,* p. 215.

INTEREST GROUPS

*Lobbying is a test—sometimes a raw test—of the judgment
and integrity of political officeholders, both elected and appointed.*

—Eugene McCarthy[1]

A traditional means of prompting governments to respond to the demands
of a particular segment of society is through interest-group activity.[2] An
interest or pressure group is an association of likeminded or similarly
situated individuals who organize for the purpose of obtaining favorable
governmental policies. Pressure groups are usually quite narrow in their
area of concern, laboring only to influence policy directly affecting their
welfare. This attempted persuasion is popularly known as "lobbying," and
a good portion of it is carried out by a paid agent, a "lobbyist," whose duty
it is to represent the interests of the pressure group before the government.
(The name *lobbyist* has its origins in the nineteenth-century practice of
group representatives "buttonholing" elected officials in the corridors of
Congress in behalf of their employers.)

The concept of lobbying is one which historically has not elicited a
favorable image. Only recently has the commonly held association between
lobbying and overt bribery or generally unethical behavior disappeared.
A rather interesting example of the distasteful flavor associated with pressure-group activity was articulated by the United States Supreme Court in
its unanimous opinion deciding the case of *Trist v. Child,* which branded
lobbying as a public wrong:

> *If any of the great corporations of the country were to hire
> adventurers who make market of themselves in this way, to procure
> the passage of a general law with a view of the promotion of their
> private interests, the moral sense of every right thinking man would
> instinctively denounce the employer and employed as steeped in
> corruption and the employment as infamous.*[3]

Lobbying has never numbered among those categories of preferred occupations which mothers dream their sons will enter.

However, the negative connotations of interest groups have recently
been significantly reduced. In part this has been due to social science
research which has demonstrated that such charges as flagrant bribery
and unprofessional standards have little factual basis, but are exaggerated
inventions.[4] Furthermore, there has been an increased awareness of the
positive role played by pressure groups. There is little doubt that interest

groups constitute a key linkage between the people and the government. The needs and opinions of functional interests are made known to political actors in a way that is not possible through the popular election system. It is through pressure-group activity that minority interests have their greatest impact on policy output.

Interest groups, of course, are not representative in the sense of reflecting the opinions of the people at large. By definition pressure groups promote the interests of their members only. Essentially this means that lobbies perform a linkage function exclusively for those who see fit to organize in the hope of advancing or protecting their own interests.

Interest groups can be classified into four categories. First, and perhaps most powerful, are the economic lobbies. These associations have as a primary goal the economic gain of their membership. Obvious entries in this category are the AFL/CIO, National Association of Manufacturers, farm organizations, veterans' groups, and the professional associations. The second group might be described as ideological interest groups, those concerned with the promotion of an ideal or belief. The National Council of Churches and the American Civil Liberties Union are two examples. Governmental associations constitute the third category. State and local governments often organize for the purpose of expressing their positions to the national government. The National League of Cities is one such organization. The final classification includes those groups seeking to improve the lot of minorities, such as the National Association for the Advancement of Colored People and the Anti-Defamation League. Any given interest group might easily fit under more than one of these groupings, depending upon the breadth of its activities. For example, the American Medical Association has both economic and ideological objectives.

The effectiveness of a pressure group in convincing the government to respond to its needs depends upon the resources of the group and how well these resources are employed. The two major raw resources which make interest groups strong are economic wealth and electoral power. Governmental bodies, especially Congress, are quite susceptible to overtures made by pressure groups which are able to extend (or withhold) large campaign contributions and those which boast of huge memberships that can be converted to votes at election time. The successful use of these resources can be seen in the operations of the wealthy petroleum lobby and the mass-membership labor unions. In addition, such factors as the prestige or status of the group and the expertise of its representatives enhance the potential power of a pressure group.

Interest groups attempt to influence governmental policy-making wherever possible. Lobbying is not restricted by institutional boundaries or organization charts. What an interest group is unable to accomplish in one governmental arena, it may try in another. Lobbying, of course, is most commonly associated with Congress. And, in fact, a good portion of interest-group activity takes place in the national legislature. Lobbyists continually keep in contact with congressmen, present research reports, testify at committee hearings, and maintain channels of communication with congressional staff. The objective of this activity is to keep the interest group's position in a favorable light and to insure that access is always available.[5]

Lobbying the executive bureaucracy follows the same pattern as interest-group activities in Congress, a continuous flow of information and consistent efforts to maintain access.[6] In much the same manner as congressional lobbyists concentrate on representatives predisposed to their cause, administrative lobbyists spend the greatest portion of their time on agencies which may have a direct effect on their clients. For example, farm groups work closely with the Department of Agriculture and unions maintain relationships with key personnel in the Department of Labor.

Lobbying activity directed at the courts must assume a different approach. Expectations of the judicial role directly prohibit pressure-group tactics commonly used in the legislative and executive processes. A lobbyist cannot approach a judge in his chambers and attempt to sway the judge's opinion on pending litigation. Such behavior would show flagrant contempt for the dignity of the judiciary. Because the courts have been specifically designed to be insulated from just such attempted influence, pressure-group activity must assume a profile which is legitimately within the bounds of judicial norms. This restricts interest-group efforts to participation in court suits. The lobby may actively support a party to a dispute with financial aid and legal assistance or may participate as a "friend of the court" in cases which may affect the group's interests. The American Civil Liberties Union and the National Association for the Advancement of Colored People are quite active in lobbying the judicial branch in this manner.[7] Interest groups may also affect the judiciary by entering the selection process. Labor and civil rights groups were major forces behind the Senate's rejection of President Nixon's nominations of Clement Haynsworth and G. Harrold Carswell to be Associate Justices of the United States Supreme Court.

Finally, interest groups often take their cause directly to the people, hoping to create public support for their objectives. The anticipated result of this strategy is to affect the government through public opinion. A pressure group may conduct an expensive public-relations campaign to promote itself. In recent years the trucking and rail industries particularly have followed this course.

Because of the important function played by interest groups in linking selected publics to the government, various proposals have been made to alter the activities and structure of the lobbying process. These reforms have concentrated on the techniques, representativeness, and effectiveness of interest groups. The selections reprinted below examine these interest-group reform attitudes.

The most traditional change which has been suggested revolves around the regulation of the activities or techniques of lobbyists. Those who have supported such regulation have been fearful of possible undue influence and shady dealings by representatives of interest groups. Reformers, however, have won only a partial victory in the battle for regulation. This victory primarily came with the passage in 1946 of the Federal Regulation of Lobbying Act.[8] This act requires public disclosure of lobbyists' activities, but enforcement of relevant provisions has only been sporadic.

In any event, it is doubtful that any regulation of lobbyists' techniques will encourage fundamental change. Lobby groups are generally in business not to make a better America, but purely to advance self-interest. This means that powerful pressure groups are too often effective at the expense of the public. For example, the petroleum lobby has generally achieved its goals, but a substantially pollution-free environment—in short, the common goal—has not been one of them. The Nader Report on the Federal Trade Commission has demonstrated this precise point:

> But the highway-automobile lobby is too strong for the weak willed FTC. This group, which has foisted miles of needless concrete on the nation at the expense of much needed mass transportation, consists of automobile manufacturers, highway contractors and subsidiary industries including the tire producers.[9]

David Hapgood's "The Highwaymen" demonstrates the disproportionate share of influence which a single economic interest can wield.

The major cause of this situation is the absence of countervailing interest groups.[10] Private groups are successful because there are no public interest groups to offset their power. For example, there is an American Medical Association, but no American Patients Association. The primary factors behind the failure to develop public interest groups are the same inhibitors of direct action (see Part One)—lack of interest and citizen apathy. At the very core of interest-group reform ideas lies the need to create public interest lobbies to initiate organized opposition to certain private interest groups. Dale Freeman's "The Poor and the Political Process: Equal Access to Lobbying" fully discusses proposed reforms in this area.

Finally, reformers have been interested in strengthening those few public interest groups that have attempted to affect governmental policy-making. To accomplish this end, analyses of successes and failures of interest-group efforts have been conducted in an endeavor to arrive at a formula for success. Tom Kahn's "Why the Poor People's Campaign Failed" discusses the weaknesses of one fledgling interest group working for social change and its unsuccessful attempt to convince the national government to respond fully to its members' needs.

THE HIGHWAYMEN

David Hapgood

Robert Moses had a vision. As he bestrode Manhattan Island, the master builder of New York gazed out over Long Island to the east and New Jersey to the west. Long Island was Moses country, lacerated with highways he had built. These highways dumped great masses of cars into Manhattan in the morning and brought them back at night, tides flowing at Moses's command. New Jersey was not part of Moses's domain, but the authorities were sympathetic; the rumor was that they intended eventually to convert their state into a 600-lane highway.

With both Long Island and New Jersey paved over, Manhattan would remain as a bottleneck. The island was clearly intended by nature to be a highway interchange and parking lot for its neighbors' cars. Moses, whose many jobs included that of City Construction Coordinator, had striven mightily for that goal with his tunnels and bridges and highways. But much remained to be done. People still occupied the space needed for cars.

So it was that Robert Moses designed the Lower Manhattan Expressway. It would connect the highways in New Jersey and Long Island via the East River bridges and the Holland Tunnel under the Hudson River. Cars and trucks would find it easy to cross the island; suburbanites could drive more quickly to city offices. And that was only the beginning, for Moses's vision foresaw four or five more expressways across the island. These projects would add to Moses's renown as the man who poured more cement than Pharaoh ever dreamed of. In the minds of those who believe that traffic should have the right of way over people, the plans were reasonable.

The Lower Manhattan Expressway was first drawn on the city map in 1941. In August, 1969, it was erased from the city map. This was the outcome of almost thirty years of political guerrilla warfare in which the residents of lower Manhattan won a rare victory over highway interests.

The battle of lower Manhattan was only the oldest of about two dozen conflicts over city highways that have broken out in recent years. Other skirmishes in Washington, D.C., Cambridge, San Francisco, New Orleans, and Nashville have escalated into what the press now calls national "highway revolt" in the cities.

That revolt pits the people who live in cities against the second most powerful lobby in the United States. (Everyone concedes first place to the military-industrial complex.) The lobby whizzes along on a superhighway it has paved for itself through the jungles of politics at the local, state, and national levels. There are almost no toll gates on that superhighway, and few red lights. The growing numbers of citizens who want to see more such controls installed have little reason to be hopeful. Despite occasional victories like that of lower Manhattan, most battles against city highways have been lost, mainly because it is the lobby, not the people, that has government support.

And no wonder. Money is the lifeblood of politics, and the richest blood that flows in the veins of state and local political organizations is derived from highways and their economic side effects. Nothing generates more financial return, legal or otherwise, to those in office than highway construction. Washington is the greatest source of highway-construction money, and it is unlikely that any official who wants to stay in Washington will put too many obstacles in the path of that money to the states. The conflict between those who do not want highways cutting into the cities and those who have a vested interest in seeing to it that city highways get built can only intensify. The stakes are very high, and not just in money, for the contest over federal highways involves, in a real sense, control of a large part of the American political process.

Congress gave the lobby its mandate in 1956 with the funding of the Interstate Highway Program. That program, the most precious jewel in the crown of the highwaymen, was set up in 1944. It was only modestly funded until 1956, when Congress decided that 90 per cent of the funds for the program's 41,000 miles of highway should come from the federal government. The total cost will exceed $60 billion. This is said to be the largest public-works program in history—which should ring an alarm in the minds of anyone familiar with public-works programs.

The financing of the Highway Program was a classic raid on the Treasury. In the annals of lobbying, the highwaymen who executed this coup deserve to be listed alongside those Chinese contractors who convinced the Ch'in emperors to build the Great Wall of China. There are certain similarities between the two operations.

The Great Wall was supposed to keep out Mongol invaders. The highway lobby's trump card was the claim that what it got Congress to call the "National System of Interstate and Defense Highways" would serve to move military units in case of war—making opposition to it seem somehow unpatriotic. Thus, the Lower Manhattan Expressway presumably would have made it possible to move troops up from New Jersey in the event that the Russians were foolish enough to invade Fire Island. The Great Wall did not keep the Mongols out, but the Chinese kept on building it over the centuries. Similarly, the interstate highways would be of no use in a 24-hour nuclear war, but, in 1968, Congress added on another 1,500 miles to the system. Doubtless, the Great Wall lobby in its time, like its American counterpart now, argued that the economy would go into a tailspin if the local contractors were deprived of work.

The arrangement by which money would be made available to finance the highwaymen's mandate was the lobby's greatest accomplishment. This arrangement, which cynics call the Ever-Normal Trough, requires that all revenues from the federal gasoline tax—now 4 cents a gallon—and other highway-related taxes (tires, spare parts) be set aside for highway construction alone. Instead of having to engage every year in the kind of undignified scramble for federal money that takes place over the Rivers and Harbors Appropriations bill, the highway lobby draws its sustenance from a trough that is refilled automatically every year without legislative appropriation. The act of filling the trough does not even appear in the federal budget. Money just pours into it at an annual rate of nearly $5 billion.

In a moment of inspiration, Congress named this device the "Highway Trust Fund." The idea is that the taxes are paid by people who use the highways and must be held in sacred trust for more highways. To use the money for any other purpose, the argument goes, would be to violate that sacred trust. Representative Jonathan Bingham (D-N.Y.), one of the small band of guerrillas who resist the highwaymen, asked not long ago what would happen if the principle of the Highway Trust Fund were to be applied to the federal tax on alcoholic beverages. Would the alcohol tax be spent only on building bars?

The lobby is both powerful and sophisticated. In contrast to its military-industrial big brother, the highway lobby is more local in its concerns, for the crucial decisions about highway routes, designs, and contracts, though subject to approval by the Bureau of Public Roads, are made at the state level, not in Washington. The lobby is an amorphous coalition; its influence upon Congress is often exerted through local political organizations.

The interests that benefit from highway construction are the most visible part of the lobby. They include the building contractors and the businesses which supply them with materials like asphalt, stone, and cement. Trucking companies are important. So are tire manufacturers. Among the unions, there are the building trades and the teamsters. Then there are the oil industry, whose sales go up with every mile driven, and the auto industry, which needs more roads on which to deploy its products. These last two giants are not so single-minded in their devotion to construction as are the other parts of the lobby. They have other interests, like repelling Ralph Nader and staving off further cuts in the oil depletion allowance.

But there is more to the lobby, for highways are not all there is to highway construction. The nineteenth-century "robber barons" who built the railroads across the United States made their fortunes not *on* the railroad but *by* it, on land suddenly made valuable by access to the railroad. The same is true of highways: more money is often made on the adjoining land than on construction of the roads themselves. So the most powerful thrust behind a highway is often not the men who will build it but the land speculators and developers who will exploit it.

In rural areas, where the land is undeveloped, money is made simply by new access to property. The highway comes through, land values sky-rocket, and speculators graze where cattle used to feed. Holiday Inns and gas stations sprout alongside the concrete. Almost everyone wants the high-way to come through or by his land. In the case of limited access roads, the struggle centers on the location of interchanges and exits, for that is where the property becomes most valuable.

In built-up areas, where the urban highways are being constructed, land manipulation is somewhat different. Here, the highway serves as a kind of explosive that blasts the pattern of land use. Urban highways typically are routed through low-density neighborhoods of one- and two-story buildings, neighborhoods that are ripe for development into high-density use: industry, commerical buildings, high-rise housing. Without a highway, development may be impossible because of zoning or the diffi-culties involved in assembling many small properties, or both. The highway literally acts as a blockbuster, smashing the neighborhood and scattering its inhabitants. Those who pick up the pieces can put them to profitable use.

Making money on highways requires political influence. The influence is used to get the highway routed through or by property you own, or it is used to find out where the highway is going before this knowledge becomes public. The officeholder has this inside information and can, if he wishes, pool his knowledge with a speculator's capital. Look at the route of a highway and the location of its exits, and you see a map of local political influence. Here is an orange-roofed restaurant on land recently bought by the county chairman (or, if he is timid, by his brother); over there ("Two Minutes From Freeway" reads the sign) is a shopping center owned by a man who, in turn, owns a public official. The recent Mafia investigations in New Jersey turned up the fact that a state senator, in partnership with a reputed Mafioso, owned land in the path of an onrushing federal highway. The investigators also learned that the alleged Mafioso had received almost $400,000 from the state for a tract needed for a highway, a tract for which he had paid $30,000. "Fair market value" is what the state is supposed to pay for land condemned for a highway; but fairness, of course, is in the eye of the state appraiser.

State and local officeholders have everything to gain from highway construction, on which they can get more bang for a taxpayer's buck than from any other kind of spending. For some, the return comes in the form of campaign contributions, which are legal; for others, it comes in the form of kickbacks, which are not. The contractors who build the road, and their suppliers, can be counted upon to express their gratitude in a form as concrete as the road itself. The land speculators will also chip in, if, indeed, the officeholder himself does not have a piece of the action. The delightful fact that highways need constant maintenance provides a third source of income. Each spring, the chosen contractor goes out to fill the potholes with tax money. Before too many years have passed, the spending on maintenance has exceeded the original cost of construction.

Furthermore, the profit to contractor and officeholder on highway work can be increased to the extent that competition can be prevented. Seldom has this tactic been as fully documented as it was by Arthur J. Holland, who served from 1959 to 1966 as mayor of Trenton, N.J., and is now a research specialist at the Rutgers University Center for Urban Studies in nearby New Brunswick. In 1956, Holland, then a young city official and candidate for the city commission, decided to take on the highwaymen by announcing that Trenton was paying too much for its street-paving work.

Paving work is done under specifications laid down by the municipalities. The "specs" dictate the kind of materials to be used and even the maximum distance from which they may be obtained. Buried in the technical jargon of the Trenton specs, Holland discovered, was a pot of gold. The prime beneficiary of that gold was the nearby Kingston Trap Rock Company, which quarries rock and makes building materials.

The specs required that building materials be obtained from a source not more than eleven miles from the City Hall of Trenton. As the alert reader may already have guessed, the eleven-mile limit reached just past Kingston's quarry. (The late Louis Josephson, the Trenton City counsel, was vastly amused by the boldness of that eleven-mile limit. "I asked them why exactly eleven miles," Josephson used to chuckle. "And you know what they actually told me? 'You have to draw the line somewhere'—that's what they said!")

Trenton's specs also restricted contractors to certain kinds of aggregates. (Aggregates, usually stone, are used for the road base as well as the surface.) In addition to trap rock, contractors were authorized to use granite or gneiss, neither of which was available within the eleven-mile limit. But they were not permitted to use gravel or dolomite or slag—all available, and all good enough for other municipalities. Thus, they could use only trap rock, and no one supplied trap rock except Kingston.

Arthur Holland then collected figures from around the state to find out what the Kingston monopoly was costing Trenton. It turned out that while Trenton was paying $14-15 a ton for its aggregates, the five other major cities in New Jersey were paying an average of $10.66. The smaller communities around Trenton were paying only $10.14. Holland also found that the elimination of competition on aggregates permitted the inflation of other parts of the paving bill. He compared the low bid offered on a Trenton street-paving job with the low bid on a job in Newark that was similar in all respects. These were the figures for the items other than aggregates:

	Trenton	*Newark*
Bituminous concrete (per ton)	$13.00	$9.00
Concrete base (per sq. yd.)	$ 4.90	$2.70
Excavation (per sq. yd.)	$ 1.10	$ .50
Preparation of sub-grade (per sq. yd.)	$ .40	$ .14
Concrete sidewalk (per sq. ft.)	$ .80	$ .50

The Newark prices were 29 per cent lower, and the Trenton low bidder would have been higher than all five of the contractors who bid in Newark. ("What do they steal in Newark?" cynics wondered.) At Newark prices, Holland calculated, Trenton would have saved $1 million over the previous ten years.

Political influence can be used to rig the specifications in other profitable ways. The "easiest way to steal," according to Holland, is to substitute cheaper or fewer materials than the specs require. Holland ordered borings in a Trenton street and brought up cheaper, forbidden dolomite (brought in by the contractor, Holland learned, from outside the eleven-mile limit) instead of the expensive trap rock required—and paid for—by the city. The danger that the street will show evidence of inferior work can be avoided by seeing to it that the specifications call for more elaborate paving than is necessary. (Trenton, for example, once specified an eight-inch base for an alley, while other cities only use six inches.) If the specs call for eight inches of trap rock, the contractor may try to fudge by putting in six inches of dolomite. Since the six inches of dolomite are an adequate base, there is no risk that the street will crumble and expose the disparity to public notice. The difference between what the city pays for and what it gets is pure gravy for the contractor and his friends in City Hall —except, of course, for the payment that must be made to the inspectors who supervise the work.

Rigging the specifications to prevent competition and permit stealing just adds frosting to the already rich cake of the Interstate Highway Program. For years, until the Highway Program tried to penetrate the cities, the lobby and its friends in government enjoyed that cake at their leisure. Who, after all, had reason to oppose them? When they are working outside the metropolitan areas—and only 6,000 of the federal system's planned 41,000 miles are urban—the highway builders do a job that is useful and often necessary. Across most of the United States, the motor vehicle (car, truck, and bus) is still the essential form of transportation. Some of the roads see precious little traffic—these are the four-lane highways from nowhere to nowhere—but even they provoke no great objection. Highways slicing through open country may destroy the environment, raising howls from conservationists, but they do not harm anyone's personal interest.

Quite the contrary. Property owners usually scramble to get their patches of woodland in front of the bulldozer in hopes of catching Howard Johnson's eye. The car-owning population sees a new highway as a benefit to itself. Any possible complaint a citizen might raise about how his tax money is spent is muffled by the Interstate Highway Program, for it allows everyone to use that fatally corrupting argument: the money's going to be spent anyway, so let's get our share of it.

The acceptance of highways rests also, of course, on the American love affair with the automobile. For most of us, the car is not just a means of transportation; it is a way of life, an essential status symbol, an object of conspicuous consumption, the vehicle to freedom. The young American male achieves his manhood when he gets his driver's license—remember? Our acceptance of the auto and the highway is ultimately self-perpetuating: more highways are built, public transport withers, and the auto does indeed become a necessity as well as a luxury. James Scott of the Highway Research Board, an arm of the National Academy of Sciences, cites a recent opinion study showing that many Americans have "close ego-involvement with the automobile as a way of life." Scott goes on to contend that mass transit will have to offer the consumer status as well as economy if it is to compete successfully with the automobile.

Popular opposition to the highwaymen did not begin until state and federal highway planners made the decision that the highways would extend not merely *to* the cities, but *into* them. Inevitably, this meant bulldozing people rather than pasture, and people in great numbers. Nor, as city-dwellers were quick to realize, was this for the city's benefit; rather, it was for the convenience of its suburban neighbors. Suburbanites own cars and want to drive to the city to work or to play (the railroad they used to ride is falling apart). But city-dwellers have no reason to drive to the suburbs. It is true that truckers and downtown stores benefit in the short run from city highways. But highways through the city destroy neighborhoods, increase traffic congestion on city streets, and further poison the air we breathe.

"What was love in the countryside began to look like rape in the city," wrote Louise Campbell in *City,* a magazine published by Urban America. In city after city, people have decided to fight the highways. Often, they also have to fight their own elected officials who cannot resist the temptation of those easy highway dollars or the pressure from the local political-business establishment. Many of these officials are minor. Some are not. The fiercer the battle, the higher the official it forces to take sides, since conflict tends to move decision-making upward. The public and private powers that line themselves up to march on the side of the lobby can be formidable.

Nowhere was this more evident than in the battle over the Lower Manhattan Expressway. Robert Moses is gone at last from the New York power structure, but the forces he represented are still there and are heavy with clout. Although Mayor John V. Lindsay killed the project, Expressway advocates included New York's most powerful men and institutions.

One was Harry Van Arsdale, the city's leading labor chief; he likes anything that provides work for the building trades. (Murray Kempton once wrote of the building trades that they have "never given the slightest cause for confidence that they would not pave over their parish priest if they were assured that the project would take a year and pay $3.50 an hour.") Another Expressway supporter was David Rockefeller, president of the Chase Manhattan Bank and perhaps the single most powerful man in New York. In the Wall Street financial district, just south of the Expressway's proposed route, people were less interested in construction of the Expressway than in the possible side effects. Smashing the neighborhoods of lower Manhattan would make valuable land available for high-rise office buildings. In anticipation, land prices doubled in the immediate area, though nearby they hardly changed. The 30-year shadow cast by the prospect of the Expressway has had the effect of raising land values while creating blight; no one wants to improve his property if he thinks it is going to be torn down.

The *New York Times* raised its powerful voice in support of the Expressway, although the *Times* has usually opposed the highway lobby and its works. Mayor Lindsay was on different sides at different times. As a Congressman, he was strongly against the Expressway. After he became Mayor, and after the Expressway was redesigned to be depressed rather than elevated, he came out for it. Finally, Governor Nelson Rockefeller, David's brother, was for the Expressway.

The opposition hardly seemed a fair match for the organization and power behind the Expressway. It came chiefly from citizens in the path of the proposed construction. The Expressway would have cut a slice through the ethnic mosaic of New York. Starting at the East River, the route would have gone through the Lower East Side, once the city's great Jewish ghetto and now a multi-racial cauldron, through Chinatown and Little Italy, and finally alongside Greenwich Village which, contrary to its reputation, is inhabited by people who are upper middle class—and very verbal.

The people of these neighborhoods fought their Thirty Years' War against the Expressway with the leadership of, among others, author Jane Jacobs, whose book *The Death and Life of Great American Cities,* shook the city planning establishment to its concrete foundations. The people, organized in shifting alliances, managed the unlikely feat of beating the Expressway. They won because they took advantage of a new issue—air pollution.

The city had made a study of the amount that the Expressway would be likely to produce, but it refused to admit that the study had been finished. Writer Mary Perot Nichols began asking in the *Village Voice* why the report was being kept secret, and Edward I. Koch, then a city councilman and now a congressman, finally forced the city to give him the report. Then he turned it over to the Scientists' Committee on Public Information, a volunteer group. The scientists issued a statement warning that air pollution would "cause the physical collapse of some people near the Expressway."

That statement, with its scientific imprint, provided fresh ammunition for the neighborhood groups; they started wearing gas masks to public meetings on the Expressway. Then, in the summer of 1969, some luck came their way. In June, Lindsay was beaten for renomination in his party's primary by a conservative, John J. Marchi, while another conservative, Mario Procaccino, was winning the Democratic primary.

Lindsay thus became the candidate of the small Liberal party. He was looking for support, and liberal Democrats were looking for someone to support. A bargain was struck: Lindsay came out against the Expressway, and the Expressway was taken off the map, presumably for good.

Other cities have won occasional battles against the highwaymen. New Orleans finally defeated the "expressway named destruction"—an elevated highway alongside the French Quarter—originally designed by a consultant from New York named Robert Moses.

But only one city in the United States—San Francisco—has developed anything approaching a *tradition* of victory over the highwaymen. Drawing perhaps on the vigilante spirit of their roaring past, San Franciscans beat off the highway builders and, in a magnificent gesture, tossed $280 million in federal funds back into the highway trough. The exact spot at which the highwaymen were repelled is marked by the Embarcadero Freeway, which hangs in mid-air, unfinished, in downtown San Francisco. Someday, there will be a statue there. The San Francisco Bay Area has embarked on a major new mass rapid transit system reaching out into the suburbs, in recognition of what everyone believes who isn't paid to believe otherwise: there are faster, cleaner, cheaper ways than the auto for moving people in and out of a city. Even Mayor Joseph Alioto spoke heresy: "We don't think we owe that much to the automobile." But, despite these examples, the highwaymen usually win.

Those who would like to believe that the power of the highway lobby may finally be diluted by the power of the federal government have little cause for optimism. The kind of attention being paid the problem by Congress, notably in the case of Washington, D.C., elicits nothing but cheers from the lobby. Since Congress controls the District of Columbia's budget, the freeway fight in Washington pits the opposition, mainly black ghetto residents, not only against the suburbs of Washington but also directly against the Congress of the United States.

The capital is already riddled with highways: 30 per cent of its land is occupied by roads, a percentage even higher than that of Los Angeles. Still unsatisfied, the highway builders set out to build more freeways from the suburbs, for the convenience of federal employees who live out of town. The planners proposed an $800 million package, of which the most disputed parts proved to be the Three Sisters Bridge across the Potomac and the North Central Freeway leading to the Maryland suburbs. The bridge would destroy nearly fifty-four acres of public land and defile historic sites on both sides of the Potomac. The North Central route has shifted with the political wind. The original route was along Wisconsin

Avenue, where traffic surveys said it should be. But that is well-to-do white territory, so the route was shifted further east, to go through low-income black neighborhoods. Congress even voted a law banning freeways west of 12th Street, on the white side of the racial dividing line. This is basic highway strategy: go where the clout is least. (One reason for not going into the commercial district is that the city would lose the taxes of businesses forced out by a highway.)

"Through the park or the ghetto" is the urban highway planner's slogan. In Washington, they tried both—North Central was at one time routed through Rock Creek Park. The blacks, no longer docile, rose in opposition, using tactics ranging from persuasion to disruption to fight the highway package at countless meetings. They call North Central "a white man's highway through black men's bedrooms." This description is entirely accurate—black homes would be destroyed for the benefit of white commuters—and it applies to many of the disputed city highways.

Congressional reaction to this revolt in its backyard was swift and brutal. The House inserted in the annual highway bill a section ordering the District to build Three Sisters and North Central. President Johnson intervened on the side of the District and blocked that dictate. But William H. Natcher (D-Ky.), chairman of the District Appropriations Subcommitte, insisted that his subcommittee would vote no funds for Washington's subway system—planned for several years—until construction of the highway package is under way. The District paid the highwaymen's ransom: finally the Council buckled under in the summer of 1969. The City Council, which had previously voted 8 to 0 against the freeway, acknowledged the political realities by agreeing to accept the freeway as the price for getting the subway. "This one smoked out the highway lobby," one observer commented. "They had to take off the velvet glove and use the mailed fist."

Congress has other ways of expressing its loyalty to the highwaymen. In 1968, $4.4 billion for highways poured into the Ever-Normal Trough, while Congress appropriated $140 million for mass transit. That 30-1 ratio is a fair representation of how the House votes on highway bills. (The House, where money bills originate, is the key body on highways.) When dissidents like Bingham or Richard (Max) McCarthy (D-N.Y.) of Buffalo offer a bill that the lobby dislikes—the one it hates most would permit diverting some of the money flowing through the trough to mass transit—they are supported by about a dozen other members of the House. The attempt to force the District of Columbia to build highways, perhaps the lobby's baldest act of the recent past, was opposed by only three of the thirty-four members of the House Public Works Committee —McCarthy, Jerome R. Waldie (D-Calif.), and Fred Schwengel (R-Iowa). McCarthy has been described as a congressman who "has kept his capacity for indignation even though he's on the Public Works Committee." McCarthy speaks with relish about the horrified reaction of his colleagues to Bingham's bill, which would have allowed cities to use "trust" money for any kind of transportation. "Like burning the flag!" McCarthy chuckles.

The Nixon Administration's strategy seems to be to appease the city dwellers at the lowest possible cost. Secretary of Transportation John A. Volpe is a highway enthusiast, but it was his decision to abandon the New Orleans expressway. Nixon and Volpe are also pushing a mass-transit program that, though token, is still a lot more than Washington has done in the past. Their program would provide $300 million for mass transit in 1971—almost twice the current amount—and up to $1 billion in 1975. Of course, Congress would have to appropriate the money, and the Nixon-Volpe team opposes a mass-transit trust fund as much as they favor the highways' Ever-Normal Trough. Besides, their mass-transit program would provide only two-thirds federal funding, whereas the highway program, with its 90 per cent federal funding, will remain irresistible to most construction-hungry city officials.

Yet it is true that the odds against those who oppose urban highways today are somewhat less than they were in Moses's day. Optimists point out that America's love affair with the automobile may be passing out of the honeymoon stage, thanks in part to Ralph Nader. Criticism of the automobile itself and of the highway establishment is appearing more and more frequently in the national media. Nothing has done more for that trend than Jane Jacobs's landmark book, which inspired the middle classes to take up arms in a battle that had been fought only by the people in the path of the bulldozer.

The planning of city highways is being changed somewhat by the "urban design concept team." The idea, devised by Baltimore architect Archibald Rogers, is to bring into the planning process, typically monopolized by engineers, such men as environmental scientists and sociologists. Rogers conceived of this tactic for his own city, then beset by plans for three federal highways, one of them originally laid out by, of course, Robert Moses. The group assembled through Rogers's efforts got a $4.8 million grant from the Department of Transportation to redesign Baltimore's highways in such a way as to make them as sound as possible—environmentally. The idea is becoming fashionable; similar teams are at work in Chicago and Brooklyn.

But these are victories in a losing war. Even the urban design concept team has severe limitations; the Baltimore group could reduce the destruction but not block the highway entirely. "Design concept" deals with how a highway is built, not whether—and whether is where the crunch occurs. The highway lobby does not care how a highway is built, elevated or depressed, as long as it is built, and as long as the city's dependence on the automobile and truck is increased.

A large battle over the future of the entire Interstate Highway Program is shaping up . . . , and the lobby has already begun preparing for that fight. The precipitating factor is the expiration date of the "trust fund." Created in 1956, the trust fund was originally due to expire in

1972; it has already been extended to 1974. No one can expect the high-waymen to give up $5 billion a year without a fight. Their first step in the campaign to keep the trough flowing after 1974 was a presentation to Congress by the American Association of State Highway Officials (AASHO) in 1967. AASHO thinks big. The United States should, AASHO told Congress, spend $285 billion on roads in the decade 1975-85. Then, having proved it can count as high as the military-industrial complex, AASHO tempered its demands: the U.S. could "partially" meet its highway needs by spending only $78 billion—two-thirds of it from the Ever-Normal Trough, the rest to be paid by the states.

The lobby is paid and professional: it has planners on tap to prove whatever needs proving. (Robert Moses's favorite planners once proved that 80 per cent of the traffic on the Lower Manhattan Expressway would be interstate and then proved that 80 per cent of it would be local.) City antihighway groups usually disappear as organizations after their own battles are lost or won. A reservoir of antihighway opinion exists among residents of threatened neighborhoods, conservationists, planners, and, most recently, environmental scientists, but up until now, nobody has tried to bring these dissidents together as a national pressure group.

The highway revolt is against the tyranny of the machine—the high-way bulldozer and the political machine that drives it. Being helpless before the highway lobby is just one form of the powerlessness that Americans increasingly resent. Seen from this perspective, the battle between city people and the highway establishment is one front in the developing struggle between those who want to redefine America and those who want to keep it the way it was.

THE POOR AND THE POLITICAL PROCESS: EQUAL ACCESS TO LOBBYING

Dale C. Freeman

INTRODUCTION

Lobbying—broadly defined as "any intentional effort to influence legisla-tion"[1]—is an essential part of effective democratic government in the United States. It provides a unique type of political expression, through which pressure groups formulate policies and seek their implementation, provide public officials with much needed information, and, by making their individual concerns well known, help to define the public interest. More generally, lobbying serves as a mechanism supplementary to the constitutionally prescribed legislative process, for resolving the inevitable conflicts among the diverse interests of society.

As a means of resolving conflicts and balancing interests, however, the lobbying mechanism has several weaknesses. In the first place, it is open to flagrant abuse. The practices of lobbyists in the nineteenth and early twentieth centuries provoked periodic scandals. Bribery and blackmail, practices which are hardly conducive to a just appraisal of competing interests, were not uncommon lobbying techniques. The calibre of lobbying activity has generally improved during this century; but abuse is still prevalent, albeit in more sophisticated guises.

Secondly, even the most legitimate forms of lobbying are somewhat covert in their operation, so that the public rarely knows what kinds of bargaining lie behind any particular legislative decision. It is not generally known, for example, how witnesses before congressional committees are selected, or how influential their testimony is. As a result the public can only apply an outcome-determinative test to the lobbying process, judging lobbying by the quality of the legislation it helps to produce, without being able to evaluate the process itself. In other words, the public has no way to discover whether the balancing function is being performed in the best possible way.

Lobbying can be defended as a beneficial device for balancing conflicting interests within society only on the assumption that all relevant interests are fairly represented in the process. The inaccuracy of this assumption in the past has been well established. A method for correcting the balance is the subject of this [article].

The connivance between elected representatives and the lobbyists of powerful special interests, and the resulting exclusion of the public interest from the process of government, were recognized early in this century. Since then there have been a number of exhaustive studies of lobbying, all of which, to one degree or another, have concluded that the interests of business and other well-financed and well-organized groups carry disproportionate weight in the legislature.[2]

> *All too often the operations of large pressure groups prevent rather than encourage the balanced compromises that are the goal of the democratic system. All too frequently the legislative contests are uneven, and in too many instances the lobbyists serve to retard rather than advance the general welfare.*[3]

The right to lobby is grounded in the First Amendment's guarantees of free speech and the right to petition for the redress of grievances. These rights are guaranteed to all citizens alike, but the disproportionate power of some private interests has such a distorting effect on the political process that many less powerful interests are excluded altogether. Representative

Buchanan, chairman of the House Select Committee on Lobbying Activities, noted in 1950 that lobbying is a "sacred right" which some make more meaningful than others. The individual consumer and the billion dollar corporation have equal rights before the law, he remarked, "but are they equal before the lawmakers?"[4]

Despite its defects, there are few who would do away with lobbying, not only because of an unwillingness to infringe upon constitutional liberties, but also out of an affirmative conviction that a fair and open lobbying mechanism can be valuable to the democratic political process. Response to the perceived inequities of lobbying, therefore, has been limited to various schemes for its modification or regulation. As we shall see, direct statutory regulation of lobbying and indirect regulation through the taxing power have been the devices relied upon to accomplish these ends. Extensive changes in the existing schemes have often been recommended, and new, more exotic, schemes have been proposed.

But these efforts have been inadequate. Lobbying abuses are still pervasive. The poor and the unorganized consumer public, the ultimate victims of these abuses, are still without viable representation in the lobbying process. This [article] considers why these efforts have been inadequate and urges a new effort on the part of Government, which can help not simply to remedy abuses, but to mold the lobbying process into an effective force for social justice in the United States.

I. LOBBY REGULATION AND THE LEGISLATIVE BALANCE

A. Restructuring Congress

The most radical proposals for curing the ills of lobbying call for an outright restructuring of Congress. These proposals proceed from the fact that the American system of geographic representation is no longer as accurate a reflection of the varying interests within the country as it once was. The economic development of the United States has created strong functional interests which transcend geographic boundaries and override regional concerns. While it may be simplistic in these days of increased racial and cultural awareness to define group interests strictly in terms of economic condition, it is undeniable that geographic proximity is no longer an accurate guide to compatibility of views, if it ever was. Because the congressional system of representation by districts does not account sufficiently for more specialized social and economic interests, lobbying had developed as a means by which these interests can be heard. Because of this, it has been suggested that the way to curb lobbying is to revise the Constitution to eliminate the geographical system of representation. More practically, it has also been proposed that Congress establish advisory councils to represent economic interests as a supplement to geographic interests.

But proposals for such functional representation have not been particularly well-received. Not only does functional representation run counter to the American political tradition, but also the task of implementing such a system would be formidable. Parliaments of industry and advisory councils have actually been adopted in Europe, but results in these countries have not indicated that a formal joining of politics and economics is an effective solution to the problem of pressure groups. And even if a system of functional representation could be implemented in this country, the same kind of imbalance which now characterizes lobbying would probably be reflected on the floor of Congress.

Another school of thought attributes the undue influence of special interest groups to the committee system in Congress. According to this analysis, the mechanics of congressional leadership tend to consolidate power in a few key men, who in turn control the operation of certain influential committees and subcommittees. By winning over one strategically placed legislator, an interest group can achieve remarkable results in Congress as a whole. The Senate and House Agricultural Committees offer a case in point. The 1968 report *Hunger, USA*, issued by the "Citizens' Board of Inquiry," concluded that

> *the composition of the Agricultural Committees of Congress— which pass upon major food assistance legislation—dictates that inevitably the needs of the poor and hungry will be subordinated to the interests of the large agricultural producers.*[5]

To avoid this situation, it has been suggested that the committee system be either substantially modified or completely eliminated. Rather than rely on committees to evaluate the merits of proposed legislation or to investigate the need for new legislation, Congress could, for example, establish a body of professional researchers to perform these functions. Comprehensive reports on each proposal would be submitted to all Senators and Representatives, who would debate the issues in full session in their respective Houses, and then vote on each particular proposal. In this way, much of the need for lobbyists as sources of information would be obviated; and the overweening influence of individual Congressmen, with its vast potential for corruption and abuse, would be reduced.

This proposal, while it merits serious consideration, has its weaknesses. The abolition of congressional committees runs counter to the jealous regard which most, if not all, Congressmen have for their powers and prerogatives. The likelihood of success for such a proposal is, thus, negligible. Furthermore, even a team of professional researchers could not be relied upon to elicit all the interests involved in a given issue. As in the present system, there would inevitably be groups whose interests were not perceived as relevant to the proposal being examined and who would, thus, still be excluded from the legislative process.

B. Registration and Disclosure

The most direct attempt to curtail the abuse of congressional lobbying has been the Federal Regulation of Lobbying Act of 1946. The weaknesses of the Act have been exhaustively discussed, and need little treatment here. It has been quite ineffective in bringing the inequities of federal lobbying under control. Many organizations which engage in extensive campaigns to influence legislation have managed to avoid registering under the Act, and many of those who do register provide such incomplete information that it is hard to draw any conclusions about the scope of their activities or the impact they have. Since 1946 there have been several congressional studies of lobbying activity, and each has produced a spate of recommendations, none of which has yet been implemented.

The Buchanan Committee reported in 1950 that "to the extent that some groups are better endowed than others, there is a disparity in the pressure which these groups can exert on the policy making process."[6] The Committee did not feel, however, that the situation called for any major revisions in the Lobbying Act. Instead, they felt that the proper control of lobbying lay in strengthening the political parties and party discipline, since it was when the parties were weak that pressure groups had the most influence. The few changes in the Act which the Committee did propose were designed principally to disclose the identity and financial participation of those who supported lobbying activity. Such information, it was felt, would enable Congress and the people to evaluate group pressures.

In 1956, a Special Senate Committee to Investigate Political Activities, Lobbying and Campaign Contributions again looked into the activities of pressure groups in the legislative process. According to Senator John F. Kennedy, a member of the committee, the ultimate goal of these investigations, and Congressional lobbying legislation in general, was to "provide sound legislative action by Congress, aided in its deliberations by the arguments, positions and presentations of *all* segments of our population."[7] In 1957, the Final Report of the Committee recommended extensive changes in the 1946 Lobbying Act. Among the major innovations of the proposed Legislative Activities Disclosure Act was an enforcement mechanism and more definite criteria of applicability. The Act included a prohibition of attempts by private individuals and groups to influence Congress through the use of spurious telegram campaigns.

The Senate Committee in 1957, like the Buchanan Committee in 1951, was convinced that full disclosure was an effective means of controlling abuses. It was their feeling that a major purpose of the 1946 Act was to begin a process of public education about "the role and responsibilities in our political system of the pressure group.[8] The committee believed that "persistent prodding through official notices and civil actions will continue the process of education well begun under the existing law."[9] They appear to have reasoned that as the public became better informed about the kinds of activity in which pressure groups engaged, the existing pressure groups would be constrained to keep their activities within acceptable limits, and other members of the public would take a more active role in "aiding" Congress in its deliberations.

It may be reasonable to assume that the prospect of full disclosure will keep most lobbyists from engaging in unfair practices; it seems unduly sanguine, however, to make the further assumption that "all segments" of our very heterogeneous society, provoked by such disclosures, will begin to make their special interests known to Congress in any meaningful way. It is generally agreed that the impact of an interest group is more or less proportional to such factors as the availability of resources (including money and access to the media), the prestige of the group and of its individual members, the degree and appropriateness of the group's organization, and the degree of cohesion it can achieve in a given situation. The consumer public in general and the poor in particular lack the prestige, organization, cohesion, and resources which they need to give their interests political viability, yet it is presumably these very groups from whom Senator Kennedy especially wished to receive "arguments, positions and presentations" as an aid to "sound legislative action."

The proposed Legislative Activities Disclosure Act of 1957 did not pass. A similar bill, proposed in 1967, met the same fate. Despite this conspicuous lack of success, there remain strong advocates of lobby regulation reform in Congress, and perhaps some changes will ultimately be made. Even those who have not supported the proposed amendments have favored some kind of reform. But statutory regulation can be effective only in protecting against abuse of the lobbying process by those already engaged in it. Regulation is not a creative process; it cannot call into being that which is not already there. Interest groups lacking the prerequisites for entrée into the political-legislative process will not be substantially aided by regulatory schemes aimed at preventing abuses.

C. Regulation by Taxation

Besides direct, statutory regulation, the other major device used by Congress to control attempts to influence legislation has been the taxing power. By allowing or disallowing deductions for specified kinds of lobbying activity and by conditioning tax status on, among other things, the extent of legislative activity, Congress has been able to influence who lobbies, in what way, and how much. Section 501(c) of the Internal Revenue Code sets out a list of organizations exempted from the income tax. Subsection 501(c) (3) exempts organizations operated exclusively for religious, charitable, scientific, educational or other similar purposes, provided that "no substantial part" of the organization's activities consists of attempts to influence legislation or participation in political campaigns. By section

170(c) (2), contributions to organizations which qualify for tax exemption under section 501(c) (3) are made tax deductible.

It is possible for organizations which engage in lobbying activity to remain tax exempt, but any group which relies heavily on private contributions for support is compelled to maintain its section 501(c) (3) status in order that donors may continue to deduct their contributions from gross income. Since most charitable institutions and organizations dedicated to public rather than private interests are in fact dependent on private contributions, the Internal Revenue Code is an effective control on the amount of activity by these groups devoted to influencing legislation.

On the other hand, Congress has also seen fit to provide incentives for lobbying by certain groups under specific circumstances. Section 162(e), a 1962 amendment to the Code, allows a deduction as an "ordinary and necessary" business expense for the cost of preparing and presenting testimony, statements, or communications before Congress or other legislative body on legislation of direct interest to the taxpayer. Deductions are also allowed for various other expenditures made in connection with this kind of activity. In recommending enactment of section 162(e), the Senate Finance Committee stated,

> It is . . . desirable that taxpayers who have information bearing on the impact of present laws, or proposed legislation, on their trades or business not be discouraged in making this information available to the Members of Congress or legislators at other levels of Government.[10]

The majority report also argued that it was illogical to allow deductions for expenses incurred in connection with judicial and administrative proceedings, but not to allow a deduction for similar legislative appearances.

The Finance Committee apparently did not perceive the even greater illogic in allowing a tax deduction to business groups for lobbying expenses while penalizing public interest groups for the same kind of activity. As Senators Gore and Douglas noted in their minority report,

> [T]he relationship of this provision [section 162 (e)] to the whole process by which our citizens seek to influence the enactment of legislation at all levels of government was not adequately considered.[11]

The inequities inherent in section 162(e) have been dramatically illustrated recently in a controversy involving the Sierra Club, a well-known conservation organization.[12] Until 1966, contributions to the Sierra Club qualified for deductions under section 170(c) (2), and the Club itself was tax-exempt under section 501(c) (3). In June of 1966, the Club placed advertisements in *The New York Times* and *The Washington Post* announcing its opposition to legislation which proposed constructions of power dams in the Grand Canyon, and urging the public to contribute to the fight against the project by writing their Congressman and supporting the Sierra Club.

Not long after these ads appeared, the Internal Revenue Service revoked Sierra's section 501(c) (3) exemption and ruled that contributions to the Club would no longer be allowed as deductions. As a result, the Club's revenues fell off an estimated $5000 per week. In the view of the IRS, the newspaper ads constituted an attempt to influence legislation and, as such, were a "substantial part" of the Club's activity. Thus, the Sierra Club was penalized for its efforts to oppose the Grand Canyon legislation. Meanwhile, due to section 162(e), the power companies on the other side of the controversy could deduct their own expenses in lobbying *for* the bill, as well as any dues paid to organizations which were used for similar purposes.

The propriety of the IRS' action in the case of the Sierra Club is questionable on a number of grounds. The case also brings out the inconsistencies and inequities in the way Congress currently uses the taxing power to regulate lobbying activity. By exempting charitable and educational institutions from taxation, and allowing tax deductions for the contributions they rely on for support, Congress indicated a desire to encourage the meritorious goals which these groups pursue. Prominent among their activities in recent years have been efforts to find a solution to such problems as racial discrimination, poverty, urban decay, and education. In recent years, Government has assumed an ever larger role in this attempt to construct a more just society, by stepping into areas of social policy formerly the exclusive domain of private social-service organizations. But the present tax laws make it difficult for charitable groups to make a rational adjustment to this fact of contemporary life.

It is deplorable that the tax laws constitute a barrier between the private charitable agencies and the legislative process, when collaboration and coordination would seem to be more fruitful for all concerned. Under the present system, any organization which, out of a purely selfless regard for the general welfare, attempts to improve the quality of federal legislation by sharing the fruits of its expertise and experience with the legislators and the public, risks losing the very tax status it relies on to insure sufficient income. Since the IRS is sporadic in its investigations, an institution runs the greatest risk when it is most highly visible, which is likely to be the time when it is struggling hardest to make its views known.

> *In the present day context, it is difficult to reconcile a law which purports to encourage private participation involving social problems with a restriction in the same law which cuts off the incentive as soon as private groups attempt too vigorously to make their views known to the one agency—the Government—whose actions far surpass in importance and scope those of all other agencies combined.*[13]

In 1959, in *Cammarano v. United States,* the Supreme Court upheld as a valid exercise of the Commissioner's rule-making power the Treasury regulations disallowing deductions as ordinary and necessary business expenses for expenditures made in attempts to influence legislation, even where the proposed legislation presented a direct threat to the taxpayer's business. A principal ground relied on by the court to justify the disallowance was the need to maintain a balance in the treatment of business and non-business taxpayers. The Court reasoned that business groups should be required to pay for lobbying activity "entirely out of their own pockets, as everyone else engaging in similar activities is required to do under the provisions of the Internal Revenue Code."[14]

In a flood of legal comment following *Cammarano,* the Court's conception of a tax equilibrium was criticized. One commentator suggested that the need to preserve an equilibrium in political-legislative restrictions between the private and public sectors might best be served by giving a liberal interpretation to the restrictions imposed on political activity by section 501(c) (3) or by eliminating it altogether, rather than by restricting business group lobbying. The response of Congress to *Cammarano* was to pass section 162(e), which benefited only business group lobbying and thereby vitiated any notion of a balance between public and private interests which *Cammarano* might have announced.

Since the passage of section 162(e), commentators have suggested a selective interpretation of the substantiality test of section 501(c) (3), repeal of the lobbying restrictions in that section and in section 170(c) (3),[15] and a modification of lobbying restrictions on charitable institutions to conform to the treatment given to business groups. These proposals all implicitly recognize the marked advantage now enjoyed by well-organized and well-financed private interests in the lobbying process, and seek to limit that advantage by enhancing the ability of less well-organized and less well-endowed organizations to compete. But like direct statutory regulation of lobbying, these proposals do little to bring into the political-legislative process those inchoate interests currently outside it. Eliminating the restrictions on political activity by non-profit groups does nothing for those people who remain unorganized and without financial support.

D. Toward Greater Participation

1. Public Lobby Organization.   One proposal which does seek to encourage wider participation in the political process by groups currently excluded is Professor Cooper's plan for a public lobby organization. This proposal would create a special new tax status for organizations wishing to engage in "public-interest" lobbying. Groups in this category would be eligible for some tax benefits, but would be subject to special protective standards. To prevent a public lobby from representing too narrow a point of view, and becoming a mere propaganda organ for aready strong economic interests, the lobby would be required to remain independent of any other organization, such as an industrial corporation, which had not passed a "public interest" test by being certified under section 501(c) (3). A public lobby could also be required to remain multi-purpose rather than concentrating on one issue. Tax benefits to any one taxpayer for contributions to public lobbies could be limited to small annual amounts to avoid the possibility of a lobby being dominated by one source of income. Benefits could also be limited to individual rather than corporate taxpayers. Further, benefits would be in the forms of a tax credit rather than a deduction, so the value of the benefit would not vary according to the tax bracket of the contributor.

The principal virtue of Cooper's proposal is that it provides at least some incentive for even the smallest taxpayer to involve himself in the political-legislative process. With a tax benefit in the form of a limited credit, the taxpayer would have a choice between sending his money to the government or sending it to a public lobby, whose purposes reflected his own concerns. Given such a choice, a significant number of people would probably opt for the tax credit, and in that way obtain at least a minimal stake in the exercise of government. Of course, there remains the problem that those with the fewest tax dollars are generally the same people whose interests are presently the most easily neglected. The tax group whose interests need the most support would be least able to take advantage of the benefits conferred by tax credits.

A more fundamental weakness of the public lobby proposal is that it fails to reach the poor non-taxpayer. Professor Cooper himself notes,

> *We must resign ourselves to the fact that any use of the tax law to stimulate the public vote is going to discriminate against non-taxpayers.*[16]

Cooper assumes that the consequences of this weakness are mitigated by the fact that, since the income tax reaches relatively low income levels, "it is reasonable to expect that the non-taxpayer groups would receive substantial benefits from the stimulated public voice."[17] But this assumption seems unjustified on a number of grounds.

First of all, it implies an identity of interest between the marginal taxpayer and the non-taxpayer. While there is undoubtedly some uniformity in the views of these two groups, particularly in the demand for improved public services, it is unlikely that those already supporting existing federal poverty programs, even with their few tax dollars, would consistently contribute to lobbies dedicated to expanding them.

Secondly, even where there is a compatibility of interest, the marginal taxpayer, as already noted, is limited in his ability to take advantage of the benefits conferred by a tax credit because of his small tax bill.

Finally, Cooper's assumption is particularly unacceptable because it emphasizes substantive results and neglects the process by which the results are achieved. Results are important, but there is a point at which even the most spectacular results do not compensate for the exclusion of substantial numbers of people from the political process. During the 1960's there has been a tremendous increase in the amount of federal money devoted to social service programs, yet there is now more unrest and discontent than ever before. Much of this dissatisfaction can be attributed to a rising level of expectation. But it also indicates that the poor cannot simply be bought off. Whatever device is used to adjust the balance between public and private interests in the political-legislative process, it must be one which does more than produce programs for the benefit of the economically depressed. It must bring "all segments of our population" into the process itself.

2. Contingent-fee Lobbying.   A second possibility for enabling people to have an impact on the legislative process, regardless of economic condition, would be to permit contingent-fee lobbying. Professional lobbyists could be paid out of the proceeds derived through their efforts. Although this kind of lobbying has traditionally been disapproved on the ground that it would encourage abusive and corrupt practices, in 1957 the Senate Special Committee to Investigate Political Activities, Lobbying and Campaign Contributions reported that ". . . it appears to us more desirable to proscribe pernicious activities on the basis of what they are and not on the basis of when and how payment is made for them."[18] Senator John F. Kennedy analogized contingent-fee lobbying to the widespread use of contingent fees in the tort field and perceived no reason to distinguish between the two practices. Both the Committee and Senator Kennedy perceived that to prohibit the practice would, in some cases, deprive the indigent of redress. As a result, the proposed Legislative Activities Disclosure Act, endorsed by the Committee, did not include any prohibition on contingent-fee lobbying; nor did the proposed amendments to the Federal Regulation of Lobbying Act introduced in the ninetieth Congress.

Unfortunately, the effectiveness of contingent-fee lobbying contracts as a means of giving the poor entrée to the political process would be limited, since the only people who could benefit from such an arrangement, aside from the lobbyists themselves, would be those who had specific claims against the Government, collectible only by special act of Congress. The poor, as a class, would still be excluded, and their interests still neglected.

In sum, it is apparent that the major thrust of the efforts so far to reform lobbying has been to perfect the lobbying mechanism by developing a more equitable balance among the conflicting interests already represented in the political-legislative process. Insufficient attention has been paid to the groups outside the political process which, because they lack the necessary organization, cohesion, and resources, find it impossible to enter. It is not a sufficient answer to say that there are individuals and groups of strong social consciousness who are prepared to lobby on behalf of the poor. In a democratic society, government is not simply a matter of ends; the means are equally important. The past year has seen the beginning of a movement to bring more "power to people," to democratize the political process down to its very roots. Lobbying, as an integral part of the political process, must also be made more democratic. All interest groups, including the poor and the consumer-public, must be given genuine opportunities to influence legislation through the lobbying process. It is the thesis of this [article] that the obligation to provide such opportunities lies with Government, which can successfully fulfill its obligation only by providing direct support for lobbying activities.

II. PUBLIC SUBVENTION OF LOBBYING

In *Slee v. Commissioner,* in referring to provisions of the 1921 Revenue Code allowing deductions for contributions to organizations operated exclusively for religious, charitable, scientific, literary or educational purposes, Judge Learned Hand declared that

> *political agitation as such is outside the statute, however innocent the aim. . . . Controversies of that sort must be conducted without public subvention; the Treasury stands aside from them.*[19]

Thirty years later, in *Cammarano v. United States,*[20] Justice Harlan invoked the wisdom of Hand and stated that the Treasury regulations contested in *Cammarano* were "a further expression of the same sharply defined policy."[21] Whether the policy against public subvention of activities to influence legislation is as "sharply defined" as the Court seemed to think is open to question, but, if we assume *arguendo* that there is such a policy, it can be challenged on a number of grounds.

In 1967, in his message to Congress on campaign financing, President Johnson declared that:

> *Public participation in the processes of government is the essence of democracy. No Government can long survive which does not fuse the public will to the institutions which serve it. The American system has endured for almost two centuries because the people have involved themselves in the work of their Government, with full faith in the meaning of the involvement.* But Government itself has the continuing obligation second to no other—to keep the machinery of public participation functioning smoothly and to improve it where necessary so that democracy remains a vital and vibrant institution.[22]

President Johnson's words were written as a preamble to a proposal for the financing of presidential campaigns by permanent Congressional appropriation, but they also provide an eloquent statement of the need to bring all Americans into the political process, and of the duty of Government to take definite steps in that direction.

Since 1930, when Judge Hand first disapproved public subvention of attempts to influence legislation, the role of the federal government in providing for the public welfare has expanded dramatically. Such programs as Social Security, Old Age Assistance, and Workmen's Compensation, commonplace today, were regarded then with suspicion and distrust. The Government is now involved in a variety of activities, involvement in which would have been unthinkable only a short while ago. A proposal for publicly supported lobbying thus seems far less heretical today than it would have in the days of Judge Hand. The notion of the government's paying to have itself lobbied seems even less implausible when one recalls that Neighborhood Legal Services throughout the country, funded by the Office of Economic Opportunity, are constantly bringing suit against local, state, and federal officials and frequently winning.

Another consideration which undercuts Judge Hand's policy against public subvention of "political agitation" is that the quality of lobbying has changed since 1930. The old fashioned type of lobbyist who sought to coerce or corrupt Congress in behalf of his private clients is not the problem he once was. Rather than direct contact, lobbyists today rely heavily on the printed word as a means of pursuing legislative aims. In fact, the increasing reliance on the mass media to mold public sentiment may be the most significant contemporary development in pressure group activity. Although direct contact is still a useful technique, the emphasis is increasingly on grassroots campaigns designed to stimulate public opinion and thus to influence the legislators indirectly. A natural concomitant of this development is an increased public awareness about current issues. As interest groups work to stimulate public opinion in favor of their viewpoint, they in effect educate the people about the problem involved. Of course the information the public receives is likely to be slanted, but too flagrant distortion runs the risk of exposure and discredit, and competing interests presumably provide or could provide the other side of the argument.

The educational aspect of grassroots lobbying, and the increasing use of this technique among pressure groups, provide another reason for public subvention of lobbying activity. The Senate Special Committee believed that a major purpose of the 1946 Lobbying Act was public education about "the role and responsibilities in our political system of the pressure group."[23] But the Act has not stimulated the broad-based participation in the political-legislative process which the Senate Committee hoped for, and the need for such participation is even more acute than it was in 1957. Education of the public remains a prerequisite to any meaningful participation. For the Government to assume this educational function directly would be impossible; the issues are too numerous and too varied. Those people whose interests are most intimately affected by the issues concerned are potentially the most qualified to educate others about them. The Government can contribute to this kind of public education indirectly, by providing financial support for the right kind of lobbying activity.

It has been suggested that a program of federally-subsidized lobbying would result in increased pressures on policy making and would for this reason be undesirable. A recent study of congressional lobbying reported that "Congressmen see interest groups as having a helpful and legitimate role in the legislative process," which is that "of providing information, opinion, and support."[24] If public subvention of lobbying activity increases pressure on policy-making by increasing the flow of information and opinion to the legislator and multiplying the interests in his constituency with which he must contend, then it is difficult to see such pressure as undesirable.

Finally, it should be noted that public support of activity to influence legislation is not really an innovation. Section 162(e) of the tax code, with its deduction for lobbying before Congressional committees, represents an indirect form of such federal subsidy. Similarly, the fact that section 501(c) (3) prohibits only "substantial" political activity by charitable institutions is an admission that Congress has not been absolutely opposed to the idea of using public funds to support lobbying by approved organizations. Another precedent can be seen in the law reform projects handled by OEO-funded legal services. Federal money is used by these groups to "educate" the public and local legislators about the need for legislation which they have drafted. The educational activity of these legal service operations bears a striking resemblance to the lobbying activity of interest groups.

Such precedents are an indication that Congress has perceived a need for keeping its members informed about the issues of concern to their constituents. In 1966, Senator Abraham Ribicoff remarked in hearings before the Senate Subcommittee on Executive Reorganization, of which he was Chairman, that

> ... we are passing laws and spending money to deal with all these problems [of poverty], but our information is poor. We don't even understand the problem. I do not see how we are ever going to straighten this out until we understand the problem.[25]

Thus, it would be in the interest of Congress and the American governmental process to institute a system of publicly-supported lobbying activity designed to elicit the kind of concerned and informed public opinion which Senator Ribicoff sees as essential.

III. THE VOUCHER SYSTEM: A SPECIFIC SUGGESTION

Once the principle of public support for lobbying has been accepted, how should it be implemented? The 1967 hearings before the Senate Finance Committee which followed the President's Message on Campaign Financing elicited discussion of the various considerations involved in developing a mechanism for publicly financing political activity.[26] The Committee heard extensive testimony on several different proposals for presidential election-campaign financing. President Johnson's proposal called for direct appropriations by Congress; others suggested tax deductions or tax credits for campaign contributions. The use of such tax incentives found favor with a number of witnesses.

A more promising approach, advanced by Senator Lee Metcalf, involves the use of vouchers. Under this plan, Treasury vouchers would be distributed to taxpayers, who would send them to the political party of their choice. The party would then redeem each voucher at the Treasury for one dollar. Testimony before the Finance Committee brought out several advantages in this plan over the direct appropriation method. This plan, for example, makes the individual citizen responsible for sending his own voucher to the party of his choice, a feature which encourages individual choice and participation.[27] A system of direct appropriation would not offer the same encouragement. Senator Long, Chairman of the Finance Committee, observed that vouchers could be made available to all citizens twenty-one or over, thus further eliminating inequities based on wealth.[28] Another advantage, noted by Senator Joseph Tydings, is that it avoids the need to secure annual congressional appropriations and gives more power to the people.[29] Finally, Mr. George Agree of the Association for the Democratic Process, observed that the number of vouchers received by a party

> *would depend on the vigor of the respective collection efforts, but this fact would enormously benefit the political process. Both parties would be encouraged to get down to the grass-roots, with an across-the-board stimulation of political interest and activity.*[30]

If the basic features of the Metcalf voucher plan could be adapted to the lobbying process without sacrificing any of its advantages it would do a great deal to democratize further the political process. Providing a voucher to all voting-age citizens would afford to "all segments of our population" increased influence in the political-legislative process. A citizen, with a voucher in hand, would be induced to consider which of his alternatives could benefit him the most. Interest groups, anxious to attract vouchers, would have to compete for them in terms of substantive achievement. The need for vouchers would be an incentive for interest groups to educate the public about the issues with which each is concerned and to inform them about recent developments. Finally, the prospect of broad-based financial support might induce latent interest groups to organize into a more effective political instrument.

Financing the political activity of interest groups through the use of vouchers would of course present difficulties, both administrative and substantive. It is not the purpose of this [article] to make a detailed proposal as to how all these difficulties could or should be solved. But solutions are available.

The first difficulty lies in trying to decide which people are to get vouchers. One of the main virtues of the plan is that its benefits need not be restricted to taxpayers. But assuming vouchers are made available to all voting-age citizens, should they be restricted to registered voters? To do so would give an incentive to lobby groups to encourage and assist in voter registration. On the other hand, there are still many areas where registration is extremely difficult, due to racial or economic discrimination. In these areas, limiting vouchers to registered voters would tend to cut off people most in need of them. Until such time as all citizens have an equal opportunity to register, it would seem preferable to make vouchers available to all citizens of voting age, registered or not.

A second difficulty with vouchers is the problem of distribution. Should each eligible recipient be mailed a voucher or should vouchers be made available at convenient distribution centers? A system of direct mailing runs the risk of omitting eligible recipients. The use of distribution centers might encounter the same problem with discrimination that hampers voter registration efforts, although this danger could be minimized by using a federal agency, such as the post office. Perhaps a combination of the two methods would provide the most satisfactory assurance that all eligible citizens would receive vouchers.

The next difficulty is to determine what organizations should be eligible to collect vouchers and cash them. Clearly some standards would have to be established to avoid the possibility that dishonest or deceitful groups could obtain public funds for personal ends. The standards would have to be reasonably objective and easily applicable to insure that interest groups desiring to collect vouchers would not be denied permission because of political pressure or the private prejudices of the administrator. A list of standards, to be set by Congress, should include limitations on the uses to which public funds could be put. In this way Congress could insure that publicly supported lobbying activity was principally devoted to public education and not to private coercion. Another standard might require an administrative structure adequate to insure that a publicly supported lobby remains open and accountable to the people whose vouchers support it. For example, a lobby group might be required to have a formal mechanism for receiving and responding to the suggestions and grievances of its constituents.

If an interest group qualifies to receive vouchers, should there be any limit on the number of vouchers the group can cash? If vouchers are distributed to all citizens of voting age, the amount of federal money potentially available for lobby support would be considerably in excess of 100 million dollars. It is conceivable that a handful of groups might attract a substantial percentage of that money, and then use it to bombard the public with educational material. It could be argued that if such a large number of people choose to support a particular lobby with their vouchers, it is no more than just to allow that lobby to spend it. On the other hand, if the primary purpose behind public subvention of lobbying activity is to correct an imbalance in the political-legislative process and to encourage expanded participation in that process through public education, then an absolute limitation on the amount of public money available to any one group would seem justifiable.

Related to the problem of whether or not to limit the voucher funds available to a group is the question of how to handle private contributions. A person cannot be prevented from giving his own money to an interest group whose ideas he supports. But should an organization which receives such private donations also be eligible to collect vouchers and cash them at the Treasury? A proposal made by Senator Albert Gore in connection with political campaign financing would accord political parties an option for public or private financing. Private support would be encouraged by allowing a tax deduction of one-half of a political contribution up to $100. Public support would be available for those parties willing to forgo private donations. This proposal might also serve the needs of lobby financing. An interest group would have the option of relying on its private supporters or refusing such contributions and accepting only vouchers.

Another possibility would be to allow a lobby group to collect and redeem vouchers so long as the total of public and private contributions did not exceed a specified maximum. This plan, however, might meet some administrative difficulty in coping with the problem of a late private contribution which puts an organization's total funds over the stated maximum. Should the organization then be required to turn back Treasury vouchers equal to the amount by which total funds collected have exceeded the maximum? Such a requirement might induce lobby groups to conceal such late contributions. On the other hand, the absence of an effective ceiling would mean that even groups with relatively easy access to private resources could receive federal subsidies.

This administrative difficulty points to a more general weakness of the voucher plan, also noted by Senator Williams with respect to the Metcalf plan for campaign financing, namely that it is "wide open for abuse."[31] There is, for example, the possibility that vouchers would be counterfeited or that bona fide vouchers would be stolen. Organizations might attempt to buy vouchers for cash, at less than the one dollar redemption value. Proper security precautions would probably be enough to keep counterfeiting and theft to a minimum. Besides, the small cash value of single vouchers would make such activities comparatively unattractive, considering the risks involved. Similarly, any lobby organization which tried to secure vouchers by offering a cash premium would have to operate on such a large scale to make the venture worthwhile that it would be easily detected.

Probably the most common kind of abuse would be the misuse of legitimately acquired funds. An illustration might be the use of vouchers to finance a fraudulent telegram campaign to persuade some congressman that his constituency supported a particular piece of legislation. The best safeguard against this is the technique nominally utilized by the Federal Regulation of Lobbying Act, full disclosure. The Lobbying Act, of course, has been conspicuously unsuccessful in bringing lobbying abuses to light; nevertheless, the principle of using publicity or the threat of disclosure to keep lobbyists in line is sound. By requiring an organization to submit a full report of its income and the ways in which money was spent before it can be certified eligible to collect and cash Treasury vouchers in the following year, it would be possible to keep a check on the kind of abusive practices most likely to appear under the voucher plan.

IV. CONCLUSION

It has been the purpose of this [article] to raise the issue of publicly-supported activity to influence legislation rather than to provide a blueprint for implementing such a policy. That there is an imbalance in the impact which private and public interest groups have upon the legislative process has long been recognized. But the techniques for coping with this situation, both those already tried and those which have been proposed, are almost invariably designed to develop a more equitable balance among the conflicting interests already represented within that process. The more fundamental problem of how to draw the currently excluded segments of society into the political process in a meaningful way, has generally been neglected. The problem has been especially neglected in the area of lobbying, which is today acknowledged as an integral part of democratic Government. The supreme obligation of Government to improve the machinery of public participation in the political process, requires that Government take bold, affirmative steps to afford all our citizens an opportunity to be heard in the legislatures of the land, not only through their votes, but also through their lobbies. Public subvention of lobbying activity, properly implemented and regulated, is a sound policy which could do much to expand the frontiers of social justice in the United States.

WHY THE POOR PEOPLE'S CAMPAIGN FAILED

Tom Kahn

It was only a few years ago that Michael Harrington wrote, in *The Other America,* that a chief characteristic of the poor was their invisibility. The white middle class had designed its neighborhoods and traffic arteries to bypass the slums; the combined forces of urban renewal and the private housing market operated to push the poor, especially Negroes, out of view and into more densely packed ghettos. Thus there grew up a physical and cultural barrier which, it was agreed, had to be penetrated if the nation's conscience was to be awakened.

Between the publication of *The Other America* and the appearance of Resurrection City in Washington this year, a great deal happened, and it is doubtful that the poor can any longer be described as invisible in the old sense. To be sure, they have not been integrated into the economic mainstream, there is still little daily contact with the affluent majority (except in laboratory settings), and there has certainly been no basic shift in power relations. But if the poor still do not exist for us as real individuals, their collective condition has nevertheless been thrust actively into the political arena. Every schoolboy knows that there are poor people in America, that a disproportionate number of them are black, that they live in deteriorating slums and ghettos, and that there is among them a growing militance and indignation; he knows as well that there is an urban crisis in this country which is characterized by high unemployment in the slums, disorder in the schools, crime, violence, and dope in the streets. And he also knows, if he is at all alert, that there is evident today a measure of organized effort in behalf of the poor that, while still meager and ineffective, goes beyond what might have been predicted a short time ago.

Now it seems appropriate to question the notion, implicit in so much meliorist thinking, that the recognition of a problem is its solution. The affluent majority, once shown the face of poverty, can react in alternative ways. After all, to make a not irrelevant comparison, peace in Vietnam is the stated (and probably genuine) goal both of those who advocate unilateral U.S. withdrawal and of those who call for a military victory. Similarly, all are agreed that poverty in America must be eliminated, but while one approach to the problem is to work for guaranteed jobs and income, another is to conclude from recent events that the poor are their own worst enemy, and that they must be repressed into respect for law and order as a precondition for receiving any advances that the future might hold. There is, in short, nothing in the faces of the poor themselves that will necessarily inspire the sympathy or supportive political action of the majority; poverty can just as easily inspire fear and revulsion.

These thoughts have been occasioned by the Poor People's Campaign of 1968, a project which has been attacked more widely, and with more contempt, than any "radical" action in years—with the *possible* exception of the incredible New Politics Convention in Chicago [in 1968]. It is precisely for this reason that one hesitates to discuss the Poor People's Campaign seriously—which necessarily means critically. Nonetheless, the discussion must take place, for the campaign embodied ideas and techniques that have been evolving over the past five years, that therefore speak directly to our political and social experience in those years, and that, finally, are likely to manifest themselves again and again in the crucial months ahead. The discussion properly begins with some notes on the history of the Poor People's Campaign, and in particular on the role played in the campaign by Bayard Rustin. For if the Poor People's Campaign failed to produce its desired impact—and most agree that it did—then the reasons for that failure, as well as its ultimate significance, must be traced in large measure to the debate which took place last April and May between Rustin and the campaign leadership.

II

Late in 1967, when Dr. Martin Luther King first put forth the notion of a Spring Protest in Washington, he and the Southern Christian Leadership Conference had already experienced several disappointments in their effort to transplant their Southern-born movement to the Northern ghettos. They had so far been unable to duplicate in the big cities of the North the relatively swift and dramatic victories they had won in the South. For one thing, the high-flown, basically optimistic rhetoric of the Southern Baptist minister failed to penetrate the bitter alienation and social breakdown of the big ghettos. Then, too, the opposition was politically much more sophisticated, often showing a deceptively amiable countenance; the Daley machine in Chicago was a far different animal from Bull Connor. Above all, the changes being sought were socio-economic in nature, and hence far less easily attainable through traditional non-violent, direct-action methods, than had been, say, the desegregation of public accommodations, a relatively straightforward political goal.

SCLC was not the only civil-rights organization confronted by these problems, but in some ways it was the one least suited to adjust to them. The Congress of Racial Equality, originally dominated by white pacifist-radicals, was going through a series of internal upheavals, and engaged in turning toward various versions of black nationalism in search of a base in the black community. The National Urban League, long regarded as the most conservative of the civil-rights groups, had fashioned a more militant image under the leadership of Whitney Young, while maintaining its ties with enlightened big business. The NAACP, with some four hundred fifty thousand members (the great majority of them black), was continuing to shoulder the legal burden but turning its attention increasingly to economic issues. (Perhaps because it is made up of some one thousand six hundred chapters throughout the country, the NAACP can vary its strategic emphasis in a functional way at the local level, without requiring sudden alterations at the national level.)

Unlike these organizations, SCLC existed as the extension of one man, Dr. King. It had, and has, no membership, no regularly functioning groups (as opposed to projects) in local communities. Consequently, when SCLC workers entered a community, they often appeared as "outsiders," and were unable to attract an enduring following loyal to SCLC. The "membership" of SCLC, like that of SNCC, is its staff, now reported at 125 full-time workers. But whereas an organization like SNCC could throw out its founding leadership and, with the election of a Stokely Carmichael or an H. Rap Brown, transform the organization from top to bottom, SCLC obviously could not.

In short, the structure of SCLC and the towering figure of its leader precluded it from making the changes undertaken by other civil-rights groups. (I leave aside here any evaluation of these changes.) But the pressures and frustrations that were building up in the entire movement were felt in SCLC as well. The Chicago project of 1966 had clearly failed, and the mass media, searching out "authentic" voices of the violent ghetto, were increasingly spotlighting young black militants. Inevitably, some of the SCLC staff became restive, worried that they were losing touch with the new currents and fearful that their own inspirational gifts were becoming obsolete. (As anyone knows who has known Southern Baptist ministers, each and every member of the SCLC leadership believes that his role is divinely inspired and divinely to inspire.) The presence of Dr. King served to prevent these frustrations and internal conflicts from erupting into public view. But there is evidence that the declining morale of the SCLC staff was in the back of his mind as he made plans for the Poor People's Campaign of 1968.

From the beginning, the plans were not very clear, and a debate on tactics took place among the members of King's "think tank"—an informal group outside of the SCLC structure that met irregularly at King's request. One member of the group was Bayard Rustin, the leading tactician of the civil-rights movement and now executive director of the A. Philip Randolph Institute, whose relationship with King dated back to the Montgomery Bus Protest in the mid-50's.

In a detailed three-page memorandum to King dated January 29, 1968, Rustin outlined a series of suggestions for the strategy and tactics of the Spring Protest (as it was then called). He proposed that the project center on economic questions, and that the aims be stated in two parts, the first encompassing long-range demands "not necessarily expected to be obtained now, such as guaranteed income for those who cannot work and public works at decent wages . . . for those who can," and the second dealing with immediate demands for "jobs, housing, welfare, and passage of a strong civil-rights bill."

In urging a list of specific, "realizable" demands, Rustin argued that

> . . . *failure to achieve some major victories in the nation's capital at this time will, I believe, increase frustration nationally. These demands should be broad enough to insure some of them being won soon. . . .*

> *I do not believe it is possible to attract sufficient numbers to the nation's capital unless, far in advance, the strategy and tactics have fully been made clear to all concerned. We are not now in the period we were in in 1963, at the time of Selma, Birmingham, and the March on Washington, when there was absolute clarity in everyone's mind as to objectives. . . . Not only do I feel it is essential that those being called into Washington know precisely what they are being called into, but I believe it is important that those in Government should have a very clear picture of aims, strategy and tactics.*

Thus the issue of specific as opposed to general demands—an issue that was later to flare into public controversy—was raised by Rustin as early as January of this year. In the same memorandum, Rustin argued against the use of disruptive tactics in Washington:

> *Given the mood in Congress, given the increasing backlash across the nation, given the fact that this is an election year, and given the high visibility of a protest movement in the nation's capital, I feel that any effort to disrupt transportation, government buildings, etc., can only lead, in this atmosphere, to further backlash and repression.*
>
> *Such tactics will, I believe, fail to attract persons dedicated to nonviolence but, on the other hand, attract elements that cannot be controlled, and who on the contrary will converge on the project with a variety of objectives in mind other than those of civil rights. . . .*
>
> *I believe you should address a series of mass meetings across the country outlining clearly your plan, in order to set the tone for the Washington demonstration in advance so that certain elements would have no excuse for converging on Washington without clarity. I sincerely believe that unless this is done, many individuals could become severe problems once they are in Washington.*

These excerpts effectively refute the charge, subsequently made, that Rustin had pooh-poohed the whole idea of the project. In fact, his memo recommended a number of concrete and positive tactical steps that King might take to safeguard the project from the dangers Rustin foresaw. For he did have deep reservations about the project and candidly told King so. "There is in my mind," he wrote, "a very real question . . . whether SCLC can maintain control and discipline over [the Spring Protest] even if the methods used are limited to constitutional and nonviolent tactics."

Two months later, Martin Luther King was assassinated. Rustin, shattered by grief, flew immediately to Memphis to organize the march begun by King on behalf of the sanitation workers. He brought the young militants, who had disrupted the earlier King march, into positions of responsibility as marshals; the resulting demonstration was a massive, inspiring tribute to the slain leader. Returning home to New York three sleepless days later, Rustin experienced one of those grotesque assaults by which certain publicists of the New Left earn their daily bread—a *Village Voice* article by Jack Newfield denouncing him for opposing King's Poor People's Campaign.

While in Memphis, Rustin had told Rev. Ralph David Abernathy, King's successor, that he would be available for consultation on the logistics of the Poor People's Campaign. In the ensuing weeks the Campaign hit snag after snag. There were delays in getting contingents out of the South, and the first groups to arrive in Washington found arrangements incomplete at Resurrection City. In mid-May, harassed and frazzled, Abernathy telephoned Rustin and implored him to take over responsibility for the one-day Mobilization in support of the Poor People's Campaign, then scheduled for May 30. Rustin resisted, on the grounds that there was opposition to him in the SCLC staff and that his entry might stir internal bickering which Abernathy could ill afford so soon after succeeding King. (In a meeting of the "think tank" two years earlier, Rustin had incurred the wrath of some SCLC staffers by arguing against King's going into Chicago.) Abernathy was not to be dissuaded, however. He pledged that Rustin, as national coordinator, would have full authority over the Mobilization, and said he would see to it that the SCLC staff cooperated. Finally, Rustin agreed to meet with Abernathy and his key aides in Washington on May 19.

Rustin, accompanied by his assistant, Norman Hill, went to the meeting with a set of fourteen points which were his precondition for accepting Abernathy's request. He stipulated, among other things, that he have full authority for the Mobilization, including selection of staff and marshals; that the Mobilization be postponed to mid-June; that there be no disruption of government functions on the day of the Mobilization; that participation in the Mobilization be based on adherence to democracy, integration, and the strategy of nonviolence; and that "in addition to stating the broad objectives of the Poor People's Campaign for guaranteed jobs and income, the one-day Mobilization will project specific concrete demands. It will be made clear that these demands do not represent the full programs of the SCLC."

The fourteen points were agreed to, and on May 24 Rustin and Abernathy held a press conference to announce Rustin's appointment as national coordinator and the postponement of the Mobilization to June 19. In Abernathy's presence Rustin reiterated that "the Mobilization will not content itself with defining general social goals. It will make specific demands which can, and must be, immediately translated into law by congressional action and Executive order."

What Rustin had in mind became clear nine days later when he issued, under his and Abernathy's names, the official Mobilization "Call." The "Call" covered the general long-range goals of the Poor People's Campaign under an "Economic Bill of Rights" that would guarantee full employment, decent wages, and an adequate income for the unemployed. It went on to list specific "attainable" demands to be made to the Congress and the President—e.g., creation of one million public service jobs; adoption of the Housing and Urban Development Act; repeal of punitive welfare restrictions; collective bargaining rights for farm workers; more funds for anti-poverty programs; expanded food distribution; etc.

There was an immediate favorable reaction on Capitol Hill, as the "Call" gave congressional liberals some concrete legislative goals to work for. It was clear that the Poor People would not be allowed to remain in Washington indefinitely; the liberals were hoping that if the Campaign could achieve some victories, a graceful withdrawal could be effected. Publication of the "Call," along with news of Rustin's appointment, also brought in support from unions, church groups, and liberal organizations, which had earlier been uneasy over the prospect of confusion and possible violence in Washington.

The fears entertained by these groups were not entirely groundless. On the day before the Abernathy-Rustin press conference, eighteen Campaigners were arrested in an unscheduled demonstration at the office of Wilbur Mills, chairman of the House Ways and Means Committee, an indication that SCLC was having trouble controlling the Campaign. It was also having trouble with its own staff. On the day the "Call" was issued, Rev. Hosea Williams, an Abernathy lieutenant, proclaimed at a rally: "The picnic is over. . . . The police want to use those billies. Well, we're going to give them a chance."

While Rustin's New York office was preparing newspaper ads, printing instruction manuals, and getting endorsements and bus commitments from national organizations, the Washington situation continued to deteriorate. Two days after the issuance of the "Call," Hosea Williams called a press conference and denounced the document as "a bunch of jazz and foolishness." He said it was "unauthorized" and asserted, furthermore, that Rustin was merely a "public-relations man" for the Mobilization. On the same day, one hundred demonstrators confronted Attorney General Ramsey Clark at the Department of Justice. In words similar to those used by Hosea Williams at the rally on June 2, one of the demonstrators shouted: "Mr. Ramsey Clark, you better tell the police to get their guns ready because we're ready. For every one of us you kill in Resurrection City, ten cities are going to burn, 'cause we ain't got nothing to lose."

The next day, in response to Williams's statements, Rustin released the full text of the 14-point agreement to the press and insisted that the "Call" had been cleared with Rev. Abernathy and the Executive Vice-President of SCLC, Rev. Andrew Young. Meanwhile, the press reported Abernathy as saying, "I did not authorize and neither did I issue" the "Call." Apparently forgetting one of the fourteen points he had agreed to, Abernathy added, "I do not think it is comprehensive enough to cover the demands of the Poor People's Campaign. I go along with some of his

[Rustin's] ideas, but I think it's got to be broader." Abernathy made no comment on Hosea Williams's charge that Rustin had no authority over the Mobilization.

Rustin's phones were flooded with calls from people whose participation in the Mobilization had been predicated on the assumption that he would be in charge. Some groups indicated they would suspend activity until some clarification were offered. Federal authorities refused to give final approval to the line of march until it became certain that Rustin or someone else had authority to sign contracts. Meanwhile, Rustin had been trying for three days to reach Abernathy by phone, by telegram, and through intermediaries—without success. Then, one June 6, Rustin announced he was suspending his role in the Mobilization pending word from Abernathy affirming the fourteen points and Rustin's authority. (During this time, it was learned, Abernathy was tied up in all-night staff meetings at which a principal topic was the firing of Rustin—reportedly a move demanded by representatives of CORE and some peace groups.)

Finally, the next morning, Abernathy called Rustin and offered to convene a press conference to reaffirm Rustin's full authority as national coordinator. Rustin proposed that the press conference be preceded by a meeting which would include Hosea Williams and several other SCLC staff members who were known to be hostile to Rustin's role. Unless they were a party to the agreement, Rustin felt, there would be no way of putting a stop to their sniping. Abernathy argued that Rustin's proposal would weaken his position as the leader of SCLC, and he reiterated that he could keep his staff in line. Rustin replied that he thought Abernathy would be ill-advised to risk internal conflict by trying to discipline his staff and that in any case he, Rustin, did not want to be a cause of factionalism within SCLC. This impasse having been reached, Rustin told Abernathy that he was resigning, but that he would be available, behind the scenes, to help in any way Abernathy wanted. (In the following days, Rustin turned over all of the Mobilization bus lists and files to Sterling Tucker—Washington director of the Urban League, whom Abernathy had appointed as Rustin's successor—and sent $4000 he had raised to SCLC for the sound system in Washington.)

The Monday following his resignation, Rustin attended a meeting of liberal organizations, which had originally been convened to discuss Mobilization plans for July 19. He explained his reasons for resigning, but declined to participate in the ensuing discussion about what these groups should now do.

III

It is not easy to evaluate a demonstration like the June 19 Mobilization. Indeed, the value of any large demonstration is not to be measured solely by its immediate results. Also important is its effect on the participants—on their morale and on their willingness to work harder once they have returned home. Reactions, whether friendly or hostile, can take a while to register.

Yet it must be said that there is so far little evidence that the Mobilization made an impact. Although a turnout of fifty thousand people—the official estimate—is not to be sneered at, it is not momentous in these days of giant rallies. Inevitable comparisons have been made with the March on Washington of 1963, which drew nearly a quarter of a million people. It is true that the Mobilization had much less time in which to prepare, but it also enjoyed more initial support than did the 1963 March. Whereas the Kennedy administration had tried to get the March called off, the Johnson administration was favorably disposed to the Mobilization, albeit for its own reasons (it hoped that the June 19 rally would afford the residents of Resurrection City an opportunity to withdraw with dignity). Nor did the '63 March have the open support of an organized bloc of liberal congressmen like the one which worked with SCLC. Finally, the constituent organizations of the civil-rights movement had, since 1963, become more experienced in the techniques of mobilizing their members for rallies and demonstrations.

The point here is not that the Mobilization was inferior to the 1963 March but that it did not live up to its own potential. A number of organizations that had planned to send large delegations finally dispatched only token representation. Nor was there a large turnout from Washington itself, where the majority of the population is black.

On Capitol Hill, the impact of the Poor People's Campaign was hardly productive of beneficial results. Perhaps nothing could have moved the 90th Congress to act—not even the assassination of Robert F. Kennedy had induced it to pass adequate gun-control laws—and certainly many of the congressmen who harangued against the Campaign needed no excuse to oppose aid to the poor. Nevertheless, the fact remains that if the Campaign were to win substantial victories, it would have had to serve as a massive lever of support for the liberal faction in Congress. This, in effect, was the role of the 1963 March in winning passage of the 1963 Civil Rights Act. But the Campaign actually served the opposite purpose. It not only became an embarrassment to congressional liberals but, in the view of many Washington observers, it diverted attention away from the crucial battle over appropriations—including appropriations for poverty programs—that was then being waged in Congress. Instead of calling the nation's attention to this debate, the Poor People's Campaign succeeded in focusing attention mainly on itself and on the residents of Resurrection City. And that was the most damaging effect of all.

"Resurrection City itself," said *Newsweek,* "conceived as a model of communal living, had fallen into a true-to-life squalor—an ill-housed, ill-fed, self-segregated, absentee-run slum afflicted with low morale, deepening restiveness, and free-floating violence." A poignant account, printed in the New York *Post* on June 20, came from Alvin Jackson, who resigned as chief security marshal for the Mobilization:

> *There is rape, robbery, and cuttings every day, and there is nothing we can do about it even if we catch the guys who did it. . . . There are about 20 guns in Resurrection City. There are lead pipes, knives, and Molotov cocktails in there. . . . The reason they leave is that men are getting tired of coming home from a day's picketing to find their belongings stolen or their wife raped.*

Not even the most cynical observer can deny that one of the greatest resources of the civil-rights movement has been its moral capital, its "soul power." Resurrection City was dubbed the "City of Hope." Rev. Andrew Bevel of SCLC had described the Poor People's Campaign as "political group psychiatry." In his words, "Sometimes in psychiatry the patients get mad and run away. This time we are not going to let the patients get mad and run away. We're going to make them well, man. We're also educators, and when people are educated and get rid of their emotional problems, they will hear us" (New York *Times,* May 19).

A month later, as if in reply to Bevel, *The Wall Street Journal* could say:

> *. . . as the reports of rape and robbery at Resurrection City began to seep out, not only were the public's fears of violence confirmed but an even stronger emotion came into play. After all, the Campaigners were people who were condemning American society, in toto or in part, as "racist" and "sick." And what values were they offering as substitutes? Not equality and justice, but robbery and rebellion against all authority by any means.*

It is easy for sophisticated liberals and radicals to dismiss this as self-righteous moralizing from the ruling class. And it must be said, in this connection, that nothing that occurred in Resurrection City was as contemptible as the outcry of those right-wing congressmen who demanded that this transplanted microcosmic slum be torn down, but who are perfectly content to let the nation's real slums—of whose misery and pathology Resurrection City was but a symbol—remain intact. But then again, I have seen the contrary argument advanced—that precisely the most progressive development of the last five years has been that the "real" Negro has come to the surface, with all his scars and hostilities painfully visible. According to this argument, which I have had repeated occasion to hear, the Poor People's Campaign was "more real" and "more true" than the 1963 March because it forced white America to see the conditions of ghetto life, not an idealized image of cheerful black-and-white togetherness.

There is a sense in which this argument rings true, for it speaks to a certain naive, idealized integrationist view of the Negro which is dangerous because it is so easily bruised by an acquaintance with reality; and once bruised, it can rapidly turn into its ugly opposite. But if we are to proceed with this style of reasoning, it is appropriate to scrutinize another stereotype which is equally dangerous—that of the heroic slum proletariat.

Too many radical intellectuals have transferred to the lumpenproletariat the sentimental image of the proletariat that was fashionable in this country in the 1930's. Today's lumpenproletariat, like yesterday's worker, is viewed by these thinkers as an inherently progressive social force. In my own view, the proletariat had, and has, many more "progressive" virtues than does the lumpenproletariat—that is, if the word "progressive" is shorn of its romantic foolishness. The working class, as Daniel P. Moynihan has pointed out, possesses an often overlooked social cohesiveness, a class identity, a culture and a moral system based largely on its more stable economic role. The lumpenproletariat lacks these qualities because it is not quite a class at all but a collection of sub-groups divided by ethnic, racial, linguistic, and geographical factors.

In any case, and more to the point, I am not sure that classes are progressive—or reactionary—in and of themselves, but only in relation to their social roles. If we leave aside life-style preferences for the moment, the working class may be said to be progressive in that it seeks, with varying degrees of success, to democratize the distribution of social wealth. Or, if you prefer, the bourgeoisie can be considered progressive in that it has revolutionized technology. (Needless to say, each of these classes can have—indeed, does have—reactionary features as well.) The standard is the transformative effect on society itself.

Now, the lumpenproletariat can be progressive to the extent that, by pressing its own demands for a larger piece of the action, it succeeds in reducing or abolishing poverty and inequality in society as a whole. Yet because it is a sub-class, internally fragmented and extremely marginal to the political process, the lumpenproletariat is the least capable of playing an independent role. It must choose from among the directions laid before society by other social forces. In terms of political action, this means some kind of coalition.

There is, to be sure, one superficially "independent" role that the lumpenproletariat can play—a nihilistic battle against society itself that involves massive rioting, burning, looting, killing. But behavior of this kind can only redound to the advantage of other forces. In the United States, where urban guerrilla warfare will not be endured, the response will be repression and a turn to the Right. Such a turn to the Right, toward the forces of reaction, is already obvious.

Thus, it is not enough to "tell it like it is," to rub the noses of the affluent in the pathology of the slum. It is especially not enough when society as a whole is confused and divided, when liberal forces are disoriented, the backlash is growing in severity, and when extremism at both ends of the spectrum takes on profoundly anti-civil-libertarian, almost Fascist, features. At such a time the paramount need is for clear programmatic alternatives and for tactics that will maximize the size and cohesion of the democratic liberal-radical forces. Measured by the extent of that need, the Poor People's Campaign, whatever its other achievements, was a failure.

NOTES: INTEREST GROUPS

Introduction

1. Eugene McCarthy, "A Senator Looks at the Lobbies," *New York Times Magazine,* August 9, 1962, p. 17.

2. For general discussions of interest groups and lobbying see Lewis Anthony Dexter, *How Organizations Are Represented in Washington* (Bobbs-Merrill, 1969); Harmon Zeigler, *Interest Groups in American Society* (Prentice-Hall, 1964); Abraham Holtzman, *Interest Groups and Lobbying* (Macmillan, 1966).

3. *Trist v. Child,* 21 Wallace 441, 451 (1874).

4. See, for example, Lester W. Milbrath, *The Washington Lobbyists* (Rand McNally, 1963).

5. For a discussion of lobbying and legislatures see Malcolm E. Jewell and Samuel C. Patterson, *The Legislative Process in the United States* (Random House, 1966), especially chapter 12.

6. Marver H. Bernstein, *The Job of the Federal Executive* (Brookings Institution, 1958).

7. Clement E. Vose, "Litigation as a Form of Interest Group Activity," *Annals of the American Academy of Political and Social Science,* 319 (September, 1958), 20-31; Clement E. Vose, "NAACP Strategy in the Covenant Cases," *Western Reserve Law Review,* 6 (Winter, 1955), 101-145.

8. "Public Disclosure of Lobbyists' Activities," *Fordham Law Review,* 38 (March, 1970), 524-535.

9. Edward F. Cox, Robert C. Fellmeth, and John E. Schulz, '*The Nader Report*' *on the Federal Trade Commission* (Richard W. Baron, 1969).

10. Stephen V. Monsma, *American Politics: A Systems Approach* (Holt, Rinehart and Winston, 1969), pp. 340-341.

Dale C. Freeman

1. House Select Committee on Lobbying Activities, General Interim Report, H. R. Rep. No. 3138, 81st Cong., 2nd Sess. 6 (1950): "In the final

analysis, there are only two practical guages of lobbying activity—intent and some substantial effort to influence legislation The means employed are secondary. . . ."

2. Final Report of the Special Committee to Investigate Political Activities, Lobbying and Campaign Contributions, S. Rep. No. 395, 85th Cong., 1st Sess. (1957) [hereinafter Senate Lobbying Report].

3. J. Deakin, *The Lobbyists* (1966) p. vii.

4. General Interim Report, *supra* note 1, at 65.

5. *Citizens' Board of Inquiry into Hunger and Malnutrition in the United States, Hunger USA* (1968), at 81.

6. General Interim Report, *supra* note 1, at 64.

7. J. F. Kennedy, "Congressional Lobbies: A Chronic Problem Reexamined," 45 *Geo. L. Rev.* 535 (1957) at 567 (emphasis added).

8. Senate Lobbying Report, *supra* note 2, at 72.

9. *Id.*

10. S. Rep. No. 1881, 87th Cong., 2nd Sess. 22 (1962).

11. *Id.* at 414.

12. The facts related herein with regard to the Sierra Club controversy are drawn substantially from Borod, "Lobbying for the Public Interest— Federal Tax Policy and Administration." 42 *N.Y.U. L. Rev.* 1087 (1967).

13. Borod, *supra* note 12, at 1117.

14. 358 U. S. at 513.

15. Cooper, "Taxation of Grassroots Lobbying," 68 *Colum. L. Rev.* 801, 842-46 (1968).

16. *Id.* at 847, n. 221.

17. *Id.*

18. Senate Lobbying Report, *supra* note 2, at 79.

19. 42 F. 2nd 184, 185 (2nd Cir., 1930).

20. 358 U.S. at 498.

21. *Id.* at 512.

22. "President's Message on Campaign Financing," 24 *Cong. Q. Almanac* 135A (1967) (emphasis added).

23. Senate Lobbying Report, *supra* note 2, at 72.

24. A. Scott and M. Hunt, *Congress and Lobbies: Image and Reality* 58 (1965).

25. *Hearings before the Subcommittee on Executive Reorganization of*

the Senate Committee on Government Operations, 89th Cong., 2nd Sess. pt. 5, at 1115 (1966).

26. *Hearings on Political Campaign Financing Proposals before the Senate Committee on Finance,* 90th Cong., 1st Sess. (1967).

27. *Id.* at 244.

28. *Id.* at 357.

29. *Id.* at 415.

30. *Id.* at 360-61.

31. *Id.* at 471.

Part Three
LEADERS AND DECISION-MAKERS

THE PRESIDENCY

> *Speculative writers have sometimes traced the origins of*
> *government to a monarch in the forest who gathered in his person*
> *all power. At length wearing of his responsibilities, the*
> *hypothetical potentate delegated some of them to followers who*
> *eventually became "courts," and shared others with a more*
> *numerous body of subjects who in due time organized themselves*
> *into a "legislature." The indefinite residuum, called "executive*
> *power," he kept for himself.*

—Edward S. Corwin[1]

Three English reporters concluded their analysis of the 1968 presidential election with a pointed reminder concerning human fallibility:

> *The president is an elected politician. He gets elected, in real-*
> *ity, as best he can. . . . But the president is not only an elected poli-*
> *tician. He is also magic. He is the monarch, emblem, and protector*
> *of national unity, defender of the American faith. And so the gap*
> *opens between the rhetoric and the reality. It is not enough that he*
> *should be a decent, honorable, sensible man who has succeeded, as*
> *Disraeli said when he became Prime Minister, "in climbing to the*
> *top of the greasy pole." He must be the divinely ordained leader.*
> *But the ordination of Richard M. Nixon was not divine. It was, as*
> *we have tried to show, extremely human.*[2]

It is widely assumed and probably correctly that Americans are particularly prone to excessive admiration of their political institutions (if not necessarily of particular incumbents), and popular attitudes toward the presidential office are perhaps even further removed from a necessary critical perspective than are attitudes toward Congress or the Supreme Court. Indeed, political analysts can usually be counted on to refer, in properly hushed tones, to the enormous respect and "legitimacy" which the presidential office commands.

The bases of popular attitudes toward the presidency are not difficult to fathom. There have been, after all, a number of distinguished Presidents, including even some twentieth-century incumbents. There have also been some mediocrities and incompetents, if not outright rogues, in the White House, but the mythical and mystical qualities of the office appear to have survived them with little damage.

The presidency is, of course, an important and powerful position, but it is usually drowned in a sea of superlatives. Depending upon the writer's perspective and flair, the President is described as the most power-ful man in the country, the free world, the entire world, or in all history. The burdens of the office are usually described as similarly unique—the toughest job in the country, the world, and so on. In addition, the President is chief of state, and this means that an enormous amount of pomp and heraldry attends the office on a daily basis. It would take a saint not to succumb to all this sooner or later, and few politicians are burdened with a modest ego or a sense of irony. The White House has become, as George Reedy puts it, the "American Monarchy."[3]

The realities of presidential power have never received the public understanding which they deserve. There are, indeed, some rather ex-traordinary limitations on a president's legislative, administrative, and political powers. Unlike a British prime minister, he cannot count upon majority support in the legislature for his programs. He is, as presidential memoirs and biographies continually emphasize, constantly struggling to control and direct the bureaucracy, usually with little success. His partisan activities, which are necessary, are viewed as demeaning or illegitimate by many citizens.

At the same time, presidential power is, in certain areas, virtually unchecked. The executive's independent warmaking power has defied simple legislative or even constitutional solution. The President is the authoritative and indeed the only voice of the government of the United States. He can and does monopolize political news coverage. He speaks for his national party and controls its organization. In the realm of for-eign policy, the public accords the President dominance, favoring a man "who will make his ideas prevail even if Congress or the public should oppose him."[4]

This last point is particularly important. There appears to be a curi-ous, if not inexplicable, divergence in public attitudes toward presidential power.[5] Support for presidential preemption of foreign policy-making is based upon public perceptions of legitimacy as well as expertise. The President has the constitutional responsibility to conduct relations with other nations. In the words of the Supreme Court, he is "the sole organ of the Federal government in the field of international relations . . ."[6] More-over, the President has intelligence sources and information not available to Congress. In particular, he can draw upon and direct the twin instru-ments of foreign policy—the military and the diplomatic establishment. Thus the public appears willing to accept the notion that the President should be allowed to fulfill his responsibility for conducting foreign rela-tions without excessive congressional or popular interference, the essen-tial result of such interference being to give aid and comfort to whatever enemies happen to exist on a given issue. This assumption of a rightful presidential superiority has received wide endorsement. Few seem pre-pared, at any rate, to argue that the principle of "politics stops at the water's edge" is mischievous and dangerous. With respect to domestic affairs, public attitudes are quite different. The public accords Congress legitimacy, and opposition to presidential policy is viewed as healthy.

In sum, the presidency today is a misunderstood office. People expect too much from it, and their expectations create hazards for the successful conduct of democratic politics. Thomas Cronin's perceptive summary of what he terms the "textbook presidency" is a useful illustration of these expectations:

Omnipotence:

> *The president is the strategic catalyst in the American political system and the central figure in the international system as well.*
>
> *Only the president is or can be the genuine architect of the United States public policy, and only he, by attacking problems frontally and aggressively and interpreting his power expansively, can be the engine of change to move this nation forward.*

Moralistic-Benevolence:

> *The president must be the nation's personal and moral leader; by symbolizing the past and future greatness of America and radiating inspirational confidence, a president can pull the nation together while directing us toward the fulfillment of the American Dream.*
>
> *If, and only if, the right man is placed in the White House, all will be well, and, somehow, whoever is in the White House is the right man.*[7]

There is, of course, a price to be paid for all of this. The selection by Henry Fairlie analyzes the costs of idealizing a political office. Mr. Fairlie believes that the presidency has a marked inclination toward "the most refined of all absolutist systems," that of "Caesaro-papism." Having had considerably more experience with monarchs than Americans, the British are somewhat more sophisticated about the relevance of spiritual matters to politics. Thus it was Harold Macmillan, a former Prime Minister, rather than an American president, who had the good sense to say, "If people want a sense of purpose, they should get it from their archbishops."

If the President does indeed have trouble keeping contact with the real world, there are factors other than popular attitudes which contribute to his insulation and isolation. The essay by George Reedy deals with the President's relations with the press. Reedy, who was press secretary to Lyndon Johnson, asserts that the press is the most effective means for keeping the President in touch with reality, but that most Presidents misunderstand the role of the press and resent its criticisms. The Nixon administration, for example, has provided numerous illustrations of Reedy's thesis concerning the antagonism between the President and the press. The positive public response to some of the more virulent attacks on the press, moreover, suggests that there is limited public understanding about the critical role which the press must play.

Another criticism of presidential government concerns the weakness of political opposition. James MacGregor Burns' essay suggests that the most important future requirement of the presidency is an effective national opposition—what he calls a Shadow Presidency. As with the press, most administrations tend to treat the opposition's criticisms as irresponsible and somehow illegitimate. If an institutionalized and effective opposition could be maintained, alternative policies could be presented to the public.

According to George Reedy, "A president's most persistent problem in staying in touch with reality lies in his staff."[8] This is one aspect of a larger problem examined by a farsighted constitutional scholar, Edward S. Corwin, more than three decades ago. According to Professor Corwin, presidential power is dangerously personalized—first, because presidential leadership depends essentially upon "the accident of personality"; second, because "there is no governmental body that can be relied upon to give the President independent advice and whom he is nevertheless bound to consult."[9] The selection by Professor Corwin discusses his proposal for stabilizing presidential leadership, a proposal which deals with the advisory problem suggested by George Reedy and which also provides a suggestive mechanism for improving relations between the President and Congress.

THOUGHTS ON THE PRESIDENCY

Henry Fairlie

I have never understood why radicals in England object to the banal clichés which the Queen normally utters to her subjects. The English, after all, fought a civil war, executed one king and sent another king packing, precisely to be sure that monarchs in the future would not say anything which had any meaning. They then made doubly sure of this by giving the crown to a Hanoverian who could speak barely a word of English. When the Queens' consort to-day, a man of continental upbringing and notions, accentuated by an education at Gordonstoun, does say something in public which appears to carry some meaning, both Parliament and the press call for the executioner: only a 20th-century half-heartedness prevents the Duke of Edinburgh's head from rolling. It could, indeed, be said that the reason why the English fought their passionate, but still rather scholarly, civil war, and laboriously carried through what deserves to be known as the Inglorious Revolution, was primarily to make certain that those on the throne, and those near the throne, would not communicate intelligently with their subjects, but only with pedigree cattle, horses, and gun dogs.

So unused is an Englishman to the idea that a Head of State can do and say things of political importance that he is at something of a disadvantage (or is it an advantage?) when he contemplates a Presidency, whether the Presidency of the Fifth Republic or the Presidency of the United States. He does not really understand an elected and powerful Head of State. President Lebrun, in his frock coat, comes much more easily in his range of vision than President de Gaulle; and an English friend of mine likes to observe that *Mrs.* Calvin Coolidge seems to him very much what an ideal Head of State should be. Whenever there has been a national crisis (real or supposed) during my stay in America, I have found myself worried by the interventions and appearances of the President. Who, I always want to know, is speaking? The Head of State? The Commander-in-Chief? The head of a temporary administration? The temporary head of a political party? It is never quite clear; at least, I am never clear. All right: "Hail to the Chief." But what chief, I ask, and chief of what?

THE IMPROBABLE UNITED STATES

I first observed [a] President of the United States on my first Saturday in this country. It was in March, 1965, just after the disturbances at Selma, Alabama, and he was giving a televised press conference in the Rose Garden of the White House. The impression which it made will never

leave me, especially the extraordinary discordance between the decorous-
ness of the surroundings and the almost Barnum and Bailey vigour with
which the whole ceremony—for a ceremony it was, and was intended to
be—was conducted. I remember turning to an English colleague, who had
been in America for some time, and asking him why the American journalists stood when the President entered, a salute which no English journalist would give to any politician. "Because, you fool, he is the Head of
State," my colleague whispered back. "But he is not to-day," I answered.
"He is a party leader announcing a new party policy." Two days later,
to my utter amazement, this same party leader was allowed to address
a joint meeting of both Houses of Congress, again conferring on a party
policy something of the dignity which only a Head of State can offer.

It will seem to some that I am labouring an obvious and not very
important point. I can only answer that the combination of Head of State
and party leader is to me the most improbable feature of what I regard as a
most improbable political office. Indeed I would, after two years, still find
it hard to explain why the United States exists at all. I can find no manifest
reason why it should have been the destiny of this subcontinent to become,
and remain, one nation, under God or not. Nor can I find any satisfactory
explanation of how this same nation survived the colossal strain of the mass
immigration which took place in the last quarter of the 19th century, and
the first twenty years of this. (When I read Richard Hofstadter's *The
Paranoid Style in American Politics*, my first and main reaction was, not
that there have been so many "kooks" on the American political scene,
but that there have been so few, and especially that there were so few
during and immediately after the period of mass immigration.) The real
miracle of the United States—and the source of its perpetual fascination
over the minds of other peoples, "more powerful than the eloquence of
Mirabeau or the sword of Napoleon," as Archibald Alison said in 1883—
is its mere existence; and, the more I ponder this improbable existence, the
more I am convinced that *one* key to it lies in the most improbable of its
political offices: the Presidency.

In fact, when I have gone back, with the slight experience of the
United States which I have so far accumulated, to a rereading of *The
Federalist*, I find in it this same awareness of the improbability of the whole
business in which the constitution-makers were engaged. *The Federalist*,
indeed, draws much of its power from the fact that it is a series of prudent
essays on the improbable; and when I describe the Presidency as an improbable office in an improbable country, it is, of course, the fact and the
nature of federalism (itself an improbable form of government, quite alien
to English concepts, even though the English did assist in creating federal
governments in Canada and Australia) which is attracting and holding my
attention.

It was David Hume who foretold that the fruitful combination of the
two ideas of representation and federation would enable—would *alone*

enable—popular government to adapt itself to a vast continent. An outside observer, on his first encounter with it, must be allowed a little bemusement at the fact that the combination has worked, that the attempt was ever made, and that the achievement is so far there to see.

A MYTHICAL INSTITUTION

First, however, there is demolition work to be done. A myth has been created since the Second World War—and is again being fostered—that the Presidency has become and is becoming "institutionalized." It is a myth worth destroying, for it is already distorting political observation. The truth is the opposite. There is no high political office which is less institutionalized.

I take an institution to be a body—an establishment, if one likes; I happen to dislike—which has a corporate existence of its own, independent of its supreme (but temporary) office-holder (or office-holders). A permanent civil service, as strongly entrenched, as formally and informally assured of its position, its influence, and its powers as is the English civil service, is quite clearly an institution. So, now, is the English monarchy; for, although the personality of the monarch may play some part in determining what she says and does (and, especially, how), it is obvious now that the heart of the monarchy lies, not in the person of the monarch, but in the office of her Private Secretary, which has built up, by precedent piled minutely on precedent, a body of rules and conventions which are self-perpetuating. To make the point amply clear, one can say that the English cabinet is an institution, that it has been "institutionalised" in the office of the Secretary to the Cabinet—but that the office of prime minister is not a political institution. Nor is the office of President of the United States.

The myth that the Presidency is being "institutionalized" is based, as far as I understand it, on the following claims:

1. That the President's personal staff, the formidable array of special assistants and counsellors in the White House, represents a qualitative, and not merely a quantitative, change in the character and activity of the Presidency;

2. That various traditional activities of the President—for example, his relations with Congress—have been "institutionalized" in a particular office in the White House: for example, Lawrence O'Brien's while he was there, and even now that, formally, he is not there;

3. That the Presidency, through various instruments, such as the rapidly developing Bureau of the Budget, has "institutionalized" its relationship with the various government departments and agencies;

4. That a body of White House lore is being built up, perpetuating itself in successive Presidencies, and exemplified by the close contact

which was established, between November, 1960 and January, 1961, between the staff of the out-going President in the White House and the (constitutionally nonexistent) staff of the in-coming one.

That is it; and, for the life of me, I cannot see that it adds up to saying much more than that the President does many things which the President did not do before, and needs a larger staff to help him. One specific claim I intend to keep separate, because it helps to make a separate and important point: namely, that the activities of the Bureau of the Budget, the Council of Economic Advisors, and the Office of Scientific Advisor to the President together constitute a form of "institutionalizing."

THE WHITE HOUSE STAFF

I have to admit that there is, at first, the charm of novelty about the special assistants and counsellors who have become such a much-publicized element of government in the past [few] years. The roll-call of these Presidential assistants since 1961, is, indeed, stirring: Theodore C. Sorenson, Arthur M. Schlesinger, Jr., Lawrence F. O'Brien, McGeorge Bundy, Carl Kaysen, Richard Goodwin, Jack J. Valenti, Bill D. Moyers, Walt W. Rostow, John P. Roche. . . . the list is extensible, the names well known. But one must beware of being seduced by the publicity which has attended them, and which some of them have done much to create. ("While few of us had a 'passion for anonymity,' most of us had a preference in that direction," says Sorenson in *Kennedy*, words which one would like to believe contain a dash of deliberate irony.) On the whole, glamour and publicity are unreliable evidence of influence and power.

Yet it is as such that they are taken, for example, by Theodore H. White:

> *The White House [under Kennedy] was a community. The politics of America were discussed not only at the White House and in its offices but were chewed over for hours in the evenings and over weekends by men who were transfixed by their participation in the thrill of power. . . . It was as if, under Kennedy, a fourth branch had been added to the traditional trio of executive, legislative and judicial branches. The new fourth branch was the policymaking branch of government.*

It is a startlingly naive remark. Yet the leap which White makes—the leap from a description of the atmosphere which Kennedy's White House staff brought with them to the claim that a new political institution had been created, a new branch of government—is much the same as that made by other observers who argue that the increased number of special assistants and counsellors to the President, and the proliferation and variety of their roles, represent an "institutionalizing" of the Presidency.

It is with no disrespect that I suggest that the nearest parallel, in previous systems of government, to the nature of these men and their role, is to be found in the eunuchs who wielded such power and influence in many of the ancient empires. Eunuch rule, in the Chinese or the Turkish, in the Roman or the Mogul, empires was the most straight-forward device which emperors found for keeping power in their own court, away from a bureaucracy or an aristocracy (or even an army) which might challenge them. The eunuchs accumulated power and influence and wealth, and one T'ang eunuch gathered so large a hoard of gold and silver, jewels and silks, that thirty carts were needed for thirty days to move them—without his even writing a biography of his emperor.

The usefulness of this parallel is that it emphasizes the personal nature of the relationship between the President and his special assistants and counsellors. The ancient emperors wanted men whom they could trust— and who could be trusted more than those of poor origins, whom they had mutilated for their convenience and peace of mind, and then raised to the highest positions? The system and the methods are not precisely the same to-day, but the degree of personal dependence remains. "Kennedy wanted his staff to be small, in order to keep it more personal than institutional," Sorensen says, and then, in a vital and emphatic passage, he hammers the point home:

> . . . *From the outset he abandoned the notion of a collective, institutionalized Presidency. He ignored Eisenhower's farewell recommendation to create a First Secretary of Government to oversee all foreign affairs agencies. He abandoned the practice of the Cabinet's and the National Council's making group decisions like corporate boards of directors. He abolished the White House practice of White House staff meetings and weekly Cabinet meetings. He abolished the pyramid structure of the White House staff, the Assistant President-Sherman Adams-type job, the Staff Secretary, the Cabinet Secretariat, the NSC Planning Board and the Operations Coordinating Board, all of which imposed, in his view, needless paperwork and machinery between the President and his responsible officers. . . . He relied instead on informal meetings and direct contacts—on a personal White House staff, the Budget Bureau and ad hoc task forces, to probe and define issues for his decision. . . .*

Both Sorensen and Schlesinger emphasise that the special assistants in the White House, in those days, were for the most part *generalists*, whereas the most obvious attribute of "institutionalizing" is *specialization*, the codification of areas and boundaries of responsibility, the strict observance of precedent and record (as in the minutes of English cabinet meetings), and an almost hierarchical accountability.

None of these features of an institution, of "institutionalizing," was present in President Kennedy's White House staff; and, although something of the air, of the atmosphere, of the wide-ranging generalist . . . disappeared, none of them [was] present in President Johnson's White House staff, either.

It is absurd to talk of the "institutionalizing" of the Presidency through the White House staff, when that staff is liable to be changed from top to bottom with each change of President, and certain to be changed from top to bottom with a change of President which also involves a change of party; when men make the office, as Lawrence O'Brien emphatically did, as McGeorge Bundy did in a way very different from that of his successor, and as John Roche [did] in a way very different from that of his predecessor; when the President can reach out and recruit almost at whim, as President Johnson did when he plucked back McGeorge Bundy during the Middle East crisis; and when the men themselves may resign almost at whim, as in the gradual withdrawal, between 1964 and 1966, of most of the "Kennedy men."

It will, I hope, eventually be seen why I regard the noninstitutional character of the Presidency as of such importance. For the moment, it is enough to say that the Presidency, as *organised in the White House,* seems to me a form of unencumbered, arbitrary, personal rule. "Institutionalization," precisely because it is based on precedent and hierarchy and codification, is the very opposite of arbitrariness; and it is with the arbitrary nature of the Presidency that I am at this point concerned.

AN INSTRUMENT OF POLITICAL WILL

The other supposed evidence of the "institutionalizing" of the Presidency can be disposed of quickly. It was President Eisenhower who first established a special office in the White Office to handle its relations with Congress. It was Lawrence O'Brien, under President Kennedy and then under President Johnson, who transformed that office into a formidable operation. But I must insist that the existence of this office, and others similar to it, is no evidence of "institutionalizing," *unless* it can be shown that it has changed the nature of the President's relationship with Congress, or the sanctions which either President or Congress can employ, or the nature of the Presidential *act* itself. The evidence is already in. It has done none of those things.

First, under President Eisenhower, the office became more a channel for Congress (i.e., Senator Lyndon Johnson) to run the White House rather than *vice versa*; while, under President Kennedy and President Johnson. it became the channel for O'Brien to work prodigious miracles in the art of directing by subtle indirection. In other words, it is the character of the President, and the character which he gives his Presidency, which has determined the role of the office—which is the very opposite of "institutionalization."

Secondly, the noninstitutional character of the office could not be clearer . . . when it [could] hardly be said to exist outside the person of the Postmaster-General, who [was], of course, Lawrence F. O'Brien. In fact, there is some evidence that, faced with a difficult 90th Congress, President Johnson [increasingly fell] back on more traditional channels of communication with Congress, and . . . even bothered to remember that his Vice-President [was] also President of the Senate.

Thirdly, if the offices in the White House are made partly by the men who hold them, and partly by the character of the President and his Presidency, they are also made partly by situations and events. The handling of the 90th Congress in 1967 was an entirely different political task from the handling of the 89th in 1965, or the 88th in 1963. All these considerations, which apply to the legislative office in the White House, apply equally to all its other offices. With a new President, with the end of the war in Vietnam, with the definition of different national "goals," the organisation of the White House would immediately look very different from its organisation under President Eisenhower, President Kennedy, or President Johnson, when the "institutionalizing" of the Presidency is supposed to have occurred. We are not, in fact, gazing on an institution at all, but on an arbitrarily flexible instrument of political will.

D.O.D. AND B.O.B.

The rapid development of the power of certain departments and agencies— the Bureau of the Budget[1] and the Department of Defense are the most obvious—is clearly an important example of "institutionalization." But the "institutionalizing" of what? It is this question which must be considered carefully, for it is not enough to show that these agencies have become more effective instruments of the political will of the President. If the claim that the Presidency is being "institutionalized" is to be sustained, it has to be shown that their own "institutionalization" has significantly altered the conditions in which the Presidential will operates: that it has significantly altered the character of the Presidential act.

Robert McNamara's assertion of the power of the Department of Defense over the established Service departments [was], of course, an indirect assertion of the Presidential power within his administration. But I am not in the least clear how significant this assertion [was]: how much of it [was] merely a reflection of the character of McNamara himself, of his "special relationship with the President," and of the wholly unmanageable nature of the war in Vietnam. I am not prepared to say, from my own observation, that the . . . character of the relationship of the President with his Service departments and his Service chiefs would survive the removal of any of these factors; that there has yet been an institutional change amounting (which is the argument I am contesting) to a constitutional change. (It is worth noticing, here, the role of the Department of Justice under Robert Kennedy: because of his personal relations with the President, even the most acute observers talked about it as an arm of the Presidency. But it was R. F. Kennedy who was the arm; not the Department.)

Similarly, the very significant development of the Bureau of the Budget . . . has obviously made the potential effectiveness of the Presidency much greater. Although President Truman relied on it, and therefore strengthened it a great deal, its nearly "institutional" development began, as so much else did, with President Eisenhower, in his attempt to create a Presidency which dispensed with the necessity for a President. (In much the same way, as is too seldom pointed out, the genius of his "military" leadership in the Second World War was to try and remove the necessity for generals. One always gets the impression from his memoirs that he could not understand why it was necessary to have a Bradley or a Patton or a Montgomery actually at the front.) From one Presidential memorandum—a significantly institutional method of proceeding—the Bureau of the Budget has moved, with the same pertinence and determination as the clerical bureaucracy under the medieval English kings, into feudal domains which previously seemed impregnable, and do not yet seem ripe to fall.

The extension of the activities and power of the Bureau of the Budget is the most obviously unexplored political development in the history of the United States in the past quarter of a century. Perhaps it is because it seems a dull subject: it is as "dull" as ditchwater, teeming with microbe, insect, and reptile life. Tadpoles, in the Bureau of the Budget, are frogs the next day—and all by virtue of the scribbled memoranda which are the hallmark of all institutional power, in any system, in any age. Climbing the steps of the Executive Office Building to visit the Bureau of the Budget is very like what it must have been to call on the scarcely known men who constituted the [obstinate] bureaucracy of Henry II. At any moment, when they talk of Commerce or Agriculture or Health, Education and Welfare as if these were part of a rebellious (ecclesiastical or lay) baronage, one expects to hear the cry, "Who will rid me of this turbulent priest?"; and one would not be in the least surprised if five knights rode immediately down Pennsylvania Avenue to butcher the department heads in the sanctuary of their departments.

The instruments of pain which the Bureau of the Budget has devised in its battle with the feudal departments of government are many and terrible. The whole mysterious eschatology (for so they represent it, as a doctrine concerning last, or final, matters) of cost-effectiveness has become an almost sublime machine of torture, which the Inquisition would not have disdained. Moreover, the Bureau is reaching, not only to the obvious feudal domains, the hitherto largely independent departments or agencies, but beyond them to the Congressional committees with whom the departments have elaborately feudal relationships of mutual right and obligation. There is no doubt, in fact, that the power of the Bureau of the Budget has changed so much in recent years that a proper Whig (if any were left) in a proper Whig assembly (if any still existed) would introduce a motion simply announcing that its power has increased, is increasing, and ought to be diminished. But I am still not certain that the change has been a radical institutional or constitutional one. . . .

THE DOORKEEPERS

Lastly, there is no evidence that any White House lore, any body of precedent or rules or conventions, is being built up, to be passed on from one Presidency to the next. The passage from Sorensen's *Kennedy*, which has been quoted above, makes it amply clear that President Kennedy ripped apart the elaborate White House staff system which President Eisenhower had constructed, and established another which suited his own needs, methods, and appetites. The peculiar circumstances of Presi-dent Johnson's succession, and especially the retention, for a number of months and, in some cases for years, of many of President Kennedy's own staff, concealed an equally personal reorganization. It was not merely that Valenti and Moyers, for example, were hardly the same kind of men as Sorensen and O'Donnell; it was that what was asked and expected of them were different. No description of the roles of Valenti and Moyers—the scope and manner and impact of their activities—would bear any institutional relationship to the roles of Sorensen and O'Donnell.

Similarly, to-day, now that Valenti and Moyers have gone, who would be bold enough to try and define, in sensible institutional terms, the role of Marvin Watson? That he is a powerful and influential doorkeeper (as was O'Donnell, as was Moyers) does not say enough. In every system of government, there have been people intelligent enough to realize that keeping the monarch's door is a source of power. It was not for nothing that, in the Middle Ages, the period in all history which has been most fertile in the creation of political institutions, the most powerful official was frequently called by the title of chamberlain (*chamber:* room; *-ling:* one concerned with); and it is no surprise, therefore, to find that, in as personal a system of government as the Presidency, the office of chamberlain still exists.

But the doorkeeper, as eunuch after eunuch in the ancient empires, and busy cleric after busy cleric in the Middle Ages, quickly discovered, can make the most flexible use of his opportunities. His post, in other words, is not an institutional one at all; it depends far too much on personal influence and opportunity; and the White House is pre-eminently a staff of competing doorkeepers.

Goosey, goosey, gander,
Whither shall I wander?
Upstairs and downstairs,
And in my lady's chamber.

The nursery rhyme, it is believed, had a precise political application when it was composed. It still has, to-day, a general political application: not least in the Executive Mansion of the President of the United States of America.

DISGUISING CONSTITUTIONAL CHANGE

Still, it is said, one cannot brush aside, in this way, the cumulative "institutionalization" which is represented, not only by the Bureau of the Budget, but by the Council of Economic Advisors and the Office of the Scientific Advisor to the President. There is no intention, here, of brushing aside anything that happens within the Executive Office Building, behind its 900 Doric columns, at the head of its four heroic cantilevered staircases. Henry Adams called the building itself "an architectural infant asylum." That the offices within it are not political infant asylums hardly needs stating.

I have dealt with the Bureau of the Budget, and acknowledged possible evidence of "institutionalization" there. (One of the obvious signs is the attractiveness of the Bureau to *career* civil servants in Washington. It can, more or less, pick and choose; and its staff has the positive bearing of an elite corps, much as Strategic Air Command once used to have in the armed services.) But, for all its obvious importance, it is hard to describe the Council of Economic Advisors as an "institution." If, as I have said, I am to recognize an institution, I wish to be shown a body whose *functions* and *attitudes* and *methods of procedure* exist, and remain very much the same, independently of the actual persons who staff them, or the actual politicians to whom they are responsible. I have followed, as closely as possible, some of the internal debates which have taken place about economic policy during the time I have been in the United States, and which have resulted in Presidential economic decisions of varying timeliness and effectiveness. But the bodies which, in these debates, have acted as "institutions," with permanent habits of address have been—lo and behold!—the Treasury and the Federal Reserve; and, of course, to meet members of the Federal Reserve System, not merely in its head-quarters in Washington, but scattered across the states, is to realise exactly what a formidable institution it is.

As for the Scientific Advisor to the President, and his office, their importance has declined as rapidly as it rose, during the period when science seemed to be the breastplate of the New Frontier. It may, of course, regain its importance, in new conditions, under another President; and its office, certainly, will survive, if only because the scientific community in the country expects it, and wants it. It has clients, in short, just as much as Commerce or Agriculture has always had them; and as even the Council of Economic Advisors may be said to have them now, among those who do not find the Treasury or the Federal Reserve congenial channels for expressing their interests or their opinions. These client relationships help to emphasise that the new arms of the Presidency are important, not because they represent its "institutionalization," but because they are a response to the expansion of its functions, and especially of the functions *it is expected to perform,* either by client bodies (e.g., the scientific community) or by the public at large. An expansion of functions *may* be a result of "institutionalization," and they *may* result in "institutionalization": this is the two-way story of all great bureaucracies. But a significant expansion of functions is the expression, primarily, not of institutional, but of constitutional change. Function, in a political process, is best defined in terms of expectation: of what people (either in the general public or as specific bodies) expect this or that part of the political process to do. In short, the powers of the constitution are redistributed because the expectation of performance by different bodies under the constitution has been redistributed. "Institutionalization" is a euphemism for disguising profound constitutional change.

A last example may be given. It could be said—it is said—that the President's supervision of foreign policy is being increasingly "institutionalized": in the National Security Council, for example, and almost physically in the Operations Room. But one should notice one feature of this development. The State Department itself increasingly leans on those in the White House who are concerned with foreign policy. The State Department itself has a heightened expectation of, not only what the White House will do, but what the White House should do. This raised expectation might seem, at first, to be only an internal, institutional, redistribution of functions. But is it much more. It is the result of a general—public— expectation of the role and powers of the President in a situation (only 25 years old) in which the definition of the national interest abroad and the creation and execution of a national policy abroad have become (as they were not before) such an unavoidable function of the political process, and one of such magnitude, that it is the Presidency which is expected to bear and perform it.

The change (like all the changes discussed), if it is institutional at all, is only secondarily so. It is primarily a constitutional change; for, a constitution may define functions, but it is itself made by expectations.

PRESIDENTIAL ENERGY

Some of the importance of Richard E. Neustadt's *Presidential Power* was that it was a restatement of the entirely personal, entirely accidental, entirely improvising nature of the supreme political office in the United

States, this nature being unavoidable because it is confronted, not only by Congress, but by a score of other repositories of power and influence usually (as has been said) "in combat postures." He never boldly takes it on, but he is restless with the idea of an "institutionalized" Presidency. Machiavelli wrote a prescription for the "new men" of the "new prince." Neustadt, in terms suitable to our more commonplace age, but with similar anticipation, wrote a prescription for the "new men" of the "new president."

Properly and significantly, Neustadt directed his attention (in the three central chapter headings) to: Persuasion; Reputation; Prestige. None of them is an institutional quality. None of them can be "institutionalized." In fact, Neustadt was writing about exactly what Hamilton and Madison and Jay wrote about in *The Federalist.* The two most remarkable features of *The Federalist,* in its discussion of the Presidency, are, first, that they discussed it so little and, secondly, that the only really extended discussion of its nature (Nos. 70-77) is a discussion of Presidential *energy.*

"The necessity of an energetic executive . . ."; "energy as the most necessary qualification . . ."—it was on this that Hamilton (they were Hamilton's papers) fixed his mind. And so (not surprisingly, for he was writing at the end of President Eisenhower's artful, but not fully satisfying, exercise in relaxed government) did Neustadt; and so, of course, did President Kennedy.

It is impossible to ignore his Uncompleted Presidency. I have not the slightest doubt that much of its importance derives from the fact that it was uncompleted: that now, and for ever more, it can be maintained that, given two full terms, this exceptionally gifted politician could have moved, convincingly and successfully, to the full realization of his policies and his hopes. I have to demur, if only on the grounds I have already suggested: that inaction is the only inexhaustible form of political energy. But the Uncompleted Presidency has enabled a constitutional legend to be created. The legend is that the personal energy of the President can overcome the energy of the other political bodies in the country whose primary interest is either in inaction or in different action. An Uncompleted Presidency is necessary to such a myth because it means that no final account can be rendered, that no final adding up of the credit and debit columns can be made. It means that the benefit of the doubt can be given to exaggerated and even exotic claims.

Would President Kennedy's second term have been the record of achievement which Sorensen and Schlesinger and Neustadt (in the after-word to *Presidential Power*) ask us to believe? I doubt it, and I am grateful for their spirits that the disillusionment never came: disillusionment, not with the man, but with the capacity of the office. How much would Lincoln have handled Reconstruction? It is the question which I never cease to ask myself as I pass the Lincoln Memorial, and watch the tourists taking their snapshots with their Polaroids. He might well have handled it superbly, but one must be given leave to doubt it. In a list of the ten greatest men the world has ever known, Lincoln would be my only confident entry as a politician (except, possibly, Elizabeth I who, in difficult and alarming circumstances, created a nation and the idea of nation which were to flower for another three and a half centuries). Yet, even our awareness of the vast achievement of Lincoln depends partly to-day on the fact that it was an Uncompleted Presidency, that the final account could never be rendered.

WRITTEN AND UNWRITTEN CONSTITUTIONS

The energy of the Presidency, actual and potential, must be the starting point. But, before going any further, it is necessary to advance two further suggestions on which the rest of my argument depends, especially since they are suggestions which I would not have advanced so confidently without an experience of Presidential government in the United States.

First, it is about time that we abandoned the fruitless distinction between "written" and "unwritten" constitutions. The more experience one has of political systems—whether direct personal experience of those existing to-day, or the indirect personal experience of reading oneself into the political adventures of the past—the more it is clear that, however useful to the English Whigs, at their moment in the 17th and 18th centuries, the contrast between "written" and "unwritten" constitutions is dangerously false.

England is supposed to be the great exemplar of a country with an "unwritten" constitution. As I have tried to convey already, there could be no more absurd falsity. Its constitution is written in an indescribable number of bureaucratic memoranda, of judicial decisions, and of political precedent, all of them written. Against all the traditional Whig propaganda, I would argue that England is not, and cannot be, subject to arbitrary and personal rule precisely because its constitution is written in a thousand-and-one scraps of paper.

The American constitution is supposedly written: and yet it needs, now, massive commentaries to explain, not merely what it means, but what it is. It has been wrenched this way and that, mostly by the Presidency and the Supreme Court, until it has become impossible to know what the constitution is merely by reading it. Since the farthest years, when the Supreme Court made its first confident assertion of the scope of federal law and federal authority, to the nearest years, when we have witnessed another such confident assertion, it has been abundantly clear that the constitution of the United States is no more "written", in the conventional sense, than that of England. From Lincoln's invocation and generous interpretation of the war power of the President, to President Johnson's employment of the war power without even a declaration of war, there has been no reason for regarding the constitution of the United States as anything but custom-made (a phrase, in America, of pleasing ambiguity)— and custom-made, sometimes, by presidential tailors with very sharp and long scissors.

POPULAR WILL AND REPRESENTATIVE ASSEMBLIES

Secondly, it is time that we rid our minds altogether of the idea that, in our age, the poular will or the popular voice find their true or convincing or authoritative expression in representative assemblies. It is certainly not true of France, which has returned, with an equanimity born of indolence, to its (revolutionary *and* Napoleonic) belief that government is "the incontrovertible agent of the . . . organic people." It is certainly not true of England, where representation has ceased to be a serious consideration in the political system, and the nature of the constitution is, with only marginal restraints, plebiscitary in its nature, a direct transference of power taking place from the people to the government. It is a *little* more true of the United States, because the two Houses of Congress can still exercise considerable restraints; but the fact remains that the popular will, in any energizing form, is again transferred directly from the people to the executive.

It was L. S. Amery who, in England, first cleared out the rubbish which the Whig propagandists had left in the attics of most constitutional textbooks. The executive, he said, had always been the "initiating, directing, energizing" influence in the constitution. Search as one may, there is no alternative to it being the same in the United States. (The Supreme Court, by its interpretation of the constitution, can also be an "initiating and directing and energizing" influence; but, when it is so, it is because it is asserting the scope of the federal magistracy, judicial and executive.)

It is not strange that the idea of the executive as the energetic and energizing influence in a political system should crop up in both *The Federalist* and Amery's *Thoughts on the Constitution*. The idea of an initiating and directing executive is essential to the notion of the national state; and where it has always, in England, reflected what Dicey called the "omnipotence and undisputed supremacy throughout the whole country of the central government," it must increasingly come to reflect the same in the United States, whatever the distribution of powers in its constitution. It is essential, also, to the notion of democracy; for the one inescapable fact about a democracy is that its appetite for government is insatiable. "On, on and on—up, up, and up"—to use Ramsay MacDonald's favourite flourish of rhetoric—it goes: free enterprise creates the popular motor car; free citizens buy it; and, in a trice, both free enterprise and free citizens are demanding federally supported highways to be built through their states. The conservative critics of democracy in the 19th century were right in their forebodings: merely by allowing rein to insatiable popular appetites, strong government would become inevitable.

At the height of the city riots in 1967, Bill D. Moyers called, publicly, for Robert McNamara to be made *tsar* in charge of clearing the city slums and ghettoes. Popular appetite had been expressed—there is no doubt that much of the looting was the simplest expression of the simplest appetites— and immediately came democracy's only response to popular appetite: the request for a *tsar*.

After Hiroshima and Nagasaki, Earl Long buttonholed one of the most violent supporters of state rights in Louisiana. "What are you going to do now", he asked, "now that the Feds have the atom bomb?" It was an extreme example, but a dry recognition, of the "omnipotence and undisputed supremacy throughout the whole country" of a national and democratic government, even under the "written" constitution of the United States. A strong executive, *The Federalist* continually argued, is threatened by "the maxims of republican jealousy." Who is jealous, now, of the power of the federal executive, when popular appetites want what only it can supply, because it "has the ships, it has the men, it has the money, too"?

"AS ONE PEOPLE . . ."

I do not wish it to be thought that, in my ignorance of American politics, I am not aware of the pluralist nature of American society, and the remnants of pluralism in its constitution. I am merely asserting that the executive energy which a national and democratic state needs for its survival is now to be found only in the federal executive and the federal judiciary. I know that it is possible to point to individual states, individual governors, individual mayors who still give fitful demonstrations that executive energy does not yet reside solely in Washington, D. C. But this is not enough. The more energetic, for example, that the schemes of Mayor Lindsay of New York City and Governor Rockefeller of New York State become—the more ambitious in their objectives, and the more extensive in their scope— the larger and more urgent become their pleas for federal help and federal money. In short, the multiplication of interests now able to mobilise in such a way that they have direct access to the central government, in order to press their demands on society, is not going to result in a corresponding diversity and complexity of political institutions and activity, but only in the strengthening of one institution and one kind of activity: not in a variety of "plebiscites," but in one plebiscite.

Where, then, does the source of energy of the Presidency reside? Quite obviously, it resides, first, in the actual and symbolic importance of the fact that he is the "Head of State." "America has no more solemn rite than the inauguration of a President," says Arthur Schlesinger, Jr. in his introduction to a collection of the inaugural addresses of the Presidents of the United States:

> *Every four years since 1789 the austere ceremony has suspended the passions of politics to permit an interlude of national reunion . . . the nation listens for a moment as one people. . . .*

To whom?

[In 1952] Edward Shils observed the coronation of Elizabeth II, and then wrote a brilliant sociological essay explaining its meaning and its relevance. He was, in fact, bowled over by the ceremony, and by the mood it created (or appeared to create). In every stage of the medieval ritual, he found an exact, contemporary social significance: the Queen stripped, at the beginning of the ceremony, of all her apparel, until she stands in nothing but a plain white shift, the image of a frail and powerless human being, only then to receive the Robe, the Sword, the Orb, the Sceptre, the Crown, the symbols of authority and majesty, *from other hands*, from the spiritual and temporal representatives of the nation and of God. Shils was so excited by the whole business that he cheerfully recorded the fact that, according to the Metropolitan Police, there were no pickpockets in the crowds on Coronation Day. Even the criminal classes, so it seemed, were moved by the coronation to regard themselves, for one day, as members of society. Even they had listened "for a moment as one people."

I do not know whether crime abates every fours years, on Inauguration Day, in Washington, D. C. But I do believe that the character of the Presidency is such that the majority of the people can be persuaded to look to it for a kind of leadership which no politician, in my opinion, should be allowed, let alone invited, to give. "If people want a sense of purpose," Harold Macmillan once said to me, "they should get it from their archbishops": a remark of recognizably English accent, finely delimiting the area of politics. This delimitation is essential to a free society, and it is the most obvious mark of a society that cares more for other things than freedom that its political leaders try to give the nation, the people, "a sense of purpose," and so justify any interference with their private pursuits, inclinations, and morals.

CAESAROPAPISM?

The Presidency seems to me to be a seed bed for, and already to have in it some of the seeds of, the most refined of all absolutist systems: Caesaropapism. Some American political scientists have tried to persuade me that it is really a constitutional monarchy, stuck more or less where the English monarchy was stuck in 1688. But no one (except Macaulay, writing his absurd eulogies a century and a half later) ever looked for "a sense of purpose" to William III, a tedious *statdholder* from the Netherlands. It was the true achievement of the Whigs to make the English monarchy dull and boring (and rather vulgar as well) and, in the process, to eliminate all concern with national and moral purpose from English politics—which does not mean from English society—for ever.

The Presidency, as we are coming to know it, is very different. When, some time ago, I expressed the view that President Kennedy reminded me of Justinian, it was drawn to my attention that another English journalist, Patrick O'Donovan of the London *Observer*, had, while he was in Washington, compared President Johnson with Justinian. I do not think this coincidence can be altogether dismissed. Historical analogies can, of course, be pushed too far. But Americans are either unable or afraid to make them at all; and, as a result, they sacrifice some of the perceptions these can offer. O'Donovan made his comparison in 1965, when President Johnson seemed to be an Emperor on the Potomac; and both he and I were commenting on the energy, equal to Justinian's, which two successive Presidents appeared to be bringing to the overdue business of the consolidation of an empire. The more I [considered] the work of the Presidency [during the past several years], the more it [seemed] to me to be embarked on a consolidation (or codification) of imperial (or federal) law and administration, with the purpose of creating, as Justinian set out to do, a commonwealth of citizens under one law, all of them persuaded of the ultimate justice, in doctrine and in practice, of the regime to which they consent.

If this interpretation is correct, then the position of the President as Head of State is going to become of increasing importance. Of all the multiple facets of Caesaropapism—instructive even to-day, because it attempted to work out the relations between people, emperor, pope, and God, in one constitution—the one which matters here is that it managed to achieve a surprisingly convincing combination between the *ascending* and *descending* theories of government: between the belief that power is conferred from below by the people, and the belief that it is conferred from above, by a superior force, i.e. God. The throne in the Byzantine Empire was elective: the people were the electors, and they could take the crown away. Indeed "the legal right to revolution" was recognized, and was voiced, for example, by the Patriarch, Nicholas Mysticus, in the 10th century. But—and it was by this trick that the Byzantine Emperors sustained themselves for so long—the people were also the Christian Commonwealth, and when they gave their assent to the Emperor at his coronation, they in fact acknowledged him as the representative of the Christian Commonwealth, and therefore as the Viceroy of God. His power having been given to him from below, the Emperor then exercised it as being confirmed from above. It was a brilliant device.

THE ORGANIC PEOPLE

More and more, it seems to me, the Presidency in the United States, having originally received power from below, according to an *ascending* theory of government, will act, and is already acting, according to a *descending* theory, as if power is confirmed to it from above by the law, the nation, the allegedly manifest (one is tempted to say, revealed) goals of the organic people. This is a recent development, and my description will be resisted by those who still emphasise the atomised nature of American society: a society of expectant capitalists and their institutions, able to buck the power of the state. I can only reply that I think their picture is already out of date (as both extreme right and new left instinctively recognise). The enmeshing of big business and the universities with the federal government hardly fits their picture. It fits the portents I am trying to describe here.

In England, the myth is still sustained that the executive is continually subject, from day to day, to a reaffirmation of assent from below, through the votes of the House of Commons. In practice, this is no longer true. But the myth is still useful. Although Harold Wilson from time to time [tried] it, no Prime Minister can announce a policy in the House of Commons (which is the only place he can announce it) as if he were a national leader, the Head of State; for there, opposite him, is the Opposition, representing half of the nation, and ready with a motion of censure and rejection. We know, anyhow, that the real Head of State is not there, but at the race-course, and the majority of the "organic people" are there, in spirit, with her.

In contrast, of course, President de Gaulle, having had power conferred on him from below (he [used] the mandate like a coronation), . . . proceeded to act as if it had been confirmed to him from above: as if he were "the incontrovertible agent . . . of the organic people," the repre-sentative of *la France douce*—or rather, these days, *la France aigre*. Similarly, the President of the United States increasingly acts, in day-to-day matters, under the same claim, that he represents a superior national will—a claim which, in a moment of national crisis, President Lincoln felt bound to assert. (In terms of political theory, Lincoln claimed to represent a national will, the *real* will, even, of the organic people, at a moment when it could reasonably have been claimed that both national will and organic people had been shown not to exist. But he won, and so we know him to be great.)

I must emphasize again that I am fully aware of the countless bodies of interest which exist in this country, able to resist and obstruct the claims of the Presidency to exercise the national or popular will. But the fact remains that these bodies, even when they are organized in the two Houses of Congress, cannot and do not claim to represent the organic people. In fact their strength lies in the quite opposite claim: that they represent the people divided into separate and local interests, its organic unity destroyed. Again, therefore, the constitution of the United States might seem to combine two opposite theories of government: organic and inorganic representation of the people. But, in the modern age, no national state, and no democratic state of any size has been able to face the problems of government without, in practice, falling back more and more on the theory that a direct transference of power takes place from the people to the executive, that there is a direct transformation of popular energy into executive energy. In the United States, the difference in the political theory is evident in the difference between the methods of the New Deal and those of the Great Society. Roosevelt, for all his improvisation and his creative political genius, really manipulated the traditional political system. But the instinct of the administration of President Johnson has been to wrench both the theory and practice of the federal constitution almost to the point of annihilating it.

Of course, the effort has had more failures than successes. Of course, President Johnson . . . encountered the inexhaustible reserves of inaction and obstruction which separate and local interests possess in a country as large as the United States. But the effort, in future Presidencies, will continue. The theory of the American constitution needs urgently to be restated in terms of the democratic, and not liberal, assumptions which now prevail in the Western world. But political theory, in the United States, is not taken very seriously.

THE NEED FOR POLITICAL THEORY

There are several obvious results of the working of the American Presidency in these conditions. In the first place, people come to expect too much of it: no sooner is a need demonstrated, an appetite expressed, than there is a demand for a presidential *tsar*. Secondly, and of course related to the first, the federal government itself tries to do too much: thus, there is a profound constitutional, as well as any political or personal, reason why the [Johnson] administration [burdened itself] with so many tasks. Thirdly, the available talent in the country, if attracted to public service, drifts more and more to the federal government, thus weakening all other sources of executive energy. Both the exaggerated elevation which the "new men" felt in the presidency of Kennedy, and the exaggerated disappointment so many of them [felt] in that of his successor, are explicable in terms of the "new presidency" itself, what is demanded of it and what it expects to do, and of the constitutional assumptions which increasingly support it.

Constitutions do matter. We spend far too much time these days examining political institutions—hence making the faulty analysis of an "institutionalized" Presidency—instead of the constitution which determines the relationship between them. Moreover, in examining constitutions, political theory is ultimately the only true assistance. If I have concentrated, in this article, on the combination of roles in the Presidency, it is because I believe that that combination lends itself, as in France, to the kind of distortion of a liberal constitution which the appetites of a democracy in a national state always demand: to the elevation of the descending over the ascending theory of government.

I am new to the Presidency. I have deliberately emphasized, perhaps over-emphasized, the one aspect of it which has most forcibly struck me: the elements in it which could lead to a form of Caesaropapism (which is a very different matter from the simple Caesarism which has always been feared to lie latent in the American Presidency, not least by the English Whigs in the early 19th century). In my edition of the *Encyclopaedia Britannica*, the article on Justinian is still the one composed by Lord Bryce. "Justinian's age," he says, "was quite unequal in intellect to so vast an undertaking as the fusing on scientific principles into one organic whole of the entire law of the empire." They are words of warning, worth addressing to the "new men" of our own age. (Was there not a hint of such a warning in Aaron Wildavsky's "The Political Economy of Efficiency" in *The Public Interest,* Summer 1967?) For, with all my selection and over-emphasis, I would add in conclusion that there is no aspect of the Presidency which does not seem to me to invite, as urgently, the assistance of political theory. The difference, in organization and role, between the national parties, on which the President relies, and the state and local parties is an obvious area in which political theory can offer illumination. So is the whole of the nominating (and, indeed, electing) process, which no longer performs, in theory or practice, what was originally expected of it.

When the two principles of representation and federation, which Hume said would alone enable a popular government to adapt itself to a vast continent, are to-day so changed and weakened, one can indeed question whether the federal constitution, as originally conceived, will survive. I am convinced only that its condition is critical, and that it requires, not only empirical observation, but the kind of political theory which makes even the prudent *Federalist* timeless.

THE PRESIDENCY AND THE PRESS

George E. Reedy

Of the few social institutions which tend to keep a president in touch with reality, the most effective—and the most resented by the chief beneficiary—is the press. It is the only force to enter the White House from the outside world with a direct impact upon the man in the Oval Room which cannot be softened by intermediary interpreters or deflected by sympathetic attendants.

This state of affairs does not arise out of any special integrity on the part of the press which, after all, is an institution manned by human beings subject to the same forces that govern human conduct generally. Neither does it spring from any unusual defenses or counterforces working against manipulation on the part of the president. It is simply a matter of the press function, which is to inform the public of the president's actions. No matter how sympathetically that function is performed, a foolish act will appear foolish, an unpopular act will arouse antagonism, and an act in conflict with previous actions will appear contradictory.

The significant impact of the press upon the president lies not in its critical reflections but in its capacity to tell him what he is doing as seen through other eyes. This is a service which, though little appreciated, is indispensable, as it will rarely, if ever, be performed by any other medium. Virtually all other communications that reach him will be shaped either directly or indirectly by people who wish either to conciliate or antagonize the chief executive. In either case, the contents of the message and the manner in which it is phrased will be governed as much by the sender's judgment of how best to produce a desired effect upon the recipient as by the substantive matters with which the sender deals.

Many newspaper stories and a much higher number of columns are written solely for their impact upon the president. Newspapermen are not exempt from the universal urge to shape history—or even to curry favor with an important element in their livelihood. But the newspaper itself is addressed to the public. If it is to survive, it must, on a daily basis, offer a reasonable presentation of events within certain bounds of accuracy and perspective. It cannot dedicate itself solely to the edification of one man, no matter how important that man may be. And while it can rearrange facts or interpret them in the best or worst possible light, its ability to *change* facts is severely limited as long as any degree of competition remains.

Presidents have considerable leverage with which to manipulate part of the press and all try to do so with varying degrees of success. The principal source of the leverage is the unusual position of the president as one of the very few figures in public life who has in his exclusive possession a type of news virtually indispensable to the social and economic security of any reporter assigned to cover the White House full time. This category of newsworthy material consists of the president himself—his thoughts, his relationship with his friends and employees, his routine habits, his personal likes and dislikes, his intimate moments with his family and his associates. The fact that these things constitute "news" of a front-page variety gives the president a trading power with individual newsmen of such magnitude that it must be seen at close quarters to be credited.

There is no other official of the government who can make a top headline story merely by releasing a routine list of his daily activities.

There is no other official of the government who can be certain of universal newspaper play by merely releasing a picture of a quiet dinner with boyhood friends. There is no other official who can attract public attention merely by granting an interview consisting of reflections, no matter how banal or mundane, on social trends in fields where he has no expertise and in which his concepts are totally irrelevant to his function as a public servant.

It is not too hard for any other high official of the government "to make news." But, with the exception of notorious scandal, he can do so only through activities which bear a direct relationship to his official function. A secretary of state can command headlines by denouncing the Soviet Union, but no one really cares about his views on dogs. A secretary of labor can inspire widespread interest by commenting on a nationwide strike, but only in his hometown is any newspaper likely to print a picture of him playing with his grandson. An attorney general will receive respectful attention when he delivers an opinion on crime in the streets, but no reporter will be credited with an exclusive for revealing that he prefers Scotch to bourbon. As the interest of correspondents in government officials extends primarily to their *public* acts, it is not possible for those officials to monopolize the release of their activities. Consequently, the press can approach such officials on the basis of a total independence which cannot be sustained by those who cover the president. It is not at all unusual for newspapers to assign correspondents to cover cabinet agencies who are personally at odds with the heads of the agencies, but any responsible editor will have long second thoughts before assigning to the White House a man or a woman who has personally incurred presidential wrath or even the dislike of secretaries in the press office. Sometimes, long second thoughts will result in the assignment of the offending reporter anyway. But such occasions are rare.

The temptations inherent in this situation to "trade out"—to swap golden nuggets for "good" stories—are so overwhelming that few, if any, presidents of the modern era have been able to resist. It is taken for granted in the Washington press corps that there are certain "favorite" reporters who have "an in with the old man," as it is impossible for this state of affairs to be concealed for any great period of time. The press corps, in the early days of any administration, watches nervously for the first signs of a story that begins "the president is known to feel" or "the president has told close associates." There is a constant jockeying for a position which will permit the correspondent to deliver to his paper a set of exclusive photographs of the president and the First Lady walking in the White House garden (pictures taken by the official White House photographer). And the competition among the television networks for exclusive film reaches heights of savagery.

Any president would be well advised to resist the opportunities that are held forth so temptingly. Many presidents have been so advised. But it is not yet recorded that the advice has been accepted. The rewards of "trading out" are immediate and apparent. The penalties, which follow inexorably, are far down the road—so far down, in fact, that when they are exacted, it is difficult to trace back their origins. Every president who has played favorites has suffered in the long run. It is doubtful whether any of them will ever accept the truth of that statement. To understand it, it is necessary to back up for a moment and analyze the problem of presidential press relations.

A president's press problems are really quite simple. He does not have to make any extraordinary effort to attract attention. All channels of public communication are open to him any hour of the day or night. Every word that he utters will, sooner or later, find its way into print. If he does not like the paraphrases used by writing reporters, he can always take to the airwaves and the electronic media will deliver his exact language, with his own intonations, into every American home. He can keep newspapermen at his side twenty-four hours a day, if he so chooses, and he can depend upon their listening to his every argument. There is no other human being on the face of the globe who has any comparable facilities for projecting every thought, every nuance, that is in his mind.

Theodore Roosevelt considered the White House "a bully pulpit" and more than fifty years later an assistant wrote the phrase into a speech by Lyndon B. Johnson. It is likely that, left to his own devices, Johnson would have thought in terms of a magnificent stage—and the transition from pulpit to stage is one of the more significant trends in modern history.

A pulpit is a platform for persuasion and exhortation. A stage is a setting for a presentation which may or may not carry a message. It can be an instrument for education and leadership or an attention-getting device for entertainment.

As a stage, the White House has no equal in the electronic age. It is equipped with props that cannot be matched by Hollywood, Broadway, and Madison Avenue combined. It is staffed by technicians capable of solving the most difficult electronics problems in the wink of an eye. And above all, it has the faculty of commanding the instant and total attention of television networks that dominate the largest audience in all history.

In no other field is the power of a president so immediately apparent as in his relationship with the television networks. His slightest wish is treated as an imperial [decree] and no press secretary ever has to ask for time on the air. He need indicate only that the president will be available.

During the Johnson administration the networks went so far as to staff a highly expensive TV room in the White House with warm cameras manned throughout the working day. This gave the president the potential of appearing live on nationwide networks at a few minutes' notice, and the fact that he used the facility only rarely did not deter television executives from meeting high weekly bills for its operation.

Presented with instrumentalities like this, the average public-relations man planning an industrial or political campaign would, with justification, consider himself in seventh heaven. He would regard as absolutely ludicrous an assertion that he had a "press problem" (although he might be tempted to leave this impression with his client). And he would be absolutely correct. The reality is that a president has no press problems (except for a few minor administrative technicalities), but he does have political problems, all of which are reflected in their most acute form by the press.

Why, then, do presidents spend so much time discussing with their confidants—and sometimes with the public—their "press problems"? Why, then, have the relationships between presidents and the press over the years traveled such a rocky road? The answer involves some complicated and subtle points which no one comprehends completely but which are worthy of study not just in terms of the press but in terms of the presidency itself.

There is a deep-seated human tendency to confuse unhappy news with unhappy events and to assume that if the news can be altered, so can the events. This tendency is particularly accentuated among monarchs. . . . Peter the Great strangled the courier who brought him the tidings of the defeat at Narva. John F. Kennedy (or at least someone on his staff) cancelled the White House subscription to the *New York Herald Tribune*. The two acts were closely related and differed only in the degree of retaliation available to the two men.

At stake is a twentieth-century form of the word magic of primitive society. There is a widespread tendency to assume that the qualities that words represent can somehow be transferred to objects, regardless of their content. Thus, the advertising man holds, as an article of faith, that any stale idea will become "exciting" if the word "exciting" is drummed into the human consciousness a sufficient number of times by the electronic media. And similarly, it is assumed that a man somehow becomes "dedicated" and "forward looking" if he can just persuade people to associate the two adjectives with his name in print.

The techniques of word magic are unquestionably successful when they are applied to commodities which are necessities of life and which do not differ essentially from competing commodities, such as soap. Whether they apply in a more sophisticated environment is questionable. And whether they can override objective facts is something that has yet to be demonstrated. A president deals in objective facts. If the nation is at war, he must draft young men to risk their lives in battle. If the nation embarks on great projects, he must tax the people in order to finance the federal activities. When he makes the promises that all political leaders make in moments of euphoria, he arouses expectations that will not be quieted except through fulfillment.

It is only in George Orwell's world that war can be labeled peace; brutality labeled justice; economic misery labeled prosperity. Within the White House itself, of course, it is possible to apply much of the Orwellian formula with a high degree of success. No assistant or secretary has ever yet won an argument with a president—and very few have tried. It is entirely possible within the walls of 1600 Pennsylvania Avenue to create a universe that is utterly to the liking of the principal occupant. He will not go so far as to alter all facts. But he can be certain that the facts will be brought to him in the most sympathetic of forms and with the harshest blows softened. Within this atmosphere, the only grating note comes from the newspapers and the electronic media which are produced on the outside and which are not subject to rewriting. The *Congressional Record* and the White House record can be "corrected"—but not, at least at present, the record of the Fourth Estate.

Unfortunately for the mental peace of presidents, events cannot be altered significantly by control over the printed word—at least not for any extended period of time. While the White House does have at its command instrumentalities for manipulating the press, they are effective only in regard to adjectives, not to the hard, substantive news that is the ultimate shaper of public opinion. Furthermore, the more successful the manipulation, the less useful becomes that part of the press which has been manipulated.

This situation arises out of the principal communications problem that faces every president—maintaining believability. The very factors that give the chief executive his tremendous advantage in the field of public relations also give him his greatest problem. It is simply that he is covered around the clock, with every word taken down and filed somewhere. Consequently, he is under the compulsion—if he is to be believed—of making his actions fit his words. Both his words and his actions make an extremely deep impression. He can lose the confidence of the people very quickly when the two do not coincide.

In this respect, a president is subjected to rules and to tests which do not apply to other types of political leaders. A senator can announce his ringing support of law and order in the streets of our cities without any fear of embarrassment over the future trend of crime statistics. But a president who makes the same statement must follow it up with action against muggers, thieves, and rapists and if the crime statistics do not go down, he is in trouble. A governor of a state can take a firm stand on cleaning up air pollution, and if the atmosphere remains foul he can explain to his constituents that the cause is the noisome discharge of sulphur-laden smoke from across the state line and there is nothing he can do about it. But a president who assumes a similar stance can never convince the American people that the problem is beyond his control.

In assessing a president, there is a deeply ingrained public assumption that his choices are determined by what he wants to do and what he does not want to do and he is, quite rightly, not accorded the benefit of the doubt when reality fails to measure up to his predictions. This is a very harsh test indeed, but there is a simple answer—presidents need not open their mouths until they have thought their way through the problem and devised workable solutions for which they need not apologize. It would be a great day for the country if this were to become the rule, but that is one day which will never arrive.

Idle words are a luxury in which no president can indulge. Of course, every presidential inauguration has been preceded by a campaign in which the promises are, at the very least, extravagant. Fortunately, the beginning of a term is marked by a public willingness to give the new president every opportunity, and if he uses this "honeymoon period" to establish his credibility, he can look forward to a relatively secure eight-year tenure in office.

The classic story of the gap between promise and performance goes back to the political grand master Franklin D. Roosevelt. In the 1932 campaign he promised the American people that he would cut governmental spending and balance the budget—a foolish promise which was forgotten almost immediately after the New Dealers entered Washington, frantic in their desire to deliver some relief to the depression-stricken populace. A torrent of spending measures spewed out of the Capitol in the famous "100 Days" of FDR. Republicans, as soon as they recovered from their shock over the magnitude of their defeat, launched a campaign to remind Mr. Roosevelt publicly of his promises to cut spending. The principal promise had been made in a speech in Pittsburgh, and after a few days of particularly vehement GOP attack, Mr. Roosevelt called in his adviser Judge Samuel Rosenman and asked him to study the speech and produce an explanation. Mr. Rosenman returned in a matter of hours and said: "Mr. President, there is only one way to explain this speech. Deny that you ever made it!"

Fortunately, Mr. Roosevelt was still in the "honeymoon" period and the problems confronting the American people were so great that no one really cared about budget cutting. He was never again, however, granted such leeway and he quickly learned to match words with action and to forgo statements, or at least make them so fuzzy that they were incomprehensible, when he clearly lacked the resources to back his promises. . . . Mr. Roosevelt was a remarkable man who learned even from his own mistakes. This is one trait that few of his predecessors or his successors emulated.

Furthermore, the influence of a president is so great that people very soon identify those who are known as his "spokesmen." He eventually finds thoughts and programs attributed to him solely because they appeared in the columns of "pet" newspapermen. When those newspapermen move to his defense in print, their explanations of his actions are suspect and discounted in the opinion of presidential observers.

It is actually dangerous for a newspaperman to have a close personal friendship with a political leader. Such unfortunates find themselves identified as "sycophants" regardless of how scrupulous they are in handling their contacts. One of the outstanding examples is the columnist William S. White, a man of massive integrity, whose fortunes declined under the Lyndon Johnson administration simply because of a friendship with the president which dated back more than thirty-five years. White, whose politics were far more conservative than those of the president, found that he could not write as forcefully as he wished on many subjects without embarrassing the White House because his words were interpreted as emanating from the Oval Room. His circulation actually picked up when Johnson left the White House because people started to read him for what *he* was saying rather than for what they thought the *president* was saying, and he had a natural audience for his point of view.

Even more important is the fact that since manipulation of the press involves favoritism to some newsmen it inevitably creates antagonism among others. There is an old political rule which is generally stated: "Every time a man does a favor he makes nineteen enemies and one ingrate." Obviously, favors cannot be done for every member of the press or they would become meaningless. For every newspaperman who is placed in an advantageous position, several others must be placed in a disadvantageous position. Every president who plays the game inevitably winds up with more enemies than friends.

Basically, however, the long-standing antagonism between presidents and the press has deeper roots than the childish games that the White House usually plays with the Washington press corps. It is more validly traced to the fundamental dichotomy of interest that exists between newspapermen and politicians. No amount of manipulation can ever produce newspapers that are satisfactory to political leaders, or politicians who are satisfactory to newspapermen (unless George Orwell's nightmare, in which politicians had the capacity not only to produce newspapers but to rewrite the newspapers of the past, comes to fruition). A few words are necessary on this point.

Politicians, as a class, are dedicated to changing the world. With very few exceptions, they have in their minds some bright and shining ideal which is so obviously superior to what exists that it seems to be reality, with the actual world around them merely some kind of an aberration. Newspapermen, on the other hand, are held, to some degree, to the facts. They can play with adjectives; they can arrange the facts in any order that suits their convenience; they can give their prejudices full sway. But it is still their principal mission to present the world as it is. The two points of view are fundamentally incompatible.

Since the politician is oriented toward changing the world, he is constantly in a search for help. He divides the people with whom he must deal into friend or foe—those who have a "constructive" attitude and those who are purely "aginners." To have any force and effect as a political leader, he must be a partisan. And no partisan ever seized and maintained a position of power on the basis of self-examination and inner doubts. An

Adlai Stevenson could arouse the respect and admiration of millions of people, but, like Hamlet who never became king, he never became president and it is doubtful that there is any conceivable set of circumstances under which he would ever have achieved the prize.

It is an article of faith with most politicians that any newspaper item even remotely touching upon the government was written through partisan inspiration, not just because it happened. The concept that there are professional standards which determine news leads and news placement is alien to their view of society.

In justice, it must be recognized that a large proportion of political stories originate with a choice morsel leaked to the press for a partisan purpose. The Washington reporter who does not play Democrats off against Republicans and vice versa is simply ignoring a fundamental tool of his trade and is not destined for success. An occasional plug in return for a hot item is considered within the bounds of ethical conduct.

But the politician's view of the press is not limited to recognition of this obvious aspect of the game. He refuses to concede that there are events which will find their way into newspapers without any partisan help whatsoever. Moreover, he is incapable of crediting newsmen with the ability to make simple deductions unassisted by people with an ax to grind.

An illustrative incident which stays vividly in my mind took place in the late 1940s when I was a reporter for the United Press. The Democrats had just recaptured Congress after two years of Republican domination and the interregnum had produced some interesting shifts in the Democratic hierarchy. Among other things, the inexorable workings of the seniority system had placed Representative William L. Dawson of Illinois in the top spot on the House Executive Expenditures Committee. Since Mr. Dawson was the first Negro to be in this position since Reconstruction, this was news by any standard, particularly as the committee had broad investigative powers. Furthermore, there were a number of Southern members in the group.

A poll of the committee was practically a reflex action. My first call was to a Southern congressman. My question was simply whether there would be any trouble. The response was a snarl: "When did [some name unknown to me] reach you?" I was completely taken back—even more so when I discovered that the congressman, with whom I had reasonably cordial relations, was referring to a small-town lawyer who was building an opposition political machine in his district. He accepted my statement that I had never heard of his foe but remained unshaken in his conviction that someone had "told" me there would be trouble or I would not have phoned him. His conviction was reinforced later in the day when he was called with the identical query by members of other wire services and newspapers. This, to him, was proof of conspiracy, not simply evidence that professional newsmen were reacting to a professional standard of judgment. (It should be added that the committee poll disclosed no opposition to Mr. Dawson and the stories that were written merely stated that he would become chairman.)

There are very few politicians who do not cherish privately the notion that there should be some regulation of the news. To most of them, "freedom of the press" is a gigantic put-on, a clever ploy which has enabled publishers as an economic group in our society to conduct themselves with a degree of arrogance and disregard of the public interest that is denied to other groups. The "ploy" has succeeded to an extent where it cannot be challenged publicly and therefore must be accorded formal deference. But the deference is purely formal and rarely expressed with heartfelt enthusiasm.

If censorship ever comes to the United States, it will explode out of the frustrations of a political leader convinced that the public good is being thwarted by self-serving reporters distorting the news. It will be the culmination of the natural political instinct to extend to the press the same standards he applies to the rest of society—does this help or hurt a worthy cause? The crusader is much more likely to sound the death knell of free expression than the cynic.

The great game of politics is a highly personal pursuit in which official activity and social amenities are inextricably intermingled. A politician really does not expect a fellow human being to sell his soul for a handshake or a free barbecue. But he is always hurt and bewildered when the recipient of the shake or the beef responds in a mood that he interprets as antagonistic. This attitude is extended not only to other politicians but to businessmen, professionals, clergymen, and the press. It is impossible for newspapermen—even those who are psychologically disposed to walk in the footsteps of the world's oldest profession—to respond on every occasion with what the political leader regards as an appropriately grateful reciprocity. Therefore, in the politician's mind newspapermen are invariably guilty of "ingratitude." Furthermore, politicians look to members of the press to be "constructive," to help them put across worthwhile programs for the betterment of humanity. It should be added, in all justice, that this is strikingly similar to the attitude of civic leaders, who always begin any crusade for municipal betterment by calling upon the editor of the local newspaper and asking him to "get behind" it.

The concept of a "constructive reporter" is a contradiction in terms. A newspaperman who selects his stories on the basis of "the national interest" is actually doing the national interest a disservice. He has no business making such decisions. The closest he can come to it and still remain true to his trade is to report what others conceive to be "in the national interest." This is a point which no successful politician can grasp.

Frequently, newspapers themselves fail to grasp the point. The classic case is the downplaying by the *New York Times* of the projected invasion of the Bay of Pigs in Cuba. Here was an instance where those who decided to temper the news were thoroughly convinced that they were acting "in the national interest" because if they featured the story, the invasion would have been called off. They did not feature the story, the invasion did take place, the result was a debacle because of inadequate planning, and American prestige dipped to a new low.

This, of course, will not serve in the slightest to convince political leaders of the future that newspapers should place reporting of the news ahead of what they consider to be "the national interest." It is impossible for them to think otherwise. The political leader who rises to the top moves through a world which is sharply delineated between those who are helping him; those who are opposing him; and those who are uncommitted but can be swung in any direction. His success has been based upon the manipulation of these three groups to achieve what he regards as fulfillment of the national interest—and such manipulation is, in most instances, entirely legitimate. The whole political process would break down and democratic government would be impossible without the existence of men skilled in this art. To persuade them that the press should be an exception would be pushing their credulity beyond human limits.

Furthermore, the politician is a human being subject to the normal tendency to overgeneralize from his own experiences. He knows that some members of the press can be manipulated. Therefore, he assumes that those who resist his blandishments have simply been reached first by a competitor. He is consciously encouraged in this belief by the newspapermen who "play ball" with him.

The importance of a "source" can be measured not only by its news value but by the degree of its exclusivity. To maintain his position in his industry, a reporter must display professional competence in judging and presenting the news. But to advance, he must also demonstrate a capacity to obtain information unavailable to others—or at least available only on a restricted or delayed basis. There are both positive and negative paths that can be followed in achieving this capacity, and the artful journalist is capable of following both courses.

The positive path is to persuade important newsmakers that they can have confidence in the manner in which the reporter will handle a story. The newsman presents himself as one who will not divulge off-the-record material; who will not embarrass his informant by identifying his source; who will not twist the facts to present an event in an unfavorable light. This approach is vital to a successful reporting career and is not to be disdained.

The negative path is consciously to feed the paranoia that characterizes virtually every politician to some degree. A few words of sympathy over the unfair treatment by the "Eastern press" (or the liberal press or the conservative press) is an effective method of slamming doors against competitors. An important leader who can be persuaded that his journalistic "friend" is the lone holdout against a "press conspiracy" can serve as a meal ticket for many years.

Since the press as a whole cannot be "won over" by tactics which political leaders regard as legitimate, it is inevitable that newspapermen eventually become the "enemy." In addition, they also become the personification of all the frustrating forces that make the life of a president so difficult. Therefore, over a period of time, it is certain that the political leader will vent his spleen against the press, never realizing that what he is really doing is venting his spleen against the whole intractable environment that surrounds him. It is a very easy matter to find legitimate grounds for criticizing the press. It is a less easy matter to realize that all these grounds apply to the world generally.

Every president has his collection of inaccuracies in press coverage and is willing to regale his listeners by recounting them for hours. Seen in perspective, these inaccuracies are usually trivial and reflect merely the fact that reporters are human beings who are bound to make errors under the constant pressure of reporting world-shaking events almost as soon as they happen. An objective evaluation would be that the degree of accuracy with which the news is reported is astounding when it is contrasted with the conditions under which it is gathered. But a politician smarting under the lash of public criticism is not very likely to be objective.

Every president has his horror stories of press arrogance. But press arrogance is merely a reflection of public arrogance. Almost every American feels qualified to give the president advice on the most complicated and subtle questions of economics, law, and international relations. It would be surprising if newspapermen were exempt from this universal temptation.

Every president can recite valid examples of press bias and is entitled legitimately to some sympathy for the manner in which he is treated by opposition newspapers. But the assumption that bias is a journalistic characteristic rather than a condition of humanity is a distorted view of the universe. When a man enters politics, he undertakes to deal with *all* human characteristics and it is not an acceptable alibi to cite some of them as overwhelming. If press bias were an absolute bar to political success, this nation would never have had an Abraham Lincoln, and Franklin D. Roosevelt and Harry S. Truman would have been denied second terms.

In reality, the problem of a president in dealing with the press is precisely the same as his problem in dealing with the public at large. But no president can find it within his ego to concede that he has failed in any degree with the public. It is far more satisfying to blame his failures on the press because his problems then can be attributed to a conspiracy. He can blame the "Eastern press," the "Republican press," or the "liberal press." He then does not stand indicted within his own consciousness (the most terrible court of all) as having failed. He was merely the victim of vindictiveness on the part of a selfish group and his failure can be attributed to the meanness of others rather than to his own inadequacies.

In the mythical world of philosopher-kings, the press policies of the White House would be very simple indeed. They would consist solely and simply of according all media equal access to whatever information was available. The philosopher-king would realize that the press is merely a part of the public, even though it is charged with some special functions in the nation's economy. Unfortunately, we do not live in the world of philosopher-kings and it is unlikely that we ever will.

CREATIVE PRESIDENCY, SHADOW PRESIDENCY

James MacGregor Burns

People were freely predicting at the time of Lyndon Johnson's inaugural in January 1965 that the nation was headed for a modern era of good feelings. The President himself had said after his election that the country had reached a new "consensus on national purpose and policy." He was quite right—the nation had indeed reached a consensus over the goals of freedom and equality. But these are not the only problems that occupy men, and history warned that eras of apparent good feelings could conceal heats and ferments that would erupt in turbulence and strife years later.

And an unblinking look at the world and the nation in the mid-sixties disclosed a profusion of interlaced problems, any one cluster of which could occupy a people's energies: at home the problems of rapidly changing group and class and generational relationships, education, urban disorder, mounting crime rates, social anomie and alienation, automation, political apathy, along with the more old-fashioned issues such as transportation, farm subsidies, labor-management relations, tax reform, monopoly and administered prices, medical care; and abroad, nuclear proliferation, the continuing and in many areas deepening poverty of tens of millions, the population explosion, the disruption of old rural cultures and the flood of people into the restless cities, the fragmentization of Africa, the social unrest of Latin America, communist expansion in Asia, along with the week-to-week "little" crises, any one of which could explode into a major one.

It was impossible in the mid-sixties to predict in what forms these problems would emerge with the passage of time. One might speculate, though, that many of the most crucial domestic problems might revolve around certain old but still compelling value-questions. Given the trends in the nation that one could predict with the greatest certainty—huge population increases in the urban and suburban areas, accelerated social mobility, a constantly enlarging and increasingly homogenized middle-class population, a decline in ethnic solidarity and variety—one might guess that once the old problems of equality and freedom had been subdued, sharper questions might emerge over the possibilities of individuality and privacy in a mass culture. If the past century has seen the early tension and later partial reconciliation of values of liberty and equality, we might be at the threshold of an age increasingly preoccupied with the relation of liberty and fraternity, of privacy and community, of the individual and the group. If in past years we have been concerned with mainly quantitative problems—the amount of goods and services produced and how they were distributed—we might be more occupied in the future with the quality of American life in a great, affluent, complacent, and perhaps mediocre society.

The quality of American life—this is not a new phrase nor a new political issue. It is older than Jefferson's dreams and as young as the Great Society. No one has defined the hope and the promise better than President Johnson. "The great society," he proclaimed at the University of Michigan in May 1964, "is a place where every child can find knowledge to enrich his mind and enlarge his talents. It is a place where leisure is a welcome chance to build and reflect, not a feared cause of boredom and restlessness. It is a place where the city of man serves not only the needs of the body and the demands of commerce, but the desire for beauty and the hunger for community.

"It is a place where man can renew contact with nature. It is a place which honors creation for its own sake and for what it adds to the understanding of the race. It is a place where men are more concerned with the quality of their goals than the quantity of their goods. But most of all, the Great Society is not a safe harbor, a resting place, a final objective, a finished work. It is a challenge constantly renewed, beckoning us toward a destiny where the meaning of our lives matches the marvellous products of our labor."

The crux of the problem is whether a system of presidential government so perfectly adapted to, and so largely facilitative of, quantitative liberalism—that is, of the augmentation and fairer distribution of goods— can redefine its purpose and shift its strategy in order to embrace new values with their implications for changes in means and instrumental goals. Such a shift calls for much more than making the White House into a showplace of the arts, or awarding medals to heroes of culture, or bestowing presidential recognition on private cultural enterprises. It means a concerted and sustained and expensive effort to impart values like those of Johnson to the barren lives of millions of Americans, middle class as well as deprived. It means diverting the kind of resources into cultural, recreational, and educational activities that we have in the past poured into economic recovery, or even into national defense. And such an effort might be controversial and even unpopular. Many Americans would oppose it and deride it; by its very nature such an effort would bring foolish blunders and mishaps that could be easily caricatured; and certain ventures—perhaps an effort to improve the quality of commercial radio and television—could precipitate clashes with powerful interests.

Above all, the shift from the pursuit of quantitative to qualitative goals would call for comprehensive, sustained, and broadly unified policies—in short, for planning. Effective planning is impossible except in the context of at least a rough ordering of values, instrumental goals, and means. It will be as important to have clearly thought out, long-range priorities in this respect as it would be in planning increased productivity. Winston Churchill once said that "those who are possessed of a definite body of doctrine and of deeply rooted convictions upon it will be in a much better position to deal with the shifts and surprises of daily affairs than those who are merely taking short views, and indulging their natural impulses as they are evoked by what they read from day to day."[1] Considering the intractable nature of the many human problems implicit in the quest for a qualitatively great society, Churchill's remarks are as relevant to a cultural strategy as to a foreign or economic.

Presidential government is a superb planning institution. The President has the attention of the country, the administrative tools, the command of information, and the fiscal resources that are necessary for intelligent planning, and he is gaining the institutional power that will make such planning operational. Better than any other human instrumentality he can order the relations of his ends and means, alter existing institutions and procedures or create new ones, calculate the consequences of different policies, experiment with various methods, control the timing of action, anticipate the reactions of affected interests, and conciliate them or at least mediate among them. If as Hubert Humphrey has said, we need not a planned society but a continuously planning society, the Presidency provides strong and versatile tools for that purpose.

Still, we must acknowledge that the Presidency has become an effective planning agency for reasons of chance as well as volition. In this century the Presidency has been the center of the conflict between labor and capital and later between segregationists and civil rights forces; it has steeled its will and its ideology in the struggles against Nazi tyranny and communist expansion. After a century of planless growth the Presidency found its place as a key part of the American system of ends and means. The question is whether presidential government can detach itself enough from set ideas and existing institutions and old ways in order to embrace new goals. With leadership, to quote Selznick . . . , "the problem is always to *choose key values and to create a social structure that embodies them.* The task of building values into social structure is not necessarily consistent, especially in early stages, with rules of administration based on economic premises. Only after key choices have been made and related policies firmly established can criteria of efficient administration play a significant role. Even then, the smooth-running machine must accept disturbance when critical problems of adaptation and change arise."[2]

To define new goals, to fashion new institutions to realize those goals, to avoid both utopianism and opportunism, to build popular support without improper manipulation, to allow for flexibility of means and redefinition of ends, and always to elevate purpose over technique—all this is the test of creative leadership. It will be the test of presidential government in the years ahead. To define leadership in this way is to see the importance of a number of proposals that have been made to strengthen the Presidency and hence to enable the President to reshape institutions and processes: four-year terms for Representatives (to bring presidential and congressional constituencies into closer correspondence); the granting of full power to the President to control executive department organization; finding means of attracting the highest talent to the executive department, especially to its major staff positions; efforts to bring into the policy-making process intellectuals with creative and innovative gifts; providing the President with greater discretionary power over fiscal policy, including the item veto and the granting of authority to change tax rates within certain limits; and above all, the further strengthening of the elected leadership of Congress so that it can act more quickly and comprehensively in harmony with the President. But the greatest need of presidential government does not lie in this kind of reform. We can expect many of these changes to take place in any event as the Presidency becomes increasingly institutionalized. Indeed, some are already taking place, in substance if not in form. Some of them at best will simply speed up transitions that already are under way—for example, greater presidential control of fiscal policy.

The greatest need of the Presidency in the years ahead will not lie in internal changes, important though these are, or even in its relations with Congress. The greatest need will be an opposition that challenges presidential values, presidential methods, presidential institutions, that is eager to take power and to present its own definition of the national purpose.

Of all the vital elements of American democratic government the national opposition is the most disorganized, fragmented, and ineffective. As a responsible opposition to the President, Congress is an almost total failure. Hostile Senators and Representatives bombard the White House from all directions. Typically they fail to advance alternative proposals and hence they do not provide the voters with an idea as to how the opposition would govern if it got the chance. The congressmen usually prefer to play the game of bargain and even various forms of genteel blackmail with the President rather than to criticize forthrightly and dramatically. No wonder that Presidents in recent years have been far more sensitive to criticism in the press than on Capitol Hill.

There are good reasons for the debility of the opposition. In part it is a simple reflection of the power of presidential government. "The aggrandizement of the President, especially by the electronic media," as Key has said, "has made the dispersed minority leadership one of low public visibility."[3] The main difficulty is the bifurcation of the opposition into the presidential and congressional parties. Once the presidential candidate—the presidential party's leader—has made his strenuous campaign and lost, he then becomes "titular" leader of the whole party. This is a polite term for shelved or even repudiated. For once the campaign is lost, the congressional party leaders try to assume the opposition role. They hold formal and visible positions from which to conduct the attack, while the titular leader usually has no formal position to fall back on, as in the cases of Stevenson in 1956, Nixon in 1960, and Goldwater in 1964. But the congressional party cannot carry the burden of militant leadership, because of its own internal divisions, its separation between the House and the Senate, and its lack of institutional structure (as compared with the Shadow Cabinet in Great Britain). If the opposition party has lost the Presidency but still controls one or both branches of Congress, as in the case of the Democrats after 1956, it lacks the advantage of being completely in the opposition; it suffers from having a modicum of power and responsibility. If the opposition party lacks control of Congress as well as of the White House, it has a poor forum from which to appeal to the public and virtually no machinery to support a focused and sustained attack on the government.

The impotence of the opposition becomes more serious as presidential government becomes more powerful. No matter how benign a government may be, it will be tempted to manipulate public opinion, to try to dominate the flow of opinion, to cover up mistakes, and to cast doubt on the patriotism or at least the honesty of outside critics. The more that government represents a consensus, or claims to, the more tempted it may be to succumb to some of these tendencies. Above all a consensus government may become flabby and complacent and lose the cutting edge of energy, initiative, and innovation. The . . . tendencies toward excessive concern with technique . . . can cause a government to lose direction and momentum unless the opposition holds it to its promises and threatens to oust it from power.

The problem is especially acute in the United States because of the lack of well organized and programmatic parties. This is less of a problem for the President because, as we have seen, he has built up his own presidential party to provide him with an electoral footing and other political resources. The opposition presidential party, lacking a President and having to make do with a titular leader, is not anchored in an organized mass following and a militant cadre. It must improvise—and that in turn encourages a similar opportunism and absence of direction in the presidential establishment.

The greatest need of the American Presidency is a potent and competitve Shadow Presidency. At the very least the opposition party should establish some kind of collective leadership modeled perhaps after the

Democratic Advisory Council of the 1950's, to give the presidential party a strong voice. More than this, it should experiment with an annual or biennial convention or conference both to choose a top leader and to renovate its program. The failure of the opposition to take this primitive step is not due to any innate difficulty but mainly to the divergent constituencies and institutional jealousies of the congressional party, which wants to dominate the opposition role even though it fills that role so feebly. Ideally there would be an annual convention, a dependable system for collecting adequate funds, a large national staff with regional and state units under it, an effective propaganda apparatus, and talented, articulate, and highly visible leadership. Whatever the exact form, it is clear that the opposition party today has a rare opportunity to exercise Jeffersonian leadership—that is, to build a new political institution.

Even more important, the opposition party must display creative leadership in defining its own version of the national purpose. It is not for outsiders to lecture the opposition party as to the goals it might propose, but one must note the great opportunity that may lie before it. If presidential government as shaped by liberals for egalitarian purposes cannot shift its own strategy toward qualitative goals, if presidential government under Democratic party leadership may be hobbled by its own success, then the opposition could seize the initiative. American conservatives have long been interested in the now intensifying problems of individuality and community, identity and alienation, liberty and fraternity, innovation and tradition, equality and hierarchy. As Clinton Rossiter has argued, they have not blinked at the hard questions about man in society. And it was under Abraham Lincoln and Theodore Roosevelt, both Republicans, that the nation first addressed itself most directly to problems of the quality of American life. In executing one of the oldest of political and military strategies—shifting the very grounds of the combat—modern conservatives can come to grips with liberal Democracy and its presidential establishment.

Perhaps all this is unnecessary—perhaps we can give in to the acknowledged rewards and virtues of presidential government, without worrying much about competition, criticism, alternatives, and the tasks of an opposition. But a great people will not be content long to float in such a slack tide. At the conclusion of his study of a group of working men in an eastern city—a group that was not technically a cross section of a larger population but may be highly indicative of social trends—Robert Lane wrote: "The man of Eastport has no cathedral building in his air space to raise his sense of importance and mission; he is not engaged anywhere in a struggle against want or fear or squalor in such a way as to engage his mind and take him out of himself; he is not, like the Italian Fascists who were his uncles, rebuilding a glorious Roman history; manifest destiny, the conquering of a continent, are parts of a history not quite his own, and anyway they refer to completed tasks. What shall he do that will call out the greatness in him? Against the background of a great purpose, he might measure the political system and say whether or not it is just. But he has no way to conjure up such a vision, and hence no way to take the measure of his society."[4]

THE PRESIDENT AS "DICTATOR" VERSUS THE PRESIDENT AS LEADER—A NEW TYPE OF CABINET

Edward S. Corwin

The growth of presidential participation in legislation, and indeed the vast expansion in recent decades of the President's role in all the departments of national power, invites our attention afresh to a question repeatedly raised regarding the presidency in the past, but never with more insistency than in recent years, or for more cogent reasons. This is the question whether the presidency is a potential matrix of dictatorship; and, if it is, whether there is a remedy.

"Dictatorship," I hardly need point out, is a word with a highly ambiguous connotation, so much so in fact that I propose to dismiss it at the outset in favor of a less colorful word, "domination." "A nation," it has been well said, "does not have to have a genuine dictator in order to suffer some of the evils of too great executive domination." Imagine an historically minded member of Congress seeking nowadays to emulate Henry Dunning's exploit in 1781 of bringing George III's domination of Parliament to an end and with it, ultimately, British resistance to American independence. It would be the part of such a member to move a resolution declaring that "the power of the President has increased, is increasing, and ought to be diminished," and he would have little difficulty in making out an arresting case.

First off, he would point out that impeachment, the weapon that the Constitution provides against presidential "high crimes and misdemeanors," is, as Jefferson, early discovered, a "scarecrow," and that to galvanize this scarecrow into life would be to run the risk of reducing the presidency to a nullity, as almost happened in 1868. Then, noting the decision in *Mississippi v. Johnson* shortly after the Civil War, he would assert, and quite correctly, that the President has no judicially enforcible responsibility either for nonperformance of his duties or for exceeding his powers. Congress's power of the purse, to be sure, still offers, he would concede, an obstacle to presidential usurpation that only an outright *coup d'état* could entirely overcome. Nevertheless, as Dr. Wilmerding points out in his volume on *The Spending Power,* not only have Presidents been able repeatedly to break over statutory controls on expenditure, but such controls are usually much abated by Congress itself in times of emergency, exactly when expenditures are heaviest and presidential dominance is at its zenith. Indeed, generalizing from what happened during the Great Depression, the honorable member might urge that congressional largess in such situations, by the hold that it gives the executive branch on millions of votes, enables the President to tighten his hold also on Congress, and so creates a vicious circle whereby Congress pays for its own slow enslavement. And, continues our orator, when war activates the President's powers as Commander-in-Chief, the situation is still more disastrous from the point of view of opposing the power of the purse to presidential dominance. The sums that Congress is at such times under every compulsion to vote are colossal. The needs that they are designed to meet are forcefully represented, and are believed by the public, to be most urgent, while itemization is put out of the question by the demands of military secrecy; and unexpected turns in the military situation can aggravate all these difficulties. Moreover, the criticism that overworked congressional committees of varying competence can offer to the demands of the executive branch under such conditions will be haphazard in the extreme. An item of $50,000 may get more consideration, and certainly far better informed consideration, than a presidential demand for billions.

Turning then to the course that constitutional interpretation has taken more and more pronouncedly in consequence of our participation in two world wars and under the stimulation of economic crisis, our fictioned Dunning will sketch a system of constitutional law that attributes to Congress a legislative power of indefinite scope and the further power to delegate this indefinite power to the President *ad libitum,* and attributes to the President in his own right an indefinite power to proclaim "emergencies" and thereby appropriate an indefinite "aggregate of powers" in meeting them. At the same time he will show that the President, not without judicial encouragement, has been able to cut loose from the two most important controls that the Constitution originally imposed on his direction of foreign policy. With our four greatest wars directly ascribable to presidential policies, the exercise by Congress of its power "to declare war" has become, he will assert, an empty formality; while by means of the executive-agreement device the President has emancipated himself from his constitutional partner in pledging the national faith.

And at this point our hypothetical member will perhaps devote a word or two to the advantages that a President today enjoys in appealing to the multitude. Propaganda, he will point out, once the casual art of a gifted few, has been within recent times converted into a skilled technique supplemented by the most ingenious gadgets of mechanical science. Today the

President of the United States can at any time request that the nation's broadcasting channels be cleared so that he may "chat" with the people, and the request will be granted pronto, for are not all the available frequencies allocated to companies on federal licenses that terminate every six months? Besides, every member of his administration is a propagandist and has access to the radio at will, although a first-class radio voice may not be the heaven-sent gift of all.

The picture is unquestionably overdrawn in some of its details. Thus, if it is true that impeachment is no longer to be reckoned with as an effective weapon in the arsenal of liberty, this is partly due to the fact that Presidents have in the past kept pretty clear of courses that might make people think seriously of so extreme a discipline. Again, although there is no court entitled to order a President to perform his duties or to enjoin him from exceeding his powers, the subordinates through whom he must ordinarily act do not share his immunity in this respect; and his orders are at all times subject to judicial inquiry into their validity when anybody bases on them any claim or justification whatsoever. Also, his subordinates are, ordinarily, liable at any time to be summoned before a congressional investigating committee and put to the question regarding their official conduct.

Nor is it by any means the fact that Congress's control of the purse strings is ineffective as a restraint on the executive branch. On the contrary, it is potentially a highly effective restraint, which with improved machinery within the power of Congress to provide could be made actual. Again, our orator did not find it to his purpose to mention that in the "concurrent resolution" a device today exists by which sweeping delegations of power to the President can be recalled by the houses without the necessity of obtaining presidential consent; and other lesser exaggerations or omissions might be indicated were it worth while.

Moreover, that is a seriously contracted point of view from which presidential domination appears as solely a *menace* to democratic institutions. Why, in the face of our democratic institutions, has presidential domination attained its present proportions? Must not this development be considered as a fulfillment in a measure of those institutions, and as an answer to some demand from public opinion, on which by hypothesis they are grounded? Without doubt, such is the fact, and especially as regards presidential leadership in legislation. Nor is it difficult to identify this demand: it is the demand that government assume an *active* role in matters of general concern, and especially in matters affecting the material welfare of the great masses of the people.

We are, then, not free to blame presidential leadership as such for those intrusions on "liberty," as it has sometimes been understood, that present expanded theories of governmental function entail. This at least must be conceded. We are free, on the other hand, to ask whether presidential leadership, as we know it, is as good an instrument of the demand that brought it into existence as conceivably it might be. Presidential leadership sets itself the task of guiding legislation; and the critics are numerous who say that it does the job badly. To make the indictment more specific, it is asserted that presidential leadership is discontinuous, not to say spasmodic; that it is too dependent on the personality of the President rather than on the authority of the office; that it is often insufficiently informed, especially as regards the all-important matter of administrative feasibility; and, finally, that the contact between the President and Congress is most faulty, being, in fact, at the mercy of either's whim. These contentions also have too much obvious validity to make it worth while to attempt to refute them or even to qualify them nicely.

In short, we are confronted, not with a *single* problem, but with *two* problems: first, that of bringing presidential power in *all* its reaches under some kind of institutional control; secondly, that of relieving presidential leadership in the legislative field of its excessive dependence on the accident of personality and the unevenness of performance that this involves. Is it possible that these two problems admit of a common solution? At least, so far as they do it is evident what form the solution must take: the *provision, namely, of some kind of improved relationship between President and Congress.*

It is not irrelevant in this connection to recur for a moment to the argument that the President's Committee on Administrative Management advanced nearly two decades ago in support of its recommendation that the independent agencies be brought within the departments whose heads compose the President's Cabinet. It was on these agencies, the argument ran, that the most novel, most controversial, most interesting activities of the national government had been lodged in recent decades, with the result that the President had been constrained to look increasingly outside the Cabinet for advice in shaping his legislative program. But let the Committee's recommendation be adopted, the argument continued, and the President would be forced, or at any rate would have incentive, to return to the bosom of his "official family" instead of consorting with this, that, and the other anonymous adviser or dispenser of happy ideas. Thus, on the one hand the Cabinet would be revitalized, and on the other hand the President would become "the spokesman for the 'administration' in the real sense of the word, not merely the interpreter of his own fancies." He would be at all times what he had always been in times of his greatest power, the representative of the public.

The argument overlooked certain facts, one of which is that "kitchen cabinets," far from being recent phenomena, on the contrary long antedate the first "independent agency." Nor is the reason far to seek. It is because the Cabinet seraglio has been recruited from an early date on principles that make it fairly certain that an active presidential imagination will frequently stray beyond its decorous precincts. One of these—the one of chief importance for the present discussion—is the idea that the heads of the great majority of the departments ought to be administrative experts, or at least capable of quickly becoming such. Unfortunately, an expert in a particular area of governmental activity is not likely to possess the breadth of outlook most desirable in a political adviser, or the time or inclination to interest himself in the problems of other departments or of the country at large. And obviously the Committee's proposal to increase his departmental duties was badly calculated to overcome these handicaps, if that was one of the ends in mind. The argument overlooks the fundamental distinction between Politics and Administration, between determining *what* government ought to do and *how* it should do it, and the exigent need of a President for responsible counsel in relation to the former. It overlooks, too, the considered opinion of competent critics that, even as an agency for the development of a unified *executive* policy among its own membership, the Cabinet has today "become an administrative anachronism."[1]

Other plans for stabilizing presidential leadership, while also pivoting on the Cabinet, are directed primarily to the problem of creating a permanent link between the President and Congress. The least radical of these would give the Cabinet members the right to attend the houses in order to participate in debate on matters of official interest to them and impose on them the obligation of doing so in order to impart information desired by the houses. The proposal, far from raising any constitutional difficulties, has the countenance of early practice under the Constitution. The first volume of the *Annals of Congress* records that "Secretary for Foreign Affairs Jefferson attended agreeably to order, and made the necessary explanations." Actually, it was Secretary for Foreign Affairs Jay, for this was on July 22, 1789, and Jefferson did not become Secretary of State till March 1790. Secretary of War Knox later visited the Senate Chamber with the President on at least one occasion, . . . and by himself on two others. The Act of 1790, organizing the Treasury Department, provided that the head of the Department should digest plans for improving the revenue and public credit and "make report and give information to either branch of the legislature, in person or in writing, as may be required," etc. That Hamilton, the first Secretary of the Treasury, was never asked to report in person was due . . . to the opposition of the rising Jeffersonian party as voiced by Madison.

And so matters rested till near the end of the Civil War, when George H. Pendleton of Ohio began an agitation, the principal result of which was a report many years later by a distinguished Senate committee supporting the idea both on grounds of policy and of constitutionality; and since then at least four future or past Presidents are on record as having expressed themselves in its favor. Why then has the suggestion never produced tangible fruit? Chiefly because most of the legislative work of Congress is done by committees, and before such a body a head of department can always obtain a far more satisfactory hearing than would be conceivably possible before either of the houses in open session. Conversely, if it is

Congress that is seeking information, it can do so through the investigatory process much more effectively and thoroughly than by the wasteful and pretentious methods of parliamentary interpellation.

We come now to a more radical proposal: *simply that the President should construct his Cabinet from a joint Legislative Council to be created by the two houses of Congress and to contain its leading members.* Then to this central core of advisers could be added at times such heads of departments and chairmen of independent agencies as the business forward at the moment naturally indicated.

That the creation of a Cabinet with legislative members would not encounter constitutional difficulties was pointed out in an earlier chapter. Nor would it amount to supplanting forthwith the "presidential system" with the "Cabinet system." The President would not become a prime minister, bound to resign when outvoted in Congress, although circumstances might arise in which it might be expedient for him to do so, as Mr. Wilson contemplated doing in 1916 in the event of Mr. Hughes's election. Nor yet would it be a figurehead like the King of Great Britain or the President of Italy, for he would still retain all his constitutional powers and prerogatives, although, again, he might choose to use them at times less for pushing a program of his own than for mediating between the programs of others, as did Washington at the beginning.

The new Cabinet would, in other words, still be a body of *advisers*. But there are advisers *and* advisers. The proposed Cabinet would comprise men whose daily political salt did not come from the presidential table, whose political fortunes were not identical with his, who could bring presidential whim under an independent scrutiny today lacking, and yet who, by putting the stamp of their approval on his proposals, would be able to facilitate their enactment into law. It would be a body both capable of *controlling* the President and of *supporting* him; of guaranteeing that the things needing to be done would be done on time, but that, on the other hand, the judgment that they needed to be done represented a wide consensus, a vastly wider consensus than the President can by himself supply.

But it may be objected that such an arrangement could not long be adhered to, or that, if adhered to, it must at times cut athwart the two-party system and so weaken the political responsibility of the President. The objection has reference to the evident possibility of the President's belonging to the party that is a minority in Congress. . . . [But] the objection overlooks the fact that the advantage supposed to accrue from President and Congress both being of the same party rarely outlasts the first two years of an administration, when indeed it lasts so long, and that some of the bitterest feuding between the two branches has often occurred when both were of the same party. It was conspicuously so in the latter days of F.D.R. . . . What kept the two branches co-operating at all was the common compulsion of a great emergency; and at such times, even under present arrangements, co-operation between President and Congress does not stop at the party line. *But why should it require a crisis to bring forth best methods, especially as with best methods operative crisis might often be avoided?* Suppose one takes the position that government is normally a species of *nation-keeping:* then it is clear that much of the fuss and fury of politics is really factitious and a sheer waste to the community; that the chief objective to be sought in political discussion, whether carried on in Cabinet council, on the floors of Congress, or elsewhere, is *consensus.* In what light does the foregoing proposal then appear?

Furthermore, it would seem that the principle of cycle holds in the matter of legislation, and especially of reform legislation, as it does in so many other things mundane. The mere enactment of laws is only the first step toward incorporating them in the social order; following it ensues a process of gradual absorption into the general institutional setup and outlook of the community; and this process is apt to be hindered rather than helped if reforms are pressed forward too fast and furiously. A wise legislative leadership will therefore reckon on a certain amount of reaction against its measures as inevitable and seek to forestall it. In such an endeavor the advice of potential political foes may easily be of more value than that of overenthusiastic supporters.

Kept within bounds, the power and prestige of the presidency comprise the most valuable political asset of the American people; they are, moreover, in a very true sense the creation of the American people. But centering as they do in a single individual who is free to advise, or to refrain from advising, with whomsoever he chooses, this power and this prestige are apt to become unduly *personalized,* thus inviting two dangers: the slowing down of the legislative process to an extent that unfits it for a crisis-ridden world in which time is often of the essence, and—in consequence—autocracy. It is therefore an additional merit of the suggestion advanced that it is calculated to meet, or at least abate, both these dangers. Effective presidential leadership is essential to the ready availability of the national lawmaking power; this ready availability reduces to a minimum the excuse for autocratic courses.

NOTES: THE PRESIDENCY

Introduction

1. Edward S. Corwin, *The President: Office and Powers* (Fourth Edition; New York University Press, 1957), p. 1.

2. Lewis Chester, Godfrey Hodgson, and Bruce Page, *An American Melodrama: The Presidential Campaign of 1968* (Andre Deutsch, 1969), p. 789.

3. George E. Reedy, *The Twilight of the Presidency* (World Publishing, 1970), ch. 1.

4. Roberta A. Sigel, "Image of the American Presidency—Part II of an Exploration into Popular Views of Presidential Power," *Midwest Journal of Political Science,* X (February, 1966), 125.

5. *Ibid.* See also Roger H. Davidson, David M. Kovenock, and Michael K. O'Leary, *Congress in Crisis: Politics and Congressional Reform* (Wadsworth, 1966), pp. 59-66, for a discussion of public evaluations of presidential and congressional performance.

6. *United States v. Curtiss-Wright Export Corporation,* 57 S. Ct. 216 (1936).

7. Thomas E. Cronin, "Superman, Our Textbook President," *The Washington Monthly,* 2 (October, 1970), 50.

8. Reedy, *Twilight of the Presidency,* p. 85.

9. Corwin, *The President: Office and Powers,* p. 312. The first edition was published in 1940.

Henry Fairlie

1. Ed. note: On May 12, 1970 the Bureau of the Budget was reorganized into the new Office of Management and Budget. The Bureau's activities, however, remain essentially unchanged.

James MacGregor Burns

1. Quoted by W. W. Rostow, "The Planning of Foreign Policy," School of Advanced International Studies, The Johns Hopkins University.

2. Philip Selznick, *Leadership in Administration* (Evanston: Row, Peterson and Company, 1957), p. 60.

3. V. O. Key, Jr., *Public Opinion and American Democracy* (New York: Alfred A. Knopf, 1961), p. 457.

4. Robert E. Lane, *Political Ideology* (New York: Free Press of Glencoe, 1962), p. 475.

Edward S. Corwin

1. Don K. Price, "Staffing the Presidency," *American Political Science Review,* 40 (December, 1946), 1168.

CONGRESS

> *Senators are part of a national phenomenon. Like successful*
> *professors who are so busy earning consulting fees that they do*
> *not teach, like successful lawyers who are so busy making contracts*
> *for the firm that they do not practice law, many senators seldom*
> *cease being candidates long enough to become legislators. Since most*
> *members of the House spend even more time being candidates,*
> *the work of the federal legislature receives astonishingly little attention*
> *from a large number of the men who are supposed to be doing it.*
>
> James Boyd[1]

During the past several years, Congress' reputation has undergone a remarkable transformation. During the early 1960's, Congress was the
favorite whipping-boy of people who claimed to be interested in responsible
government. As one former Senator states, "The trouble with Congress
today is that it exercises negative and unjust powers. . . . The heart of the
trouble is that the power is exercised by minority, not majority rule."[2]
Dominated by conservatives with a fair sprinkling of racists and an adequate number of buffoons, Congress could be counted upon for consistency.
On important domestic legislation—civil rights, aid to education, medical
care for the aged, urban development—congressional opposition was expected and, during the Kennedy administration, successful. With respect
to foreign policy, Congress was ready and willing to spend large sums for
what it called "military preparedness," and the dominant congressional
temper could best be described as aggressive nationalism.

During this period, Congress was active in developing a number of
major legislative policies and programs which were later passed under the
Johnson administration.[3] This process was largely hidden, however, and
the public image of Congress was generally unfavorable. Under such circumstances, a well-meaning president was bound to look good, at least in
comparison. As one study pointed out, public dissatisfaction with Congress
could be attributed chiefly to Congress' "dilatory handling of the lawmaking function."[4] And thus the conventional wisdom held that presidential
power was good (positive majoritarian, humane) while congressional power
was bad (negative, obstructionist). The 1964 election and its immediate
aftermath, moreover, indicated what executive-congressional cooperation
could accomplish. The Goldwater candidacy resulted in better than 2-1
Democratic margins in both the House and Senate, and the result, in the

words of *Congressional Quarterly,* was an "amazingly productive" session in 1965.

> *The scope of the legislation was even more impressive than the number of major new laws. Measures which taken alone would have crowned the achievements of any Congress were enacted in a seemingly endless stream. . . . The pace of the 1965 session was so breathless as to cause a major revision of the image, widely prevalent in preceding years, of Congress as structurally incapable of swift decision, prone to frustrate demands for progress.*[5]

The widening war in Vietnam, however, quickly cut the heart out of Lyndon Johnson's Great Society programs, and it inevitably came to dominate domestic politics. Executive-congressional cooperation on domestic policy diminished, indicating, as one writer stated, that "the 89th Congress was an aberration from a less harmonious norm."[6]

In a sense, Lyndon Johnson managed to improve Congress' standing with the public by destroying his own. During the Nixon administration, Congress has been equally fortunate. Congress gained much of the credit for reducing military spending, while the administration refused to consult with Congress prior to the Cambodian and Laos adventures. With respect to domestic policy, Congress managed to gain some initiative on tax reform, pollution control, and education, while the administration accrued liabilities from a recessionary economy. And, of course, on selected issues, such as the SST, the voting rights act renewal, or the Haynsworth and Carswell nominations, Congress (particularly the Senate) managed to look almost statesmanlike. But it was the exercise of the warmaking power that really forced a hard look at Congress, and that led many presidential defenders to wonder what they had helped to fashion.

> *Since the days of Franklin D. Roosevelt, the White House has been the mecca of academicians and lawyers dedicated to reforming and transforming the American nation, if not the world. They have volunteered their brains, their talents, and even their careers to strengthening the presidency, in the belief that only the president could realize their objectives. To many of them, Congress was the constant enemy, an enemy that not only resisted reform but constantly contrived to hamstring the president.*
>
> *But the Cambodian invasion produced the gnawing fear that perhaps they had helped fashion a Frankenstein's monster of presidential power.*[7]

Ten years ago, Congress was the problem as far as most liberals were concerned. Today conservatives are expressing similar outrage over congressional attempts to cut military spending and to curb the President's foreign policy powers. One wonders, of course, whether Congress has changed that much or whether it is simply benefiting from fortuitous circumstances.

Some changes have indeed occurred. In 1970, Congress approved its first major internal reorganization since 1946. Neither of the two traditional foci of congressional reform—the seniority system for choosing committee chairmen nor the filibuster rule in the Senate—were altered, but committee and floor operations in both houses were opened to greater scrutiny.[8] Perhaps the most important change concerned voting on amendments in the House. Previously, only the results of the teller vote were recorded. The procedure was changed so that twenty members could demand a record vote (that is, a vote on which each member's position is recorded). In 1970, under the old rule, 188 members of the House passed the SST on a non-record vote. In 1971, 420 members cast record votes, and the SST was defeated. The new rule was probably largely responsible for the SST's defeat. According to Rep. Charles Whalen, the new procedure "means that the primary factor in your voting is not whether you will please Boggs or Albert or Jerry Ford; you've got to think about what your constituents want."[9]

Moreover, a number of very powerful conservatives left Congress during the past decade, and their successors have not been able to wield the same degree of control. And, hopefully, some members of Congress have been educated by the events of the last ten years to a greater appreciation of the explosive potential of certain policy problems.

There are, nevertheless, some aspects of congressional performance which deserve continuing attention. According to Nelson Polsby, the policy-making role of Congress remains uncertain, despite the apparent turnaround of the past decade. Professor Polsby's essay provides a useful discussion of the distinctions between the two houses of Congress, and his suggestions concerning congressional capabilities are particularly appropriate, given the increasingly technical aspects of economic and defense policy.

While the Polsby essay treats congressional ethics as a separable and subordinate problem, it is probable that public assessments of institutional integrity will actually be an important determinant of future performance. The executive branch, for example, has obviously been less effective when it has lost the confidence of significant portions of the public. It is difficult to imagine Congress playing a positive policy-making role unless the public takes Congress seriously. The article by James Boyd deals with some of the more disturbing implications of congressional ethics (or lack of ethics). Congress has generally responded to its members' ethical lapses with the utmost reluctance and a sympathy for malfeasance altogether out of keeping with its characteristic self-righteousness. Mr. Boyd suggests that the problem goes beyond Congress, which it undoubtedly does, and his pessimistic assessment of popular democracy's effects on political integrity requires one to examine just what citizen responsibility actually means.

Keeping account of what occurs in Congress, however, is not an easy task. Michael Green discusses some of the reasons for poor press coverage in the House and makes some suggestions for improving it. Mr. Green's point is similar to George Reedy's analysis of the President and the press. It is virtually impossible to have responsive and responsible government if the public is largely uninformed about what government is doing. This places a very heavy burden on the media to provide adequate information, and the manner in which the media approach governmental decision-makers affects the adequacy of information.

The fourth essay is by Jacob Javits, Republican Senator from New York. Senator Javits is a member of the Committee on Foreign Relations, and he examines what has been and will probably continue to be the most critical area of executive-congressional relations—foreign policy-making. The executive branch has been generally unwilling to accept an active congressional presence on foreign policy matters. According to a recent report by a Senate subcommittee:

> *In at least one instance, security classification has been used to prevent legitimate inquiry by the proper committees of the Senate into matters which the Executive Branch did not want to discuss.*
>
> *In one striking instance, the Executive Branch, by means of the use of classification, sought to prevent any discussion in closed session by the Foreign Relations Committee, apparently because of concern over the context in which the information in question would be discussed. At issue was the placement of United States tactical nuclear weapons in foreign countries.*[10]

Senator Javits suggests that Congressional surveillance of executive defense and planning agreements must be improved. Most important, the executive branch must promote effective and continuing consultation with Congress or serious constitutional confrontations will continue to occur.

There are, of course, other obstacles to congressional responsiveness and responsibility. The seniority system and the filibuster rule, for example, are anti-majoritarian devices, and the distribution of power in the Congress does not encourage accountability. Congress has been able in the past to avoid dealing with many divisive issues, and it will probably continue to do so as long as the public acquiesces. It can be forced into action, but this will require intellectual changes outside Congress as well as structural changes within Congress. Most important, the public will necessarily have to take Congress seriously and enforce congressional accountability. Voting for congressional candidates is overwhelmingly based upon party labels, but the cohesion and effectiveness of the congressional parties are limited. One study explains these seemingly contradictory facts by focusing on the public's limited information about the parties in Congress and about individual members of Congress.

> *In the congressional election, to be sure, the country votes overwhelmingly for party symbols, but the symbols have limited meaning in terms of legislative policy. . . . The electorate sees very little altogether of what goes on in the national legislature.*

Few judgments of legislative performance are associated with the parties, and much of the public is unaware even of which party has control of Congress. . . .

What the public's response to the parties lacks in programmatic support is not made up by its response to local congressional candidates. . . . perceptions of individual candidates . . . are almost untouched by information about the policy stands of the men contesting the House seat.[11]

The internal characteristics of Congress, then, are important. But the efficacy of internal reform and even the likelihood of such reform would appear to depend upon greater public interest in and awareness of what Congress is doing. An uninterested and uninformed public will usually get the kind of government it deserves.

STRENGTHENING CONGRESS IN NATIONAL POLICY-MAKING

Nelson W. Polsby

The word is out that the Congress of the United States may have had something to do with the alteration . . . of American policy toward Southeast Asia. On the domestic scene, Congressmen can be observed taking the lead in tax reform and increasing federal appropriations for education. Consequently, it may briefly be fashionable to take Congress seriously, and perhaps those few of us who all along have been arguing this view *sotto voce* ought to say a word or two before Congress resumes its accustomed role of thwarting the domestic programs of liberal Presidents, and is once more relegated to the dustbin of historians if not of history.

To be sure it is easy enough to see why that popular guide to Washington politics, Casual Observer, finds Congress hard to understand. It is organized quite differently from the conventional bureaucracy, which Casual Observer professes to despise, but which he and his friends comprehend. Instead of having a single head, Congress looks like the hydra of Greek mythology. Instead of neatly delegating work downward and responsibility upward, Congress is a complex, redundant, not always predictable, and purposely unwieldly network of crisscrossing and overlapping lines of authority and information.

The mere contemplation of this organizational design customarily leads Casual Observer to assert overhastily that Congressional decision-making is inefficient, cumbersome, and in need of instant reform. Consider, for example, the frequently regretted fact that Cabinet officers are asked to justify certain aspects of their programs in much the same language before authorization and appropriation committees in both houses—four presentations in all. Clearly an inefficient use of a busy executive's time, according to the busy executive and his friends. Yet this same busy executive as a matter of course insists that programs coming up the line to his office be justified repeatedly to program review committees, bureau chiefs, department level staff, and departmental budget officers, and he would think nothing of justifying the program again to other interested executive branch departments, to the President and the Budget Bureau. Cabinet-level officers quite commonly make presentations, formal and informal, justifying their programs to the general public, to interest groups, to newspapermen. Why, then, does the need for Congress to hear justifications as well constitute such an intolerable inconvenience? Why should this alleged inconvenience lead to recommendations that Congress revamp its structure?

Casual Observer also finds Congress hard to fathom because the political theories that are currently available do not help him resolve some basic choices that he generally has to make in order to defend his preferences with respect to the distribution of power within the national government. Does he want a strong Congress? A strong Congress means precisely one capable of asserting its will, even though Presidents, interest groups, courts, and ephemeral majorities of public opinion may find it inconvenient. A weak Congress means less effective oversight of executive policy-making and of the bureaucracies, and such weakness diminishes the capacity of Congressmen and Senators to play the roles of critic, goad, and ombudsman. Further, he must decide whether to vest power in Congress or in the majority party within Congress. If the former, he must be prepared to tolerate coalitions which occasionally—and perhaps persistently—thwart the will of the majority of the majority party. Of such majorities are the conservative coalition—and the progressive one that unhorsed Joseph Cannon—made. If he opts for stricter party responsibility, he must accept the weakening of Congress vis-à-vis national parties, and whoever controls them—presumably quite often the President. For a long time, there were modish and unequivocal answers to these structural dilemmas, just as in the 'thirties Casual Observer's father knew what he thought of an innately reactionary institution like the Supreme Court. Now, however, while the idea of Congressional checks and balances and initiatives seems to make a little sense, it is possible to give these choices more evenhanded consideration.

The reasons why Congress and Presidents generally get along rather badly are too well known to require much reiteration. Differing constituencies arising from, on the one hand, the unit rule of the electoral college and, on the other, from the differential effects of party competition, the residuum of malapportionment, and the seniority system account for part of the conflict. So do purely institutional factors, the most important of which is the differing time scale of Presidential and Congressional careers.

President Kennedy understood this problem quite well, as the following quotation from Theodore Sorensen's book suggests:

> *"Wilbur Mills," he said one day, "knows that he was chairman of Ways and Means before I got here and that he'll still be chairman after I've gone—and he knows I know it. I don't have any hold on him."*

More generally, the argument is that the career expectations of political actors influence the rates at which they are willing to expend resources. By the standards of the operational leaders of Congress—Congressional party leaders, committee and subcommittee chairmen, their minority counterparts, and leading up-and-coming members in both parties—the career of any President is short. In the 91st Congress considerably more than a majority of both houses had already served with at least three Presidents of the United States. More to the point, the vast majority in both houses could plausibly entertain the prospect of continuing to serve on into the indefinite future. Thus, while Presidents are under a constitutional injunction to seize the day, the men of Capitol Hill—even supposing they agree with the President and his programs—must calculate the consequences of their support against future demands upon their own resources. This leads to strategic dilemmas and to disagreements between Congress and the Presidency that are scarcely touched by proposals such as the four-year Congressional term of office, which seeks to coordinate the time of election but not the terminal points of Presidential and Congressional careers.

There is no definitive, universally acceptable answer to the question of how strong Congress should be. On the whole, gains in institutional strength are likely to be had at costs in institutional responsiveness. But there are many possible mixtures of these two qualities. A legislature that is merely an arena for the registering of the policy preferences of groups organized in the society at large is obviously not the only alternative to a legislature that is totally impervious to external sentiment. There is at present no very satisfactory description of Congress which assesses the developing balance between these somewhat incompatible goals. Thus Casual Observer is also handicapped in his attempts to understand Congress because Congress itself has been changing over the years, while our descriptions and justifications for it have not kept pace.

The accepted view of what a legislature contributes to government is that it represents the people, and it is as a representative body that Congress finds its ultimate justification in our political system. The difficulty that all modern legislatures face, of course, is the tremendous increase in the scale of modern government that makes it almost impossible for individual legislators genuinely to represent the people back home in any simple or straightforward fashion. And most legislatures collectively have pretty much stopped doing so. In most parliamentary systems, they are now mindless creatures of the political parties that run them.

But Congress is an exception. Principally because of historical accidents that destroyed the temporary unity of both the national parties earlier in this century, Congress built on some nineteenth-century precedents in ways that have maintained and in some cases enhanced its independence in the political system. One major consequence of this process of institutionalization has been to shift the balance in the careers and life-styles of legislators from amateur to professional, from the status of temporary ambassador from home to that of member of the legislative group. Where Congress used to embody a popular will in some formal sense by its collective representativeness, it now does so *de facto* through the piecemeal pressures of case work for constituents, legislative committee hearings, and the appropriations process. Where representation, emphasizing the ambassadorial function, was once the characteristic, conscious activity of Congressmen and Senators, today it is deliberation, emphasizing the increasing centrality to Congressmen of their lives as members of a legislative work group and status system.

Thus in a sense Congress has been modernizing itself, through processes which have shifted the loyalties and the attention of Congressmen and Senators toward Washington and away from the grass roots, differentiated its internal functions, and professionalized legislative service.

However, we have not yet developed a fully articulate rationale for a legislature that takes this developmental path; instead we are still relying both descriptively and evaluatively on notions of representation that made more sense when Congressmen spent most of their time at home and came from relatively knowable communities.

Thus a discussion of the strength of Congress in the political system might profitably consider the ways in which the House and the Senate organize to do business, as a means of gaining insight into how a legislature can cope with the complex demands of a large heterogeneous society, including the rest of a big government. This may serve to throw some light on how or whether an effective legislature can contribute to democratic government.

As institutions, the House and the Senate differ markedly in their contemporary characters. The House is a highly specialized instrument for processing legislation. Its great strength is its firmly structured division of labor. This provides the House with a toehold in the policy-making process by virtue of its capacity to specialize and hence, in some collective sense, to provide for the mastery of technical details. House members are frequently better prepared than Senators in legislative conferences, and usually have the better grasp of the peculiarities of the executive agencies they supervise. This is a consequence of the strong division of labor that the House maintains: members are generally assigned to one or two committees only. Floor debate is normally limited to participation by committee members. There is an expectation that members will concentrate their energies rather than range widely over the full spectrum of public policy.

Patterns of news coverage encourage specialization. General pronouncements by House members are normally not widely reported. Senators, because they are fewer, more socially prominent, and serve longer terms (hence are around long enough for newsmen to cultivate) and allegedly serve "larger" districts, can draw attention to themselves by well-timed press releases almost regardless of their content. One result of all this publicity (among other things) is that the Senate is increasingly the home of presidential hopefuls, and this of course tends to generate still more Senate publicity. Some years ago I inquired of the chief of an important Washington news bureau if there was an imbalance between House and Senate news coverage. His response (bowdlerized) was: "The House! Look at them! There's no presidential timber there at all."

The maintenance of a perennially timberless ecology like the House is difficult because it cannot entail excessive centralization of power. Decentralization of power is necessary for the House to sustain its capacity to cope with the outside world through its complex and specialized division of labor. The House's major career incentive is the opportunity accorded a tenth to a fifth of its members to possess the substance of power in the form of a committee or subcommittee chairmanship or membership on a key committee. At present seniority acts as a bulwark of this incentive system by guaranteeing a form of job security at least within the division of labor of the organization. Without decentralization of power there would quite likely be no incentive for able men to stay in the House; without able men (there are few enough of these at any rate) there would be no expertise. Without mastery of subject matter, initiatives taken and modifications made in public policy are capricious, responsive largely to prejudice, or ineffective, or failing that, detrimental.

The essence of the Senate is that it is a great forum, an echo chamber, a publicity machine. Thus "passing bills," which is central to the life of the House, is peripheral to the Senate. In the Senate the three central activities are cultivating national constituencies; formulating questions for debate and discussion on a national scale (especially in opposition to the President); and incubating new policy proposals that may at some future time find their way into legislation.

Where the House of Representatives is a large, impersonal, and highly specialized machine for processing bills and overseeing the executive branch, the Senate is, in a way, a theatre where dramas—comedies and tragedies, soap operas and horse operas—are staged to enhance the careers of its members and to influence public policy by means of debate and public investigation.

In both the House and Senate the first commandment to newcomers is "specialize." But this means different things in each house. "Specialize" to a Representative means "tend to your knitting": work hard on the committee to which you are assigned, pursue the interests of your state and region. Consider, however, the consequences of these well-known features of Senate organization: Every Senator has several committee assignments. Boundaries between committees are not strictly observed. On the floor, quite unlike the House, virtually any Senator may speak for any length of time about anything. Thus the institution itself gives few cues and no compulsions to new Senators wondering what they should specialize in. For the Senate, specialization seems to mean finding a subject matter and a nationwide constituency interested in the subject that has not already been preempted by some more senior Senator.

It is a cliché of academic political science that, in legislative matters, it is the President who initiates policy, and Congress which responds, amplifying and modifying and rearranging elements that are essentially originated in the executive branch. Not much work has been done, however, on following this river of bills-becoming-and-not-becoming-laws back to its sources. Where do innovations in policy come from *before* the President "initiates" them?

It appears that a great many newly enacted policies have "been around," "in the air" for quite a while. In the heat of a presidential campaign or later, when a President wants a "new" program, desk drawers fly open all over Washington. Pet schemes are constantly being fished out, dusted off, and tried out on political leaders. There is often a hiatus of years, sometimes decades, between the first proposal of a policy innovation and its appearance as a presidential "initiative"—much less a law.

It is certainly not generally true that policy innovation begins with a presidential message to Congress. For behind each presidential message lurk months of man-hours of work and sometimes years of advocacy and controversy. The two great fountainheads of new policy seem to be, first, generally acknowledged "problems" producing the demands upon government that spur bureaucrats to ad hoc problem solving. This often later has to be codified or rationalized as "policy." Second, a longer range buildup in the society of something that at first is not generally conceded to be a "problem." Those who see it that way may formulate demands upon the government in the guise of a "solution." This initiative may first be taken by a professor, or by staff professionals attached to an interest group, or by a government "expert." On rare occasions, experts attached to a Congressional committee will initiate a policy. More often, I think, Congress is in on the beginning of a policy innovation because it provides the first sympathy for an innovation concocted by outside experts.

Many of our most important policy innovations take years from initiation to enactment. Surely the idea of Medicare, to take an obvious example, was not "initiated" by the Johnson administration in the 89th Congress. Proposals incorporating its main features had been part of the Washington landscape since the early Truman administration. Medicare, like other great policy innovations, required *incubation,* a process in which men of Congress often play very significant roles. Incubation entails keeping a proposal alive while it picks up support, or waits for a better climate, or while a consensus begins to form that the problem to which it is addressed exists. Senators and (to a lesser extent) Representatives contribute to incubation by proposing bills that they know will not pass, making speeches, making demands for data and for support from interest groups favoring the proposal. Sometimes a sympathetic committee chairman can be persuaded to allow hearings on such a proposal. This focuses public attention, mobilizes interest groups for and against, and provides an occasion for the airing of a proposal's technical justifications. Policy incubation is, of course, not exclusively a Congressional activity; lobbyists may plant stories in the press, organizations may pass resolutions, professors may write books and articles. Most major policy innovations have been incubated by methods such as these.

The net effect of the Congressional process of incubation in any event is to develop a sense of community among far-flung interest groups that favor the innovation by giving them occasional opportunities to come in and testify. It provides an incentive for persons favoring the innovation to maintain up-to-date information on its prospective benefits and technical feasibility. And it accustoms the uncommitted to a new idea.

Thus the Senate is in some respects at a crucial nerve end of the policy. It articulates, formulates, shapes, and publicizes demands for significant policy innovation. Proposals to increase the structuredness of the Senate, to force germaneness in debates, to tighten committee assignment procedures, and reduce the number of assignments per Senator, misunderstand the nature of the Senate and the contribution it uniquely makes to the political system. What is needed in the Senate is as little structure as possible; its organizational flexibility enables it to incubate policy innovations, to advocate, to respond, to launch its great debates, in short, to pursue the continuous renovation of American public policy through the hidden self-promotion of its members.

I do not mean by this to suggest that Congress is entirely self-sufficient in the policy-making process, or that all demands on Congress are equally well treated. Far from it. In order finally to make new policy, Congress generally does need the power of the Presidency to set priorities and focus the energy sufficient to mobilize the successive majorities that law-making requires. A presidential priority is a tremendous advantage in clearing away obstacles, but the President's support is usually purchased at a price: the proposal becomes his. This is not merely a matter of credit, although who gets credit is no trivial matter. It also affects the substance of policy. The executive branch begins the process of bargaining by including some features of a proposal and dropping others, adding bait here and padding there. In some cases (e.g., foreign aid, civil rights) executive branch control over bargaining is tight and continues right through the legislative mill. In others (e.g., surtax, Medicare) influential members of Congress establish which provisions will survive and which will be sacrificed. Sometimes (e.g., the bill establishing a Department of Housing and Urban Development in the Kennedy administration) the most significant battle is precisely over who will control the bill.

But even with the President behind a bill, and despite years of Congressional incubation, the mortality rate for "new" proposals is high. Most Congressional policy-making takes place under adversary circumstances. Thus Congressional decision-makers ordinarily cannot enjoy the luxury of examining alternative means to stipulated ends. In an adversary process ends are not stipulated but contested. Agreement on means is often sought as a substitute for agreement on ends. Ends are often scaled down, pulled out of shape, or otherwise transformed. In short, from the standpoint of an outsider who cares about one or more pressing problems in society, the Congressional process of policy-making looks chaotic at best, perversely insensitive at worst.

If the perception of chaos is largely an optical illusion, the perception of insensitivity may not be. Insensitivity, slowness to register some kinds of new demands, exists in Congressional policy-making and is not altogether curable. It can come about because the strength of a demand in society as it is felt by an outsider has no counterpart equally strong within the Congressional process itself. Sometimes Congress does not reflect "needs" as defined in the society at large because Congress is malapportioned, or because the "wrong" sorts of people dominate the relevant committees. In this fashion a wave of short-run, intense demands might break futilely across the superstructure of any stable organization. Given the stately metabolism (fixed terms of office, staggered Senatorial elections) decreed for it by the founding fathers, Congress could hardly be expected to operate efficiently with respect to short-run demands in the best of circumstances.

A second source of Congressional insensitivity to innovation is of course the fact that many urgent demands are pressed upon Congress by groups with whom Congressmen—and quite often the bulk of their constituents—simply disagree. Not all righteous causes are popular. And, as a matter of fact, not all momentarily popular causes are necessarily righteous. Congressmen often have a keen appreciation of this.

It may be said that Congressmen are more concerned than they should be with popularity. But this constraint on their judgment is the result of the fact that they are popularly elected. They must ask who will get the credit or the blame for public policies. They must know who is for what and how strongly, because these matters affect not only their own future efficacy but also the present chances that a majority can be assembled.

Is there a practical alternative to a process of legislative policy-making in which alternative policies are put to stringent tests of internal political acceptability? If the internal politics of the institution did not matter, the legislature would be a mere arena, a place for forces as they exist in the outside society to contend. The group that captures such an organization may find it marginally useful in pressing claims upon leaders situated elsewhere since victory in some arenas can give legitimacy to a cause. But as an organization develops independent power and internal structure at the same time that it begins to devote a portion of its resources to self-maintenance, it also develops a measure of insensitivity. To require total responsiveness of a legislature is to require it to be powerless.

Although Congress has developed institutional strength within its political system to a degree unrivaled by most contemporary legislatures, it does not follow that nothing can be done to increase its sensitivity to social problems, or increase its effectiveness within the logic of its own developing character. To me the reason most reform proposals are uninteresting is not because reforms are necessarily less appealing than the status quo, but because they are usually addressed rather arbitrarily to "needs," and typically neither needs nor solutions are discussed within the context that includes the relevant features of the ongoing system.

A number of meritorious reforms have been suggested that do not bear on the operations of the Congressional collectivity except insofar as the general reputations of all members are affected by the transgressions of a few. Reforms bearing on conflict of interest, disclosure of income, and other such matters do not materially affect the strength of the institution except as the institution's strength is mirrored in its general reputation.

Problems of Congressional morality cannot really be addressed responsibly without considering comparable problems in the private sector. Even under the new tax law American taxpayers will be giving rather substantial subsidies, far exceeding in their magnitude salaries and perquisites furnished Congress, to certain privileged persons and industries—most conspicuously oil companies and banks. How relevant is it to condemn Congressmen for allegedly taking "junkets" at taxpayer expense while in the private sector all manner of extravagance is routinely charged off to "business expenses" as a tax dodge? When Congress recently voted to raise Congressional salaries the news media were generally outraged. The fact is, considering the weight of their responsibilities, even at the new rates, Congressmen are far from overcompensated. It is necessary for them to maintain out of pocket two bases of operation. Their campaign expenses are not deductible as business expenses. Consider, also, the compensation of men in positions of comparable responsibility in the private sector. I doubt that the top 535 men in the automotive industry, or on Wall Street, or in television make do with the equivalent of salaries of $42,500 plus small change in the way of stationery allowances, inexpensive haircuts, a few overseas junkets, and occasional trips home on military aircraft.

All this provides no excuse for Congressmen not to bring themselves within the scope of the conflict-of-interest laws as they presently apply to political executives. This may be more technically difficult than it sounds, since like the everyday activities of the Secretary of the Treasury, their votes touch everything, so no investment of capital is immune to a conflict-of-interest problem. There are, however, enough violations of propriety to make the problem worth thinking about.

Important as these matters are for public morality, they do not touch the institutional life of Congress. I want to list three suggestions that are pertinent to the functioning of the collectivity. They embody changes in present arrangements, but do not disturb most existing institutional values except in ways I shall describe.

First, a scheme for mandatory retirement. Mortality is a melancholy fact, which comes upon us in different ways, and at different rates of speed.

Most modern organizations protect themselves against its creeping effects by requiring the retirement of members after a certain age is reached. Congress now has a generous pension plan that works no economic hardship upon most members forced into retirement by electoral defeat. Instead of relying wholly upon local party systems to replace ailing, failing, and senile members, Congress should protect the efficiency and integrity of its functioning by providing for mandatory retirement at a stated age. If on college campuses these days thirty years of age seems about right for this purpose, perhaps for Congress the age seventy is suitable.

It will be argued in opposition to this proposal that many valuable persons make Congress their second career, and Congress would be depriving itself of much-needed maturity and good judgment in legislative affairs; that no similar impositions are contemplated for other political officers, and thus that the proposal is inequitable; and that the proposal places an unnecessary requirement upon electors in states and districts.

All three objections lack weight. The first ignores the extent to which Congress is presently a young man's game though, to be sure, a young man's waiting game. Men who arrive in Congress past the age of fifty-five rarely have a chance to accumulate sufficient seniority to acquire institutionally-based influence. This proposal would over the short run, in fact, give some older new arrivals more of a chance to shine, since it would clear the most senior men out of the way at a predictable rate. But it would not materially affect the incentive system as it currently applies differentially to men of different ages.

The second objection, that the proposal is inequitable, has no merit with respect to the executive branch, since the President's term of office is strictly limited by other means, and other political officials serve at his pleasure. As for the judicial branch, I have no desire to reopen the issue of court packing, but neither have I any objection in principle to the imposition of mandatory retirement upon all federal judges.

Finally, there is the matter of the protection of the interests of voters. Presumably, if they want to send elderly Representatives and Senators to Congress, they should be allowed to do so. I merely assert a competing interest, one that has grown in importance over the years, namely the interest that Congress has as an institution in maintaining a membership sufficiently vigorous to conduct its increasingly demanding business successfully. Surely each Congressional district and each state contains more than one potential Congressman or Senator, so the disability the requirement of mandatory retirement places on the voters of each district must be regarded as minimal. A more impressive objection is that the proposal is unconstitutional. This was not fully apparent until the Supreme Court decided Powell v. McCormack last year, holding that Congressmen could be excluded from sitting only if they failed to meet qualifications specified in the Constitution. It now appears that it will take remarkable agility at textual construction by future courts or two-thirds votes by each House of Congress respectively to expel in individual cases, or a Constitutional amendment, in order to give effect to a general retirement scheme.

The second suggestion has to do with the improvement of technical knowledge available to Congress. Congress gets technical knowledge principally from committee staff personnel who make themselves knowledgeable in the subject matter coming before them. But while the executive branch has systematically been engaged in professionalizing its means of technical understanding over the past decade or more, Congress on the whole has not done so. It is romantic for Congressmen to think of themselves as not in need of expert and detailed explicit analysis because they are "generalists." Generalism is too often a genteel name for ignorance. The professionalization of economic forecasting and defense procurement in the executive branch led to tremendous increases in the power of political decision-makers to identify options and choose among them. This is precisely the capacity many Congressmen feel they are losing. And, if they choose to do so, they can professionalize their own committee staffs, thereby increasing the efficiency of their explicit analytical activities and enhancing their own knowledge and power.

To "professionalize" entails continuous contact with a community outside the world of Capitol Hill. Professional men—economists, operations researchers, psychologists, and so on—maintain standards of performance by knowing and participating in their professional communities. Typically, nowadays, the top economists of the executive branch—the men who formulate fiscal policy, antitrust policy, international trade policy, and so forth—are first and foremost professional economists. Their loyalty to professional standards means (in general) that the options presented to political executives will be feasible and technically sound.

Typically, Congressional committees are staffed by means of an older, less effective process of patronage. This produces loyal service and, by the standards of an earlier day, highly competent service. But unswerving loyalty to the chairman is seldom enough to produce technically informed criticism of executive proposals, sophisticated insight into alternatives, or sensitive awareness of emerging problems in the world. Yet these are what Congress needs. Hence, two corrective proposals. Committees should be encouraged to constitute outside advisory groups to advise the chairman on the technical competence of the work the committee is receiving from its staff. Secondly, more extensive exchanges for one- or two-year hitches of service should be instituted between Congressional committee staffs and comparable staff in the executive branch, private business, labor unions, social service organizations, and universities.

The purpose of these proposals is to bring to bear upon explicit policy analysis on Capitol Hill the standards—and the considerations—that are commonly employed in policy analysis within the executive branch and elsewhere in society. Steps such as these will not necessarily bring Congress into harmony with the executive branch in areas where they now disagree, since there is no reason to suppose that a large number of disagreements over national policy are based on ignorance—though some may be. These disagreements should be resolved. Other disagreements may occur if Congress chooses to equip itself with more professional analytic personnel, since not all executive branch proposals are free from controversy even when they are grounded in thorough professional knowledge. Thus more professionalism in explicit analysis can assist Congress in finding disagreements and weak spots in executive branch recommendations and can increase the probability that Congress itself can initiate policy. These proposals, therefore, genuinely attempt to strengthen Congress rather than to weaken it.

My third suggestion is a simple endorsement of Representative Morris Udall's proposal to elect House committee chairmen at the start of each Congress. Udall's plan is not a return to king caucus. Rather, it provides for the selection of committee chairmen from a slate of the three most senior members of the majority party to be elected by secret ballot by all majority caucus members, with the ranking member on the minority side to be picked by a similar process in his caucus. This provides an institutional hedge against a too-arbitrary chairman, or one who is incapacitated or hopelessly out of step with his colleagues, without wholly vitiating the advantages of seniority or placing chairmanships in the hands of some centralized authority.

I have mentioned that the great advantage of the seniority system is that it decentralizes power in the House of Representatives by creating multiple centers of policy influence and increasing the number of good Congressional jobs. This adds to the incentives of the Congressional career. Proposals to centralize power must always be weighed against the damage they may do to this incentive system. Effective legislatures in world history have been fragile and rare. In most places and at most times legislatures have been little more than arenas for the registering of organized group interests or electoral colleges for cabinets. The Udall plan has the advantage of even further decentralizing power—to Congressional party rank and file—rather than placing it in the hands of party leaders, and thus this plan increases the general level of incentives for House members to make careers in the House.

These proposals recognize that institutions must provide means by which they can respond to outside demands, yet at the same time retain the capacity to exercise independent choice. They recognize the peculiar contributions the House and the Senate make, individually and together, to American politics, and seek to enhance the participation of these institutions in the processes of policy-making by improving their capabilities rather than destroying their power.

THE RITUAL OF WIGGLE: FROM RUIN TO REELECTION

James Boyd

This is the era of the impeached Congressman. As of this writing [September 1970], one Member is in jail, two are under indictment, a former Member was just convicted in Trenton, one has been censured, one expelled, four defeated after ruinous press exposés, and several are being held in protective custody by the Attorney General. And if the ratio of detected to undetected offenders is as low within Congress as without, there lurks a batallion of nervous legislators, each of whom feels a premonitory twinge every time he reaches for the morning newspaper.

Among the intelligentsia, an impugned legislator is as much ridiculed as the streetwalker was until Dostoyevsky explored her whys and found a saint. Perhaps we dote too much on the shady politician's final bequest to us—the poisoned meat or the polluted water or the tax hike or the sandy cement that causes our neighborhood school to cave in—to properly savor the brighter scenes of his act. Recall Adam Clayton Powell on Bimini, hiding out from the law with Miss Ohio; or Hugh Addonizio lamenting to the judge that being on trial for extortion all day was impeding his reelection campaign by limiting him to nighttime rallies; or Senator Dodd daring God to strike him dead if he were lying, while colleagues inched out of range; or the great Dirksen, at Governor Stratton's trial, telling the jurors that it was perfectly proper for Stratton to pocket the campaign funds and not pay taxes, because if the first lady were to appear regularly in public, didn't she needs lots of corsets and step-ins and frillies? So even when you consider the poisoned meat, the act is still funny. Besides, we're going to get the crash landing anyway, so why not enjoy the sleight-of-hand and the feats of levitation while we're airborne?

And what we enjoy we study. We go to the circus and laugh at the clowns; if we are of an inquiring bent we begin to notice that what at first appeared as madcap foolery is in fact the unfolding of a painstaking art, and our mirth becomes tinged with understanding, respect, admiration. So it is with our apprehension of the indicted solon. Old Porky up there on the platform amid the red, white and blue bunting—weeping his heart out after avowing his innocence before God, while the wife and kids embrace him and the crowd cheers—is not the slob he seems. Off the stand he is quite sensitive and stoic. Study him from month to month as he fends off conviction and wriggles toward reelection: you will see that what at first seemed spontaneous idiocies, the desperate acts of an inferior man at bay, are instead integrated parts of a ritual as exacting and delicate as the hand fluttering and eye rolling of the Balinese dancer.

When Congressman James Michael Curley, a cultivated man who read Shakespeare aloud in the evening, chose upon his release from prison not to slip quietly home but rather to be met by five brass bands, it was not that he was uncouth. He was grappling with the enigma of modern politics: how to be at once both a defendant and a candidate. The politician cannot run for office and at the same time plead insanity or take the Fifth or turn state's evidence. As defendant, he must hide from snoopers and process servers; as candidate, he must be everywhere accessible and seem to confront all accusers boldly. As defendant, he must be secretive, devious, sullen; as candidate, open, forthright, gregarious. As defendant, he must measure his every word; as candidate, perjury is a way of life. Even as he enters into stipulations with the prosecution, he must shout his innocence. He teeters through the minefield with one eye on the jury and one on the public, and so to the undiscriminating it looks like an elephant's ballet. But there is logic and precision to it all.

The moment which launches all the bawdy gaucheries to come is always a solemn, interior one. Usually it begins on the telephone. Senator X phones his office one morning and young Foster tells him in a squelched voice that Jack Anderson has exploded a stinkbomb in his 600 newspapers—the slush fund, the Swiss bank account, the works. The Senator's strength drains out in a puddle. He slumps in a flaccid heap and stares glassily at the accusing phone; the knowing place in the pit of the stomach sinks into infinity. Helpless tears come and hysteria ferments. It is the moment of maximum hazard to a political career; a too-defiant denial, a tell-tale dodge, an injudicious admission can in a flash proliferate into a major investigation and undo 30 years of patient conniving. The Senator's glazed eyes conjure up newspaper headlines, the dock, the recall of Congressional credit cards, the cell door clanking shut. But it need not be so. Of all the colleagues to drink from this cup in the past 10 years, only one, Representative Tom Johnson, actually did a stretch. Most escape with nothing lost save honor. They laugh again, prosper, and get reelected. And those who don't, if you study it, have invariably botched up their defense by straying from the rules and precedents carefully developed by the elders.

Rule 1. *Admit nothing until you know the worst; if it looks like a one-shot affair, hide till it blows over.*

The redeeming facet of a scandal is that people soon forget. Yesterday's tax evader, Robert E. Tehan, is today's federal judge in Milwaukee. Who remembers now that in 1964 Senators Sparkman and Smathers went through their secular Gethsemanes when their peculiar banking and investment ventures were headlined during the Bobby Baker hearings? No one, except the keeper of newspaper morgues, because they did not rush forward to testify and clear their names. They played possum, there was no follow-up of any consequence, and today they remain esteemed public figures. When Congressman John Dent was shown by *The Wall Street Journal* to have violated the Corrupt Practices Act, he yawned, remained incommunicado for a spell, and his seniority still accumulates. Senator Dirksen was for years hounded by reporters for the details of his fabulous law practice in Peoria, which somehow commanded fat retainers from many of our greatest corporations; but he'd always shush-shush the reporters with his mock curlicued wrath and he took those details to the grave. Now they are planning statues in his honor.

One of the more effective non-defenses was made by Julian G. Sourwine, chief counsel of the Senate Internal Security subcommittee. It was shown at a Senate hearing in 1967 that Sourwine had knowingly passed a check for $2,500 that bounced in a Las Vegas bank. Morever, he had duped a Senator into endorsing the check, and the Senator eventually had to make it good. This was a rather delicate matter, for Sourwine was and is the chief Senate watchdog against security risks in government, people who, for instance, get in such desperate financial straits that they write bad checks in four figures. Had the matter received a second day of publicity it might have been farewell for Sourwine, but the foxy old Red-fighter just shut off the phone switchboard and hid for a while; and the charge faded, uncontradicted but forgotten.

Sometimes, of course, circumstances just won't permit waiting out the squall. Sometimes reporters have the answers instead of just the questions, or the blow may fall in the middle of a campaign, or it may be so explosive that one has to respond. For such occasions, study the following rules.

Rule 2. *If you must speak out—confess to what is known, evade what is unknown, and cry.*

The ritual of the bogus public confession of the no-longer-hidable has been popular ever since Grover Cleveland publicly confessed to bastardy. On the day, Cleveland, who theretofore had been known mainly for drinking beer in the back rooms of Buffalo saloons, became "Mr. Integrity." No one remembers the President Cleveland who sent troops into Chicago to help the railroads beat up starving strikers; all that remains is the sturdy image of the benign old walrus who owned up and made his support payments.

Senator Richard M. Nixon's 1952 Checkers performance is perhaps the classic in this genre. Up on slush fund charges, he confessed frankly to having received a puppy for his infant daughters and to having kept his wife in a cloth coat; his slush fund disappeared in a flood of congratulatory telegrams, never to reappear. On a tawdrier but nonetheless effective level, Thaddeus Dulski, chairman of the House Post Office and Civil Service Committee, just broke down and bawled when it was revealed in 1967 that he had accepted an $11,000 purse from the postal unions and the third-class mailers while he was authorizing legislation to raise postal salaries and cut third-class rates. His tears washed away the suspect $11,000, and nothing more has ever been heard of it.

Rule 3. *If at all possible, give the money back—or at least give it to someone.*

According to his defense counsel, Senator Thomas Dodd was in jeopardy of a long prison term if the Senate convicted him, as was recommended unanimously by its Ethics Committee, of having fraudulently charged the government for travel expenses actually paid by others. So Dodd gave back the $1,767 to the Senate disbursing office, and the Senate dropped the charge by a vote of 51 to 45. Emboldened, Dodd offered to refund any of the $116,000 in campaign contributions he had diverted to his personal use, if the donors asked. "Even if I have to sell my shirt," he said. But that one didn't wash and the Senate censured him 92 to 5. Apparently, the offer wasn't imaginative enough. He should have consulted John Byrnes or Seymour Halpern of the House. Congressman Byrnes was shown in 1964 to have helped obtain a favorable tax ruling for the Mortgage Guaranty Insurance Corporation and to have then bought restricted stock on advantageous terms not available to ordinary citizens. Five days after exposure, Byrnes announced that he was giving the stock to Scholarship, Inc., for aid to deserving youths. Case closed. In 1969, Seymour Halpern, ranking Republican on the House Banking Committee, was revealed by reporter Jerry Landauer to have put himself $100,000 in hock, mostly in unsecured loans to banks which were vitally interested in matters before Halpern's committee. The documentation was so airtight it made even reporters feel sorry for Halpern, an amiable man with a beautiful young wife and a flair for high living. But the Congressman rose to the challenge with a virtuoso application of Rule 3. He announced that he would pay back the loans by auctioning off his prize collection of famous signatures, the passion of his life which he had been devotedly gathering from early childhood. What more could be said?

Rule 4. *If partial confession and restitution fail to stem the headlines, arrange a quickie exoneration from a semi-respected source.*

The traditional sources are (a) the House Speaker, (b) the respective chairmen of the Senate and House Ethics Committees, or (c) the Attorney General. Milton Friedman has observed that all regulatory agencies soon become fronts for the malefactors they are supposed to regulate; certainly this is true in the Congress. There are so many precedents here that the difficulty is to sort them out for the model most appropriate to the occasion.

Less than 24 hours after Representative Dulski was accused, Speaker McCormack summarily cleared him without a look at the documents. Career saved.

When it was disclosed that Senator George Murphy was one of the politicians being subsidized by California tycoon Patrick Frawley— Frawley gave Murphy unrestricted credit cards, paid half his rent, and threw in $20,000 a year; Murphy in turn watched movies for Frawley on a special screen Frawley had installed in Murphy's apartment—the Senator immediately produced a statement from Senate ethics watchdog John Stennis that there was nothing improper about this arrangement. Before that, Chairman Stennis turned in the same verdict for Senator Edward Long of Missouri. *Life* had revealed that for years Long had been receiving a $2,000 check each month from M.A. Shenker, attorney for imprisoned Teamster boss James Hoffa. Long contended this was "shared fees" for several cases he was helping Shenker with, but no proof was ever published that this was so—nor was any explanation given why the "shared fees" always amounted to $2,000 a month. It was messy, but after a private probe Chairman Stennis declared "not guilty."

Before Stennis, the ethics watchdog was Senator Everett Jordan of North Carolina; who presided over the Senate investigation into Senate aide-in-chief Bobby Baker. In that inquiry, it turned out that so many Senators were tangled up with Baker's finances that it was almost impossible to investigate Baker without probing them, too. Almost but not quite. First, Senator George Smathers was discovered to be mixed up with Baker in a real estate deal that reportedly returned $75,000 to Smathers on a $9,000 investment. Jordan heard Smathers out in chambers and found "nothing improper." He certainly wasn't going to investigate Smathers, he said. The next day he summarily exculpated former Senator Lyndon B. Johnson. But this piecemeal approach was making the committee look ridiculous and the Senate nervous, so Jordan issued a blanket amnesty for all Senators who had been or might ever be involved with Baker. "This committee," he said, "is not investigating Senators."

The House Ethics Committee is even more reliable in time of need. In its five-year suzerainty over 435 Congressmen, it has yet to find one needful of investigation. Its staff director is an ex-lobbyist who is not even an attorney.

Apparently, all ethics committees are destined for this fatuous role. When the labor movement had its flirtation with probity, wise old John L. Lewis guffawed from the start; and on the first anniversary of the A.F.L.- C.I.O.'s Committee on Ethical Practices, Lewis wired an inquiry, "Have you found any ethical practices?"

Unfortunately, clearances so routinely obtained begin to lose public credence. Attorney General John Mitchell has rushed in to fill the void.

Does the U.S. Attorney for New Jersey announce he is probing alleged ties between the underworld and Senate candidate Nelson Gross? Mitchell quickly announces that there is no such investigation and what's more there won't be one.

Does the U.S. Attorney for Maryland ask for an indictment of a contractor who a grand jury found had entered into bribery negotiations with several prominent Congressmen? Mitchell says nothing doing and sees to it that the grand jury presentment is suppressed.

Are 21 G.O.P. finance chairmen in open violation of the Corrupt Practices Act for failing to report where they got their money? Not interested, says Mitchell.

Does the Internal Revenue Service, after a two-year investigation, recommend that Senator Dodd be indicted for criminal income tax evasion? Mitchell gives Dodd a letter of exoneration to read at his campaign rallies.

Are a dozen corporations, from Delaware to California, indicted for making illegal contributions to Members of Congress? It is so arranged that the corporations may plead *nolo contendere* without the identity of the Members being revealed.

We touch here upon the greatest boon in our legal system—the blocked indictment. There is no appeal from the prosecutor who refuses to prosecute or the investigating committee which refuses to investigate. However grisly the facts, they are harmless in locked vaults; of course, come the close roll call, one may feel an inclination to vote with the side that holds the keys.

Rule 5. *If the unpleasantness persists, use the "stranger in paradise" routine: You can't help it if goodhearted friends have an urge to shower you with gifts or if lucky fate strews your path with roses.*

People accept the fact that politicians, like movie actors, live in a world where fantastic things happen. When John Doe contracts for house renovations, the bill is usually twice what the work is worth, not half. Yet, he'll believe House Whip Hale Boggs' story that the construction company with the House Office Building garage contract just happened to charge him $21,000 for $45,000 worth of home improvements—because Congressmen live in a world where those things happen. Whenever John Doe buys stock it goes down; but he is not so jaundiced by that as to discredit the explanation of Representative Multer that his windfalls in banking investments were just lucky breaks that had nothing to do with his being a member of the House Banking Committee.

The favorite "stranger in paradise" device is the "very close friend" who is always doing wonderful things for you and expecting nothing in return. Take the wife's vacation syndrome: when ex-Congressman Addonizio was confronted with checks signed by other people for his wife's vacation he was unperturbed. "Just a very close friend," he shrugged. If John Doe had a friend who offered to pay for *his* wife's vacation, he'd start to worry about it; but for a Congressman's or a mayor's he accepts it. Representative Giaimo of Connecticut collected $32,000 in 1966 as a tax-free gift from a group of friends who wanted to pay tribute to his public service. Now John Doe never had anyone pay him a cash tribute, let alone tax-free. But he is not intolerant of Giaimo's explanation; the Congressman was renominated without difficulty and is a favorite for reelection. "Just a close friend" is a phrase which echoes through Congressional history: Senator Birch Bayh's Florida vacations, Dodd's Oldsmobiles, the turnpike bonds of Congressmen Herlong and Watts, Happy Chandler's swimming pool, the dozens of testimonial purses raised in Washington each year from friends who happen to be lobbyists. It's a warming phrase when you're caught with something that muckrakers outside the charmed circle say you shouldn't have.

Rule 6. *Insist that you would have done the same favor for any constituent.*

There's a problem here, admittedly. The gift of stock or the home renovation job was just explained by Senator X as the generous, disinterested act of a very close friend. Now it is asked why Senator X officially intervened to get that friend a pardon or a tax loophole. Special favors for friends? No. With as much aplomb as possible it must be argued that any constituent, had he but asked, would have received the same favor.

Jim Curley was in trouble once for violating the Civil Service Act by taking a classification test under an assumed name. When hecklers would taunt Curley with it, he was not in the least defensive. "A man came to my door seeking help," he would intone, jutting his jaw toward the crowd. "He needed a job. His children were hungry. But he couldn't pass the examination because he had no education. So I took that test for him and he got that job. And thereafter he held his head up among men and his family was nourished. And I want every citizen of Massachusetts to know that I would do the same for you and *you* and You and YOU—" until the crowd would explode in a frenzy of adulation.

The giants of the past are departed; yet in small ways they can be emulated. When headlines proclaimed that Congressman Giaimo had set up a Caribbean vacation cruise at government expense for a man who turned out to be a racketeer, he calmed the flap overnight. There was nothing unusual, Giaimo explained; he would gladly arrange the same cruise for any of his 461,086 constituents. There's a logical flaw in this, as in the old campaign promise to give every American boy and girl a Harvard education. But the history of these things is that people don't look that closely.

The only caveat here is: don't carry the definition of "constituent" too far. At the recent trial of Martin Sweig, aide to Speaker McCormack of Boston, Congressman Leggett of California was called by the defense to bolster up Sweig's contention that it was an accepted practice to give New York lobbyists the run of one's offices, phones, and secretaries. Leggett testified that he regarded the whole United States as his constituency and had no hesitancy about letting any constituent use his office or telephone on behalf of commercial clients. This seemed a bit much to the jury. One of the jurors later confided to *The New York Times,* "After hearing him, it is my opinion they should investigate *all* the Members of Congress."

Rule 7. *At the moment of deepest personal disgrace, announce for reelection.*

In other lands, the exposed statesman commits hari-kari or resigns; here he declares his candidacy. Nixon turned his 1952 slush fund explanation into an election rally; Powell always reannounced after each brush with the law; on the day of his Senate censure, Dodd declared for a third term; John McCormack's first public response to the Voloshen-Sweig indictment was to re-up for the Speakership.

There are three reasons. One, even the rumor of a possible vacancy 10 years ahead of schedule excites the animals in the party hierarchy back home; a quick announcement keeps them in line. Two, as long as one is in office and seems likely to stay there, he has the Indian sign on the prosecution; no one believes, for instance, that Senator Daniel Brewster would ever have been indicted for bribery had he been reelected instead of defeated in 1968. Three, the thought of one's constituency as a jury of last resort sitting above the real jury, even above the Supreme Court, is a comforting one. So as the indictments come down, the far-sighted politician will keep reiterating that the real verdict won't come in until the people vote several years from now. After all, that's a jury he's always fooled in the past.

Rule 8. *Set up a series of endorsements by prominent churchmen.*

The predilection of the American church for mountebanks has been known to discriminating politicians since at least 1858, the year of the Lincoln-Douglas Senate campaign. Both candidates were citizens of Springfield, Illinois, where they were personally known to all the clergy. Douglas was a braggart, a boozer, a man facile with truth and money; Lincoln was humble, a teetotaler, a man of almost fanatical veracity, the fellow who walked all those miles to return the penny. The issue was the most important moral question ever before the nation—the extension of human slavery. Douglas was for it, for reasons of political expediency; Lincoln was against it and stated his opposition in the most exalted spiritual terms ever heard in partisan debate. It was inevitable, therefore, that 21 of the 23 Protestant pastors of Springfield endorsed Douglas over Lincoln and that the Catholics of Illinois voted almost unanimously for Douglas—the winner.

Since then, the politician in trouble has intuitively turned to the church, knowing that whatever the accusation, a cardinal can be found to pose with, a Protestant pulpit is open for a guest sermon, a denominational college is ready with an honorary degree, a Communion breakfast is in need of a speaker. All this lends a patina of innocence.

When Truman aide Matt Connelly was convicted, a great dinner was held in his honor, presided over by the Archbishop of Boston. Such gambits paled a bit in the latter day of the Truman Administration, when too many indicted officials told juries that they were Papal Knights of Malta with credentials from Pope Pius XII. But it quickly revived.

The case of Senator Robert Byrd of West Virginia, now the Senate's third ranking Democrat, is illustrative. In the midst of an early campaign for Congress, Byrd's puritanical, idealistic, patriotic image, which had made him the odds-on favorite, suddenly was drenched with a pail of garbage. It was revealed that in happier days he had been a wine-bibber, a Ku Kluxer, and a draft dodger. But Byrd, dressed in clerical black and with the face of an accolyte, had been a preacher of the gospel, had conducted a noted radio Bible school that reached half of rural West Virginia, and regularly elevated his rallies with poetry readings of "The Touch of the Master's Hand." The parsons rose as one to his defense. His conversion to temperance, brotherhood, and war was certified as genuine and the unpleasantness blew over.

But Members in trouble need not assume that proof of reform or even contrition is at all necessary to gain ecclesiastical endorsements. Adam Powell was once the most conspicuous sinner in America. He had kicked out his wife and confiscated her income. He had been proved a forger who regularly traveled to vacation spots under an alias, with lady friends under aliases, all at government expense. He had been found guilty of lying about an old woman in Harlem and had refused to pay damages. He was perpetually in contempt of court. He was a fugitive from justice, and his every entry into New York to preach his Sunday sermon was accompanied by national speculation as to whether or not he would get out by sundown or be arrested. He had abandoned his Congressional duties and openly reveled in his beachcomber's tryst with Miss Corinne Huff. And he was impenitent; worse even, he flaunted his sins as religious acts. "Keep the faith, Baby," he would say, raising his glass.

By January, 1967, when the House of Representatives had to formally question Powell's credentials, who was left to defend him? The Church, of course. The Greater New York Baptist Ministers Conference, the New York City Presbyter, the National Council of Churches, announced resolutions of support for Powell. The Reverend Walter Fauntroy demanded a national work stoppage in his behalf. Powell, they all said, had been a great chairman, an inspiring symbol to blacks. And besides, his morals were no worse than the other Congressmen's.

Rule 9. *It's time to pick a scapegoat.*

The scapegoat, or decoy, is the *sine qua non* of all major political scandals. It's undignified but essential.

The routine decoy is the opposition political party. You are being persecuted by political enemies who want to discredit you and take away your seat. This was, in essence, the response of Senator Vance Hartke to press reports that he was under federal investigation for accepting a bribe.

But blaming "politics" is too flabby a scapegoat to really win the public. Better results are obtained by crying "yellow journalism" and charging a frame by the "power hungry media." The late Drew Pearson made a marvelous decoy because so many Congressmen had been burned by him that the latest third-degree casualty to be wheeled onto the Floor always had a majority on his side. The following attacks on Pearson illustrate the statistical and the oratorical methods. Senator George Smathers: "I join two Presidents, 27 Senators, and 83 Congressmen in describing Drew Pearson as an unmitigated liar." The late Senator Kenneth McKellar: "Pearson is an ignorant liar, a pusillanimous liar, a peewee liar . . . a revolting, constitutional, unmitigated, infamous liar!"

Better even than being the hapless victim of the press is to be a martyr, for then you are being tortured not for your indiscretions, but for your virtues. A young Congressman with larceny on his mind should get into the field of anti-Communism. Congressman J. Parnell Thomas, jailed for taking salary kickbacks, remained a martyr to the end to those who were sure he was framed by the Communist conspiracy he fought so energetically. To millions, Senator Joe McCarthy, too, was censured for his anti-Communism, not for evading committee inquiries into his finances. Roy Cohn uses his Red-hunting kudos at all his fraud trials. Dodd, who was the victim not only of the Reds but of a sex ring that infiltrated his office, still draws applause in New Haven when he says, "I may well be the only honest man in Congress. . . . I am the most maligned figure in human history."

Once the case reaches the hearing room or the courtroom, a personal scapegoat must be arraigned—the chief witness for the state. It was *he* who did what he says *you* did. This is the inviolable rule of Senator Russell Long, defender of impeached Senators. Long on witness Michael O'Hare: "That crook, that thief, that liar, that scoundrel, that bandit . . . that murderer!" Long on witness John Sullivan: "Danny Brewster never took that money. These charges were made by a former employee who is trying to divert attention from his own conduct."

Rule 10. *If newsmen persist, bolder moves are advisable: issue a statement requesting an official investigation.*

Rule 11. *Threaten a multi-million dollar libel suit against your accusers but don't file it; if you must file it for tactical reasons, withdraw it before it gets to trial.*

These rules are closely related and should be discussed together. "X" has been accused. If he is innocent, he can just open his books to the public, answer all questions from the press, and use the vast media resources at his disposal to propagate his vindication. If not innocent, the mock investigation and libel suit enable "X" to seem to be doing the same thing, while actually doing nothing of the sort. As soon as "X" has announced these moves, he can with virtuous air refuse to answer all further questions from the press.

Suggested release: "I have placed the matter before the proper authorities. I have brought suit to clear my name. Under the American system of jurisprudence, it would be contumacious for me to discuss this litigation in the press, so I am forced to withhold all further comment, no matter how much it pains me, until proceedings before the proper tribunal commence."

This statement will get you through an entire campaign; after a few days, the reporters will even stop asking.

The three most suitable agencies to demand investigation from are, depending on the locus of your clout, the F.B.I., the House Ethics Committee, and your local grand jury. All three can proceed only in secret. None can investigate without a nod from the higher-ups, and even then the findings can't be published. Even if on the level, the typical political investigation takes years to complete; all that time you can pose as a maligned innocent awaiting justice. If once in a hundred times a runaway grand jury, an oddball U.S. attorney, or an overwrought committee counsel gets out of hand, the Attorney General or the chairman has the last word and can keep the lid on.

As for the libel suit, a mere threat of it may achieve the objective. Timing is the key element. The *Life* exposé on Governor James Rhodes of Ohio, a 1970 Senate candidate, came in May, 1969. Rhodes made the standard move and said he'd sue. But if he had sued then, the case might have been called up for trial or preliminary deposition before the Senate campaign was over and he'd have to either take the stand and answer questions or back out ingloriously. So he waited almost a year to file suit. That way, the case couldn't possibly come up until after the election. In the meantime, he was ostensibly confronting his accusers.

Senator Dodd's libel strategy is instructive for the victim of a protracted imbroglio. With tremendous fanfare, Dodd filed a $5 million, 14-count suit in 1966 against Pearson and Anderson—truly a man defending his reputation! But at each critical stage of the litigation he would quietly withdraw various of the counts; thus Pearson's attorneys could not depose Dodd under oath concerning them. Dodd could not win anything this way, of course; his case was disappearing like a tube of baloney in a meat slicer, but a political libel suit is brought for pretense, not money. Eventually, all 14 counts were withdrawn. But Dodd's ingenuity persisted. Abandoning the charge that he was the victim of lies, he now pleaded that others had invaded his privacy and taken information with which he could have made money himself. All told, the courts were tied up for three years without one public cross-examination. Dodd eventually lost out on all counts, but in the meantime he appeared to his followers to be stoutly defending his honor while in fact he was dismantling piece by piece the suit he himself had brought.

Artful dodgers have filled the records with precedents, but the most brilliant evasive tour de force in American annals was the 1968 finesse by Congressman Cornelius E. Gallagher of Bayonne, New Jersey. He was in the midst of his reelection campaign when the Time-Life empire boffed him. Gallagher was a collaborator with the Mafia, *Life* said, was a partner in business ventures with underworld boss Joe Zicarelli, had used his Congressional office to further the business and personal interests of Zicarelli, had used political muscle to squash a gambling probe in Bayonne, and had been linked to the underworld in the tapped phone conversations of gangland figures. As if this wasn't enough, *Life* also alleged that a paid murderer and convicted extortionist with the macabre name of Kayo Konigsberg had, under Mafia orders, removed from Gallagher's cellar the body of one Barney O'Brien, a small-time hood. *The New York Times* reported that these revelations stunned even Members of Congress. So grotesque were they, in fact, that the Hudson County Democratic organization, which regularly ingests scandal without belch, panicked and demanded the death penalty—that Gallagher resign "within three days" both as its candidate for Congress and as delegate to the upcoming Democratic National Convention.

But Gallagher did not panic. Who among the captains of history can claim such perfection under fire as the embattled Gallagher now displayed? Immediately, he invoked Rules 2, 4, 5, 6, 7, 8, 9, 10, and 11. He redeclared his candidacy. With no cardinal available on short notice, he sought an endorsement from Governor Richard J. Hughes. He then requested a grand jury investigation and a House Ethics Committee probe. He announced plans for a libel suit against *Life*. He confessed to certain harmless business ventures with close friends and said that whatever he had done for Zicarelli he would do for any constituent. He described *Life* as "a modern court of inquisition." A House colleague, Congressman Charles Joelson, roughed up Attorney General Ramsey Clark over the disclosed wiretraps.

Within 72 hours, though not a fact had changed, the contretemps was resolved. Governor Hughes declared Gallagher to be "a very great man, a wonderful man." The Hudson County Democratic organization reversed itself and announced united support for Gallagher; Boss John V. Kenney, alias "The Little Guy," declared that by asking for a grand jury probe and announcing a libel suit Gallagher had shown the organization he would prove his innocence. Attorney General Clark said he knew nothing about any references to Gallagher in any Mafia wiretaps. On the campaign trail, Gallagher was cheered as never before; petitions were circulated to dissuade him from resigning; he was overwhelmingly re-elected. What does it matter today that Gallagher never filed the libel suit that caused "The Little Guy" to revoke excommunication? Or that the grand jury probe never began and never could have begun because, as Hudson County prosecutor Tumulty announced, "the statute of limitations had already expired" on all charges made by *Life*. Or that the House Ethics Committee investigation never materialized? Or that Ramsey Clark was wrong and the Justice Department did have Mafia tapes and they did mention Gallagher? What counts is that in the moment of maximum danger, Gallagher was ready with his precedents.

Rule 12. *When judicial proceedings become inevitable, claim constitutional immunity.*

A scandal that survives to Rule 12 must be recognized as truly dangerous. The grand strategy has failed; now one must try to worm out on technicalities.

The Constitution provides that Members of Congress cannot be interfered with by anyone on their way to Washington nor held accountable for anything they say on the Floor. These safeguards were intended to banish fear and thus protect the integrity of Congress, but they have been gradually converted into protections against prosecution for theft, fraud, bribery, extortion, felonious assault, and lascivious carriage.

The modern phase began when two New York cops surprised Senator Warren G. Harding of Ohio in a hotel room with nubile Nan Britton, who was later to write a book about her illegitimate child entitled *The President's Daughter*. Threatened with arrest for fornication, carnal knowledge, and drunk driving, Harding awed the local police by charging contempt for the U.S. Constitution. He was released and journeyed on undisturbed, his peccadillos remaining undisclosed until he was our martyred President. In recent years, new constitutional theory has been proclaimed by Congressmen Powell, Johnson, and Dowdy.

Powell established the doctrine that no person elected to Congress can be excluded for any reason other than failure to meet the requirements of age, residence, and citizenship. Johnson got a Supreme Court reversal of his conviction for conspiracy to defraud on the grounds that part of his defrauding was done on the Floor of the Congress where he was immune (but he was retried and convicted for off-the-Floor activities). John Dowdy of Texas is today the chief constitutionalist in the Congress. Indicted early this year for bribery and perjury, Dowdy asked dismissal on the grounds that any briberies and perjuries committed by him in the performance of his duties were ipso facto beyond the reach of the policeman's knout; he also asked for change of venue, from Baltimore to Texas, where he may be tried not only by his peers but by his constituents. At this writing, Dowdy has lost the early rounds, but the appeals process has scarcely begun and will consume many years.

Rule 13. *During trial or impeachment proceedings, observe all the traditional formalities listed below:*

(a) From now on, never appear in public without your wife. Be sure your entire family, including pre-school children, attend every court session. The spectacle of your wife and children being subjected to all the evidence of your wrongdoing day after day will distress the jury and incline them toward pity for you. Although the experience may cause emotional damage to younger children, psychiatry can repair that later. Right now, it's go for broke.

(b) Feign illness and a sort of stunned vacuity, as if the indignity of it all is too much for your sensitive nature; this glazed mien is a must as groundwork for a convincing loss of memory when you take the stand. Loss of weight, a sickly pallor, a cane, the general look of a man about to break are mandatory if one is to create the "hasn't he already suffered enough" atmosphere.

(c) When questioned by the press in the hallways, emphasize how you welcome the chance to clear your name, how you asked for this trial, how the only thing that bothers you is the suffering it's inflicting on your family, how you'd still go after the Reds if you had it all to do over, how glad you'll be when the verdict is in and you can back to your duties.

(d) Employ the "partial expert"—the hired C.P.A. to give a tidied statement of your net worth, the paid handwriting expert to testify that it was *not* your signature after all, the tax consultant (retired) who will swear he told you not to list those testimonial purses.

(e) If convicted, abandon all dignity and beg for mercy. Congressman Johnson petitioned the court not to send him to prison on the grounds that the resultant indignity would so affront his honor as to cause him to commit suicide.

(f) If, despite this plea, you are sentenced to prison anyway, follow Johnson's example and announce you are getting the warden to assign you to the V.I.P. hospital. That way, you will be constantly attended by doctors, and subsequently remembered not as a jailbird but as a patient.

(g) Don't despair. Remember that Congressman Tom Lane won reelection after he was convicted. So did Jim Curley and Adam Powell. Besides, there is always the probability of a presidential pardon. It has been the custom for the President to let all convicted politicians out of jail every year at Christmas time, when the public is preoccupied and forgiveness is in the air. Late in the Administration of President Johnson, yuletide pardons were so numerous that the custom began to get a bad name and was suspended temporarily. But Attorney General Mitchell has persuaded President Nixon to reinstitute it.

The foregoing has been set down not as a how-to-do-it tract for charlatans, nor as a guide for detecting the falsehoods of guilty men, though I suppose perverted minds could misuse the information for both purposes—just as a chemistry book could be misused to construct a bomb or an illustrated text on gynecology exploited for erotic pleasure. My purpose is scientific and philosophic.

I set out in the beginning to show that from an exposed Congressman's first laryngitis attack to his Christmas Eve release from jail and subsequent strategy meeting to plan the next campaign, he acts out of folk wisdom known only to politicians. The ritual, partly glimpsed here, is preserved by Congressional elders, and all Members in trouble master it by rote. To prove this point, I shall cite the travail of a man as different from an ordinary Congressman as a swan is from a hippopotamus. My object is to show that even in this case the ritual was followed without deviation down to the most banal detail. I refer to the misfortune of Senator Edward Kennedy. Recall the steps by which a patrician gentleman with the most sophisticated advisers in the West defended himself exactly as would the commonest Boston pol:

After the private moment of despair the panic and hiding in the Shiretown Inn; the cryptic statement to the police; the precipitate smuggling out of the body, before autopsy, to a jurisdiction beyond reach of subpoena; the long period incommunicado at Hyannisport while the Kennedy proconsuls hammered together a plausible story; the appearance at the Kopechne funeral wearing a neck brace and the vague reports about a brain concussion; the rumors from the Compound about a stunned listlessness; the clandestine negotiation with friendly authorities to set up a traffic violation as the charge; the guilty plea to that charge which cut off all public proceedings; the suspended jail sentence; the television broadcast in which what was publicly known was confessed and the rest glossed over; the announcement for reelection with the added refinement of a plebescite by mail; the public welcoming of an investigation when it finally became unstoppable; the assurances that all the facts would be aired at the proper time while stealthily maneuvering to block any public airing; the involved constitutional gimmickry which added up to the Senator's claim to personal immunity; the "reluctant" refusal to answer reporters' questions on the grounds of protecting the dignity of the court; the hiring of "partial experts"—this time air bubble experts; the public concern for "getting this over so I can get back to my Senate duties" while privately employing every possible instrument of delay; the loss of memory and the lying under oath (in the opinion of Judge Boyle); the brilliant series of technicalities on which the serious charges which might have been brought were one by one eliminated. And now the careful period of rehabilitation, the press build-up that the Senator has become serious, cut down on drinking, is dieting and exercising, and no longer is activated by pretty girls. Not a pirouette missed in the elephant's ballet.

Examined individually, how gross, ignominious, and transparently fraudulent these maneuvers are; but in the aggregate, how efficacious! How many times did you chortle as Teddy lumbered preposterously with his subterfuge? But look at the results: the Senate Majority Whip post retained, reelection assured, credibility damaged but salvageable, presidential prospects rising, a climate irresistibly building in which it begins to seem unsportsmanlike to bring up Chappaquiddick. In another year or two the whole affair will dissolve into the morning mists off Martha's Vineyard.

The basic premise behind a ritual so manifestly successful ought to tell us something important about our society. In my opinion, it is this: in American public life there is no sense of honor, no concept of it, no expectation of it, no reward for it. Wherever honor exists it is an unrequired discipline a man imposes on himself for private reasons. This is the reverse side of the blessing of popular democracy, and may yet turn that blessing into a curse.

We are a country of Falstaffs and the shrewder politicians all know it. Many civilized nations have soldiers who will shoot down unarmed civilians; in America they are lionized in their home towns, praised by Congressmen, and favored by a clear majority in the Gallup Poll. Many nations have cops who bludgeon unarmed adolescents and fire machine guns into the windows of the girls' dormitory; there they are extolled by their governor and have fan clubs organized and bumper stickers printed in their honor. Many nations have district attorneys who stage an occasional massacre and then dramatize the scene on television as self-defense; here, when such a creature is exposed as a calculated liar, he not only keeps his job but begins to dream of the governorship. Many nations have legislators who are shown to lie, cheat and steal; here church synods, panels of distinguished citizens, and ideological movements pass resolutions praising them. Such egalitarian buffooneries are the key to our political process. Once the politician masters this, he will face his indictments with equanimity.

The difficulty in catching on to this reality has unfairly retarded the political progress of our more recent arrivals, particularly those of ethnic strains which retain a hereditary respect for "face" and personal dignity. Signs abound that this handicap is passing. Having learned the rules, Greeks, Jews, Poles, and Japanese are regularly winning reelection to Congress; and recently 100,000 Italian-Americans held a mass rally in New York to protest police repression of the Mafia.

OBSTACLES TO REFORM: NOBODY COVERS THE HOUSE

Michael Green

Behind the closed, guarded doors leading to the House chamber one Wednesday morning several months ago, a dramatic and unexpected confrontation took place. Occurring at what was to have been just another routine monthly meeting of the House Democratic caucus, a customarily tepid conclave which normally fails to summon the interest of the Congressmen themselves, the confrontation totally bypassed the press. Even had the doors not been closed, reporters most likely would have shown scant interest. Conversely, had they been interested, the closed doors would have been no bar to their extracting ample accounts of developments inside.

But that morning, events unfolded in a public vacuum. Not only were they dramatic, they were politically significant—a first early signal of the determined, open rebellion by a few House reformers that was to break out two months later in defiance of the institution's customs and leaders. The issues raised were important to the country. The frustration and anger voiced against the House establishment revealed a sudden new boldness, not quite like the kind of militancy in evidence before, pushing back the boundaries of political civility in the chamber which in the past had always marked the acceptable outer limits to demands for change by young reformers.

Even without such hints of significance, the confrontation was in itself newsworthy. Out of the sea of anonymity which engulfs most Congressmen most of the time, and nearly all junior Congressmen nearly all of the time, an obscure, previously conservative and well-behaved, two-term Congressman from California named Jerome R. Waldie stepped forward and was recognized. For the next few amazing moments, he gave 78-year-old Speaker John W. McCormack a dressing down to his face, in front of his assembled colleagues, that was without contemporary precedent and shocked all in attendance.

The charge was "a dismal lack of leadership." The tone, though sternly polite and dignified, was unmistakably personal. The immediate criticism centered on the Speaker's attitude toward Administration policy on Vietnam, but went beyond it to question the performance of all in the House leadership and the antiquated procedures that had made the House seem as obsolete in the last third of the 20th century as any institution in society.

Predictably, the reaction by McCormack and by those faithful party regulars who habitually attend him was one of outrage. The reaction of the public was non-existent. For good reason: not a line appeared in the nation's press the following morning. Nor on the television screen that evening. Nor anywhere the day after, nor the day after that, save for one afternoon daily clear across the country, which buried the story on an inside page at the bottom in one of the back sections.

Nearly a week passed before Congressional reporters finally stumbled across the story by accident. Even at that late date, the confrontation was considered significant enough to rate as news, and Washington papers carried several accounts. But the story might just as easily have never appeared.

Ordinarily, the failure of the press to discover and report this solitary incident when it occurred might be dismissed as an understandable omission, given the multitude of events that compete for a reporter's attention and energy and all the judgments which must be made at various levels as to the value of an event as news.

But an examination of the position now occupied by the House in the political life of the country, in relation to public awareness of it and concern over it, and specifically to the need for reform, suggests a chronic failure by the press that goes far deeper than any single oversight. It extends to the coverage of all kinds of activities in the House, whether related to reform or otherwise, with serious implications for the future of the democratic process itself.

At a recent press conference, Representative Allard K. Lowenstein (D.-N.Y.) warned that if the House were to become any more ignored than it was already, it would become as obsolete as the House of Lords and the country would simply evolve into government by Presidential decree.

If the public is without alarm, perhaps it is because Lowenstein's words went virtually unreported, as had Waldie's confrontation with the Speaker. And even had his warning been heard, could it be said the press had so prepared the public that it might have understood the meaning of his words?

The disturbing truth is that the increasing irrelevance of the House in American life is attributable at least in some proportion to the degree to which its activities and people remain a mystery to the public, and that the hope for urgently needed reforms is doomed in large part by this same public ignorance. The current state of general House coverage by the press is a key ingredient in the despair Congressional reformers feel over their chances for success in the uphill battle they face. At least some of them though not impolitic enough to say so publicly, now see the issue of reform in the House as being inseparably intertwined with the need for change in the coverage the press gives to Congress. Without changes in press coverage, they hold out little hope for the kind of public pressure which alone might drag the institution into the modern world.

The larger casualty of the present state of affairs is the political process itself. At a time when the system is beset on all sides by accusations of unresponsiveness, often made in violence, the elected representatives supposedly closest to the people are among the least known officials in Washington, and the institution that in theory most directly links the people to government is furthest removed from their eyes and comprehension. Is it any wonder, in words Waldie used to challenge the Speaker, that "no one really looks to the House or its leadership as an authority or as a hope in this trying period for our country"?

Examples of the great Congressional coverage gap extend to a disturbing array of issues and events. The conclusions to be drawn can only be disheartening.

The press has failed to keep the public abreast of even the basic developments related to the reform effort.

For the past year, a subcommittee of the House Rules Committee considered legislation to modernize some of the antiquated House procedures. Its work went virtually unreported. Without the stimulus of public pressure, the subcommittee soon abandoned all substantive proposals for reform. It decided not to deal with the questions raised by the seniority system, lobbying practices, conflict-of-interest, secret committee meetings, unrecorded votes, and similar basic issues. It is doubtful many in the country even knew the subcommittee existed or that legislation was being drafted. Certainly, few constituents knew how their own Congressmen stood on these issues in testifying before the subcommittee. By the time legislation was actually drafted, the determination of reformers to add meaningful amendments on the floor existed without the benefit of public comprehension and support. Coverage by the press was too minimal to have any effect.

The press has failed to show the real forces at work and to chronicle the shifting alliances for and against change.

The champions of House reform in prior years have looked curiously pale of late. When Waldie followed up his initial confrontation with the Speaker with a challenge at a subsequent caucus, in the form of a "no confidence" resolution against the House leadership, the old reformers shunned him. Similarly, when the once-militant Democratic Study Group offered a mild resolution calling only for a study of the seniority system even that move was thought too bold by many of the older champions. Rep. Morris K. Udall (D.-Ariz.), who challenged McCormack for the speakership only a year ago, suggested privately it was not the right time to make waves. He hopes to bid for the speakership again next year. The aging, autocratic committee chairmen found unexpected allies in their moves to prevent the reorganization bill from ever reaching the floor, even with its watered-down and largely meaningless proposals. Such old-time labor liberals as Representatives James G. O'Hara (D-Mich.) and Frank Thompson (D-N.J.) shifted uncomfortably at the thought of the rules subcommittee bill emerging. Their exaggerated fear was a possible move on the floor to split the House Labor and Education Committee and pack the new labor panel with anti-union conservatives, a move few thought was really in the works or would have a serious possibility of success, anyway. Conservatives, in turn, feared liberal amendments from the floor aimed at introducing meaningful House reform.

The strange posturing and maneuvering by the reformers of old was disturbing, but, thanks to the press, their reputations as champions of change have remained untarnished. Their fearful whispering not to "make waves" stayed a private affair. Their evolution within the system they once confronted openly and subsequent replacement by a newer group of young militants standing in the shoes they once wore, went unreported by the press.

The press has failed to pursue its own as well as the public interest.

One of the few real hopes of bringing about eventual reform in the House has centered in efforts to open it up to public scrutiny. Perhaps the single most important proposal considered by the rules subcommittee was to permit live TV coverage of the House and its committees. It was fitting and ironic that the proposal was rejected by the subcommittee in a private session behind closed doors. But the proposal's enemies were not numbered from just among the ranks of the House power structure, which prefers not to have the public view what goes on. The opponents included the writing press.

Samuel J. Archibald, Director of the Washington Freedom of Information Center, run by the University of Missouri School of Journalism, tried in vain to mobilize editors and publishers to support the proposal. He found "no interest at all" among working newsmen in the House Press Gallery, most of whom strongly opposed it. He found "very minimal interest" on the part of various editorial and publishing associations— "very minimal." The death of the proposal, and the deeper issues involved in its rejection, were virtually ignored by all media, including television news itself.

The press has failed to show the average Congressman as he really is.

The anonymity of those Congressmen opposed to reform, who remain unknown both to the country at large and to their own constituents, is a special aspect of the perennial failure to achieve reform. If a few colorful, entrenched committee chairmen like L. Mendel Rivers (D-S.C.) head of the Armed Services Committee, have received wide publicity, the bulk of anonymous Congressmen who support the antiquated system have not, even in their own districts. They include a wide variety of types, each opposing change for his own reasons. Many do not think of themselves as anti-reform. Rather, they see no need for it, some professing genuine astonishment at the reformers' complaints.

A Democratic colleague of Waldie's from California serves as an example. Rep. John J. McFall, 52, with 14 years in Congress, is one of those honest, amiable, pleasant-faced members whose name and status are always lost on observers in the Congressional gallery, if not to most of his colleagues as well. A "zone whip" for the Democratic leadership, assigned to keep tabs on members in a limited geographical area on important votes, he also heads the party's research activities in the House, though in seniority he still ranks well down the list on the Appropriations Committee. Well-liked by colleagues of all persuasions, he is a part of the comfortable existing order. It was McFall who helped put together McCormack's rebuttal to Waldie's charges.

Sitting back in his office swivel chair recently, head down on his chest, thumbs rotating around each other on his lap, feet spread apart and socks drooping around his ankles, McFall expressed honest puzzlement over the reformers' complaints. "I really don't understand what they're talking about," he said. "I really don't understand. I really don't."

That, say the reformers, is no small part of the problem. But it is not one likely to ever be considered in McFall's home district. For the seven terms he has served in Congress, his actions affecting the lives of all in the country, no newspaper in his district or outside of it has reported, either regularly or occasionally, his actual day-in and day-out performance in the midst of Congressional life as it really is. His attitudes, maneuverings, relationships, and thoughts remain unknown to the public. John McFall's socks have never drooped in his hometown paper. In fact, when he very nearly lost his last reelection campaign, it was not because he had displeased his constituents but because, a post-election survey showed, so many of them didn't remember quite who he was. So it is, to a greater or lesser extent, with most members of Congress; they are known to editors and readers back home only by their press handouts and occasional visits. Who they really are and what they really do over a period of 14 years is not "news."

The press imposes its own self-censorship.

At a recent press conference crowded with reporters, Speaker McCormack, third in line for succession to the Presidency, blew his top. Turning on a reporter who had written a matter-of-fact, even sympathetic account of McCormack's years in Congress and current troubles, the Speaker denounced the newsman as "a goddamned sonofabitch." The reporters seemed stunned. None was sufficiently stunned, however, to write anything about the outburst. No one seemed sure exactly why, except perhaps that McCormack is an old man, given to frequent outbursts these days over both real and imagined slights, and it did not seem the tasteful thing to do.

All the foregoing provides only glimpses of the deeper and more basic problem, which is that the average Congressman lives and works today far from the beaten path of press coverage; and the abuses of the system he either fights or engages in, and the failure of the system in dozens of its intricate parts, are far removed from the attention of the public and any possible response from it. Because the press never shows the system and its participants to the public, pleas for reform can only fall on confused ears, producing hesitation and uncertainty in place of loud demands for action. In a recent interview, Allard Lowenstein asked incredulously: "Do you know that we were not allowed to have a roll call vote on whether to deploy the ABM? And that on the Vietnam resolution the President wanted passed because it was vital to his plan for peace, there were no hearings, and discussion was limited to four hours—which averages out to 30 seconds a member—and there was no way to introduce amendments? And we've voted on amendments to bills that appropriate billions of dollars without having the amendments *explained,* let alone discussed?

"If only the country understood what goes on! But the whole procedure is designed to make that impossible."

It is clear the country does not know what goes on and that the system does make it impossible. It is also true that for all practical purposes, the press is a part of that system.

The relative absence of Congressional coverage today has many causes. In part, it reflects the low esteem to which the House itself has fallen in relation to the Senate and to the other branches of government, with a corresponding reduction in its news priority. The secrecy of the House, which bars reporters from committee sessions where billions of dollars are allocated, plays a major role, as does the sheer bulk of the institution.

Yet, it can be argued that the House is now the last, best hope of democracy as a participatory process, and therefore the most important institution of all—important as both a cause and potential remedy of the feeling of political impotence which afflicts the American body politic.

But the Congressional press corps is poorly equipped to serve as a bridge for bringing the House into the arena of modern life. The fault is both physical and attitudinal, resting more with press management than with the reporters assigned to Washington, most of whom function at a high level of competence within the restricted news spheres.

In physical terms, most medium-sized dailies in the country either maintain ludicrously understaffed bureaus or, most often, no bureau at all to cover local Congressmen on the Hill. They rely on wire copy. Here the deficiency in coverage is most obvious. For by the nature of a wire service reporter's preoccupation with the major news event of the moment, there is neither the opportunity nor the inclination to be concerned with the average Congressman. All the dailies back home receive is mimeographed press releases from the Congressman's own Washington office.

The result is a yawning gap in coverage more serious than is generally known. The fact, for example, that not a single major newspaper in the San Francisco-Oakland area, with its millions of people, maintains a Washington bureau is regarded as something of a scandal among Hill reporters themselves. Even when a paper maintains a bureau, however, the appearance is likely to be deceiving.

One California newspaper chain maintains a two-man bureau. But the two reporters are assigned to cover a total of nine Congressmen, two Senators, the Departments of Interior, Agriculture, HEW, and HUD, and occasionally the White House. Quite obviously, there is no time to do the job that needs doing. Another newspaper chain, based in Michigan, has one man to cover eight Senators and countless Congressmen for newspapers in four states spreading as far west as Oregon. The story is the same.

Even where a major newspaper or news service maintains a large bureau, the average voter may find it no easier to discover what his Congressman is doing and what he is really like. *The Los Angeles Times* has nearly two dozen reporters in town. But an esoteric publishing philosophy which stresses the more occult and ivory-tower dimensions of major stories leaves local Congressmen and their maneuverings as dimly reported as ever and the House as mysterious.

The attitude of publishers and news editors back home is primarily responsible for the failure of coverage in Washington. They have a highly ritualistic view of governmental coverage which holds unquestioned sway year after year and in its own way is as unresponsive to the times and as impervious to change as other hardened institutions of society, including the House itself.

What is generally omitted from coverage of Congress, almost alone of the categories of people and events with which a newspaper regularly deals, is journalism that might portray Congressional life so as to engage public interest. The human face of Congressmen and their aides, in all the day-to-day expressions of their small human foibles and unreported triumphs, mirror the forces at work in the population as a whole. They color the story and, in so doing, reveal it. But the public is not allowed to know this story. Readers are told only in dry, clipped accounts the numerical fate of legislation. They are shown the final score, seldom the action itself. The smells and faces and humanity of the players is lost to them and with it the opportunity for interest. The daily weather report is more interesting to the public and seemingly has more demonstrable relationship to their lives.

Journalistic tradition holds certain kinds of writing appropriate only to certain categories of coverage. Thus, there is business writing and sports writing, governmental coverage and garden columns, and the one is not to be confused with the other. Red Smith belongs on the sports pages. No one wonders what magic interest might be aroused in the public if he suddenly began covering Congress and appeared on the front pages. By the same token, if the present style of government reporting were extended to the coverage of sports events, the American people would lose interest in sports overnight. If Broadway Joe Namath's socks are seen to droop, millions of Americans via the press will hang on the unravelling threads. But for their news about government, the American people must suffer the dullest, driest, and most dehumanized accounts being published in the English language. Perhaps, as will be argued, the average Congressman is just not all that interesting or glamorous. But certainly there must be potential in someone like Dapper Dan Flood (D-Pa.), the Shakespearean actor-turned-Congressman, with his twirled villain's mustache, dark glasses, Gaylord Ravenal voice, and white buck shoes, who controls billions of dollars in appropriations every year. Unfortunately, there appear to be no Damon Runyons now assigned to the Congressional press corps who might be equal to him. It is doubtful anyway that a distant editor trained to the present type of coverage could be persuaded by his reporters that Dan Flood actually exists.

The tradition of journalistic drabness in governmental coverage is not very old. It was not so long ago that William Allen White could report from the thick of political action or H.L. Mencken could freely dismiss a Congressman as a "boob" in his coverage. When Mark Twain was covering Congress for a time in the last century, one account began, "Dear Reader: Suppose that you were a Congressman. And suppose that you were a thief. But I repeat myself." Well, they don't write like that anymore.

It is high time that we started writing about the House as it is. What happens in Congress is a deadly if silent war within our political boundaries; we need more Ernie Pyles to cover it by living, eating, and getting shot at alongside the political troops while writing about combat conditions. Perhaps the confusion and puzzlement the average citizen now feels might be replaced by comprehension and involvement. At least government would have a face. The electorate would need not seek after strange devils to explain the mysterious coming of political winds. The process, by being human, would become rational, and even to lost souls in forgotten cities all things might seem possible within the system as it was meant to be.

If the possibility or even certainty exists of abuse by politically motivated reporters in providing this kind of intimate coverage, one also needs to ask the price of public apathy and Congressional unresponsiveness. It may still be easier to balance subjective coverage between reporters of different political hues than to rebuild Detroit.

In the current state of governmental coverage, the public has long since given up trying to understand elected behavior. Voters in a district, of course, may always hold their own Congressman accountable. But perhaps he has publicly supported the legislation they favor, as a majority of his colleagues may have, and yet it has died in the murkiness of some closed committee room—if he was in that room, his constituents need never know how he voted. It should be of little wonder that the system breeds despair and that the average citizen feels politically impotent.

It would not be accurate to say the press has failed utterly to communicate the need for change. The public has a general awareness by now, due to constant repetition over the years, that a seniority system that places aging, Southern autocrats in charge of powerful committees somehow works to the disadvantage of the country as a whole. It grasps, as well, the issue involved in the continued rule or non-rule of McCormack, third in line at age 78 for succession to the Presidency. The symbol here is powerfully visual. Particularly when McCormack sits behind the President at televised State of the Union messages, the gaunt visage of a man who has simply become too old for the job he holds conveys an unmistakable conclusion.

But the crisis of the House requires more than vague public uneasiness in order to be resolved. It requires intimate public knowledge, day by day, of the deeper evils of the system as it functions on a primary level and of the manner in which those evils are worked. This, in turn, requires a scope and depth and humanity of coverage on a continuing basis that so far shows no signs of appearing.

It requires, in the end, an urgent understanding by citizens that they alone have the power to force the institution to become responsive, not only in terms of the great social problems facing the country, but, first, in reshaping its own procedures to meet those problems. Somehow, it has not occurred to constituents who make their voices heard in Congress on a myriad of issues from crime to taxes that they have the power to influence the House toward its own reform. Somehow, it has escaped their notice that the way the House conducts its affairs is as much their business as any other issue and has great longrange impact on their lives. This is the real failure of the press.

What is required for public understanding is that coverage honor the truism set forth by Honoré de Balzac when he observed: "Men are so made that they can resist sound argument, and yet yield to a glance."

It should be the daily job of the press to record not only the bills that are moved and the votes that are cast but the glances that are exchanged and the human motivations that are behind them. Only then will the art of governmental reporting imitate life as it is with all its potential for change.

THE CONGRESSIONAL PRESENCE IN FOREIGN RELATIONS

Jacob K. Javits

In the field of foreign policy the constitutional powers delegated under Articles I and II to the Congress are keyed to the phrase "advise and consent." However, in America's greatest moments of external crisis the emphasis has been on "consent." The exercise of the right to advise has, on many occasions, been less than welcome to the executive recipient of Senatorial recommendations.

No sooner had President Washington launched the nation's first Administration than he found the advice of the Congress so abusive that he strode from the Senate chamber swearing "never to return to this place." And Secretary of State John Hay summed up his bitter experiences at the hands of the legislative body in the late nineteenth century by observing: "A treaty entering the Senate is like a bull going into the arena. No one can say just how or when the final blow will fall. But one thing is certain—it will never leave the arena alive."

Much has changed in the intervening period. A "strong presidency" has evolved into a national institution welcomed in this century by most Americans. That welcome is a response to the quickened pace of communications and the apparent need for the country to act immediately and with decisiveness in the ever recurring crises of contemporary foreign policy.

The American people began to learn in Theodore Roosevelt's day to focus their attention on the White House as the seat of national power and policy in foreign affairs. The potential for this attitude to flourish has of course always existed in the constitutional powers granted to the President. His role as Commander in Chief and his mandate to "conduct the foreign policy of the United States" have from the beginning carried the possibility for an assumption of authority and an exercise of power that exceeds the principle of the equal but separate powers of the three branches of government.

Only in this century, however, has that Presidential potential grown to such dramatic proportions that it threatens to precipitate a crisis in constitutional relationships. For the right to advise as well as to consent implies a two-way relationship. The constitution-makers in Philadelphia, on the basis of their own experience with the British Crown, wished to assure a reciprocal and consultative function affecting the Legislative and Executive Branches. Yet a few short years later, the problems of the second half of the twentieth century were foreshadowed in the reaction of President Washington to the Senate in his first and only visit there.

Other Presidents since have given evidence of agreement with our country's first Chief Executive. The failure of President Wilson to include Republican members of the Foreign Relations Committee in his deliberations on the Treaty of Versailles led, finally, to the destruction of the League of Nations and in some degree perhaps to the outbreak of the Second World War. Senator Lodge's antipathy to the Treaty may or may not have been changed by a Wilsonian overture. The question of motivation is not critical. The point is that the Senate was not asked to advise and, tragically, it did not consent. In the years that followed we protected ourselves from what Churchill described later as "the gathering storm" by insulating ourselves with the illusion of "normalcy." Today, those of us who exercise high executive and legislative power can no longer rely on such an illusion. The most ill-informed citizen knows that any new storm carries with it the threat of nuclear war.

II

Television so charges responses that a recent book is entitled "The Living Room War." In sharply defined focus the horrors of the present war are brought in living color to bemuse the evening hours of "an audience" of millions. There is justified unease in the hearts of the American people. The President who is chosen to lead us and the Senators and Congressmen chosen to represent the people must reflect an awareness of that unease and must act to eliminate, where possible, the reasons for its being. Today, Viet Nam is the essence and the symbol of that unease.

President Nixon himself recently remarked on his awareness that his own views of the Viet Nam situation are at odds with what he called the country's "leadership communities." The most important segment of that leadership community, in terms of its power to act and to restrain, is within the United States Senate. If the country is to extract itself from the morass of Viet Nam, then the President and the Senate must act in common and not in dissension and struggle. It is time now for the Congress to reassess its own role in terms of what it has and has not done and what it should do in the future to assure the free debate that is indispensable to our ultimate decision—the product of free institutions. That debate must seek the national interest ahead of partisan advantage. Every element of foreign policy must be totally debated, and the "loyal opposition" is under special obligation to see that this occurs.

It is highly questionable whether the Truman Doctrine, the Marshall Plan, and even UNRRA could have taken place without the leadership exercised in the Senate by Senator Vandenberg's Foreign Relations Committee and the acceptance of that leadership by the country at large. Dean Acheson, in his recent memoirs dealing with his years as Secretary of State, presents in pungent fashion his own account of the relationship between the State Department and the Vandenberg Committee. While the tone of Dean Acheson's recollections differs sharply from the attitudes expressed in Senator Vandenberg's memoirs, they are in full agreement on the essential factors that dominated that key period in postwar policy-making. The Presidential power was exercised in close consultation with the Senate Committee on Foreign Relations. That committee, in turn, helped to amend and shape policy so that it could in good conscience be supported by the Congress before the country at large.

Today, debates about the Viet Nam war, the defense budget and domestic priorities are bringing about an even more powerful role for the Congress in foreign affairs. We have all seen this happening and most view it as a healthy sign; the probing, the questioning, the suggesting, the delving into national security requirements with the same scrutiny which the Congress always has given to domestic affairs have met with general approval. Yet, in themselves, these do not add up to a new role for the Congress in foreign policy. They represent but a beginning of a new assertiveness and a new activism by the Congress, the basis of which has always existed in terms of constitutional authority. The Congress over the last ten years has not asserted this authority because of the preëmption of the role by the Executive Branch and because the Congress tended, albeit all too willingly, to bow to the allegedly superior secret information of the President.

A major function of the Congress with respect to the great issues of foreign policy and national security is that of shaping as well as articulating public opinion. In a democracy such as ours, governmental action is possible only within parameters defined by public attitudes and opinions. In the major Senate foreign-policy debates of the very recent past—Viet Nam and ABM—we have learned that the development and public presentation of new information and interpretations bearing on the great issues is a vital Congressional function as well as a potent instrumentality in asserting legislative prerogatives and responsibilities.

There certainly was vigorous debate within the Executive Branch concerning the ABM issue, but it was, perforce and properly, a debate conducted *in camera* and it was before a jury structurally oriented heavily toward the military viewpoint. The countervailing views of distinguished scientists, outside experts and qualified public men were brought to bear on the question only as a result of Congressional initiative. The same has been true to a lesser extent with respect to the Viet Nam war.

Until the recent Congressional challenges, the Administration has enjoyed an overwhelming predominance in the field of national security information and interpretation. We have learned and will put to good use, I am convinced, the practicality as well as the necessity of meeting the Executive on roughly equal terms with respect to relevant information and interpretation.

A salutary by-product has been the evolving capacity of the Congress to handle, rather than be intimidated and manipulated by, the problem of "classified" information upon which Administration decision-makers rely so heavily. In the course of hearings on the ABM it became apparent that classified information is sometimes made available on a highly selective basis by Administration witnesses. Diligent and imaginative probing often uncovers additional classified information which supports opposite conclusions. Moreover, we have learned that intensive Congressional scrutiny of so-called classified information can lead to the declassification, with Administration concurrence, of relevant information which has remained classified more for the sake of bureaucratic convenience than for legitimate national-security reasons.

It is the discovery and development of alternative viewpoints about "secret" information which makes the greater use of closed-door sessions of the Senate and House a potential instrument of greater Congressional effectiveness in foreign policy. Attendance invariably is high at secret, closed-door sessions at which the full range of classified information can be presented and submitted to critical cross-examination by proponents and opponents of a particular measure.

Of perhaps even greater usefulness is the technique evolved during the Viet Nam and ABM debates of bringing differing interpretations and recommendations dramatically but responsibly to the public's attention. An alternative case, differing from that presented by the Administration, has been articulated with great effectiveness before Congressional committees both by Senators and by distinguished public witnesses whose knowledge, judgment and experience carry great weight. I believe that this is a technique which the President and his senior Cabinet advisers should welcome. It can materially enhance the quality of decision-making and the efficacy of policy implementation, to the President's advantage, for the nation ultimately will judge the President on performance rather than on rhetoric. Moreover, in our system as contrasted to the parliamentary system, major revision of Administration-sponsored legislation does not represent the threat and the challenge to the government which similar action would do to the British Government, for instance.

III

The road to greater Congressional participation in foreign policy is marked by the choice of key issues for public examination. We have not yet addressed all the basic foreign and national security issues other than Viet Nam and the Anti-Ballistic Missile system. Because of this concentration of effort, two misimpressions are developing: first, that we in the Congress only criticize and have little that is positive to offer; and second, that we tend to oppose most of the Administration's present foreign and security policy. Neither is true. Unfortunately, our criticisms may continue to be mistaken for a broadside on the present U.S. role in the world until we forge a new concept of Congressional-Executive relations on foreign policy and a new more relevant foreign policy.

The catalyst for defining the new relationship has been and is obviously Viet Nam. The war there brings us face to face with a policy dilemma in the separation of powers under the Constitution. The war is being carried out under the President's powers as Commander in Chief. There was no declaration of war by Congress. Only a Sense-of-the-Congress Resolution backs him; and that is terminable by resolution of both Houses. Who, then, shall decide when substantively there is to be war? This dilemma, and the uncertainty it creates about the responsibility for war, points up the need to find a new "check and balance" in the Congressional role in foreign policy—a "check and balance" that is adaptable to modern "undeclared" war.

The Congress has yet to question effectively the powers of the Commander in Chief to dispose American forces overseas as he sees fit. President Eisenhower in 1958 landed Marines in Lebanon. President Johnson in 1965 poured 20,000 U.S. troops into Santo Domingo. Both assertions of military power came without declarations of war. We were considerably more fortunate in each case than we have been in Viet Nam, for the Executive's objective was achieved both times without the horrifying material and human costs we are paying in the present conflict. It is my judgment that as unfortunate as is the Viet Nam conflict, it would be even more so if Congress had declared war. The Viet Nam action issues from executive decision; it is not a commitment of the national honor.

If the Congress had declared war, a tremendous complex of international agreements, a whole area of international law would have been invoked in such fashion as to unloose unforeseeable consequences. Public opinion might very well have required the bombing of Haiphong harbor and probably a land invasion of North Viet Nam. There are those who assert that our Viet Nam involvement should have been offered to the Congress in the context of a proposed declaration of war and that, if faced with such a prospect, we would not have become involved in the conflict as we did. I, for one, am glad that no such declaration was sought or given. The power to declare war is an ultimate Congressional power to commit the nation. The power not to declare war is a legitimate check on foreign policy.

Members of the Senate were among the first to sound the call for a reassessment of America's commitment in Viet Nam. As sentiment against the conduct and the nature of the war rose in intensity, the Senate itself provided the principal forum for the expression of views ranging from dissent to the presentation of alternative action. Whatever the merits of the individual positions assumed by my colleagues throughout these last difficult years, it is my view that political scientists will record the role of this Senatorial opposition as one of the high points in the history of the Senate as a great deliberative body.

No matter what the ultimate outcome in Viet Nam, a somber warning note has been struck. Not only has policy been brought into question, but the institutions of policy-making themselves. When a policy loses public support and proves non-viable, and when, nevertheless, the institutions of government either support or do not change that policy, the validity of the institutions as well as the policy is called into question. An individual President may fall in the wake of adverse public opinion, but if we are to preserve the fabric of our society, we must assure ourselves that the *institutions* of the Presidency and the Senate retain their viability. Under the stresses of the Viet Nam war this relationship has been subject to strains unparalleled within the last century.

The United States Senate, notwithstanding objections voiced within its chambers to the course of American policy in Viet Nam, was so used during the Johnson Administration as to find itself a Presidential echo rather than an independent voice. As Commander in Chief, President Johnson was in absolute control of all information relating to the course of the war. That control was a key factor in the overwhelming adoption of the Tonkin Gulf Resolution. When confronted with the Commander in Chief's assessment that American troops are under attack by a foreign enemy, few Senators will take it upon themselves to refuse to support an effective response. To do so would be against the national interest as it has been understood since the inception of the Republic.

But today there are many who think that the Congress was mis-informed or inadequately informed as to what actually occurred in August of 1964 in the Gulf of Tonkin. A mutual distrust between the President and his principal legislative advisers in the area of foreign affairs has grown steadily. Senators today are inclined to cast a jaundiced eye on Presidential assessments, and, unfortunately, even on assertions of fact. This distrust of the exercise of the executive power can lead to a reassertion of Congressional authority and, hopefully, renewed coöperation between the President and the Senate—or it can push us toward a stalemate of wills.

Mr. Nixon's assumption of the Presidency provided us with the opportunity to extricate ourselves from the Viet Nam conflict. In the months since he took office he has not yet given adequate evidence of responding to a mandate that he himself acknowledges to get us out of the war. He told the nation in May: "I do not criticize those who disagree with me on the conduct of our peace negotiations. And I do not ask unlimited patience from a people whose hopes for peace have too often been raised and then cruelly dashed over the past four years." And yet his immediate response to the October Moratorium offered no fresh evidence of response to the dissent on Capitol Hill. The President, in his November 3 address, made no mention of any Congressional policy role in his plan to end the Viet Nam war; yet if we are at last to free ourselves of Saigon's "veto" on the Vietnamization of the war, the Congress will have to stand with the President in the decision. The enormous pressures being exerted on the President by those involved in the war or who favor its prosecution are not conducive to patience with criticism, no matter how constructive it is in its intent or application.

Nevertheless, we in Congress—even of the President's own party—must continue to criticize when necessary in order to fulfill our mandated role. It has been suggested by Representative Jonathan Bingham . . . that increased Congressional surveillance of military expenditure is not only a necessity today but gives promise of being an even weightier factor in future sessions of the Congress. The increasing complexities and expenses of weapons systems are too often causative factors in the evolution of policy. It is the case of the cart before the horse, and some of us at least have been awakened to the need for putting them back into proper position. But military spending and weapons systems are only one element in the shaping of foreign policy.

While we in Congress must continue to permit the Executive to determine the direction of that policy, we must insist more forcefully that he provide his reasoning and justification so as to discern where day-to-day actions, unglamorous in detail but substantive in effect, may carry the country. We must also exercise vigilance to assure that foreign policy is not being made for us in the Defense Department, the intelligence agencies or elsewhere by such faits accomplis as contingency plans, the deployment of forces or the location of bases, which deprive us effectively of our voice in foreign policy. It is here that Congress can act as both a restraining and as an informing influence, and, where appropriate, as an affirmative partner with the Executive.

Of course, the first prerequisite for the best functioning of our constitutional system in foreign policy is a knowledgeable and sensitive President who wants to coöperate with the Congress in foreign policy. This is perhaps the best assurance that the Congress will do its part and that the coöperation will work.

In any case, the Congress must fulfill the full dimension of its constitutional role. In order to reassert its proper place, we must consider enlarging some of its capabilities. The Executive Branch has at its disposal the largest and best equipped staff in the world. If Congress is to fulfill its responsibilities adequately, it, too, needs a staff—larger and of better quality than exists today. In an age when we spend billions on atomic arsenals we must allocate resources to those endeavors which will hopefully make those arsenals obsolete.

IV

There is, fortunately, an element of foreign policy in which Congress has continued to play a leading role throughout what we have come to think of as an era of executive dominance.

Section VIII of Article I of the Constitution empowers Congress to "regulate Commerce with foreign nations" and to "lay and collect Taxes, Duties, Imposts, and Excises." The powers and responsibilities of the Congress in this field have grown in importance throughout the postwar period and I look to a similar growth in the decade of the 1970s.

There has been a vast increase in international trade, and investment problems will loom as large as trade problems in the 1970s. Continuing international monetary problems have sharply challenged the very foundations of our international monetary system, which is based on gold. The year 1970 may see significant changes. The problems of an inward- or outward-looking Common Market and the expansion of this economic grouping also loom large, as do those of better integrating the powerful Japanese economy into the Western system. The world's North-South standard-of-living gap is a problem of such magnitude that its bridging cannot be conceived of in terms of presently existing institutions and developmental assistance programs. These problems dictate the need for a more coördinated approach to the issues of foreign economic policy within the Congress and the Administration as well as between Congress, the Administration and international organizations. The time may come when it will be necessary to create a new department of cabinet rank to handle the issues of foreign trade and aid, technology and U.S. private investment; there will be a parallel need for new committees within both Houses of the Congress to deal with the new legislation and new approaches that will be required.

The future will be built on what we are doing now, and here again the Congress is in the forefront. In the very near future, the Joint Economic Committee (JEC) of the Congress, of which I am the ranking Minority member, will open hearings on a wide range of trade issues facing this nation. It should be recalled that similar hearings were a prelude to the Kennedy Administration's introduction of the Trade Expansion Act in the early 1960s—the truly historic legislation which formed the cornerstone of our trade policy during this decade. Hopefully, these hearings will again lead the way into the 1970s.

The Joint Economic Committee has also pioneered in other crucial areas which will be of increasing importance in the years ahead. Certainly its groundbreaking hearings regarding the economy of Mainland China did much to correct myths and misinformation which had accumulated during the emotional McCarthy years in the 1950s and to stimulate new and more realistic thinking. It is clear that our relations with Mainland China must evolve over the years in a way so as to increase commerce and cultural and educational interchanges. The ideological and military-oriented approach of the Defense and Commerce Departments relates not to the future but to the receding past. The State Department shows signs of going the other way, however.

Congressional innovation must extend to economic détente with Eastern Europe. The recent Senate passage of the Export Expansion and

Regulations Act—even over some Administration opposition—is a first step in our agenda for the 1970s. Paralleling the vital search for a modus vivendi in the field of strategic weaponry, we should undertake a search for positive moves in the fields of monetary affairs, aid and trade, general economic relations and the coordination of developmental assistance efforts. We should very much hope that over the next decade the Soviet Union would consider joining established international trade and financial agencies such as GATT, the IMF, IDA and the IBRD, and regional trade and financial organizations.

If these and other foreign-policy objectives are to be achieved, a dialogue between the Executive and Legislative Branches must occur in such style as to ensure meaningful responses on the part of each. Many years ago, as an undergraduate at New York University, I debated in the negative a resolution moving the adoption of a parliamentary form of government for the United States. NYU won the debate, but experience has since moved me somewhat closer to the position of my opponents from CCNY. Although the parliamentary form as practiced in other countries would introduce into the American society an element of instability we can ill afford—outweighing the value of its flexibility and sensitivity— there are elements within the parliamentary system we might in practice adopt.

In the Executive Branch only the President is elected; the Secretaries of State and Defense, the agency and department heads are responsible to him. Every Congressman has a specific constituency to which he is responsible and responsive. The Congress must reassert itself in the formation of foreign policy so as to avoid the bitterness of future Viet Nams in which its constituents suddenly find themselves reluctant participants.

Perhaps we could initiate the practice of interpellations—where at "closed-door" Senate sessions members of the President's Cabinet might find it possible to appear and to be as responsive to questions from the floor as Cabinet members are obliged to be in such sessions in the House of Commons, and as they are when testifying before Congressional committees. Such a parliamentary interchange would help participants counsel each other about information which otherwise would have to be taken on faith.

In any event, hard questions must be asked of the executive agencies. Since the early days of the Presidency, executive privilege has been asserted by the Executive Branch. Presidents from Washington to Nixon have each, on occasion, refused to provide the Congress with information deemed privileged by the President. That information is often requisite to intelligent assessment of a given policy issue. But its denial to the Congress by the President is hallowed by long and effective precedent.

Increased surveillance of executive defense and planning agreements overseas is required of the Congress. Too few Americans are aware that the treaty-making process has eroded to a point where the "executive agreement" has tended to eliminate the Senate's concurrence as a component of national arrangements with foreign powers. In 1968, 57 treaties were concluded and 226 executive agreements were made in the name of the United States Government. Those executive agreements, no matter what their purpose, abrogate in effect the Senate's rights and obligations. We must, at the very least, subject them to a more intense scrutiny than we have in the past. Secret agreements between the Executive Branch and foreign powers have become all too frequent in recent history, as the Senate Subcommittee on Military Security and Commitments Abroad is finding in its current investigations.

In 1968 we learned that our highest military authorities had assured General Franco of a continuing American military presence on Spanish territory, as part of the bases agreement. Even more recently it was disclosed that in 1965 the Thai Government and the American Military Mission in Thailand signed a "contingency military plan." That arrangement, ostensibly agreed to under the SEATO umbrella, pledged assistance of an order that should have come only with Congressional authorization. Recently, Secretary of State Rogers, in a statement before the Foreign Relations Committee, diluted the effect of that agreement. But seven years ago we were told by Secretary of State Rusk that Thailand was "vital to the national interest of the United States and to world peace."

We must assure ourselves in the future of a continuity of national attitudes in foreign relations rather than the breaks that inevitably come when arrangements are made without adequate constitutional authority. There is a case for executive agreements, but they should be reconciled to the Senate's power to advise and consent—that is, the Senate must be made privy to them.

The whole Senate will probably have to sit with increasing frequency with the "doors closed" in secret session. There have been three occasions in this session of the Senate—twice on the ABM, once on military spending—when we have taken such action. To date, however, this procedure has been infrequent enough to warrant headlines when it occurred. I suggest it should become part and parcel of the process by which we advise and consent. Only then can we exercise full moral suasion on the President to take us into his confidence sufficiently to comprehend some of the policies initiated in the White House. Such secrecy is often held to be repugnant to the democratic process. But in our time it may well be one of the tools which can assist its survival.

"Meaningful consultation," a phrase used by Senator Ervin in the recent debate on the National Commitments Resolution, is a key to the changing role Congress must play in foreign relations. The nearly 5,000 international agreements reached by the Executive since 1946 have done much to shape the nature of America's position in the world. We must assure ourselves that in the future the American people through their elected representatives will have considerably more to say about the nature of that position.

The National Commitments Resolution places the Senate on record as follows:

> *Whereas accurate definition of the term "national commit-ment" in recent years has become obscured: Now, therefore be it Resolved, That (1) a national commitment for the purpose of this resolution means the use of the armed forces of the United States on foreign territory, or a promise to assist a foreign country, gov-ernment, or people by the use of the armed forces or financial re-sources of the United States, either immediately or upon the hap-pening of certain events, and (2) it is the sense of the Senate that a national commitment by the United States results only from affir-mative action taken by the Executive and Legislative branches of the United States Government by means of a treaty, statute, or con-current resolution of both Houses of Congress specifically provid-ing for such commitment.*

In order to meet the obligations inherent in that resolution, we must move more closely to a sharing of day-to-day responsibility with the Executive.

Essentially, the constitutional role of the United States Senate in foreign policy is consultative. Our powers are not comparable to those of the Presidency. The one weapon we have, the control and authorization of appropriation—the power of the purse—must necessarily be used with the greatest discretion. It is my view that only in a situation in which the President is completely resistant to the national will, as expressed by an overwhelming vote of the Congress, should this power be brought to bear. For as we call upon the President to respect the rights of the Legislative Branch we must, even in times of stress, respect his. The use of such power in foreign policy through denying appropriations implies a rejection of the American President almost as stunning in its implications as a vote of no confidence under the parliamentary system—which thereby ousts the government. It would, in all probability, make it very difficult there-after for the President to perform the executive function in foreign-policy areas having little or nothing to do with the case in point, *e.g.* the Viet Nam conflict.

We must be aware of the potential for disaster in conflicts between the branches of the Federal Government. It has been a great source of strength and gratification to me and to my colleagues that our efforts—particularly with respect to Viet Nam and the nuclear arms race—have elicited such strong and broad popular support from the people we represent. But, wherever and whenever possible, the Executive and the Legislative Branches must respect each other's rights and sensibilities. This being said, it is essential that we face up to the difficult prospect that some day the President of the United States may interpret his executive powers in foreign affairs in a way that directly conflicts with the way Congress interprets its own obligations. If that day comes, the Congress will have to consider seriously the cut-off of funds for purposes to which the national constituency is opposed.

I hope that day never comes. That is why I feel so strongly that the National Commitments Resolution is a watershed in the American experience. I see this resolution as a concrete response to the desire, perhaps I should say the demand, of the American people that the Senate play its full role in the national security field, especially with respect to national commitments.

I see this resolution as a signal to the Executive Branch that it must adjust itself psychologically and procedurally to a new reality—the reality that the Senate will not again shrink from its responsibilities or yield its constitutional power with respect to national-security issues and the solemn undertaking of national commitments.

If the Executive Branch responds to that signal, the danger of constitutional crisis will pass as have so many other fevers of the American spirit. For more than a century this nation has avoided a governmental stalemate. We must continue to do so. We in the Congress must avoid throwing the gauntlet down before the Executive. But we must also have in return greater respect by the President for the advise-and-consent function of the Congress and specifically of the Senate. For in the remainder of the twentieth century we must live together if we are to live at all.

NOTES: CONGRESS

Introduction

1. James Boyd, "A Senator's Day," in Charles Peters and Timothy J. Adams, eds., *Inside the System* (Praeger, 1970), p. 113.

2. Joseph S. Clark, *Congress: The Sapless Branch* (Harper Colophon, 1964), p. 17.

3. See, for example, James L. Sundquist, *Politics and Policy; The Eisenhower, Kennedy, and Johnson Years* (Brookings Institution, 1968).

4. Roger Davidson, David Kovenock, and Michael O'Leary, *Congress in Crisis: Politics and Congressional Reform* (Wadsworth, 1966), p. 57. See also Chapter One for a very good discussion of the realities of congressional reform.

5. Congressional Quarterly, *Politics in America* (Third Edition; May, 1969), pp. 62-63.

6. Stephen K. Bailey, *Congress in the Seventies* (Second Edition; St. Martin's, 1970), p. 103.

7. John Averill, "Eating Crow at Mike's," *Washington Monthly,* 2 (September, 1970), 49.

8. In 1971, the House Democratic Caucus opened the door to a minor adjustment of the seniority system, and the Republicans promised even more significant changes when and if the party gained control of the House.

9. *Washington Post* (June 20, 1971).

10. U.S. Senate, Committee on Foreign Relations, Subcommittee on United States Security Agreements and Commitments Abroad, *United States Security Agreements and Commitments Abroad, Volume II,* 91st Congress, p. 2432.

11. Donald E. Stokes and Warren E. Miller, "Party Government and the Saliency of Congress," in Angus Campbell, *et al., Elections and the Political Order* (Wiley, 1966), pp. 209-210.

THE JUDICIARY

> *To distrust the judiciary marks the beginning of the end of society. Smash the present patterns of the institution, rebuild it on a different basis . . . but don't stop believing in it.*

Honoré de Balzac[1]

During the debate over the ratification of the U. S. Constitution the authors of the *Anti-Federalist Papers* expressed considerable reservations over the proposed judiciary, observing that those who would be vested with the judicial power were "to be placed in a situation altogether unprecedented in a free country." A critical examination of the courts which the opponents of the Constitution urged in 1788 was never really carried out, much to the chagrin of the abolitionists of the 1850's, economic liberals in the 1930's, southerners in the 1950's, and conservatives in the 1960's. There is little doubt about the great powers held by the American judiciary. It can strike down state and federal statutes found repugnant to the Constitution, negate executive commands and administrative orders, punish summarily those who treat the court with less than due respect, and establish procedural regularities which other governmental officials must follow. No other democratic society allows so much authority to rest in the hands of non-elected political actors, unaccountable to the will of the citizenry and confined only by self-restraint and exceedingly vague notions of the judicial role.

The function of the federal judiciary is primarily to settle in a fair and impartial manner cases and controversies arising under the laws of the United States and secondarily to act as a check against the executive and legislative branches. The courts provide the most effective means of accomplishing one of the stated objectives of the Constitution, to establish justice. If the judiciary is to operate successfully it must be responsive to legitimate claims and demands articulated in the form of law suits. Should the courts consistently fail to respond adequately to well-founded petitions the purpose of the judicial process flounders and reform is necessary.

There are those who complain that the responsiveness of the judiciary to the pleas of certain elements of society has been entirely too exaggerated. The Supreme Court has been criticized for becoming too activist in its crusade to right the wrongs of our country and for disregarding traditional legal restraints. These contentions are not entirely without merit. The Supreme Court has probably induced more social change during the past two decades than any other governmental body. The Court has radically altered race relations, drastically changed principles of representation, championed protections against law enforcement abuses, and clearly drawn a line between church and state. The Court has displayed a willingness to protect the rights of minorities far beyond anything envisaged by the framers.

However, when discussing the responsiveness of the federal judiciary one should always keep in mind three basic points. First, courts are by nature quite passive institutions. Judges, unlike officials in the legislative and executive branches, cannot initiate governmental action. Before courts are able to adjudicate a matter, a suit involving the issue must be filed. The responsiveness of the judiciary depends first upon participation by individuals or groups in litigation. No matter how badly a judge might wish to decide a legal issue he cannot do so unless a dispute arises concerning that question.

Second, a judge is always faced with competing demands. The American adversary system of justice dictates that courts may only settle questions presented by opposing parties which arise from a real dispute. Both litigants urge the court to respond positively to their arguments. The judge's decision resolves the dispute in favor of one of the parties involved. Therefore, the judiciary is always responsive to someone's demands. The question, then, becomes not whether the courts are responsive, but to whom do they respond.

Third, it is a common but rather serious mistake to evaluate the judiciary solely on the basis of the United States Supreme Court. This emphasis on the apex of the judicial system has become known as the "upper court myth." While the Supreme Court may be the most visible and the most prestigious court, it handles only a minute portion of the total federal caseload. The real work of the judiciary is performed by the federal trial courts, the United States District Courts. These lower tribunals are found in each state and are staffed by some 400 judges. Most cases end with a determination at this trial level. Appeals from the District Courts are taken to one of the eleven Courts of Appeals, which serve as a buffer between the trial courts and the Supreme Court. The Supreme Court itself primarily decides only those appeals which in its discretion appear worthy of disposition by the highest court in the land. Therefore, while the Supreme Court might seem to be an agent bent on promoting social justice, it would be presumptuous to assume that the lower courts automatically share this reformist attitude.

Although the federal judicial system is considered to be far superior to its state counterparts, the courts of the national government remain beset with major flaws. Most of these problems have infected the federal judiciary for quite some time, but the battle for judicial reform is a comparatively recent phenomenon.[2] At the risk of oversimplification the major problems confronting the judiciary may be reduced to three: the inability of the federal courts to cope with a mushrooming caseload, the quality of decisions rendered, and the ethical conduct of judicial personnel.

Chief Justice Warren Burger's 1970 State of the Federal Judiciary Address is an excellent treatment of the current condition of the judicial machinery. Over the past several decades the number of suits filed in federal courts has exploded. Congress, failing to respond to this condition by creating significantly more judgeships, staff, and technological assistance, has stood idly by witnessing the judicial branch smothering under the sheer weight of its own workload. The business of judging has ground to a near halt. Periods of several years between the filing of a suit and its disposition are now quite commonplace. The comment of the Chief Justice that we are operating a judicial system in a supermarket age with cracker-barrel corner grocer methods may well be an understatement. George Washington might collapse upon realizing the extent to which the presidency has evolved, but John Marshall could reassume the Chief Justiceship with little more adjustment than might be provided by a two week refresher course in Constitutional Law. Burger's suggested reforms are intended to bring the federal judiciary into the twentieth century.[3]

The problem of quality of decision-making to a great extent flows from the inefficient manner in which the federal judiciary is operated. The overwhelming caseload of the lower federal courts means that insufficient amounts of time and resources can be devoted to cases filed. In order to help clear the dockets judges and prosecuting officials take as many shortcuts as reasonably possible. This has spawned in criminal cases the "plea copping" system (also known as "bargain justice" or "plea bargaining") explained by Leonard Downie, Jr. in his essay on "Crime in the Courts: Assembly Line Justice." This system centers on the procedural quirk which provides that if an accused pleads guilty to a charge, no trial takes place, only a short sentencing session.[4] For every suspect who pleads guilty the court is spared a long, involved trial, and the docket is cleared more quickly. Informal pressures are present which promote guilty pleas. Often if the accused will agree to plead guilty, the court in return will reduce the charge to a lesser offense or agree to impose a relatively light sentence. The plea copping arrangement is detrimental in two ways. First, for the guilty the imposed punishment may be too light to deter or rehabilitate the accused from committing subsequent crimes (assuming that our penal systems do actually deter and rehabilitate). Second, and most important, the innocent is pressured into pleading guilty to a crime he never committed for fear of receiving a much harsher sentence if the case is fully tried and his innocence is not established.

A second area of decision-making in which the judiciary has acquired a dubious record is in its treatment of the poor. The Supreme Court has been quite receptive to claims of indigents over the past several years showing a marked shift from its 1837 statement characterizing the poor as a "moral pestilence." The Warren Court, for example, ruled that indigents have a right to a free trial transcript to aid in preparations of appeals[5] and that indigents have a right to be represented by state provided counsel in criminal actions.[6] The Burger Court has continued this tradition by holding that the poor cannot be jailed for inability to pay traffic fines[7] and that indigents must be accorded access to divorce courts even if they are unable to pay court costs.[8] But even with these decisions the poor are disadvantaged in court. Jerome Carlin, Jan Howard, and Sheldon Messinger discuss the plight of the poor before the judiciary in "Civil Justice and the Poor." First, the law itself is often biased against those of the lower economic classes, a fact which should not be too surprising given the social backgrounds of the lawmakers sitting in Congress and the state legislatures. Second, the poor receive generally inferior legal representation. Expert legal counsel is employed by those who are blessed with fat pocketbooks. The poor tend to be represented by overworked, generally young and inexperienced legal aid attorneys, who, although zealous, are no match for law firms working in behalf of more economically comfortable clients. The result is a lack of judicial responsiveness to the claims of the poor.

The final major concern of students of the judiciary has been the matter of judicial ethics, a subject which prompted Jonathan Swift to note:

> . . . *judges are persons . . . picked out from the most dexterous lawyers, who are grown old or lazy; and have been biased all their lives against truth and equity, lie under such fatal necessity of favouring fraud, perjury and oppression, that I have known some of them refuse a large bribe from the side where justice lay, rather than injure the faculty, by doing anything unbecoming their nature or their office.*

Although few would argue that Swift's words describe the federal bench today, the problem of ethical behavior of the judiciary merits considerable discussion.

Historically, American judges have been assumed to be ethically sound unless some outrageous form of misbehavior (for example, receiving a bribe) was discovered. During their tenure on the high bench, Supreme Court judges have often carried on outside activities.[9] Many lectured, wrote, and held professorships. Various judges served as informal presidential advisors, writing speeches, planning political strategy, and even handling the personal financial affairs of the Chief Executive. Several jurists served on presidential commissions, such as Chief Justice Warren's chairmanship of the commission to investigate the assassination of President John Kennedy. John Jay and John Marshall held the positions of Chief Justice and Secretary of State simultaneously. Samuel Chase campaigned for the passage of the clearly unconstitutional Alien and Sedition Acts. Justice Miller waged an effort to have his brother-in-law appointed to the Court. Salmon Chase campaigned for the Democratic presidential nomination. Justice Jackson served as chief prosecutor at the war crimes trials at Nuremberg. And Chief Justice William Howard Taft, perhaps the most blatant of all, was apparently unable to refrain from becoming involved with every political scheme that happened along.[10] Ethical breaches occurring in the lower federal courts have been more mundane, lacking an element of political intrigue.[11] The most common offenses have been excessive drunkenness and siphoning off bankruptcy case funds for personal use.

In recent years, however, standards of judicial propriety have become much more restrictive. President Johnson's nomination of Justice Abe Fortas to be Chief Justice was not approved by the Senate primarily because of alleged unethical conduct. Fortas served as a close personal advisor to the president. Futhermore, his acceptance of an excessive $15,000 payment for teaching a seminar at American University and $20,000 from the foundation of a man later found guilty of securities manipulation destroyed any chance of Senate confirmation. President Nixon's nomination of Court of Appeals Judge Clement Haynsworth to be Associate Justice of the high court suffered a similar fate. Haynsworth was charged with conflict of interest based on his business activities while sitting on the bench. The Senate rejection of his nomination indicates that such conflicts of interest made the nominee unfit for service on the Supreme Court.

But the question of judicial ethics is far from solved by two actions of the United States Senate. The American Bar Association's Canons of Judicial Ethics (ironically written under the chairmanship of William Howard Taft) provided the only real statement delineating the ethical role of the judge. The Canons are a reasonably complete list of "dos and don'ts" for the judge, but only personal adherance enforces them. For example, Judge Haynsworth should have paid more attention to Canon 26 ("a judge should abstain from making personal investments in enterprises which are apt to be involved in litigation in the court") and Canon 33 (". . . avoid such action as may reasonably tend to waken the suspicion that his social or business relations or friendships constitute an element in influencing his judicial conduct.") Robert B. McKay, Dean of the New York University School of Law, discusses the subject of judicial ethics in his "The Judiciary and Non-Judicial Activities."

THE 1970 STATE OF THE FEDERAL JUDICIARY ADDRESS

Chief Justice Warren E. Burger

When President Segal and the Board of Governors of this Association invited me to discuss the problems of the federal courts with you, as leaders of the legal profession, my mind turned at once to one of the great statements on the problems of the administration of justice. That was Dean Roscoe Pound's famous speech to this Association at its meeting 64 years ago this summer. He said then that the work of the courts in the 20th Century could not be carried on with the methods and machinery of the 19th Century.

If you will read Pound's speech, you will see at once that we did not heed his warning, and today, in the final third of this century, we are still trying to operate the courts with fundamentally the same basic methods, the same procedures and the same machinery he said were not good enough in 1906. In the supermarket age we are trying to operate the courts with cracker-barrel corner grocer methods and equipment— vintage 1900.

I would not be warranted in coming here today if I spent our very limited time reminding you what is good about our courts, or about the splendid and dedicated judges and others, most of whom are overworked to make the system function. I wish the public could know what the Association has accomplished first in the support of public defender programs and now more recently in providing free legal services for people long unrepresented in civil matters. My responsibility today, how-ever, is to say to you frankly—even bluntly—what I think is wrong with our judicial machinery and what can and must be done to correct it in order to make the system of justice fulfill its high purpose.

The changes and improvements we need are long overdue. They will call for a very great effort and they may cost money; but if there are to be higher costs they will still be a small fraction, for example, of the 200 million cost of the C-5A airplane since the entire cost of the Federal Judicial System is 128 million dollars annually. Military aircraft are obviously essential in this uncertain world, but surely adequate support for the Judicial Branch is also important.

Wall Street experts recently estimated that American citizens and businesses spend more than 2 billion dollars a year on private security and crime control. Aside from the ominous implications of such private policing in a free society, just think what 2 billion dollars could do for public programs to prevent crime and enforce law. That is where such support belongs.

More money and more judges alone is not the primary solution. Some of what is wrong is due to the failure to apply the techniques of modern business to the administration or management of the purely mechanical operation of the courts—of modern record keeping and systems planning for handling the movement of cases. Some is also due to antiquated, rigid procedures which not only permit delay but often encourage it.

I am confident that if additional costs arise in the process of making needed changes and improvements in the management of the judicial system, Congress will support the Courts. But judges must demonstrate the needs clearly. Congress is harassed with demands for more appropriations for more and more new programs, each of which is labeled a high priority. We must first show Congress and the public that we are making the best possible use of what we already have and it is here that improved methods and skilled management techniques will count. These additions of equipment and personnel will cost relatively little in relation to the whole budget.

You know that in this brief report I can do no more than touch highlights and more detailed treatment of these problems must follow. I hope we can provoke debate—even controversy—to explore and test what I have to say. With increasing urgency every one of my distinguished predecessors from Chief Justices Taft and Hughes to Chief Justice Earl Warren have pressed these matters, but today I place this burden squarely on you, the leaders of the legal profession, in common with all judges. If the 144,000 lawyers you represent in 1,700 state and local bar associations will act promptly, you will prevent a grave deterioration in the work of the federal courts. And you should remember Justice Vanderbilt's warning that these tasks are "not for the short-winded."

In the federal courts today the problem areas are essentially in large cities. Here we find in the judicial system no more than a reflection of the complexities created by population growth and the shift to large urban centers. The problems exist where the action is.

In Maine, for example, there is only one federal District Judge and literally not enough for him to do. As a result he has, for 15 years or more, accepted assignments to go to courts all over the country where help was desperately needed. Many judges in the less busy districts have done the same. It is in the large centers that both civil and criminal cases are unreasonably delayed and it is there that the weaknesses of our judicial machinery show up.

How did this situation come about in the face of numerous additional judgeships added by Congress in the past 30 years?

When we look back, we can see three key factors:

First, the legal profession—lawyers and judges—did not act on Dean Pound's warnings to bring methods, machinery and personnel up to date.

Second, all the problems he warned about have become far more serious by the increase in population from 76 million in 1900 to 205 million in 1970, and the growth of great cities and increase in the volume of cases.

Third, entirely new kinds of cases have been added because of economic and social changes, new laws passed by Congress and decisions of the courts. All this represents the inevitability of change and progress.

In his 20th Century, wars, social upheaval, and the inventiveness of Man have altered individual lives and society. The automobile, for example, did more than change the courting habits of American youth— it paved the continent with concrete and black top; it created the most mobile society on earth with all its dislocations; it led people from rural areas to crowd the unprepared cities. The same automobile that altered our society also maimed and killed more persons than all our wars combined and brought into the courts thousands of injury and death cases which did not exist in 1900. Today automobile cases are the largest single category of civil cases in the courts.

All this ferment of wars, mobility of people, congestion in the cities, and social changes produced dislocations and unrest that contributed to an enormous increase in the rate of crime. In a free society such as ours these social and economic upheavals tend to wind up on the doorsteps of the courts. Some of this is because of new laws and decisions and some because of a tendency that is unique to America to look to the courts to solve all problems.

From time to time Congress adds more judges but the total judicial organization never quite keeps up with the caseload. Two recent statutes alone added thousands of cases relating to commitment of narcotics addicts and the mentally ill. These additions came when civil rights cases, voting cases and prisoner petitions were expanding by the thousands.

Meanwhile criminal cases, once a stable figure in the federal courts, were increasing. Added to that the records show that in all federal district courts the time lapse in criminal cases from indictment to sentence has doubled.

To illustrate some of the changes, consider just a few figures:

From 1940 to 1970:
—Personal injury cases multiplied 5 times;
—Petitions from state prisoners seeking federal habeas corpus relief increased from 89 to 12,000;
—During this period Congress increased the number of judges by 70%, while the total number of cases filed in the federal district courts nearly doubled.

But the increase in volume of cases is not by any means the whole story. Experienced district judges note that the actual trial of a criminal case now takes twice as long as it did 10 years ago because of the closer scrutiny we now demand as to such things as confessions, identification witnesses, and evidence seized by the police, before depriving any person of his freedom. These changes represent a deliberate commitment on our part—some by judicial decision and some by legislation—to values higher than pure efficiency when we are dealing with human liberty. The impact of all the new factors—and they are many and complex—has been felt in both state and federal courts.

The Criminal Justice Act of 1964 guaranteed a lawyer for criminal defendants—at public expense for the indigent—and along with it appeals at public expense. The Bail Reform Act of 1966 authorized liberal release before trial without the conventional bail bond. Each of these Acts was an improvement on the existing system, but we can now see what was produced by their interaction in a period when crime was increasing at a startling rate. The impact was most noticeable in Washington, D. C., where federal courts handle all felony cases. Defendants, whether guilty or innocent, are human; they love freedom and hate punishment. With a lawyer provided to secure release without the need for a conventional bail bond, most defendants, except in capital cases, are released pending trial. We should not be surprised that a defendant on bail exerts a heavy pressure on his court-appointed lawyer to postpone the trial as long as possible so as to remain free. These postponements—and sometimes there are a dozen or more—consume the time of judges and court staffs as well as lawyers. Cases are calendared and reset time after time while witnesses and jurors spend endless hours just waiting.

If trials were promptly held and swiftly completed, and if appeals were heard without delay, this would be less a problem, and perhaps debates over preventive detention would subside. But these two Acts of Congress came in a period when other forces including decisions of the courts were making trials longer, appeals more frequent and retrials commonplace. We should not be surprised at delay when more and more defendants demand their undoubted constitutional right to trial by jury because we have provided them with lawyers and other needs at public expense; nor should we be surprised that most convicted persons seek a new trial when the appeal costs them nothing and when failure to take the appeal will cost them freedom. Being human a defendant plays out the line which society has cast him. Lawyers are competitive creatures and the adversary system encourages contention and often rewards delay; no lawyer wants to be called upon to defend the client's charge of incompetence for having failed to exploit all the procedural techniques which we have deliberately made available. Yet the most experienced defense lawyers know that the defendant's best interest may be served in most cases by disposing of the case on a guilty plea without trial.

A new category of case was added when it was decided that claims of state prisoners testing the validity of a state conviction were to be measured by federal constitutional standards. As a result federal district courts were obliged to review over 12,000 state prisoner petitions last year, as compared with 89 in 1940.

There is a solution for the large mass of state prisoner cases in federal courts—12,000 in the current year. If the states will develop adequate post conviction procedures for their own state prisoners, this problem will largely disappear, and eliminate a major source of tension and irritation in State-Federal relations.

There is another factor. It is elementary, historically and statistically, that systems of courts—the number of judges, prosecutors, and of courtrooms—has been based on the premise that approximately 90% of all defendants will plead guilty leaving only 10%, more or less, to be tried. That premise may no longer be a reliable yardstick of our needs. The consequence of what might seem on its face a small percentage change in the rate of guilty pleas can be tremendous. A reduction from 90% to 80% in guilty pleas requires the assignment of twice the judicial manpower and facilities—judges, court reporters, bailiffs, clerks, jurors and courtrooms. A reduction to 70% trebles this demand.

This was graphically illustrated in Washington, D.C., where the guilty plea rate dropped to 65%. As recently as 1950, 3 or 4 judges were able to handle all serious criminal cases. By 1968, 12 judges out of 15 in active service were assigned to the criminal calendar and could barely keep up. Fortunately few other federal districts experienced such a drastic change, but to have this occur in the national Capital, which ought to be a model for the nation and a show place for the world, was little short of disaster.

Changes in the laws that are part of what we call the "revolution in criminal justice," which began as far back as the 1930's, have brought this about. Anyone who questions these changes must recognize that until the past two decades criminal justice was the neglected stepchild of the Law.

There is a widespread public complaint reflected in the news media, in editorials and letters to the editor, that the present system of criminal justice does not deter criminal conduct. That is correct, so far as the crimes which trouble most Americans today. Whatever deterrent effect may have existed in the past has now virtually vanished as to such crimes.

If ever the law is to have genuine deterrent effect on the criminal conduct giving us immediate concern, we must make some drastic changes. The most simple and obvious remedy is to give the courts the manpower and tools—including the prosecutors and defense lawyers—to try criminal cases within 60 days after indictment and let us see what happens. I predict it would sharply reduce the crime rate.

Efficiency must never be the controlling test of criminal justice but the work of the courts can be efficient without jeopardizing basic safeguards. Indeed the delays in trials are often one of the gravest threats to individual rights. Both the accused and the public are entitled to a prompt trial.

The addition of 61 new federal district judgeships by Congress within recent weeks is the result of efforts which began 5 years ago. Since it takes time to fill these important positions and new judges do not reach peak efficiency at once, their full impact will not be felt for a long time. We see therefore that the additional judges, needed in 1965, were not authorized until 1970. We cannot solve our problems by meeting needs 5 or more years after they arise. The time to plan for 1975 and 1980 needs is now, and I hope this can be accomplished, not simply by adding more judges, but by the more efficient use of judicial manpower and greater productivity through improved methods, machinery, management and trained administrative personnel.

Meanwhile, not a week passes without speeches in Congress and elsewhere and editorials demanding new laws—to control pollution, for example, and new laws allowing class actions by consumers to protect the public from greedy and unscrupulous producers and sellers. No one can quarrel with the needs, nor can we forget that large numbers of people have been without the protection which only the lawyers and courts can give.

The difficulty lies in our tendency to meet new and legitimate demands with new laws which are passed without adequate consideration of the consequences in terms of caseloads. This is dramatically illustrated in the current budget of the Office of Economic Opportunity. Congress has granted that program 58 million dollars for legal services. That 58 million is a sound commitment to an underprotected segment of our people whose rights have suffered because they could not afford a lawyer. Few things rankle in the human breast like a sense of injustice. Whether the problem is large or small in the abstract it is very large to the person afflicted. We should applaud Congress for taking that step. But cases cannot always be settled by lawyers and the burden thus falls on the courts. This allowance for Office of Equal Opportunity legal services is almost half of what is allowed for the operation of all the courts in the federal system. Here again we have an example of a sound program developed without adequate planning for its impact on the courts.

What this all adds up to is that for at least 50 years the federal court system has experienced the combination of steadily increasing burdens while suffering deferred maintenance of the total judicial machinery—and added to that, much of the machinery has long been obsolete. The foresight of Congress in creating the Federal Judicial Center for research and study of court problems 2 years ago is one of the few bright spots in the past 30 years.

Now we must make a choice of priorities. When we want to dance we must provide the musicians and the public may well be called upon to pay something more for the federal judicial system to increase its productivity. But neither costs nor the number of judges can be held down if the caseload is steadily enlarged.

To prepare for this report to you, I asked every federal judge for suggestions. The hundreds of replies reflected a note of frustration and even anguish at the daily management and administrative burdens that drained time and energy from their primary duty to dispose of cases. That was the common denominator and the common complaint. Federal judges are today in somewhat the position of members of Congress a generation ago, before the Reorganization Act which gave adequate staffs to the Members and to the important committee work of the Congress.

The business of litigation is highly complex. To assemble all the necessary individuals is not as simple as TV shows depict. It actually involves the very difficult task of bringing together a judge, 25 or more prospective jurors, lawyers, witnesses, court reporters, bailiffs and others, at the same place at the same time without lost motion. The absence or tardiness of a single person will delay the entire process and waste untold time. Countless citizens serving as jurors have been irritated with the inefficiencies of the courts because they find themselves watching TV in the Juror's Lounge rather than hearing cases in court.

The management of busy courts calls for careful planning, and definite systems and organization with supervision by trained administrator-managers. We have at least 58 Astronauts capable of flying to the moon, but not that many authentic court administrators available to serve all the courts in the state and federal systems. The federal courts need immediately a court executive or administrator for each of the 11 circuits and for every busy federal trial court with more than 6 or 7 judges. We need them to serve as the "traffic managers," in a sense as hospitals have used administrators for 40 years to relieve doctors and nurses of management duties. We are almost half a century behind the medical profession in this respect.

In basic principles, it is indeed essential that we maintain our links with the past and build carefully on those foundations because they are a result of thousands of years of human experience in the evolution of the law. There is great value in stability, predictability and continuity. But the procedures of the law ought to respond more swiftly—as hospitals and doctors, farmers and food distributors have changed their methods. Yet the major procedural change of this Century was the development of the Federal Rules of Civil Procedure a generation ago. Except for those Rules, Thomas Jefferson of Virginia, Alexander Hamilton of New York and John Adams of Massachusetts would need only a quick briefing on modern pleading and the pre-trial procedures in order to step into a federal court today and do very well indeed. We see, therefore, that the judicial processes for resolving cases and controversies have remained essentially static for 200 years. This is not necessarily bad, but when courts are not able to keep up with their work it suggests the need for a hard new look at our procedures.

If the picture I have been painting seems melancholy, I must in fairness touch on a few brighter sides—but sadly there are only a few.

In recent years ferment stimulated by Roscoe Pound, Vanderbilt of New Jersey, Parker of North Carolina—to name only three now gone—has brought on widespread growth of Judicial Seminars, Institutes and Study Centers that have contributed much and we owe a great debt to my colleague, Justice Tom Clark, who has worked tirelessly on improvements in both state and federal courts.

Perhaps one of the most significant developments in a generation is the creation this year—under the leadership of this Association along with the American Judicature Society and the Institute of Judicial Administration—of the Institute for Court Management at the University of Denver. Here for the first time is a place where court administrators can be trained just as hospital administrators have long been trained in schools of business administration.

Sadly even these bright spots emphasize how painfully slow we are to supply what courts need. The price we are now paying and will pay is partly because judges have been too timid and the bar has been too apathetic to make clear to the public and the Congress the needs of the courts. Apathy, more than opposition, has been the enemy, but I believe the days of apathy are past.

As to the future I can do no more than emphasize that the federal court system is for a limited purpose and lawyers, the Congress and the public must examine carefully each demand they make on that system. People speak glibly of putting all the problems of pollution, of crowded cities, of consumer class actions and others in the federal courts. Some of these problems are local and we should look more to state courts familiar with local conditions.

Let me list some major steps for the future—steps to begin at once:

1. The friction in relations between state and federal courts presents serious problems in both the review of state prisoner petitions and other cases. I strongly urge that in each state there be created a State-Federal Judicial Council to maintain continuing communication on all joint problems. Such a body could properly include a member of the highest state court, the chief judges of the larger state trial courts and the chief judges of the federal district courts. In some states such bodies have already been created on an informal basis.

2. State and federal judges should continue their cooperation with the American Bar Association to establish and maintain standards of conduct of lawyers and judges that will uphold public confidence in the integrity of the system we serve.

3. We should urgently consider a recommendation to Congress to

create a Judiciary Council consisting of perhaps 6 members, one-third appointed by each of the three branches of government, to act as a coordinating body whose function it would be to report to the Congress, the President and the Judicial Conference on a wide range of matters affecting the judicial branch. This Council could (a) report to Congress the impact of proposed legislation likely to enlarge federal jurisdiction; (b) analyze and report to Congress on studies made by the Judicial Conference and the Federal Judicial Center as to increase or decrease in caseloads of particular federal districts; (c) study existing jurisdiction of federal courts with special attention to proper allocation of judicial functions as between state and federal courts; (d) develop and submit to Congress a proposal for creating temporary judgeships to meet urgent needs as they arise. Some state legislatures authorize such appointments based on a formula of population and caseloads in order to adjust promptly to population changes in rapidly developing areas; (e) study whether there is a present need for three-judge District Courts and whether there is a present need for federal courts to try automobile collision cases simply because of the coincidence that one driver, for example, lives in Kansas City, Kansas, and the other in Kansas City, Missouri; (f) continue study and examination of the structure of the federal circuits that are now based largely on historical accident and are unrelated to the demands of modern judicial administration and management.

4. The entire structure of the administration of bankruptcy and receivership matters should be studied to evaluate whether they could be more efficiently administered in some other way. Pending studies on this problem should be pressed to conclusion.

5. Over the years various statutes and decisions of courts have altered many aspects of criminal procedure. Meanwhile some of the states have experimented with innovations and have developed new procedures to improve justice. Since Congress is now considering an entirely new federal criminal code we should soon undertake a comprehensive re-examination of the structure of criminal procedure to establish adequate guidelines reflecting adjustment to the new code, judicial holdings, and the experience of the states.

6. The system of criminal justice must be viewed as a process embracing every phase from crime prevention through the correctional system. We can no longer limit our responsibility to providing defense services for the judicial process, yet continue to be miserly with the needs of correctional institutions and probation and parole services.

7. The whole process of appeals must be re-examined. It is cumbersome and costly and it encourages delay and it takes too long. Some courts, notably the overworked 5th Circuit, have developed procedures to screen out frivolous appeals. Finality at some point is indispensable to any rational—and workable—judicial system.

8. We made a wise choice in guaranteeing a lawyer in every serious

criminal case but we must now make certain that lawyers are adequately trained, and that the representation is on a high professional basis. It is *professional* representation we promise to give—nothing more—and always within accepted standards of conduct. This Association has now provided lawyers with comprehensive and authoritative standards and it is up to the courts and the bar of every state to make sure they are followed.

I have necessarily left some subjects untouched and others undeveloped but I hope I have imparted a sense of urgency on the problems and needs of the courts. I hope also I have made my point that it is not simply a matter of more judges but primarily better management, better methods and trained administrative personnel.

A sense of confidence in the courts is essential to maintain the fabric of ordered liberty for a free people and three things could destroy that confidence and do incalculable damage to society:

That people come to believe that inefficiency and delay will drain even a just judgment of its value;

That people who have long been exploited in the smaller transactions of daily life come to believe that courts cannot vindicate their legal rights from fraud and over-reaching;

That people come to believe the Law—in the larger sense—cannot fulfill its primary function to protect them and their families in their homes, at their work, and on the public streets.

I have great confidence in our basic system and its foundations, in the dedicated judges and others in the judicial system, and in the lawyers of America. Continuity with change is the genius of the American system and both are essential to fulfill the promise of equal justice under law.

If we want to maintain these crucial values we must make some changes in our methods, our procedure and our machinery, and I ask your help to make sure this is done.

CRIME IN THE COURTS: ASSEMBLY-LINE JUSTICE

Leonard Downie, Jr.

The elderly lawyer pushed through the swinging gate in the dark wooden railing separating court officials from the public and walked up and down past packed rows of spectators. He was dressed for the racetrack, where he intended to spend the afternoon, in an orange and green sport coat, bright green slacks, and soft white leather shoes, and his clothes were a flash of unexpected color in the drab, stuffy, downtown courtroom.

It was 10 o'clock on an August morning in Recorders Court, which is the criminal court for the city of Detroit. In many ways, the scene could have been any criminal courtroom in the United States.

"Jackson," the lawyer called out. "Sam Jackson."

He was trying to find a client he had seen only once before, months ago, when he had been appointed to defend the man for a $100 fee from the state of Michigan. On that first day, he stood briefly beside Jackson as he was arraigned and a date set for his trial. Until this morning, when a courtroom clerk handed him a copy of the official court "paper" for the case, the lawyer had done nothing more.

"Jackson," he called again.

A slightly built black man in a polo shirt and work pants rose hesitantly a few rows back in the audience. Sam Jackson, a sometime laborer and truck driver, had, his past record showed, been connected off and on with gambling and dope. Arrested nearly a year earlier for possession of a concealed pistol, found when a police detective stopped and searched his car, he had been free since then on bail while waiting for his trial. Today, he was one of many defendants, mostly black, crowded together with relatives and friends in the worn wooden pews of Courtroom No. 8.

To these benches and to the barred cells hidden behind the courtroom are brought each day scores of men and women charged with felonies: murder, rape, robbery, burglary, serious assault, the sale or possession of narcotics, and the illegal possession of a weapon. Many, like Jackson, wait a year or longer to be tried. But, for most of them, trial before a judge and jury never comes.

"Jackson?" the lawyer asked, pushing down his glasses to peer at his client. "Okay, okay; sit back down. I'll be with you in a minute."

Turning, he walked through the gate again toward a cluster of perhaps 30 policemen, all in street clothes, standing and gossiping idly near the empty jury box on the left side of the courtroom. In the confusion and cacophony that characterize the criminal courtroom scene, the policemen were balanced by a swirling, changing mass of as many men opposite them. These are the criminal lawyers, most of whom work in Courtroom No. 8 every day. Their only clients, whose fees are usually paid by the state, are those assigned to them by the court. Some keep dingy offices in squat, grimy buildings across narrow Clinton Street from the Courthouse; others have no offices at all and operate out of the courtroom itself. Known collectively as the "Clinton Street bar," they carry no briefcases and seldom consult lawbooks; their case preparation consists of marking trial dates in dog-eared datebooks and scanning court papers hurriedly on the day a case comes up. Jackson's lawyer is one of the more flamboyant Clinton Street barristers.

By this time, as the lawyer passed by, the judge was already seated on his perch atop a two-tiered wooden platform, surrounded by clerks, bailiffs, and other functionaries shuffling through and stamping papers just below him. Save for the two or three persons standing immediately before him to conduct business, nobody seemed really aware of the judge's presence. Lawyers, policemen, clerks and others criss-crossed noisily in front of his bench, streamed back and forth through the swinging gate, and generally kept up an ocean's roar of conversation that crashed around the pronouncements of the judge, occasionally drowning out his words altogether.

"Detective Sanders," Jackson's lawyer loudly addressed a policeman in a gray suit. "You got the Jackson case?" The policeman, recognizing the attorney from past dealings, nodded. "Good," said the lawyer, still several feet away. Then, ignoring the judge nearby, the lawyer shouted the question that, in Recorders Court, takes the place of trials, juries, legal rules, and the rest: "Hey, Sanders, what can you do for me today?"

Coming together in the middle of the courtroom, the lawyer and policeman began to haggle amiably over what reduction the government might make in its charge against Jackson if he agreed to plead guilty, rather than go to trial before a jury. If convicted of the felony charge by a jury, Jackson would be given a prison sentence of several years. The law required it. The policeman suggested to the lawyer that the charge could probably be reduced to "failure to present a gun for licensing," a misdemeanor carrying a penalty of only 90 days in jail, *if* Jackson agreed to plead guilty immediately. Together, the lawyer and detective Sanders then crossed in front of the judge to join a line of other attorneys and policemen that stretched to a back room occupied by the prosecutor, who is himself seldom seen in the courtroom.

Case by case, the prosecutor and each lawyer, usually joined by the policeman involved, hammer out a bargain for a guilty plea, similar to the one that Jackson's lawyer was seeking. If the accused agrees to admit guilt, rather than insist on a trial by jury, the government reduces the charge against him, often seemingly assuring the defendant of a lighter sentence. Thus, a man charged with armed robbery, which carries a mandatory 20-year prison sentence, might plead guilty to unarmed robbery or attempted robbery, and receive a sentence of a few months or years in prison. Another, charged with burglary, might "admit" to attempting "unlawful entry." The changes are not made simply to fit the facts of the crimes involved; usually, the robber *had* used a gun, or the burglar *had* succeeded in getting inside a house and carrying off an armful of valuables. Instead, the change is made to induce the defendant to trade the possibility of a long prison term (against a chance for freedom if acquitted by a jury) for the promise of a shorter sentence.

In Sam Jackson's case, the prosecutor readily agreed to the bargain offered by the lawyer and policeman. The lawyer came out, found Jackson again, and took him into the bustling hallway outside the courtroom.

"I got you 90 days," he told Jackson enthusiastically. He did not refer at all to the crime itself or to his client's actual guilt or innocence. "It's a good deal. You have a record; you go to trial and get convicted on the felony and you're in trouble."

Jackson nodded agreement.

"Remember," the lawyer cautioned as the men started back inside the courtroom, "don't hem and haw in front of the judge, or he might insist on a trial."

Jackson's turn came quickly. He stood mute while the judge, a shrunken man in his sixties, sorted through papers on his desk and read out the defendant's name and address and the charge originally placed against him. A court stenographer recorded everything on a stenotype machine.

"The prosecutor has signed a statement that he will accept your plea of guilty to a lesser charge," the judge announced, in words familiar from uncounted other cases. Then, like a clergyman leading a litany, with Jackson responding at appropriate pauses, he intoned, "You are pleading guilty because you are guilty?"

"Yes, sir."

"No one has threatened you, or promised you anything?"

"No."

"No one has induced you to plead guilty?"

"No."

"You understand your constitutional right to a trial, and you are freely waiving that right?"

"Yes."

Turning sideways in his overstuffed swivel chair to stare out a soot-clouded window, the judge wearily recited, as he had again and again already that morning: "Let the record show that counsel was present, that the defendant was advised of his rights and that he understood them, and that the defendant waived his right to trial by jury or this court, and that he freely withdrew his plea of not guilty and entered a plea of guilty." The stenographer took it all down. The judge swiveled around again and sentenced Jackson to 90 days in jail.

Plea bargaining is what the lawyers call it.

No trial. No jury of peers. No exhaustive search for truth. No exacting legal rules. Only empty, sometimes dishonest words substituted for the reality of "due process" guaranteed by the Constitution.

A lawyer who knows next to nothing about his client or the facts of the crime with which he is charged barters away a man's right to a trial, and, along with it, the presumption that a defendant is innocent until proven guilty—the presumption on which the American system of criminal justice rests.

A prosecutor who knows little more about the case than what a policeman tells him hurriedly trades off one of American society's most important responsibilities—the responsibility for providing for those charged with criminal acts a full hearing and the levying of appropriate sanctions upon those convicted of crimes against that society. The judge, who has abdicated his authority to bartering lawyers, acquiesces in all this and sanctifies it for "the record." Everyone pays lip service to justice. But everyone's true faith is in expediency.

And why not? An indifferent public has allowed the system to become overwhelmed with work: too many cases for too few judges, too few lawyers, too few clerks. An uncaring legal community has failed to modernize the system to cope with the inundation. How else can the system survive, except by trying to dispose of cases as fast as it can?

Plea bargaining instead of trials is the answer in crowded criminal courts across the nation. In New York, prosecutor and defense attorney haggle over guilty pleas in front of the judge's bench in frenetic whispers between cases. In Chicago and San Francisco, the bargaining is often done in polite confidential conferences, sometimes in the judge's chambers, with his participation. In Washington, D.C., brisk and businesslike plea bargaining is conducted in small glass-enclosed cubicles in the prosecutor's office before the case goes to a judge. In Dallas, prosecutors bargain directly with incarcerated defendants through jailhouse bars. According to the best estimates, at least 90 per cent of the persons "convicted" in American courts are never proven guilty at all. Instead, they plead guilty without trials.

Everyone in the system, including the judge and the defendant's own lawyer, offers inducement or exerts pressure for a guilty plea to save the time and trouble of a trial. If the prosecutor is not empowered to reduce the charge, the judge makes it clear that his sentence will be lighter for a guilty plea. Those who insist on a trial, the most basic of constitutional rights, are openly punished by prosecutors and judges with maximum charges and harsh sentences.

Sometimes, the judge takes a leading role in the bargaining process. In one routine case in Chicago's criminal court, selection of a jury began at 10 a.m. for the trial of a young Mexican-American charged with selling heroin to an undercover agent. As the tedious process of interviewing jurers dragged on into late morning, the judge suddenly interrupted and asked the opposing lawyers: "Do you want a conference in this case?"

In Chicago, that's the signal to begin bargaining. The prosecutor and lawyer followed the judge out of the courtroom to his chambers and, once inside, the prosecutor offered to reduce the charge to possession of heroin. The judge, noting that it would be the youth's second conviction for that offense, said that he would sentence him to a minimum of five and a maximum of 10 years in prison if he would plead guilty. (In Illinois, where most sentences include both a minimum and maximum time, the maximum for a second narcotics conviction can be life imprisonment.)

The defense lawyer, a law professor who frequently volunteers to defend indigent suspects free of charge, refused the deal. "Too much time," he said about the proposed sentence.

"Look," the judge warned him, "if that man is convicted by a jury, I'll give him 20 years. You take some of my time; I'll take some of his."

But the lawyer refused to give in. The three returned to the court-room. Most of another hour went to interviewing jurors, and lunch time neared. The prosecutor called the lawyer over with him to the judge's bench, saying in an anxious undertone, "Look, I'm busy. I've got another case to be tried this afternoon. How about two to 10 years?"

The judge inclined his head in agreement. But the defense lawyer countered with two to five years. (Reduction in the maximum end of the sentence can mean earlier parole.) The judge thought a moment, grimaced, and gave in. The defendant pleaded guilty.

Most often, a prosecutor starts off the plea bargaining process by charging defendants in ways designed to produce compromises. In Cleveland, Ohio, and Washington, D. C., for instance, a defendant is regularly charged with a slew of offenses covering a single crime: a bank robber is indicted for armed robbery, theft, one charge of assault with a deadly weapon for every customer and teller he pointed his gun at, possession of an illegal weapon, and so on. In California, under a strange old law, a technical charge of kidnapping is thrown in for good measure if the robber orders victims at gunpoint to move around, lie down, or open a safe. If the defendant in these or similar situations pleads guilty, all the charges but one are dropped. What happens if he chooses not to plead guilty? In Cleveland, if a defendant insists on a trial and is convicted, the judge often metes out for each charge separate sentences that must be served one after the other. Under Ohio's law for minimum-maximum sentences, this prac-tice leads to such absurdities as a sentence of 12 to 240 years in prison (one to 20 years for each of 12 charges) given a woman convicted of embezzling union funds.

In places where the prosecutor habitually levies only one charge for a crime, usually the strongest suitable for the circumstances, prosecutors and defense attorneys—especially public defenders, who are also paid by the government and work alongside the prosecutor in court every day—operate on informal understandings that certain charges will always be reduced to certain lesser offenses. In California, for instance, according to a recent study by the University of California Center for Legal Studies, burglary is usually reduced to petty theft, assault with a deadly weapon to assault without a weapon, and molesting children to loitering at a school playground. In cities like Detroit and Chicago, where armed rob-bery frequently becomes unarmed robbery if the defendant pleads guilty, the decision to plead is called "swallowing the gun." In Washington, D.C., the distinction between a plea of felonious assault and to simple assault, which is a misdemeanor, often is based on the number of stitches required to close the victim's wounds. In New York City, four of every five defendants originally charged with a felony wind up pleading guilty to a misdemeanor.

"We are running a machine," a Los Angeles prosecutor has told one researcher. "We know we have to grind them out fast." A Chicago prosecutor vows: "I'll do anything I can to grind them out fast."

So, frequently, will the defendant's own lawyer, whether he is a public defender or privately retained, with the result that, on almost any day in a big city criminal court, a defendant can be seen disavowing before a judge a guilty plea arranged by his lawyer.

Such was a typical case on a typical day in San Francisco's Superior Court. Three defendants in a burglary case were supposed to plead guilty in exchange for being placed on probation. Their lawyers had made the arrangements with the judge in his chambers. But when the defendants themselves came before the judge from the lockup, one insisted that he was not guilty. "This is not what I expected," his lawyer, a public defender, said sheepishly, as the judge ordered a date set for a trial. On the way out of the courtroom, the public defender apologized to the lawyers for the other two defendants that their scheme had gone awry. "The best laid plans of mice and men," he muttered. "That guy doesn't know what is good for him."

In Detroit's Recorders Court, where only three of every 100 criminal defendants is ever tried by a judge or jury, the plea bargaining system is merely a little more overt than elsewhere. Once a deal is made, every formal rule and safeguard is blatantly twisted to accommodate it. Thus, on the same morning that Sam Jackson made his guilty plea for failure to present a gun for licensing, a man charged with burglary decided to plead guilty to attempted unlawful entry. He was questioned by the judge about when and where the crime took place, as Michigan law requires if there is any doubt about accepting the plea in lieu of trial.

"Where did the offense occur?" the judge asked.

The defendant was silent. Clearly, he did not know or could not remember. The judge picked up a police report and read off an address. "Is that the one?" he asked.

"Yeah, that sounds like it," the man answered.

The judge then read off a time, a date, and a list of items stolen from the house identified. The defendant said it all seemed to sound right. The judge accepted his plea.

"Why are you pleading guilty?" another judge, G. W. Crockett, asked another defendant, a 20-year-old with a bushy Afro hair style, on another day.

"To get off," the youth answered matter-of-factly.

"What?" demanded Crockett, a black man who has been something of a dissenter and unsuccessful reformer in Detroit's Recorders Court.

"I want to get probation," the young man said. "I want to get out of jail." (He had been imprisoned 150 days awaiting trial.) "They said I could get out this way, that you'd give me probation. Besides, I didn't really rob anybody. I just took some reefers off that woman's bed. I was visiting there. We were friends. I just slipped them out. I didn't pull any knife like they said."

Crockett, an ebony-skinned man with graying hair, shook his head. The youth had been charged with armed robbery. The prosecutor decided to allow him to plead guilty to larceny, a misdemeanor, so that he would be eligible for probation or a sentence of only a few months in jail, instead of 20 years in prison.

"I don't know," Crockett said, his voice rueful. "Either you committed a crime or you didn't. Just reducing the charge doesn't make much sense. We need more facts. But what can I do?" He accepted the plea and put the youth on probation.

A tough-looking young white man, more than six feet tall and heavy-set, came before Judge Crockett next. He was pleading guilty to attempted felonious assault.

"But it says here," Crockett interrupted, reading from the police report, "that you hit a man repeatedly with a beer bottle."

"It was just an argument," the defendant protested, and he described a sidewalk altercation in front of a cafe. First there were angry words, then he hit the other man with a beer bottle that he had carried out of the tavern with him. The victim was knocked to the ground.

"And then what happened?" Crockett asked.

"He got back up, so I hit him again," the man explained. "After a few more times, he didn't get up any more."

Crockett quieted loud laughter in the courtroom and stared straight ahead for a moment, seeming to search with anxious eyes for help in making sense of what he was hearing.

"And I understand that the victim nearly died," he said, more to himself than anyone else. "*Attempted* assault," he repeated, drawing out the word "attempted" very slowly. Yet Crockett had to accept the plea. He had the prosecutor's signed statement accepting it, sealing the bargain. There was no other alternative. The system had decided.

The next defendant, a young black man in a blue suit whose bearing was uncharacteristically refined for Recorders Court, told Crockett that he was a college student from Detroit attending school in Alabama, where he kept a gun to protect himself. Driving back home with friends, he left the gun under the floor mat in the back seat of his car, where he had always kept it at school. As he drove through a white Detroit neighborhood, he recounted, his car was stopped by policemen, who said he was speeding but gave him no ticket. Instead, they frisked him and his friends and searched the car, found the gun, and charged him with illegal possession of a concealed weapon.

In many ways, the student's case was similar to Sam Jackson's, except that this youngster had no prior police record. He was formally admitting guilt to the charge of not presenting the gun for registration.

Crockett appeared disturbed. "If the facts are what you say they are, you should not be pleading guilty," he told the youth. "Those policemen had no right to search you or your car—that is, *if* you are telling the truth. Without a trial, without questioning the policemen or other witnesses, I have no way of telling.

"That's what's wrong with this system," Crockett's voice rose. "If you're telling the truth, you shouldn't be convicted of anything. And what those police did should be brought out into the open. But without a trial, I have no way of knowing if you're lying or not. This way, there is no review of this practice of police just pulling people over and going through their cars. That's why these things go on every day here, because we have vacated our responsibilities."

Always, in plea bargaining, compromises are struck between guilt and innocence. Little connection is made between who the accused person is, what took place that led to his arrest, what happens to him in the courtroom, what is done with him next. Decisions on whether to free a convicted man on probation or how long he should instead be sentenced to prison are based most often on what must be done to seal a bargain for a guilty plea, rather than on whether or how a guilty person should be punished or rehabilitated. In fact, nobody can be certain that innocent persons are not being convicted, nor, more frequently, that habitual criminals are not being let off lightly. The first possibility undermines the very foundation of our legal system. The second increases daily disorder in society by reinforcing in the wrongdoer a smug certainty that the law is something he need never really respect.

But plea bargaining is not the only shortcut to justice practiced regularly in criminal courts today. Many thousands more cases—in many places, half the court's serious criminal cases—never get even as far as the plea-bargaining stage. The defendants charged in them—innocent and guilty alike—are arbitrarily set free before a trial, in effect acquitted by default, because the overburdened system cannot accommodate them.

Under pressure to keep the judge's case calendar as light as possible, the prosecutor drops charges against defendants wholesale before the cases can reach the judge. These decisions, made by a young assistant prosecutor, usually overworked and inexperienced, are most often based on a quick glance at police reports of arrests. Summarily, he tosses out cases that seem too "weak," cases involving charges such as a husband's beating his wife that seem too "cheap," those involving as defendants neat-looking, middle-class people who seem "respectable" and not likely to get into trouble again.

Frequently, perhaps, the prosecutor is dispensing admirable justice and saving the system from needless further congestion. But nobody ever knows for sure. The prosecutor makes no investigation of his own before acting. Most often, no judge reviews his decision.

In their turn, some judges throw out still more cases in large lots when they reach them in the coutroom. The judges, too, base their decisions on no more than a look at a court paper or a remark from a prosecutor or defense lawyer.

Other defendants, usually the often-convicted and knowledgeable, win freedom simply by out-waiting the courts. Patiently, they endure delay after delay arising as a natural product of the overloaded system, and then they have their lawyers stall still longer with procedural tricks and requests for postponements that nobody has time to challenge. In the end, witnesses who have come back to court again and again stop showing up, or, as the months pass, even the most conscientious among them find that their memories fade. Judges and prosecutors become impatient with musty cases that further bog down their operation; a carefully timed request by the defense lawyer, often on the day when witnesses are not there, is enough to persuade them to throw the case out.

There still are trials. But when a rare criminal trial does take place before a judge, or a judge and jury, it is as often as not a shadow drama of the real thing, played out by poorly prepared lawyers before obviously uninspired judges (who sometimes conduct their more productive guilty plea business off to the side of their bench while the trial is in progress). Seldom, except for the most complicated, serious, or glamorous cases, has the prosecutor or even the defense lawyer (who have crowded schedules of their own) planned what he was going to do in advance. Sometimes, the judge has to coach the prosecutor or defense lawyer, or both, to ask questions of witnesses or make motions they would not otherwise have thought to do themselves. Or, conversely, the harried judge must work to speed up the case, reminding the lawyers not to "stall" with questions or arguments that seem unrewarding to him, and prodding a jury that spends more than an hour or two deliberating its verdict. Lawyers for both sides in the chaotic Manhattan branch of New York City's Criminal Court say that a long trial there is any that lasts more than 10 minutes.

In several cities, including Baltimore, Cleveland, and Chicago, persons charged with misdemeanors—vagrancy, disorderly conduct, simple assault, gambling, shoplifting, and other petty thievery—are usually not represented by lawyers when they are tried. In Baltimore's Municipal Court, not even a prosecutor is present for criminal cases. The arresting policeman, who often looks uncomfortable doing it, must present the government's evidence to the judge and sometimes point out information favorable to the defendant that otherwise would be overlooked. The judge must ask the questions that a prosecutor or defense lawyer would ask, suggest the arguments, if any, that they might make, and, in the end, decide the outcome of the case. There is no jury, no court reporter, not even a court clerk. Legal rules are treated nonchalantly, and such usually inadmissable evidence as hearsay testimony often is allowed.

The assumption that anyone accused of a crime in the United States has a right to a full adversary trial of his guilt or innocence—with well-prepared advocates for each side, carefully overseen by an able, evenhanded judge, searching diligently for the truth and satisfying all legal rules and safeguards—is fundamental to our system of justice, and to the general populace's confidence in it. Yet, with few exceptions, this concept has become little more than a still-celebrated myth or both folklore and formal jurisprudence. Not only in Perry Mason dramas, but also in real life appellate court decisions, the body of criminal law, and urgent legal controversies, the myth is still believed to represent reality. As a result there is little in the way of formal rules, high court pronouncements, or even informed legal or public opinion to ensure that justice is done in the way that men and women are actually "tried" every day in American courts.

Instead, everything is left up to the criminal court bureaucracy, which, like its counterparts throughout government and private commerce, is concerned first with its own day-to-day survival. Judge, prosecutor, defense attorney, policeman, and clerk are working partners struggling to keep their heads above water as the flood of cases rises unceasingly. Is it not natural that, for them, expediency should take precedence over justice, eventually becoming one and the same with it in the minds of the bureaucrats?

Only a few voices from within raise any alarm. A bar association in New York City condemns "mass assembly-line justice" that rushes defendants into guilty pleas "in violation of their legal rights." A New York state appellate judge warns that "instant justice" is "converting our courthouses into counting houses." An exasperated Washington, D.C., city judge, now chief judge of the General Sessions court there, complains that criminal courts have become "factories where defendants are quickly processed like so many sausages."

"Wherever the visitor looks at the system, he finds great numbers of defendants being processed by harassed and overworked officials," the widely respected legal educator and researcher, Edward L. Barrett, Jr., has written. "Suddenly, it becomes clear that for most defendants in the criminal process, there is scant regard for them as individuals. They are numbers on dockets, faceless ones to be processed and sent on their way. The gap between theory and reality is enormous."

Indeed, momentous Supreme Court decisions and currently fashionable public and legal debates over criminal law and the rights of the accused are simply irrelevant to what actually happens each day inside the courtroom. In many cities, judges and lawyers never bother to explain to defendants (as appellate courts have instructed them to do) the various constitutional rights they can invoke to protect them in court. Despite high court rulings on the right to a lawyer, many defendants still do not have one, or else they wind up with courthouse hangers-on of dubious ability who can get no other clients.

The admissability at a trial of a confession obtained by police is perhaps the most debated public issue concerning criminal courts, but it is essentially a moot question in a system in which 90 per cent of those convicted admit guilt anyway, in the courtroom. Appellate court decisions and legal controversies over what evidence can be used against defendants when they are tried are virtually meaningless when few defendants are ever actually brought to trial. Accusations that judges are too lenient or harsh on criminals, or too pro- or anti-police, assume powers that judges often no longer exercise in deciding guilt or innocence, or even fixing sentences, in many criminal cases.

Mass production criminal justice in the United States dates back at least to before the first national surveys of American courts in the 1920's and 1930's began to document and decry the gradual disappearance of adversary justice in criminal courtrooms. ((No systematic study has ever been made of the workings and consequences of the mass production processes that have evolved, such as plea bargaining.) But expediency has not necessarily meant efficiency. Quite to the contrary. In many cities, the court system's traditional disorganization and the avalanche of work now crashing down onto it seem to be leading inevitably to the day when the criminal court machinery may grind to a standstill.

"They are just spinning their wheels now," observes one veteran lawyer about New York City criminal courts, which he, as an official of the Vera Institute for Justice, a non-profit legal reform "think tank," is studying and trying to improve.

"People talk about the criminal courts breaking down," he says. "The fact is, here at least, they *have* broken down. But nobody wants to admit it."

The volume of criminal cases in New York City's court system has more than doubled in a decade, and each judge must face as many as 200 serious criminal cases each day. One of the most respected jurists on the bench of Criminal Court in Manhattan, Simon Silver, abruptly resigned in late 1969 because he was "fed up with congestion."

"I feel I cannot give the cases the real attention they're entitled to," Judge Silver said when he decided to step down after 22 years' service as a magistrate and judge before his current term expired. "As each case comes up, a judge should have the time to listen to the lawyers, to evaluate the situation, to determine whether violence is involved and must seriously be considered. The defendant's background should be explored, and the reasons for his actions. Sudden emotional flare-ups should be treated differently from crimes that seem to be chronic.

"At present, I find that I cannot dispose satisfactorily of more than 15 cases a day. The rest [usually 100 to 200 or more] are adjourned [postponed to another day], and that creates a heavier backlog. I have to spend more time on adjournments [setting dates for future hearings of the postponed cases] than in listening, considering, and disposing."

Despite the haste with which many other criminal court judges run through cases, there are on any given day more than 7,000 criminal defendants in jail awaiting their turn in court in New York City. In

Detroit, Cleveland, Chicago, and Washington, D.C., defendants often must wait a year or longer for their cases to be tried or otherwise concluded. In Lynn, Massachusetts, [near the end of 1969], a man charged with armed robbery was finally ordered freed unconditionally after the state failed to try his case within the two-year limit set by the state constitution.

The criminal courts are the neglected stepchildren of already overcrowded, undermanned, niggardly financed, and hopelessly antiquated state and local systems of trial courts. In New York City, some criminal court judges must conduct court in converted clerks' offices and judges' robing rooms. In Baltimore, Cleveland, and Chicago, among other places, most misdemeanor cases are tried in makeshift courtrooms located on the upper floors of old police stationhouses, while the police continue doing business downstairs. These rooms are like those of old tenements, with exposed pipes, peeling paint, falling plaster, and exposed wood. Only second-hand accessories and an old desk for the judge make them officially courtrooms. There is seldom room for half the participants to sit.

In Chicago, felony cases are tried in the deteriorating Cook County criminal court building adjacent to the notoriously rundown county jail. Its badly lit, acoustically impossible, poorly maintained courtrooms provide a stark contrast to the bright, well-designed, extravagantly furnished modern courtrooms provided for the city's well-heeled civil case lawyers and litigants in the new 30-floor, glass and steel Civic Center building downtown. In city after city, the criminal court is kept separate, in older buildings and rundown neighborhoods, from the rest of the trial courts and their silk-suited barristers who operate in the better downtown districts. Nowhere do the criminal courts have enough judges or supporting personnel. Methods for scheduling cases and keeping records (usually all by hand) have remained largely unchanged since courts were first established in the American colonies.

Criminal court is where the chief judge sends rookie, hack, or senile judges who cannot be trusted with complicated civil cases. The majority of the private-practice lawyers appearing before them are counterparts of Detroit's Clinton Street Bar (called "Fifth Streeters" in Washington, D.C., for instance, and the "Baxter Street Bar" in New York City). They wait for judges to appoint them to cases, or they prowl the halls soliciting work from defendants and relatives of defendants who pass by. If they are not paid by the local or state government, management of their clients' cases is built around efforts to extract money from defendants or relatives. The client is told pointedly that the quality of service depends on the fee. If time is needed for the money to be raised, the lawyer has the case postponed in court. Judges knowingly cooperate in this fee collection effort by postponing the case without reason when a lawyer gives the signal. In New York, the attorney always tells the judge he needs time to locate a witness, a "Mr. Green."

The derelicts who seek and often find peaceful repose on the front steps or inside the corridors of criminal court buildings in city after city make the message clear: criminal court is for the dregs of society and the lowly of the legal community.

The absence of much concern, scrutiny, or help from the outside reinforces in criminal court bureaucrats a profound cynicism and resistance to criticism and change. The malaise eventually overtakes even many of the young and idealistic newcomers joining the staffs of the prosecutor, public defender, or the probation office chief.

This "hostile attitude toward 'outsiders' " is actually a "defensiveness" on the part of courthouse bureaucrats who must each day satisfy the demands of assembly-line disposal of intolerably large caseloads by legal "shortcuts, deviations, and outright rule violations adopted as court practice," observes Abraham Blumberg, a noted lawyer and sociologist who has been studying mass production justice from a new perspective.

"Fearfully anticipating criticism on ethical as well as legal grounds, all the significant participants in the court's social structure are bound into an organized system of complicity," Blumberg has written. "Breaches and invasions of 'due process' are institutionalized, but are, nevertheless, denied to exist."

The conspiracy leaves out the defendant.

"Accused persons come and go in the court system," Blumberg has pointed out, "but the structure and its personnel remain" day in and day out. To keep going, to survive the pressures of the workload, and to avoid facing the injustices they are party to, "they must preserve their own relations and interaction at all costs.

"The client becomes a secondary figure in the court system. He may present doubts, contingencies, and pressures which challenge or disrupt . . . but they are usually resolved in favor of the organization. Even the accused's lawyer has far greater professional, economic, and other ties to the various elements of the court system than to his own client. In short, the court is a closed community."

Nowhere is Blumberg's analysis better documented than in New York City's Criminal Court in lower Manhattan. There, in a dingy, tomb-like building filled each day with milling throngs, can be found typical, if sometimes extreme, examples of the distortions of justice that assembly-line processing produces at every stage in the criminal court system.

The nerve center of Criminal Court is Part 1-A. Through it, during daytime and evening sessions, passes a daily procession of 200 to 500 defendants arrested that day or the night before for every kind of crime, making their first appearance in court. Most are represented at this initial hearing by lawyers from the Legal Aid Society, a quasi-public defender supported by the city and private donors. Those who can afford it hire their own lawyers—frequently from the Baxter Street Bar—before their next date in court, if there is one.

The pandemonium in Part 1-A is unique even for a criminal courtroom. Defendants on bail, victims of and witnesses to crimes, and others fill the wooden benches and line the walls. Dozens of policemen, in plainclothes with badges pinned on suits, sports shirts, and windbreakers, scurry about, retrieving defendants for their cases from the public pews or the lockup behind the court, bringing them and their papers before the judge, and returning them after each case. The scene in front of the judge is a constant jumble of people bumping into one another as defendants, policemen, and witnesses for each case come and go. The pace is so rapid-fire that the judge himself often has time only to check his calendar and set dates for cases to be continued to another day. Most of the talking is done by a bailiff called the "bridgeman," who in each courtroom of Manhattan's Criminal Court, stands just below the judge on the bottom level of the two-tiered platform.

"Numbers 104, 105, 106, 107, 108, and 109, step up here," a swarthy, dark-haired, gruff-voiced bridgeman shouts in calling a case with six defendants arrested for possession of narcotics. "Hurry it up, hurry it up."

The defendants squeeze between the prosecutor and the Legal Aid lawyer in front of the judge. Policemen and witnesses crowd around them. The two lawyers operate in shifts with other prosecutors and defenders. Each stands for about an hour in front of the judge, taking cases as they come. The prosecutor knows nothing about a case until it is called and he sees the court papers for the first time. Sometimes the Legal Aid lawyer has interviewed defendants briefly through the bars in the lockup, or he is given a scanty fact sheet by another defender who saw the prisoner.

In a rapid tobacco-auctioneer's sing-song style, the bridgeman reads the formal charge against the defendants so fast it can barely be understood.

"Put up your hands," the bridgeman orders the policemen who made the arrest. Under New York law, they must swear to the veracity of the charge they filed. They stick up their right hands, but they are not really paying attention to the bridgeman; they are explaining their case in whispers to the prosecutor. The Legal Aid lawyer leans over to try to overhear them. The bridgeman rattles off the oath: "Officers, doyou swearthatthisistheaffidavityousigned?" No response, but it doesn't matter. "Put your hands down," the bridgeman growls.

"All right, QUIET in here," he interrupts himself to shout. "Shut that door back there."

"Howdya plead, howdya plead?" the bridgeman demands of the Legal Aid attorney, a young blonde woman. She frantically asks a few whispered questions of some of the defendants and turns to the prosecutor to confer with him.

"Let's go, let's go," the bridgeman barks. "Officers, Number 110, Stanton, is next. Have the prisoner ready. We've got to move along."

After a few more words with the Legal Aid lawyer, the prosecutor announces that charges against four of the men will be dropped. There is no explanation why. A date is set for the trial of the other two, who plead not guilty.

"All right, all right, you can go," the bridgeman tells the four who were let go. "Hurry it up." The other two men are to be returned to the lockup, but the bridgeman first has to advise them of their rights. This is his most practiced speech, a series of run-together sentences delivered without looking up as he sifts through his papers for the next case:

> *Youunderstandyouhavetherighttoanattorneyortherighttoanadjournmenttoprocureone. Ifyoudonothavethefinancialresourcestoaffordanattorneythecourtwillappointoneforyou. Youalsohavetheright tocommunicatefreeofchargebytelephoneormailwithanyofficerofthe court.*

His voice rises:

"All right, put the prisoners away. Take them away."

Already, he is calling the next case. "Number 110. Stanton. Let's go. Step to the other side of your attorney, mister. Hands out of your pockets. Officer, put your hand up."

Frequently, defendants and witnesses are rushed away by the bridgeman before they understand what was decided about the case or when and where they are to return to court for the next hearing. In many cases, nothing more is done than the setting of a date for trial. Other cases are dismissed by the prosecutor, usually with no reason given. Occasionally, a guilty plea is arranged on the spot after a whispered conference in front of the judge. The judge passes sentence right away.

In one case, the Legal Aid lawyer announced that her client wanted to plead guilty to assaulting a policeman. But the defendant said he "didn't hit nobody." The judge ordered a date set for trial.

No case lasts more than five minutes. Many are over in 60 seconds.

During a break, one young prosecutor, just out of law school, said he likes the system. "It becomes routine," he explained with some pride. "You can look at the first couple of lines on the [police] complaint and tell what the case is about, what the state can prove. The defense attorney is equally skilled. You just learn to think quickly on your feet. It's fascinating. I enjoy it."

From Part 1-A, cases go to myriad other branches, depending on the nature of the charge, supposedly to be tried. But most of the branches are mere clerking operations in which dates are set by the judges for further postponements of the cases. The prosecutor is waiting for the defendant to agree to plead guilty. The defendant is trying to outwait the government and have the case dismissed. The excuses for delays run the gamut, but nobody believes them or cares. By court rule, after several postponements, the judge marks the next excuse the "final" one for the defendant or the government. But that means nothing. Cases wind up marked "final, final, final" against the defendant or government, and still another postponement is granted. Witnesses, told they must show up each time the case is scheduled, are forced to return to court five and six times on the average, often only to find the case dismissed or the defendant pleading guilty. Only five of every 100 cases are eventually tried by a judge. "If even 10 per cent ended in a trial," one prosecutor says, "the system would break down."

The judge's main function in courtroom after courtroom is merely to consult a calendar and order "Pick a date" for each case to be post-poned to. Baxter Street lawyers seem to limit their practice to asking judges for delays and pleading their clients guilty. They buttonhole new prospects in the halls and confer with current clients in the aisles of courtrooms even as the judges are conducting business.

Occasionally, a trial is held. Most defendants in trials are represented by Legal Aid lawyers. Often, the defender and the prosecutor are friends and carry on playful banter during the brief trial. They make agreements on many issues beforehand, to save time. Their case presentations are austere.

In one such trial, a middle-aged Puerto Rican man with a wife and two children was charged with indecent exposure at a subway station— the complaining witness was a secretary whom he had annoyed. The prosecutor, a pretty young woman with long brown hair, coud not resist smiling and joking with "Bill," the Legal Aid lawyer, during the 15-minute trial. The case was already a year old and had been postponed nine times. Both the defendant and the secretary were tense and confused as they tried to recall the incident. The prosecutor cleverly trapped the defendant into a mistake about the time of an alibi. The judge was persuaded and found the man guilty.

"Your talents were wasted on that one, Bill," the prosecutor told the Legal Aid lawyer as the case ended.

"I tried to get him to plead guilty to loitering months ago," Bill explained. "But he wouldn't do it."

Avoiding "unnecessary" trials, processing the sausages with the bridgeman's "Let's go, let's go" haste and determination, ignoring the fates of defendants and crime victims alike, blotting them out as human beings: this is the business of New York City's Criminal Court and its counterparts across the face of the country. The necessity to move cases quickly is the central task. Determining guilt or innocence, deciding on the treatment of offenders, and dealing with those in the public who are dragged into the process are all secondary matters. Means are shaped not in accordance with the constitutional ideal of justice, but rather to satisfy the ends of the bureaucracy in its daily battle with caseloads.

A committee on minimum standards for criminal justice of the American Bar Association has, for instance, given plea bargaining insti-tutional legitimacy by declaring that "conviction without trial will and should continue to be a more frequent means for the disposition of criminal cases." The system "cannot operate effectively unless trial judges in fact grant charge and sentence concessions to most defendants who enter a plea of guilty."

This is one of the committee's conclusions in a recent report on plea bargaining, made without any real study of the process. Yet, later in the same report, the committee virtually contradicts itself by insisting that judges should still consider "rehabilitative, protective, or deterrent" purposes in passing sentence, and should not impose heavier than justified sentences whenever "the defendant has chosen to require the prosecution to prove his guilt at trial."

The public has not been consulted; the Constitution has not been amended; but someone has here adopted a different standard for justice than the one that has always been a first lesson in civics for school children. Imagine, a defendant *requiring* the government to prove his guilt at trial.

What can one conclude but that David Burnham, the award-winning crime reporter for *The New York Times,* was right when he summed up the experienced visitor's disgusted reaction to what is happening today in criminal courts? Describing Manhattan's Criminal Court, he in effect described every other: "the most cynical place in the world."

CIVIL JUSTICE AND THE POOR: ISSUES FOR SOCIOLOGICAL RESEARCH

Jerome E. Carlin, Jan Howard, and Sheldon L. Messinger

THE CHARACTER OF LAW AFFECTING THE POOR

It has long been argued that the law is not a neutral instrument, but rather that it is oriented in favor of those groups or classes in society having the power to bend the legal order to their advantage. The contention is that today as in the past the law primarily serves to protect and enhance the rights and interests of property holders and those in positions of wealth and authority. Three types of bias are considered: (1) favored parties; (2) dual law—*de jure* denial of equal protection; (3) *de facto* denial of equal protection.

Favored Parties

The law frequently favors certain parties or roles in a relationship, and the poor, are less likely than the rich to be found in these roles. Thus, substantive and procedural law benefits and protects landlords over tenants, and lenders over borrowers. Let us examine these two examples of favored party bias in the law.

Landlord-Tenant. The common law has generally promoted the interests of the landlord against the tenant; this has had a special impact on poor tenants living in slums. According to traditional legal doctrine the tenant's obligation to pay rent is independent of his lessor's covenants to repair and maintain the premises. Thus, unless there are statutes to the contrary, the tenant cannot withhold rent as a means of compelling landlord compliance with health and safety codes or contractual obligations. This posture of the common law has particular relevance to the poor because they often live in vermin-infested substandard housing where landlords perpetually fail to provide needed services and repairs.

To correct some of the injustices resulting from strict application of the common law the courts have developed the fiction of a constructive eviction by the landlord when his breach of contractual obligations denies the tenant beneficial use and enjoyment of the premises. Thus, under certain circumstances the tenant may be permitted to abandon the premises without further liability. However, as Fossum puts it: "The right to move out is an empty one for the people in the slums."[1] This fact has prompted some to argue that the court should recognize a tenant defense of failure of consideration when landlords violate their obligations. Then the tenant could either rescind the contract and abandon the premises or pay a pro rata reduction in rent. Giving tenants this option would be a step toward equalizing protections of the law.

> *It has been observed that tax law benefits the slum landlord to the detriment of the tenant. Julian Levi contends that, "If the tenement is old and in bad condition, allowable depreciation under the Internal Revenue Code will be high; while poor condition and deterioration will be recognized by the real estate tax assessor as the occasion for reducing appraised values."[2]*

Procedural law as well as substantive law may be biased in favor of the landlord. For example, New York requires a violation of record before tenants can invoke certain defenses against landlords who have failed to provide essential services. This requirement may subvert the rights of tenants because of the difficulties involved in establishing an official record of violation. Thus, it is agrued that the court should look to the actual condition of the dwelling, not simply to violations of record.

Public housing laws are also said to be biased against the tenant. According to Cloward and Elman:

Legislation is written in such a way as to deny tenants any of the rights commonly associated with tenancy in private housing. Apartments can be inspected at will by management; leases are month to month; eviction can occur without recourse to the courts.[3]

Sparer contends that in some places the housing authority reserves the right to evict without giving any reason whatsoever.

Borrower-Lender. In the consumer area favored-party bias is perhaps mostly clearly seen in the creditor-debtor relationship. With respect to laws governing interest rates it has been observed that "such interest ceilings as legislatures impose on retail installment credit and small loans . . . are set at the behest of credit extenders and without study."[4] Further, the contention is that "few states have any real penalties for usury,"[5] that generally the sanctions are too mild to discourage illegal lenders. Usury laws may also be rendered ineffective by exemption provisions. According to Brunn such provisions in the California constitution exempt almost everyone professionally in the business of lending money. Moreover creditors can obtain special state permits or licenses which allow them to charge more than the basic usury rate. Neal argues that most lenders today have such permits. "Banks, credit unions, loan companies, finance companies, and even retailers, now can charge more than the simple interest rate defined as 'tops' under state usury codes."[6]

There are many other loopholes favoring the creditor. For example, credit extended by a seller is not generally subject to the provisions of interest and usury statutes, the theory being that the vendor is not engaged in lending money but in selling goods. The credit charge is supposedly not interest. It merely represents the difference between the cash price and the installment price.

Laws concerning remedies for missed payments may also favor the creditor. In some jurisdictions, he is allowed two remedies—repossession and deficiency judgment. Some observers believe this gives an unfair advantage to the creditor.

Dual Law—De Jure Denial of Equal Protection
A second kind of bias is seen in the development of separate and unequal systems of law for the poor and for certain racial minorities. As a result, many lower class whites and Negroes are in effect relegated to a position of second-class citizenship. Such persons are denied *de jure* the protections and benefits which the law provides for middle and upper class whites. To the extent that *de jure* discrimination arises from or is supported by "state action," it may of course be challenged under the Fourteenth Amendment.

According to tenBroek there are two separate systems of family law, one for the poor and one for those in comfortable circumstances. The rules differ with respect to property and support relations of husband and wife, creation and termination of the marital relationship and responsibility for the support of relatives. His contention is that the family law of the rich is "civil family law," created, developed and administered by the courts— not designed in either substantive provision or judicial administration to meet the needs of the poor. The family law of the poor is public law, administered largely through state and local non-judicial agencies, and more concerned with minimizing the costs of relief than maximizing the rights and interests of recipients. TenBroek asks whether a dual system of family law is less unequal than school racial segregation, generating among recipients a feeling of inferiority that may affect the hearts and minds of the poor in ways unlikely ever to be undone.

The dual law argument applies to welfare law in general. In considering many types of welfare programs (e.g., public assistance, unemployment insurance, public housing), Reich contends that the government has one set of rules for dispensing benefits to the poor and another for dispensing largess to the rich (*e.g.,* licenses, subsidies, contracts). He argues that entitlement to government largess is less likely to be protected as a right when the recipient is poor, and concludes that this constitutes a denial of equal protection under the federal constitution.

The classic cases of dual law affecting the poor are laws which discriminate against Negroes and other racial or national minorities. Such laws have a special impact on the poor, because many of them are non-white. As a result of government action, *de jure* discrimination against Negroes has been appreciably reduced, but it is still a widespread phenomenon. Segregation of public schools will continue to be legal in many localities of the South for some time to come. And the court has ruled that tax exempt private schools can discriminate if the founder of the charitable trust specified discrimination as a condition of the trust. In certain sections of the South the semi-official Parent-Teachers Associations exclude from membership all parents and teachers from segregated Negro schools and they do so legally. Private hospitals can discriminate or segregate unless public subsidies are involved. And discrimination in employment is illegal only in industries covered by fair employment laws. . . .

De Facto Bias

A third type of bias in the law may be termed *de facto* bias. On paper the law treats rich and poor alike, but in fact the correlates of poverty make equality impossible. Ehrlich suggests that *de jure* equality may actually accentuate *de facto* inequality. He argues that "the more the rich and the poor are dealt with according to the same legal propositions, the more the advantage of the rich is increased.[7]

De facto bias is pervasive because so many correlates of poverty such as indigency, ignorance or insecurity can serve as barriers to justice. In essence it is bias by default. It represents a failure of the law to take into account the differential capacity of rich and poor to realize the protections and benefits which the law provides.

A number of illustrations of *de facto* bias can be given. In each case a law that is impartial on its face with respect to social class is biased in its effects.

New York's highly restrictive divorce laws are presumably applicable to all classes in society. In practice, however, they are more likely to prevent the poor, than the rich, from legally terminating their marriages, because poor people lack the resources to obtain out-of-state divorces. According to O'Gorman a "migratory divorce" is one means of evading the proscriptions of New York law, but he says:

> Since a migratory divorce is usually more expensive than one secured locally, this pattern of evasion is not equally open to all New Yorkers. If the state laws are easily avoided by financially independent residents, they can be avoided by others only at some sacrifice, and avoided not at all by those with low incomes. In this sense, the laws impinge differentially on the population; they are more binding on some groups than others.[8]

As a result the poor may resort to either a fraudulent New York action or more commonly desertion. Equality might be achieved by restricting the freedom of the rich (*e.g.,* by New York's refusing to recognize the legality of certain out-of-state divorces) or by increasing the options of the poor (*e.g.,* by making New York divorces easier to obtain).

Laws which specify the conditions under which legally enforceable bargains may be made are often biased against the poor. George Brunn maintains that while an inequality of bargaining power underlies all transactions of buying and borrowing, the poor are especially disadvantaged. They lack the information, training, experience and economic resources to bargain on equal terms with sellers and lenders. Thus the common law which embodies the *laissez faire* rule of the market place—let the buyer beware—is biased against the poor because they find it especially difficult to beware of abuses in the market place.

The draft law illustrates *de facto* bias in the law as we have defined it. Poor persons are less likely to have jobs which qualify them for deferment on occupational grounds, and they are less likely to be students. Moreover, they are less likely to know about the legal status of conscientious objector and to be articulate enough to qualify for that status.

Several tests are suggested for identifying and analyzing *de facto* bias; these may provide grounds for challenging the validity of laws that are biased in fact. (1) *Latent intent:* Where the real although hidden purpose of the law is to discriminate against the poor or other disadvantaged groups, this is a blatant case of *de facto* bias. (2) *Knowledge of effect:* Where those responsible for making and enforcing the law are cognizant of its discriminatory effects but make no effort to reduce them, *de facto* bias is highlighted. (3) *Prior law as a contributing factor:* Where the barrier to equal protections or benefits is itself the result of prior laws there is a clear link between *de facto* and *de jure* bias. Kaplan contends that *de facto* segregation in schools may be unconstitutional as long as the segregated housing pattern resulted from state action (*e.g.,* "where a city council had by ordinance compelled Negroes to live in certain areas"). (4) *Egalitarian thrust of the law:* Where the law explicitly seeks to provide protections and benefits on an egalitarian basis, the failure to consider extra-legal obstacles to this end clearly subverts the purpose of the law. In this situation there may be an affirmative duty to mitigate *de facto* bias. (5) *Instrumental importance of the protection or benefit:* Where the inaccessible protection or benefit would be instrumental for the achievement of other legal rights and privileges, the discriminatory consequences of *de facto* bias are magnified. Thus, it is especially important to counter the incapacity of the poor to retain counsel. Similarly it is more important to repeal a poll tax than a fishing tax. (6) *Relevance of barrier to legitimate purpose:* Where the poverty-relevant barrier to benefits can be shown to have a legitimate purpose, one can argue that the *de facto* bias in the law is justified. The more relevant the barrier is to a legitimate purpose, the more justified the barrier becomes. Thus, if the purpose of barriers to voting is to achieve an informed electorate and if we assume this purpose to be legitimate, literacy tests become more justifiable than poll taxes.

A difficult question is how to distinguish between *de facto* bias and a failure to eliminate poverty. At some point the task of negating bias in the law becomes a task of changing the condition of the poor. The complexity of the problem can be seen in the case of *de facto* segregation in schools, a problem combining poverty and race. Since *Brown v. Board of Education* many have argued that Negroes have a right to be educated in integrated schools and that any law which establishes school boundaries in a manner that results in *de facto* segregation is a biased law. Typical plans to end *de facto* segregation attempt to deal with the effects of segregated housing (*e.g.,* bussing students across town); a more revolutionary approach might make housing patterns themselves the focus of concern. This would go further toward changing the condition of the poor.

Remedies

To counter and abate *de facto* bias, two approaches may be used: (1) *The poor may be given special benefits* to make the law work for them as it works for the rich. For example, they may be given free legal representation or the right to waive court costs. The barriers the rich overcome naturally are artificially removed from the poor. (2) *The rich may be penalized* as a means of equalizing benefits and protections. Thus, in most if not all small claims courts no one can have a lawyer. The practice of "reverse discrimination" combines the two approaches. Where the benefit is scarce, the special prerogatives given the disadvantaged may in effect penalize the advantaged. Giving Negroes temporary job preference may be a means of achieving overall equality, but in the short run it penalizes whites.

Because of their powerless position often the most effective remedies for the poor are those which allow a *collective* challenge of the status quo to combat institutionalized abuses which no single individual could effectively call into question. Thus, in the struggle for civil rights the mass demonstration has been an important tool for rallying public support and for welding the Negroes themselves into a politically effective movement. In the struggle for decent housing the rent strike has at times been an effective means of holding landlords accountable.

But a basic limitation of the law is its inability to treat the problems of the poor as essentially collective or class phenomena. The law has been slow to recognize and remedy the collective problems of slum tenants, low-income buyers and borrowers and public assistance recipients. And it has been slow to respond to the collective problems of Negroes in gaining full citizenship.

Only recently, for example, has Congress acknowledged that such barriers to voting as literacy tests are obstacles that discriminate against Negroes collectively. The individualistic posture of the law appears to be changing. In a number of recent decisions federal courts have upheld the right of Negroes to engage in collective protest (marches, sit-ins, etc.), in some instances sanctioning demonstrations which were alleged to disturb the peace or to violate trespassing laws. A further example is the court's decision in the *Button* case which encourages the disadvantaged in general to band together in pursuing their legal interests.

As we suggested above, the problem of remedying bias in the law shades into the problem of remedying poverty itself. Effecting *legal* equality becomes at some point a problem of effecting *social* equality. The effectiveness of law as an instrument for meeting the needs of the poor depends largely on its success in eliminating poverty, in moving the poor out of their deprived status. Today this is an important goal of law. It stems from an enlarged conception of the rights of man and a changing conception of the role of government in providing, protecting and implementing these rights. It also stems from the belief that poverty is caused by large impersonal forces in our complex industrial society, not by the poor themselves. Reich argues that "when individuals have insufficient resources to live under conditions of health and decency, society has obligations to provide support, and the individual is entitled to that support as of right,"[9] and he adds that in our highly organized, institutional and bureaucratic society the avenue of providing basic rights to the poor must be through law. What is involved here is a view of law as a positive, affirmative force for change, not simply a reactive process. This approach is evidenced in such programs as medicare, the war on poverty, and voter registration for Negroes.

Laws do not simply reflect the way men are treated in society; they influence the character of that treatment. When laws are biased against the interests of a particular group or class of people their deprived status is given official sanction. This is most obvious in the case of dual law, where the poor are officially relegated to a position of second-class citizenship. But favored party and *de facto* bias are perhaps even more pervasive and their impact more important. Thus, the law itself serves to define and maintain the position of the poor. . . .

LEGAL REPRESENTATION AND THE POOR

The more fully developed a legal order, the greater the need for persons capable of formulating and challenging the reasons upon which the authority of claims, decisions or actions is based. The specialized responsibility for carrying out these critical functions may be located in a variety of social roles. In the Anglo-American system of law this responsibility has traditionally been assumed by the legal profession. Study of the role of the legal profession in relation to the poor directs our attention to the wide variation in the character and quality of legal services provided different classes in society.

Character of Legal Service for the Poor

Existing studies indicate that the poor are least likely to use lawyers, that when they do they generally have access to the least competent and least responsible members of the bar, and that such assistance as they are provided is generally of a quite limited character. Let us consider first the services provided the poor by private attorneys.

Surveys conducted in several states indicate that about two out of three lower class families have *never* employed a lawyer, compared with about one out of three upper class families. A recent study of lawyers in private practice in New York City found that less than five per cent reported the median income of their individual clients to be under $5,000 a year, although half the families and unrelated individuals in New York City had incomes under this amount. Conversely, 70 per cent of the lawyers reported that the median income of their clients was over $10,000, yet less than 10 per cent of New York's families and unrelated individuals received incomes that high.

The relatively few private attorneys available to the poor tend to be the least well trained and the least likely to conform even to the minimal standards of the bar. These lawyers are invariably at the lower end of the profession in quality of training and level of academic achievement, and because of the insecurity of their practice they are most likely to succumb to temptations to exploit clients.

Legal services rendered the poor are apt to be restricted in scope and limited in effectiveness. Cases are not usually accepted unless there is a clear cause of action and a fairly certain return—that is, unless the case in effect pays for itself. A personal injury case handled on a contingent fee basis is the prime example. Because fees are usually small, when poor clients are accepted, lawyers are ordinarily reluctant to devote much time or energy to their problems, and there is usually little incentive to go much beyond the case as presented. Legal service is characteristically too little and too late. The poor man usually waits too long before seeking legal help; if he comes to a lawyer at all it is generally after he has been arrested, after his goods have been repossessed or after his wages have been attached. Because the poor are financially insecure, their lawyers are often under considerable pressure to seek quick settlements. There is rarely any interest in raising or pursuing legal principles that would have relevance beyond the case at hand.

To supplement private legal representation special agencies have been created for the express purpose of extending legal services to the indigent. These include assigned counsel and public defender systems in criminal cases and Legal Aid in civil cases. With respect to the representation of criminal defendants, there is considerable evidence to suggest that neither the assigned counsel nor public defender system as now constituted is capable of providing adequate service to the indigent accused. A large proportion of poor defendants (particularly in misdemeanor cases) are not represented at all. Moreover, when counsel is provided he frequently has neither the resources, the skill nor the incentive to defend his client effectively; and he usually enters the case too late to make any real difference in the outcome. Indeed, the generally higher rate of guilty pleas and prison sentences among defendants represented by assigned counsel or the public defender suggests that these attorneys may actually undermine their clients' position.

Legal Aid organizations have been seriously handicapped in meeting the vast potential need for legal representation among the poor and in dealing with the cases that are actually handled. Resources are grossly inadequate. Less than 4 million dollars was spent in 1963 to finance the operations of all Legal Aid organizations in the United States handling civil cases. This figure represents less than two-tenths of one per cent of the total expenditures for legal services in the United States in 1963. Largely because of its meager resources Legal Aid has just barely managed to keep up with the expanding population. In 1963 it was processing about the same number of new cases per thousand population as in 1916. Lacking sufficient staff and funds, legal aid organizations have been understandably reluctant to extend or advertise their services. Rather, there is a marked fear of opening the flood gates, of becoming swamped with new cases. Furthermore, high caseloads frequently lead to a mass processing of cases and thus to routinized, perfunctory service. Three out of four accepted applicants for Legal Aid receive only a single brief consultation; only a minimal amount of time is given to the investigation of facts, to legal research and drafting of legal documents and to court work. Many offices, in fact, are incapable of handling cases that require extensive investigation or time-consuming litigation. The situation is further aggravated by low salaries, high turnover in personnel and in-adequate direction "by disinterested or inactive boards of directors." There is little time or incentive to enter into a contest over legal principles, to make or alter law or to combat institutionalized sources of injustice.

The effectiveness of Legal Aid is also limited by its vulnerability to pressure from local bar and business interests which are its principal financial supporters. The local bar insists upon a strict application of financial eligibility requirements to insure that all cases are excluded that might possibly yield a fee to a private attorney. As a result, close to a fifth of all applicants to Legal Aid are annually rejected on financial grounds. Pressure from local businessmen has led to the exclusion of bankruptcy cases in many Legal Aid offices, and it has resulted in a reluctance to press claims against local merchants, landlords and others whose interests would be threatened by more vigorous representation. The tendency, therefore, is for Legal Aid to become a captive of its principal financial supporters who may well be considered its real clients. This leads to a cautious, passive and accommodative posture on the part of Legal Aid attorneys.

It is also important to note that Legal Aid attorneys often conceive of legal service to the poor as a charity or privilege rather than a right. This paternalistic orientation is most evident in the handling of divorce cases. The general view is that divorce is a luxury that should be granted only if the client is deemed morally deserving or if it is absolutely neces-sary "to protect either the wife or the children from immediate or threatened physical harm, or moral jeopardy."[10] Otherwise, it is felt separation would be an acceptable alternative.

This view of the poor client as incapable of knowing his own best interests—as an irresponsible and immature person—not only undermines the dignity and self respect of the client but it also weakens the capacity of Legal Aid attorneys to recognize legal rights and to seek effective legal solutions. For the poor client, Legal Aid often becomes another line to wait in, another humiliating experience and a further reminder that the law is unresponsive to, if not opposed to, his interests. The experience of the poor with Legal Aid and the effect of this experience on their attitudes toward and willingness to use the law deserve serious study.

Functions of Legal Representation

What are the functions lawyers might perform that would result in more effective representation of the poor? The following catalogue of functions reflects the need to move beyond the kinds of service the poor have so far been receiving to a much closer approximation of the wider range of services enjoyed by the more advantaged segments of the society.

Asserting legal rights which, although recognized in law, remain unimplemented.

Claims and defenses available to the poor often remain unasserted because of the absence of counsel. State housing codes which require landlords to provide heat, water and electricity and to keep the premises free of vermin are frequently violated by slum landlords. Without counsel poor tenants cannot realistically be expected to force compliance. Fraud and misrepresentation in the sale of consumer goods and illegal collection practices could be challenged on the basis of established legal doctrine, but without the assistance of counsel the poor consumer is virtually without recourse; indeed, his very inactivity as well as the inappropriateness of his actions may lead him into further trouble:

> *The slum dweller who buys unwisely can hardly be expected to know his liabilities or his rights of recourse against his seller, even if firmly established under law. He does not understand that he must pay for goods even though repossessed, that unrelated possessions can be attached for nonpayment of the purchased goods, or that additions for court costs, marshals' fees, and interest can multiply the original debt.*
>
> *Often he mistakenly believes his legal remedy against a fraudulent seller is to stop paying.*[11]

In the area of public welfare those who might be eligible for assistance are often improperly denied aid, and benefits may be illegally delayed or terminated. Moreover, some authors believe that methods for determining fraud sometimes lead to unconstitutional invasions of the right to privacy. It is unlikely that such abuses will be remedied so long as the poor lack competent legal representation.

Facilitating the development of legal rights in areas where the law is now vague or biased.

> *The poor live in a legal universe which has, by and large, been ignored by legal scholars. Low visibility decisions decide their destiny; official discretion determines their fate; and rights, even with lawyers to assert them, take a destructively long time to ascertain and vindicate.*[12]

Lawyers are obviously needed to develop rights that are now only weakly recognized, to help clarify and fashion the law to allow the poor a greater measure of the protections and benefits that the law could be made to provide. Furthermore, as we have seen, much law tends to be biased against the poor, and competent representation might not only serve to "delay or nullify its operation" but may also "prompt reassessment and change."[13] Accomplishment of these tasks requires skilled advocates to present the interests and claims of the poor before a myriad of decision makers. This would include careful preparation of legal arguments before appellate tribunals and effective lobbying in administrative and legislative bodies.

Bringing pressure to bear to increase the fairness and reasonableness of adjudicative procedures and to insure more positive and sympathetic implementation of legal policies.

One of the basic contributions lawyers can make to the administration of justice is to insist upon adequate procedures for safeguarding the right of parties to a fair hearing and reasoned judgment. As noted in the Report of the Joint Conference on Professional Responsibility:

> *In a very real sense it may be said that the integrity of the adjudicative process itself depends upon the participation of the advocate . . . The institution of advocacy is not a concession to the frailties of human nature, but an expression of human insight in the design of a social framework within which man's capacity for impartial judgment can attain its fullest realization.*[14]

Because the poor rarely have the assistance of a skilled advocate they have little protection against the frequently capricious exercise of official discretion. Competent advocates for the poor would help remedy this situation. They could also increase the responsiveness of agencies to the special needs and interests of the poor and encourage more active and effective implementation of the law on their behalf.

Assisting in the creation of contractual relations and legal associations to maximize the opportunities and benefits the law provides.

It is this activity more than any other which permits the marshalling of the resources of the law for the realization of common interests and aspirations.

> *In our society the great bulk of human relations are set, not by governmental decree, but by the voluntary action of the affected parties. Men come together to collaborate and to arrange their relations in many ways; by forming corporations, partnerships, labor unions, clubs and churches; by concluding contracts and leases; by entering a hundred other large and small transactions by which their rights and duties toward one another are defined.*

> *Successful voluntary collaboration usually requires for its guidance something equivalent to a formal charter, defining the terms of the collaboration, anticipating and forfending against possible disputes, and generally providing a framework for the parties' future dealings. In our society the natural architect of this framework is the lawyer.*[15]

Lawyers serving well-to-do individuals or large business clients devote the major portion of their energies to the performance of these tasks. In representing poor clients, however, lawyers rarely if ever assist in establishing contractual relations or other forms of legal association. Nevertheless, this kind of representation could be of vital significance to the poor by helping to provide them with an organizational base for more effective participation in and use of the legal order. As will be noted below, legal competence is related to and also supported by political or civic competence. Similarly, legal representation may be seen as political as well as legal in nature. Lawyers not only help to assert and establish claims of right, they also provide a voice for their clients in the decision-making process; and the latter is often an essential precondition for the former. It has been observed that, "the power to create legal relationships is a form of political power."[16] By helping to organize the poor the lawyer in effect serves to enlarge their political competence, and this in turn may further enhance their capacity for more effective use of the law.

Conditions Leading to Inadequate Representation

The functions of the lawyer outlined above are only rarely performed for the poor either by private attorneys or by lawyers specially charged with serving the indigent. What are the conditions that prevent the legal profession from extending and enlarging its services to the poor? The answer lies partly in the fact that the poor lack the competence and resources that would allow them to obtain more adequate representation. We must also consider, however, certain structural characteristics of the legal profession and the traditional orientation of lawyers to clients and their problems.

Structure of Rewards. Success in the legal profession as in other occupations is largely measured by the size of one's income. Since the financing of legal services still rests primarily on the principle of fee for service, the poor man is generally an undesirable client. The size of the anticipated fee is not only a factor in the decision to represent a client, it also affects the quality of service provided—for example, decisions about type of action, place of jurisdiction and preparation of the case.

Prestige in the legal profession is also a function of the class and ethnic background of the lawyer's clientele and certain characteristics of the clients' legal problems. High status clients who provide a continuous supply of legal business involving challenging legal problems are considered the most valued clients. In these respects the poor have little to offer. Among the salient features of a lower class clientele are: (1) the presence of clients from ethnic and racial minorities; (2) lack of resources leading to little incentive to treat their problems as other than "cut and dried" legal cases; (3) the non-recurring character of the legal problems ordinarily brought to the lawyer (like personal injury, divorce, crime) leading to a highly unstable and insecure practice, and (4) the necessity of contact with those levels of the administration of justice that are least likely to welcome vigorous presentation of the client's case and most likely to require compromise of ethical standards. As a result lawyers generally make every effort to move beyond this kind of practice and bitterly resent their inability to do so. In short, for most lawyers a lower class clientele is a mark of failure.

Party Initiative. The reluctance of lawyers to serve the poor also stems from the commitment of the legal system to party initiative, which requires the lawyer to wait upon the presentation of a case or claim before taking action. This does not mean that lawyers must adopt an entirely passive posture. They reformulate issues and facts, recommend certain courses of action and discourage others. It does mean, however, that the client has the responsibility for bringing his case to the attention of the lawyer. The Canons of Ethics deem it unprofessional for a lawyer to solicit "employment by circulars, advertisements, through touters or by personal communications or interviews not warranted by personal relations,"[17] and they forbid lawyers from stirring up litigation by "seeking out those with claims for personal injuries or those having any other grounds of action in order to secure them as clients, or to employ agents or runners for like purposes."[18] A basic assumption of these canons is that parties are competent to initiate claims. But this is not ordinarily true of the poor.

We may well ask why lawyers should not "stir up litigation." The police and prosecuting attorneys do this for the criminal courts; what would happen were lawyers to do so on the civil side? Should solicitation be prohibited if lawyers are thereby able to inform persons of their legally protected rights? What of moving a community to protest en masse some common legal grievance: is this the proper work of attorneys? What is it that is thought to be lost if a more active orientation were adopted? Are these beliefs well grounded?

Focus on the Particular Case or Controversy.   Lawyers tend to restrict their attention to the case at hand and to the particular parties to the controversy or action. This reflects in part the preference of the common law tradition for counseling in specific controversies between defined interests on a case by case basis. And the case-method of instruction still employed by most American law schools undoubtedly reinforces this traditional orientation. The legal problems of the poor, however, characteristically arise from systematic abuses embedded in the operation of various public and private agencies, affecting large numbers of similarly situated individuals. Effective solution of these problems may require the lawyer to direct his attention away from a particular claim or grievance to the broader interests and policies at stake, and away from the individual client to a class of clients, in order to challenge more directly and with greater impact certain structural sources of injustice. Consequently, if the lawyer conceives of the poor man's problems as basically separate and individual he may achieve at best only a temporary and limited accommodation of a particular grievance without altering established policies and institutionalized practices. Thus, an attorney representing a welfare recipient may consider it unwise for his client to appeal a decision on eligibility so long as a satisfactory informal adjustment is offered by the welfare agency. He may, however, be turning down an important opportunity to challenge and possibly alter a particularly harsh regulation or rule adversely affecting many other welfare recipients.

It may be necessary, therefore, to supplement or replace individual representation with other forms of advocacy that would serve to aggregate the demands of the poor and allow for more planned presentation of claims to give the poor a more meaningful voice in the legal process and greater leverage in the promotion and protection of their interests. These other forms of representation might include: *organizational advocacy*— legal services provided to an organization representing the common or collective interests of a group, or made available to members of the group through its intervention; and *strategic advocacy*—issues selected and generated for the purpose of challenging established practices and for pressing recognition of new rights.

Although rarely employed on behalf of the poor, these forms of advocacy are by no means new. Labor unions, trade associations and corporations have for some years secured the services of lawyers to represent and support the legal interests of their members. The newly acquired legitimacy of group legal practice as a result of recent Supreme Court decisions will undoubtedly increase the use of such arrangements. Moreover, the test case (a form of strategic advocacy) is a widely recognized and not infrequently employed device for developing new law. What changes in the organization of the legal profession would be necessary to bring these forms of legal representation to the poor? What problems would lawyers face in carrying out these tasks? For example, how can the collective interests of the group be championed effectively without sacrificing possibly conflicting interests of particular members?

Conceptions of Legal Relevance.   A lawyer is trained to view persons and events in the light of certain standards of legal relevance. In order to perform his job well the lawyer must be able to translate facts, issues, and problems into legal facts, legal issues and legal problems. This task is made easier when the client speaks the same language as the lawyer and when the matters brought by clients fall into clearly established categories, or are at least presented in ways that are readily translatable. The poor ordinarily do not speak the same language as lawyers, and their problems are least likely to fit into convenient legal categories. Problems with welfare, landlords or local merchants often do not appear to the lawyer as constituting a clear cause of action for the poor client. The attorney's legal training has prepared him to deal with creditor's rights, not debtor's rights; to represent clients before federal regulatory agencies, not before a local welfare agency or police department; to handle stock options and executive pension funds, not unemployment insurance benefits.

It follows, therefore, that although lawyers may readily acknowledge that the poor have problems, they may be reluctant to define them as legal problems. Indeed, there is a tendency to conceive of their problems as basically social or psychological, calling for therapy rather than justice. Moreover, even when a legal problem is detected the attention of the lawyer may shift to some other, more "fundamental," yet non-legal level of concern. The tendency to conceive of the problems of the poor as essentially non-legal is evident among Legal Aid lawyers. The adoption of this perspective weakens the lawyer's capacity to recognize legal rights and seek legal remedies; it also provides him with a seemingly legitimate rationale for perfunctory service and for his reluctance to serve the poor as a lawyer.

Federal Intervention: OEO's Legal Service Program

With passage of the Economic Opportunity Act of 1964 the federal government has assumed responsibility for financing legal services for the poor and for setting policy standards to guide the organization and provision of such services. The orientation of the OEO legal service program represents a major break with the philosophy of traditional Legal Aid. This is indicated by: (1) the importance placed upon the establishment of neighborhood law offices to increase the accessibility of legal services to the poor; (2) the requirement that the poor be represented on the governing board of the legal service agency to enhance responsiveness to client needs; (3) the adoption of a more aggressive stance in promoting the collective as well as individual interests of the poor, including the use of legal advocacy as an instrument of social change; and (4) concern for insuring the independence of the legal service organization from those vested interests that might be threatened by more vigorous representation of the poor.

Evaluation of the federal program provides a unique opportunity to explore more fully many of the issues that have been raised in this section of the paper. In particular, we are led to inquire into the various dimensions of effective legal service and the social arrangements that would implement effectiveness. What conditions, for example, are likely to support or undermine the independence of the legal service agency? It will be important to consider in this regard the organizational history of the agency, the political struggles and compromises in establishing the agency and the resulting structure of control.

Furthermore, what are the conditions that are likely to promote a more vigorous style of representation? To what extent will this commitment be eroded by the inevitable pressures of practice and ever-increasing caseloads? To what extent will involvement in a multi-service center increase the risk of reducing potential legal problems to social welfare problems? To what extent will pressures from vested interests lead to the adoption of a more cautious and accommodative posture?

A factor that will undoubtedly be of major importance in the development of the program is the attitude of the bar. As in the case of Legal Aid there appear to be a number of lawyers who fear a loss of business as a result of extending free legal services.

A more important and pervasive fear is that the bar, especially the organized bar, will lose control over the provision of legal services to the poor. The OEO requirement of "maximum feasible participation" of the poor has been interpreted to mean that the governing boards of these programs should include at least some representatives of the poor. A number of lawyers, including many officials of Legal Aid, bitterly resent this demand. At the National Conference on Law and Poverty in June of 1965 the president of the National Legal Aid and Defender Association indicated that many legal aid societies would withdraw from the OEO program if they are required to reorganize their board of directors to admit "members of the poor and representatives of the poor."[19]

To what extent, then, will the bar itself interfere with the development of the program, or reduce it to a mere extension of the conventional type of Legal Aid service? A more fundamental question, perhaps, is whether it is possible to establish a government-supported legal service program dedicated to stimulating social change, particularly when the changes that are being sought will affect the structure and operation of agencies of government itself?

Important questions are also raised as to the character of the legal service agency. Does the traditional type of private law office (particularly the small, neighborhood office) provide a useful model for agencies serving the poor? It may be necessary to explore and experiment with different forms of organization, different methods of allocating work, new types of specialization. The establishment of a centralized research and planning staff may well be called for to implement the broader, strategic goals of the program. Further, what organizational tools can be devised for processing a large volume of cases? How much of the work of the agency can be routinized without imperilling the effectiveness of the services provided? What functions might be delegated to law students, or perhaps to sub-professionals?

POVERTY AND LEGAL COMPETENCE

Throughout this essay we have said that the poor enjoy fewer of the benefits and protections of the law than the rich. We have attempted to identify some of the conditions of this phenomenon, focusing principally on certain characteristics of the legal system and those who operate the system. We must also take into account the readiness and ability of poor persons to use the law. What qualities are required, and under what social conditions are they likely to emerge?

One view of the citizen's role in the legal system stresses his capacity to evoke favorable consideration from officials in the application of established rules. We would suggest another image of the competence required to use the legal system, one that emphasizes the ability to further and protect one's interests *through active assertion of legal rights*. We call the relevant ability "legal competence." The legally competent person will want and expect government officials to take his interests into account in both their dealings with him and with others; but he will see their propensity to do so as closely connected with his own actions. The competent subject will take initiative. Moreover, like other practical men, he is concerned with creating, preserving and expanding his capacity to initiate action. He may expect government officials (and others) to accord him "equal treatment" and "serious consideration," but he will continuously lay a basis for this expectation through his own actions.

As we see him, the competent subject will see law as a *resource* for developing, furthering and protecting his interests. This is partly a matter of knowledge. The competent subject will be aware of the relation between the realization of his interests and the machinery of law making and administration. He will know how to use this machinery and when to use it. Moreover, he will see assertion of his interests through legal channels as desirable and appropriate. This is not to say that he will view law as omni-relevant, as a sort of all-purpose tool. He will be aware of the limits of law. But it is important to stress that he will not be hostile to extension of the rule of law. When he believes it proper, he will make an effort to bring his interests under the aegis of authoritative rules. This will call for "a creative act of influence" that will affect the content of official decisions.

It is implicit in what we have said that the competent subject will have a sense of himself as a *possessor of rights,* and in seeking to validate and implement these rights through law he will be concerned with holding *authorities accountable to law*. With respect to the latter, Almond and Verba contend that in seeking favorable rulings from legal and other government authorities the subject may appeal to "the set of administrative rules that are supposed to guide the action of the government official, or he may appeal to his considerateness."[20] We suggest that the legally competent subject does more than appeal to the considerateness of officials; he *insists* that official actions and decisions be consistent with authoritative rules.

In doing so he changes or reinforces his relationship to those who make and administer law. He changes it in a direction compatible with the rule of law, for his manner of winning "consideration" tends to reduce his dependence on the good will and whims of those who govern. The competent subject demands that there be *reasons* for official decisions and actions, and that these reasons be consonant with both "reason" and "law." Power, however benevolent, is not for him its own justification.

In sum, it is evident that "legal competence" is a complex quality. Broadly speaking it would appear to consist of one part *awareness* and one part *assertiveness*. The legally competent person has a sense of himself as a possessor of rights, and he sees the legal system as a resource for validation of these rights. He knows when and how to seek validation.

Beyond this, the legally competent person takes action: he not only "knows his rights" and how to validate them, he turns to the legal system and uses it when his interests can be served by doing so. In the process, he tends to extend the rule of law.

THE JUDICIARY AND NONJUDICIAL ACTIVITIES

Robert B. McKay

The quality and the integrity of the American judiciary has never been higher than today, and judicial sensitivity to ethical considerations continues to rise. But the public seems almost more mistrustful of the legal system in general, and the judiciary in particular, than ever before. How can this be? The explanation is not difficult. The ethical expectations of the public have risen even more rapidly than have the perceptions of the judges of what is now expected of them. Standards of judicial behavior, not seriously challenged when the incumbent was Chief Justice John Jay, John Marshall, or William H. Taft, or during the tenure of many Associate Justices from the earliest to some of the most recent, are no longer acceptable to the legal community, to the public in general, or to the United States Senate. Presidents Johnson and Nixon learned this lesson the hard way, as did Justice Fortas and Judges Haynsworth and Carswell. Lower federal courts and state courts have similarly developed more acute perceptions of what is and what is not permissible conduct for members of an appointed or elected judiciary.

The more relaxed standards of yesterday are no longer acceptable. But this relatively abrupt change in attitude creates problems. As a result of this new zeal for a higher ethic in performance of the judicial function, some judges are charged with wrongdoing where there is no fault by any standard, and others are held responsible for failure to meet a standard never before demanded, and only now in the process of formulation. However unfortunate this may be for judges caught in the middle of an evolving ethical standard, the *system* should benefit from the opportunity to raise standards to a level that contemporary society will not only tolerate but demand. New standards of judicial conduct, now being developed, must satisfy two broad objectives. On the one hand, the standards must be appropriately demanding to the end that justice is facilitated in every possible way. At the same time the standards must ensure that the judges are not unnecessarily separated from the communities they serve in strait-jackets of judicial isolation.

The problems have been given too little attention in the past, and they are not easy. But appropriate solutions must be found. The purpose of this discussion is to enumerate some of the questions and to suggest some permissible limits to the nonjudicial activities of sitting judges. Specifically, an effort will be made to differentiate between quasi-judicial activities, which are likely to be tolerated or even encouraged, and extra-judicial activities, which are likely to be forbidden or at most tolerated. I leave to others in the Symposium the related questions of disqualification and conflict of interest, including proposals for disclosure of financial interests.

I—SOME ANCILLARY ISSUES OF JUDICIAL ADMINISTRATION

Preliminarily, it is important to establish that definition of the permissible limits for nonjudicial activities is closely related to other issues involving the judiciary and judicial administration. Outside the scope of this paper, or even this Symposium, but inescapably relevant to questions of judicial ethics are at least the following:

1. Selection of Judges. So long as most judges outside the federal judicial system are elected on a partisan basis, necessitating political campaigns and election expense, it is idle to pretend judicial insulation from the most venal of all extra-judicial influence, the favor of the political leader or the momentary passion of the electorate. Nothing is more central to judicial integrity than selection of judges on the basis of merit rather than political preferment.

2. Judicial Pay Scales. So long as a substantial number of states compensate the judges of their highest courts at less than $25,000 per year (often with inadequate retirement plans) and provide even less for judges in the lower courts, those charged with the drafting or enforcement of ethical standards for judges are likely to remain tolerant of compensation for nonjudicial activities. Ethical sensitivity is not quick to rise above economic need.

3. Overcrowded Calendars. Almost without exception in the large urban centers, and to a surprisingly large extent in more modest-sized communities as well, justice delayed is the rule rather than the exception. Whether the fault lies with permissive rulings on criminal procedure, defective court management, or too few judges, the result is the same. The system is discredited; and the harried judge is less likely to be concerned with the niceties of judicial propriety than with the pressing need to relieve pressure on a crowded docket.

4. Lack of Respect for the Courts. Large segments of American society are disenchanted, and worse, with the world in which they find themselves. The judicial system is a natural and vulnerable target for the disaffected. When there are complaints about the integrity of judges, suspicion turns into conviction that justice is not to be had in the courts. Disrespect for the courts is taking new and more virulent form in increasingly contemptuous conduct in court and even physical disruption. Even more alarming is the widely shared mistrust of the judicial system as a whole. It is evident among minority groups, the poor, and even among some of the best educated of our youth who increasingly voice their lack of faith in the courts and in the law itself.

II—THE FUNCTION OF ETHICAL STANDARDS

In General. The standard that will guide the future conduct of judges is clearly not the standard that applied even in the recent past. The nomination of Abe Fortas as Chief Justice of the United States, the withdrawal of the nomination after certain disclosures, his resignation after further disclosures, and the rejection by the Senate of the nomination of Judges Haynsworth and Carswell to the Supreme Court made inevitable the recasting and tightening of previously ill-defined concepts of what conduct is permissible and what is not for judges outside their official duties.

Because the danger of overreaction is severe, it is important at the beginning to consider carefully the interests that are involved and the price that is paid for any limitation upon the outside activities of judges. It would be easy, but intellectually lazy, to hold that the sole business of judges is judging, that all else is at least distracting, and that accordingly a judge should avoid all nonjudicial activities that might either be time-consuming or influence his opinion on matters that come before him. The argument proves too much. If a judge is to live in *this* world and not in the isolation of a sequestered juror, he is constantly shaping his views on all kinds of matters that may come before him. The perceptions of a judge are influenced by conversations with family, friends, and colleagues; by his choices among the competing news media; his preferences in recreational activities; and even his tastes in clothes and hair styles (the long or short of it).

Skeptics may well charge overkill at this point, for of course no one suggests that judges cut themselves off from family, friends, and colleagues. But anything short of that impossible dream is unlikely to accomplish the objectives of those who seek immunization of the judiciary from all the opinon-shaping forces that surround them. It is at least arguable—and I for one would so argue—that a judge is likely to be a better dispenser of justice if he is aware of the currents and passions of the time, the developments of technology, and the sweep of events. To judge in the real world a judge must live, breathe, think, and partake of opinions in that world.

The dangers of over-involvement in the so-called real world are also great, not only in the perceptions of the public, which are important, but in reality as well. The hazards to guard against are three: (1) participation in outside activities so extensive that the time and energy available for the primary obligation are measurably impaired; (2) participation in out-of-court activities that may lead to actual bias or the appearance of prejudgment of issues likely to come before the court; and (3) actions that impair the dignity and esteem in which the court should be held. Because of the close relationship among these it may be helpful to give examples, which will in turn be refined in the concluding section of this paper with detailed enumeration of the types of quasi-judicial and extra-judicial activities that raise questions of judgment as to permissibility.

By Way of Illustration. Active participation by judges in the affairs of the day, whether advice to Presidents, service on special legislative commissions, or the more homely tasks of arbitration and partisan political activity, has been accepted as a matter of course until almost the present moment. Justices of the Supreme Court of the United States, surely no less sensitive to judicial proprieties than other judges, have indulged in all these activities—and then some. . . . More than half the Justices who have ever sat on the Court have participated in extensive nonjudicial activities, including many that would now be unacceptable—most without any effort at concealment and without embarrassment, for there was no thought the conduct was wrong.

Who can doubt that Chief Justice Taft and Justices Brandeis and Frankfurter felt no impropriety in offering advice to Presidents of the United States? Surely, each regarded his special role as presidential adviser with a mix of obligation and privilege. No one has come forward with supportable evidence of improper influence upon any judicial opinion arising out of these private exchanges. And yet there are few individuals, if any, who will now defend this practice of the recent past. One wonders why. These and other confidential relationships were never hidden, yet there was no public outcry until the Johnson-Fortas relationship acquired the ill-sounding sobriquet of "cronyism." Was the practice always ill-advised, or is this but another example of overreaction to a transitory public passion? My speculation is that the public indignation in this case is not transient, but will remain open to ready rekindling if further disclosures should be made in cases not now known. In this instance, at least, the public opinion is correct; the practice of judicial advisement on matters of state is not tolerable. It is difficult to believe that in a nation of more than 200,000,000 people the President cannot do without the advice of members of the federal judiciary. When President Franklin Roosevelt needed the services of Justice Byrnes as "Assistant President," the Justice resigned from the Court (and none too soon by present standards; during his brief tenure on the Court he regularly advised the President). And when President Lyndon Johnson wanted Justice Goldberg to become Ambassador to the United Nations, Goldberg too resigned. President Truman, however, did it the other—and wrong—way. He nominated Fred Vinson to be Chief Justice, presumably without any thought by either that their close relationship need be interrupted in any way; and apparently it was not.

The surprising fact is that there is little precedent to guide the legislative and judicial hands that are now seeking to define standards adequate for a present that already seems far removed from a chronologically recent past. Federal statutes are not particularly helpful, and the precipitate rulings of the Judicial Conference of the United States in 1969 and 1970 provided more confusion than guidance. Similarly, state statutes and court rules are generally inadequate. And the Canons of Judicial Ethics are completely unavailing in their bland counsel in favor of nonspecific virtue and their vague caution against unidentified wrong. To determine why the legal system has not provided more satisfactory guidance, it becomes necessary to review briefly the limited, and discouraging, history of efforts to identify the permissible limits on nonjudicial activities and then, more hopefully, to examine the prospects for the better day that now seems likely.

III—LEGISLATIVE AND JUDICIAL REGULATION OF NONJUDICIAL ACTIVITIES: A RECORD OF FAILURE

Probably there is universal agreement with the common-sense wisdom of Lord Coke's statement that no man shall be a judge in his own case, but that standard offers little guidance beyond the conscience of each individual judge. It was scarcely more useful in the search for fairness in the courts of the eighteenth and nineteenth centuries than when Lord Coke wrote in the seventeenth century.

The earlier more casual views on the permissible range of judicial conduct become more understandable when consideration is given to eighteenth and nineteenth century attitudes about the law, lawyers, and judges. In the early days of the Republic there simply weren't many lawyers, and almost none were trained in university law schools. Accordingly, it is not surprising that most judges were not lawyers and depended for their livelihood principally on income from nonjudicial activities. As the number of lawyers increased in the early decades of the nineteenth century, their prestige plummeted until the nadir was reached during the Jacksonian era. By the middle of the century, many states had removed all requirements for admission to practice on the theory that law, like any other trade, should be open to the competition of the market place.

The first demand for higher standards of professional conduct came from Roscoe Pound in his 1906 speech on "The Causes of Popular Dissatisfaction with the Administration of Justice." Moved in part by that speech, the American Bar Association drafted the Canons of Professional Ethics, which were approved in 1908; but no separate rules were prepared for judges at that time. Subsequent movement was slow, as described in a 1969 report of the American Judicature Society:

> [R]esolutions presented at the ABA's 1909 and 1917 conventions calling for the appointment of a committee to draft a set of Judicial Canons were quickly forgotten. Many felt such canons were unnecessary; that the real issue was judicial competency rather than honesty. Others believed it was not the proper role of the Bar to impose standards on the judiciary, feeling that such canons would more appropriately be developed within the judiciary.
>
> It is likely that matters would have rested in this state of inertia for many more years had it not been for the public admission of a certain Federal District Court Judge [Kennesaw Landis] that he was supplementing his $7,500 federal salary with $42,500 a year for legal services rendered as a national commissioner of the baseball associations. Powerless to bring sanctions against him under the Professional Ethics Canons, delegates attending the 1921 ABA Convention could only vote a resolution of censure.[1]

An American Bar Association Committee was then designated to propose standards of judicial ethics. Under the direction of Chief Justice Taft, the committee formulated proposals that were approved by the ABA in 1924 as the Canons of Judicial Ethics. Since that time official recognition has been given to the Canons in forty-three states, sometimes with local variations.

In 1969, after several years of study the ABA approved a new Code of Professional Responsibility to replace (and vastly to improve) the 1908 Canons of Professional Ethics. The next step, now under way, is to formulate new standards of judicial ethics. An ABA Committee on Standards of Judicial Conduct was appointed in 1969. Known as the Traynor Committee, the body presented its Interim Report, confined to the more controversial aspects of judicial ethics, to the 1970 annual meeting of the ABA in St. Louis. A final report is anticipated in 1971 with action by the ABA possible as early as the summer of 1971.

The American Bar Association has been the pacemaker in the establishment of standards of judicial conduct, and most states have been content to adapt the ABA-proposed Canons to their own needs. Now, however, there is considerable activity by other bodies. Both Congress and the Judicial Conference of the United States have demonstrated increased interest in the development of standards for federal judges. Several state legislatures have enacted legislation, and the highest appellate courts in other states have adopted new codes of judicial conduct.

Curiously, the division of responsibility between court and legislature in the regulation of judicial ethics seems never to have been worked out in any systematic way. The absence of thoughtful analysis of this crucial matter is illustrative of the general inattention to the question of developing standards of judicial ethics. Even at the federal level, where the separation of powers is said to be a principle of constitutional dimension, there is no clear differentiation between what is permitted and what is forbidden to Congress and to Court (or Judicial Conference). Indeed, for most purposes Justices of the Supreme Court and judges of the lower federal courts look to the ABA Canons of Professional Ethics for guidance, even though the Canons have never been specifically made applicable to the federal judiciary except as federal judges are members of the bar of states that have adopted the Canons. Thus, for example, when the propriety of Justice Fortas' nonjudicial activities was questioned, the ABA Standing Committee on Professional Ethics did not hesitate to inquire into possible violation of the Canons or to conclude that there was a "clear violation," citing eight separate canons "bearing on the Fortas question."[2] Similarly, when the Haynsworth, Carswell, and Blackmun nominations were under consideration, the ABA Standing Committee on the Federal Judiciary, in approving the qualifications of each candidate, reviewed questions of prior conduct in terms of consistency or not with the Canons of Judicial Ethics.

A majority of the Supreme Court has recognized, at least in dictum, that standards of conduct can be imposed on federal judges. But Congress has dealt with few of the issues, and then not comprehensively. Only three statutes, all in title 28 of the United States Code, are important for present purposes: section 144 provides for disqualification for "personal bias or prejudice"; section 454 prohibits the practice of law; and section 455 provides for disqualification of a judge in any case in which he has a "substantial interest." Proposals now before Congress would go considerably further, but still do not purport to offer a comprehensive code. Title IV of the Judicial Reform Act defines conflicts of interest exclusively in terms of financial interest and requires the filing of financial statements. The other principal proposal now before Congress, in the Judicial Disqualification Act of 1970, proposes amendment to section 455 of title 28 (interest of justice or judge) and to section 144 of title 28 (bias or prejudice of judge).

The Judicial Conference of the United States has dealt with questions of ethics at most episodically. Its principal concern has been for the regulation of nonjudicial activities, but here, too, without any suggestion of comprehensive regulation, a matter apparently still left to the American Bar Association. In 1963, for example, the Judicial Conference dealt with a single question, the propriety of service by federal judges as officers or directors of corporations, forbidding such service on for-profit corporations, but allowing continued service with not-for-profit corporations.

On June 10, 1969, the Judicial Conference, upon the recommendation of its Committee on Court Administration, adopted a resolution prohibiting the acceptance of compensation, whether in the form of loans, gifts, gratuities, honoraria, or otherwise, for nonjudicial services. The resolution provided, however, that a judge might accept such compensation if, upon application to the judicial council of his circuit, it was determined that the services would not interfere with the judge's judicial duties and would either be in the public interest or were justified by exceptional circumstances. Where judicial council approval was secured, public disclosure was required of the services rendered and the compensation received.

At the same meeting a second resolution required each judge to file with the Judicial Conference an annual statement of investments and assets held at any time during the year; a statement of income, including gifts and bequests; and a statement of liabilities. The Conference also directed its Committee on Court Administration to begin the formulation of comprehensive standards for the conduct of federal judges, a project never undertaken or apparently even considered. The risk of concurrent development of inconsistent standards became apparent two months later when the ABA created the Traynor Committee with a mandate similar to that given the Judicial Conference's Committee on Court Administration. The possible conflict was at least postponed, probably removed, when Justice Traynor suggested that the Judicial Conference suspend "any further action on all the resolutions adopted in June . . . so that the Conference . . . may have the benefit of the research and work of this Committee."[3]

The June 1969 resolutions of the Judicial Conference were criticized by some lower federal court judges, by some legal educators, and in some editorials. One widely quoted comment was that of Judge Irving Kaufman, President of the Institute of Judicial Administration, and Professor Delmar Karlen, Director of the IJA. In a letter to the members of the IJA they said on May 28, 1969 (before announcement of the resolutions of the Judicial Conference):

> *In view of the growing concern about outside activities of judges, we think it important to reaffirm the principle that judges should not become monastic, but should continue to work with the organized bar and the law schools of this country in efforts to improve the administration of justice. Judicial reform is no more a sport for the weak-hearted than it is for the short-winded. If judges should falter now in face of the agitation of the moment, most of the motive power behind court reform would be lost.*

When the Judicial Conference met on November 1, 1969, it modified the earlier resolutions by suspending the requirements of prior judicial council approval and public disclosure. The Conference also adopted a resolution requiring federal judges to report to the Conference any extrajudicial compensation exceeding $100 in any quarterly period. The resolution further provided that the Chief Justice designate a panel of three federal judges to review the reports, which were to be kept confidential except to the extent that the panel concluded that they should be brought to the attention of the Conference. These resolutions were also criticized, particularly in newspaper editorials which described the modification, particularly the nondisclosure features, as a "retreat."

Finally, on March 18, 1970, the Judicial Conference announced a further change, reversing the June 10th resolution that had required federal judges to file annual returns. The new rule requires semiannual statements of income for extra-judicial income in amounts of $100 or more, including income from lecturing, teaching, and writing. Under this rule federal judges are also required to list gifts worth more than $100 received by them or any member of their immediate household, as well as any "interests" in parties to cases in which they "knowingly participated."

During essentially the same period a number of state legislatures, state courts, and state bar association groups investigated the need for revision, usually tightening, of ethical standards. Amended Codes have been adopted in Illinois and Wisconsin, and proposals for change are being studied in Florida, Maryland, New Jersey, and New York, among others.

IV—THE VARIETIES OF NONJUDICIAL ACTIVITY: SOME COMMENTS

In considering limitations that should be imposed on the nonjudicial activities of judges, the reasons for permission and prohibition should be kept clearly in mind. Although the problem has been discussed before in this paper, it may be useful to summarize, now more briefly, the risks and the benefits.

Nonjudicial activities, whether quasi-judicial or extra-judicial in nature, should not be allowed if there is a substantial likelihood that the undertaking will

1. interfere with the performance of official duty;
2. interfere, or seem to interfere, with the impartiality of the participating judge; or
3. impair the dignity and prestige of the judicial office.

Where these hazards are not involved, there are reasons to permit, even to encourage, nonjudicial activities if their performance will

1. help to prevent judicial shortsightedness arising from loss of contact with the world outside the court;
2. continue the education and development of essential skills in law and judicial administration; or
3. enrich and educate the audiences to which the judge lectures, writes, or teaches.

Even if these ultimate values are accepted, however, the drawing of lines between virtue and fault in particular instances is by no means an automatic process. The most well-intentioned judge needs standards tested in experience in order to inform his conscience in deciding among alternative courses of conduct. Even though all choices may be equally legal, the appearance of propriety or not may vary considerably from one alternative to another.

To facilitate discussion it should be helpful to differentiate, as does the Traynor Committee, between quasi-judicial and extra-judicial activities. Although some activities in each class should be permitted and some discouraged, the considerations are sufficiently distinct to justify separate analysis.

1. Quasi-Judicial Activities. This category includes those activities of judges that are not part of their assigned duties, but are related to the judicial function through efforts to improve judicial administration, to accomplish law reform, or to inform other judges, lawyers, or the general public about the nature of law or the substance of its component parts. Although no judge should be required to engage in quasi-judicial activities, the fact is that competent performance of some of the activities identified below is often helpful in bettering judicial performance and increasing public understanding of the judicial function.

a. Lecturing, Teaching, and Writing. Probably no statue or rule of court categorically forbids teaching, writing, or lecturing on legal, or even nonlegal, subjects. The issue, only recently surfaced, is whether judges can be compensated for their work. The Rules of the Judicial Conference of the United States of June 10, 1969, later suspended, and still later reversed, came very close to such a prohibition, permitting the acceptance of compensation only upon a finding by the judicial council of the circuit that the service would be in the public interest or was justified by exceptional circumstances, and that it would not interfere with the performance of judicial duties. Even after the bar was lifted, many federal judges have declined invitations they would otherwise have accepted at law schools and at gatherings of lawyers and judges in a context of continuing legal education. Others, continuing to lecture, to teach, and to write, decline even modest honoraria that are readily available to others for similar service, thus making judges less equal than other lawyers.

The point requires little elaboration. The simple fact is that good sense seems to have been restored on this point. Similarly, the new Illinois Rules, which categorically forbid compensation "of any kind" for all other nonjudicial activities, specifically exempt "reasonable compensation for lecturing, teaching, writing, or similar activities."

The Traynor Committee, after learning that the majority of law schools which responded to a committee questionnaire relied on judges as teachers, lecturers, or moot court judges, concluded in paragraph 2(a) that a judge "may speak, write, lecture, teach, or participate in seminars on matters pertaining to the law and the legal system," and that he could receive "reasonable" compensation as defined in paragraph 7 (Compensation and Expenses) of the Committee report.

The conclusion reached by the Traynor Committee is sound. Judges, lawyers, law students, and the public interest would suffer if these fruitful exchanges were silenced. Judges should not be made second-class citizens.

b. Law Reform Advocacy.   No one is better qualified to speak on law reform and questions of improvement in judicial administration than judges. Even though the efforts necessary to accomplish significant change are often substantial, no barrier should be raised against judicial participation in such activities beyond assurance that the obligations of judicial office are met. A good case could even be made for the proposition that judges have an *affirmative* obligation to work for improvement in judicial administration.

Canon 23 (Legislation) of the present Canons of Judicial Ethics offers a general license for judges to offer advice on legislative change (presumably including administrative, executive, and judicial reform as well). The rationale of the Canon is that the judge has "exceptional opportunity to observe the operation of statutes, especially those relating to practice, and to ascertain whether they tend to impede the just disposition of controversies. . . ." The Traynor Committee recommends more specific treatment, dividing the question of legislative counseling into separate categories that are treated differently.

The Committee would allow a judge to "consult with legislative and executive bodies and officials on matters of judicial administration" [paragraph 2(b)]; but "in drafting legislation and in other activities directed to improvement of the law, the legal profession, and the administration of justice," the recommendation is more restrictive. The Committee would allow participation in the latter activities only "under the auspices of a bar association, judicial conference or other non-partisan organization" [paragraph 2(c)]. The Committee's limitation is intended to prevent "the 'one man' judicial crusade by means of legislative appearances [and to protect] the judge from legislative pressure to appear as an individual and give his views on proposed legislation." As thus explained, the distinction drawn between individual advocacy in relation to judicial administration and group advocacy in other matters of law reform is understandable. But confusion may remain as to the difference between "judicial administration" in paragraph 2(b) and "the administration of Justice" in paragraph 2(c).

2. Extra-Judicial Activities.   Few if any judges confine themselves to the courtroom, law library, chambers, and the privacy of home. The loneliness and isolation of judicial life, to some extent necessary and desirable, become more tolerable to the kind of person best suited to the bench when coupled with the opportunity to engage in quasi-judicial activities of the kinds suggested above. But the questions do not end there. Few judges, upon accepting judicial office, want to cut themselves off entirely from friends at the bar and in public life or to terminate all private pursuits from which they derived satisfaction. Again the question is to determine which activities and which social or professional relationships may safely be continued without dilution of either the appearance or the reality of full and fair devotion to the cause of justice.

a. Practice of Law.   Nearly all observers agree now that the private practice of law should be forbidden to full-time judges. Even so, this represents a change from the standard of Canon 31 of the present Canons of Judicial Ethics which allows private practice where judicial compensation is not "adequate." Uncertainty continues, however, whether a limitation on "private practice" should exclude such related activities as executorships, trusteeships, and arbitration proceedings.

Ordinarily, one would have thought that the perimeters of private practice were fairly well understood. But questions were raised in the case of Justice Fortas whether the $20,000 annual fee he first accepted from and then returned to the Wolfson foundation involved the practice of law. He answered that at most he was committed to advice, including but not limited to legal advice. No resolution of the question was reached because Justice Fortas resigned before an answer was required. The question is important, however, because charges have also been advanced against Justice Douglas. If he was engaged in the practice of law, a federal "high misdemeanor" has been committed. . . .

More troublesome are the subordinate questions as to whether a judge can perform some of the duties often done by lawyers, but which do not necessarily require legal skills, such as executorships, trusteeships, and arbitration proceedings. Canon 27 is vague but generally permissive unless the performance of the duties of an executor or trustee

> *would interfere or seem to interfere with the proper perform-ance of his judicial duties, or if the business interests of those rep-resented require investments in enterprises that are apt to come before him judicially, or to be involved in questions of law to be determined by him.*

The Traynor Committee recommendations are more restrictive, denying fiduciary service "except for the estate or person of a member of his family," and even then with further limitations. Surely the principle is sound, particularly as softened by the recommendation in paragraph 10(a) of a grandfather clause to permit continued service in a fiduciary capacity by a judge in office when revised rules take effect "if the interests involved and the time demands are not substantial. . . ."

Canon 31 of the Canons of Judicial Ethics authorizes judges to serve as arbitrators for compensation. The Traynor Committee, recognizing that the free-and-easy standard there set forth would not be consistent with other more restrictive rulings of the Committee, concludes that a judge "may serve as an arbitrator only under extraordinary circumstances" (paragraph 9). But why should it be permitted at all? There are no family or personal reasons, as in the limited exception to the rule against fiduciary service; and there is no public interest to be served by having a judge rather than another serve as arbitrator.

b. Business and Charitable Activities.   There is now general agreement that a judge should not, in the words of the Traynor Committee recommendation, "engage in business or serve as an officer, director, or advisor of any business organizations" [paragraph 6(a)].

Many judges serve as officers, directors, and trustees of not-for-profit organizations; many others prefer not to be involved. Most observers would leave the matter where it stands, to the discretion of the individual judge. But there are limits, which are well identified by the Traynor Committee in paragraph 3 of the committee report:

> *A judge may participate in civic and charitable activities so long as they do not reflect adversely on his impartiality or interfere with fulfillment of his judicial duties. A judge may serve as an officer, director, trustee, or advisor of a nonprofit organization— educational, religious, charitable, fraternal, or civic—subject to the following limitations:*
>
> *(a) He should not serve if it is likely that the organization will be substantially engaged in proceedings in his court;*
>
> *(b) He should not serve if doing so will divert substantial time from his judicial duties;*
>
> *(c) He should not engage in raising or investing funds, except that he may endorse efforts to obtain funds for an organization devoted to the improvement of the law or the administration of justice.*

c. Partisan Politics.   There is only one possible justification for any judge's involvement in partisan politics. The sad fact is that most judges are still elected and so must participate in the political process at least to the extent necessary to gain and retain office. Appointive judges, including all the federal judiciary, are fortunately separated from the political process upon confirmation and should thereafter have nothing to do with partisan politics, whether by holding party office, participating in election campaigns, endorsing candidates, or soliciting funds. For judges who must seek partisan endorsement and political support, including financial, the problem is more difficult. It is not always easy for a judge to remain aloof from politics because his own position is involved. Nevertheless, in the public interest the prohibition should be as nearly total as possible. When an effective rule against political involvement is stated and enforced, judges should be relieved of many pressures that they must now endure.

The Traynor Committee states the principle with admirable succinctness in paragraph 8.

> [*A judge*] *should not engage in political activity except to the extent necessarily involved in obtaining or retaining judicial office through an elective political process. A judge may represent his country, state or locality on ceremonial occasions and in connection with educational and cultural exchanges.*

Illinois Rule 70 is more explicit.

> *A judge shall not (a) hold any official position or office in a political party, shall not serve on any party committee or act as a party leader, and shall not take part in political campaigns except when he is a candidate for elective judicial office; (b) become a candidate for a federal, state or local non-judicial elective office without first resigning his judgeship. A candidate for a judgeship shall not personally solicit or receive campaign contributions, but should establish some method which will not involve him in the direct solicitation of funds.*

d. Public Service.   It has been common in the past for judges to accept appointment to commissions, boards, and other public service positions. The practice has been particularly tenacious at the Supreme Court level where Presidents have frequently drawn upon the prestige of membership on the Court to accomplish some difficult assignment or, more cynically, for personal political advantage. The Appendix shows how common the practice has been at the Supreme Court level, from the occasions on which President Washington sent Chief Justice Jay abroad to negotiate with foreign nations to the instance of President Johnson's insistence that Chief Justice Warren preside at the investigation into the assassination of President Kennedy. These episodes and many others diminished the prestige of the Court; and the result could scarcely have been otherwise. Whenever issues that are highly visible and sensitive are entrusted to a public commission for resolution or recommendation, the results are unlikely to satisfy all the critics, perhaps none. Participation in such a process by members of the judiciary is less likely to settle a troublesome public issue than to lend credence to the all-too-common charge that the courts are part of the political process. The charge becomes hard to deny when five members of the Supreme Court of the United States sit as members of an electoral commission, and each vote is consistent with the advantage of his own party, as happened in 1877 in the Hayes-Tilden dispute.

Even apart from the possible charge of political involvement, if the nonjudicial assignment is important, it requires time and energy, necessarily involving some interference with performance of official duty. Justice Jackson's year-and-a-half absence from the Court when he was the principal prosecutor at Nuremberg was an embarrassment to the Court. Chief Justice Warren's solution in connection with the investigation of the Kennedy assassination was scarcely better when he sought to perform two crucial tasks concurrently. That Warren succeeded as well as he did is a testimonial to his capacity, not to the merit of the idea.

The state codes do not seem to deal directly with the point. The Traynor Committee is also not explicit, although the sense of the recommendations appears to be against such service.

It should follow inevitably from what has been said above that private counseling or advice to members of the executive or legislative branches should not be tolerated, whether under the guise of a friendship continued from the past or under the harsher rubric of "cronyism."

e. Personal and Social Relationships.   Apart from bland advice that a judge is entitled to retain pre-court friendships, what can be said that is helpful? Probably not much, but the Traynor Committee in paragraph 5 puts it gracefully, with a minimum of embarrassed posturing, as follows:

> *A judge should not allow his social relations or friendships to influence, or appear to influence, his judicial conduct. He should not knowingly permit others to trade on the impression that they have special influence with him. He should not testify as a character witness unless he is convinced that his testimony is essential to a just result.*

CONCLUSION

Chief Justice Roger Traynor, speaking to the Second Circuit Judicial Conference in September 1970, said that the ABA Committee on Standards of Judicial Conduct does not aspire to rewrite the Ten Commandments, to annotate the seven deadly sins, or to prescribe a legislative code to forbid judges from hijacking planes, trains, buses, or other means of transportation in interstate commerce. More prosaically, efforts to define standards of judicial conduct should not even be regarded as attempts to legislate morality. The problem is not one of coercing recalcitrant judges with the whip of threatened sanctions. The objective of improved standards is rather to provide guidance for judges who wish to conform to standards that will enlarge public confidence in the judicial process. Judge Irving Kaufman hit the right note, also speaking at the Second Circuit Judicial Conference, when he suggested that a code of judicial conduct asks judges to submit "to ethical dialogues rather than to penal directives."

The definition of appropriate standards of judicial conduct is only part of the task of restoring public confidence in the judicial system. The selection of judges must be removed from politics; judicial pay scales must be made adequate; and delay in the courts must be reduced. While those problems are being overcome, it is important at the same time to advise judges what conduct is expected of them. Some standards will be cast in terms of proscription, even providing sanctions for abuse; but most should be in the form of guidelines to inform the conscience of the judge who wishes to conform his conduct in every respect to the appearance as well as the reality of impartial service to the cause of justice.

NOTES: THE JUDICIARY

Introduction

1. Quoted in Arthur Selwyn Miller, "Public Confidence in the Judiciary: Some Notes and Reflections," *Law and Contemporary Problems,* 35 (Winter, 1970), 69.

2. The American Judicature Society is an exception to this absence of crusades for judicial reform. It has concentrated on this task for the past sixty years, too often, however, failing to gain sufficient support for change.

3. For another example of proposals for reforming the judicial machinery see Judge Griffin B. Bell, "Toward a More Efficient Appeals System," *Judicature,* 54 (January, 1971), 237-244.

4. For other "plea copping" studies see Abraham Blumberg, *Criminal Justice* (Quadrangle, 1967) and Donald J. Newman, "Pleading Guilty for Considerations: A Study of Bargain Justice," *Journal of Criminal Law, Criminology and Police Science,* 46 (1956), 780-790.

5. *Griffin v. Illinois,* 76 S. Ct. 585 (1956).

6. *Gideon v. Wainwright,* 83 S. Ct. 792 (1963).

7. *Tate v. Short,* 91 S. Ct. 668 (1971).

8. *Boddie v. Connecticut,* 91 S. Ct. 780 (1971).

9. See, for example, "Non-Judicial Activities of Justices of the Supreme Court: A Selective Summary," *Law and Contemporary Problems,* 35 (Winter, 1970), 27-36.

10. For a good treatment of Taft's activities on the Court see Walter F. Murphy, *Elements of Judicial Strategy* (University of Chicago Press, 1964).

11. Joseph Borkin, *The Corrupt Judge* (Clarkson N. Potter, 1962).

Jerome E. Carlin, Jan Howard, and Sheldon L. Messinger

1. J. Fossum, "Rent Withholding," 53 *California Law Review* 314 (1965).

2. J. Levi, *The Legal Needs of the Poor: Problems Relating to Real*

Property, paper read at the National Conference on Law and Poverty, Washington, D. C., June 23-25, 1965.

3. R. Cloward & R. Elman, "Poverty, Injustice and the Welfare State: How Rights Can Be Secured," 202 *The Nation* 264 (March 7, 1966).

4. G. Brunn, *Legal Aspects of the Rights of Creditors and Debtors,* p. 8; paper presented at a Seminar on Research Needs in Consumer Economics, Sept. 11, 1964, Univ. of Calif., Berkeley.

5. See C. Neal, *The Known and Unknown in Consumer Credit,* p. 8, *ibid.*

6. See *Id.* at 9.

7. E. Ehrlich, *Fundamental Principles of the Sociology of Law* 238 (1936).

8. H. O'Gorman, *Lawyers and Matrimonial Cases: A Study of Informal Pressures in Private Professional Practice* 11-13 (1963) at 22-23.

9. See C. Reich, "Individual Rights and Social Welfare: The Emerging Legal Issues," 74 *Yale Law Journal* 1256 (1965).

10. J. Carlin and J. Howard, "Legal Representation and Class Justice," 12 *U.C.L.A. Law Review* 415 (1965).

11. P. Wald, *Law and Poverty 1965* 27-28 (1965).

12. E. Cahn and J. Cahn, "The War on Poverty: A Civilian Perspective," 73 *Yale Law Journal* 1317 (1964).

13. *Id.* at 1341.

14. "Report of the A.B.A. Joint Conference on Professional Responsibility," 44 *A.B.A. Journal* 1159, 1160-61 (1958).

15. *Id.* at 1161.

16. E. Cahn & J. Cahn, *supra* note 12, at 1339.

17. Canon 27 of the Canons of Professional Ethics of the American Bar Association. See H. Drinker, *Legal Ethics* 316-17 (1954).

18. Canon 28. *Id.* at 319.

19. T. Voorhees, *Legal Aid—Current Needs and New Directions* 6, paper delivered at the National Conference on Law and Poverty, Washington, D.C., June 24, 1965.

20. G. Almond and S. Verba, *The Civic Culture* (1965), p. 168.

Robert B. McKay

1. American Judicature Society, Report No. 8 (June 1969).

2. *The New York Times,* May 21, 1969, at 1, col. 4.

3. Letter from Roger J. Traynor to Chief Justice Warren E. Burger, Oct. 27, 1969, quoted in Ainsworth, "Judicial Ethics—The Federal Judiciary Seeks Modern Standards of Conduct," 45 *Notre Dame Law,* 470 (1970) at 475.

THE BUREAUCRACY

*We see indecisive politicians posing as resolute statesmen
and the "authoritative source" who blames his misinformation on
"situational imponderables." Limitless are the public servants
who are indolent and insolent; . . . and governors whose
innate servility prevents their actually governing.*

—Laurence J. Peter and Raymond Hull[1]

The subject of the federal bureaucracy is not one which the average student of American politics approaches with particular relish. Such an attitude is indeed understandable. The administration of the national government appears devoid of any romantic qualities. It does not operate in the politically charged atmosphere of Congress, wield the awesome power of the presidency, or benefit from the majesty of the courts.

Yet the bureaucracy is important, if for no other reason than the cold fact that its activities affect the daily lives of Americans more than any other governmental institution. The pervasive quality of bureaucratic impact is easily demonstrated. We drive automobiles meeting federal safety requirements on federally administered highway systems. We are transported by federally inspected air, bus, and rail transportation, which operate on federally approved routes, for which we pay federally established fares. We eat foods grown under federal subsidy programs, processed under federal inspection, and packaged and advertised according to federal policies. We listen to the federal weather reports on federally regulated radio and television. We communicate on federally controlled telephone systems and pay rates partially set by the federal government. The federal postal system delivers our federal tax returns, social security checks, and induction notices. We attend federally aided educational institutions, often benefited by federally administered scholarship programs. When ill, we may be admitted to federally supported hospitals and take federally approved drugs. The ways in which the bureaucracy touches our lives constitute an almost endless list.

Because of the major influence which the bureaucracy has over our lives the question of its responsiveness has often been raised.[2] Theoretically the bureaucracy responds to the will of the people only indirectly. The administrative agencies are designed to carry out in a somewhat neutral manner the policies of the popularly elected Congress at the direction of the elected President who serves as chief administrator. There is no established direct line of communications between the people and the administrators.

Historically, reforming the bureaucracy has taken as its principal goal the removal of partisan politics from administrative behavior. Such modifications in the administrative process were desperately needed due to the excesses of the "spoils system" originally initiated during the tenure of President Andrew Jackson. Under Jackson's "common man" philosophy, government employment became a reward for political support. The bureaucracy was filled with partisans with no regard for individual competence. Administrators became responsive primarily to the will of their political parties. To cope with this situation Congress approved the Civil Service Act in 1883. The goal of this program was to select bureaucrats on the basis of quality rather than partisanship. Today over 90 percent of federal employees are covered by merit system regulations. An additional measure, the Hatch Acts, prohibited certain federal employees from participating in the affairs of political parties.

As successful as these reforms may have been they leave untouched several problems plaguing the administrative arm of the national government. The bureaucracy is a multi-billion dollar conglomerate, employing almost three million civilians (many of them highly trained professionals) working in thousands of departments, agencies, bureaus, and offices. Countless decisions are reached each day at all levels of the administration, very few of which are brought to the attention of the public. The bureaucratic machine is hounded by complexity and impersonality. Inefficiency is evident. In order to reduce this problem of inefficiency, various proposals have been submitted calling for restructuring the bureaucracy. Most of these, including President Richard Nixon's 1971 governmental reorganization plan, amount to little more than redrawing organization charts. Without more fundamental change increased responsiveness to public needs will not occur. Peter F. Drucker's essay, "The Sickness of Government," explores the major problems currently confronting the bureaucracy. He discusses the impotence of governmental action in both domestic and foreign policy areas, the obstructive influence of bureaucratic norms, and finally suggests changes to make the administrative branch of government more effective.

However, to have a bureaucracy which responds to the legitimate needs of the public more than mere efficiency is necessary. Some form of institutional communications between the people and the administrators is required. Because of their own failures to achieve responsiveness, Congress and the President often do not supply the theoretical citizen-bureaucrat linkage. Yet the bureaucracy itself does not appear eager to establish a working relationship with the populace. The "credibility gap" so frequently discussed in recent years describes well the attitude of the average citizen that governmental officials are unwilling to disclose fully details about their activities. Anthony Lake's "Lying around Washington," which appears below, provides interesting insights into the problem of credibility in United States foreign policy. Unless administrators begin engaging in honest communications with the voters it will be most difficult to achieve any semblance of bureaucratic responsiveness.

Given the lack of citizen input into the bureaucratic process, the question of to what or to whom do the administrative departments currently respond naturally arises. To a certain extent the bureaucracy must conform to the will of Congress and the President. On Congress all administrative agencies must depend for program authorization and for all important appropriations. No head of any agency can risk the possibility of legislative reprisals for wandering too far afield from congressional wishes. The President, of course, holds the power to direct the various executive departments within the limits set by Congress. Over certain departments, those concerned with national defense and foreign policy, the chief executive exercises particular control. Yet it is the exception rather than the rule for the President or Congress to ride roughshod over an administrative agency. The vast majority of actions taken by the bureaucracy are not strictly monitored, and agency personnel are normally given wide discretion.

Often, however, the bureaucracy seems to respond to considerations of self-interest. Frequently this self-interest is personal in nature. This perhaps is what Murray Edelman had in mind when he noted that "In their obsession with the state, men are of course obsessed with themselves."[3] Few administrators, if any, will acknowledge that their offices are no longer functional or necessary. Rare is the bureaucrat who will voluntarily support the notion that his agency be merged into another for reasons of efficiency. Bureaucratic agencies thus tend to pursue self-perpetuation, to seek new work when tasks originally assigned them are completed. Ad hoc agencies tend to become permanent ones. Budget requests are always for increases. Often bureau heads will control their agencies as if they were lords over feudal fiefdoms and establish powerful positions unassailed by presidents or congressmen. The long tenures of General Lewis B. Hershey, former head of the Selective Service System, and J. Edgar Hoover of the Federal Bureau of Investigation have been severely criticized on just this account.

Self-interest also commonly takes the form of promoting pet concerns. The heads of agencies become advocates for their own programs or programs sponsored by client pressure groups (see Part Two). Cabinet officials are placed in a situation of competing with other department heads for presidential and congressional favor.[4] Disputes arise over program priorities. Which should have preference, for example—a request of the Department of Defense for a new missile system, or HUD's proposed housing program? While on the surface inter-agency competition may not appear dysfunctional it often becomes so. Such administrative lobbying may occur in the form of wasteful and sometimes illegal public relations campaigns. More important, the agency which prevails in inter-agency competition may do so in ways detrimental to the public interest. An interesting example of such public-relations campaigns was the subject of the controversial 1971 CBS documentary, "The Selling of the Pentagon," which exposed the huge sums of public funds expended by the military for the sole purpose of promoting its own programs and image.[5] In their essay on "Statutory Restraints on Administrative Lobbying: 'Legal Fiction'" Richard L. Engstrom and Thomas G. Walker analyze the subject of bureaucratic self-interest expressed in the form of attempted influence over Congress. An interesting aspect of this problem is that such bureaucratic self-promotion openly occurs in the face of federal law prohibiting it.

The final selection which appears in this section on the bureaucracy, Louis M. Kohlmeier's "A Proposal for Reform," concerns itself with the regulatory agencies of the federal government. These deserve special mention because of their importance in the regulation of commerce and consumer affairs and because of their special status as being independent of the executive branch hierarchy. These agencies control such important areas as use of atomic energy, transportation systems, communications, monetary policy, labor relations, unfair trade practices, and securities transactions. Most were created after events indicated the inability of industries to regulate themselves. The Securities and Exchange Commission, for instance, was created in 1934 following the stock market crash. Yet the regulatory agencies are not always as effective as they might be. Too often they are captured by interest groups representing the very concerns the agencies were designed to regulate. Kohlmeier's essay is a proposal to modify these important agencies and to make them more responsive to public needs.

THE SICKNESS OF GOVERNMENT

Peter F. Drucker

Government surely has never been more prominent than today. The most despotic government of 1900 would not have dared probe into the private affairs of its citizens as income tax collectors now do routinely in the freest society. Even the tsar's secret police did not go in for the security investigations we now take for granted. Nor could any bureaucrat of 1900 have imagined the questionnaires that governments now expect businesses, universities, or citizens to fill out in ever-mounting number and ever-increasing detail. At the same time, government has everywhere become the largest employer in the society.

Government is certainly all-pervasive. But is it truly strong? Or is it only big?

There is mounting evidence that government is big rather than strong; that it is fat and flabby rather than powerful; that it costs a great deal but does not achieve much. There is mounting evidence also that the citizen less and less believes in government and is increasingly disenchanted with it. Indeed, government is sick—and just at the time when we need a strong, healthy, and vigorous government.

There is obviously little respect for government among the young— but the adults, the taxpayers, are also increasingly disenchanted. They want still more services from government. But they are everywhere approaching the point where they balk at paying for a bigger government, even though they may still want what government promises to give.

The disenchantment with government cuts across national boundaries and ideological lines. It is as prevalent in Communist as in democratic societies, as common in white as in nonwhite countries. This disenchantment may well be the most profound discontinuity in the world around us. It marks a sharp change in mood and attitude between this generation and its predecessors. For seventy years or so—from the 1890's to the 1960's— mankind, especially in the developed countries, was hypnotized by government. We were in love with it and saw no limits to its abilities, or to its good intentions. Rarely has there been a more torrid political love affair than that between government and the generations that reached manhood between 1918 and 1960. Anything that anyone felt needed doing during this period was to be turned over to government—and this, everyone seemed to believe, made sure that the job was already done.

The Fabians in Great Britain or the German Social Democrats started their love affair with government before 1900. It became general with World War I when government, using taxation and the printing press, had mobilized social resources way beyond what anyone earlier would have thought possible. When the Great Depression hit, a decade later, everyone immediately turned to government as the savior. It is pathetic to recall the naïve belief that prevailed in the late 1930's—such, for instance, as was preached in one of the best-sellers of the depression years, *To Plan or Not to Plan,* by the British Labour economist Barbara Wooton. The book's author, honored by the British government with a life peerage as Lady Wooton, is still alive and active; but nothing is more remote from us today, or less appealing, than the messianic innocence of this fervent love letter to government. All it says, and it says it on every page, is: "Utopia is here—all that's needed is to take everything away from the wicked, selfish interests and to turn it over to government." World War II reinforced this belief. Again, government proved itself incredibly effective in organizing the energies of society for warfare.

DISENCHANTMENT

But now our attitudes are in transition. We are rapidly moving to doubt and distrust of government and, in the case of the young, even to rebellion against it. We still, if only out of habit, turn social tasks over to government. We still revise unsuccessful programs over and over again, and assert that nothing is wrong with them that a change in procedures or a "competent administrator" will not cure. But we no longer really believe these promises when we reform a bungled program for the third time. Who, for instance, any longer believes that administrative changes in the foreign aid program of the United States (or of the United Nations) will really produce rapid world-wide development? Who really believes that the War on Poverty will vanquish poverty in the cities? Who in France believes that one more commission on administrative reform will really change the system? Or who, in Russia, really believes that a new program of incentives will make the collective farm productive?

We still repeat the slogans of yesteryear. Indeed, we still act on them. But we no longer believe in them. We no longer expect results from government. What was torrid romance between the people and government for so very long has now become a tired, middle-aged liaison which we do not quite know how to break off but which only becomes exacerbated by being dragged out.

What explains this disenchantment with government?

We expected miracles—and that always produces disillusionment. Government, it was widely believed (though only subconsciously) would produce a great many things for nothing. Cost was thought to be a function of who did something rather than of what was being attempted. There is little doubt, for instance, that the British, in adopting the "free health service," believed that medical care would cost nothing. All that such a health service can be, of course, is a form of "pre-paid" medical care.

Nurses, doctors, hospitals, drugs, and so on have to be paid for by somebody. But everybody expected this "somebody" to be somebody else. At the least, everyone expected that under a "free" health service the taxes of the rich would pay for the health care of the poor. But there never are enough rich people around to carry the burden of any general service.

All such plans are, in effect, taxation and compulsory saving that force the individual to pay for something whether he wants it or not. This is their whole rationale, and it is not necessarily a bad rationale. But the illusion persisted that government could somehow make costs go away and produce a great deal for nothing—or at the expense of only an affluent minority.

ABOLISHING "VESTED INTERESTS"

This belief has been, in effect, only one facet of a much more general illusion from which the educated and the intellectuals in particular have suffered: that by turning tasks over to government, conflict and decision would be made to go away. Once the "wicked private interests" had been eliminated, a decision as to the right course of action would be rational and automatic. There would be neither selfishness nor political passion. Belief in government was thus largely a romantic escape from politics and from responsibility.

One root of this argument was a hatred of business, of profit, and, above all, of wealth. That motives other than the desire for monetary gain could underlie self-interests and that values other than financial values could underlie conflict did not occur to the generation of the 1930's. Theirs was a world in which economics seemed to be the one obstacle to the millennium. Power did not appear in their vision—though this blindness in the decade of Hitler and Stalin is hard to imagine, let alone to understand. C. P. Snow's description in *The Masters* (1951) of the conflict for power within the "self-less" and "disinterested" small community of an Oxbridge college profoundly shocked the sensibilities of a generation that had grown up believing that conflicts were always motivated by economic self-interest and could be avoided by eliminating gain, that is, by nationalizing the economy.

One need not be in favor of free enterprise—let alone a friend of wealth—to see the fallacy in this argument. But reason had little to do with the belief in government ownership as the panacea. The argument was simply: "private business and profits are bad—*ergo* government ownership must be good." We may still believe in the premise; but we no longer accept the *"ergo."* Thus, the Labour government felt committed in 1967 to renationalize the British steel industry (just at the time when, ironically, the industry was on the verge of long-term decline, and when, therefore, take-over by government meant the highest possible windfall profit for the shareholders). But it immediately declared that the industry would have to be run for profit. It put in as chief executive the purest of arch-capitalists, Lord Melchett, heir to one of the world's greatest industrial fortunes (his grandfather and father founded and built Imperial Chemical Industries), a hereditary peer and a topflight investment banker, in addition to being a life-long Tory! By contrast, less than twenty years earlier, when steel was first nationalized in Britain by an earlier Labour government, an ideologically "pure" trade-union stalwart had been the chief-executive-designate.

There is still a good deal of resistance to the responsibility of politics, and resentment of the burden of political decision. Indeed, the young today want to "drop out" altogether—in a frightening revival of the hostility to responsibility that made an earlier young generation, forty years ago, so receptive to totalitarian promises and slogans. But no one, least of all the young, believes any longer that the conflicts, the decisions, the problems would be eliminated by turning things over to government. Government, on the contrary, has itself become one of the wicked "vested interests" for the young.

A CASE OF NONPERFORMANCE

The greatest factor in the disenchantment with government is that government has not performed. The record over these last thirty or forty years has been dismal. Government has proven itself capable of doing only two things with great effectiveness. It can wage war. And it can inflate the currency. Other things it can promise, but only rarely accomplish. Its record as an industrial manager, in the satellite countries of Eastern Europe as well as in the nationalized industries of Great Britain, has been unimpressive. Whether private enterprise would have done worse is not even relevant. For we expected near-perfection from government as industrial manager. Instead we only rarely obtained even below-average mediocrity.

Government as a planner has hardly done much better (whether in Communist Czechoslovakia or in de Gaulle's capitalist France). But the greatest disappointment, the great letdown, is the fiasco of the welfare state. Not many people would want to do without the social services and welfare benefits of an affluent, modern, industrial society. But the welfare state promised to do far more than to provide social services. It promised to create a new and happy society. It promised to release creative energies. It promised to do away with ugliness and envy and strife. No matter how well it is doing its jobs—and in some areas, in some countries, some jobs are being done very well—the welfare state turns out at best to be just another big insurance company, as exciting, as creative, and as inspiring as insurance companies tend to be. This explains why President Johnson's spectacular performance in enacting the unfinished welfare tasks of the New Deal failed to make him a hero with the public.

The best we get from government in the welfare state is competent mediocrity. More often we do not even get that; we get incompetence such as we would not tolerate in an insurance company. In every country, there are big areas of government administration where there is no performance whatever—only costs. This is true not only of the mess of the big cities, which no government—United States, British, Japanese, or Russian—has been able to handle. It is true in education. It is true in transportation. And the more we expand the welfare state, the less capable even of routine mediocrity does it seem to become.

I do not know whether Americans are particularly inept at public administration—though they are hardly particularly gifted for it. Perhaps, we are only more sensitive than other people to incompetence and arrogance of bureaucracy because we have had, until recently, comparatively so much less of it than other people. In any case, we are now appalled to realize that, during the past three decades, federal payments to the big cities have increased almost a hundred-fold for all kinds of programs, whereas results from this incredible dollar-flood are singularly unimpressive. What *is* impressive is the administrative incompetence. We now have ten times as many government agencies concerned with city problems as we had in 1939. We have increased by a factor of a thousand or so the number of reports and papers that have to be filled out before anything can be done in the city. Social workers in New York City spend some 70 or 80 per cent of their time filling out papers for Washington, for the state government in Albany, and for New York City. No more than 20 or 30 per cent of their time, that is, almost an hour and a half a day, is available for their clients, the poor. As James Reston reported in *The New York Times* (November 23, 1966), there were then 170 different federal aid programs on the books, financed by over 400 separate appropriations and administered by 21 federal departments and agencies aided by 150 Washington bureaus and over 400 regional offices. One Congressional session alone passed 20 health programs, 17 new educational programs, 15 new economic development programs, 12 new programs for the cities, 17 new resources development programs, and 4 new manpower training programs, each with its own administrative machinery.

This is not perhaps a fair example—even of American administrative incompetence. That we speak of "urban crisis," when we face a problem of race, explains a lot of our troubles. But in other areas, the welfare state has not performed much better. Nor is the administrative mess a peculiarly American phenomenon. The daily press in Great Britain, in Germany, in Japan, in France, in Scandinavia—and increasingly in the Communist countries as well—reports the same confusion, the same lack of performance, the same proliferation of agencies, of programs, of forms—and the same triumph of accounting rules over results. Everywhere, rivalry between various agencies is replacing concern with results and with responsibility.

POWER WITHOUT POLICY

Modern government has become ungovernable. There is no government today that can still claim control of its bureaucracy and of its various agencies. Government agencies are all becoming autonomous, ends in themselves, and directed by their own desire for power, their own narrow vision rather than by national policy.

This is a threat to the basic capacity of government to give direction and leadership. Increasingly, policy is fragmented, and execution is governed by the inertia of the large bureaucratic empires, rather than by policy. Bureaucrats keep on doing what their procedures describe. Their tendency, as is only human, is to identify what is in the best interest of the agency with what is right, and what fits administrative convenience with effectiveness. As a result the Welfare State cannot set priorities. It cannot concentrate its tremendous resources—and therefore does not get anything done.

The President of the United States may still be the most powerful ruler—more powerful than either the prime ministers of parliamentary regimes dependent upon a majority in parliament, or the dictators who can be overthrown by conspiracies against them among the powerful factions within their totalitarian apparatus. And yet even the President of the United States cannot direct national policy any more. The various bureaucracies do much what they want to do. The Anti-Trust Division of the Department of Justice, for instance, has been making its own policies and pursuing its own course these last twenty years, with little concern for what the incumbent President believes or orders. The Soil Conservation Service and the Bureau of Reclamation, the Forestry Service and the Weather Bureau, the Federal Trade Commission and the Army Engineers have similarly become "independent" rather than "autonomous."

Not so long ago, policy control by the political organs of government could be taken for granted. Of course there were "strong" and "weak" presidents as there were "strong" and "weak" prime ministers. A Franklin Roosevelt or a Winston Churchill could get things done that weaker men could not have accomplished. But this was, people generally believed, because they had the courage of strong convictions, the willingness to lay down bold and effective policies, the ability to mobilize public vision. Today, a "strong" president or a "strong" prime minister is not a man of strong policies; he is the man who knows how to make the lions of the bureaucracy do his bidding. John Kennedy had all the strength of conviction and all the boldness of a "strong" president; this is why he captured the imagination, especially of the young. He had, however, no impact whatever on the bureaucracy. He was a "strong" president in the traditional sense. But he was a singularly ineffectual one. His contemporary, Mr. Khrushchev in Russia, similarly failed to be effective despite his apparent boldness and his popular appeal. By contrast, bureaucratic men who had no policies and no leadership qualities emerge as effective—they somehow know how to make red tape do their bidding. But then, of course, they use it for the one thing red tape is good for, i.e., bundling up yesterday in neat packages.

This growing disparity between apparent power and actual lack of control is perhaps the greatest crisis of government. We are very good at creating administrative agencies. But no sooner are they called into being than they become ends in themselves, acquire their own constituency as well as a "vested right" to grants from the treasury, continuing support by the taxpayer, and immunity to political direction. No sooner, in other words, are they born than they defy public will and public policy.

INTERNATIONAL IMPOTENCE

The crisis of government domestically is nothing compared to the crisis of government as an effective organ in international life. In the international arena, government has all but disintegrated. The "sovereign state" no longer functions as the effective organ for political tasks. This is not happening, as the liberals had always hoped, because a political world community has transcended the narrow, petty boundaries of national states. On the contrary, the national state is everywhere in danger of collapsing into petty, parochial baronies—whether French Canada or an independent Flanders, Biafra in West Africa or self-governing Scotland.

To our grandparents, around 1900, it was clear that the trend ran toward larger government units. It was clear to them that the national state created political organisms capable of effective cooperation in international society. This had been the lesson of nineteenth-century history. Indeed the century closed with the last "unification," though an imposed one: the taking over of the Boer Republics of South Africa by the British and their incorporation into the British Empire.

Since then, the process has been one of steady fission. It began in the Balkan wars, which, undertaken to create larger unified countries, ended by creating more small ones. It has accelerated ever since. Even Czechoslovakia, the most successful of the new countries created in World War I, proved incapable of becoming the effective agent of unification but was torn apart by the strife of the national minorities—German, Hungarian, and Slovak—that refused to be "unified."

Not one of the new countries established since World War II has so far created the unified nation that, to the nineteenth century, was so obviously the end point of history. Instead we are getting tribal splinters, pretending to be national states, imposing on their citizens all the costs of a national state, driven by all the jealousies, resentments, and pride of a national state—but incapable of being an effective organ either of domestic government or of the international community. Increasingly, we are fragmenting the world into governmental pygmies, each endowed with tremendous power vis-à-vis its citizens, each perfectly capable of tyranny, but incapable of governing.

In 1900 there were fewer than fifty sovereignties in the whole world —twenty in Europe and twenty in the Americas, with the rest of the world having fewer than a dozen. World War I increased the number to about sixty. Now we have more than 160, with new "mini-states" joining the ranks almost every month. Only on the American continents has there been no splintering of sovereignties. There are twenty-odd sovereignties of 1900 still, by and large, the political reality of today (except in the rapidly fragmenting Caribbean area). Some of the new sovereignties are very large countries: India, Pakistan, Indonesia. But most of them are smaller than the Central-American countries an earlier generation contemptuously dismissed as "banana republics," and much too small to discharge the minimum responsibilities of sovereignty. Today we have scores of "independent nations" whose population is well below a million people. Indeed we have some whose population is hardly as large as a good-sized village.

At the other end of the scale, we have the "super-powers" whose very size and power debar them from having a national policy. They are concerned with everything, engaged everywhere, affected by every single political event no matter how remote or petty. But policy is choice and selection. If one cannot choose not to be engaged, one cannot have a policy—and neither the United States nor Russia can, in effect, say: "we are not interested." The "super-powers" are the international version of the welfare state—and, like the welfare state, incapable of priorities or of accomplishments. The super-powers, therefore, invariably over-react—as Russia has done in the satellite countries and as the United States has done in the Congo, in Santo Domingo, and perhaps in Vietnam. Yet they under-achieve. Their might, although great enough to annihilate each other— and the rest of us into the bargain—is inappropriate to the political task.

This means that decisions in the international sphere can no longer be made in an orderly and systematic fashion. It is no longer possible for any decision to be arrived at by negotiation, consultation, agreement. It can only be arrived at by dictation or by exhaustion. Although force has, therefore, become infinitely more important in the international system, it has become infinitely less decisive—unless it be the ultimate force of a nuclear war that might destroy mankind.

Decisions are also no longer effective. No longer can they be expected to be carried out. In the international sphere, we have the same divorce of policy from execution that characterizes domestic government.

We get more and more governments. But all this does is to increase costs. For each of these sovereignties has to have its own foreign service, its own armed forces, and so on. And no government, whether its territory spans the continents or is smaller than one city block, can any longer discharge the first duty of government: protection from, and defense against, attack from outside. It is perfectly true that most of the new "mini-states" are political absurdities, defenseless against the threat of instant annihilation. But so are the "super-powers" in this age of nuclear "over-kill." With nuclear weapons being easy to make and, in effect, available to the smallest and weakest country, there is no "defense." There is only—questionably—"deterrence" by the threat of retaliation. But if government cannot defend its people, the first reason for the very existence of government has gone.

This may be regarded as gross exaggeration. It certainly is not the picture the older generation still sees. But it is, increasingly, the reality. It is the situation to which we react. And the young people who are not, as we older ones are, influenced by the memories of our love affair with government, see the monstrosity of governments, its disorganization, its lack of performance, and its impotence rather than the illusions the older generation still cherishes and still teaches in the classroom.

WHAT GOVERNMENT CANNOT DO

Yet never before has strong, effective, truly performing government been needed more than it is in this dangerous world of ours. Never before has it been needed more than in our pluralist society. Never before has it been needed more than in the present-day world economy.

We need government as the central institution that expresses the common will and the common vision, and enables each organization to make its own best contribution to society and citizen while expressing common beliefs and common values. We need strong, effective governments in the international sphere so that we can make the sacrifices of sovereignty needed to give us working supra-national institutions for world society and world economy. We cannot wait until we have new political theory or until we fully understand this pluralist society of ours. We will not recreate the beautiful "Prince Charming" of government, or the all-wise economist-king of Barbara Wooton's *To Plan or Not to Plan*. But we should be able to come up with a competent, middle-aged professional who does his work from nine to five and does it well—and who, at least, is respected as a "good provider," though the romance has long gone out of him. In the process, government may shed the megalomania that now obsesses it and learn how to confine itself to realistic goals.

Certain things are inherently difficult for government. Being by design a protective institution, it is not good at innovation. It cannot really abandon anything. The moment government undertakes anything, it becomes entrenched and permanent. Better administration will not alter this. Its inability to innovate is grounded in government's legitimate and necessary function as society's protective and conserving organ.

A government activity, a government installation, and government employment become immediately built into the political process itself. This holds true whether we talk of a declining industry—such as the nationalized British coal mines or the government-owned railroads of Europe and Japan. It holds equally true in Communist countries. No matter how bankrupt, for instance, the Stalinist economic policies have become in Czechoslovakia, Hungary, or Poland, any attempt to change them immediately runs into concern for the least productive industries, which, of course, always have the most, the lowest-paid and the least-skilled—and, therefore, the most "deserving"—workers.

The inability of government to abandon anything is not limited to the economic sphere. We have known for well over a decade, for instance, that the military draft that served the United States well in a total war is immoral and demoralizing in a "cold war" or "limited war" period. No one defends our present system—yet we extend it year after year on a "temporary" basis. The same inability to abandon applies to research projects supported by government. It holds true as soon as government supports the arts. Every beneficiary of a government program immediately becomes a "constituent." He immediately organizes himself for effective political action and for pressure on the decision-maker.

All institutions, of course, find it hard to abandon yesterday's tasks and to stop doing the unproductive. All of man's institutions—and for that matter, all men—are committed to what they are used to and reluctant to accept that it no longer needs doing or that it does not produce results. But government is under far greater pressure to cling to yesterday than any other institution. Indeed the typical response of government to the failure of an activity is to double its budget and staff.

WELFARE, FARMS, AND DEPRESSED AREAS

Nothing in history, for instance, can compare in futility with those prize activities of the American government, its welfare policies and its farm policies. Both policies are largely responsible for the disease they are supposed to cure. We have known this for quite some time—in the case of the farm program since before World War II, in the case of the welfare program certainly since 1950.

The problem of the urban poor is undoubtedly vast. No city in history has ever been able to absorb an influx of such magnitude as the American cities have had to absorb since the end of World War II.

Wherever it happened in the past, there was the same collapse of family, community, and local government—in the cities of England in the late eighteenth century when the Irish came in; in the cities of North America around 1840, again with the coming of the Irish; in the cities of continental Europe later on, as for instance when the Czechs started to migrate in large numbers into the Vienna of the Hapsburgs in the closing years of the nineteenth century. The influx of almost 2 million rural Negroes and Puerto Ricans into New York City alone, in less than a fifteen-year period, exceeded any of these earlier migrations. It is unprecedented in the history of cities.

But we certainly could not have done worse if we had done nothing at all. In fact, the nineteenth-century cities that did nothing, did better. And so, these last twenty years, has São Paulo in Brazil, which, inundated by similar floods of rural, illiterate Negroes, fresh from serfdom, did nothing—and is in better shape than New York City.

Our welfare policies were not designed to meet this problem. They were perfectly rational—and quite effective—as measures for the temporary relief of competent people who were unemployed only because of the catastrophe of the Great Depression. Enacted in the mid-1930's, the relief policies had essentially finished their job by 1940. But being government programs, they could not be abandoned. Far too massive a bureaucracy had been built. The emotional investment in these programs and in their slogan had become far too great. They had become "symbols" of the "New Deal."

Small wonder, then, that we reached for them when the entirely different problems of the 1950's arose, that is, when the rural Negro moved into the core city in large numbers. And small wonder that these programs did not work, that instead they aggravated the problem and increased the helplessness, the dependence, the despair of the Negro masses. But all we could do when relief failed to relieve was to double the budget and to double the number of people engaged in filling out forms.

The farm program tells the same story. It was designed—also in the 1930's—to save the family farmer and to restore his economic and social health. Instead it has subsidized his replacement by large, heavily capitalized and highly productive "industrial farms." This may well be a more desirable result than the one the farm program was meant—and is still meant—to produce. But it was abysmal failure in terms of the program's announced objectives. Yet the program goes on, with an increased budget, and increasingly perverse consequences.

Lest this be read as a criticism of the American government, let me add that this experience knows no distinction of race, creed, or nationality. The depressed-areas policy in Great Britain dates back to the 1920's. In all that time it has not restored to economic health one single "depressed area." But it has effectively penalized the shift of labor to areas of higher productivity, higher wages, and better jobs. It thereby has slowed growth in the healthy regions. Yet whenever it is realized that the "depressed areas" are still depressed, the budget goes up.

GOVERNMENT AND MISMANAGEMENT

Government is a poor manager. It is, of necessity, concerned with procedure, just as it is also, of necessity, large and cumbersome. Government is properly conscious that it administers public funds and must account for every penny. It has no choice but to be "bureaucratic"—in the common usage of the term. Every government is, by definition, a "government of paper forms." This means inevitably high cost. For "control" of the last 10 per cent of any phenomenon always costs more than control of the first 90 per cent. If control tries to account for everything, it becomes prohibitively expensive. Yet this is what government is always expected to do. And the reason is not just "bureaucracy" and red tape; it is a much sounder one. A "little dishonesty" in government is a corrosive disease. It rapidly spreads to infect the whole body politic. Yet the temptation to dishonesty is always great. People of modest means and dependent on a salary handle very large public sums. People of modest position dispose of power and award contracts and privileges of tremendous importance to other people—construction jobs, radio channels, air routes, zoning laws, building codes, and so on. To fear corruption in government is not irrational. This means, however, that government "bureaucracy"—and its consequent high costs—cannot be eliminated. Any government that is not a "government of paper forms" degenerates rapidly into a mutual looting society.

The generation that was in love with the state, thirty and forty years ago, believed fondly that government would be economical. Eliminating the "profit motive" was thought to reduce costs. This was poor economics, to begin with. It is worse public administration. The politician's attention does not go to the 90 per cent of money and effort that is devoted to existing programs and activities. They are left to their own devices and to the tender mercies of mediocrity. Politics—rightly—is primarily concerned with "new programs." It is focused on crisis and problems and issues. It is not focused on doing a job. Politics, whatever the form of government, is not congenial to managerial organization and makes government defective in managerial performance.

We have built elaborate safeguards to protect the administrative structure within government against the political process. This is the purpose of every civil service. But although this protects the going machinery from the distortions and pressures of politics, it also protects the incumbents in the agencies from the demands of performance. Of course, we maintain officially that civil-service tenure is compatible with excellence. But if we had to choose, we would probably say that mediocrity in the civil service is a lesser evil than "politics." As far as the judiciary is concerned—where we first created "independence"—this is certainly true. How far it is true in administrative agencies is debatable. A good many people have come to believe that we need some way of rewarding performance and of penalizing nonperformance, even within civil service.

Still, the premium within government will be on not "rocking the boat" in existing agencies, that is on no innovation, no initiative, but rather on doing with proper procedures what has been done before. Within the political process attention will certainly not be paid to the on-going routine work, unless there is the publicized malfunction of a "scandal." As a result, management of the daily work of government will remain neglected. Or be considered a matter of following "procedure" and of filling out forms. By excelling as a manager, no one in politics will ever get to the top, unless at the same time he builds his own political machine, his own political following, his own faction.

We can—and must—greatly improve the efficiency of government. There is little reason these days to insist on "10 per cent audit," for instance. Modern sampling methods based on probability mathematics actually give us better control by inspecting a small percentage of the events. But we need something much more urgently: the clear definition of the results a policy is expected to produce, and the ruthless examination of results against these expectations. This, in turn, demands that we spell out in considerable detail what results are expected rather than content ourselves with promises and manifestos. In the last century, the Auditor General became a central organ of every government. We learned that we needed an independent agency to control the daily process of government and to make sure that money appropriated was spent for what it was intended for, and spent honestly. Now we may have to develop an independent government agency that compares the results of policies against expectations and that, independent of pressures from the executive as well as from the legislature, reports to the public any program that does not deliver.

We may even go further—though only a gross optimist would expect this today. We may build into government an automatic abandonment process. Instead of starting with the assumption that any program, any agency, and any activity is likely to be eternal, we might start out with the opposite assumption: that each is short-lived and temporary. We might, from the beginning, assume that it will come to an end within five or ten years unless specifically renewed. And we may discipline ourselves not to renew any program unless it has the results that it promised when first started. We may, let us hope, eventually build into government the capacity to appraise results and systematically to abandon yesterday's tasks.

Yet such measures will still not convert government into a "doer." They will not alter the main lesson of the last fifty years: *government is not a "doer."*

WHAT GOVERNMENT CAN BE

The purpose of government is to make fundamental decisions, and to make them effectively. The purpose of government is to focus the political energies of society. It is to dramatize issues. It is to present fundamental choices. The purpose of government, in other words, is to govern. This, as we have learned in other institutions, is compatible with "doing." Any attempt to combine government with "doing" on a large scale paralyzes the decision-making capacity.

There is reason today why soldiers, civil servants, and hospital administrators look to business management for concepts, principles, and practices. For business, during the last thirty years, has had to face, on a much smaller scale, the problem that government now faces: the incompatibility between "governing" and "doing." Business management learned that the two have to be separated, and that the top organ, the decision-maker, has to be detached from "doing." Otherwise he does not make decisions, and the "doing" does not get done either.

In business this goes by the name of "decentralization." The term is misleading. It implies a weakening of the central organ, the top management of a business. The true purpose of decentralization, however, is to make the center, the top management of business, strong and capable of performing the central, the top-management task. The purpose is to make it possible for top management to concentrate on decision-making and direction, to slough off the "doing" to operating managements, each with its own mission and goals, and with its own sphere of action and autonomy.

If this lesson were applied to government, the other institutions of society would then rightly become the "doers." "Decentralization" applied to government would not be just another form of "federalism" in which local rather than central government discharges the "doing" tasks. It would rather be a systematic policy of using the other, *the nongovernmental* institutions of the society—the hospital as well as the university, business as well as labor unions—for the actual "doing," i.e., for performance, operations, execution.

Such a policy might more properly be called "reprivatization." The tasks that flowed to government in the last century, because the family could not discharge them, would be turned over to the new, nongovernmental institutions that have sprung up and grown these last sixty to seventy years.

REPRIVATIZATION

Government would start out by asking the question: "How do these institutions work and what can they do?" It would then ask: "How can political and social objectives be formulated and organized in such a manner as to become opportunities for performance for these institutions?" It would also ask: "And what opportunities for accomplishment of political objectives do the abilities and capacities of these institutions offer to government?"

This would be a very different role for government from that it plays in traditional political theory. In all our theories government is *the* institution. If "reprivatization" were to be applied, however, government would become *one* institution—albeit the central, the top, institution.

Reprivatization would give us a different society from any our *social* theories now assume. In these theories, government does not exist. It is outside of society. Under reprivatization, government would become the central social institution. Political theory and social theory, for the last two hundred and fifty years, have been separate. If we applied to government and to society what we have learned about organization these last fifty years, the two would again come together. The nongovernmental institutions—university, business, and hospital, for instance—would be seen as organs for the accomplishment of results. Government would be seen as society's resource for the determination of major objectives, and as the "conductor" of social diversity.

I have deliberately used the term "conductor." It might not be too fanciful to compare the situation today with the development of music 200 years ago. The dominant musical figure of the early eighteenth century was the great organ virtuoso, especially in the Protestant North. In organ music, as a Buxtehude or a Bach practiced it, one instrument with one performer expressed the total range of music. But as a result, it required almost superhuman virtuosity to be a musician.

By the end of the century, the organ virtuoso had disappeared. In his place was the modern orchestra. There, each instrument played only one part, and a conductor up front pulled together all these diverse and divergent instruments into one score and one performance. As a result, what had seemed to be absolute limits to music suddenly disappeared. Even the small orchestra of Haydn could express a musical range far beyond the reach of the greatest organ virtuoso of a generation earlier.

The conductor himself does not play an instrument. He need not even know how to play an instrument. His job is to know the capacity of each instrument and to evoke optimal performance from each. Instead of "performing," he "conducts." Instead of "doing," he leads.

The next major development in politics, and the one needed to make this middle-aged failure—our tired, overextended, flabby, and impotent government—effective again, might therefore be the reprivatization of the "doing," of the performance of society's tasks. This need not mean "return to private ownership." Indeed what is going on in the Communist satellite countries of Eastern Europe today—especially in Yugoslavia—is reprivatization in which ownership is not involved at all. Instead, autonomous businesses depend on the market for the sale of goods, the supply of labor, and even the supply of capital. That their "ownership" is in the hands of the government is a legal rather than an economic fact— though, of course, an important one. Yet to some Yugoslavs it does not even appear to be incompatible with that ultra-bourgeois institution, a stock exchange.

What matters, in other words, is that institutions not be run by government, but be autonomous. Cooperatives, for instance, are not considered "capitalist" in the Anglo-American countries, although they are "private" in that they are not run by government. And the same applies to "private" hospitals and the "private" universities. On the other hand, the German university has traditionally been almost as autonomous as the American "private" university, even though—as is the case with European universities generally—it is a state institution.

Reprivatization, therefore, may create social structures that are strikingly similar, though the laws in respect to ownership differ greatly from one country to another and from one institution to another. *What they would have in common is a principle of performance rather than a principle of authority.* In all of them the autonomous institution created for the performance of a major social task would be the "doer." Government would become increasingly the decision-maker, the vision-maker. It would try to figure out how to structure a given political objective so as to make it attractive to one of the autonomous institutions. It would, in other words, be the "conductor" that tries to think through what each instrument is best designed to do. And just as we praise a composer for his ability to write "playable" music, which best uses the specific performance characteristics of French horn, violin, or flute, we may come to praise the lawmaker who best structures a particular task so as to make it most congenial for this one or that of the autonomous, self-governing, private institutions of a pluralist society.

THE SPECIAL ROLE OF BUSINESS

Business is likely to be only one—but a very important—institution in such a structure. Whether it be owned by the capitalist, that is, by the investor, or by a cooperative or a government might even become a secondary consideration. For even if owned by government, it would have to be independent of government and autonomous—as the Yugoslavs show—not only in its day-to-day management, but, perhaps more important, in its position in the market, and especially in a competitive capital market.

What makes business particularly appropriate for reprivatization is that it is predominantly an organ of innovation; of all social institutions, it is the only one created for the express purpose of making and managing change. All other institutions were originally created to prevent, or at least to slow down, change. They become innovators only by necessity and most reluctantly.

Specifically, business has two advantages where government has major weaknesses. Business can abandon an activity. Indeed it is forced to do so if it operates in a market—and even more, if it depends on a market for its supply of capital. There is a limit beyond which even the most stubborn businessmen cannot argue with the market test, no matter how rich he may be himself. Even Henry Ford had to abandon the Model T when it no longer could be sold. Even his grandson had to abandon the Edsel.

What is more: Of all our institutions, *business is the only one that society will permit to disappear*. It takes a major catastrophe, a war or a great revolution, to allow the disappearance of a university or of a hospital, no matter how superfluous and unproductive they might have become. Again and again, for instance, the Catholic Church in the United States attempts to close down hospitals that have ceased to be useful. In almost every case, a storm of community nostalgia forces the supposedly absolute bishop to retract his decision.

But when the best-known airplane manufacturer in the United States, the Douglas Company, designer and producer of the DC3 was in difficulty in 1967, neither the American public nor American government rushed to its rescue. If a competitor had not bought the company and merged it into his operations, we would have accepted the disappearance of Douglas—with regret, to be sure, and with a good deal of nostalgic rhetoric, but also with the feeling: "It's their own fault, after all."

Precisely because business can make a profit, it *must* run the risk of loss. This risk, in turn, goes back to the second strength of business: alone among all institutions it has a test of performance. No matter how inadequate profitability may be as an indicator, in certain respects, it is a test for all to see. One can argue that this or that obsolete hospital is really needed in the community or that it will one day again be needed. One can argue that even the poorest university is better than none. The alumni or the community always have a "moral duty" to save "dear old Siwash." The consumer, however, is unsentimental. It leaves him singularly unmoved to be told that he has a duty to buy the products of a company because it has been around a long time. The consumer always asks: "And what will the product do for me tomorrow?" If his answer is "nothing," he will see its manufacturer disappear without the slightest regret. And so does the investor.

This is the strength of business as an institution. It is the best reason for keeping it in private ownership. The argument that the capitalist should not be allowed to make profits is a popular one. But the real role of the capitalist is to be expendable. His role is to take risks and to take losses as a result. This role the private investor is much better equipped to discharge than the public one. We want privately owned business precisely because we want institutions that can go bankrupt and can disappear. We want at least one institution that, from the beginning, is adapted to change, one institution that has to prove its right to survival again and again.

If we want a really strong and effective government, therefore, we should want businesses that are not owned by government. We should want businesses in which private investors, motivated by their own self-interest and deciding on the basis of their own best judgment, take the risk of failure. The strongest argument for "private enterprise" is not the function of profit. The strongest argument is the function of loss. Because of it, business is the most adaptable, and the most flexible of the institutions around. Therefore, it is the one best equipped to manage.

INTERNATIONAL REPRIVATIZATION

Reprivatization is still heretical doctrine. But it is no longer heretical practice. Reprivatization is hardly a creed of "fat cat millionaires" when Black Power advocates seriously propose making education in the slums "competitive" by turning it over to private enterprise, competing for the tax dollar on the basis of proven performance in teaching ghetto children. It may be argued that the problems of the Black Ghetto in the American city are very peculiar problems—and so they are. They are extreme malfunctions of modern government. But if reprivatization works in the extreme case, it is likely to work even better in less desperate ones.

One instance of reprivatization in the international sphere is the World Bank. Though founded by governments, it is autonomous. It finances itself directly through selling its own securities on the capital market. The International Monetary Fund, too, is a case of reprivatization. Indeed, if we develop the money and credit system we need for the world economy, we will have effectively reprivatized the creation and management of money and credit that for millennia have been considered the prime attributes of sovereignty.

Again, business is well equipped to become the "doer" in the international sphere. The multinational corporation, for instance, is our best organ for rapid social and economic development. In the Communications Satellite Corporation (COMSAT) we are organizing world-wide communications (another traditional prerogative of the sovereign) as a multinational corporation. A socialist government, the Labour government of Britain, has used reprivatization to bring cheap energy to Britain—in contracts with the multinational oil companies for the exploration and development of the natural gas fields under the North Atlantic Ocean. And the multinational corporation may be the only institution equipped to get performance where the fragmentation into tribal splinter units, such as in the "mini-states" of Equatorial Africa, makes performance by government impossible.

But domestically as well as internationally, business is, of course, only one institution and equipped to do only one task, the economic one. Indeed it is important to confine business—and every other institution—to its own risk. Reprivatization will, therefore, entail using other nongovernmental institutions—the hospital, for instance, or the university—for other, noneconomic "doing" tasks. Indeed, the design of new nongovernmental, autonomous institutions as agents of social performance under reprivatization may well become a central job for tomorrow's political architects.

TOWARD A NEW POLITICS

We do not face a "withering away of the state." On the contrary, we need a vigorous, a strong, and a very active government. But we do face a choice between big but impotent government and a government that is strong because it confines itself to decision and direction and leaves the "doing" to others. We do not face a "return of laissez-faire" in which the economy is left alone. The economic sphere cannot and will not be considered to lie outside the public domain. But the choices of economy—as well as for all other sectors—are no longer *either* complete governmental indifference or complete governmental control. In all major areas, we have a new choice: an organic diversity in which institutions are used to do what they are best equipped to do. In this society all sectors are "affected with the public interest," whereas in each sector a specific institution, under its own management and dedicated to its own job, emerges as the organ of action and performance.

This is a difficult and complex structure. Such symbiosis between institutions can work only if each disciplines itself to strict concentration on its own sphere and to strict respect for the integrity of the other institutions. Each, to use again the analogy of the orchestra, must be content to play its own part. This will come hardest to government, especially after the last fifty years in which it had been encouraged in the belief of the eighteenth-century organ virtuosos that it could—and should—play all parts simultaneously. But every institution will have to learn the same lesson.

Reprivatization will not weaken government. Indeed, its main purpose is to restore strength to sick government. We cannot go much further along the road on which government has been traveling these last fifty years. All we can get this way is more bureaucracy but not more performance. We can impose higher taxes, but we cannot get dedication, support, and faith on the part of the public. Government can gain greater girth and more weight, but it cannot gain strength or intelligence. All that can happen, if we keep on going the way we have been going, is a worsening sickness of government and growing disenchantment with it. And this is the prescription for tyranny, that is, for a government organized against its own society.

This can happen. It has happened often enough in history. But in a society of pluralist institutions it is not likely to be effective too long. The Communists tried it, and after fifty years have shown—though they have not yet fully learned—that the structure of modern society and its tasks are incompatible with monolithic government. Monolithic government requires absolute dictatorship, which no one has ever been able to prolong much beyond the lifetime of any one dictator.

Ultimately we will need new political theory and probably very new constitutional law. We will need new concepts and new social theory. Whether we will get these and what they will look like, we cannot know today. But we can know that we are disenchanted with government—primarily because it does not perform. We can say that we need, in a pluralist society, a government that can and does govern. This is not a government that "does"; it is not a government that "administers"; it is a government that governs.

LYING AROUND WASHINGTON

Anthony Lake

An American jet is shot down deep within a Communist nation. The U.S. government claims the plane was collecting data on the weather. Would you believe it? Would anyone?

Many did believe it in May, 1960—until the government reversed its claim and came clean about what the U-2 had really been doing. In the immediate wake of the government's admission that it had lied, the *Wall Street Journal* ran a sadder-but-wiser editorial on the incident's lesson:

> "... it is going to be hard to convince people hereafter that explanations from Washington can be taken at their face value.
> ... So we have been caught not only in a rather provocative act but also in dissembling. The one can be explained as a piece of bad

judgment. The explanation for the other will come harder. No one will argue, we suppose, that this country has done anything different from what the Russians do all the time. . . . The difficulty is that we have told others and ourselves we are different. . . . And now the sad part is that this image, which has been one of the strengths of America, is now sullied by our own self-righteous zeal that led us to believe that anything we choose to do is right."

To press critic A. J. Liebling, this editorial "sounded like the beginning of wisdom."[1] It also helped mark the beginning of a decade in which the nation lost much of its faith in the word of its government.

What is worth recalling today about the U-2 incident is not that the government tried to lie about it, or even that the President's press secretary, when asked what lessons he had learned, replied, "Don't get caught." It is that now, [little more than] a decade later, we would not be surprised by such a lie. As Liebling noted, until 1960 it had been "a badge of loyalty to accept the official version of such episodes." The press almost universally believed the government's first explanation that the U-2 was a weather plane which had strayed off course, and so reacted strongly when the government recanted. Today, a similar lie would be received neither with such credulity nor, upon exposure, with such outrage. Reporters would complain to press secretaries, a few editorials would be written (mostly for partisan political effect), and the lie would merely add a few more yards to an already yawning credibility gap.

Before 1960, Washington's pronouncements on national security were given the benefit of the doubt. Since then, the government has been publicly caught out in enough deceptions, even on the most important issues, to raise strong doubts in the minds of most informed Americans about the value of the official word.

LITTLE LIES AND BIG SECRETS

There have been the flat lies—for example, the initial explanations of the U-2's mission, the lie by an unwitting Ambassador Stevenson at the United Nations concerning U.S. involvement in bombing raids on Cuba before the Bay of Pigs invasion, and petty mistruths about the President's and other officials' schedules.

There have been still more misleading statements—not quite lies, but partial revelations of the truth deliberately designed to fool the public into believing what the government wants it to believe. These must be considered the functional equivalent of lies, whether or not a court of law would convict the government of perjury. The public does not read the fine print in government statements, and when it is fooled the result is the same loss of confidence which follows a flat lie. The explanations surrounding the invasion of the Dominican Republic in 1965 provide a good example: while our troops were there partly to "protect American lives," as Washington first described their mission, the more important objective quickly became apparent—intervention in local politics.

Another example, though it concerned a smaller matter, was President Johnson's statement at a press conference in March, 1967, that there was "no truth" to reports he was looking for a successor to Ambassador Lodge in Saigon. Five days later he announced that Ellsworth Bunker would succeed Lodge. The President's press secretary then explained that, since the President had already found Bunker, he was not actually "looking for" a successor. President Johnson had not lied, but only in the most literal sense.

The government's passion for secrecy is less dramatic than its lies and demi-truths, but the result can be the same—loss of public confidence. Washington is secretive about important things. It refused for forty-four days to admit the loss of an H-bomb (later recovered) when a B-52 bomber and jet tanker collided over Spain on January 17, 1966. The facade of silence was maintained in spite of almost immediate general knowledge of the bomb's loss. Witness this dialogue at the Defense Department reported by [The] New York Times:

> REPORTER: *Can you tell me whether you've located the missing bomb?*
> BRIEFING OFFICER: *I don't know of any missing bomb, but we have not positively identified what I think you think we are looking for.*

More recently, the Nixon Administration initially kept secret the raid on the prisoner-of-war camp at Son Tay, 23 miles from Hanoi, on November 21, 1970. The raid was admitted a few days later, however, as part of a denial of the North Vietnamese claim that the U.S. had dropped bombs during that weekend in the Hanoi area. (We had announced "protective reaction" air strikes against North Vietnam limited to the area below the nineteenth parallel, far to the south of Hanoi.) Defense Secretary Laird, in making the denial, said that the only American activity above the nineteenth parallel had been the raid on the POW camp and diversionary action by Navy planes dropping flares. The Administration said that the sounds of bombing heard by people in Hanoi, as well as any civilian casualties in the vicinity, must have been caused by the explosion of wildly fired North Vietnamese antiaircraft missiles. This line was maintained briefly, and then came another revelation by the Defense Department; U.S. planes actually did carry out bombing and strafing attacks on military sites in the area in support of the Son Tay raid. In other words, the North Vietnamese claim of U.S. bombing raids near Hanoi was basically correct, and the initial U.S. denial was a misrepresentation.

Secrecy enshrouds small things as well. One investigator found in 1968 that secrecy labels had been placed on the amount of peanut butter consumed by our armed forces (lest we tip off the nation's enemies to the degree of our military preparedness), as well as on "a twenty-year-old report describing shark attacks on shipwrecked sailors; a study of the modern adaption of the bow and arrow; a scrapbook about atomic energy compiled from newspapers and magazines by a group of college students; and a report on the use of public funds to send border inspectors to rifle and pistol matches."[2]

A DAMAGED DREAM

The existence of the credibility gap is well known. Examples of deceptions abound. But the consequences and causes of the problem have received surprisingly little attention.

The government's credibility is more than a moral issue. It is more than a political problem for the party and President in power. It is a problem of such fundamental importance, having such complex institutional causes, that it deserves far more thought and discussion than it has been given. During the past decade the government's information policies have been debated and decried primarily by the press and the political opposition. They should be of greater concern to all citizens, and particularly to government officials themselves.

In the long run, in our open society, if the government often lies it will get caught—especially when it lies about subjects of vital concern. The consequent loss of confidence in the government's word carries costs to our political system, and to the government's ability to function domestically and internationally which far outweigh any conceivable short-range advantages the lies might seem to promise.

To be believed is (to some extent) to be trusted. Not to be believed— the present condition Washington often faces before the world and the American people—threatens the character of representative democracy. Even the strongest democratic government on earth must be gravely damaged if its own citizens do not believe it; essential dialogue and confidence between the public and the institution of government is lost. Restoring the credibility of our government is not a subsidiary or technical issue; it is, in fact, essential to overcoming many of our troubles at home and abroad.

Public suspicion about official statements has contributed to the government's increasing inability to lead the country. For most Americans, the federal government at the beginning of the 1960's was, for good or ill, the physical and psychological leader of the attack on our social problems. Today, the government is more often an object of disinterest, distaste, or outright hostility, especially by our younger citizens. In his 1970 State of the World Message, President Nixon said that "many of our young people . . . see life as lonely conformity lacking the lift of a driving dream." The deceptions of the past decade make it hard for the government to provide any part of that dream. Few educated people in their mid-twenties have been able to watch news broadcasts or read newspapers since junior high school without coming to regard a governmental statement with the same suspicion as a cigarette commercial.

THE GOOD WITH THE BAD

Apart from domestic damage, the credibility gap has hurt our foreign policy. Miscalculation as a result of uncertainty about the real meaning of Washington's words is an everpresent danger. Distrust of the government's statements about its purposes in committing American military forces abroad now limits the government's ability to gain public approval for many of its foreign activities. This applies even to small-scale actions which just might presage American military involvement. Examples: U.S. civilian aid programs in countries which might become "new Vietnams," and the loan of three C-130 aircraft to the Congolese government in 1967. If the Executive is to build greater support for the aid program, or enhance its ability to take strictly limited actions in a crisis, it must find a way to persuade the public and Congress that limited activities are, in fact, limited—and will remain so. Critical suspicion of its motives and intentions, both in the Congress and in a large segment of informed public opinion, will otherwise continue to constrain all our foreign activities, the good with the bad, the safe with the reckless, and the small with the large.

The government's reaction to this constraint during the past decade has been precisely the wrong one. Rather than attempting to restore public confidence in its explanations so it could act when action might clearly be needed, Washington has resorted to verbal overkill and deception. The public was inundated by hyperbolic statements about progress in Vietnam as criticism of our involvement there grew during the mid-sixties. Falsely optimistic claims can trap the government by creating illusory public expectations of success. The government cannot later allow these public illusions to be destroyed without domestic political damage. It therefore comes under great pressure to commit more resources and prestige to faltering programs in order to justify past optimism or at least put off the day of reckoning. This was one of the patterns which drew us ever deeper into Vietnam.

Some of the Johnson Administration's rhetorical bad practices were continued in the Nixon Administration, most notably during the Cambodian incursion of April-May, 1970. Whatever the wisdom of the President's Cambodian decision, the rhetoric in which he wrapped its announcement was unwise. The dimensions of the consequences of not sending American troops into Cambodia were overstated: "If, when the chips are down, the world's most powerful nation . . . acts like a pitiful, helpless giant, the forces of totalitarianism and anarchy will threaten free nations and institutions throughout the world." Such overstatement increased the scope of our commitment to the Cambodian government; it played on the fears of those in the nation who are most apt to see dangers and conspiracies in every world event; and it therefore helped convince many critical listeners, who have come to reject so uncomplicated a view of the world, that there could be no truth to what the President said or might say later on the subject. The announcement itself thus deepened the emotional division in the nation which was bound to follow the President's decision.

Similarly, President Nixon's claim before his October 7, 1970 speech on Indochina that this would be "the most comprehensive statement ever made on the subject" by any President made some critics more than usually skeptical about what he actually did say during a speech that was hardly "comprehensive," whatever its other merits.

U.S. reporters in Cambodia saw and reported U.S. planes flying direct combat support for Cambodian government troops in early August, 1970. It was an apparent refutation of President Nixon's June 30 statement that after July 1 the only operations by American planes in Cambodia would be "interdiction" missions against the movement of enemy troops and materials which threatened U.S. troops in Vietnam. When confronted with these reports, the government fell back on deceptive word games. There were, spokesmen cautiously allowed, "ancillary benefits" of our interdiction campaign. But the President's statement was still, they said, both accurate and the official policy. Secretary Laird argued that, "it depends on what you refer to as interdiction." He suggested that the widely reported air strikes by seven U.S. planes 900 feet in advance of Cambodian troops at Skoun—strikes called in by a Cambodian ground controller—were part of an interdiction campaign aimed at preventing the Communists from reopening sea supply routes through Cambodian coastal towns. (Skoun, as reporters then noted, is thirty-five miles northeast of the Cambodian capital, Phnom Penh; the nearest coastal village is eighty miles southwest of Phnom Penh.) Five months later, on January 20, 1971, Secretary Laird dismissed previous government positions as "semantics," admitting that the U.S. provided both "some airlift" and "air support" for Cambodian and South Vietnamese units fighting in Cambodia. News photos of U.S. servicemen surreptitiously in Cambodia, wearing civilian clothes, clouded the issue further. It is precisely incidents like this one which make many Americans suspicious of *all* their government's activities abroad.

SPIRALING DISBELIEF

This spiral of public disbelief, official rhetoric and misleading news management to overcome it, greater public disbelief as a result, more rhetoric, etc., etc., has so debased the language of debate on foreign policy that it is hard to discuss the issues—even in private—in anything approaching an objective manner. It is hardly surprising that many citizens, of differing philosophies, simply shut their ears and close their minds whenever they hear words like "commitment," "intervention," "just," "honorable," and even "peace."

Misleading public statements also cause great damage within the government itself. Richard Neustadt has observed, "The tendency of bureaucratic language to create in private the same images presented to the public should never be underrated."[3]

Moreover, when a false public image is presented, it corrupts debate within the government. An official who makes a misleading public statement is likely to defend it inside government as well, lest he appear uncomfortably cynical. His private doubts about the statement are suppressed. And when he has thus committed himself publicly, subordinates are inhibited from making embarrassing arguments that he is wrong. Lower-level reporting and analyses also begin to reflect the false public image.

In addition, the public line is all that many officials hear about issues with which they are not intimately concerned. As they learn over time how dishonest the government has been on these issues, their cynicism about the government's information policies, and their view of the public and press as manipulable objects, grow. And this, in turn, reinforces cynicism on the question of how honest *they* need to be when drafting public statements on matters for which they are responsible.

CAUSE BEFORE CURE

We must seriously consider the causes of the government's disturbing loss of credibility in the 1960's if there is to be any rational basis for attempted cures. Secrecy and falsehood have not been historically peculiar either to the U.S. government or to the last ten years. *All* governments throughout history have lied. *All* have had an obsessive concern for secrecy. On November 9, 1775, the Continental Congress resolved:

> ". . . That every member of this Congress consider himself under the ties of virtue, honour, and love of his country, not to divulge, directly or indirectly, any matter or thing agitated or debated in Congress, before the same shall have been determined, without leave of the Congress; nor any matter or thing determined in Congress, which a majority of the Congress shall order to be kept secret."

But our government's credibility has seldom been so much in question as during the past decade. Part of the reason is that the public is better informed. Television has made a major contribution to this phenomenon, especially in its newscasts on the war in Indochina. The war itself was the issue on which the government's record of intentional and unintentional fabrication was worst—and with the most tragic consequences. And the television explosion (in 1953, about 46 percent of U.S. homes had television; by 1965, about 94 percent; today, almost every American home is so blessed) meant that millions of Americans were able to see their government's misstatements confounded in dramatic detail.

In November, 1967, General Westmoreland gave a joint session of Congress a glowing picture of military progress in Vietnam. President Johnson was equally up-beat about the pacification program in his State of the Union Message on January 17, 1968. A week later, Americans were watching the enemy's massive Tet offensive on their television sets. High officials could argue the offensive was a great enemy defeat; but on television it was a crushing denial of our government's progress reports.

Another reason why the circumstances of the 1960's made the government's credibility problem particularly acute derives from basic shifts in public attitudes toward U.S. foreign policy generally. Largely, but not only, because of the bad experience in Vietnam, the Congress and informed public became during this decade far more sensitive to the nature and scope of U.S. activities abroad. In 1954, for example, apparently accurate reports—and U.S. government denials—of a CIA role in the overthrow of the Arbenz government in Guatemala raised little outcry here among the public or in the Congress. As the 1960's saw more attention and criticism given to government activities which had been accepted or disregarded during the 1950's, officials reacted by making greater efforts either to hide their programs from public scrutiny, or to protect them by misrepresenting their true character. In the process, the ability of the public and Congress to pass reasonable judgment on these programs suffered.

Some journalists became less willing to grant the government the benefit of the doubt during the 1960's, and by their stories contributed to the gap. But reporting the government's performance, warts and all, is their job. The way to narrow the gap is not to ask reporters that they be more understanding of the government's problems, and therefore be less critical of its shadings of the truth. The cure lies in changing, insofar as possible, those factors which determine the government's performance. This requires a realistic understanding of why the government sometimes lies and why it apparently lied more often in the 1960's than before.

WHY OFFICIALS LIE

No simple "devil" theory can explain it. Some critics have blamed the whole problem on President Johnson. The press did become highly suspicious of him; and, like his successor, he came to office with his own suspicions and distrust of the Eastern press. But the gap had begun to grow before he took office, and in any case the President is simply the most important, not the only, government spokesman. The bulk of governmental statements are made by other men, usually the White House and departmental press spokesmen, who act largely on the basis of guidance supplied by middle- and upper-level officials. Every morning the various bureaus and offices in the State and Defense Departments, as well as the National Security Council staff, hurriedly prepare guidance for the State, Defense and White House late-morning or mid-day foreign affairs press briefings. The press offices coordinate their planned announcements and responses in a conference telephone call just before the briefings begin. The more important items are approved by senior officials. The President sees only the very most important or politically tendentious among them.

Some officials undeniably do enjoy "managing" the news, particularly those officials who are most given to the belief that "reading the cables" gives the official an expertise which no private citizen could have. Most government officials concerned with foreign policy share this elitist prejudice to some degree. But the other side of the coin is that they are so busy reading the cables, they have little time to reflect upon and keep up with the broader analyses of American foreign policy produced outside the Executive branch.

To conclude simply that power in Washington has absolutely corrupted the members of the Federal bureaucracy, however, is to conclude that nothing can be done short of destroying that power. In fact, most officials would rather stick to the truth. They take no pleasure in misleading the public. But when dealing with the press, many believe they are forced to prevaricate by apparently compelling pressures. These pressures are of two kinds: substantive pressures generated by national security or domestic political considerations, and the pressures on any individual who wishes to succeed in and be loyal to his organization. (In addition, officials sometimes lie unwittingly as a result of simple governmental ineptitude. Phil G. Goulding's fascinating book, *Confirm or Deny,* describes in grisly detail how low-level mistakes produced the government's unwitting lie when denying the U.S. overflight of a French atomic installation in 1965. Our mistaken public denial in 1967 of the Soviet Union's charge that our planes had strafed its merchant ship *Turkestan* in the harbor of Cam Pha, North Vietnam, was caused by a cover-up in the Air Force unit involved in the incident.)[4]

Much of the secrecy and most of the flat lies on foreign affairs are produced by the first of these pressures: considerations of "national security." To paraphrase Sir Henry Wotton, a press secretary becomes, in these cases, an honest man who is asked to lie at home for his country.

THE CLAIMS OF "NATIONAL SECURITY"

"National security" as a rationale for public deception gained particular power during the 1950's and 1960's. The importance of secrecy about technological developments in strategic weaponry explains only a small part of the reason why. More important was the psychology of the cold war. It is revealing that in 1955 Robert Cutler, long a Special Assistant to President Eisenhower, entitled his defense of secrecy in government, "Some Considerations Affecting the Publication of Security Information *in Time of Propaganda War"* (emphasis added). The U.S. public's right to information was seen, in this view, entirely in a cold war context; public discussion at home was to be subordinated to the requirements of effectively opposing Communism abroad.

The demands of "national security" also inhibit revelations which would embarrass us before world opinion or damage our relations with other states. In trying to maintain secrecy about our lost H-bomb in Spain we were acting at the request of the Spanish government. Our government decided that we could not violate that request. If we did, we would add to the burden on the Spanish government caused by our own mistake in losing the bomb; we would prejudice Spanish cooperation with our efforts to find it; and we would further sour Spain's attitude toward our air bases there. We therefore went ahead and looked ridiculous to our own public for the sake of our interests in Spain.[5] Similarly, the Thai government prevented for some months our admission that U.S. planes on combat missions were using bases in Thailand, although it was a fact well known to the American press. We apparently feared losing the use of the bases if the Thai request was not honored.

An argument might be made that there are some things the United States must do abroad for its security which, if they were revealed, would be opposed by important segments of the American public, or even by a majority of the electorate. This argument could be applied, for example, to the effort to provide surreptitious tactical air support for Cambodian troops. Such secrecy also allows greater flexibility: if you don't admit you are doing something, you can stop doing it without loss of face. But the public, and often the Congress, has no voice in deciding whether such actions are actually in the U.S. interest. And when the truth comes out, the government is more embarrassed than if it had been frank all along.

In many cases the demands of national security do dictate secrecy. It would be dangerous to reveal the exact nature and positions of our strategic deterrence force. It would be tragic to destroy a secret peace negotiation by publicizing it. Even open covenants are most likely to be successfully arrived at secretly. Some things cannot be said publicly without very seriously embarrassing a foreign government and our relations with it. At a less important level, it is hard to argue that the President or other senior officials should publish their schedules in advance when traveling to potentially dangerous areas—although private advance notice to the press, for their convenience, might be given.

The choice between frankness and evasion can thus be agonizing when national security is thought to be at stake. In the last decade, however, the choice has too often been falsehood. In nearly every case where our national interests, or what we thought were our interests, would have been even slightly damaged by revelation of the truth, the immediate demands of the moment seemed to indicate the necessity of telling a lie or keeping silent. And when choosing between the latter, the government has too often misled the public instead of simply refusing to say anything when it couldn't tell the truth. In making these choices, officials failed to recognize the Chinese water torture effect each lie had on public credulity and public support.

DOMESTIC POLITICS

The other substantive pressure for prevarication is the desire for domestic political advantage. In its "guidance" for reporters, the government tries to persuade the press and public that the Administration in power is aware of almost every petal falling around the world, and that it never makes a mistake. The President is deified. He is almost always portrayed as working—even when in reality he is getting the rest so essential to his well-being. President Eisenhower's "working vacations," even on the golf course, are a case in point. In addition, the President is almost always portrayed as "following events closely"—even at those times when he is not informed, either because the significance of the events doesn't warrant it or because nobody knows the facts.

Events are also interpreted for the press in the most advantageous way. When reporting on the President's meeting with six Kent State students on May 6, 1970, Press Secretary Ron Ziegler (whom Robert Semple of [The] New York Times has described as being "as honest as any press secretary has ever been") tried hard to leave the impression that the six had reported to the President that student unrest had been caused by campus problems. Reporters had to drag out of him the fact that the students had also mentioned Vietnam and Cambodia as contributing causes. As Ziegler first tried to portray them, the students' views would have been helpful to a President trying to weather the political storm following his Cambodian decision.

Given the diversity of political views within the Federal bureaucracy, it is surprising how seldom its officials make public statements—on or off the record—which would be politically embarrassing to the party in power. Why does the same official who learned to live with the budgetary numbers games of a Democratic administration now accept just as easily the different numbers games of the Republicans? Why do officials usually hew to the government's public position or remain silent even when they know it is misleading? The explanation lies in the nature of the Federal—or any—bureaucracy. Even the most intelligent, high-minded official invariably believes he must toe the government's public line—for his personal success, his professional effectiveness, and, paradoxically, his own sense of honor, require it.

BUREAUCRATS AND NEWSMEN

As anyone in any organization knows, success and even survival in a pecking order require good relations with the inhabitant of the next level up in the hierarchy. There are few more formal pecking orders than a career service which distinguishes among ranks—such as the armed forces and the Foreign Service. Demonstrated loyalty to one's boss is the *sine qua non* of bureaucratic success. It is usually possible to disagree with him in private, but woe betide the official who embarrasses his immediate superior before the public or before *his* superior.

The safest course is therefore to avoid the press, to say only what one's boss would say, or to speak frankly only off-the-record or so anonymously that no one will know who it was who said what. (Sometimes subordinate officials are simply ordered to have no dealings with the press whatever— although not as often as many reporters believe.) When the official takes one of these tacks, the result is either more secrecy, more dissemination of the party line, or a confusing story in which the public is left to guess just how authoritative the unnamed "government source" really is.

A more admirable side to bureaucratic loyalty is that anyone who is dedicated to his job—and the level of dedication in the Federal career service is generally quite high—must feel guilty about undercutting the discipline of his organization and betraying the trust placed in him by his boss. It can be difficult for the individual who opposes decisions or statements made by his superiors, but remains silent, to decide whether his act of loyalty is (1) unwarranted subservience or, instead, (2) the discretion necessary to a smoothly functioning government. For no government can govern effectively if every employee who disagrees with a program attacks it in public.

Some disaffected officials resolve this problem by saying nothing publicly, or finally quitting their jobs. Others publicly support policies with which they disagree, trying to use the credentials of loyalty they thus obtain to put forward their private case for opposition more strongly—a particularly dangerous form of "the effectiveness trap." Its real effectiveness is limited by the fact that the official may be trapped privately by his public position. And, more important, the effect of his public statements may outweigh any amount of countervailing private argument.

There is another dimension to these questions of loyalty. When the government is under attack, an official naturally feels drawn to defend it, even if he agrees with the substance of the attack, much as criticism acceptable within a family is intolerable from an outsider. This reaction is fortified by a natural urge to strengthen one's own organization against others. One weapon in this struggle is official secrecy. As Max Weber wrote, "Every bureaucracy seeks to increase the superiority of the professionally informed by keeping their knowledge and their intentions secret. Bureaucratic administration always tends to be an administration of 'secret session': insofar as it can, it hides its knowledge and action from criticism . . . Bureaucracy naturally welcomes a poorly informed and hence a powerless parliament— at least insofar as ignorance somehow agrees with the bureaucracy's interests."[6] Now, in the age of mass media, secrecy has been joined in the Executive's arsenal by manipulative "news management."

None of this means, of course, that no official ever disloyally gives information to the press. But unauthorized statements or *sub rosa* leaks are seldom the result of refusal to go along with the government's news management. Too often, they represent news management of a different kind. Some leaks are made to strengthen a pet project, often with misleading arguments and facts. Others are made when a specific organization within the government feels threatened or short-changed—as with leaks by some members of the military services whose loyalty to Army, Air Force or Navy is greater than their loyalty to the government as a whole.

THE TIME FACTOR

Finally, the pressures of time add to the likelihood of misleading statements. A foreign event or crisis often first comes to an official's attention on the press ticker. The official cables are still being encoded, sent, received, decoded and distributed. As the ticker item arrives, the press in Washington demands the government's comments and more facts, each reporter competing for speed with the others. If the government delays until it can get more facts, it is accused of deviousness or incompetence. The government press spokesmen require immediate guidance. Officials therefore react more quickly than they should. They try to downplay the story, in the hope that the problem will go away. They try to make all comments fit previous statements of the government's policies, since that seems the safest course, even though, on reflection, the event abroad might warrant changing past policies. Simple mistakes of fact are made in the heat of the moment. Under such pressure, tactical considerations loom very large, and only an exceptional official can be expected to remember the longer term consequences of shading the truth.

All of these pressures on the government to be secretive, misleading or flatly mendacious—i.e., the demands of national security, domestic political advantage, and bureaucratic survival—are increased proportionately by the importance of the issue. The stakes involved in public statements on hot issues are largest, so it may be more "dangerous" in those cases for the official to be frank with reporters or for the government to be frank with the public. In a crisis, information within the government is more severely limited, to guard against leaks. Time pressures usually increase as the press competes more strenuously for scoops. It is thus on precisely those issues where public interest is greatest that the government's record of veracity tends to be worst.

REDUCING THE GAP

No one should expect that the government can or will be completely open about all its activities and policies. If the public ever became satisfied with its access to the government's inner thoughts and workings, one would have to conclude either that the press and Congress had sold out to the Executive branch, or that the Federal bureaucracy, the President's interest in domestic politics, and our relations with foreign nations had all ceased to exert their pressures on the government's information policies. Some tensions are healthy among a press, a Congress, and an Executive, which, after all, have different roles and interests.

The problem is not simply one of increasing or reducing the amount of accurate information available to the public. The crux of the matter is trust—that is, belief by the press and public that the government is doing everything it responsibly can do to inform the public adequately and honestly. Such trust requires two things. There must be more understanding by the press and public of the real problems which inhibit the government as a whole, and individual officials, from complete candor on certain issues, especially those involving important national security considerations. At the same time, it is unreasonable to expect this understanding to blossom until the government begins to demonstrate that it is not hiding behind the shield of national security when it need not and, more important still, that it is not trying to take unfair advantage of the press in order to mislead the public. In short, it is time for the Executive branch to mend its ways.

Most students of government-press relations have concentrated their attention, and their hopes for reform, almost entirely on the press and Congress.[7] The Executive, they assume, compulsively and consistently lies, and always will. Congress and the press, they argue, must be stronger and more aggressive in ferreting out and publishing the Executive's secrets and deceptions.

Congress and the press should, indeed, responsibly do much more to help keep the public accurately informed. But the ability of most reporters to avoid being "managed" by the government is limited by increasingly intense press competition for straight news and inside stories. The reporter who gets into print first is rewarded by his editor; the reporter or columnist who writes the most favorable article after an official background interview is the one most likely to be rewarded by the government with future interviews. The best reporters resist these pressures: they take time to be right, and take a close look at the inside dope they are given. The reputations of some critical columnists force government officials to meet with them without the *quid pro quo* of a favorable story. But competitive pressures for speed and "inside" information will always make most of the press highly dependent on the government's interpretation of events.

Those members of the Congress and the press who do try to help close the credibility gap can do so only by publicizing it and catching the Executive in its deceptions, in an effort to influence its future behavior. This is necessary, but does not add directly to public confidence in the government's word. Since the press and Congress cannot by themselves solve the problem, primary responsibility for narrowing the gap must be taken by the Executive branch itself—or there will be no real progress.

TOWARD CREDIBILITY

The most important change in furthering this end is one that cannot be accomplished by administrative fiat: government officials must learn to remember how damaging a lie or misleading statement is in the long run, even if it looks like the least bad solution in immediate situations. The President and his topmost associates bear an immense responsibility in this regard. They set the tone; their statements become the holy writ at lower levels of government. A change in attitude at the top is far more important than any procedural innovation, for it would shape the government's day-to-day performance as nothing else could. More specific measures would also help:

The government should carry out a program of identifying and releasing information which is now secret but need not be.

The government should more often say nothing at all when truly serious considerations of national security forbid a frank statement. Lest its silence on specific questions or rumors be construed as confirmation, it might establish a list of subjects on which it would never, on principle, comment—e.g., secret negotiations. Debate between press and government over the list would be more healthy than current ambiguities.

No government official should ever be asked by his superiors to give a speech supporting policies with which he disagrees. Such requests are now considered natural, even "good politics." They should be considered an abuse of the official's loyalty and the government's good word.

Press briefings by senior officials should more often be on the record, so their names and reputations are directly involved in the accuracy and consistency of their views and the "guidance" they give reporters. Off-the-record and background interviews cannot be totally discarded. They are useful for diplomatic trial balloons, and they also provide many news sources. But they should no longer be the rule rather than the exception.

The authority of press spokesmen should be strengthened within the government, and their accountability for the government's credibility increased commensurately. They now receive guidance, often at the last minute, from officials whose primary constituencies are either foreign (a State Department desk officer), political (a White House aide concerned with domestic affairs), or both (most senior foreign policy officials). The spokesmen try to get guidance which is as complete and accurate as possible. But frequently there is no time, or they are simply ordered to follow a less-than-candid line. As a result, they sometimes wittingly or unwittingly have to peddle misleading information. It is time that more recognition be given within the government to what should be the press spokesmen's most important constituency—the public, and its belief in the government's word. The spokesmen should be given strengthened bureaucratic authority to reject misleading guidance. They should also be included in all important meetings and information channels, so they are kept as well informed as possible.

Finally, the press should accept less critically statements by the government that it will defer comment on an event or issue until it has more facts. The government should resist pressures for quick comments, waiting until it has both its facts and the time to reflect a bit on their implications.

No one who is concerned with the course of events within the United States, or with the ability of our government to govern and represent us abroad, can doubt the urgent necessity of greater confidence between our government and ourselves. It cannot act effectively without public confidence. And the public cannot give support, or counsel through informed debate, when it is uncertain about the facts which the government presents. The constraints on our foreign policies of a suspicious public and Congress will not be relieved by more deceptions, which only produce greater suspicions.

What is needed is release of more information to the public, and a better understanding of what the rules of the natural conflict between press and government must be. The press should understand that the government cannot always tell all. And the government should understand that every unnecessary secret, or consciously misleading statement, is more costly in the long run than whatever tactical benefit it might seem to bestow. When both begin to follow these principles, mutual confidence can be built, and the natural tension between government and press will work for the nation's benefit rather than against it. The essential first step is for the government to realize that it cannot lead the public while misleading it.

STATUTORY RESTRAINTS ON ADMINISTRATIVE LOBBYING— "LEGAL FICTION"

Richard L. Engstrom and Thomas G. Walker

The question of federal regulation of lobbying activities has undergone considerable scrutiny by students of public law. The attention which the subject has gained is indeed justified, for it brings to the surface problems both legal and political in nature. The legal literature contains numerous discussions in this area, including research on improving the legislative process through pressure group restrictions, the history of federal lobbying statutes, the effectiveness of such restraints, and the various types of interest group activities.

However, as sound as this previous work has been, the treatment of lobbying has suffered from narrowness of scope. Too often the discussions on federal regulation have dealt only with the activities of private parties and their paid representatives. An example of this can be seen in James H. Tilbery's examination of lobbying at the federal level:

> Consequently, today the term lobbying embraces three general areas of activity for the purpose of defeating or influencing passage of legislation: (1) citizens expressing individual opinion on legislation; (2) citizens organized into groups for the purpose of expressing collective opinion on legislation; and (3) the paid legislative agent, against whom most lobbying regulation is directed.[1]

This emphasis upon the activities of private interest groups has caused us to neglect studying what may well be the most effective lobby in the United States—the executive branch of the national government.

Since the 1950s every executive department has had a departmental level office with the explicit function of lobbying the United States Congress. In their activities these bureaus and agencies frequently operate as large pressure groups with their own resources similar to those of the private interest organizations. Through liaison officials these departments maintain direct contact with congressmen and congressional staff. Offices of public affairs or public information afford a department the opportunity to engage in "indirect lobbying," using official publications and educational materials as a means of manipulatng public and clientele group support for the department's particular interests. The more than three million federal civilian employees in the nation constitute a huge reservoir capable of exerting influence upon the United States Congress.

Congress has not failed to recognize the existence of the executive branch as an interest group and has passed legislation to restrict the activities of governmental lobbies as well as those of private pressure groups. This article examines the legislative history of congressional attempts to regulate administrative lobbies, the effectiveness of this body of law, and discusses the potential enforcement agents of these statutory restraints.

I

The history of the United States Congress is replete with examples demonstrating the determination of that body to guard against encroachments by the executive branch into the legislative arena. As early as 1913, Congress began acting with suspicion toward the growing bureaucratic influence over the legislative process. In that year an act was passed stipulating that "No money appropriated by any act shall be used for the compensation of any publicity expert unless specifically appropriated for this purpose."[2]

In 1919, Congress enacted the most significant piece of legislation regulating administrative lobbying, the *Lobbying with Appropriated Moneys Act*.[3] The law, in part, reads as follows:

> *No part of the money appropriated by any enactment of Congress shall, in the absence of express authorization by Congress, be used directly or indirectly to pay for any personal service, advertisement, telegram, telephone, letter, printed or written matter, or other device, intended or designed to influence in any manner a Member of Congress, to favor or oppose, by vote or otherwise, any legislation or appropriation by Congress, whether before or after the introduction of any bill or resolution proposing such legislation or appropriation; but this shall not prevent officers or employees of the United States or of its departments or agencies from communicating to Members of Congress on the request of any Member or to Congress, through the proper official channels, requests for legislation or appropriations which they deem necessary for the efficient conduct of the public business.*

Anyone in violation of this statute is subject to possible fine, loss of employment and imprisonment.

Passage of the *Lobbying with Appropriated Moneys Act* was a response to administrative behavior in the closing days of the previous Congress. At that time congressmen had been bombarded with "thousands upon thousands"[4] of telegrams which had been initiated in Washington by administrative officials who, at public expense, had wired out urging people to telegram representatives in support of various appropriations measures.

The debate on this law clearly demonstrates the intention of Congress to proscribe behavior of this genre and to regulate various forms of administrative lobbying. Chief spokesman for the bill, House Appropriations Committe Chairman James W. Good of Iowa, argued that the act would:

. . . prohibit a practice that has been indulged in so often, with-
out regard to what administration is in power—the practice of a
bureau chief or the head of a department writing letters through-
out the country, sending telegrams throughout the country, for this
organization, for this man, for that company to write his Congress-
man, to wire his Congressman, in behalf of this or that legislation.[5]

Regarding such administrative attempts to influence Congress, Representative Good stated that "it was never the intention of Congress to
appropriate money for this purpose, and section 5 of the bill will absolutely put a stop to that sort of thing."[6] Representative Edward E. Denison
of Illinois manifested the House's understanding of the bill by declaring
that the proposed legislation "simply prohibits employees or officials of
the Government from using public funds in communicating to Congress."[7]
Quite obviously it was the feeling of Congress that it was improper for
employees of the government to use public funds in expressing their
support of various programs or policies.

In 1939, Congress again felt the need to curtail administrative advances into the legislative process. The executive agencies had begun
printing and distributing publications in support of New Deal legislation
with the purpose of increasing public approval for such programs. Congress responded to this form of indirect lobbying by passing an act prohibiting governmental agencies from mailing free of postage any books,
documents, pamphlets, and similar material unless they had first received
a request for them.[8]

In addition, since 1951 Congress has attached to a number of appropriations bills one of the following clauses:

No part of any appropriation contained in the Act shall be
used for publicity or propaganda purposes not authorized by the
Congress.[9]
No part of any appropriation contained in this Act, or of the
funds available for expenditure by any corporation or agency in-
cluded in this Act, shall be used for publicity or propaganda pur-
poses designed to support or defeat legislation pending before the
Congress.[10]

The Congress has also placed explicit limitations upon the amount of funds
made available for some departmental liaison activities.

A review of the legislative history in this area of law clearly reveals
that Congress has formally sought to restrain administrative influence over
legislative matters. The passage of a statute, however, does not insure the
realization of its aims.

II

Administrative lobbying has not only remained unrestricted in the face of prohibiting statutes, but has become openly institutionalized. This is evidenced by the creation of congressional "liaison" offices within the various executive departments. The reason for this bureaucratic freedom in conducting legislative campaigns is simply the total nonenforcement of the statutory prohibitions. There has never been a prosecution resulting from the anti-executive lobbying laws, nor in the fifty-seven year history of this legislation has there been an indictment based upon its provisions.

On only one occasion have the federal courts even cited the anti-lobbying statutes. In the case of *Angilly v. United States*,[11] a United States district court in New York upheld the dismissal of a customs inspector charged with illegally withholding a number of entry documents and related funds. The *Lobbying with Appropriated Moneys Act* was cited by the court only to support the validity of the dismissal procedure. This lone example of judicial consideration of this body of legislation was in no way directly related to enforcing the anti-lobbying provisions of the federal law.

The rather thorough lack of enforcement has rendered the intended curbs totally ineffective. Speaking to this point J. Leiper Freeman has explained:

> *Actually, these laws might be viewed predominantly as examples of legal fiction in our government today. They do not abolish bureaucratic lobbying or public relations activities. Their major consequences are that bureaus and agencies must call their public relations staffs information or education units, and administrative "lobbying" is required to conform to certain protocols of liaison, reference work, public reporting, public speaking, and testifying in reply to congressional inquiry.*[12]

Although these statutes have been ineffective, congressional discontent over certain administrative techniques does flare up occasionally. Congressman Thomas B. Curtis of Missouri, during the 1965 hearings of the Joint Committee on the Organization of the Congress, called the practice of using federal employees and facilities to lobby the Congress "scandalous,"[13] Congressman Frederick Smith of Ohio once declared that "every bureaucrat should be put in jail for lobbying to put his schemes through Congress,"[14] Edward deGrazia explains that congressional criticism occurs when liaison activities become too open, when they are "crude" and "obvious," and when the executive branch threatens rather than renders favors and services.[15]

What constitutes liaison activities which are sufficiently "crude" and "obvious" to cause a critical response? One of the more recent criticisms from Capitol Hill occurred during the Senate hearings on the nomination of Abe Fortas to be Chief Justice. The Department of Justice prepared a twenty-seven page study of Fortas' opinions, concluding that the work of the Justice "deserves extremely high marks." This study, inserted into the record by Senator Philip Hart, prompted the Senate Judiciary Committee to ask the Justice Department to defend its preparation of the memorandum, as well as Senator Sam Ervin to remark, "The Department of Justice has started propagandizing the Committee."[16]

Congressman H. R. Gross of Iowa wanted the Secretaries of Defense and State prosecuted for co-signing letters sent to congressmen pressing for adoption of a foreign aid bill in 1963. In 1962, Congress criticized Secretary of Health, Education and Welfare Anthony Celebrezze for spending $3,562 of public funds in sending telegrams to legislators asking their support of a bill to aid higher education. Members of the House and Senate committees having jurisdiction over Indian affairs once took the publicity tactics of Commissioner of the Bureau of Indian Affairs John Collier to their respective chamber floors. Collier had used the bureau's official publication, *Indians at Work*, to organize support for his policies. The legislators used statements from the publication as examples of ". . . unfair and unwarranted use of public facilities and of official status."[17] In 1950, Secretary of Agriculture C. F. Brannon was criticised by Congress for delivering speeches in various cities on the purposes of the "Brannon Plan" and how it would alleviate many of the farmers' problems.

Few congressmen have attacked the general practice of administrative lobbying or have attempted to answer a basic question, as once posed by Congressman Clarence J. Brown of Ohio, "whether the bureaucracy should rule through pressure?"[18] The criticisms of most congressmen have not centered on the general principle of the propriety of such pressure activity. Criticism seems to be expressed only when a legislator is opposed to the policy being advocated by the administration, not when the lobbying tactics are used in support of a position he too advocates. For example, when the issue of establishing the Department of National Defense was before Congress, President Truman told the service officials to cease lobbying against it. The opponents of its establishment then cried that the experts were being muzzled. V. O. Key explains that:

> *Attacks on administrative action are usually part of a campaign against a specific piece of legislation. Phrased in extravagant language, they are designed to discredit the administrative agency by branding it as a lawbreaker.*[19]

The House Select Committee on Lobbying Activities of the 81st Congress, while conducting a study on pressure group behavior, also considered the question of executive lobbying activities. That committee came to the rather startling conclusion that in its belief the existing laws prohibiting lobbying by executive agencies were meeting the situation. This committee report again emphasizes that a majority of congressmen react to the particular issue with which the lobbying tactic is connected and not the general principle of such lobbying.

III

There are three governmental organs which have the power to enforce the anti-executive lobbying statutes. The Department of Justice is responsible for initiating prosecutions. The General Accounting Office conducts independent examinations of the manner in which the executive branch discharges its financial responsibilities. The Government Operations Committees of Congress conduct investigations into the administration and operations of the executive departments. However, the fact remains that none of these agencies have ever made an active attempt to enforce the statutory provisions, nor do they express a desire to commence such enforcement.

A spokesman for the Department of Justice informed one Congressman that he could be assured that the Department would undertake prosecution under the provisions of the *Lobbying with Appropriated Moneys Act* whenever the facts warranted such action. Yet such proceedings have never been initiated. The Justice Department has even ruled that this statute cannot be interpreted to prohibit any executive agency head from using department facilities to address an unsolicited letter to members of Congress concerning pending legislation.

Such behavior on the part of the Attorney General's Office is indeed understandable. The Justice Department is a member of the president's executive family along with the other departments and agencies falling under the control of the Chief Executive. As such the Department is not likely to embarrass the administration by filing charges against various executive officials for illegal lobbying activities. That there is competition among departments and differences of opinion over interests and priorities is well known, but the historic 1943 dispute between Vice President Henry Wallace and Commerce Secretary Jesse Jones over the wartime procurement programs serves as a lesson in excessive intra-administration strife.

The problems which render Justice Department enforcement unlikely are not encountered by the General Accounting Office, which is an arm of the Congress and not part of the executive branch. Even so, this agency has also proven ineffective in applying restraints on executive lobbying activities. In regard to the *Lobbying with Appropriated Moneys Act,* the G.A.O. claims that it lacks enforcement authority. The statute contains fine and imprisonment provisions which are criminal in nature, and, therefore may only be enforced through judicial action. It is the policy of the G.A.O., when encountering information which indicates that a federal criminal law has been violated, to furnish such information to the appropriate criminal law enforcement agency (the Department of Justice) and to the particular department involved.

What becomes of this information when the Department of Justice receives it? The experience of one congressman clearly explains:

> Some years ago I took on a case involving a very flagrant violation of this section (section 1913 of Title 18, United States Code) by the Civil Service Commission. The Comptroller General's report indicated that in his opinion there was a violation, and he turned the file over to the Attorney General. Nothing further was heard. I wrote the Attorney General, and then wrote the Comptroller General. The final bit of correspondence indicated that the Comptroller General could do nothing to make the Attorney General prosecute, and the Attorney General, with some very specious legal reasoning, indicated that in his opinion the law was unconstitutional anyway.[20]

The G.A.O. does, however, have authority to enforce the provisions against publicity and propaganda contained in the appropriations acts. Its action here is limited to the mere recovery of the amount of the money improperly expended. It has interpreted these provisions as prohibiting the use of appropriated funds for personal services and publications intended to affect the course of legislation "by molding public opinion,"[21] and has stated that the provisions are "directed toward precluding activities and expenditures of an extraordinary nature not related to the normal operating functions of a Governmental agency."[22] The G.A.O. is in a dilemma in enforcing these restrictions because there are no clear guidelines as to what constitutes inappropriate behavior. Comptroller General Elmer B. Staats explained:

> The reason for this is that agencies are authorized and, in some cases specifically directed to keep the public informed concerning their programs. Where such authorized activities involve, incidentally, reference to legislation pending before Congress, it is extremely difficult to draw a dividing line between the permissible and the prohibited.[23]

The G.A.O. has, therefore, operated under the belief that it cannot disregard administrative determinations of what is appropriate unless the activities are clearly extraordinary.

The G.A.O. will not act upon its own initiative in enforcing these lobbying restraints, but only upon congressional requests. Its justification for such a policy is that

> In view of the minimal possibility for making a possible violation stick and of the minimal amounts of appropriated funds that are generally involved, we have not seen fit to devote our already overburdened audit staff to the task of specifically searching out possible violations of these statutes.[24]

In recent years the G.A.O., at the request of legislators, has conducted several investigations into suspected violations of those propaganda and publicity provisions. On one occasion it did conclude that the executive activities constituted such a gross violation that enforcement could be effected. In the remaining investigations, it decided that the behavior in question was not sufficiently in the nature of propaganda or publicity to fall under statutory proscription.

The case in which it determined a violation concerned the Post Office Department's attempt to defeat the Cunningham Bill in 1960. This bill, passed by the House, would have prohibited the Department from placing first class mail aboard air liners when the volume of air mail did not fill the space available—a practice presumably causing loss of revenue to the rail-roads. The Department distributed letters which opened:

> *WOULD YOU PAY FOR TWO SEATS ABOARD AN AIR LINER AND USE ONLY ONE????*
> *Of course you wouldn't but that's just what Congress will ask you to do should it enact the Cunningham Bill. . . ."*

After entering a request that the receiver in turn write or wire his Senators to press for the defeat of this bill, the letter ended with "PLEASE HELP US TO HELP YOU!"

The Department also made available to local newspapers an editorial in which it described the reasoning behind the Cunningham Bill as "a specious argument." Again an appeal was made for "all those who are interested in providing quicker and better mail service" to write their Senators in opposition. The G.A.O. ruled that these activities were "a clear exhortation on individual Congressmen."[25] Even though the activities were found to be in violation of statute, no action was taken because the amount of funds involved was small and commingled with proper expenditures. The G.A.O. explained that the cost of auditing the expenditures would have greatly exceeded the amount that could have been recovered.

The Government Operations Committees of both chambers of Congress also have the authority to enforce the anti-executive lobbying statutes. This authority stems from the responsibility of these committees for conducting comprehensive examinations into the activities of the executive branch. Yet no enforcement action has been undertaken. Two factors may contribute to this condition: 1) the value congressmen place on services provided them by the executive departments, and 2) the partisan nature of the congressional committee system.

There are many demands placed upon congressmen which the individual legislator cannot personally satisfy and which his office is not equipped to handle. Often the representative must rely on outside assistance, and a large portion of this outside assistance is provided by the administrative bureaus. One major area in which this is especially true concerns the problem of acquiring sufficient information. One freshman congressman has been quoted as saying:

> *We have to know too much. We have to make too many de-*
> *cisions. There is a tremendous problem in international relations*
> *and congressmen are constantly involved in this. But in addition*
> *we are supposed to know all about domestic activities—about edu-*
> *cation, water pollution, small business problems, dams, etc. No*
> *matter how hard working and conscientious a congressman is, no*
> *matter how much homework he does, he just can't master these*
> *problems. We just don't have the time to keep informed properly.*[26]

The impressions of this representative have been corroborated in sev-
eral studies. One of these was conducted by Dartmouth's Public Affairs
Center in the summer and fall of 1963. A random sample of eighty United
States Representatives was asked the following question:

> *Now, what are the most pressing problems you face in trying to*
> *do your job as a Congressman—what are the things that hinder you*
> *in your tasks? (and) What are the most pressing problems which pre-*
> *vent Congress from doing what you think it ought to do?*

Each congressman was given a quota of ten responses which the Center
grouped into fourteen categories. Seventy-eight per cent of the legislators
had a response placed in the category entitled "Complexity of decision-
making; lack of information."[27]

One of the primary sources of information available to the legislator is
the executive branch. This is especially true when the congressman is of the
same political party as that of the president. The departments often provide
representatives and committees not only with valuable information, but
also with documents, prepared speeches, and strategy suggestions. The
executive agencies may render other services to the individual congressman by assisting him in meeting the diverse demands of his constituents.
These constituency demands may include such requests as inquiries for
information, aid in locating federal employment, or assistance in guiding a
citizen's case through the adjudicative process of an administrative agency.
The success of a congressman in these areas may well be dependent upon
the quality of his working relationships with the various executive departments. Overlooking administrative advances into the legislative arena may
be seen as quite an inexpensive price to pay for maintaining open channels
of communications with these bureaus. A congressman, whether acting
alone or within a committee, is not apt to reveal violations of the anti-
administrative lobbying statutes at the risk of straining his relationships
with the very departments which provide him with so much valuable
assistance.

An additional obstacle to congressional enforcement of the administrative lobbying restrictions is the partisan make-up of the Government
Operations Committees. The problem arises when the majority of the
committee members are of the same political party affiliation as the president. It is not an easy matter to convince such a majority to conduct an
investigation which may discredit their party's administration. Presidential

support may be very important to the individual legislators, and it is not probable that they would risk the alienation of the president by criticizing the lobbying activities of the Chief Executive's administrative officials.

Various measures have been introduced to alter this partisan situation. A bill by Congressman Robert H. Michel proposed that the chairman and majority of each committee belong to a major political party other than the president's. Another proposed reform was put forth by Congressmen Thomas B. Curtis, Durward G. Hall and James C. Cleveland. In their supplemental views to the Monroney-Madden Report they recommended the creation of a Committee on Procedures and Policies in both Houses of Congress with "the power to examine into and report back to the Congress on the expenditure of Federal funds by the executive branch to insure they are spent efficiently and in accordance with the law." Membership on these committees was to be divided equally between the majority and minority parties, and the chairmen were to be members of the minority party.

The Government Operations Committees themselves do not provide conditions which would encourage enforcement of the anti-executive lobbying laws. The committees have not taken an active role in this area, and once the business of a congressional committee becomes firmly established there will be no major change in its activities without the presence of powerful stimuli to prompt such a modification in committee work. The Government Operations Committees must compete for their members' time and attention with the more attractive committees of which they may also have membership, as well as the almost overwhelming daily demands upon a congressman's resources. The problem of "illegal" administrative lobbying is not likely to provide a stimulus of sufficient strength to prompt these committees into the active enforcement of the relevant statutory restraints.

The situation faced by the legislator is not such that one would predict congressional enforcement of the restrictions on executive lobbying. It is doubtful that the advantages accruing to the individual congressman from attempts to enforce the limitations will outweigh the potential risk involved. This partially explains why congressmen tend to object to executive lobbying only when they also object to the substantive issue being promoted by the lobbying tactics, for only in such situations do the potential advantages reach sufficient magnitude to warrant the action. Notwithstanding this hesitancy on the part of congressmen to press the point, administrative departments are sensitive to possible congressional reactions. Congressional criticism, then, although rarely brought to bear, does provide a potential means of enforcing the intended statutory restraints.

IV

Restrictions have been promulgated by Congress which were intended to curb the lobbying tactics of both private groups and the bureaucratic officials of the executive branch of the federal government. In reality the restraints placed upon pressure manufactured by the executive branch have been even less effective than the restrictions upon private interest groups. It is quite obvious that Congressman Good's 1919 prediction that the *Lobbying with Appropriated Moneys Act* would "absolutely put a stop" to such activities has not become a reality. The provisions contained in this body of law have simply never been enforced. The General Accounting Office, in its desire to avoid entanglement in the political arena, does not enforce them on the grounds that it would be uneconomical and impractical. Other possible enforcement authorities, including the Justice Department, congressional committees and the members of Congress, have found enforcement contrary to their own interests. Enforcement, however, is not impossible. Congressional criticism may be the most effective potential vehicle for restricting such proscribed activity, for every administrative agency is dependent upon Congress for the authorization and funding of department programs. Yet as conditions exist today, this entire legal area may be viewed as a classic case in "legal fiction."

Nonenforcement, of course, is certainly not unique. There are numerous examples of laws which remain on the statute books and are not enforced, but usually because they are outdated and, therefore, insignificant. However, a strong case may be built for the argument that laws restricting administrative lobbying are far from antiquated. Rather, these statutes become more "modern" as bureaucratic influence continues to grow. This position would undoubtedly include the ethical and philosophical objections to such practices. If one considers administrative lobbying an unwarranted executive transgression on legislative powers and believes it improper for popularly elected lawmakers to be pressured by bureaucratic officials, then it would be quite justifiable to conclude with Representative Curtis that the present situation is "scandalous" and dysfunctional to our governmental process.

A counter argument may be advanced based upon evidence of practical governmental operations. From this viewpoint the restraints on executive lobbying are indeed antiquated. They were designed to preserve a form of government which has since passed—the strict separation of legislative, administrative, and judicial powers. The dividing lines between these branches, especially the legislative and executive, are today exceedingly fine. The complexity of the governing process today does not allow Congress simply to make the laws and the executive to enforce them. From a very pragmatic viewpoint, the administration, with its sophisticated means of gathering information and its ability to design appropriate programs and policies, must not only be able to provide Congress with objective information, but must also have the freedom to advocate the passage or defeat of legislation. Those of this mind would conclude with Ernest S. Griffith that the "network of informal liaison relationships is one of the keys to the successful operation of our Constitution."[28]

The worth and propriety of executive lobbying may well be debated by those interested in questions of public law, democratic theory, and governmental operations. But regardless of the normative judgment one ultimately makes, the fact remains that, in the face of statutory provisions to the contrary, what is probably the most powerful lobby in Washington continues to operate relatively unrestricted.

A PROPOSAL FOR REFORM

Louis M. Kohlmeier, Jr.

Given the present state of domestic economic affairs, probably the worst that Americans can expect in the immediate future is higher taxes, higher prices, more traffic jams, more blackouts and more old movies on television. Highway contractors, those members of Congress who own TV stations and the Washington lawyers who know a way through the mazes of government will get richer. Negroes who expect equal job opportunities will grow more frustrated and the rest of us will become more confused.

The efforts to adapt big government and big business to the Constitution will continue apace. The regulators will meet together in the Administrative Conference of the United States to attempt to reform themselves. There may be an American Ombudsman, that officer of government invented by Scandinavian Socialists so that frustrated citizens have a place to register their complaints against the bureaucracy. The Supreme Court will continue to search the Constitution for words that give new meaning and vitality to individualism and economic freedom. Contrariwise, there will be efforts to adapt the Constitution to big government and big business. Rexford Guy Tugwell has written no fewer than thirty-two drafts of a new Constitution. Tugwell as a young man was one of President Franklin Roosevelt's New Deal brain trusters and as an older man he has felt "an uneasy sense of something wrong" in the relationship of the old Constitution and the new reality of economic and social responsibility and authority vested in the central government.

All these efforts to adapt reality to the Constitution or to write a new Constitution more in keeping with reality are unlikely anytime soon to assuage public frustrations, remedy old conflicts in federal programs and bureaus or discipline total federal spending to some system of priorities. Consequently, Congress will continue to shift to the President, his Council of Economic Advisers and his executive branch departments more responsibility for governmental efficiency and economic security and Congress will delegate piecemeal to the President and those who serve at his pleasure more authority to fulfill his responsibilities. It seems unlikely that a President anytime soon will emerge as the dictator whom Justice Frankfurter in 1952 said could come forth from the accumulation of presidential power, no matter how disinterestedly that authority was gained. America was sufficiently bothered by the precedent of Franklin D. Roosevelt's four terms so that it ratified the Twenty-second Amendment in 1951 to bar a future President from more than two full terms in office.

If the near-term threat of dictatorship in America may thus be dismissed, certain other risks cannot. It remains to be seen whether the President, his economic advisers and his great departments can succeed where Congress and its regulatory agencies have failed. The executive branch, by and large, is not now as defenseless as are the regulators against pressures brought by special-interest segments of the population and against commitment to special private causes. The pressures bear on the great departments, some of which tend in time to become advocates of broad special-interest groups. The Department of Labor is regarded by all concerned as the voice of organized labor; the Department of Commerce is the accepted advocate of business; the Department of Agriculture is the spokesman for as well as subsidizer of farmers. But these departments are advocates of very large special-interest groups which, because they are not of a single view on matters of competition, subsidy and so forth, expose department officers to varying points of view. And, most importantly, their advocacies are not unduly objectionable to the public at large because cabinet secretaries are subject to the discipline of the President whose constituency embraces all the people.

If the President and his executive branch are now reasonably secure against the pressures and commitments that have plagued the regulators, they may not remain so. The experience of the democracies of western Europe suggests that increased centralization of power within government generates its own pressures and problems. Big business and big labor are capable of generating big political pressures that do not necessarily assist efficient government planning. Issues of mechanization, full employment and higher wages in industries such as transportation, communications, steel and automobiles that have been cartelized or nationalized tend to be resolved more by political than economic means, and if they are not resolved, big labor is capable of general strikes that paralyze a nation. Government, industry and labor relationships in the United States do not yet parallel those in Europe. But neither is America as far from Europe as it once was. General Motors says industry and government should work "not as adversaries, but as allies," and government no longer disagrees.[1]

The alternatives to a continuation of the present trend of public frustration and government inefficiency resolved through growing centralization of authority in the President are not simple. But neither are alternatives an unexplored miasma. President Kennedy proposed an alternative in the transportation area when he called not for the transfer but for the repeal of much of the Interstate Commerce Commission's authority to regulate rates. He was inconsistent in that he proposed to rely "more on competition" and antitrust law concerning railroad rates but he used the informal persuasive powers of his office, rather than antitrust law, to prevent steel and other price increases. Perhaps he did not, in his own mind, act inconsistently; his means varied but the ends he sought were lower prices. John Kennedy was, obviously, a pragmatist.

His contribution was to state the problem and offer an alternative solution. "We must begin," he said, to resolve the conflicts and inefficiencies in transportation programs or face the certainty of "even more difficult and costly solutions in the not-too-distant future."[2] Some of those who served President Kennedy, such as Newton Minow, added the thought that agencies such as the Federal Communications Commission should be abolished and their responsibility and authority redistributed among the three constitutional branches of government. Taken as a whole, the Kennedy era was tentative and groping, but it rejected the cynicism that the only thing history teaches is that it teaches nothing. Certainly the need for greater efficiency in the administration of each federal program and for establishment of some scheme of priority among programs, applicable to federal spending and manpower resources, are greater now than when Kennedy spoke. At the end of its time, the Johnson Administration counted no fewer than 435 federal social and economic programs, compared, it said, with 45 at the time President Kennedy came to office.

Big government and its counterparts in industry and labor will not disappear; they were responses to the demands of the people in an era of industrialization and urbanization, for economic security and abundance. Blind condemnation of bigness, no less than blind affirmation, is of no help. If the needs of governmental efficiency and priority are to be met, and balanced anew with doctrines of economic freedom and individualism, bigness must be disciplined through a redistribution of powers among the three constitutional branches; a re-evaluation of the relationship between the federal government and the states and a reaffirmation of antitrust law as the best and only means this nation has discovered to assure economic freedom and economic individualism. The Constitution is not outmoded as a charter of government and of liberty. The competitive free enterprise system, enforced by antitrust laws, is not incapacitated as the most efficient means men have found to assure consumers the lowest prices, the greatest technological progress and the best allocation of resources.

The independent regulatory agencies as they presently exist, should be abolished, and the powers of each should be carefully reexamined. Those promises and powers in their laws which do not conflict with competitive principles and antitrust statutes should be distributed among the three branches; those that do conflict should be repealed. In redistributing those powers which are retained, consideration must be given to the question of whether some tasks, assumed by Washington in pursuit of the general welfare of the entire nation, can more effectively be performed by state and local governments, alone or in a new form of partnership with the federal government. Washington must treat all who are subject to its laws and beneficiaries of its programs with equality and uniformity. That fundamental constitutional requirement inhibits effectiveness of centralized planning in a nation as large, populous and variegated as is the United States. The transportation requirements of New York are not the same as those of Nashville and Tucson. The Federal Trade Commission admittedly has not been able to effectively police the retail advertising of all merchants on every Main Street and one FCC member has said, "Federal efforts alone can never be successful."[3] If Washington delegates or shares its tasks, it must also share its tax revenues. The most promising method is block grants to the states; Washington would, for example, grant to each state a proportionate sum for transportation purposes and allow the state to decide where and how to spend the money. Federal authority and money cannot be shared in areas of exclusive federal jurisdiction, such as navigable waters and airways. But federal funds, shared or not, should not be used to subsidize private corporations.

In the redistribution of powers among the executive, legislative and judicial branches of the federal government, each branch would be charged with larger economic responsibility and authority.

The authority of the President must in some degree be commensurate with his responsibility and both must be disciplined. Unlimited responsibility without some amount of authority invites irresponsibility and invasion in matters of private rights involving prices and wages. If Congress insists that the President bear responsibility for full employment and full purchasing power, then he must have a voice in authority for making monetary policy, which now is vested in the Federal Reserve Board. Perhaps efficiency also requires that he have the authority to raise and lower income tax rates within a limited range prescribed by Congress. But his authority should be confined to power that is narrow in its range of discretion and uniform in its application. He should not, formally or informally, exercise authority over prices charged by private corporations or wages negotiated by labor unions. Nor should his Council of Economic Advisers promulgate price and wage guidelines. The role of the council should be to advise the President, in the exercise of his authority and in his recommendations to Congress, and to coordinate the enforcement and administration of law by the great departments of the executive branch.

Congress is the least efficient, and most democratic, of the three branches. It is a committee of more than five hundred and its composition is more or less constantly changing. It has devised a permanent supporting structure consisting of professional committee staffs, the legislative research services of the Library of Congress and the executive branch monitoring functions of the General Accounting Office. But Congress apparently is inherently incapable of itself regulating the nation's commerce or else it would not have created the independent regulatory agencies and, more recently, enacted the Employment Act and created the Council of Economic Advisers. Having charged the President with responsibility, and having now begun to enlarge the authority of the executive branch, Congress should have no great difficulty in removing the regulators and reapportioning their powers.

Congress doubtless will remain the least efficient branch, but certainly it can be strengthened. Members of the most democratic branch should receive at least $100,000 annually, plus expenses, for their services. They should not need private incomes; the repeal of the regulators' powers over industrial pricing and entry into the business will remove from the lawmakers' reach the temptation to use public office for private gain. Congress could further be strengthened if the Constitution were amended to provide four-year terms for members of the House of Representatives, as President Johnson suggested. The proposal for terms longer than two years has merit and if it is adopted consideration also should be given to limiting a representative or senator to no more than two, or perhaps three, consecutive terms. What is good for the President may be good also for members of Congress. Moreover, a limitation on length of service would eliminate, or alleviate, an objectionable feature of congressional committee organization: the seniority system which permits elder legislators to unduly dominate the work of Congress.

The judicial branch long has been the third of three, insofar as size and money are concerned. Lower federal courts perennially are weighted down by dockets of cases awaiting trial and their work loads would be greatly increased by abolition of independent agencies whose formal decisions take the place of federal district court decisions and which are appealable directly to a federal circuit court of appeals. Congress has recognized the problem of overloaded dockets to the extent of creating some new federal judgeships and a few federal district courts of specialized jurisdiction, such as the United States Court of Claims and the United States Court of Customs and Patent Appeals. If the regulatory agencies are abolished, it must create more. It could reconstitute the National Labor Relations Board as a labor court. It should create at least one additional specialized court, to be known as the commerce court, to decide antitrust cases as well as enforcement actions in such matters as food and drug labeling, fraud in the sales of securities and transportation industry safety violations. These specialized courts would decide cases brought by the executive branch or by private citizens, or by the executive branch on behalf of private citizens, as the Justice Department now brings suits to open employment opportunities to Negroes. The commerce court might be constituted from out of the Federal Trade Commission. But the judges of all such courts would have lifetime tenure and be subject to the discipline of the Supreme Court; they would not have the power to both make law and decide it, as the regulatory agencies now do.

There is no constitutional solution to the problem of the regulators other than to abolish them, as they now stand, and redistribute those powers which constitutionally may be exercised by the three branches. The Constitution created a government of the people and the people gave their sovereignty only to officers whom they elected and judges to whom they gave lifetime tenure.

Regulators are extensions of the legislative branch but it would be totally inconsistent and wholly impractical to elect regulators to four-year or other terms. Congress created the agencies for the very purpose of removing the regulation of commerce from politics and substituting independent expertise for political partisanship. There is no reason to believe that popular election of regulators would not further intensify the politics of regulation and deny expertise and independence.

To confer upon the regulators, as they now exist, lifetime tenure also would be inconsistent and impractical. The Constitution, in granting tenure to judges, denied them the power to decide issues other than those brought before them in cases and controversies. Judges cannot reach out to make law where they feel law should be made; it was the purpose of regulation by independent agency to do precisely that. Judges do, of course, make law, but it is subordinate to and contained by statute law written by Congress. To confer upon the regulators something less than lifetime tenure, say terms of ten or twenty years, might make them more efficient but it also would be an unsatisfactory compromise. It would deny them lifetime tenure, which is the only real badge of independence, and it would make them more arbitrary in the exercise of powers which are essentially political, and which for that reason are constitutionally apportioned to the legislative, and most democratic, branch.

To transfer the regulators and their powers intact to the executive branch would confer upon the President powers which, as the Supreme Court has said, would be so discretionary in form and so arbitrary in effect as to be unconstitutional.

Abolition of the agencies, it must be emphasized, does not mean abandonment of specific federal promises of the lowest possible rates and prices and the greatest abundance of goods and services or repeal of the general promise of economic stability and security. It does mean restructuring of some parts of government and of industry for the purpose of improving the likelihood those promises can be fulfilled and economic freedom will not be lost.

Reaffirmation of competition as a national policy and refurbishment of antitrust law as the means of enforcing that policy are absolutely essential prerequisites to abolition of the regulatory agencies. The writing and enforcement of antitrust law never has been and never will be a pure science, economic or political. Antitrust is, as regulation attempted to be, a political policy addressed to industrial economics. The policy of antitrust is to foster competition; the policy of regulation, formal or informal, is to suppress competition. There are and will continue to be valid exceptions to the rule of competition. Natural monopolies, in the form of local electric, water and transit companies, are exceptions that will continue to be regulated under state authority. But all the exceptions that by law or habit have been created in Washington should be re-examined.

The preferences of the Defense and State Departments for big business and their implied distrust of competition rest on premises of national interest and national defense that, at best, have little relationship to the consumer interest; the Krupp steel mills of prewar Germany served similar national interests. The preferences of the regulatory agencies rest on efforts to make regulation more efficient and these efforts, as they have turned out, also bear little relationship to the consumer interest. So far as the preferences of the President and his Council of Economic Advisers are concerned, these also rest on the needs of efficiency in the attempt to secure lower prices and to foster economic stability.

The purported justification underlying all these various preferences for industrial concentration rest basically on the economic assumption that concentration is more efficient than competition as a means of securing lower production costs and, consequently, lower prices or more rapid technological advance. It is assumed that the bigger business is, the larger will be its capability of reducing production costs, lowering prices and/or engaging in research and development. The Federal Trade Commission has not addressed itself to the question of whether in fact prices decline and technology advances in direct ratio to business bigness. But the preponderance of evidence produced by economic studies at a number of universities demonstrates rather conclusively that bigness results in lower prices and greater innovation up to a point, and bigness beyond that point results in potentially monopolistic profits, rising prices and an abatement of inventive genius in corporate research and development laboratories.

It is not clear whether the point at which bigness breeds inefficiency may be reached when a corporation has $1 billion or $20 billion or $100 billion of assets. The point unquestionably varies among different industries.

Antitrust law is a useful, if not perfect, instrument for enlarging the store of knowledge concerning the public effects of industrial concentration. It can be made more useful. Enforcement by the Justice Department should be coordinated with the work of the Council of Economic Advisers. The informal efforts of the President to regulate prices and wages through the prestige or inherent powers of office would be abandoned and those ends pursued through formal antitrust actions, coordinated with fiscal and monetary policy by the Council of Economic Advisers, filed by the Justice Department and decided by the commerce court. The formal exceptions to antitrust law enacted by Congress for the benefit of the regulatory agencies should be repealed.

Antitrust law does not seek to minimize the consumer benefits of mass production; it seeks to maximize those benefits by fostering a maximum amount of competition among a reasonable number of corporations. The antitrust division of the Justice Department sought not to break up General Motors Corporation into one hundred companies, but into a half-dozen competing automobile manufacturers. The law avoids the pitfalls of regulation of industrial prices and practices by dealing with the structures of industries. It aims to foster the greatest possible amount of competition among mass producers by attempting to ensure that older companies do not dominate or monopolize an industry to the extent of frightening off potential new entrants; by barring mergers of substantial competitors; by banning price-fixing conspiracies among competitors and by guarding against the great variety of agreements with suppliers and with retailers by which producers can discriminate against competition.

The Sherman Act still is a forceful deterrent to price-fixing, and the Clayton Act, as amended by Congress in 1950 with the Celler-Kefauver Anti-Merger Law, effectively prevents horizontal mergers of direct competitors and vertical mergers of producers with their suppliers or retail customers. Indeed, the only substantial price-fixing and the only substantial mergers of direct or related competitors that remain are in the regulated industries. Federally regulated industries are not monopolies and they should be subject to the full range of antitrust remedies and they should not be the beneficiaries of federal subsidies.

Conglomerate mergers, the new vogue among regulated as well as unregulated industrialists, sometimes involve the union of disparate companies but more often are a large corporation's method of entering a related line of business which it could have entered through expansion of its own facilities. The big soap manufacturer entering the household bleach business by acquiring a bleach company is the standard example. Conglomerate mergers of this sort, in addition to sometimes involving stock transactions of questionable financial integrity, are anti-competitive in that the acquiring company is eliminated as a potential competitor. By this line of reasoning, all conglomerate mergers are potentially anti-competitive where the merger partners are large companies, each financially capable of entering the other's industry through internal expansion and thus of increasing the number of competitors in each industry.

The Sherman and Clayton Acts as written are legally adequate laws but enforcement has been inadequate. Active participation by the Council of Economic Advisers in formulation of antitrust policies and suits should result in greater enforcement effort. But, pending the council's participation, Congress can act to reinvigorate enforcement. The antitrust division of the Justice Department needs more money and manpower. The division in recent years has had an annual budget of about $7 million, which is less than half the budget of a single large regulatory agency and one-tenth the amount the government has paid in airline subsidies in a single year. After giving it more money and manpower, Congress should curtail the division's frequent consent decree settlements of antitrust suits it has brought. It has been allowed to compromise suits on the theory that, being understaffed, it thus could bring more suits. Suits should go to trial and, in price-fixing suits, businessmen no longer should be allowed to plead no-contest and thus avoid trial where the trial record can be used by private parties and by the states as the basis for triple-damage suits against the price-fixers.

Congress should further augment enforcement by enacting an absolute ban on all mergers in the future involving significant competitors—direct, indirect or potential. A significant merger could be defined as one in which one of the merger partners has annual sales or assets in excess of $100 million. Pending clarification by the Council of Economic Advisers of the points in various industries at which mass-production economies no longer yield lower prices and greater product innovation, the absolute bar would permit mergers of smaller companies and ban automatically those of larger corporations. The acquiring company in a conglomerate merger would be required to prove it is not a potential entrant, through internal expansion, in another industry. The only other exceptions to the ban would be where the acquired company was failing and would go out of business except for the merger or where the acquired company was privately held by an owner who died and, for that reason, might otherwise go out of business. But the burden of proving entitlement to these exceptions should also be placed on the parties to a merger proposal.

Antitrust law does not and should not in any way bar business bigness achieved through internal sales success and inventiveness, rather than by merger. It does not and should not prevent any corporation from entering another line of business through internal expansion, instead of merger. Industry is and will continue to be free to capitalize on economies of large-scale production and on the capabilities of managerial talents. Internal growth and expansion predictably will not result in monopoly, if a large and successful company's business remains open to new competitors.

Almost all industries in America today which are dominated by very large corporations with near-monopolistic powers—regulated industries such as the railroads and non-regulated industries such as steel and automobiles—are in fact the results of mergers which took place many years ago and which were not challenged at the time. Mergers of competitors, actual and potential, are and will be banned; in all fairness, mergers of years past that permit industry domination today should also be undone. Antitrust laws as they now exist can be applied to old mergers because Congress has applied no statute of limitations to these laws. Some economists, including a recent Assistant Attorney General in charge of the antitrust division, have suggested that Congress reach existing industrial concentrations by enacting a new law which would make it illegal for a dominant corporation to hold "unreasonable market power" in its industry.

When competition is reaffirmed and antitrust law is refurbished, there will be no need of regulators. The agencies should be abolished on a first-in, first-out basis.

The transportation area demands first attention, as President Kennedy indicated. The antitrust law exemptions that permit railroads, truck lines and barge lines to fix rates should be repealed. The Interstate Commerce Commission's controls on entry into these industries, through its power to license common carriers, and its power to approve mergers also should be repealed. Railroad and other transportation industry executives who persist in fixing prices should be subject to the criminal penalties of the Sherman Act. Antitrust law would take the place of regulatory law and there no longer would be any function for the ICC or its National Transportation Policy mandate, which is impossible of fulfillment.

The authority of the Civil Aeronautics Board to fix domestic airline fares, control entry into the industry and approve mergers should similarly be repealed. Commercial airlines are no longer an infant industry and they should by law be declared ineligible for subsidies. If these actions are taken, and antitrust law is thereby substituted for regulatory law, there will be no reason or excuse for a Civil Aeronautics Board.

The elimination of rate-fixing conferences, subsidies and controls on entry will not be so easily accomplished in areas of overseas air and ocean transportation. The democracies of western Europe, which have ownership interests in their international airlines and shipping companies and which are the mainstays of the International Air Transport Association and other rate-fixing conferences, will resist United States withdrawal. Nonetheless the United States supplies far more passengers and freight than any other nation and it should use its influence to re-establish competition on international air and sea traffic lanes.

Pan American World Airways and other U.S. companies operating international air services are not now receiving federal subsidies and they, like domestic airlines, should no longer be eligible for subsidies. To end the need for federal subsidization of construction of commercial ships, American shipping companies should be given the freedom they now are denied to build ships in foreign shipyards. To end the need for ship operating subsidies, U.S. ship lines must meet foreign-flag competition the same way other United States producers are expected to compete on the international market. Higher American wages and other operating costs must be offset by superior American technology and automation. American shipbuilders, ship operators and maritime labor for too long have lobbied in Washington intensively and successfully for subsidies with the fundamental argument that America needs its ships for national defense emergencies. Automated ships designed in America and built in foreign yards will be under American control for defense emergencies.

Coordination of the remaining federal programs involving domestic transportation will lie within the responsibility and authority of the Department of Transportation. It already has authority as well as responsibility in matters of rail, highway and aviation safety that formerly was vested in the ICC and CAB. Regulation of automobile safety was vested in the department in 1966. Regulation of safety matters in international ocean transportation should be transferred to the department; the Federal Maritime Administration, its authority to subsidize ship construction and operation having been repealed, can thus be totally abolished.

Aviation safety, on domestic and international air routes, will continue to be an important matter of Transportation Department concern. The public interest requires continued operation by the Federal Aviation Administration of the nation's air traffic control system and certification by FAA of new types of aircraft. FAA is part of the Transportation Department; its spending must be coordinated with actual levels of air traffic and with total federal spending. Airlines and other civilian users of the FAA's air traffic control and navigation system should pay their full share of the costs of operating and improving the system, through establishment of airways user charges. Federal spending to develop a supersonic commercial airliner should end. The SST should not be built until private enterprise can develop a reliably safe and commercially sound airplane and perhaps an SST should not be built even then, if the public nuisance of sonic booms cannot be substantially reduced.

Improvement of the nation's rivers, harbors and coastal waterways for navigation, flood control and generation of electricity also must remain a federal concern because these navigable waterways belong to no single state and are in exclusive federal domain. But the works of the Army Corps of Engineers must be transferred to either the Transportation Department or the Department of the Interior. Inasmuch as federal promotion of barge line transportation will be inappropriate in a new era of transportation competition, perhaps the other purposes of waterways improvements will be paramount and the works of the Engineers therefore should be transferred to the Interior Department. Control of floods, dredging of harbors and control of beach erosion and pollution certainly are proper federal concerns, but barge lines and other private interests that gain special advantage from such programs must pay appropriate user charges for the benefits received.

Federal spending for improvement of surface transportation within the United States cannot quickly be curtailed. If construction of the Interstate Highway System were stopped prior to its planned completion in 1972, millions of motorists would write irate letters to their congressmen. Federal highway construction already has gone so far that federal subsidies probably are essential to save what is left of the nation's urban and intercity surface transportation facilities. Federal spending for highways and common-carrier forms of transportation will continue to grow until 1972. But coordination, through the Transportation Department, can begin before then. The Highway Trust Fund, which defies coordination, should be eliminated and highway spending controlled by annual appropriations; highway user charges larger than those presently collected should be required of all truck lines. The federal government then should adopt a block grant program for transportation, giving to each state annually a proportionate sum, based upon population, to be allocated for urban and intercity highways, rail facilities, subways or buses. The Transportation Department would have authority to make certain that the grants are used efficiently and honestly, but state governments would have final authority to decide how and where the money is expended.

Communications services, like transportation services, involve a combination of intrastate, interstate and international responsibilities and demand new and enlightened approaches. Domestic telephone and telegraph companies are natural local monopolies whose rates and practices will continue to be regulated by the states. Long-distance telephone and telegraph services, both interstate and international, also have been monopolistic in nature and have been regulated by the Federal Communications Commission. Technology, however, has blurred the distinction the FCC has attempted to maintain between voice (or telephone) services and written communications (or telegraph) services, and technology is further blurring distinctions between wire, cable and radio as methods of carrying all types of communications. It seems entirely likely that, given free rein, communications satellites offer a relatively cheap new method of transmitting very large volumes of interstate and international communications and of opening both domestic and overseas long-distance communications to a new era of competition. If this potential of communications satellites were realized, competition and antitrust law could be substituted for regulation of long-distance services and the land-based, local telephone and other connecting services would continue to be regulated by the states.

Enlarged use of communications satellites would of course require assignment of more radio frequencies and complicate the already large problem of frequency allocation. The existing problem of allocating frequency space among users of industrial radio services, public police and fire departments and similar users and commercial broadcasters demands more comprehensive and enlightened government study and action. The responsibility for study and the authority to allocate frequency space should be transferred from the Federal Communications Commission to the executive branch. Allocation authority should be shifted to the Commerce Department, where it originated, but would better be pinpointed by transfer to the Transportation Department, which then would be the Department of Transportation and Communications.

In re-evaluating present and projected radio spectrum usage, the executive department should immediately add to the space available for satellite and other communications by moving all television broadcasting into the ultra high frequency channels, and thus freeing the very high frequency channels for other uses. The move will inconvenience television receiver owners, but no more than they already have been inconvenienced.

It will put all commercial TV broadcasters on an equal footing, increase competition in the industry, eliminate the most onerous features and politics of the FCC's 1952 master plan and perhaps even bring back to life more television networks.

Further, the executive department and Congress should reconsider the 1962 Communications Satellite Act. Reconsideration might well lead to the conclusion that competition, rather than a monopolistic government-industry consortium, is appropriate for international as well as domestic communications. They clearly should reject the proposal, made late in 1968 by a presidential committee headed by a State Department official, of a still larger government-sponsored monopoly that would own all U.S.-held submarine cable and other facilities, including satellites, for international communications. In addition, Congress and the executive branch should endorse competition by encouraging the development of cable-television and pay-television services within the United States. And the Federal Communications Commission should be abolished.

Re-examination of federal responsibility and authority in the area of energy resources also is long overdue. The inability of the Atomic Energy Commission to promote civilian uses of atomic energy, to the extent hoped, suggests that Congress again should relax governmental controls over private use and take new measures to foster industrial competition. Civilian control of atomic energy should remain, but control should be transferred to the Department of the Interior. The department could regulate safety and other aspects of private industrial usage of atomic energy. Inasmuch as the primary private use apparently will continue to involve atomic generation of electricity, it is entirely appropriate that the Secretary of the Interior become the coordinating agent of all federal programs concerning energy resources. The Federal Power Commission's authority to license the construction of hydroelectric dams on navigable waterways should be transferred to the Secretary and Congress must fix standards he is to follow in deciding whether contested dam sites are to be developed by private investor-owned utilities or by public authorities. His decisions would be appealable to the new commerce court. Federal regulation of interstate transmission of natural gas and of gas producers should be abandoned; neither transmission nor production is a natural monopoly and competition should be required in both areas through the application of antitrust law to entry into the business, to merger proposals and to rate-fixing. Regulation of electric and gas utilities, which are local distribution monopolies, should remain with the states.

Federal supervision of national banks and federal insurance of deposits in national and state banks are essentially safety functions which should be consolidated in the Treasury Department. The Office of Comptroller of the Currency, already in the department, could be renamed the Federal Banking Administration. The administrator would assume the Comptroller's authority to examine and supervise national banks. The bank regulatory authority of the Federal Reserve Board would be transferred to the administrator and the function and authority of the Federal Deposit Insurance Corporation also would be consolidated in the new office of the administrator.

The Federal Reserve Board, thus relieved of its responsibility and authority to examine and regulate member banks of the Federal Reserve System, would become solely an agent of monetary policy, adjusting the nation's supply of money and credit to its needs of the moment. The Federal Reserve System of member commercial banks would remain intact but the board should be abolished as an independent agency. It should be re-formed as a part of the executive branch and must be, if the responsibility which has been charged to the President by Congress for full employment and purchasing power is to be fulfilled. Conservative bankers assert that the Federal Reserve Board's independence is a healthy brake on the soft money and easy credit policies of some liberal Presidents. But the Federal Reserve Board has not proved itself unerring in economic wisdom either and divided responsibility and authority lead to conflict and invite irresponsibility. The President, not the board, is accountable to the intended beneficiaries of full employment and purchasing power. Authority for monetary policy should be vested in a multimember board, but the board should be part of the executive branch. Its members should be confirmed by the Senate and should serve at the pleasure of the President. It could be composed of the chairman of the Council of Economic Advisers, who also would be chairman of the new Federal Reserve Board; the Secretary of the Treasury; and the administrator of the new Federal Banking Administration.

Reform, over the long term, also should include an end to the dual system of national and state banks. Chartering of commercial banks by the federal government and the states has led to conflicting standards of competition. Chartering of new banks, which means control of entry into the business, should be left to the states alone. State law on branch banking already controls national as well as state banks and should remain. Banks are not in fact interstate businesses and should not be allowed to spread themselves across state lines. More competition among banks is desirable and antitrust law should apply to bank mergers and, to the extent possible, to other competitive matters in the banking industry.

A banking industry consisting entirely of state-chartered and state-regulated banks need not be inconsistent with a central banking system headed by the reconstituted Federal Reserve Board. State banks as well as national banks presently are members of the Federal Reserve System.

Federal jurisdiction in matters of consumer protection from false advertising, securities frauds, flammable fabrics and the like should be re-evaluated and new balances struck between federal and state authority and government regulation and free competition. Federal efforts to police hundreds of thousands of retailers and other businessmen who deal directly with consumers should be re-examined and abandoned where Washington cannot succeed. Those policing functions which the federal government can best perform, such as guarding against false advertising on national television and stock manipulation on national securities exchanges, should be transferred to a new Consumer Affairs Division in the Justice Department. The division would police consumer frauds and misrepresentations by filing suits in the new commerce court. Policing of lesser frauds and misrepresentations would be left to the states and to individuals. To assist, the federal government should provide funds in the form of state grants which would be distributed to Better Business Bureaus and similar organizations and would be used to expand the embryonic program, now administered by the federal Office of Economic Opportunity, to provide legal services to consumers who cannot afford a lawyer's fees.

The Federal Trade Commission's authority to police misleading advertising, flammable fabrics and mislabeled furs thus would be redistributed between the Consumer Affairs Division and the states. The FTC's authority to enforce the Clayton Antitrust Act would be consolidated with the same authority already existing in the antitrust division of the Justice Department. The Robinson-Patman Act amendment to the Clayton Act, which the antitrust division has almost never used, would be repealed. Hopefully, federal exemptions from antitrust laws which permit states to enact fair-trade laws also would be repealed. And the Federal Trade Commission would be abolished and made over into a part of the judicial branch.

The Securities and Exchange Commission would similarly be taken apart and abolished as it now exists. Authority to investigate fraud in the sale of securities and manipulation of stock market prices would be transferred to the Consumer Affairs Division. Its authority to control entry into the stock market business and to regulate stock exchange commission rates would be repealed. Entry would be free and mergers and commission rates would be subject to antitrust laws. Antitrust law thus reaffirmed would be employed to bar forevermore member firms of the New York Stock Exchange and other exchanges from fixing commission rates and to bestow on investors the benefits of commission rate competition. The new federal program of grants to the states for the purpose of strengthening Better Business Bureaus and other consumer protection agencies might well be expanded to also strengthen the securities regulatory agencies of New York, California and other states.

The labyrinth of federal bureaucracies that regulate labor and management relations ought to be reformed. Federal laws guaranteeing workers' right to organize, those proscribing unfair union and management practices and those written to assure democratic procedures in unions' internal affairs should be administered by the Labor Department through suits filed in the new labor court. The National Labor Relations Board can be reconstituted as the court. The Labor Department already polices unions' internal affairs, through suits filed in federal district courts. It also should assume the functions now vested in the NLRB, including the supervision of union representation elections among employees.

Federal programs now assigned to the National Mediation Board and the Federal Mediation and Conciliation Service should first be combined and then reviewed by Congress and the Labor Department. Federal mediation clearly has not been successful in transportation. Its collateral effect of stagnating labor-management bargaining, leading ultimately to compulsory arbitration, is surely undesirable. Greater reliance for mediation and conciliation might be placed on state agencies which already exist for those purposes.

Labor's basic right to organize and bargain for wages and other benefits is not an abuse of antitrust laws but organized labor should not enjoy total immunity from those laws. Unions ought not to be used as price-fixing mechanisms, either by barbers, musicians and other self-employed persons or by agreement of workers with employers. Antitrust law does and should apply to conspiracies of unions with employers for the purpose of damaging competitive employers or unions.

The Equal Employment Opportunity Commission should be abolished because it is an inefficient means of opening job opportunities to Negroes and other minority groups. Its responsibility should be transferred either to the Labor Department or to the civil rights division of the Justice Department. Suits to require employers and unions to fulfill their obligations under the 1964 Civil Rights Act would be filed in the new labor court, as they now are filed by the Justice Department in federal district courts.

The reform of the regulators will not be quick or easy. More and perhaps better answers may be found in the course of abolishing the independent regulatory agencies and subjecting their promises and powers to the discipline of constitutional doctrine and of the competitive system reinforced by antitrust laws. If those promises and powers are not so disciplined, governmental efficiency, coordination and priority will be pursued by other means. Greater economic stability and consumer security will be found, but at greater expense of economic as well as individual freedom.

NOTES: BUREAUCRACY

Introduction

1. Laurence J. Peter and Raymond Hull, *The Peter Principle* (Bantam Books, 1969), pp. 2, 4.

2. See, for example, Francis E. Rourke, *Bureaucracy, Politics, and Public Policy* (Little, Brown, 1969).

3. Murray Edelman, *The Symbolic Uses of Politics* (University of Illinois Press, 1964), p. 2.

4. Richard F. Fenno, Jr., *The President's Cabinet* (Harvard University Press, 1959).

5. This documentary prompted widespread public and governmental criticism. CBS President Dr. Frank Stanton narrowly escaped being bound over on charges of contempt of Congress when he refused to disclose information about the program to the House Commerce Committee.

Anthony Lake

1. A. J. Liebling, "The Coast Recedes," May 2 (sic), 1960, in *The Press* (New York: Ballantine Books, 1961).

2. Bruce Ladd, *Crisis in Credibility* (New York: The New American Library, 1968), pp. 188-189.

3. Richard Neustadt, *Presidential Power* (New York: John Wiley and Sons, Inc., 1960), p. 139.

4. Phil G. Goulding, *Confirm or Deny—Informing the People on National Security* (New York: Harper and Row, 1970).

5. Goulding, *op. cit.,* p. 32.

6. H. H. Gerth and C. Wright Mills, *From Max Weber: Essays in Sociology* (New York: Oxford University Press, 1958), pages 233-234.

7. For the most comprehensive reform proposals, see Ladd, *op. cit.,* chapter 10.

Richard L. Engstrom and Thomas G. Walker

1. Comment, *Lobbying—A Definition and Recapitulation of Its Practice,* 11 Ohio S. L. J. 557, 559 (1950).

2. U.S.C. section 54 (1913), as amended, 5 U.S.C. section 3107 (1967). The current statute now reads "appropriated funds may not be used to pay a publicity expert unless specifically appropriated for that purpose."

3. 18 U.S.C. section 1913 (1951).

4. 58 Cong. Rec. 403 (1919).

5. *Id.*

6. *Id.*

7. 58 Cong. Rec. 425 (1919).

8. 39 U.S.C. section 4154 (1962).

9. Departments of State, Justice and Commerce, the Judiciary, and Related Agencies Appropriations Act of 1968, Pub. L. No. 90-133, tit. VII, section 701.

10. Independent Offices and Department of Housing and Urban Development Appropriations Act of 1968, Pub. L. No. 90-121, tit. III, section 301.

11. 105 F. Supp. 257 (S.D.N.Y. 1952).

12. J. Freeman, *The Political Process: Executive Bureau—Legislative Committee Relations* 39 (1965).

13. *Hearings on the Organization of Congress Before the Joint Comm. on the Organization of the Congress,* 89th Cong., 1st Sess., pt. 6, at 1027 (1965).

14. Quoted in V. Key, *Politics, Parties and Pressure Groups* 702 (5th ed. 1964).

15. deGrazia, "Congressional Liaison: An Inquiry into Its Meaning for Congress," in *Congress: The First Branch of Government* 311 (A. deGrazia ed. 1966).

16. 26 Cong. Q. Wk. Rep. 2005 (Part II, July 26, 1968).

17. J. Freeman, *supra* note 12, at 87.

18. Quoted in D. Blaisdell, *American Democracy Under Pressure* 88 (1957).

19. V. Key, *supra* note 14, at 704. Liaison tactics have even been scored by private interest groups when used to advance a policy to which the groups are opposed. In 1962, the American Medical Association charged Secretary of Health, Education and Welfare Abraham Ribicoff with using public funds ". . . to propagandize for a bill which many people and many groups have vigorously opposed" by publishing a booklet on medical care for the aged. The association even demanded that the Attorney General determine whether this was a criminal act. *Id.* at 703. The press, too, has attacked the lobbying activities of administrative agencies. For example, when NASA offered to fly the more than 500 Senators and Representatives (along with one relative each) to Cape Kennedy to watch the launching of the Apollo 11 moon shot, one large midwestern newspaper charged that "NASA overreaches itself in its current effort—in the name of 'public information'—to lobby Congress with the taxpayers' money." *The Detroit News,* July 10, 1969 (Editorial, NASA Goes Too Far).

20. Letter from the Honorable John J. Rhodes, Arizona, to the Honorable Charles E. Goodell, New York, Sept. 30, 1967.

21. Letter from Comptroller General of the United States Joseph Campbell to the Honorable John Bell Williams, Mississippi, Sept. 28, 1962.

22. Letter from Comptroller General of the United States Joseph Campbell to the Honorable H. R. Gross, Iowa, March 20, 1962.

23. Letter from Comptroller General of the United States Elmer B. Staats to the Honorable Thomas B. Curtis, Missouri, Sept. 7, 1967.

24. *Id.*

25. Letter from acting Comptroller General of the United States Frank H. Weitzed to the Honorable John F. Baldwin, California, Oct. 11, 1965.

26. Quoted in C. Clapp, *The Congressman: His World as He Sees It* 104-105 (1963).

27. The questions and these data are reported in Janda, "Information Systems for Congress," in A. deGrazia (ed.), *supra* note 15, 409-410.

28. E. Griffith, *Congress: Its Contemporary Role* 65 (4th ed. 1967).

Louis M. Kohlmeier, Jr.

1. James Roche, chairman of the board, General Motors Corporation, in an address before the Illinois Manufacturers Association, Chicago, Illinois, December 12, 1968.

2. Message on Transportation, April 4, 1962.

3. James M. Nicholson, member of the Federal Trade Commission, in remarks before the Allied Daily Newspapers of Washington, Vancouver, Washington, May 24, 1968.

CONCLUSION: PROSPECTS FOR REFORM

> ... [*W*]*e have come to rely on a comfortable time lag of fifty years or a century intervening between the perception that something ought to be done and a serious attempt to do it.*
>
> —H. G. Wells[1]

> *Every reform, however necessary, will by weak minds be carried to an excess that itself will need reforming.*
>
> —Samuel Taylor Coleridge[2]

In this volume we have explored the problem of reforming American political institutions in order to make government more responsive to the legitimate needs of society. It is all too evident that the political system in the United States has failed to confront effectively the major problems facing the nation, and the current state of public policy is disturbing to a great number of citizens. The deterioration of our urban areas, the quality of health care, the hunger of the poor, and the probabilities of attaining a lasting world peace are hardly conducive to optimism.

The institutional reforms suggested in the preceding pages, even if immediately implemented, would not instantly alleviate the nation's ills. These reforms, however, would increase governmental sensitivity to social ills and facilitate the task of making our society more civilized and humane.

The prospects for governmental reforms are varied. Some may appear to be certain given the lapse of a few years; for others, the odds of achievement are rather poor. Campaign-spending reform, for example, seems likely, and some improvements may even be in effect by the next presidential campaign. On the other hand, changing the popular view of the presidency or creating a politically enlightened and active public are undoubtedly a long way off. Most reform probabilities fall somewhere between these two extremes.

Before governmental institutions can be reformed, three crucial prerequisites must be satisfied. Reformers must (1) muster sufficient political support for change; (2) propose changes consistent with the principles of democratic political theory; and (3) propose changes which are both practical and rational.

GATHERING SUPPORT FOR CHANGE

The first task of a reformer must be to recruit supporters to his cause in sufficient numbers to demonstrate a meaningful show of political force. For example, Democratic liberals in the House of Representatives have, over the past decade, attempted to reform the office of Speaker and to change the seniority system. They have suffered embarrassing defeats, because they have been unable to garner enough votes. There is an arithmetic of reform in cases such as this.

Yet sheer numbers alone do not guarantee success. There is overwhelming public support for direct election of the President, but the electoral college remains. Successful reform movements must have strong political leadership and organization. Opponents, almost by definition, hold strategically superior positions. It is far easier to defend the status quo than it is to change established ways of conducting government.

Furthermore, reformers must be prepared to sustain their campaigns for long periods of time and maintain their interest, if not their fervor, in spite of inevitable failures. Arthur T. Vanderbilt, former Chief Judge of the New Jersey Supreme Court, after spearheading a long but ultimately successful campaign for improvement of the state court system, observed, "Judicial reform is not a sport for the short-winded." This same description may be accurately applied to any reform of government.

Motivating individuals to participate in reform movements is not an easy assignment. Most citizens, as we have noted, do not place political activity high on their list of preferred activities. It will take rather large doses of dissatisfaction before significant segments of the public will actually work for political reform.

Nor are governmental officials readily enlisted to work for institutional reform. These political actors have a rather large stake in the status quo. There is a natural fear that supporting the reform of one governmental institution may somehow lead to the reform of one's own agency. Even reform-minded officials are apprehensive about upsetting a system which, although imperfect, has accomplished a number of worthwhile goals over the years. Unfortunately, it often seems that before reform occurs (instigated either from within or from without government) conditions must first become so dismal that change appears urgently imperative.

REFORM AND DEMOCRATIC THEORY

The American people are quite chauvinistic about their political institutions. We are a society of Constitution worshipers. Our children are taught at a very early age that this is a country with a government "of the people, by the people, and for the people." Even while strenuously objecting to certain policies, Americans are quick to defend their system of government as the best yet designed.

This basic fact, that the country almost totally accepts and supports governmental institutions should not be forgotten if reforms are to be successful. Proposed changes must fall within the basic framework of generally accepted democratic values. The far Right might well prefer a constitutional monarchy and the far Left might support government by a "peoples' revolutionary council," but neither alternative stands any chance of being adopted because of the bounds imposed by our political culture.

To make existing institutions more responsive to the needs of American society, however, does not necessitate abandoning our democratic philosophy; it only requires moving the government toward a fuller realization of democratic ideals. A seniority system in Congress which thwarts the will of the people is, in effect, an anti-democratic device. A bureaucracy which often refuses to disclose its activities fails to meet the democratic tests of accountability and responsibility. A system which allows economic interest groups to call the shots in various areas of public policy-making is a system which does not live up to its democratic premises.

REFORM AND RATIONALITY

John Ingalls once wrote, "The purification of politics is an iridescent dream." A prudent person should not expect too much from politics, but improvements can be made. Dreams alone, however, are not enough. A dream must be linked to rational blueprints for progress and hard work. Dreamers will be successful only after others have molded their dreams into hard proposals, usually many years after the philosopher has departed to his everlasting reward.

A reformer who truly wants to improve government must make his proposals in a rational and practical manner. Sloganeering used reasonably ("taxation without representation") may convey the sentiments of the reform, but it is only one weapon of a whole arsenal at his disposal. And like any other high-powered weapon, slogans ("burn, baby, burn," "power to the people") can backfire. The American people may well be apathetic, uninformed, and inactive, but collectively they are usually not stupid.

Americans perceive their political institutions as having been won only at the expense of much blood and even more sweat. They are understandably suspicious of those who would alter the form of their government. Most citizens would probably agree with Theodore Roosevelt that there is a "lunatic fringe in all reform movements." The successful reformer will realize this and will gear his campaign accordingly. Because of this, spokesmen for reforms should be individuals who are not personally obnoxious to those who are to be recruited into the reform fold. This may mean that the forces for change must appear disgustingly respectable and thoroughly American. The people of the United States, while rejecting the radical revolutionary without giving the matter the slightest thought, may listen to the reformer whose pleas are couched in rational terms.

REFORMING AMERICAN POLITICS

Any reformer who urges that political institutions should be more responsive to the will of the society is taking a calculated risk. He assumes that the American people are basically reasonable, well-meaning individuals, plagued with a certain degree of human imperfection. He also accepts a major premise of democracy, that the citizenry can make intelligent choices between alternatives and build a better society. Nonetheless, a compulsively responsive government could result in repression of minorities and other reactionary tendencies. For this reason we have repeatedly emphasized that responsive government is not one which perfectly mirrors public sentiment, but one which responds to society's legitimate needs. Reformers should not forget that the framers of the Bill of Rights placed limitations on governmental authority to protect Americans from the abuse of political power. But, neither should they ignore the importance of responsible political leadership.

Before concluding, it should be noted that reform is a continuous process, not a one-shot affair. No governmental system is ever perfect. Societal changes will always occur. Government will require periodic reform in order to keep in step with the problems confronting the nation. As Peter Marris and Martin Rein described it, "Ideas of reform, like Buddhist souls, are chained to a wheel of reincarnation, striving at each rebirth to grow toward beatitude."[3]

Reform is not easy, but the benefits of a more responsive government make the effort well worthwhile. Those reforms which will have the greatest impact on society will be the most difficult to achieve, for here interests which benefit from the status quo are most solidly entrenched. Real governmental reform will not come about until the people and their political leaders make a commitment to change. Such commitments have not occurred spontaneously in the past, and concerned citizens may do well to apply an occasional strong, political shove.

NOTES: CONCLUSION

1. H. G. Wells, *The Work, Wealth and Happiness of Mankind* (Doubleday, Doran, 1931).

2. Samuel Taylor Coleridge, *Biographia Literaria* (E. P. Dutton, 1908).

3. Peter Marris and Martin Rein, *Dilemmas of Social Reform* (Atherton Press, 1967), p. 235.